VIKING PANZERS

VIKING PANZERS

The German 5th SS Tank Regiment in the East in World War II

Ewald Klapdor

STACKPOLE
BOOKS

Published in 2011 by
STACKPOLE BOOKS
5067 Ritter Road
Mechanicsburg, PA 17055
www.stackpolebooks.com

Printed in the United States of America

10 9 8 7 6 5 4 3 2 1

Library of Congress Cataloging-in-Publication Data

Klapdor, Ewald, 1916–
[Mit dem Panzerregiment 5 Wiking im Osten. English]
Viking panzers : the German 5th SS Tank Regiment in the East in World War II / Ewald Klapdor.
p. cm.
"Original German-language edition self-published by Ewald Klapdor in Siek, Germany, in 1981 as Mit dem Panzerregiment 5 Wiking im Osten"—T.p. verso.
Includes index.
ISBN 978-0-8117-0802-9
1. World War, 1939–1945—Regimental histories—Germany. 2. Waffen-SS. Panzerregiment "Wiking," 5—History. 3. World War, 1939–1945—Tank warfare. 4. World War, 1939–1945—Campaigns—Eastern Front. I. Title.
D757.85.K5313 2011
940.54'1343—dc22

2010049261

Contents

Foreword

A history of *SS-Panzer-Regiment 5* of the *5. SS-Panzer-Division "Wiking"*[1] cannot aspire to completely cover its subject, since the necessary and relevant wartime documents are available only for some of the subordinate elements and only for certain periods of time and operations. A circular from the Federal Archives notes the following in this regard:

> The daily logs of the divisions end, for the most part, by the middle or end of 1943; only the daily logs of higher levels of command extend into 1944 and, in exceptional cases, into 1945. The daily logs of the formations and units under division level were not evacuated and were destroyed in the aerial attack on Potsdam. The files maintained in the former archives of the *Waffen-SS* are located in Czechoslovakia and are not available for use.[2]

In addition, there is a lack of well-researched summarizing accounts by former members of the regiment, with the exception, once again, of some of the subordinate units. Likewise, the documents concerning personnel authorizations, equipment, and types of ammunition are also incomplete.

✠

The original concept for this work envisioned an account of the regiment from its inception to the end, including its operations, based on original documents provided by comrades and by personal after-action reports and firsthand accounts.

1. Translator's Note: The 5th SS Armored Division "Viking." The division underwent numerous designation and organizational changes throughout the war. In its earliest incarnation, it was *SS-Division "Wiking,"* and on 9 November 1942, it was redesignated as *SS-Panzer-Grenadier-Division "Wiking."* It was further redesignated as the *5. SS-Panzer-Division "Wiking"* on 22 October 1943, a title it retained to the end of the war.

2. Author's Note: Circular of the Federal Archives/Military Archives. Translator's Note: The reader is reminded that this book was originally written in 1980, prior to the collapse of the "Iron Curtain."

The first effort soon demonstrated the inadequacies of attempting a military history of the regiment. This was due to the above reasons as well as the well-known difficulties of trying to get differing statements concerning the same event to agree. This necessitated supporting the framework of the intended history with military historical data that was unquestionable. That entailed a search for official documents that were formulated at the time of the events, recognized by competent authority and recorded (daily logs with their annexes).

In the Federal Archives in Freiburg, I received all requested help and was afforded great accommodation. I succeeded in finding access to official documents that enabled me to make authoritative statements concerning the operational points of main effort of the regiment and the division that were based on historical fact. Those operational efforts include Rostow, Ssagopschin, Malgobek, the area southwest of Stalingrad, the area around the Donez, Kowel, Brest-Litowsk and Hungary.

In order to maintain continuity from 1942 to 1945, it also seemed advisable to emphasize the activities of the division occasionally. As a consequence, there are repeated references and details concerning the other divisional formations, especially the grenadier regiments.

The historical framework that was thus created was then able to accept additions from personal diaries, letters and after-action reports. Those indispensible elements, which enliven the account, are the portal for the reader to the world of experiences and feelings of those who were the "actors" at the time and provide the necessary background for understanding the exceptional situation that war represents.

The personal diaries, letters and after-actions reports, which were written during the war, should do justice to the demands for an account that was written close to the event. The closer the written accounts are to the actual occurrences, the less likely they are to be influenced by viewpoints and knowledge that was gained later, the mixing of events or even opportunistic slanting. The firsthand accounts that have been selected portray that which had been experienced to the best of the ability of the person writing it.

The coupling of those documents along with the results of looking through official sources are presented in this work with the sole purpose of offering a useful orientation and the ability to form an opinion about a portion of the German armed forces in the Second World War and a portion of the *Waffen-SS.*

Among the postwar publications used was the work of the Soviet army general S. M. Shtemenko, who was the head of the operations section of the Soviet General Staff and the deputy chief-of-staff: *The Soviet General Staff at*

War, 1941–1945. I was unable to find a German translation of the book, so the quotations taken from it have been translated by me.[3]

In conclusion, I would like to thank Wolf Schneider for his personal diary, which gave me the courage to start this endeavor.

In addition, my thanks to comrades Hein and Dr. Renz for allowing me to use the original documents in their possession, which were helpful in portraying the events of 1944.

I would also like to thank the director of the veterans association of the regiment, my comrade Proschek, for his organizational assistance in collecting the documents.

I owe special thanks to the senior archivist of the Federal Archives in Freiburg, Meyer, and his associates for their willing and valuable support.

Finally, I thank all of my comrades who made their contributions available and took pains to help bring about this work.

3. Translator's Note: As a result, I have been forced to do several reverse translations into English. Correspondingly, they may not be entirely consistent with a word-by-word comparison of the originals. It is hoped that the basic sense of the passage is still conveyed, although much of that depends on the quality of the original Russian-to-German translation as well.

The author as an *SS-Untersturmführer.*

CHAPTER 1

The Activation and Commitment of *SS-Panzer-Abteilung 5* on the Eastern Front

THE WILDFLECKEN TRAINING AREA AND SENNELAGER

The four regiments of the *SS-Verfügungstruppe*[1] that were in existence at the start of World War II on 1 September 1939—*"Leibstandarte Adolf Hitler," Deutschland." "Germania"* and *Der Führer"*—were reinforced, expanded, consolidated and reorganized at the beginning of 1941 into four motorized divisions/reinforced brigades: *SS-Brigade "Leibstandarte Adolf Hitler," SS-Division "Das Reich," SS-Division "Totenkopf"* and *SS-Division "Wiking."*[2]

The four formations had distinguished themselves during the first year of the campaign in the Soviet Union in 1941 through operations with the larger German field army. Consequently, these successes led to the intent to provide these formations with armored elements and reorganize them into mechanized infantry divisions. In addition, more divisions were planned for activation.

✠

In the spring of 1942, there were activation elements for three tank battalions at times at the Wildflecken Training Area. The leaders of the elements, who were also designated to be the initial commanders

1. Translator's Note: The *SS-Verfügungstruppe* was the precursor of the *Waffen-SS*. In English, it has the approximate meaning of "General-Purpose Forces." Author's Note: The formations of the *Verfügungstruppe* were formally redesignated as the *Waffen-SS* on 12 March 1940 (*RGBL*, vol. I, 512, according to Paul Hausser's *Soldaten wie andere auch*, 66, hereafter referred to as Hausser).

2. Translator's Note: As with the *"Wiking"* division, the other core divisions of the *Waffen-SS* will be referred to by their honorifics.

of the battalions, were *SS-Sturmbannführer*[3] Mühlenkamp (*"Das Reich"*), *SS-Sturmbannführer* von Reitzenstein (*"Wiking"*) and *SS-Sturmbannführer* Schönberger (*"Leibstandarte"*).

As Mühlenkamp recalled after the war, it was initially an open question as to what battalion would be assigned to what division. These decisions were later dictated by circumstances. For instance, when *"Das Reich"* was pulled out of the front for reconstitution, the battalion that had been earmarked for it went instead to *"Wiking"* since it was still committed in the Mius position and was preparing to participate in the upcoming summer offensive.

A directive from the SS Main Office found in the archives of the veterans association dictates the following under Point I:

> By order of the *Führer,* a third SS tank battalion is established.
> The SS tank battalion established for *Division "Reich"* by order of directive *SS-FHA*, Organization Staff, Log Entry 830/42, SECRET, dated 11 February 1942, will bear the designation *"SS-Panzer-Abteilung 5"* and will now belong to *SS-Division "Wiking."* The 3rd SS Tank Battalion established by today's order will belong to *SS-Division "Reich"* and will be assigned to it on the day of its activation. It will bear the designation *"SS-Panzer-Abteilung 2."*[4]

The extraordinarily rapid expansion of the regiments of the *Waffen-SS* into divisions and reinforced brigades posed problems with regard to the establishment of tank formations, not only in numbers of personnel, but also in qualitative technical issues.

Movement on the battlefield in a rolling combat vehicle made of steel—something akin to the movement of a boat on a moderately choppy sea—and being directly exposed to the effects of enemy fire required more of a mental and physical adjustment than former ways of combat. The crews had to become cohesive entities in extremely tight quarters, and everyone—whether driver, radio operator, loader or gunner—determined the combat effectiveness of his tank by the degree of his capabilities in his functional area.

Command and control of the individual vehicle, as well as of the units and the battalion, had to be practiced and mastered in a short time, all under the constraint of the restricted visibility in the vehicles and the sole means of communicating, which was through radio and intercommunications systems.

Within the *Waffen-SS,* there were no replacement detachments at the time that could make the core cadre of necessary specialists for armored elements

3. Translator's Note: Major. A rank equivalency chart can be found at the back of the book.

4. Author's Note: *SS-FHA*, Organizational Staff, Log Entry 2310/42, SECRET, 18 April 1942.

available. Mühlenkamp later recalled that he received permission to search out men, noncommissioned officers and officers in the replacement detachments of the front divisions of the *Waffen-SS* who appeared to be suitable candidates as tankers and to gather them at the Wildflecken Training Area.

These men, some of whom already had front-line experience, began to arrive during the first two months of 1942. They were men from the replacement detachment of the *"Deutschland"* Regiment in Prague, the *"Germania"* Regiment in Hamburg-Langenhorn and another replacement unit in Apeldoorn (Holland).

At that time of year, the training area at Wildflecken was extremely inhospitable to tanks, since it had a snow cover of 1.5 meters, as the future commander of the 2nd Company, *SS-Obersturmführer* von Staden, noted in his diary. Correspondingly, the captured French Hotchkiss tanks, which had been designated as training vehicles for the battalion, were "stranded on the ramps (75%) and on the approach road (10%)."

Von Staden went on to write: "By 15 February, our battalion was directed to initiate courses of training . . . unbelievably punctual . . . by 19 February, we were listing the first classes . . . On 4 March, the first driver's training started and, on 12 March, the battalion was issued its first tanks."

While the initial training was getting underway, the remaining personnel decisions could also be made. According to von Staden, "the company commanders and officers that had been identified by the Main Office arrived on 10 March." The commander of the 1st Company was *SS-Obersturmführer* Schnabel, the 2nd Company *SS-Obersturmführer* von Staden and the 3rd Company *SS-Hauptsturmführer* Darges. The commander of the Headquarters Company was *SS-Obersturmführer* Gaipel. Within the Headquarters Company, the leader of the reconnaissance platoon was *SS-Untersturmführer* Martin, the motorcycle platoon *SS-Untersturmführer* Hein, the engineer platoon *SS-Untersturmführer* Schraps and the signals platoon *SS-Untersturmführer* Köntop.

The final issue of tanks took place on 27 March. The majority of the tanks earmarked for the 1st and 2nd Companies were the *Panzer III* with the longer-barreled 5-centimeter main gun of 60 calibers.[5] The enhanced performance of the longer barrel gave the type 40 armor-piercing round a muzzle velocity of 835 meters a second and the armor-piercing sabot round was even faster, at 1,198 meters a second.[6] That knowledge helped reinforce the trust of the tankers in their new weapons. The 3rd Company of the battalion, the so-called "heavy" company, was initially equipped with the shorter-barreled 7.5-centimeter main gun of 43 calibers.[7]

5. Translator's Note: *Kampfwagenkanone (KwK) 39/L60.*

6. Author's Note: Rudolf Lusar, *Die deutschen Waffen und Geheimwaffen im Zweiten Weltkrieg,* 74.

7. The vehicles were *Panzer IV Ausf. F2.*

The training on the weapons and equipment, the driver's training and the combat and field training was decisively influenced by officers on loan from the Army. The leader of the training element was *Hauptmann* Phillip. Helping him in his efforts to train the battalion were *Hauptmann* Kertscher, *Oberleutnant* Euler, *Leutnant* Böckler, *Leutnant* Rößler and a number of others. Mühlenkamp and von Staden later praised the work of those men.

By the beginning of May, the initial phase of the activation—the issuance of weapons and equipment, the driver's training and the basic training on weapons and equipment—was ended. The battalion was moved to the Stauhmühlenlager Training Area near Paderborn, where it could intensify its gunnery and field training, with the object of rapidly attaining deployment status.

On 31 May, von Staden noted in his diary that the first battalion-level exercise had ended with a pass-in-review before *SS-Gruppenführer* Krüger.[8] Krüger found words of praise for the performance of the battalion and stated "that the battalion would master any mission it was given."[9]

For the most part, the enlisted personnel, noncommissioned officers and officers who had joined the battalion had come from motorized formations and had enthusiastically embraced their new armor-related duties in the many courses. Map exercises and exercises at the unit and formation level had familiarized the noncommissioned officers and officers with the leadership principles of armor and armored formations. Their overall enthusiasm and pride in belonging to an esteemed branch of service, which they were helping to create within the ranks of the *Waffen-SS*, was palpable.

The end of the training period at Camp Staumühlen was signaled by the return of *SS-Untersturmführer* Dedelow and *SS-Untersturmführer* Flügel of the 3rd Company and *SS-Obersturmführer* Klapdor of the 1st Company from gunnery courses at the armor school at Putlos along the Baltic.

During the first few days of June, preparations were made for the rail transport of the battalion to the Eastern Front. Correspondingly, there were "farewell" socials held in the areas around the training facilities in Paderborn, Bielefeld, Ahlen and especially Bad Pyrmont.

On 9 June, the initial elements head eastward. The first tank battalion of the *Waffen-SS—SS-Panzer-Abteilung 5*—loaded on trains with its Headquarters Company and two line companies. Each of the tank companies had three line platoons with five tanks each, as well as a company headquarters section with two tanks.

8. Translator's Note: According to the *Das Reich* website, Krüger was assigned to the SS Main Office at the time. He had been the commander of the *Polizei-Division* and went on to command *Das Reich*. He committed suicide at the end of the war to avoid capture by the Soviets in the Kurland Pocket (www.dasreich.ca/kruger.html)

9. Author's Note: von Staden.

Within the heavy company, only the elements designated to have the "short" version of the *Panzer IV* also moved out. The portions of the company to be outfitted with the *Panzer IV* with the long-barreled main gun were to be sent east later. The tanks were numbered in the traditional fashion, with three numerals on the turrets, the first indicating the company, the second the platoon and the third the tank within the platoon. As with all of the other division vehicles, the tanks also bore the divisional tactical sign, the so-called *Sonnenrad,* a swastika with rounded corners.

AMWROSIEWKA

> The rail movement has already taken a week . . . back through beautiful Germany again: The Harz [Mountains], Thuringia, Saxony and Silesia. It continued on through Poland. What a contrast! Once again, those dirty, poverty-stricken villages, paths, people in tatters. Then we went into the unending vastness of Russia. Strange, but we moved along approximately the same route that we had back then during our [original] advance: Lemberg, Tarnopol. Memories and battles are in front of me. And still it does not seem comprehensible that all of that took place a year ago there. The trains were moving as if it were peacetime.
>
> Burned-down, shot-up houses; knocked-out, abandoned tanks remind us of the hardness and terrors of the previous year. Most of the farmland has been planted.
>
> We crossed over the Dnjepr at Dnjepropetrowsk. For the first time, the weather was somewhat nicer today. Up until this point, it had rained almost continuously. The entire route, especially at stops and trains stations, is crawling with children and adults, who want soap, bread and cigarettes from us in exchange for eggs.[10]

Ever since 9 June, the battalion had been on the move towards the division in its area of operations along the Mius, a river that flows from north to south west of Taganrog past the towns of Kuybyschew and Metwjewskurgan into the Asovian Sea. The river line determined the front line during the heavy fighting north of the Asovian Sea during the winter of 1941–42.

Let us continue with the author's correspondence:

> After nine days of being on the train in normal third-class passenger cars with wooden benches, we approached our immediate objective—the city of Amwrosiewka, about 70 kilometers north-northwest of Taganrog—along the Asovian Sea. One year ago, we had covered the same stretch in five months of fighting.

10. Author's Note: Letter written by the author on 16 June 1942.

Most likely, everyone felt the change last night from our homeland—from deep in the rear to the vicinity of the front. In the distance, the night was rent by sheets of lightning, the fire from the nightly artillery duels. A barely controlled feeling of trepidation was shaken off during the day by the return of light and by keeping occupied.

The offloading during the morning hours of 18 June 1942 took place in the accustomed manner. The quarters had already been prepared for us. We were once again guests in the simple Russian houses or we set up in our tents. It was an environment that seemed completely familiar to us and nothing out of the ordinary. It only appeared to have been interrupted for a short while by a stay in the *Reich.*

By 19 June, the rail transports of the battalion had arrived and offloaded. Most of the battalion took up quarters in Amwrosiewka, with the 2nd Company in Wassiljewka. Von Staden's diary for 20 June reported a commander's conference down to battalion-command level at the division command post in Uspenskaja. During the conference, the division commander[11] emphasized the special character of the division as a formation of volunteers from practically all of the northern and western European countries[12] who had devoted themselves to the same mission and the same goal. He stated that the extra demands placed on all leaders in the division were an appreciation for the respective national characteristics of the soldiers, an ability to empathize and a particularly flexible leadership style.

An overview of the military situation gave a clue as to the upcoming missions of the division. The time remaining prior to operations was to be used for continuing, expanding and perfecting training.

---

11. Translator's Note: Since the book was originally written primarily for former members of Klapdor's regiment, he assumes some familiarity with the division and its commanders. In this case, he is referring to the first and long-time commander, *SS-Obergruppenführer* Felix Steiner, who went on to increasingly higher levels of command and was one of the most decorated soldiers in the German military. He survived the war and became one of the great advocates of the *Waffen-SS* as a military force.

12. Translator's Note: One of the reasons the division fought exclusively on the Eastern Front was the fact that it had a substantial minority of foreign volunteers—primarily from Holland, Belgium and the Scandinavian countries—that were enticed into German service by the promise of being able to fight Bolshevism. The foreign volunteers were concentrated mostly in the mechanized infantry regiments, but a substantial number were also to be found in the other combat-arms formations of the division.

On 29 June, the division commander inspected the battalion in Amwrosiewka. He greeted the men as a new element in the division and an increase in its combat power that promised much success.

✠

The battalion shared quarters in Amwrosiewka with the division's field replacement battalion. Other than the nine-day interruption for the rail movement, training continued unabated. The surrounding terrain offered good opportunities for road-march training and field exercises.

In addition to the military training, there was also time devoted to sports, and the playing fields in the city saw a number of games and competitions.

There was also a "Viking Home," which presented cultural events as part of its mission to look after the forces. A variety show with both German and Russian entertainers provided the necessary relaxation and distraction. If it had not been for the Soviet nuisance bombers—referred to as the "duty bombers" or the "sewing machines"[13]—which occasionally dropped light bombs in the vicinity, such as in the "Stalin Park," but rarely caused much damage, no one would have thought he was near the front. In general, the tanker awaited the upcoming operations with confidence. The unbridled thirst for action and a certain carefree attitude are reflected in the following letter the author wrote at the time:

> Our first closer brush with the front came in the form of an invitation from the commander of the 2nd Company of [*SS-*] *Aufklärungs-Abteilung 5,* [*SS-*] *Hauptsturmführer* Schlei, to go to his command post on the anniversary of the start of the campaign in Russia. As it started to turn dusk, we moved towards the front via Uspenskaja and reached the command post on foot, a large, apparently bombproof dugout.
>
> It was a strange night. All sorts of feelings were given due course: happiness in being out at the front again; the hard winter fighting, which so suddenly transformed the large-scale, successful offensive operations of the summer of 1941 into forms of positional warfare that are so problematical for motorized formations; the feeling of unbroken strength and confidence and of finally forcing the issue at the start of the summer after a year of fighting; the discharge of this unbridled power; a little bit of cockiness.

13. Translator's Note: The German soldiers called them "sewing machines" since the nuisance bombers were usually outmoded biplanes that could only fly at night without fear of being immediately shot down. They had to throttle back so the pilot could hold the stick between his legs in order to hand-drop light-explosive munitions. The corresponding sound generated by the small engine was similar to a sewing machine.

> A battalion surgeon felt that his talents were being underutilized. He implored the commander of the reconnaissance battalion, [*SS*-] *Hauptsturmführer* Pätsch, who was also present, in that regard. He wanted to be given a troop command, no matter the circumstances. Around midnight, it was no longer possible to suppress the urge to plant a swastika flag in front of the Russian positions. A patrol "raised" the flag about 70 meters in front of the Russian lines; it then started to receive angry but unsuccessful Russian fire at first light and the following day.
>
> The predictable reaction forced us after leaving the convivial command post of the [company] to hop energetically across a stretch of terrain that the enemy could observe.

While the days in Amwrosiewka all started to flow together, there was a serious loss in the 2nd Company. Its commander, von Staden, was killed in a training accident. The tankers gave him over to the soil of the Soviet Union at the divisional cemetery, a burial area that was already quite expansive and located between Amwrosiewka and Uspenskaja. Each of the innumerable mounds of dirt held a life that had been extinguished all too early. The objective of the dead remained the goal of the living, that day and the next, only that the "tomorrow" for the living was also an uncertain one. It was clear that a large-scale offensive was soon to start.

For his part, the enemy had undertaken great measures in the southern sector of the Eastern Front in the first half of 1942 so as to exploit the setbacks that had been inflicted on the German forces that winter and take back important positions as a result of their exhaustion. In part, the Soviets hoped to achieve some operational success.

In January and February, the Soviets had attacked along both sides of the Isjum in the direction of Kharkov. The German front was pushed back 80 kilometers along a frontage of 180 kilometers. At the same time, the Soviets conducted a large-scale landing on the Crimea, which led to the loss of the Kerch Peninsula.[14]

On 12 May, a new offensive was launched on both sides of Kharkov. In the north, the Soviets met with no success, but in the south, they broke through to just south of the city. Five days later, the Soviets were encircled as the result of a German counterattack from the Slawjansk area that led to considerable

14. Author's Note: von Tippelskirch, *Geschichte des II. Weltkriegs*, Athenäum Verlag: 1956. The overview in the following paragraphs stems primarily from a synopsis of von Tippelskirch.

losses west of the Donez among twenty Soviet rifle divisions, seven cavalry divisions and fourteen tank brigades.

Just a few days prior to that, the Kerch Peninsula had been retaken (16 May). On 1 July, the strong fortress of Sewastopol was taken, with 100,000 Soviets captured.

As a result, the Soviet losses during the spring in the southern portion of the Eastern Front amounted to approximately 490,000 prisoners, as well as the capture or loss of more than 3,700 artillery pieces and 1,500 armored vehicles.

The Soviets' reserves appeared to be inexhaustible, especially when the losses of the previous year were taken into consideration: Between Kiev and Moscow, they had lost 1,300,000 men captured and 9,000 artillery pieces and 2,000 armored vehicles lost or captured. Their losses up to that point amounted to more than half of all of the entire German armed forces that had started the campaign against the Soviet Union on 22 June 1941.

✠

The tank battalion had been in Amwrosiewka ten days when the tension-relieving news arrived that the large-scale German summer offensive had started and led to a breakthrough between Bjelgorod and Kursk. Woronesch was taken on 7 July; on 9 July, *Heeresgruppe A* started its offensive. Part of the field-army group was composed of the *17. Armee,* which, in turn, had the *LVII. Panzer-Korps.* The corps consisted of the *13. Panzer-Division* and the *198. Infanterie-Division,* in addition to the *"Wiking"* Division. It was poised to strike in the area north of the Asovian Sea.

The author's correspondence continues:

> While we followed the progress of events on a daily basis with great excitement, nothing initially changed for us in Amwrosiewka. The portions of the local populace, with whom we inevitably came in contact in our quarters, were very hospitable and in no way ill disposed. Despite a certain caution overall, our conversations occasionally took on a carefree openness. In conversing with Sina, a student from Kiev who had returned to her parents, my neighbors, in Amwrosiewka, it was clear that she perceived Bolshevism as a Russian national phenomenon and as progress, which had received an unfortunate setback by our appearance. Her trust in the strength of the Russian people, the correctness of its societal structure and her self-confidence impressed us. We had entered this country completely under the influence of literature that had described the events of the revolution and filled with the horrible events in the wake of the societal restructuring in this gigantic land. In this case, it appeared that there was no wish for a return to the pre-revolutionary times.

CHAPTER 2

Attack and Pursuit across the Don, the Kuban and the Terek

ROSTOW

Towards the middle of July 1942, the battalion was alerted by the division. Its tanks were prepared for movement and positioned along the roads, camouflaged. The quarters were cleared. Everything took place quietly and in a practiced manner. The unknown adventure that was the nature of an armored engagement had been anticipated so long that it was unable to cause that unique disquiet and overbearing tension now that it was just about to start.

The battalion marched south from Amwrosiewka. After a few days of waiting in the Fedorowka area, it reached the assembly area west of Ssambek that had been designated for *Panzerkampfgruppe Gille*,[1] which had been formed for the attack on Rostow. *SS-Oberführer* Gille was the division artillery officer and the artillery regimental commander. The core of his battle group consisted of the tank battalion. It was also composed of elements of *SS-Panzer-Jäger-Abteilung 5* and the cannon battalion of *SS-Sturmbannführer* Schlamelcher. The division also formed two infantry battle groups based around the *"Germania"* and *"Nordland"* regiments.

A decisively important factor in preparing for and executing wide-ranging operations is the provisioning of the troop commanders with the necessary cartographic materials. The cartographic materials prepared by the map and survey section of the Army General Staff were supplemented, expanded, enlarged or shrunk by the cartographic sections of the field armies and corps. Each map contained a legend. In order to counter the occasional incorrect

1. Translator's Note: Armored Battle Group "Gille." Ad hoc battle groups were usually named after the officer assigned to lead them. Herbert Gille ended the war as a corps commander and one of Germany's most highly decorated officers.

or simplistic assertions made in other accounts, it should be mentioned here that the cartographic materials available to the division and the battalion were wide ranging, current and sufficient for the campaign in the Caucasus. To offer proof of this assertion, the map sheets available to commanders, including the tank battalion commander, are listed here:

- Consolidated Maps: Asow–Rostow (3rd edition of 24 July 1942); Bagajewsjaja (1st edition of 1 July 1942); Wesselyi (3rd edition of December 1942). Those were 1:100,000 map sheets that were produced by the survey section of the operations section of the Headquarters of the *17. Armee* and printed by the 517th Topographic Section (Motorized) and reprinted by the 617th Survey and Map Detachment (Motorized). The maps were based on original maps produced in 1935–37 and 1938.
- Working Map Rostow–Grossnyi (1:100,000; 1 June 1942). Produced and printed by the 602nd Survey and Map Detachment (Motorized) and based on maps produced in the Soviet Union in scales of 1:100,000 (1937/1940) and 1:500,000 (1937/1940).
- Armavir Map Sheet (1:500,000; 1 May 1942). Produced by the Map and Survey Section of the Army General Staff. Based on a Soviet map at 1:500,000 (Sheet L-38-B, Pjatigorsk [modified conic projection] and produced in 1934 by the cartographic Trust of the USSR and supplemented by material available through January 1941).
- Pjatigorsk Map Sheet (1:500,000; 1941). Based on a Soviet map in 1:500,000 (Sheet L-38-B, Pjatigorsk [modified conic projection] and produced by the General Staff of the Red Army, using materials available through January 1941).
- Alagir Map Sheet (1:50,000). Based on a Soviet map in 1:100,000 and aerial photos (as of 6 September 1942).
- Malgobek Map Sheet (1:25,000). Prepared by the survey section of the operations section of the *LII. Armee-Korps*. Printed by the 452nd Map and Topographic Section (Motorized).

The attack on Rostow was the final note in the overture to the German summer offensive, which had started on 28 June with a breakthrough through the Soviet positions between Bjelgorod and Kursk. The attack on Rostow started three weeks later.

The *17. Armee* was redesignated as *Armeegruppe Ruoff* on 8 July 1942. The field army group command issued order number 79 on 20 July. It stated in paragraph 1: "Enemy situation unchanged; it is anticipated that he will withdraw at any time to Rostow or even to the southern front as far as the sea."

Paragraph 3 read: "*Armeegruppe Ruoff* attacks early on 21 July 1941 with *Gruppe Kirchner* to capture Rostow and continues the pursuit with its remaining forces."

Paragraph 4a stated: "*Gruppe Kirchner* attacks on 21 July in accordance with the special telegraph sent on 19 July: *Armeegruppe Ruoff,* Operations, Number 2854/42 SECRET. Attack start: 0400 hours."[2]

Gruppe Kirchner, formed by a field army order issued during the evening of 15 July, was earmarked for the intended attack on Rostow. It consisted of the *LVII. Panzer-Korps* (*13. Panzer-Division* and *"Wiking"*) and the *XXXXIX. Gebirgs-Korps.*[3] They received the *298. Infanterie-Division,* the *73. Infanterie-Division* and the *125. Infanterie-Division* the day before the attack was ordered (on 20 July). In the attack order issued by *Gruppe Kirchner* at 1630 hours on 20 July,[4] the alpine corps was directed to attack east on both sides of the Ssambek. Within the *LVII. Panzer-Korps,* the *13. Panzer-Division* was ordered to cross the Ssambek and move into the village of the same name and then advance east across Hill 101.5, some 6 kilometers east of the town. The *"Wiking"* Division received the mission to follow the *13. Panzer-Division* across the Ssambek, because a second suitable crossing point was not available.

At 0400 hours, the *298. Infanterie-Division* opened the Ssambek bridgehead and expanded it to the east. At 0945 hours, the commanding general of the *LVII. Panzer-Korps* ordered the *13. Panzer-Division* to move out. In paragraph 3 of the same order, the following can be found: "The tank battalion of *SS-Division Wiking* is to be afforded right-of-way at the Ssambek Bridgehead." The division was directed to ford its wheeled vehicles at Warenowka, some 4 kilometers farther to the south.

The weather was sunny and hot. The almost unbearable heat demanded the utmost from the infantry when it marched. Within a single regiment of the *73. Infanterie-Division,* forty men were lost to heat exhaustion within a short period.[5]

---

2. Translator's Note: The German military used Middle European Time in its orders, which was two hours earlier than the local time at the Eastern Front.

3. Translator's Note: The Germans did not adopt a fixed corps structure until later in the war. Initially, corps consisted of a headquarters and headquarters staff and some corps troops, with the subordinate combat elements attached based on the mission.

4. Author's Note: Daily logs of the *LVII. Panzer-Korps.*

5. Author's Note: Daily logs of the *LVII. Panzer-Korps.*

By the evening of the first day of attack, the lead elements of the division were north of a line running Ssinjawska–Hill 107.6–Hill 116.9. The lead elements of the *13. Panzer-Division* adjoined farther north. Towards evening, the *8./Lehr-Regiment Brandenburg z.b.V.*[6] was attached to the Army division for the capture of important targets.

That same night, both the *13. Panzer-Division* and the armored group of the *"Wiking"* Division linked up in the area southeast of Alexandrowka to attack Ssulfan Ssaly and the enemy to the southwest of it. On the first day of operations, the tanks were able to advance more than 30 kilometers. Only 15 kilometers separated them from the western edge of the city of Rostow.

After hard fighting, the *13. Panzer-Division* succeeded in taking Ssulfan Ssaly and Krassny Krym on the road leading into Rostow from the northwest at noon on 22 July. The tanks of *SS-Panzer-Bataillon 5* were held up by mines and difficult terrain: "Moving through the deeply cut *Balka* is only possible in a few places, even for tanks."[7]

In the course of the afternoon, the battalion succeeded in crossing the tank ditch in the Tschaltyrskaja *Balka* southwest of Krassny Krym. By evening, it had broken through two of the three defensive belts around the city of Rostow. The defensive belts consisted of tank ditches, belts of mines, mine dogs[8] and antitank defenses. The tanks reached a line northwest of Sapadny, from which the attack objective, Rostow, appeared to be within reach the next day.

As Mühlenkamp later recalled, it was the boldness and violence of the tank attack, the terrific interaction with the engineers in the clearing of minefields and tank ditches, the taking of tank ditch passage points (some of which were undamaged), and the identification and rapid elimination of threats to the tanks that contributed to the battalion's success. Among other individual accomplishments, Mühlenkamp cited Wilde's platoon from the 1st Company, which destroyed an enemy field battery of six guns after conducting a bold envelopment after Mühlenkamp had ordered it attacked.

6. Translator's Note: The Brandenburg Instructional Regiment was the equivalent of special forces and had specially trained and language-qualified German personnel as well as indigenous personnel. A history of this formation and other special operations forces employed by the Germans in World War II can also be found in Franz Kurowski's *The Brandenburger Commandos: Germany's Elite Warrior Spies in World War II,* also published by Stackpole.

7. Translator's Note: A *Balka* was the Russian word for defile and was universally used by German soldiers on the Eastern Front. Author's Note: Daily logs of the *LVII. Panzer-Korps.*

8. Translator's Note: The Red Army conducted experiments whereby antitank mines were strapped to the backs of dogs that had been trained to go underneath armored vehicles. The Germans encountered these "mine dogs" in various sectors of the front.

The lead attack elements of the *13. Panzer-Division* were at Trud by the evening of 22 July. Early in the morning of the next day, it was involved "in street fighting with numerous antitank guns and weak enemy forces in the vicinity of Kamennolomni."[9]

At the same time, the tanks of the battalion were stopped by the last tank ditch on both sides of Sapadny, while the mechanized infantry battle groups of *"Germania"* and *"Nordland"* only made slow progress through the tough and bitterly defending enemy forces in Krym and Tschaltyr.

By noon, the last tank ditch was breached. The tanks of the battalion rolled into the western portion of the city, past bunkers in the street, barricades and roadblocks of all sorts, without encountering significant enemy resistance.

In the course of the morning, the *13. Panzer-Division* forced "a crossing over the creek southeast of Kamennolomni and pressed into the city in hard individual engagements."[10]

✠

In contrast, the tanks of the battalion left the west side of the city that afternoon, advanced along the northern banks of the Don to the west and screened towards the west southeast of Ssemernikowo and west of Nishne-Ginlowskaja and to the southwest in the direction of the Mertwyj Donez. The daily logs of the corps recorded the following during the morning of 23 July:

> Aerial reconnaissance indicates the withdrawal of the enemy across the Don west of Rostow in front of the attack spearheads of the *298. Infanterie-Division*. To prevent crossing possibilities, *SS-Division Wiking* receives the mission to advance as far as Ssemernikowo on the Don and establish blocking positions oriented to the west in the tank ditch there.

While the tank battalion and elements of the infantry battle groups of the division were largely able to prevent the crossing of the enemy over the northern arm of the delta of the Don,

> the *13. Panzer-Division* was able to take possession of the entire western portion of Rostow in the course of the afternoon after breaking enemy resistance. A combat patrol was able to capture the Russian ferry across the Don intact. Towards evening, the bulk of the division was on the Don and established contact with the forces of *SS-Division*

9. Author's Note: Daily logs of the *LVII. Panzer-Korps*.

10. Author's Note: Daily logs of the *LVII. Panzer-Korps*.

> *Wiking* that were in the area to the west of the Don bridge. The ferry traffic at Kumshenskyi [about 4 kilometers south of Ssemernikowo] could not be entirely prevented by *Gruppe Kirchner*; the necessary forces were not available.[11]

The daily logs of the corps on 24 July recorded the following concerning the conclusion of the fighting for the city of Rostow and the bridges over the Don, which were so important for continued operations:

> Russian resistance came back to life again during the night. The commander of the *13. Panzer-Division* decided—on his own initiative and before the actual order to do so reached him—to cross the Don by surprise with elements of his division and establish a small bridgehead that same night 1.5 kilometers southwest of the railway bridge. Towards morning, the division, with strong support from the *8./Lehr-Regiment z.b.V. 800*, succeeded in breaking enemy resistance and taking the bridges over the Don, as well as the railway bridge to Bataisk, intact.

The events of the two days of fighting were recorded by the author:

> On 21 July 1942, infantry formations broke through the front north of Taganrog. We were brought forward during the day of 22 July and into the night. The supply columns were pressing into the battlefields of yesterday. We crossed a tank ditch and some artificial obstacles in the terrain, which offered little cover and was not broken up. During the morning hours of 22 July 1942, we positioned ourselves in a suitable rear-slope position southwest of Ssulfan-Ssaly and prepared for our first attack. The friendly forces to the left, the *13. Panzer-Division*, was going to attack Rostow along the Ssulfan-Ssaly road.
>
> With understandable tension, we awaited the order "*Panzer marsch.*" The hatches were closed. Just like exercises conducted in the past few weeks, we rolled over the rise in the familiar W formation. The narrow vision ports restricted visibility. Off to the right and left in an imposing array, the steel fortresses rolled across the uneven ground like rising and falling boats on choppy waters. The terrain in front of us was open and easy to survey; in some areas, it was covered with high growths of grass. After a few minutes, we were in front of the first obstacle, a broad belt of mines, sometimes easily identifiable, other times not. While I hesitated a moment, uncertain what to do,

11. Author's Note: Daily logs of the *LVII. Panzer-Korps.*

the tank moving behind and to the left of me detonated a mine. The weakly armored hull was torn open, and the radio operator on the right side badly wounded.

The enemy defensive fires started up; at that moment, there was no doubt that we offered them excellent targets. Our entire attention was focused on the firing positions of the Russian antitank guns. The all-too-slowly receding initial excitement and the rocking of the fighting vehicle made it difficult to observe for targets. It was only due to pure luck and the sharp eyes of my driver that we made it through the minefield unscathed. The other vehicles also found gaps. The attack was rolling.

At that moment, I was suddenly thrust forward against the turret wall with my head. There was a crash; the tank no longer moved. It was also no longer horizontal; instead, it was slanted steeply forward. It did not seem advisable to dismount, since immobilized tanks acted like a magnet for the enemy's defensive fires. Machine-gun fire was also smacking off the armored plate of the tank. We were helpless: the turret would not traverse, no weapons could be used; nothing could be seen through the optics.

After a few minutes, the rapidly attacking tanks pulled the sound of battle along with them. I was able to dismount and saw just the back half of the tank jutting out of a well-camouflaged tank trap. The main gun had bored itself into the ground. After the Russian antitank defenses and machine guns left us completely alone, a tank from the second attack wave pulled us out of the trap. The weapons were made operational again, and we were able to reach the spearheads of the attack without incident. A wonderfully constructed tank ditch could be breached by going through on crossing points that were still intact. Prisoners started to be assembled in the ditch. We looked for the Russian artillery in the depths of the main battle area. The enemy appeared to be pulling back slowly.

In the afternoon, the middle defensive belt around Rostow was broken through with the same drive. The Russian artillery attempted to disrupt our attack position. Standing in the commander's hatch, I suddenly felt a blow to my back after the detonation of a shell. I collapsed onto my seat and later discovered a small piece of steel that apparently had run out of penetrative power.

The attack proceeded as if it were an exercise. The companies, which attacked in waves, gained ground by taking turns seeking cover and then closing up again. They eliminated resistance, sometimes by means of concentrated fires. Terrain obstacles could be bypassed, for the most part.

The commander of the 1st Company, *Obersturmführer* Schnabel, took a grazing wound to his heel while he was standing on his tank. Late in the afternoon, his tank started to spew smoke. There were no large-scale damages or losses, however.

That evening, we saw the outline of Rostow; heavy clouds of smoke were lying over the city. The refueling and reaming of the tanks lasted into the night. We tried to organize our impressions in our thoughts. We were generally confident and happy that our first operation had proceeded so well up to that point.

We had already reached the third tank ditch early in the morning on 23 July. It had been intended to protect the outskirts of the city. Since there were no passage points, one had to be created.

Engineers collapsed the walls of the ditch with demolitions. With all of the shovels on hand, the embankments were flattened out, simultaneously raising the bottom of the ditch. Early in the afternoon, the tank battalion was ready to penetrate into the city.

The enemy resistance at that location had practically collapsed. With caution, some of the turret hatches were opened, but the heads remained inside as we moved into the western suburbs. No serious resistance was encountered.

The *13. Panzer-Division* was also fighting in the city at the same time. The sounds of heavy fighting came from the eastern part, echoing across the southern banks of the Don.

Late in the afternoon, our tanks started to roll out of the city again so as to screen the raised northern banks of the Don and await the next day. We had to provide our own dismounted security. That meant that despite the physical strains of the last few days, our tank crews would not get any sleep the coming night.

But even the strictest disciplinary measures concerning the manning of guard posts in the vicinity of the enemy could not prevent posts from falling asleep. For instance, I found my good, reliable loader, Abraham, fast asleep at his guard post when I made the rounds after midnight. He was scared stiff. Both of us kept quiet about the incident.

✠

The powerful flood plain of the Don started to come into focus out of the dawning light on the morning of 24 July. Nothing blocked the view to the south and to the west. Individual swimmers and oarsmen in the mighty river were tankers of the division, who could not resist the opportunity to refresh themselves.

During the morning, the tanks rolled back into the city. They set up in a park; today was a day of rest.

A letter home written by the author on 24 July attempted to capture the impressions of the last few days:

Our debut went very well. The large number of tanks, artillery, *Stukas*, close-air support aircraft, destroyers and fighters provided a hellish concert. It was literally a rolling operation like nothing I had ever experienced before. As a result, we were outside of Rostow at noon yesterday; in the afternoon, we went in.

It was a unique feeling—something that cannot be described—that moved us when our first tanks went in. Road obstacles, barricades, bunkers. All of the window shutters were closed. Occasionally, a civilian surfaced from out of a hole in the ground; you could read the hell he had gone through over the past few days on his face.

Our first objective had been reached.

I'm am presently sitting in a park. A little bit of quiet is terrific after having spent the last few days in the tank. Despite that, there's still a bit of crashing and banging, since the Russians are bitterly defending the eastern part of the city. The rattling of machine guns . . . detonations and aircraft round out the acoustic picture, while the setting sun illuminates the city, which is enveloped in smoke and haze, in a unique manner.

Another letter:

The 25th of July was a day of rest. Nobody knew how long that situation would last. The city of Rostow had suffered terribly as a result of the fighting. Even though there are the all-too-fresh traces of fighting, there are still smoldering flames and blackened ruins and our impressions of the city at the mouth of the Don naturally burden us . . . despite all that, it appears to be a middle-European, metropolitan city, not only in its center but also at its periphery. Churches with domes, a large theater, movie houses, broad streets and multi-storied houses, just as in every large German city. New apartment buildings have been constructed on the outskirts of the city, similar to the ones we were already familiar with from the industrial cities of the Ukraine.

> Adjoining them are one-story houses of brick, wood and clay that are surrounded by picket fences.
>
> In the city, we discovered large basement rooms that were literally stacked up to the ceiling with radios. The populace probably had to surrender the devices so as not to be able to receive radio signals sent from the German side.
>
> In the outbuildings at the harbor there were welcome supplies; soap and cigarettes are especially sought items. Some of the barrels have leaked in the wine cellars; in places, you can wade in wine. In the city proper, it is deathly still after the sounds of war of the last few days. To the south, on the other side of the river, a few reports of artillery or detonations. Otherwise, just the sounds of vehicles and engines.
>
> In a letter written on 27 July:
>
> It went quiet everywhere all at once. Individual shots; *Flak* was firing its tracers into the dark skies, as if this magnificent Russian heaven filled with stars needed some sort of supplement. Even the last remaining vehicles have quieted down.

BETWEEN THE DON AND THE KUBAN

> During the early-morning hours of 28 July, the tanks of the *Wiking* Division rolled through the city of Rostow, which was still in death throes. The electrical and telephone lines above the ground cross the streets and plazas and demand special alertness on the part of the tank commanders standing in the hatches. I received a wallop in the back from a cable stretched across the street when I turned around to take a picture.[12]

Thus begins the next chapter of the battalion's history, which takes the reader across the Don, Kuban and Terek Rivers and the area leading up to Grossny, the oil region of indispensible importance to the enemy. The fighting took part as a result of Directives 41 (5 April) and 45 (23 July) at the armed forces command level. Since the operations of the summer of 1942 in the southern portion of the Eastern Front belong to one of the most exciting chapters of World War II, leading to the destruction of the *6. Armee* at Stalingrad and the ultimate loss of the Caucasus, we will treat these directives in some detail. The multifaceted opinions and judgments rendered after the

---

12. Author's Note: Author's account.

events can be better identified for their ultimate value when one goes back to the origins of the operational concepts.

Directive 41[13] provides the general intent of the operations:

> While still maintaining the original features of the campaign in the East, it is imperative that the Army hold the center sector, cause the collapse of Leningrad in the north and establish land contact with the Finns and, on the southern wing of the front force a breakthrough into the Caucasus.
>
> Based on the situation following the outcome of the winter fighting, the available forces and the transportation situation, this objective can only be achieved incrementally.
>
> Therefore, all available forces are to be concentrated for the main operations in the south, with the objective of eliminating the enemy forward of the Don so as to then take the oil regions in the Caucasian area and achieve entry into the Caucasus proper . . .

After discussing the conduct of operations in a series of attacks that follow one another and either were interconnected or supplemented each other, the directive went on to state the following in Section D of the document:

> The rapid continuation of the movements across the Don to the south to achieve the operational objectives must be conducted with an eye towards the seasonal conditions.[14]

A little more than three weeks after the start of the coordinated attacks dictated in Directive No. 41, Directive No. 45 was issued on 23 July. The continuation of operations was detailed in Paragraph II:

> Objectives for further operations:
>
> A. Army:
>
> 1. The next mission of *Heeresgruppe A* is to encircle the enemy forces that escaped over the Don to the south and southeast of Rostow and eliminate them . . .
> 2. After eliminating the enemy group of forces south of the Don, it is the most important mission of *Heeresgruppe A* to take the entire eastern

---

13. Author's Note: German Armed Forces High Command/Armed Forces Command Staff, Number 55616/42, SECRET COMMAND MATTER, Chief of Staff, *Führer* Headquarters, dated 5 April 1942.

14. Author's Note: This directive and Directive No. 45 are reproduced in Friedrich Lenz, *Stalingrad, der verlorene Sieg,* 1956.

coast of the Black Sea, thus effectively eliminating the Black Sea harbors and the enemy's Black Sea fleet . . .

To that end, the designated portions of the *11. Armee* (Rumanian Alpine Corps) are to be moved across the straits of Kertsch as soon as the advance of the main forces of *Heeresgruppe A* begins to take effect so that they can then advance along the Black Sea coastline to the southeast. A crossing over the Kuban is to be forced by an additional grouping of forces, which will concentrate all available alpine and light infantry divisions, taking the high ground at Maikop and Armavir. During the further advance of that group of forces, which is to be reinforced by the timely addition of alpine units, against the western portion of the Caucasus, all trafficable passes are to be exploited so that the Black Sea coast can be taken in conjunction with the forces of the *11. Armee.*

3. At the same time, the area around Grossny is to be taken with a grouping of forces consisting primarily of motorized formations, while a flank guard orients to the east, and some elements block the Ossetian and Grusinian military roads, preferably along the mountain passes. Following that, the area around Baku is to be taken in an advance along the Caspian Sea.
4. As ordered, *Heeresgruppe B* has the mission of advancing against Stalingrad to defeat the enemy group of forces forming there, occupy the city proper and block the land bridge between the Don and the Volga, while still establishing a defense along the Don.

Both directives unequivocally identify the offensive in the Caucasus as the main operation in the southern sector of the Eastern Front. There is no discussion of two operations of equal importance. Moreover, the establishment of defenses along the Don and movements in the direction of Stalingrad assume the character of a strategic guard mission for the northeastern flank of the Caucasus operation.

✠

On 28 July, the division and its tank battalion moved out to conduct a pursuit of the enemy south of the Don, after the divisions of the *III. Panzer-Korps* had already crossed the Don farther to the east on 26 July and had already reached the Manytsch while attacking south two days later.[15]

The mission issued to the division on 27 July at 1950 hours stated, in part:

15. Author's Note: von Mackensen, *Vom Bug zum Kaukasus*, Kurt Vowinkel Verlag: 1967.

> *SS-Division Wiking* crosses the Don Bridge at 0400 hours on 28 July 1942 with its lead elements and, advancing through Bataisk and Olginskaja, initially takes the high ground southeast of Seljanaja-Roschtscha.[16]

The attack objective was approximately 30 kilometers east of Bataisk. For the crossing of the Don, *Pionier-Bataillon 74* and *Pionier-Bataillon 203* were allocated to *Gruppe Kirchner* on 23 July and further attached to the *XXXXIX. Gebirgs-Korps.*

Although the lead elements of the division crossed the bridge at 0400 hours on 28 July, the bridge capacity proved to be inadequate. Portions collapsed and had to be reinforced. Disruptions and delays were the result. It was not until 1430 hours that the bridge was sufficiently improved—*Panzer-Pionier-Bataillon 4* was committed to help as well—that the deliberate crossing could start. Around 1800 hours, most of the division was on the southern banks of the Don.[17]

Before all that happened, however, the 1st Company of the tank battalion reached its daily objective, Seljanaja-Roschtscha, around 1500 hours. The author later wrote:

> The destroyed bridge over the Don was lying in the mighty stream. Engineers had established a pontoon bridge, over which our tanks then reached the southern banks by moving carefully and maintaining large intervals. In contrast to the large bridge, the crossings over the southern arms of the delta were taken intact by the Germans.
>
> Along the road heading east, on which we were moving, there were motorized supply columns and horse-drawn *Panje*[18] wagons of all types and sizes. Motorcycle messengers forced their way past the columns in both directions. Since the Russian roads are often known to have the advantage of being able to be widened without any extra effort—usually they were not bordered by ditches—the fact that columns were next to one another was no obstacle as long as independent changes of direction or crossing the direction of march was avoided. Approaching us and heading north were long columns of Russian prisoners with bread bags in their hands or blankets and shelter halves slung over their shoulder, not unlike an assault pack. Individual members of the local populace looked on, seemingly

16. Author's Note: Daily logs of the *LVII. Panzer-Korps.*

17. Author's Note: Daily logs of the *LVII. Panzer-Korps.*

18. Translator's Note: *Panje* was the name given to the simple Soviet peasant carts by the German soldiers.

apathetically. I thought about the student, Sina, in Amwrosiewka, who once replied to our question—Why didn't she and other Russians offer the prisoners, their fellow countrymen, something?—that the prisoners were traitors who had not fulfilled their obligation to fight to the end.

The last remaining houses of Bataisk—destroyed, for the most part—were behind us. The great wide openness, which seemed to go on without end to the south and east, swallowed us up. The growing expanse made even our compact and powerful column appear to get ever smaller. It should be mentioned that this ability to disappear in the surroundings, into whose depths we were given new missions on a daily basis, was also veiled somewhat by the thick clouds of dust and dirt that rose high in the sky, even from he smallest of vehicles.

We continued to pass marching infantry elements that had attacked through Bataisk to the south. Elements of a bicycle battalion[19] looked at us roll past with a little bit of envy. The divisional command post, which had been established around three large haystacks, was also behind us at that point. From that point forward, there was only enemy in front of us, who appeared to be withdrawing in an orderly fashion but without maintaining a cohesive front.

It appeared to get dark earlier here for some reason. We set up security in the positions we reached. The resupply of the tanks with fuel and ammunition lasted until midnight. We slept in the open or, in the best of cases, in a protective dugout shoveled out from under the tank.

On 29 July, the tanks of the division initially rolled east in the direction of Swobodnyi on the southern banks of the Manytsch so as to relieve the *16. Infanterie-Division (mot.)*,[20] which had attacked from the north and established a bridgehead there. The march objective for the division, however, was Balabanoff-Gigant, off to the southeast.

Towards noon, the avenues of advance for both the *"Wiking"* Division and the *13. Panzer-Division* were changed to avoid the march paths from crossing.[21] The *13. Panzer-Division* was directed to advance on Gigant, while *"Wiking"* was to head for Jegorlykskaja by way of Metschetinskaja. Once again, correspondence from the author captures the scene:

---

19. Translator's Note: In non-motorized infantry divisions, the divisional reconnaissance battalion was usually outfitted with bicycles in the earlier stages of the war.

20. Translator's Note: 16th Motorized Infantry Division. These were the precursors to the mechanized infantry (*Panzergrenadier*) divisions.

21. Author's Note: Daily logs of the *LVII. Panzer-Korps.*

As the sun rose, which caused the horizon on the edge of the steppes to glow, *SS-Panzer-Abteilung 5* prepared to further pursue the withdrawing enemy. The battalion was screened on the flanks by the companies of the reconnaissance battalion and given artillery support in the form of the relatively far-ranging cannon battery of a battalion of [*SS-*] *Artillerie-Regiment 5*. Its forward observers moved with the spearheads of the attack. As a result, good cooperation and rapid effectiveness was obtained.

Heavy antitank guns on self-propelled carriages accompanied our attack. Mechanized infantry[22] sat on the rear decks of the tanks so as to be immediately available.

Like the iron tip of a long-shafted spear, the armored group bore into the slowly withdrawing columns of Russians which, nevertheless, continued to escape complete envelopment.

The attainment of the day's objective was not determined by the enemy; instead, it was determined by our rate of march through corn fields, heavy vegetation on the steppe and *Balkas* without trails, which gave some of the sections of terrain the character of defiles.

We spent the night south of Metschetinskaja in the positions we had reached so as to resume the pursuit at sunrise on 30 July. Around 0900 hours, we were outside of Jegorlykskaja, which was taken by storm against heavy enemy resistance.

The enemy rearguards were a lost cause. They still attempted to get away from our tanks, which were firing on the move, even after they were within effective range of our weapons. There were occasional dramatic scenes when pursuer and pursued moved next to one another or behind one another in the same direction. Truck drivers were shot out of their seats. To the right of me, a prime mover with limbered gun moved down the slope without a driver. A few earth-brown figures rose halfway up out of the grass—an expression of terror in their faces—right in front of the steel giants.

No one took an interest in collecting prisoners. Our motto was: Forward! This form of forward assault brought about a danger that had not been counted on. There was armed enemy not only in front of us but also behind us. When several tank commanders got shot in the head, we became more cautious.

---

22. Translator's Note: Mechanized infantry was really a misnomer, since few of the mechanized infantry regiments had more than a company or battalion of armored personnel carriers (*Schützenpanzerwagen* or SPW). As a result, the infantry sometimes mounted up on the tanks, especially whenever speed was of the essence, since their trucks could not often keep pace with the tanks when moving cross-country.

Positions that had been overrun were completely cleared of the enemy. On the slope south of Jegorlykskaja, the Russians had to be smoked out of their holes individually. My tank was positioned over an angled trench. Nothing stirred inside despite repeated demands to surrender. Safety off, I carefully attempted with my pistol to look into the hole. I saw a Russian on the ground, pressed to the earth, conforming to the angle of the trench. He hesitantly raised himself with a tense expression on his face; his machine gun was underneath him. He then climbed out of the trench and trotted to the rear, seemingly distrustful with regard to his mild treatment.

Just three hours later, around 1200 hours, our tanks were positioned outside of Ssredny Jegorlyk, 20 kilometers farther south. During our march through an extended *Balka*, we were suddenly attacked by Russian fighters, whose machine-gun fire pelted the quickly closed hatches and the rear decks like hail. They could tell we were relatively helpless and did not leave us alone. After a short while, however, the scene changed. Summoned by the air-ground coordination officer attached to the division, the destroyer squadron of *Major* Döring appeared and put an end to the madness.

It was directed that Ssredny Jegorlyk be taken in a direct assault. The division commander, [*SS*-] *Gruppenführer* Steiner, moved fearlessly and directly behind the tank battalion in his light-colored dust jacket and with his small battle staff. His command post was up front. Decisions and orders were adjusted to the progress of the fighting—rapidly, with no time lapse. The artillery went into position; the forward observers registered and corrected the guns. While we were getting ready, the shells of the cannon battery were already singing above us. The Russians were ejected and fled to the rear.

We were ordered to halt on the slope south of the locality. It was a maintenance halt, which we could not understand. Standing in our turrets and observing through binoculars and the naked eye, we could observe Russian columns filing past us from the northeast to the southwest. Contrary to what we wanted to do, we were not ordered to immediately move into those rearward movements. That 30th of July had left a special impression on us young tankers. In a letter written on 31 July, I wrote:

"Yesterday was probably the nicest one so far. There were signs of unregulated flight. Among other things, we saw actual camels for the first time. That meant that Asia was slowly coming into sight. It is unbelievably hot here. On average, you are in the tank for 12 hours.

The water situation is also not the best. But those are only temporary conditions.

"The populace is by no means similar to the people in the Ukraine. Yesterday, we took Jegorlyk. Not a soul to be seen. All of them were hunkered down in their holes in the ground. I hope the mail to Germany is not nearly as long as it is in reverse. The route back to Germany becomes ever longer."

In order to reduce the time for mail by five days, next-of-kin were given airmail stamps. The letters were not allowed to be more than 10 grams, and the front side of the envelope had to be marked with two diagonal lines all the way across.

We became familiar with the living conditions of the local populace; it was the same everywhere. In the vicinity of the simple clay huts, there was a clay oven in the open, on which food was cooked. The cellars dug into the earth were amazingly cool, frequently roomy and only reachable by means of a small entry, which was not too difficult to hide. The earth cellars were serving the people as shelters and hiding places.

Our tank crews spent the night in the open behind the mechanized infantry of the *"Nordland"* Regiment, which was in front of us, and recovered from the heat and dust and dirt clouds of the day. The faces gradually became narrower. In addition to the outside temperature, there was the sticky heat inside the fighting compartment. The uniforms became more and more loose fitting. Frequently, the trousers were the only thing worn.

The menu became more monotonous. Brought forward in water buckets, boiled chicken, eggs and cucumbers were the standard meal. The chocolate taken from the "iron rations"[23] was held in especially high esteem.

Fuel and ammunition appeared to be available in sufficient quantities. Potable water became scarcer.

Riding high on our own successes, we feverishly tuned in to the radio at night for news reports. They connected us to the overall events of that summer of 1942: The armored formations of the *6. Armee* and the *4. Panzer-Armee* decided the battle in the Great Bend of the Don in their favor. A crossing over the Don had been forced at Kalatsch. Operations against the lower course of the Volga were starting. To the east of us, the *13. Panzer-Division* had forced a crossing over the

23. Translator's Note: The *eiserne Rationen* were survival rations, which were not supposed to be broken into except in cases of dire emergency. They were carried along on the fighting vehicles and theoretically provided enough food for three days.

> Manytsch at Ssalsk by conducting a wide enveloping maneuver to the east. Rommel's tanks in North Africa were driving the English before them as far as the gates of Egypt. In the Atlantic that summer, the *U-Boote*, attacking in packs, were sinking an average of 500,000 tons of shipping monthly from out of the convoys. There was success on all fronts. The will to attack and the forcefulness of the attack appeared to be shatterproof.
>
> Early on the morning of 31 July, the lead elements of the division were attacked unexpectedly in Ssredny Jegorlyk by enemy rearguards. Two Soviet battalions, supported by two tanks and rocket launchers, attacked Jegorlyk from the west and were turned back. The battalion's tanks then moved out to the south, reaching Betschanowskiy at 0915 hours and Petschanokopskoje around noon. The attack objective issued late in the evening for the next day was Belaja Glina.

The enemy was still able to successfully evade the grasp of the attackers, as indicated in the numbers of prisoners and spoils-of-war reported by the *LVII. Panzer-Korps*. From the start of operations south of Rostow until 31 July 1942, 9,000 prisoners were taken and 28 guns captured.[24] Let us continue with the first-hand account of the author:

> The enemy blocked the path of the attacking infantry on 1 August 1942 in strong and improved field fortifications around Nowo Stepnoy on our right flank. We were pivoted to the right and prepared to attack the enemy positions. While the artillery salvoes were still fixing the enemy, our tanks were already at the initial foxholes of the Russians. We overran the deeply echeloned position methodically and slowly. The infantry that were following us had difficulty in smoking the Russians out of their individual holes.
>
> About 30 meters to the left of me, the tank commanded by [*SS*-] *Scharführer* Hühnerfaut approached a dugout. At the moment when the tank appeared to be in its dead zone in relationship to the hole, a Russian in shirtsleeves rose up, tossed a bundled charge under the tank and disappeared. Before I was able to warn Hühnerfaut, the detonation took place, but it did not appear to cause any damage. The tank overran the hole, halting and collapsing it. I could not believe my eyes when the same Russian, unconcerned about the tanks that were following, appeared again, threw a second bundled charge but, once again, without damaging the running gear. A high-explosive round put an end to the actions of that brave man.

---

24. Author's Note: Daily logs of the *LVII. Panzer-Korps*.

> Our attack continued without hesitation and then started to approach a long hedge that ran perpendicular to our direction of attack. Suddenly, the branches and limbs started to move, as if storm winds had hit them. The hedge started to come apart and vehicles, which had been terrifically camouflaged up to that point, started racing rearward as moving bushes. They were superior to our tanks in terms of speed. The rounds of our main guns and machine guns were faster, however.
>
> For the first time, we captured vehicles of American manufacture.
>
> We aimed for the city of Belaja Glina in restless pursuit. The Krasnodar-Ssalsk was crossed. Freight trains loaded with war materiel and coupled behind steaming locomotives were left behind us. Like a column of ships, our tanks cut through the waving field of grain, turrets and main guns traversing. The lanes created became the march routes for the motorized columns following us. Individual houses, their straw-thatched roofs going up in smoke and flame, were the signs of a rapidly overpowered resistance. Around 1800 hours, Belaja Glina was taken.

The ambushes by scattered enemy groups against the fighting elements, as well as the supply troops, became an annoyance. They caused the division to clear the area around the town with its main body on 2 August and to reorganize its own forces. The lead tank elements were pushed forward as far as Nowo Pokrowskoje, some 15 kilometers south of Belaja Glina. Despite pressure from the corps, the armored group did not move out again until the morning of 3 August. The first-hand account of the author continues:

> The movement continued south through villages, grain fields and sunflower fields without a rest. At 1100 hours, the Kropotkin—Woroschilowsk rail line was crossed.
>
> Fourteen days ago we had still been assaulting Rostow. At this point, late in the afternoon of 3 August, we were at the great bend of the Kuban, some 250 kilometers south of Rostow, after a week of uninterrupted pursuit against a withdrawing enemy. Here, at the steep banks of the northern side of the Kuban, which changes its previous north-south route here to a westerly direction, the eye was presented with a transformed landscape. Without disruption from the enemy, the eye followed the river with its innumerable branches and twists, which surrounded small islands. Both banks were edged with broad, green belts of woods, which appeared to transition to an endless plain further to the south.

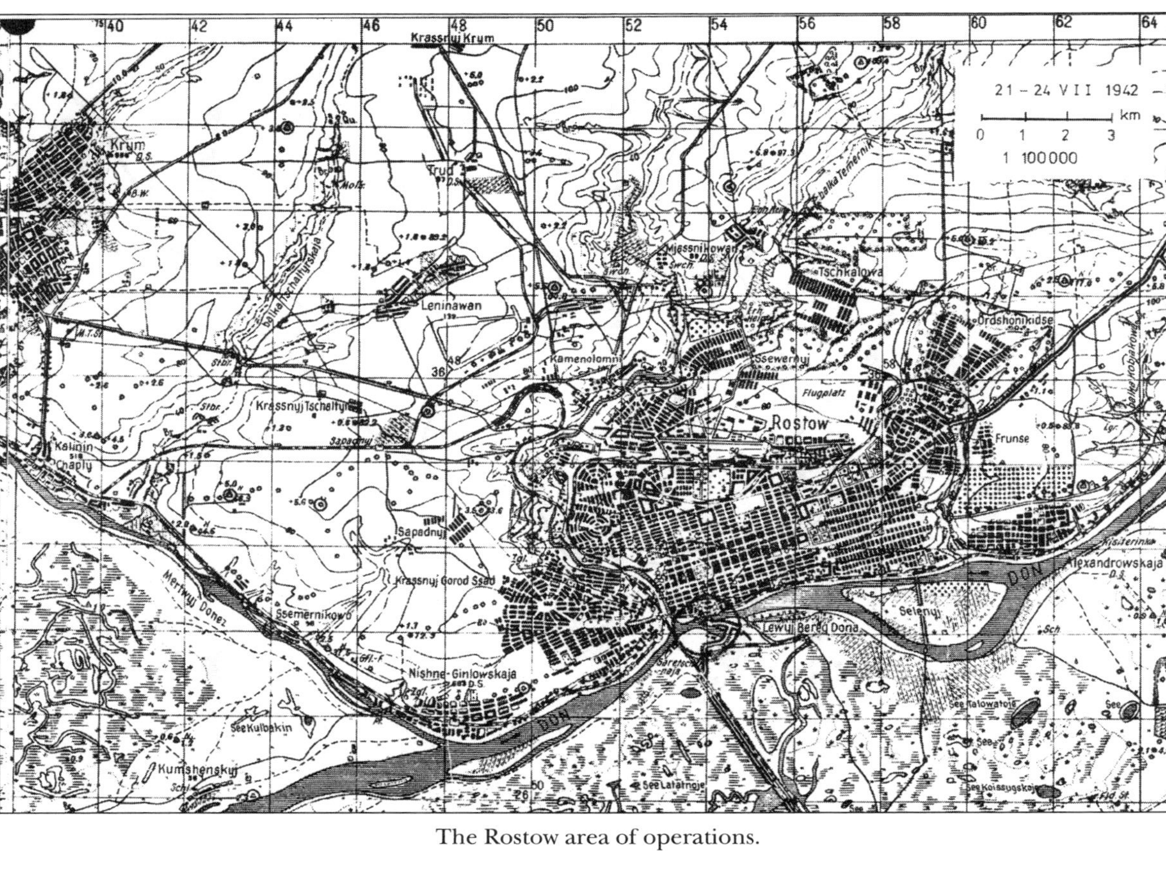

The Rostow area of operations.

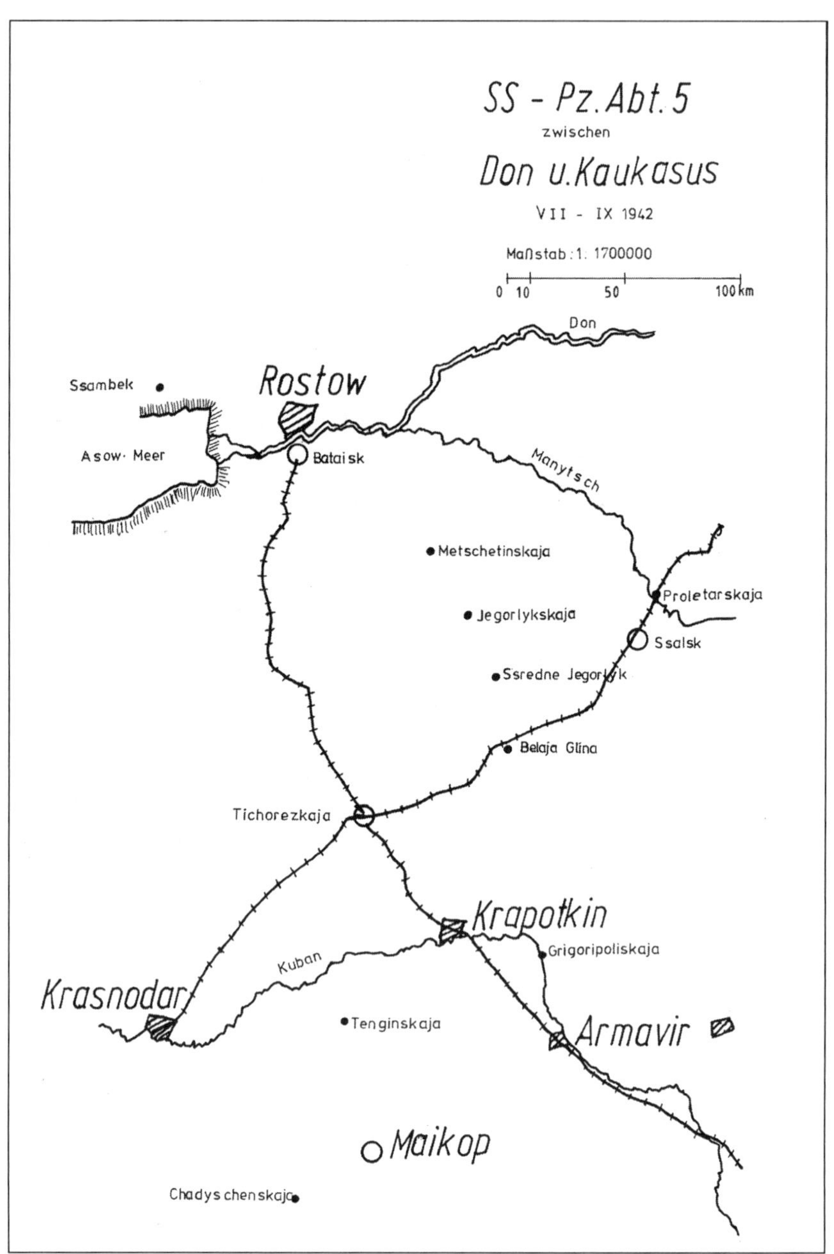

SS-Panzer-Abteilung 5 between the Don and the Caucasus.

Discussing an attack in the summer of 1942: (left to right) *SS-Hauptsturmführer* Oeck, *SS-Untersturmführer* Dedelow, *SS-Obersturmführer* Schnabel and the commander of the 1st Company.

SS-Panzer-Abteilung 5 in the attack during the summer of 1942. In the foreground is a *Panzer III* with a short 5.0-cm main gun.

22 July 1942: Prisoners are collected in the second tank ditch.

The antitank ditch is blown by prepared charges.

Combat engineers level the sides of the ditch; shovels and timber are used to fill it.

SS-Obersturmführer Klapdor's *Panzer III* with turret number *121*. In the side hatch is *SS-Unterscharführer* Brödel, Klapdor's gunner.

A *Panzer III Ausf. J* from Klapdor's platoon—*SS-Scharführer* Hühnerfaut's *124*—prepares to cross the third tank ditch. Note the divisional insignia on the right front mudguard and most of the men are wearing camouflage smocks over their field blouses, even though it is in the middle of the summer.

Tanks of the battalion enter Rostow on 23 July 1942.

An assault detachment from the *13. Panzer-Division.* This photograph is often mistakenly attributed to the fighting in Stalingrad.

Bunkers block the roads, and streets and have to be eliminated.

Destroyed bridge over the Don at Rostow.

The intact bridge over the flood plain of the Don Delta.

On 28 July 1942, the battalion's tanks rolled towards Bataisk over the engineer bridge.

THE BRIDGE OVER THE KUBAN AT KROPOTKIN

This unregulated stream, which forms a large river system with the rivers flowing towards it from the High Caucasus and interrupted the inexorable advance of the German attack spearheads for the first time, had not been crossed at any point.[25] Of the few crossing points available, none were in German hands. As a result, Kropotkin, a rail center and crossing point over the Kuban some 25 kilometers to the west of us, was the attack objective for the next day. The bridge was to be taken intact in a coup de main.

In the early-morning hours of 4 August 1942, the armored group—the *1./SS-Panzer-Abteilung 5* and the combat elements of the reconnaissance battalion, together with the grenadiers of the *"Nordland"* Regiment—rolled west. We approached Kropotkin with encountering resistance; it was unexpectedly in front of us in the early-morning hours.

The terrain sloped steeply down to the flood plain, in which the city spread itself out. We could see the train station with the naked eye; they were still shunting there. Without a doubt, the Russians were attempting to get elements of the rolling stock across the river. Our high-explosive rounds did little to disturb them. They did not reply to our fire.

But where was the bridge? We could not identify it from our positions. There wasn't a lot of time to hesitate.

The attack order from the battalion required us to move out immediately, enter the city, advance ruthlessly to the Kuban and take the bridge intact. With the 2nd Platoon of the 1st Company in the lead,[26] the tanks rolled slowly off towards the right and down a rough and graduated path into the city. There was no one to be seen either in the houses at city's edge or in the center of the city. Everything appeared to have died off . . . no obstacles . . . no resistance.

In the middle of the city, I missed the road leading to the bridge over the Kuban. While we were still trying to orient ourselves, the reconnaissance platoon of *Untersturmführer* Sepp Martin had taken over the lead. The platoons of the 1st Company then followed him in reverse order. *Sturmbannführer* Mühlenkamp, the battalion commander, had inserted himself between the two lead platoons, with the company commander, *Obersturmführer* Schnabel, in the lead. My platoon was the last one in the lead company. We left the southern

25. Translator's Note: This section consists entirely of a firsthand account by the author.

26. Translator's Note: This was Klapdor's platoon.

edge of the city behind us and, after going around a curve to the right, rolled along a raised road, sort of like an embankment, towards a bight of the river. Narrow bands of trees on both sides of the road restricted visibility. Up to this point, not a shot had been fired.

At that moment—the light *Panzer II's* must have been right next to the river—a powerful cloud from a detonation rose in front of the tank column. The bridge flew into the air and then dropped into the river.

At the same time, there was the sound of fighting. The crack of antitank rounds from antitank guns in previously hidden firing positions to the right of us and apparently on the far side of the river was mixed with the harsh bark of main guns firing up front at the approach to the bridge. Machine guns likewise started to graze the road from the right. The Russian antitank fire increased. The first two or three tanks, which halted beyond the concealment afforded by the rows of trees, were seeking cover on the left-hand side of the road. A tank just in front of the bridge halted and fired. Perhaps it was hit and immobilized. A short while later, dark smoke engulfed it; it was burning, but it continued to fire.

The neatly strung-out tanks along the road were unable to join in to the right due to the restricted visibility caused by the rows of trees. Radio communications appeared to have disintegrated. No word could be understood that was sent through the ether in this confusion. Making a snap decision, I opened my turret hatch, dismounted, jumped to the left side of the road and ran up front to the battalion commander's vehicle, protected by the vehicles on the road. The commander appeared in the carefully opened hatch and appeared enraged about the loss of the radios. He agreed to my recommendation to move the tanks to the right of the road and down into the trees so as to eliminate the enemy's antitank defenses by all available firepower and using the better visibility afforded there. The tanks directed by me deployed along the edge of the curtain of trees and let loose with such a volume of fire against the far bank that the Russian antitank and machine gun nests fell silent after a short period.

When "Old Fritz," the commander of the *"Nordland"* Regiment, *Oberführer* von Scholz, appeared a short while later, the sound of fighting had subsided substantially. He was happy how the ambush situation had been mastered quickly and vividly recalled the motorcycle company of his regiment the previous year, which I had led until I had been wounded. In the meantime, a few Russian deserters had shown up who had swum across the river.

Our mission had only been half accomplished. But even without an intact bridge over the Kuban, the rapid move and the taking of the city of Kropotkin was a success. It made the way easier into the Kuban for the following formations of the *17. Armee.*

After the commander of the 1st Company rejoined the mass of tanks with the vehicles that had pulled back to the left side of the road, we left Kropotkin that afternoon using the same route we had taken in. We admired the preparatory work of the *Luftwaffe* around the destroyed train station area. The enemy had had to leave behind freight trains loaded with trucks and artillery pieces.

TENGINSKAJA

The 1st Company then set up camp a few kilometers from the place where it had reached the Kuban the previous day. Two days of rest had been directed.

The main body of the tank company, which had been joined in the meantime by the 3rd Company, which had been rushed to the front with its long-barreled *Panzer IV's,* had advanced farther to the south on the east bank of the Kuban on 3 August, along with the reinforced *"Germania"* Regiment. After about 25 kilometers, it had rapidly reached and taken the locality of Grigoripoliskaja. There was no bridge over the Kuban there, either. In a determined move, Dorr's company of motorized infantry crossed the river in rubber rafts, covered by the artillery and tanks. Against the stubborn resistance of the Soviets, the initially small bridgehead was expanded and held.

An 8-ton pontoon bridge was brought forward and released for traffic at 0500 hours on 6 August. It turned out to be too weak and was thereupon reinforced to a 16-ton capacity during the afternoon by the corps engineer battalion.[27] The author:

> While a pontoon bridge was being brought up to Grigoripoliskaja, we were happy to be able to recover a bit. Our thoughts turned to Germany, a few thousand kilometers to the west.
>
> We heard unsettling news on the radio. Bombing raids on Hamburg and other residential areas had been conducted by the English. Ever since the start of the attack on Rostow on 22 July, we had not received any mail from the homeland.
>
> The sun made the quicksilver rise to sub-tropical temperatures here on the plains of the Kuban; during the evenings and at nighttime,

27. Author's Note: Daily logs of the *LVII. Panzer-Korps.*

however, it seemed cool to us. After the days of rest—necessary even for the maintenance personnel—*SS-Panzer-Abteilung 5* crossed the Kuban on the pontoon bridge at Grigoripoliskaja during the early-morning hours of 7 August 1942. It moved out from the bridgehead, which had already been expanded, and headed northwest to continue the pursuit of the enemy. Otrado Kubanskaja was taken around 0730 hours; the Kropotkin-Armavir rail line was crossed. We captured freight trains that were still under a head of steam. During the evening, we were 12 kilometers southeast of Tifliskaja. There were no longer any enemy forces in the great bend of the Kuban.

At first light on 8 August, the battalion resumed its pursuit to the southwest. The performance of our tanks was quite good measured against the demands placed on them the last few weeks. Mechanical issues had barely surfaced thanks to the exemplary operations of the maintenance sections up front with the companies on the battlefield and the quick completion of more major repairs by the battalion's maintenance platoon, which was superbly outfitted with personnel and equipment, under the leadership of *Obersturmführer* Sobota. In the case of smaller mechanical repairs, such as swapping out track links and torsion bars, the tank crews were trained to do it themselves.

The frontal armor on the tanks, which was no longer able to stop the larger calibers of the enemy's antitank guns and tank cannon and which was considerably less than the armor on the new Russian tanks like the T-34, was reinforced in the field by placing spare track on the front slope of the tank. The thin side armor of the *Panzer III's* represented its weakest point. It forced us to lead the tanks in such a manner that only the front of the vehicle was offered to the enemy whenever possible. That demand was especially imperative whenever a firing halt was called. The penetrating ability of our 5-centimeter main gun allowed maximum ranges of about 500 meters. In contrast, the Russian T-34, with its side armor that was nearly twice as thick, was dangerous to the *Panzer III* at 1,500 to 2,000 meters with its 7.62-centimeter main gun.

Our fighting vehicles rolled across the slightly rolling open terrain that favored armored vehicles in an inverted wedge. The interval between the group of tanks and the grenadiers that were following became ever greater. We could not prevent enemy groups from collecting behind us, moving in close order and attempting to regain contact with their main forces to the south. The situation to our rear became increasingly murky.

That morning, around 1000 hours, a cloud of dust and dirt—actually, more like a wall of dust and dirt—running perpendicular the direction of march became visible. About 15 minutes later, we identified the source. The Laba, a tributary of the Kuban, had to be several hundred meters in front of us. On the near bank, the north bank, there was an endless herd of cattle moving from north to south. It seemed the Russians were attempting to follow the exhortation to leave behind scorched earth for the enemy and to take all of their cattle to safety. He did not count on the rapidity of our advance. That herd of cattle would never cross the Laba.

While the animals were slowly trotting along to the south in front of us, the rapidly growing sounds of fighting suddenly piped up off to our right wing, sounds that immediately garnered our complete attention. Off to the right oblique, about half way to a built-up area about 400 meters away, one of our tanks was burning.

In the minutes that followed, while we were still somewhat uncertain, we were briefed: The locality to the right of us was Tenginskaja, which had a crossing over the Laba. While the tanks of the reconnaissance platoon that were off to the right of our attack wedge approached the cattle, the herd parted suddenly and a Russian antitank gun, which had heretofore been concealed by the cattle and the dust cloud, opened fire at pointblank range and knocked out two of their number. *Untersturmführer* Martin was badly wounded. The Russian antitank gun was then eliminated.

There was no doubt that Tenginskaja was occupied by the enemy. They were intending to prevent our crossing of the Laba by means of an antitank-gun belt.

In between our present location and the locality was a flat depression that parallelled the outskirts of the village, which was ringed by trees. The intermediate terrain was without cover and allowed good opportunities for well-dug-in and camouflaged antitank guns to engage our tanks.

Behind us, there was also a similarly flat depression that allowed a somewhat covered approach to the edge of the village; as a result, it determined our plan of attack: An immediate attack without waiting for the uncertain arrival of the mechanized infantry.

The turrets of our tanks were directed with attention towards the edge of the village. I reached the position with my platoon, where we had to exit the protective concealment of the depression and approach the edge of the village across the open and completely observable terrain. The direction of attack was the end of the row of trees at the outskirts, where I could make out a Russian antitank gun. It was eliminated in a short firing halt. Firing with all of our machine guns while on the move, we approached the outskirts without taking any losses.

My tank was positioned in front of the abandoned Russian antitank gun and was in the process of starting to overrun it to make it unserviceable. At that moment, there was a hard blow to the front slope of the tank. Before I could grasp that it had been a Russian antitank round that had ricocheted, our small fighting compartment was filled with the racket of an ear-deafening detonation, accompanied by a garish flash. Direct hit! Off to the right . . . no more than 50 meters away . . . around a few wooden outbuildings . . . Russians! In desperation, I attempted to have my gunner, *Unterscharführer* Brödel, traverse the turret so as to fire. Since not a word was understood—apparently, our intercom system was no longer functioning—I yanked on his right shoulder to indicate he should traverse the turret farther right. The turret did not stir. A fraction of a minute after the first hit, there was a flash right in front of me on the gun mantlet. A shot of flame . . . a terrible crack! I was able to move all of my limbs, however. But this time, the flash did not go out; it was burning inside our fighting compartment.

"Bail out . . . get out!" I opened the hatch on the commander's cupola and attempted to get out and behind the turret as quickly as possible as cover against the machine-gun fire that had started up. Despite the fact that my right arm was stiffened at a right angle as the result of a shattered joint the previous winter, I got out of the narrow, man-wide hatch quickly, only to suddenly get caught up. The cables from my headphones and throat mike were wrapped around my head and neck; in my excitement, I had forgotten to remove them.

I was able to free myself with a desperate jerk. I jumped behind the tank and was under cover there for the time being.

A few meters off to the right was a small depression in the ground, right next to the end of the row of trees. The gunner and loader, who had jumped down next to me in the meantime, raced behind me. At least we had some cover to the front in that position. Our pistols were the only weapons we had. Our radio operator had also hopped over to our hole in the meantime. Only Jupp, our driver, was still missing. Since I could find no trace of him, I ran back behind the smoking tank and discovered him unconscious underneath it.

I carefully attempted to pull him back some. The heavy burns over the entire upper part of his body made that appear an impossible undertaking, however. His only sign of life was a deep moaning. At that point, a machine-gun bullet penetrated his upper arm as well. How did he manage to get out of the tank in that condition? The engine had been turned off, as the regulations prescribed, and the key had been pulled out, as we later discovered.

In the meantime, it appeared the *Untersturmführer* Hübner must have penetrated farther into the village; the sound of the fighting was growing distant. Tanks from the company that had been following us rolled by. While the maintenance contact team was already looking after our tank—the fire had been put out and it was being towed away—we succeeded in loading our badly wounded Jupp on a vehicle as carefully as possible and moving him across the bumpy terrain to the clearing station.

Untersturmführer Martin had already been lying there for about an hour after his vehicle had been knocked out and he had been badly wounded by a round lodged in the lungs.

The surgeon had his hands full. Among others, a man came in for treatment who had shrapnel in his skin under the chin. He was as white as chalk. The shrapnel was removed, a dressing applied and he was released. The same piece of shrapnel could have literally cost him his head.

In the meantime, my head and right arm were wrapped in white dressings as a result of the bad burns. The battalion commander had me report to him and agreed with my request not to be sent to the rear. Instead, I was to move with the trains. In a few days, my tank would be ready again.

By then, in the searing midday heat, the Russian antitank-gun belt had been broken open, Tenginskaja taken, the forced crossing of the Laba achieved and the majority of the battalion on the south bank of the river by the late afternoon. The rest of the day was devoted to maintaining weapons and equipment, as well as preparing for a continuation of the attack to the southwest the following morning.

Confidence in victory and a feeling of superiority enables forces to perform unusually well; they reinforce combat power to a barely imaginable degree and are in a position of being able to replace missing materiel. In short, both are of incalculable value. During that time, we cut completely through Russian columns streaming from north to south in a series of bold attacks. We left them behind us, without worrying about what they would do next. The old maxim—

> "The enemy in front of us and friendly forces to our rear"—did not apply any more. We were starting to gradually swim along with those streams of Russian columns, with only our objective in our eyes: the Western Caucasus, the oil region of Muck and Tuapse on the Black Sea.

On that same 8 August, the battle groups of the *"Nordland"* and *"Germania"* Regiments, attacking south, reached crossing points over the Laba at Tamirgojewskaja and Petropawlowskaja, supported by the 2nd and 3rd Tank Companies. The formation of small bridgeheads was achieved by means of bold night attacks. Despite that, the enemy's demolition of the bridge at Tamirgojewskaja could not be prevented.

> During the night of 8–9 August 1942, the construction of a provisional bridge at Tamirgojewskaja by *SS-Division Wiking* was abandoned, since the few available engineer forces and equipment were insufficient. Most of the *SS-Pionier-Bataillon* was still in the reconstitution area . . .

✠

> *SS-Division Wiking* closed up to the village and bridgehead of Tenginskaja in order to move out again on 10 August 1942. The completion of the 16-ton bridge by the corps engineer battalion is not anticipated before the onset of darkness. [28]

On the morning of 10 August, the tank companies and the battle groups of the division moved out to continue the pursuit of the enemy. Tanks of the 3rd Company reached Maikop at 1400 hours as part of an advance guard. Once there, the advance guard established contact with the *III. Panzer-Korps.*[29]

Most of the tank battalion crossed the Belaja north of Beloretschenskaja. The city proper was taken at 1600 hours. The author continues:

> On 10 August, attempts to resist by a Russian Guards Cavalry Corps were thwarted, and the Belaja, a tributary of the Kuban, was crossed. In the distance, the plains came to an end; the high ground of the Western Caucasus marked the horizon. The enemy's resistance grew and intensified. The Russian artillery was no longer firing indiscriminately. Their fire missions on our lines of communication

---

28. Author's Note: Both quotes are from the daily logs of the *LVII. Panzer-Korps.*

29. Author's Note: Daily logs of the *LVII. Panzer-Korps.*

and the groupings of vehicles forced the rear-area services and the trains, where I was, to hop around the area in quite the lively fashion and change positions.

On 11 August, elements of our trains vehicles were needed for the planned operations of the *7./Lehr-Regiment Brandenburg* on the bridge over the Pschecha at Pschechskaja. The next day, the Brandenburgers raced through the Russian columns in their brown Russian gear. They caused the columns to give up any notion of resistance, and they sowed confusion and panic. At the bridge in Pschechskaja, they got rid of their Russian uniform pieces and fought in their German uniforms. A short while later, they were relieved by the grenadiers of the *"Nordland"* Regiment, who were attacking their way forward to them. The important crossing point at Pschechskaja remained intact and available for our supply columns.

While changing my dressings, the battalion physician, Dr. Standl, recommended I go to a hospital in the rear—he literally tore away the skin from my head and my arm—so as to avoid infections and disfiguring scars.

That afternoon, I rode back to the main clearing station at Tenginskaja in the staff car of the [battalion] maintenance officer, *Obersturmführer* Sobota. Although we arrived there without any contact, the head of the clearing station received us in front of his quarters, agitated and beseechingly. It just then occurred to us that there were hardly any medical personnel to be seen. According to the doctor, the Russians moved through the village the previous night in closed columns. For reasons unknown, the presence of the main clearing station remained unknown to them. It was not hard to imagine what would have been the fate of the wounded there [had they been discovered]. That day, the Russians were showing signs of wanting to attack the village. Any and everyone who could carry a rifle was at the edge of the village defending.

"You're a line officer, after all," he said, turning to me. "Help me!"

Operating on the principle that the greater the distance from the village, the less chance the enemy had for his weapons to be effective, I assembled all of the stretcher bearers and whipped up an infantry attack into the flank of the enemy, whose limits on the wings could be identified. The attack brought some relief to the brave medics in the village.

Far out in the surrounding area, we went to ground and waited on our side for the enemy. I was amazed that the enemy's rifle fire was landing very close to me despite all of the changes of position. Finally, I realized that my head, wrapped in radiant white dressing and visible from afar, offered a terrific target.

Although the Russians did not attack over the next two hours, they still remained a threat that had to be eliminated before nightfall. There was contact with the tank battalion, and a few tanks were able to drive those unpleasant neighbors away from the main clearing station.

On 12 August, an aircraft that landed and took off in the open fields transported me and other wounded to Armavir. A *Ju 52* took us on board there and by that evening we were in a well-maintained hospital in Taganrog on the Asovian Sea. There were nurses from the Red Cross. The atmosphere in that hospital in the rear area can be summed up in a few sentences. I was taken to a room that was ultimately occupied by 15 men of differing ranks and arms. To elevate the physical well-being of all of the patients—regardless of rank—the sparkling wine reserves of the hospital administration were distributed freely. The attitude of the nurses was a blessing. They were on the go from early in the morning until late at night; they were always in a good mood and had a cheerful word for everyone. A radio in the room put an end to our being cut off from the outside world. The offer of the chaplain to make use of his personal library was accepted with gratitude.

The conversations centered around experiences at the front, opinions on the outlook for success and the discussion of philosophical issues. Of great importance for each individual was the question regarding his own fate: return to a formation at the front or transfer to a hospital in the homeland and return to Germany. The attitude of a *Rottenführer* of our battalion, who was also here with head wounds, but of a more serious nature, was both impressive and unique. He loudly requested that he be allowed to stay and that he be returned to his comrades as soon as his condition allowed it. A young *Leutnant* with a round through the hand represented the opposite. His wound was healing so well that he complained when the hospital train was delayed, since no one in the homeland would believe he had sustained a wound if he only had a band-aid on his hand.

In a transition hospital, such as ours, you could see how happy each man was when he was transported back to Germany. Weeks, even months of longing were about to be fulfilled. Most of them could care less how they got back, as long as it was Germany. Many of them would be back one day to travel the same path. Some of them [voluntarily] stayed behind and were sent back to their formations, barely healed, in order to fill gaps in the line that had developed. What might have motivated them to go back? For one, it might have been inner unrest; he was looking for new experiences. An ill-defined thirst for action, even ambition might have led him to always search out danger, something whose dimensions were no longer unfamiliar to him. Others remained behind and went back because they had to. An inner obligation to their dead and living comrades forced them back to their old stations.

On 17 August, another hospital train departed for Germany. The healing process for my wounds made such good and rapid progress that I could be released back to my unit in the Caucasus on 21 August. We flew out into the dawning day at 0500 hours. Below us was the sea. Far to the east, the sun was climbing out of the broad flood plains of the Don. We flew over villages, where people were once again undergoing their daily lives. Just a few weeks ago, our tank wedges had moved through the area that now appeared so peaceful.

A staff car took me from Maikop to a completely transformed landscape. There were woods on both sides of the road, whose ends were not in sight. Instead of the dusty plains, there was countryside that reminded me of the highlands back home. At the outskirts of Maikop, the German sense of organization was present in a sign that could not be missed on the roadside: "You are heading into the mountains . . . are your brakes in order?"

Driving half an hour farther west, engineers were sawing and cutting paths through the edges of the thick woods. Signals personnel were laying telephone wire. The staff car moved more slowly up the ever-steepening road once it was across a wooden bridge that spanned one of the mountain creeks that flowed into the Belaja. From there, we could enjoy magnificent views.

Towards evening, I arrived back at the location of the 1st Company of *SS-Panzer-Abteilung 5* in Karabolinskaja.

THE WESTERN CAUCASUS

The author continues:

The overall situation for the *"Wiking"* Division had changed decisively in the days I had been gone. Although it had advanced into the mountain valleys and the remote mountain villages of the Western Caucasus after the headlong advance through the plains of the Kuban . . . although it had crossed the Maikop-Tuapse road to the south . . .

the entryway to Tuapse was blocked by the heights of the Western Caucasus—1,000 meters and higher—uncharted valleys and roaring creeks. Completely changed fighting conditions; unsuitable for tanks and motorized formations.

The 3rd Battalion of *"Nordland"* and the 2nd Battalion of *"Westland"* had been brought forward from their reconstitution areas, but the division was still bogged down.

The attack could still be launched with prospects of success by suitably equipped formations. But the *XXXXIV. Armee-Korps* was still days away by foot.[30] As a result, the enemy gained decisive days needed for intensifying his defensive efforts and for bringing up reserves.

The delaying tactics Marshall Timoschenko had ordered at the beginning of July—avoiding encirclement and not defending every foot of ground without considering the casualties—had been replaced by the demands of Stalin to stop all rearward movements. His new orders: There was only victory or death.

On 23 August 1942, we were given a demonstration of the new state of affairs in the position that we had reached that was the farthest to the west. In Chadyschenskaja, embedded in the pocket of a valley, we failed in the effort to advance farther. The detonations of the Russian shells echoed threateningly from the dark, steep slopes. There were only 60 kilometers separating us from Tuapse and from the coast of the Black Sea.

While our fantasies still played with visions of operations as far as the Turkish border—it was still not considered impossible to repeat the threat to the English Mediterranean position *a la Korps "Yilderim"* in World War I[31]—we heard about the visit of the English Prime Minister, Churchill, in Moscow while we were located in this farthest corner of the theater of war in the southern Russia. At the opposite end of the European Front, along the coastline of northern France, we heard about the destruction of the English infantry forces

30. Translator's Note: The author had identified this as the *XXXXIV. Jäger-Korps*, but there was no such type of corps in the German army. The formation in question is undoubtedly the *XXXXIV. Armee-Korps*, which was committed in the Caucasus during this time frame and had four divisions allocated to it at the time (two regular infantry divisions and two light infantry divisions).

31. Translator's Note: A reference to the obscure German operations in the Middle East in support of the Ottoman Empire in World War I, which were intended to cause the collapse the British colonial empire in that region. The support was not insignificant and it was not without effect, but the entire effort has been relegated to the footnotes of history.

at Dieppe.[32] The continuing attack between the Don and the Volga in the direction of Stalingrad was watched and discussed with growing tension.

At 1500 hours on 24 August, *SS-Panzer-Abteilung 5* left Karabolinskaja. The tanks reached Apscherowskaja, about 20 kilometers in the direction of Maikop, towards evening. There, in that mountain village along the Pschecha, a tributary of the Belaja, we set up for a longer stay. The tanks and vehicles received provisional bays constructed out of four posts, two cross beams and a roof consisting of boards, tin and hay. The richness of the Western Caucasus is manifest in its wood. The societal framework was informed by sawmills and industries devoted to processing wood and processing plants for the oil deposits. In contrast to the purely agrarian populace of the Kuban, we became familiar with industrial workers, specialists and technicians. Their mistrust and reserve were pronounced. Despite that, conversations were occasionally held with an amazing openness. The Soviet system had opened opportunities for social advancement; one trusted the strength of his own people, who could only find their own way for things and who did not need the advice and support of capitalistic countries. We were openly requested to return to Germany.

Among the few exceptions that we encountered whereby we were treated sympathetically was from a former Czarist officer, who had come to this region as a result of the chaos of the revolution and whose daughter, Tamara, was friendly to us when we were quartered in her place.

The predominately unfriendly attitude of the populace, which apparently was maintaining contact with the Russian forces, forced us to be unusually attentive and corresponding security measures. I slept with a submachine gun in my arms. There were nightly incidents of wild firing and the tossing of hand grenades.

Sunday, 30 August 1942, had something special arranged for taking care of the troops. A trip to Maikop was scheduled at 1115 hours for attending the movies. After a newsreel, which showed our own

---

32. Translator's Note: Actually, the English losses were relatively minor compared to those to the Canadian forces, which amounted to more than 50 percent of their assault forces being killed, wounded or captured (in excess of 3,000 men).

attack on Rostow six weeks ago, the movie *Wiener Blut*[33] was shown. It was in Maikop that we heard about a plan to poison bread intended for German forces. It was discovered in time and was therefore thwarted.

In addition to cultural matters during those quiet weeks, there were also official duties and actions. Öhler, Grunert, Dörre and Bahlinger—all in the rank of *Rottenführer*—were promoted to *Scharführer* on 1 September. In addition, Öhler also received the Iron Cross, Second Class.

✠

On 3 September, the achievements of the battalion received recognition and praise in the form of the award of the Knight's Cross to the battalion commander, *Sturmbannführer* Mühlenkamp. It was a welcome and justified reason for celebrating.

The nature of things in the Caucasus, the way of perceiving and thinking of things by the men who were fighting, the nature of the relationship of the "Germanic Volunteers" in the division to the mission they imposed upon themselves, cannot be illuminated any more clearly than by the following firsthand account by the Dutch volunteer, J. Hepp, whose comrades were fighting in all elements of the division:[34]

Muk, August 1942. The rapid advance through the Kuban was behind us; the front in the Caucasus was developing. Those of us in *"Germania"* were held up for a few days in the village of Muk. The Bolsheviks had set up defenses in the hilly terrain around the locality and sent us his greetings in the form of artillery shells from time to time. They also attempted to enter Muk a couple of times, but they had to pull back after a few skirmishes. At the time, I experienced something that affected me deeply not only because of what happened but also because of its symptomatic meaning. It strengthened my belief in the correctness of this struggle, in which I was participating as a Germanic volunteer. Right in the middle of the

33. Translator's Note: *Viennese Blood.* No references to the film can be found. It was apparently based on the operetta of the same name, which, in turn, was based on the waltz by Johann Strauß.

34. Author's Note: Taken from *Wiking Ruf,* Number 19, May 1953 (Hannover). Translator's Note: The *Viking Call* was the periodical produced by the division's veterans association. As is typical in many German accounts, no first name is given, only an initial.

noise of the physical violence, that sublime reality came to us all at once, both demanding and comforting, which is the actual meaning of our existence for all time.

Our antitank platoon (in the 4th Company) had found quarters in a one-story building (apparently an administrative or party building) . . . the vehicles and guns remained in the garden, well camouflaged against aerial attack. The artillery harassing fires of the Russians, which repeated themselves at regular intervals, had resulted in the windows of the rooms we had occupied having practically no more panes after the second day. In the evening, we set about closing off our living and sleeping spaces with panes that had remained intact from unoccupied rooms. Satisfied with our efforts, we looked for our sleeping places on the floor in the dark. We had barely laid down, when the Stalin organ[35] played its pretty fugue and all of our windowpanes were gone.

The next morning, just as we were just about to head out to find some panes that had miraculously survived somewhere or cardboard (our gun commander, who hailed from the Lüneburg heath, was defiantly stubborn and wasn't about to take no for an answer), when orders arrived: Form up in two hours with everything spit and polish!

Our assault packs, which had been stored for many weeks in the backpacks on the vehicle, were retrieved. While we commenced cleaning and polishing, there was a lot of speculation. Soon, however, the rumor came around: The regimental band had shown up and was giving a concert.

That was a strange, uplifting, yes, even somewhat surreal feeling, when the units all marched up from every nook and cranny of the small, primitive village as if in peacetime (fortunately, the Russian artillery had been silent for a few hours). For weeks on end, they had known nothing but combat, dust, hardship. I was in a celebratory mood as I marched along down to the bottomland of the river below the village where the "concert" was supposed to be held next to the brickworks.

Like emissaries from a better world, our comrades from the regimental band stood there with their instruments in front of the low outbuildings of the brickworks . . . musicians in field gray. I believe they were in a celebratory mood as well, fully aware of their program,

35. Translator's Note: Generic name given by the German soldier for the rocket launchers employed by the Soviets that were mounted on the back of trucks. The German equivalent was the *Nebelwerfer.*

when they saw how both the young and old soldiers, a few hundred, from differing European countries, crowded around on boards and crates and shelves of the brickworks as they placed their instruments to their mouths to play the first note.

Then Beethoven's "Egmont Overture" sounded under the sunny Caucasian skies, in the green flatland of a Caucasian mountain river; it lifted our souls skyward. That was followed by the prelude to the first act of Wagner's *Lohengrin* and other works of our European classics.

As if in deep worship at a religious service, we listened intently . . . we drank in the sounds. The bitterness of the fighting gave way more and more on the tanned faces. Our souls breathed in a sphere far removed from violence and animosity. A shot-down *Rata,*[36] a few hundred meters away, was the only thing that reminded us of the war.

A huge happiness and thankfulness swelled up in me . . . that there could be such a thing as this in the humanity that was fighting so hard . . . that something that was just as necessary as supplies and rations . . . that the nourishment of our souls could be done . . . and that these men, who had been so tuned into war and fighting, still had such a hunger for the power and value of a more tender world.

I thought to myself: How characteristic for the humanity and culture we were defending that it was not some fiery dance music, some libidinally charged dance hall tune that was brought to the men at the fighting front. Instead, it was the most sublime and challenging music that the occidental masters had created.

One does not need to worry about the soul of a community that shows such an attitude. It will survive all brutalization, all weeding over, all desecration. That was clear and comforting to me. After a short break, during which a couple of Russian aircraft circled above the plain but soon disappeared, the second part of the concert started. Lighter music was on the program at that point: Strauß, von Suppé, Mascagni and others. Our hearts were swaying to the rhythm of the "Beautiful Blue Danube" when there was a howling above us and a Russian shell impacted in our vicinity. Without skipping a beat, the musicians continued playing. We weren't about to allow a stupid Russian shell to take away our beautiful, regenerative hour! But the second one soon followed . . . and then a third. It was clear that the enemy artillery had gotten wind of our concert (from the aircraft).

36. Translator's Note: The *Rata* was an obsolete fighter aircraft that was nevertheless used by the Soviets until around the middle of the war.

> But there was no panic, no hurry to get cover. The piece was played masterfully to the end and then stopped. It was only reluctantly that we followed orders to break up. It was difficult to suddenly return to the world of war.
>
> Little was spoken as the units marched along the village paths to their quarters: Germans, Dutch, Flemish, Danes. They felt rejuvenated, enriched. And for some, it was clearer than ever before what objective these operations had.
>
> No concert has ever moved me as much as that "concert" at the front.

The author continues:

> After the weather had been uninterruptedly hot and dry following our departure from Amwrosiewka, it suddenly rained for a few days. Initially, that was a blessing, but its consequences were a thriving of flies, wasps and mosquitoes, which had to be eliminated on a daily basis.
>
> On 9 September, the 1st Platoon of the 1st Company was alerted and attached to the [divisional reconnaissance battalion] to clear up an ambush. The situation was rectified, however, without the tanks becoming involved.
>
> On 10 September, *Unterscharführer* Löblein, an experienced tank commander, returned to the unit even though his wound to the upper thigh had not healed.

In the meantime, the *97. Jäger-Division* and the *101. Jäger-Division* had closed in sector, relieved the forward elements of the division and started preparing for the continuation of the attack in the direction of Tuapse. In the middle of August, the *III. Panzer-Korps* had been withdrawn from the front around Maikop in order to attack south from the area east of Woroschilowsk towards the Terek.

At 0950 hours on 15 September, the division received a telegraphic message from the *LVII. Panzer-Korps*: Instead of the Slovenian Fast Division, *SS-Division Wiking* is to be pulled out of the line expeditiously and moved to the sector of the *1. Panzer-Armee.*

Under paragraph 4, the following could be read:

SS-Division Wiking initiates movement with the tank battalion and other available elements this same 15 September (oral orders). March route of the division: Maikop—Labinskaja—Armavir—Georgiewsk.[37]

The author continues:

We were ordered to be prepared to march at 1800 hours on 15 September 1942. During the early-morning hours of 16 September, the tanks marched in the direction of Maikop and reached Armavir that evening. The initial march objective was then to be Soldatskaja and Karagatsch by means of train.

There we encountered a completely new type of person in that gigantic country: mountain people, whose desire for freedom could not be broken, even by the Bolshevists, as could plainly be seen. They followed Islam.

Stringent orders were issued that consideration was to be taken of the mentality and feelings of those mountain peoples. There were allowed to retain their weapons. The men proudly carried a dagger on their belts. We were not allowed to enter the houses.

That meant that we bivouacked in the open or in our tents in the available courtyards of the fenced-in farmsteads. The tanks were camouflaged. My tank was parked on the front side of a house that was lived in by a man, four women and a child.

The women followed our activities with interest, but they remained reserved on the outside. In the morning, they sat in front of the house, took a sip of water out of a metal pitcher and then wet their hands and moistened their faces. Those had to have been symbolic gestures.

Late one morning, the man of the house entered through the courtyard gate, a slaughtered chicken in his right hand. He walked a few steps towards the sitting women and tossed them the chicken without saying a word. It was plucked energetically by all of them.

In general, the attitude of the locals towards us was friendly. In some instances, the men formed elements that voluntarily took up the fight on our side.

In the vicinity of the village, I discovered a neglected cemetery, whose unusual markers stood out: narrow slabs of stone, almost as

37. Author's Note: Daily logs of the *LVII. Panzer-Korps.*

tall as a man. They had Arabic-Turkish inscriptions in six rectangles arrayed over one another.

The events of the war, for which there was no shortage of unusual occurrences, provided a surprise there in Soldatskaja that demonstrated the limits to the effectiveness of orders on the one hand and the strength of human feelings to overcome barriers on the other.

One night, just before 0200 hours, I was checking the guards. The guard who was to be relieved was waiting in vain for the driver of my tank, who was the designated relief. After slowly becoming upset and not accustomed to a lack of punctuality of that type, I started to look for my driver, along with *Untersturmführer* Hübner, who had been awakened in the meantime. He was neither with his comrades nor in the tank, where you could also sleep. While looking in the tank, I noticed that the window in the front side of the house, about the height of the right-side turret hatch and right across from it, was open. A suspicion welling up in me was being suppressed at the same time by thoughts of the strict orders and the sensitivities of the locals. Simply entering the house was out of the question. We suspected a trick. Without a sound, we approached the opened window again. By chance, the beam from my flashlight entered it. For a fraction of a second, a head with tangled hair was visible. Everything remained quiet. Minutes passed. While we were still considering what to do and waited, we suddenly heard a noise on the opposite side of the house, something akin to someone jumping from a great height onto soft grass. That could only have been our missing man. After a few minutes, he then marched through the courtyard gate without demonstrating the slightest sign of wanting to say anything, such as the reason for his belated guard relief. After assuring him that the incident would remain among us, he explained the events.

The scene the next morning was quite moving. While we were getting ready to move out, the small, black-haired hostess handed my driver foodstuffs of all sorts through the opened window . . . foodstuffs that were very valuable to her.

An exercise is discussed at the Camp Senne Training Area in May 1942.

July 1942, Amwrosiewka: The 2nd and 3rd Platoons of the battalion's 1st Company prepare to be inspected by the division commander.

The village street in Amwrosiewka.

A frontline stage show at the "Viking Home" promises ninety minutes of entertainment.

28 July 1942, Bataisk: Prisoners head north while the tanks of the battalion continue south.

The friendly forces to the left, the *13. Panzer-Division,* cross the dividing point between Asia and Europe, the Manyisch Reservoir.

The battalion's tanks attacked between the Don and the Kuban in July and August of 1942, hitting the constantly withdrawing enemy and breaking all resistance. Blow: Late-model *Panzer IIIs* with the 5.0-cm L/60 main gun, effective against the T-34 at relatively short ranges.

Between the Don and the Kuban. The bottom image shows a *Marder II* (7.5-cm *Pak 40* on a *Panzer II* chassis) that was assigned to the division's antitank battalion.

4 August 1942, Kropotkin: A view from the demolished bridge over the Kuban.

The tank of *SS-Untersturmführer* Martin burns in front of the approaches to the bridge. In the foreground is the battalion commander's tank.

8 August 1942, evening in Tenginskaja: The officers of the 1st Company meet. From left to right: *SS-Obersturmführer* Schnabel, *SS-Obersturmführer* Klapdor (bandaged), *SS-Untersturmführer* Kolodzi, *SS-Oberjunker* (officer candidate) Pinnow and *SS-Untersturmführer* Hübner.

12 August 1942, along the Belaja. From left to right: Unidentified driver, *SS-Obersturmführer* Sobota, *SS-Untersturmführer* Niemann, *SS-Untersturmführer* Dedelow (in the tank hatch of the *Panzer IV*) and *SS-Obersturmführer* Klapdor (head dressing).

A *Panzer III* of the 1st Company fords a stream. Other tanks await their turn.

10 August 1942: Fording the Belaja at Beloretschenskaja. In the foreground above is a *Panzer II*, at this stage of the war used primarily for reconnaissance.

6 September 1942, Apscheronskaja: The battalion commander, *SS-Sturmbannführer* Mühlenkamp, poses with officers of the battalion after his award of the Knight's Cross to the Iron Cross. The officer in the field gray to the far right in the photograph is the *Luftwaffe* ground liaison officer.

SSAGOPSCHIN—MALGOBEK

The companies of the tank battalion were brought forward from Soldatskaja through Prochladnyj as far as the Terek, approximately 60 kilometers, on 24 September. They crossed the river and bivouacked in some tree-covered terrain on the south bank.

The main body of the division was also pushed forward on 24 September to the area around Srestowskiy-Gokinajeff-Saizoff on the north bank of the Terek. Heretofore, the *"Westland"* Regiment had been in the area northwest of Pjatigorsk, *SS-Pionier-Bataillon 5* and *SS-Panzer-Aufklärungs-Abteilung 5* in the Sspwjetskaja in the Deisoff-Krassnyj area and the *"Nordland"* Regiment in the Ssowjetsskiy area, some 30 kilometers north of Prochladnyj. While elements of the *"Westland"* Regiment's 3rd Battalion had already relieved elements of *Infanterie-Regiment 66* of the *370. Infanterie-Division* in the Terek bridgehead during the night of 23–24 September, the main body of the division crossed the river over the bridge at Chamidija, west of Gnadenburg,[38] to the south during the night of 24–25 September and the following day. The bridgehead had been taken by formations of the *LII. Armee-Korps* on 3 September. The bridgehead had been expanded to 50 kilometers in width and 17 kilometers (Nish-Kurp) and 23 kilometers (Werch-Akbasch) deep by 24 September. The corps had not had the forces necessary to further expand the bridgehead to the south against the relatively narrow ridgelines that spread out before it.

The German forces were reorganized in the bridgehead that was located in the great bend of the Terek. Coming from the southeast, the river initially turned northwest only then almost east after a bend of nearly 20 kilometers. It was the intention of the *1. Panzer-Armee* to conduct the decisive thrust of Ordshonikidse after the division had been brought forward. If the city were taken, then it would cut the lifelines of the necessary supply lines of communications along both the Ossetian and Grusinian military roads, thus creating the prerequisites for the assault on Grossny.

The terrain that had to be negotiated was marked by ridgelines of up to 100 kilometers in length running in an east-west direction. Those were natural barriers against the German attack, and they offered only a few crossing points for the German north-south advance. Correspondingly, the first operational objective of the armored field army was to open the bottleneck at Elchotowo, between the Terek and the western edge of the Mussakay Range, and the

38. Translator's Note: One of a number of ethnic German settlements in the region, most of which were ordered forcibly evacuated by Stalin at the start of the war.

bottleneck at Atschaluki, between the eastern edge of the Mussakay Range and the Ssunshen Range.

The field army had two corps at its disposal: the *III. Panzer-Korps* (*23. Panzer-Division, 13. Panzer-Division* and the *370. Infanterie-Division*) and the *LII. Armee-Korps* (*"Wiking"* and the *111. Infanterie-Division*). The *XXXX. Panzer-Korps* covered the eastern flank of the field army.

In his book, *Europäische Freiwillige,* Peter Straßner[39] describes a conversation in Pjatigorsk between *SS-Gruppenführer* Steiner and the chief of staff of the field army concerning a crossing of the Caucasus along the two aforementioned supply routes that was "ordered from above" and had as its goal the taking of the Transcaucasus. In the daily logs of the *1. Panzer-Armee,* there is not a shred of evidence for either crossing the Caucasus with mechanized forces or for the referenced conversation.

The conduct of the operations was dictated by Directive No. 45 (Paragraph A3) of 23 July. In the 22nd Individual Directive of the *Führer* at the beginning of October 1942, it was unmistakably outlined once again (excerpt):

> . . . the field army is informed that it is the intention of the German Army High Command, depending on the development of the situation at Stalingrad, to allocate 1–2 motorized formations from the field-army group to the field army. It is intended to give the field army the opportunity with them, in the spirit of issued directives, to take the area around Grossny while blocking the Ossetian and Grusinian military roads and advancing farther in the direction of Machatsch Kala [Caspian Sea].[40]

The attack of the two axes of the *1. Panzer-Armee* was time-staggered:

> The *III. Panzer-Korps* attacks on 25 September to break through the bottleneck at Elchotowo. To that end, the available artillery of the *LII. Armee-Korps* supports the *III. Panzer-Korps* by eliminating flanking movements along the east flank of the *III. Panzer-Korps.* Details are to be coordinated directly.
>
> The *LII. Armee-Korps* attacks on 26 September, with the main effort of its attack directed against Ssagopschin.

39. Author's Note: Peter Straßner, *Europäische Freiwillige,* Munin Verlag: 1968.

40. Author's Note: This extended quotation and the following one are from the daily logs of the *1. Panzer-Armee.*

The importance of that decisive fighting in the area of the Caucasus and its failure justifies a closer look at details of its preparations and execution. At 1200 hours on 24 September, the *LII. Armee-Korps* issued written orders to its subordinate divisions and troop elements. Excerpts follow:

1. The enemy forces facing the corps have already been beaten by either friendly attacks or as the result of casualty-intensive enemy counter-attacks. From an infantry perspective, they no longer possess great combat power. In contrast, the artillery defensive elements and the employment of anti-armor weapons must continue to be assumed to be strong. Mining and reinforcements to the terrain can be expected, especially directed against armored vehicles. Based on previous reconnaissance results, it is not expected that the enemy will employ large amounts of armor or stronger reserves.
2. *LII. Armee-Korps* attacks on 26 September from the area east of Nish-Kurp–southeast of Malgobek (on the Kuban), with its main effort south of the high ground Nish-Kurp–Wosnessenskaja to destroy the enemy between the two masses of high ground and to open the bottleneck at Atscaluki.

   To the right, the *III. Panzer-Korps* attacks on 25 September to open the bottleneck at Jelchotowo and advance through to Ordshonikidse . . .
3. Attacking: To the right, *SS-Division Wiking*; to the left, *111. Infanterie-Division.*

   Boundaries: Southern slope of 565–Southern exit of the Pssedach–Rasdolnoje road from the mountains (3 kilometers south of San. Sowjetskij)–Nowaja Derewna (northern outskirts).

   Missions:

   a) *SS-Division Wiking* attacks from line 320 (3 kilometers east of Nish-Kurp)–565 with a strong right wing on both sides of attack axis 408 (3 kilometers east of the northern outskirts of Nish-Kurp)–southwestern tip of Ssagopschin. It takes as its first attack objective Pssedach and Ssagopschin. A small group is to be employed echeloned right from the eastern slope of 489 (4 kilometers south of Nish-Kurp) to capture Keskem. Depending on the development of the situation, the attack of weaker forces to open the area around Malgobek from the south can be taken into consideration after the taking of Ssagopschin.

   The next objective is the opening of the bottleneck of Atscaluki by the rapid advance of mobile forces, while covering the southern flank by the taking of the Babalo and Srednjaja hills.

b) Mission of the *111. Infanterie-Division* is to take the high ground Nish-Kurp–Wosnessenskaja by attacking from the west and north. First attack objective: Area around San. Ssowjetskij . . .

4. Artillery:
Arko 140 places the *II./Artillerie-Regiment 65* and *Mörser-Abteilung 607*[41] in position to the east of Nish-Kurp in such a fashion that any efforts to flank the attack of *SS-Division Wiking* from the two ridgelines can be eliminated and the attack of the *111. Infanterie-Division* astride the ridgeline can be supported . . .
5. . . .
6. Sequence of events:
Night of 23–24 September: relief of the *I.* and the *II./Infanterie-Regiment 66* by one battalion from *SS-Division Wiking*. Relief of the *III./Infanterie-Regiment 66* by *111. Infanterie-Division.*
Night of 24–25 September: Approach and positioning of the artillery and [night of] 25–26 September: *SS-Division Wiking* in position (with main body not until the last night).
7. . . .
8. . . .[42]

On 25 September and the night of 25–26 September, the troop elements of the division reached their bivouac and assembly areas. The command staff of the division was set up to commence operations 5 kilometers west of Malgobek on the Kurp:

Bivouac area for *SS-Infanterie-regiment "Westland"* and *SS-Aufklärungs-Abteilung* directly southwest of the command post. The 2nd Battalion [of the divisional artillery] in position 1 kilometer north of the 3rd Battalion with three light and one heavy battery.

Effective tonight, the bivouac area of *SS-Panzer-Abteilung 5* is the defile 1 kilometer east of the northern portion of Nish-Kurp.

---

41. Translator's Note: *Arko 140* = *Artillerie-Kommando 140* = Artillery Command 140, which was the corps artillery headquarters. The 65th Artillery regiment was a corps artillery element and the 2nd Battalion had a 10-centimeter cannon battery and two 15-centimeter heavy field howitzer batteries. The 607th Heavy Artillery Battalion was equipped with three batteries of 21-centimeter long-range cannon. Although *Mörser* would appear to be a cognate, the German word for mortar is *Granatwerfer.* A *Mörser* was a term reserved for heavy artillery.

42. Author's Note: This extended quotation and the following one are from the daily logs of the *LII. Armee-Korps.*

Correspondingly, this meant the division positioned itself in the area around Nish-Kurp during the night of 25–26 September. It was to attack southeast towards Ssagopschin without the *"Germania"* Regiment, without the 1st Battalion of its divisional artillery and, further, without the 10th and 13th Batteries of the divisional artillery.

The attack sector was a rolling valley depression that ran from west to east with an average width of 3 kilometers. It was flanked on both sides by ridgelines that rose in terraced style and had slopes of 8 percent or more. The Soviets had developed a strong defensive system by connecting the localities on the ridge tops, which had fortress-like improved positions, and numerous antitank gun and artillery positions, which had excellent interlocking fields of fire.

That made the intended attack difficult from the very beginning. Tank ditches at both ends of the valley depression, which were very well covered, only served to reinforce that impression.

The attack plan of the division aimed at first overcoming the tank ditch, eliminating the flanking fires from the two hill positions and then breaking through into the valley with the armored group.

To that end, the 2nd Battalion of the *"Nordland"* Regiment was directed to attack the enemy on the southern slopes, while the remaining two battalions of the regiment were to take the northern slopes. After the tank ditch had been breached, the tank battalion, together with the 1st Battalion of the *"Westland"* Regiment, was to move out. For the attack on the tank ditch, the division was initially given one battery of *Sturmgeschütz-Abteilung 109*[43] in support, which was to be returned to the *111. Infanterie-Division* after taking the ditch.

Coordination was made with the friendly forces to the right, the *370. Infanterie-Division*, for it to launch its attack at the same time, provide flanking artillery support for the 2nd Battalion of *"Nordland,"* and provide flank coverage in general.

The *"Nordland"* battalions launched their attacks at 0445 hours on 26 September. They encountered an enemy who was well prepared, defended toughly, did not surrender and was supported by surprisingly strong artillery and airpower. Five hours after the start of the attack, at 0945 hours, the division was able to report that it had reached the tank ditch west of Osemyj with some elements. At the same time, the attached Army assault-gun battery was released from its attachment and returned to *Infanterie-Regiment 70* of the infantry division.

In the meantime, the tank battalion moved out. Its combat strength was 48 tanks—5 *Panzer II's*, 11 *Panzer III's* (short), 23 *Panzer III's* (long), 3 *Panzer*

---

43. Translator's Note: As there was no *Sturmgeschütz-Abteilung 109*, the author must have transposed numerals, with *Sturmgeschütz-Abteilung 190* actually being intended.

IV's (short) and 6 *Panzer IV's* (long)—and 12 self-propelled 7.62-centimeter antitank guns. The self-propelled guns were under the command of *SS-Hauptsturmführer* Oeck.

At 1045 hours, the division reported to the corps by telegraph:

> Lead tank element has bypassed tank ditch to the north. Currently engaged against toughly defending enemy in position east of the tank ditch.
>
> Likewise, the *II./Nordland* has tough enemy in front of it in front of the southern portion of the tank ditch. Tank battalion has moved out to take the enemy positions on the southern edge of the tank ditch. Three tanks lost to bundled charges.[44]

The tanks were occasionally fixed by the Soviet artillery and the tank hunter–killer teams. The 1st Company, the lead element of the battalion, lost the leader of the 1st Platoon, *SS-Untersturmführer* Kolodzi, when his tank—Number 112—received a direct hit.

Despite the enemy situation presented in the corps order, the Soviet infantry possessed amazing *esprit de corps* and a surprising stubbornness.

Three hours after the tank battalion went around the tank ditch, the division reported to the corps:

> Minefield 500 meters east of the tank ditch. Engineers are clearing. Renewed move against Ssagopschin around 1500 hours. Currently, the enemy has employed a battalion of artillery to engage the tanks.

It was typical fall weather: clear and sunny, with temperatures reaching 75 degrees. The tank battalion eventually closed up, and it forced a breakthrough around 1500 hours. The two (medium) tanks companies, augmented by *Panzer IV's* from the 3rd Company, blasted their way forward, supporting one another. The tanks attempted to protect one another from tank hunter–killer teams by echeloning themselves appropriately. Bundled charges and demolition teams were hiding everywhere. The heavy flanking fires of the medium- and heavy-caliber artillery from the southeast had a demoralizing effect.

Pockets of Soviet resistance held out in the area around the breakthrough. They had armor-defeating weapons and defended with hitherto unknown determination. *SS-Untersturmführer* Flügel, the commander of the 2nd Company, had to send tanks back to funnel the battle staff forward, a measure that was necessary for continued command and control.

---

44. Author's Note: Unless noted otherwise, the extended quotations that follow are all from the daily logs of the *LII. Armee-Korps* or its supplemental annexes.

The enemy groups stubbornly holding out behind the front—some of them even had individual artillery pieces—were so strong that, for example, they occasionally made it impossible for the friendly forces on the left, the *111. Infanterie-Division*, to bring forward ammunition and rations or to bring up the artillery, which was so necessary for the continuation of the attack.

The division summarized the results of the first day of attack in a report to the corps at 2015 hours as follows:

1. In the course of the day, the enemy forces around Osemyj, who defended extremely stubbornly in a system of positions in depth and along two antitank ditches, were broken through, and the attack by the tanks and infantry carried forward to the Ssagopschin–San-Ssowjetskij road. Heavy enemy artillery of medium and heavy caliber flanked the attack from the southeast.
2. *SS-Panzer-Abteilung 5* formed a defensive blocking position at 1800 hours north of Ssagopschin. *SS-Infanterie-Regiment "Westland,"* with its 1st and 2nd Battalions, abuts the blocking position. *SS-Infanterie-Regiment "Nordland"* is screening the right flank with its 2nd Battalion to the southwest of Osemyj, orienting east and southeast. Contact has been established with friendly forces to the right. The 1st and 3rd Battalions [of *"Nordland"*] are still engaged in tough close combat after the onset of darkness with enemy holding north of the breakthrough point.
9. . . . Losses: 4 officers and 35 enlisted killed. 5 officers and 180 enlisted wounded, of which 10 remain with their units.

At 2215 hours, the corps telegraphed the division with its mission for 27 September:

> *SS-Division Wiking* clears the area around Osemyj-Keskem-Pssedach-Ssagopschin early on 27 September, takes Keskem, Pssedach and Ssagopschin and closes up in the area around Ssagopschin so as to attack the Werch-Atschaluki bottleneck from there. The division holds back a small group of tanks to advance from Ssagopschin on Malgobek—in coordination with the *111. Infanterie-Division*—after the *111. Infanterie-Division* takes San-Ssowjetskij. The corps artillery supports the division, initially from its original positions, and then prepares to move rapidly to change positions into the area around Ssagopschin.

The attack bogged down in the fires taken from heavy weapons. The enemy's air force appeared in droves. Despite strong friendly artillery support and the repeated reorganization of the attack forces, the attack did not gain ground. The effect of the enemy's artillery, which seemed to cover the widely scattered tanks exposed in the rolling terrain, which offered little cover, was horrific. The moral duress was unsustainable. The Red Air Force joined the fight, bombing and strafing.

At 1715 hours, the division submitted this report:

> Attacks by large bomber formations between 1500 and 1630 hours. Between 20 and 30 bombers or armored destroyers; high- and low-level attacks. 2–4 German fighters were not sufficient for defense.

Later that afternoon:

> Reorganization of the artillery for the new attack could not be conducted during the day due to the effects of constant aerial attack and strong artillery from Malgobek. Similarly, the tank battalion was also unable to [reorganize].
>
> Organization and preparations for the attack against Keskem and Pssedach to take place at night. Moving out early on 28 September. Request for this day:
> a) Air support against the artillery positions at Malgobek.
> b) Heavy fighter support against the repeated low-level attacks, since the tanks as well as the artillery are in completely open terrain.

By the evening of the second day of attack, the lead elements were some 1,200 meters north of Ssagopschin. The positions of the 2nd Battalion of *"Nordland"* remained unchanged:

> The *III./SS-Infanterie-Regiment "Nordland"* has assumed responsibility for all of the left-hand sector. The *I./"Nordland"* has been relieved and has assembled behind the 3rd Battalion.
>
> *SS-Infanterie-Regiment "Westland"* is positioned with its 1st Battalion from along the swell in the ground north of Ssagopschin to the north almost to the slope of the northern ridgeline.
>
> Reinforced *SS-Panzer-Abteilung 5* with the *I./SS-Infanterie-Regiment "Westland."*
>
> The 2nd Battalion [of *"Westland"*] interspersed within the lines of the *I./SS-Infanterie-Regiment "Westland."*

> The 3rd Battalion between the 1st and 2nd Battalions [of *"Westland"*].

The large amounts of weaponry of the enemy, concentrated into the smallest of spaces, is shown by the number of weapons that were captured after the breaching of the tank ditch at Osemyj (along a sector of 1.5 kilometers) and the advance on Ssagopschin. Although there were only 133 prisoners taken from the Soviet 57th Rifle Brigade, the following were captured: 21 4.5-centimeter antitank guns; 9 7.62-centimeter antitank guns; 1 10.5-centimeter artillery piece; 22 antitank rifles; 68 machine guns; 42 submachine guns; 2 mortars; 207 rifles; and 4 trucks.

The losses in tanks corresponded to the enemy situation. The battalion reported 20 non-operational tanks on the evening of 27 September. The total losses were 1 *Panzer* II, 4 *Panzer III's* (short), 11 *Panzer III's* (long), 2 *Panzer IV's* (short) and 2 *Panzer IV's* (long). One of the *Panzer IV's* was a complete loss, while the remaining could eventually be recovered and repaired. Nevertheless, the battalion requested 10 replacement tanks from the division as replacements for the losses.

During the evening of 27 September, the Soviets conducted rolling aerial attacks on Nish.Kurp as it started to turn dark.

Based on his assessment of the course of the fighting on the first two days, the division commander recommended to the corps "to advance along the southern slope of the ridgeline with the main body of the division and its tanks in the direction of Malgobek and take it."

He felt that the taking of the high ground around Malgobek was the key for the success of continued operations. The corps thought otherwise and stated "that the main effort of the operations is to remain on the southern wing and in attacking southeast towards the important bottleneck at Nish-Atschaluki." At 2315 hours, it gave the following mission to the division for 28 September:

> Exploiting the morning fog, *SS-Division Wiking* takes Ssagopschin with as strong a force as possible and advances further from there towards the high ground of Babalo-Ssrednjaja.

In paragraph 3 of the same order, there was a reminder: "The strained ammunition situation requires the sparing use of ammunition!" It was a comment that was barely comprehensible at that phase of the attack, especially in light of the inadequate aerial support.

In the three days that followed, the grenadiers and tank crews of the division wrestled for the hotly contested Ssagopschin, which they were unable to take. As had been ordered by the corps, the morning ground fog was used to neutralize the flanking fires and the fires from above.

The reinforced 2nd Company of the tank battalion then moved out to attempt a breakthrough by going around the northern part of Ssagopschin and attacking that decisive obstacle from the east. The infantry battalions also attempted to exploit the thick fog and enter the Soviet positions. The tanks broke through the Soviet positions. In addition to the undiminished and continued tough resistance, there was yet another surprise: The fog lifted unexpectedly. Brilliant sunshine allowed the Soviet defenders to bring their weaponry to full bear. Despite that, the tanks succeeded in blocking the Grusinian military road east of Ssagopschin. The following morning, however, they were forced to fight their way back to the infantry because of blocking positions in their rear that the Soviets had established during the night. In the process, they succeeded in turning back a large enemy immediate counterattack and knocking out 12 tanks in the process (1 KV-I, 6 T-34's and 5 Mark III's[45]).

Apparently ignoring the success of the friendly forces to the right—the *III. Panzer-Korps* was gaining ground—the Russians in front of the division continued to reinforce their elements on 29 September. At 0950 hours, aerial reconnaissance in the area west and southwest of Malgobek identified 50 enemy tanks. During the afternoon, it was further reported that "additional troop elements and armored vehicles (400–500 motorized vehicles and approximately 25 tanks were observed) have been identified in the Wosnessensskaja-Ssagopschin area."

Early in the morning, the division briefed the corps that it was of the opinion that the attack was only possible without heavy losses if

1. Aerial superiority is achieved through the employment of stronger friendly airpower.
2. The enemy artillery is eliminated as a threat by taking the area around Malgobek.

Once again, the corps disapproved the division's recommendation to take Malgobek: "The axis of advance continues to be towards the southeast and Hill 181 (Babalo) and the bottleneck at Werch-Atschaluki."

45. Translator's Note: The last was of British manufacture and provided to the Soviets through Lend-Lease arrangements. The British designation was Valentine. The Russians appreciated the reliability and relatively thick armor of the Valentine but were less impressed with the puny 2-pounder gun. It was used for infantry support.

The tension between the division and the corps grew as a result of the differing opinions on how to conduct the fight. The mission for 30 September sent to the division by telegraph at 2200 hours stated the following:

> *SS-Division Wiking* punches through the zone of villages bounded by Keskem-Pssedach-Ssagopschin by concentrating all of its infantry and artillery combat power and takes the area around the fork in the road 4 kilometers east of Pssedach as a prerequisite for the continued attack on the Babalo-Ssrednjaja high ground.

✠

At this point, we will provide some personal perspective concerning the round of fighting just described by presenting the firsthand account of former *SS-Sturmmann* Neumann, a tanker in the 2nd Company of the tank battalion:

> 26 September 1942: *SS-Infanterie-Regiment "Westland"* had been attacking the tank ditch southwest of Nischnyj-Kurp since 0700 hours; we crossed it at 1000 hours. A few tanks were lost to mines. Vehicle 112 received a direct hit from artillery.
>
> We were under extremely heavy artillery fire for four hours and were exposed to constant attacks from the Russian air force. At 1500 hours, we moved out and broke through the enemy infantry positions, advanced towards Malgobek, which was about 2 kilometers off to the left and on dominant high ground from us. A few 7.62-centimeter antitank guns were put out of commission. *Untersturmführer* Perthes was killed by a round to the head; *Obersturmführer* Wörner was wounded in the head.
>
> When it started to turn dark, we rolled behind a slight swell in the ground, screening all around us. We were all by ourselves; the infantry could not be brought forward, since there was still Russian infantry between us.

✠

> On the morning of 27 September, we discovered that the Russians had positioned an infantry and antitank outpost on our open right flank during the night. We attacked with a platoon and destroyed the outpost, which turned out to be a Russian battalion. We remained concealed, widely dispersed, behind a swell in the ground all day

long. We were covered by artillery from Malgobek, the high-ground position that dominated everything.

The second night started. As was demonstrated during the attack movements of the following day, 28 September, the Russians had reinforced their mine obstacles in front of us, which stretched from Malgobek to just shy of Ssagopschin, during the night. It should be noted that they left a wide lane [through the mines] so as to lay the groundwork for their use of tanks. They intended to carry out the attack parallel and to the right of us and then directly into our deep right flank. That would have separated us from our neighboring division, the *13. Panzer-Division.* An additional proof of those intentions was the positions of a forward outpost to the right on 27 September, which was intended to cover the attack movements. But things turned out differently.

It was 28 September. The darkness gave way to the light of a new day. Thick fog covered the terrain around us and barely allowed 20 meters of visibility. Weapons and tanks were ready to go. The last preparations for the upcoming fight were made. We were informed that the 2nd Company and elements of the 3rd Company had the mission of blocking the Russian route of retreat, Ssagopschin–Nisch-Atschaluki, so as to prevent the withdrawal of Russian heavy weapons and take Ssagopschin. The motors were turned over; we moved out. The company immediately spread out and stopped after a few hundred meters. Figures could be seen in the gray of the fog. A company from *SS-Infanterie-Regiment "Westland"* approached and mounted out tanks. A short conference among the unit leaders gave us time to make our own observations. Was the fog to our advantage or did it make our advance more difficult? In any case, we all felt that our tank company had received a mission once again of which we all could be proud.

The command of *"Panzer marsch"* tore us out of our thoughts. We were attacking.

After a little bit of movement, our optics and vision ports fogged up. Thick drops of water, formed by the fog, were hanging on them as well, making observation even more difficult. The cursing grew loud. Straining, pairs of eyes searched the veil of fog to find something. All in vain! You could only see right in front of you. The mounted infantry had to watch twice as hard to avoid being surprised. And so we continued to roll on. Our tanks spooked their way into the fog like eerie shadows. An edge-of-your seat view of a tank attack!

Suddenly, the fog became thinner. Occasionally, we could get a clear few hundred meters' glimpse of the terrain. It came as a total surprise when the fog lifted completely. The banks of fog were behind us. Radiant sunshine made everything bright and clear.

The Russian infantry lines were broken through rapidly. We quickly gained ground.

"*Achtung!* Enemy tanks in the depression 1,500 meters at 3 o'clock." I could clearly hear those words on the radio in the tank, even though I was not wearing headphones. Our first encounter with enemy tanks. Everything in us was tense. Would we be able to take out a few of them? Commands soon echoed down into the fighting compartment from the tank commander. I laid out antitank rounds. In between, I found some time to take a glance out of the side vision slot. Right! In the depression off to the right, there were some 25 tanks to be seen at the stated distance. Unmistakable. They were moving rapidly towards our lines.

Suddenly, there was a whistling sound overhead. Antitank gun or tank main gun?

We moved ahead rapidly. "*Achtung!* 1 o'clock . . . 400 meters . . . enemy tanks!" So it was tanks after all! I rapidly rammed the antitank round into the breech. A few of our own vehicles had already opened fire. The Russians were still firing. Our tank had identified a target. "Fire when ready!" The first round was already out of the gun. Seconds of great tension passed. The reports of our main tank guns that were taking a firing halt next to us could be heard. "It's burning!" Our tank commander announced with an excited, but happy voice. Our first "kill." But our elation could only last so long; new fire commands were issued as we continued to move forward. When I cast another quick glance out of the vision slit, I saw two Soviet tanks stationary and smoking at the end of a high, dried-out field of sunflowers 200 meters away at 2 o'clock. But we were still being engaged by either antitank guns or tanks. Our commander called out: "Vehicle 231 is burning!"

Damn! Fortunately, we saw the crew bail out. The platoon leader, *Untersturmführer* Nicolussi-Leck, switched tanks. A smoke column announced the knocking out of another Russian tank. It had hit 231 in the engine compartment, thus causing the rapid fire. Now it had been his turn.

Over the radio, I heard about the fourth Russian tank knocked out. We were elated and satisfied.

In the meantime, the mass of enemy tanks on our right flank had stopped and was stationary, doing nothing. They had been surprised by our advance and terrified by the knocking out of the four tanks, all of which turned out to be T-34's.

As we later figured out, we had caught the last portion of a wedge of a Russian tank formations that had attacked . . .

Our company commander exploited the confusion of the Russians. We advanced farther into the valley appearing in front of us, which was bounded on the left and right by dominant high ground. To the right was Ssagopschin; off to the left, Malgobek rose on dominant high ground. At the beginning of the fighting, our infantry had to dismount; it was conducting its engagements in small groups. Nevertheless, we quickly gained ground and approached the tank ditch through the antitank-gun and antitank-rifle fire. It was a dried out riverbed that was quickly set up as a tank ditch.

Crossing it turned out to be extraordinarily difficult for us. *Oberscharführer* Bachschuster was killed in the process by artillery shrapnel. The remaining vehicles were able to get across safely.

By then, we had advanced far past Ssagopschin. We swung to the right so as to advance on our attack objective, the Ssagopschin–Nisch-Atschaluki road. Our lead platoon immediately made contact with some more Russian tanks that were positioned on that road. After a short while, a few of them were on fire. The enemy pulled back to a slope and remained stationery about half way up. We reached the road and blocked it. We then had a little bit of time to reflect on our great success, since everything was initially quiet around us. The Russians were not doing anything. They had been completely surprised and were totally confused.

We were proud when we heard the final tally of "kills." It was six T-34's and five English Mark III's. Two other T-34's had been immobilized. We were all elated.

As I discovered later, we had run into the lead elements of a second Russian tank battalion, which had been the reserves of the other battalion and was to be committed into the fight in case of stronger resistance. But our advance had separated the two tank forces of the Russians.

In order to better identify the approach of vehicles, our company commander had one platoon move forward on the left side of the road. When that happened, an antitank gun immediately started firing; the platoon was engaged. After a short while, the platoon leader reported the destruction of two 7.62-centimeter antitank guns. But he was also being engaged by two tanks, which he was unable to engage with the 5-centimeter main gun, since they were too far away. As a result, he was ordered to move somewhat back from the road again.

Our company, together with the elements of the 3rd Company, then formed a semi-circle, screening in the direction of the road. For a long time, nothing happened. In the distance, we could see Russian trucks leaving Ssagopschin, kicking up great clouds of dust.

An order then came down that the swastika [aerial recognition] flags were to be removed and the vehicles well camouflaged. The Russian air force soon appeared above us with 18 aircraft. They had identified us, but had not attacked. Apparently, they did not recognize that we were German tanks and confused ours with theirs, since the silhouettes and types could not be identified as a result of the camouflage.

The platoon leader of the 2nd Platoon made the best of the critical moment by standing on his turret and waving skyward towards the aircraft with both arms. Most of the tank commanders followed his lead and the machines actually turned away from Ssagopschin. The incident enlivened our spirits. But there was an even bigger surprise coming. We thought we were seeing things when they dropped their bombs over Ssagopschin, which was still in Russians hands. That wasn't too hard to take. While we were engaged in a lively conversation concerning the grotesque situation, we were interrupted by the report of guns in the distance. What was going on? Unbelievable . . . what in the world was going on that day? The Russians had started firing with their artillery from Malgobek into Ssagopschin. Apparently spurred on by their aircraft, the Russian artillerymen did not want to take second place in making it as difficult as possible for the hated enemy to advance into [the town]. In reality, they were engaging their own formations, which had been positioned there all along. At that point, our artillery also made its presence known . . .

The Russians must have been completely confused. Hadn't their heavy weapons identified us? We attributed it to the fact that their signals communications must be bad, and we hoped that our infantry and antitank forces would soon come forward to occupy the ground we had taken.

Suddenly, a Messerschmitt fighter appeared above us. It swung past us and then started a low-level approach. The Messerschmitt strafed us. Since we were in no position to identify ourselves as German tanks, this happened a couple of times.

Completely unexpected, a few antitank rounds whistled overhead. The source could not be identified. The two T-34's halfway up the slopc also opened fire on us, without our main guns being able to reach that far [with effective fire].

All of a sudden, there was a rush approaching us. The impacts of heavy Russian artillery could be felt between us. We were being engaged from all sides. We had to change positions; we rolled back a bit. But the impacts went along with us. The reports from an 18.2-centimeter battery could be clearly distinguished. It was firing at us from an open-field position. It was a damned tricky situation. The bastards were registering on us. The impacts came ever closer. Depending on where they landed, we moved back and forth. The shells exploding right next to our tanks made an ear-deafening racket. In between, there was the whistling sounds of the antitank guns and the tank main guns. Dust and dirt penetrated the interiors of the tanks; shrapnel smacked with a clang against the steel walls of the tank. It was a terrible strain on the nerves, sitting there in the middle of artillery fire without being able to do anything, hearing the report of the guns and then waiting for the impacts. There was no getting around the feeling of confinement in the tank.

Some time passed that way. Then our company commander decided to roll into the tank ditch to get out of the beaten zone of the artillery. Carrying out his orders proved to be extraordinarily difficult, however, since the Russians immediately shifted their fire to the spot where the first tank entered the ditch. Despite that, all of the vehicles made it through without a problem.

We were able to catch our breath there. We were concealed by the ditch up to our turrets, meaning that we could no longer be engaged. It was at that point that we started to realize how bad the air was in the tanks. It was more than a lift to the spirits to be able to breathe fresh air through the opened hatches. We camouflaged our vehicles and quickly took stock of the battle damage. While some of the tanks had a mudguard shot off or a torsion bar was lost due to shrapnel, our tanks were operational again after a short time. Shot-up track links were soon replaced. The company commander went from vehicle to vehicle to check on the wounded.

I looked at my watch; it was 1600 hours. We had been in the ditch for an hour. The commander's vehicle was in constant radio contact with the battalion and the division. Our infantry had moved out, but it was only making slow progress in the face of strong resistance. As a result, we waited for the arrival of darkness.

It was 1630 hours. The day slowly drew to a close with the onset of darkness. We placed our submachine guns at convenient locations and were ready to go in our hatches. About an hour went by without anything happening. Suddenly, I heard rustling behind me . . . the fire from a submachine gun was already headed in that direction. I fired as well. We could hear the sounds of Russian from there. Someone called out something that we could not understand. We employed our limited Russian and told the Russians to come our way immediately.

A few figures appeared in the darkness, which we pulled down into the ditch. There were 17 men. They were immediately taken to the company commander and interrogated with the help of an interpreter.

On edge, we listened intently to every sound. Headlights could be seen in the distance. The Russians were driving around there without a care in the world.

After a while, orders arrived directing us to move out of the ditch by platoon and, as a company, set up an all-round defense in the open. That would allow a better defense in case of any close-in attacks.

The guards observed intently from the turrets. The sounds of moving Russian trucks could be heard all the time. Over the radio, the general praised our company commander for his successful advance.

Three battle-damaged tanks moved back with the wounded under the cover of darkness. The time went by. Cool fog rose, which gave us the shivers. We changed the guard posts hourly. It was 0400 hours in the morning. The guards heard engine and track sounds. Tanks? The company commander was awakened. Without a doubt, it was Russian tanks. They were moving right tin our rear. After a short while, the track sound died. The Russians had blocked our path and inserted a blocking position with their tanks between us and our own infantry. The company commander summoned his platoon leaders and ordered everyone to get ready. The engines were fired up, and we moved out.

The outline of the tank moving ahead of us in the fog was hard to make out. We halted. At the same moment, we could hear the report of a main gun. It was not clear whether it represented one of ours being knocked out or an enemy tank. We moved out again. After a short distance, we rolled past a smoldering tank. It was a Russian KV-I. A large hole gaped in the turret. One of our *Panzer IV's* had delivered the destructive direct hit at pointblank range against the Russian tank, which was part of the blocking position. After about 200 meters, there was a whistling sound between us. We were being engaged on two sides by antitank guns. It was also difficult to make them out. That meant only one thing: move through even faster!

Antitank rifles were also barking. Our driver strained to see the tank moving ahead of us. Just don't lose it in the fog! The barking of the antitank guns, which had erupted so suddenly, ceased just as quickly. It appeared we had made it through the enemy's blocking position. Since we were in a column, we had only engaged one of the blocking tanks.

Another halt. Did the lead elements encounter the enemy again? But we found out that we had reached our own lines. They were elated to see us there. They had followed the progress of our fighting and seen the Russian countermeasures. Unfortunately, we had a wounded man in tank 212. An antitank rifle firing at pointblank range had penetrated the hull and wounded the loader in the foot . . .

We would never forget that 28th of September and the morning of the 29th. . . . Only one word would be needed in the future to conjure up that engagement before our eyes: Ssagopschin.

The attack objective for 30 September for the division was once again Ssagopschin. The division reported a failed attack once again that afternoon:

At 0550 hours, the *I./SS-Infanterie-Regiment "Nordland"* moved out on the right, with the *II./SS-Infanterie-Regiment "Westland"* in the center and the *I./SS-Infanterie-Regiment "Westland"* on the left. The *III./SS-Infanterie-Regiment "Nordland"* was positioned along the right flank with a screening mission. The two right battalions were able to achieve success initially, around 0730 hours. The enemy, who is very well equipped with heavy machine guns and other automatic weapons and who is in well-prepared field fortifications, which are supported by heavy artillery and rocket launchers, covered the attack from all positions from elevated positions.

He is flanking the attack from the left with approximately five batteries east of Malgobek, as well as two batteries [firing] from the direction of Pssedach. As a consequence of the stubborn defense, the attack bogged down.

The reserve battalion, the *III./SS-Infanterie-Regiment "Nordland,"* was brought forward to the left of the *I./SS-Infanterie-Regiment "Nordland,"* so as to continue the attack with the main effort on the right in the sector of *SS-Infanterie-regiment "Nordland."*

An immediate counterattack from the locality in approximately company strength was turned back by the *I./SS-Infanterie-Regiment "Westland."* Towards noon, the *I.* and *II./SS-Infanterie-Regiment "Westland"* turned back a counterattack of approximate battalion size, supported by four tanks.

The attack sector is exceptionally unfavorable because of its sunflower fields and heather wildflowers, which prevent the employment of heavy weapons in any deliberate fashion and any type of overview. Movements of enemy infantry along the right flank have been identified.[46]

Within the area of operations of the *III. Panzer-Korps*, the *13. Panzer-Division* had bogged down outside of Elchotowo:

The *370. Infanterie-Division* is reorganizing its badly decimated formations and, with its right wing, has turned back several enemy immediate counterattacks against the dominant high ground east of Werch.Kurp. The division has lost 210 men in just one infantry regiment alone in two days of fighting for that high ground.[47]

Even under those circumstances, the field army continued following its original intent and agreed completely with the assessment of the situation that the *LII. Armee-Korps* had developed:

It continues to be the case that the decision rests with *SS-Division "Wiking,"* with its relatively strong forces, in that it has to take the bottleneck at Nish-Atschaluki, which is so important to the enemy, if the friendly attack on Ordshonikidse is to remain fluid.

In the daily logs of the *1. Panzer-Armee*, there are some observations that address the composition of the division with European volunteers and alleged difficulties in command and control. To support that absurd assumption, the

46. Author's Note: Daily logs of the *LII. Armee-Korps.*

47. Author's Note: This passage, the next one and the information on the table are from the daily logs of the *1. Panzer-Army.*

following foreign composition of the division is recorded in the daily logs of the field army:

Origin	Officers	Noncommissioned Officers and Enlisted Personnel
Dutch	3	929
Flemish	—	124
Danes	8	316
Norwegians	—	126
Swedes	—	7
Swiss	—	9
Finns	12	575
Totals	23	2,086

The total number of European volunteers in the division on 1 October 1942 was thus 12 percent of the total authorized strength of the division (17,648 men).

On the morning of 1 October, the corps ordered a temporary stopping of the attack on Ssagopschin after the division reported at 0910 hours:

> That it had not succeeded in breaking through the main battle area at Ssagopschin and taking the locality. It considers a continued frontal advance against the locality as not possible . . . [48]

Furthermore, *General* Ott, the commanding general of the *LII. Armee-Korps*, was informed at the division command post at noon on the same day that it would not be possible to hold the limit of forward advance because of the nature of the terrain. The commanding general replied emphatically

> that the defense was only a temporary one until new forces for a continuation of the attack had arrived. For that reason, when the attack is continued in several days, no terrain was to be surrendered which would have to be retaken in heavy fighting. The commanding general expressly forbade the commander of the *"Nordland"* Regiment, which was employed outside of Ssagopschin, to shorten the front by 2 kilometers, despite numerous requests [of the latter].

48. Author's Note: This passage and the next one are from the daily logs of the *LII. Armee-Korps.*

SS-Oberführer von Scholz, the regimental commander, had based the failure of the attack and the request to pull back his forces 2 kilometers on a written description of the terrain that he had had prepared. The text of that document is reproduced here to deepen an understanding of what happened at the time:

> The attack has to be conducted as a pure infantry attack, doing without the support of heavy infantry weapons.
>
> A broad grain field stretches towards Ssagopschin on both sides of the Pssedach-Malgobek road and to the east of it. It slopes down towards Ssagopschin in a broad plain, transitioning into bottomland about 500 meters wide.
>
> To the east of the bottomland, the terrain climbs in terrace form in the direction of Ssagopschin. The series of positions erected by the enemy start at the edge of the terraces and runs several hundred meters east in the direction of Ssagopschin. It consists of numerous, small nests that flank one another.
>
> The terraced terrain [in front of Ssagopschin] is vegetated with a thick matting of gorse.[49] It does not allow the rifleman to fire with his light weapons.
>
> Support by heavy infantry weapons is only possible out of the depression west of the Pssedach-Ssagopschin road, since every position [suitable] for heavy weapons on the forward slope of the grain field can be observed by the enemy batteries in Malgobek and can be shot to pieces there without any possibility of self-defense.
>
> The use of heavy machine guns to support the attack would not be possible from the grain field or from the depression in front of the grain field, because no fields of fire would be available, since it would be prevented by the grain plantings and the gorse. Artillery support could only be provided from a position that was located 7 kilometers from the forward lines. There are no other options, since the remaining terrain around Malgobek can be observed without any obstruction and the attack batteries in their positions would be shot to pieces without having the opportunity to fire.[50]

During the night of 1–2 October, the division commander ordered a shortening of the front by 2.5 kilometers—in defiance of the orders from the

49. Translator's Note: Any of several spiny shrubs of the genus *Ulex,* especially *U. europaeus,* native to Europe and having fragrant yellow flowers and black pods. Also called *furze, whin.* (www.thefreedictionary.com/gorse)

50. Author's Note: Annexes to the daily logs of the *1. Panzer-Armee.*

corps—after he had convinced himself of the correctness of the regimental commander's assessment by going to the terrain in question himself. By pulling back, he created the necessary prerequisites for combat during the time given over to defense.

Geheim!

Rundbild

Aufgenommen am: 10 10 1942

Standpunkt: Grabenstellung auf Anhöhe
1½ km nördl Straße Nish Kurp-Ssagopschin

rechts: 84 607
hoch: 48 200

Aufnahme und Auswertung durch
Vermessungsabteilung 602 (mot) 1

Cover text for the panoramic photograph on the pages that follow:
SECRET!
Panorama Photo
Taken on: 10 October 1942
Location: Trench line on the high ground 1.5 kilometers north of the Nish-Kurp–Ssagopschin road
Right: 84 607
Up: 48 200
Taken and evaluated by *Vermessungs-Abteilung 602 (mot)*

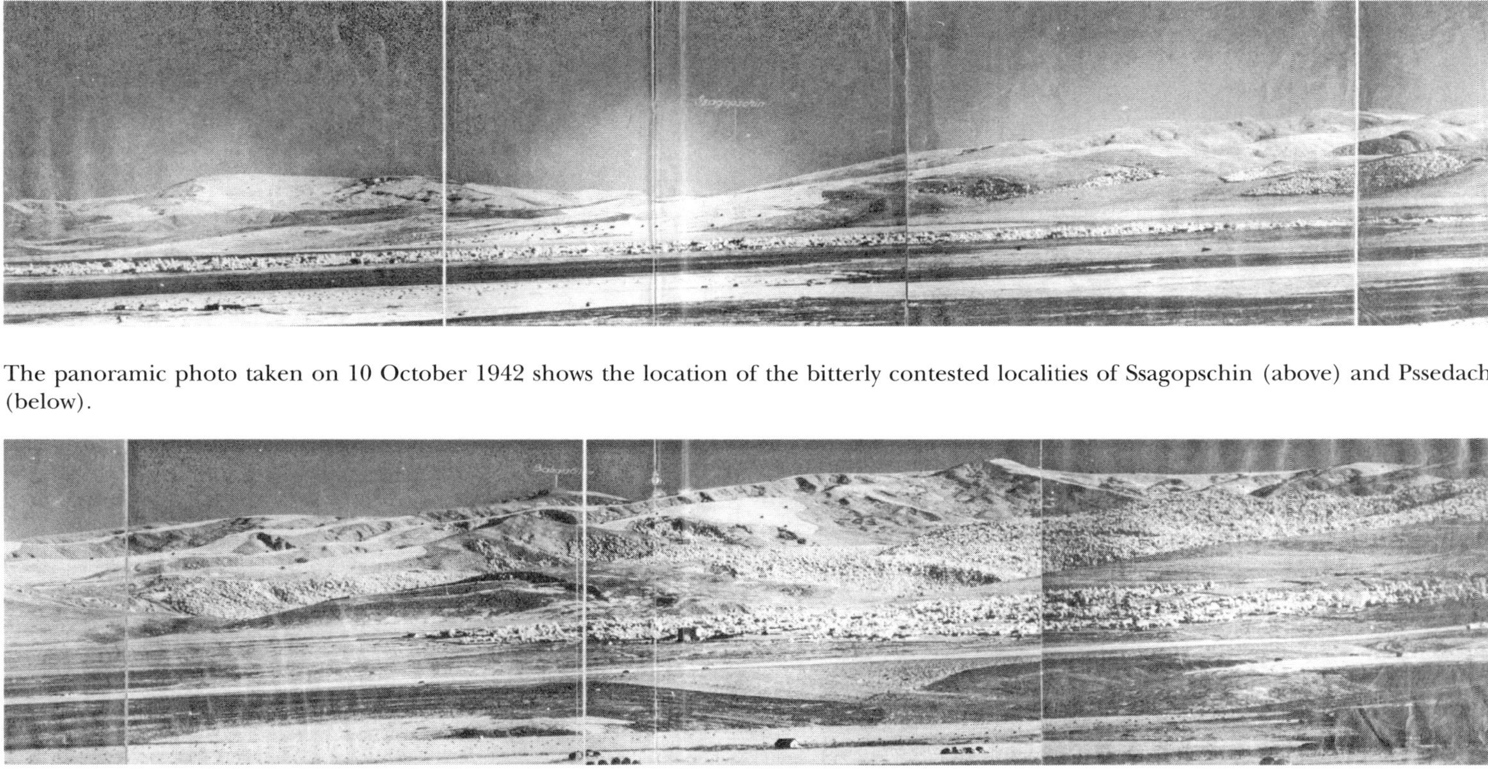

The panoramic photo taken on 10 October 1942 shows the location of the bitterly contested localities of Ssagopschin (above) and Pssedach (below).

September 1942, the Caucasus: The commander of the 3rd Company, *SS-Hauptsturmführer* Darges, in his *Panzer IVG.*

A captured flag bearing the images of Stalin and Lenin.

A *StuG III Ausf. G.* In 1944, two companies of the *Panzer* Regiment were equipped with this vehicle instead of the *Panzer IV.*

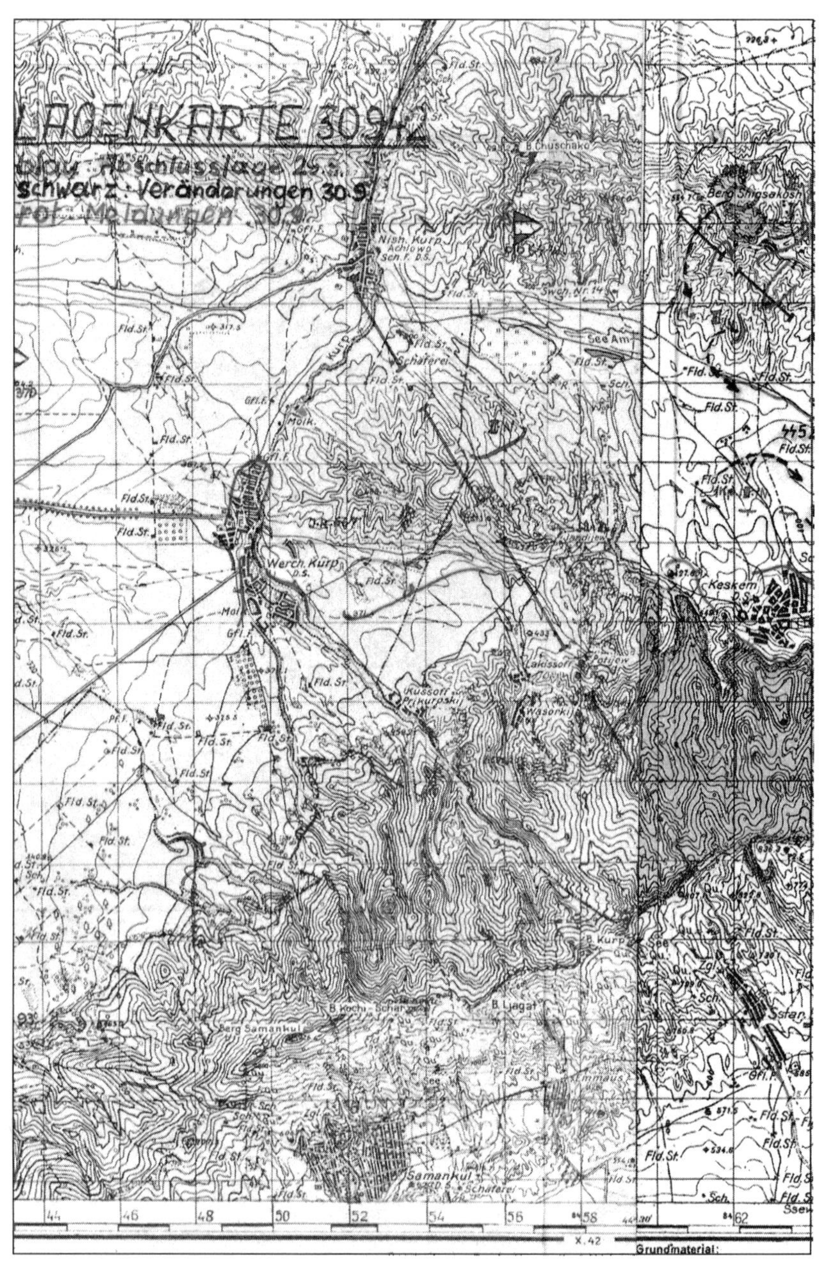

Situation map of the *LII. Armee-Korps* on 30 September 1942.

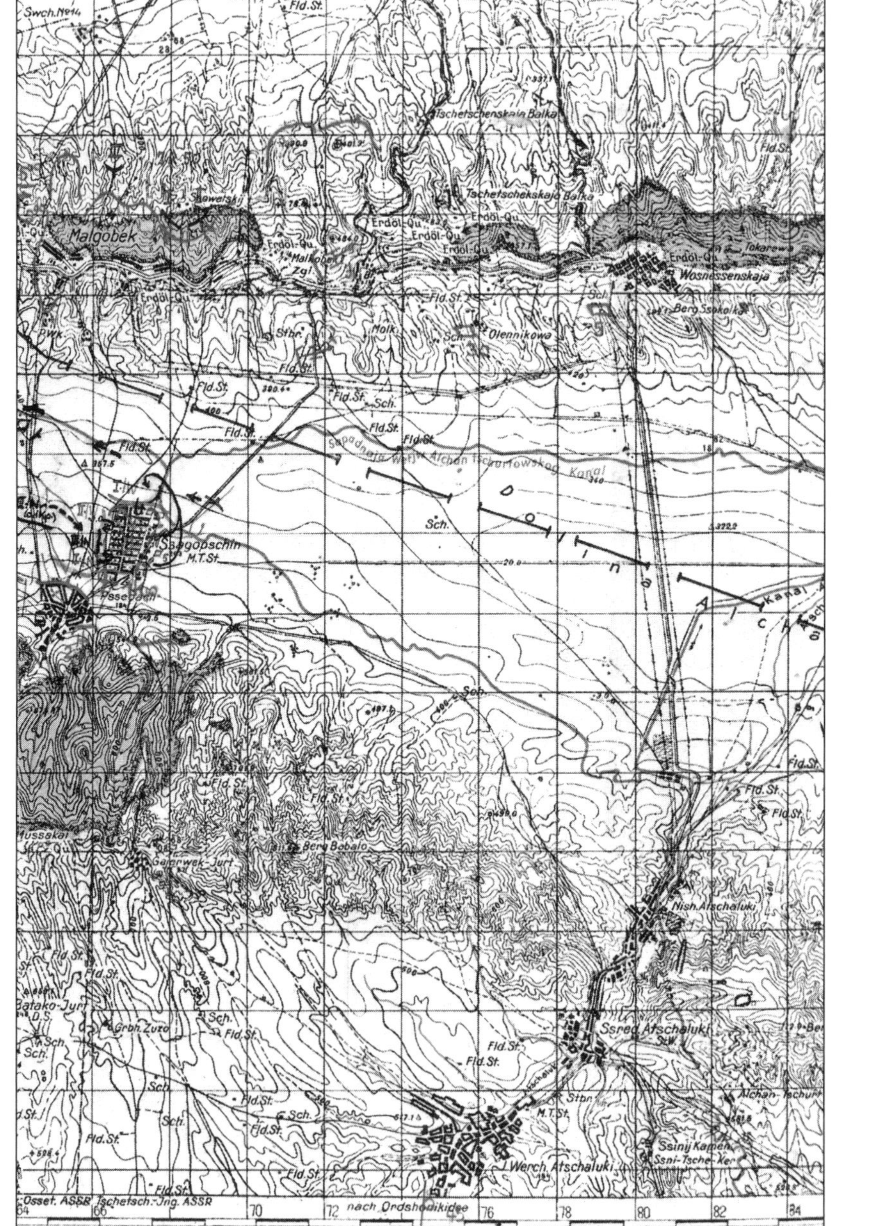

Swch.Nr14
Fld.St.
Tschetschenskaja Balka
Tschetschekskaja Balka
Malgobek
Erdöl-Qu.
Wosnessenskaja
Tokarewa
Berg Ssokolka
Olennikowa
Sch.
Ssagopschin
M.T.St.
Kanal
Berg Bobalo
Nish. Atschaluki
Ssred. Atschaluki
Werch. Atschaluki
Alchan-Tschurt
Ssinij Kamen
Ssni-Tsche-Ker
Batako-Jurt
Grbh. Zuzo
Osset. ASSR Tschetsch.-Jng. ASSR
nach Ordshonikidse
66
70
72
76
78
80
82
84

MALGOBEK—REFERENCE POINT 701

For the attack on Malgobek, which was scheduled to be launched in the next few days, the *"Germania"* Regiment, which had arrived from the Western Caucasus during the morning of 2 October, was attached to the *111. Infanterie-Division.*

The division commander was informed by the corps that no air support would be available for the planned assault. *SS-Gruppenführer* Steiner thereupon stated that he thought the attack could not be executed and that he would report the matter to *Reichsführer-SS* Himmler.

Those events further complicated relations between the division and the corps. The intended bypassing of the chain-of-command is a military matter, as is the shortening of the forward lines that Steiner had ordered, and these were reported to the field-army group by the field army, and the latter requested that circumvention of the chain-of-command be forbidden by the field-army group. It also requested that the field-army group issue a warning to the division commander that it was first necessary to obtain approval of the next senior headquarters prior to pulling back the front lines.[51]

At 0830 hours on 3 October, the 2nd Battalion of the *"Nordland"* Regiment attacked the crests of the dominant high ground 5 kilometers southeast of the southern edge of Nish-Kurp. It took the crests at 0930 hours, eliminating the 4th Battalion of the Soviet 57th Rifle brigade. Ninety prisoners were taken in. That attack provided some relief to the friendly forces to the right, the *370. Infanterie-Division,* which had lost the northern portion of Werch-Kurp the previous day. The regiment from the infantry division that had been employed there had taken 136 casualties.

During the morning of 3 October, the 2nd Company of the divisional engineer battalion closed the gap between the 2nd and 1st Battalions of the *"Nordland"* Regiment.

The maintenance services of the tank battalion had not been idle and, working feverishly, had succeeded in making more than 34 tanks operational by the evening of 3 October: 4 *Panzer II's,* 10 *Panzer III's* (short), 15 *Panzer III's* (long), 1 *Panzer IV* (short) and 4 *Panzer IV's* (long). In addition, six self-propelled guns were also reported as operational.

After a relatively quiet daytime on 4 October, preparations were continued into the night of 4–5 October for the attack on Malgobek. After some reorganization, the 2nd Battalion of the *"Nordland"* Regiment was

51. Author's Note: Daily logs of the *1. Panzer-Armee.*

positioned for attack on the left wing of the division. Taking its place on the right wing, adjoining the 2nd Company of *SS-Pionier-Bataillon 5*, was the division's reconnaissance battalion.

The field army promised the corps that 7 or 8 *Stukas* would support the attack. The corps attack order dated 2 October read in part:

> 2. *LII. Armee-Korps* attacks on 5 October with the objective of opening the bottleneck at Ssagopschin by advancing on the ridgeline in the direction of Malgobek-Wosnessenskaja and creating the prerequisites for the subsequent attack on the bottleneck at Ataschaluki.
> 3. Combat missions:
> a) *SS-Division Wiking* (minus the reinforced *Germania* Regiment) presses forward with its right wing in the direction of Keskem. The center of the division holds its current positions, fixing the enemy there by continuous combat raids supported by artillery and feigning the intention to attack. The left wing of the division joins the attack of the *111. Infanterie-Division* along the ridgeline, with the objective of taking the start of the road from Ssagopschin to the northeast on the ridgeline.
> b) The *111. Infanterie-Division,* with the attached reinforced *Germania* Regiment (including 3 light and 1 heavy battery), attacks along the ridgeline on both sides of the main road and takes the hilltop fortress of Malgobek. First attack objective: the narrow-gauge railway running from the north to the high ground.[52]

Supported by 45 batteries, the center and right wings of the *111. Infanterie-Division* attacked at the designated time of 0430 hours on 5 October. This was followed by the left wing of the *"Wiking"* Division after a short interval. Under clear skies and temperatures that reached 77 degrees Fahrenheit, the attack slowly but surely gained ground. Contrary to expectations, the enemy's artillery support was light. After nine hours of tough struggle, approximately 2.5 kilometers of ground was taken and, with it, the attack objective. At 1530 hours, the reinforced *"Germania"* Regiment was in the western outskirts of Malgobek and on the jutting height of the part of Malgobek known as "Crude Oil."

---

52. Author's Note: This entry and all remaining quotations until further notice are from the daily logs of the *LII. Armee-Korps.*

> The attack was supported by *Stuka* attacks, which provided palpable support. The enemy put up a tough defense in field positions that had been improved with heavily fortified bunkers . . .
>
> The *II./SS-Infanterie-Regiment Nordland* took the southwestern portion of Malgobek in hard fighting. Several immediate counterattacks, conducted by Russian armored forces with a total of some 20 tanks, were turned back. 10 enemy tanks were knocked out. The *I./SS-Infanterie-Regiment Westland* took the left wing as far as the portions of the locality taken by the *II./SS-Infanterie-Regiment Nordland.*

The enemy tanks knocked out by the tank battalion were all British Mark III's. Eight of them were burnt out; two were immobilized. The battalion suffered the loss of two *Panzer III's* (short), four *Panzer III's* (long) and two *Panzer IV's* (long). In addition, one self-propelled gun was knocked out. Of the tanks, one *Panzer III* (long) was a complete write-off. The personnel losses from those days weighed heavily on the battalion. The 1st Company had no more officers. The company commander, *SS-Obersturmführer* Schnabel, as well as two officer candidates, Pinnow and Gräbert, were killed. *SS-Untersturmführer* Hübner and *SS-Untersturmführer* Wilde had been wounded.

On the evening of 5 October, two events occurred that made the continuation of the attack more difficult. *Stukas* could not be "made available by the field army" for additional operations "since the [German Army High Command] had earmarked them for another area." In addition, the division was directed to control the amount of artillery fire, since it "is far too much. On 5 October, the division fired 2,600 light field howitzer and 600 heavy field howitzer rounds."

By contrast, it was stated that the *111. Infanterie-Division* had only fired 1,073 light field howitzer rounds, neglecting to mention that all of the corps artillery had supported the infantry division's attack, including *Kanonen-Abteilung 711* and *Mörser-Abteilung 607.* It was a hard-to-understand warning, coming in the midst of an attack operation of decisive importance in extremely difficult terrain. Yet it was also an indicator of the problems supply troops were having in keeping up with demand and the increasing burden being borne by the soldiers in the front lines—with the enemy enjoying the exact opposite, since his logistics lines of communication were growing shorter.

On 6 October, the *"Germania"* Regiment, together with *Angriffsgruppe Tronnier* from the *111. Infanterie-Division,* assaulted and took the locality of Malgobek. All of the enemy's immediate counterattacks were turned back:

> On the left, the *II./SS-Infanterie-Regiment Nordland* took the locality of Reference Point 642 and the hill just to the northeast. Its left wing is

> positioned next to the *I./SS-Infanterie-Regiment Germania* in the group of houses; its right wing is in contact on the edge of the locality with the *I./SS-Infanterie-Regiment Westland,* which had advanced along with its left wing.
>
> The *II./SS-Infanterie-Regiment Nordland* brought in 120 prisoners.

In order to reinforce its left wing, the division pulled the 3rd Battalion of the *"Nordland"* Regiment out of position on the right wing and inserted it for attack between the 1st Battalion of the *"Nordland"* Regiment and the *"Germania"* Regiment. The attack objective was the ridgeline east of "Crude Oil," where the enemy had reinforced his positions in the meantime. Around 0800 hours, the Soviets smashed into the attack of the 2nd Battalion of *"Nordland,"* which had just gotten underway, with 12 tanks. The tank battalion, which was positioned behind the mechanized infantry, committed a company of tanks and its attached company of self-propelled guns in an immediate counterattack. Towards noon, the Soviet thrust had been turned back; one enemy tank was destroyed.

> The *III./SS-Infanterie-Regiment Nordland* (main effort) moves out from the hill southeast of Reference Point 693 at 1300 hours in conjunction with the *I./SS-Infanterie-Regiment Germania* in the direction of Reference Point 701.

The ridgeline on both sides of that point was the thorn in the flesh for the friendly forces to the left. Those friendly forces did not butt up to the forces of the division, and they were being taken under fire by the Russians' heavy weapons on their right wing.[53]

The Russians were continuously being reinforced. An enemy column consisting of approximately 1,000 men and numerous motorized and horse-drawn vehicles was identified 5 kilometers east of the forward lines around noon. Infantry, supported by tanks, was observed advancing from the southeast.

The *111. Infanterie-Division* requested the commitment of *Stukas* to relieve the hard-fighting infantry:

---

53. Author's Note: It should be pointed out that Reference Point 701 was not Hill 701, which is indicated in some writings. It was a target reference point for artillery purposes, facilitating communications by means of shorthand for important areas and targets, as opposed to having to use grid coordinates. There was no high ground of 701 meters between Malgobek and Wosnessenskaja.

> After coordinating with the commander of [*Nahaufklärer-Geschwader*] *1*, a bombing run was to be conducted by reconnaissance aircraft of the Close-Range Reconnaissance Squadron against the enemy in front of the *111. Infanterie-Division, Infanterie-Regiment 70, Germania* and the *III./Nordland*. Unfortunately, the attack did not take place, since the reconnaissance aircraft had to drop their bombs instead on Ssagopschin due to the enemy's heavy antiaircraft defenses [over the target area].

Although engineer assault parties penetrated into the enemy's defensive system shortly before the onset of darkness, the attack proper bogged down.

The next morning, the *"Germania"* Regiment broke through the enemy's position and advanced as far as the western edge of Malgobek II. At the same time, the enemy was ejected from the patch of woods along the hill road. The woods were cleared of the enemy as far as its eastern edge. The next day, the simultaneous attacks by the 3rd Battalion of *"Nordland"* (north) and the 2nd Battalion of the same regiment (west) met with no success. About 400 meters south of the hill road, they were forced to ground by several 44-ton KV-I's. Without *Stuka* support, the tank battalion was unable to engage that type of fighting vehicle. It was not anticipated that there would be any air support, however.

An attack planned for 10 October against Reference Point 701 was preempted by a deliberate Soviet attack with strong forces supported by tanks. According to statements made by line-crossers, a new division had been brought forward, as well as the 15th Tank Brigade with Mark III tanks. The tank battalion received new orders: "*SS-Panzer-Abteilung 5* is prepared to counterattack in the event enemy pressure lets off."

At the time the order was issued, the battalion had 34 operational tanks at its disposal. In vain, the enemy ran up against the German positions for three days without breaking into the main line of resistance. This was despite strong aerial support. On 12 October, 18 Soviet bombers, escorted by fighters, conducted four bombing runs on Malgobek and the positions on the high ground. At the same time, however, *Generaloberst Freiherr* von Richthofen, in charge of *Luftwaffe* support in the southern sector of the Eastern Front, was at the command post of the *LII. Armee-Korps*. He stated "that the commitment of large air formations has not been planned in the immediate future, since they continue to be tied to the fighting in Stalingrad."

On 14 October, the Soviets flew two bombing runs and strafing attacks with 33 aircraft against the German forward lines.

✠

On 14 October, the tank battalion had more than 30 operational tanks. By then, it had lost seven tanks to battle damage, but the maintenance services had also repaired and returned several vehicles.

On 14 October, the last remaining battalion of the *"Germania"* Regiment, the 3rd Battalion, rejoined its parent formation, arriving from the Western Caucasus. It relieved *Infanterie-Regiment 50* from the *111. Infanterie-Division,* with the result that it rejoined its parent regiment on the ridgeline.

The capture of the enemy's positions at Reference Point 701 was ordered for 15 October so that the situation south of the hill road could be finally cleared up. Late in the afternoon, the ridgeline defined by Reference Points 699 and 701 was taken and occupied after hard close-in fighting that received flanking fire from enemy tanks and heavy weapons. It was lost two times in immediate counterattacks conducted by Russian tanks. It had not been possible to bring the necessary antitank weaponry forward in time. The seesaw fighting lasted into the darkness. The enemy finally gained the upper hand.

For the next day, 16 October, it was ordered that Reference Point 701, Malgobek II and Hill 478.8 (1 kilometer north of Malgobek II) be taken once and for all.

The chances of success and the planned execution of the mission that afternoon were seen in such a completely different light by the commanding general, *General der Infanterie* Ott, and the two division commanders, *Generalleutnant* Hermann Recknagel and *SS-Gruppenführer* Felix Steiner, that the former felt compelled to issue the following telegraphic directive to them on the morning of 16 October:

> The attack on Hill Reference Point 701, the village of Malgobek II and Hill 478.8 takes place today. If the authority or the willingness to fight on the part of the subordinate leaders is not sufficient, I request the esteemed division commanders to personally take the place of the regimental commanders and conduct it.
>
> /signed/ Ott

✠

The reinforced 3rd Battalion of the *"Nordland"* Regiment, the battalion composed of Finns, and elements of the tank battalion attacked in the afternoon. After two hours of hard fighting, the ridgeline at reference Point 701 fell to the German forces at 1730 hours. An immediate counterattack conducted by 17 Russian tanks from the southeast was successfully turned back.

That same day, along the ridgeline in front of Malgobek II, a battle group from the *111. Infanterie-Division,* composed of the *"Germania"* Regiment and *Gruppe Tronnier,* wrested the hilltop village from the enemy after tough fighting. The forces then stormed Hill 478.8. As it started to turn dark, the enemy launched an immediate counterattack with the equivalent of two battalions, and the enemy force succeeded in regaining control of the hill. The following day, *"Germania"* stormed the hill again and, after several hours of fighting, took it once and for all.

The enemy conducted counterattacks all of the following day against the newly won positions of the 3rd Battalion of *"Nordland."* The enemy's efforts were supported by tanks. All of the attacks were turned back, with three enemy tanks knocked out by the tanks of *SS-Panzer-Abteilung 5.*

With the fighting on 17 October, the division's offensive efforts in the Ssagopschin-Malgobek came to an end. The division transitioned to the defense in the positions it had won. Effective 18 October, the tank battalion became the corps reserve. Based on a request from the division, the corps decided against moving the tank battalion to the Malgobek-Kurp area, and it remained in the Nish-Kurp sector, where living quarters had already been prepared and could be occupied. The divisional engineers, which were also designated as a corps reserve, remained in the same area as well.

The outcome of German operations in the Terek area was determined primarily by four factors:

1. The estimate of the enemy situation—the strength and combat power of the opposing forces as well as the strength of the reserves available to the enemy—as outlined in paragraph 1 of the corps order of 24 September 1942, was far removed from reality.
2. The terrain estimate, with regard to the employment of armor and as prepared by the corps, was in contrast to the estimate formed by the responsible commanders of the division. It was not until after the con-

clusion of the fighting, which was both casualty intensive and without success, that the corps chief of staff changed his assessment during a briefing at the command post of the *1. Panzer-Armee* on 27 October: "Based on the experience of the corps during the recent fighting, an attack through Ssagopschin on Atschaluki has little prospect of success, if not impossible, without first capturing the dominant ridgeline at Wosnessenskaja, since it can be strongly flanked from the ridgelines to the north and south. The hill terrain northwest of Atschaluki is most likely especially difficult and ill suited for armored formations . . . Even the *13. Panzer-Division* had characterized this axis of attack at one point as ill suited for it. It was for that reason that this division was not employed in the direction of Elchotowo at the time."

3. It is difficult to comprehend how such an important operation could be conducted without air support. There are no indications in the daily logs of either the *LII. Armee-Korps* or the *1. Panzer-Armee* of pressure being exerted on the highest levels of command for the kind of air support that was needed and desirable.
4. Similarly, the bottleneck in the supply of artillery ammunition is also difficult to understand. There was a suitable railway branch line that ended only a few kilometers behind the front. The bottleneck made the offensive in the Terek comparable to an automobile that is supposed to move but already has its brakes applied.

The men of the tank battalion improved the dugouts in Nish-Kurp that they had been assigned. It goes without saying that the men were thinking of spending the winter in the Caucasus and wanted to be prepared for it. As early as 12 October,

> the field army had issued an order concerning measures to be taken for winter preparations. In general, it should be noted that it cannot be assumed that a deep blanket of snow in the operational area of the field army north of the Caucasian Highlands during the winter will stop the operations of motorized and infantry formations that do not have equipment enabling winter movement for lengthy periods. That said, the forces in the field must also be prepared to conduct the fight on the move by means of skis and sleds in cases of snow, as well as ensure resupply. Each infantry and armor division, as well as *SS-Division Wiking*, is ordered to establish a formation composed of all branches that is capable of winter movement. To that end, the

divisions will be issued winter equipment—increased in number and improved over the previous winter—in the form of sleds, *Akjas*, skis and snow mounts for all of its heavy weapons.[54]

The intent of the German command at the time can be seen in the introduction of a specially formed corps headquarters element, the so-called *Seekommando Xerxes*, under the command of *General der Flieger* Helmuth Felmy, which had been earmarked for manning the harbors on the Caspian Sea. It was a volunteer force comprised of 2,200 men, with Arabs, Palestinian Germans and Foreign Legionnaires, among others. Partially comprised of motorized elements, the formation was seen as a welcome reinforcement for the *1. Panzer-Armee*, whose combat power could be used to screen its flanks. That mission was a disappointment to Felmy, however, and he wrote to the German Armed Forces High Command on 28 October:

> I therefore am worried that an employment of the corps headquarters and its formations will lead to such high attrition that it will no longer be in position to be employed in the Near East in the spring . . . [55]

Ssagopschin and Malgobek were turning points in the events of the southernmost front of the German armed forces. In place of delaying actions and wide-ranging withdrawals by the enemy, a determined will to defend had surfaced at the edge of the vital oil fields and on the flank of the equally important supply routes to the Soviet forces coming from Iran.

American help through the Persian Gulf, which reached the southern portion of the desperate fighting conducted by the Soviets, became appreciable for the first time. According to estimates by the German General Staff, the assistance coming through the Persian Gulf during the period from May to November 1942 amounted to some 100,000 tons.

In order to put those numbers in perspective, it should be pointed out that the main German tank employed in that sector, the *Panzer III*, weighed 22 tons. The supplies being flown into Stalingrad at the time averaged 137 tons daily. That was a total of only 4,000 tons a month.

The commander of the tank battalion later wrote:

> It was during the fighting down in the Caucasus that American weapons appeared in large numbers for the first time. Some Russian

54. Author's Note: Daily logs of the *1. Panzer-Armee.*

55. Author's Note: Friedrich Lenz, *Stalingrad, der verlorene Sieg,* 158, 187, 190.

> tank units were equipped entirely with Shermans, American Dodge trucks and jeeps. Even the uniforms that the Russian soldiers wore, especially the equipment issued to the Russian alpine forces, were of American origin. Even the rations that we pulled out of the rations containers on knocked-out fighting vehicles were American.
>
> The only thing left on the Russian soldier that was Russian was the soldier himself. Everything else was of American origin.[56]

In the face of the inadequate aerial support for the offensive of the *1. Panzer-Armee,* the employment of enemy airpower became ever more important. In the German reports available concerning the fighting, there is no mention of the strong Soviet airpower in the Grossny area being identified by German aerial reconnaissance.

The English military history, Basil Liddell Hart, wrote the following concerning the German failure:

> An important factor in the failure was that the Russians had hundreds of bombers stationed at the airfields in the vicinity of Grossny. . . . As a result, the Russian bombers were able to harass Kleist's field army without interference.[57]

At this point, mention should be made of the medical services of the tank battalion. They underwent their first large-scale baptism of fire during the heavy fighting for Ssagopschin and Malgobek. The battalion surgeon, *Dr.* Standl, has provided a firsthand account of the organization of his section, the conditions under which it operated and the fighting up through its conclusion at Malgobek:

> The medical section of *SS-Panzer-Abteilung 5* had the following composition: one battalion surgeon and one assistant battalion surgeon; one senior medical orderly (in the rank of *SS-Hauptscharführer*); one medical orderly (in the rank of *S-Unterscharführer*); three stretcher bearers; one driver for the *Sd.Kfz. 15*; one driver and one radio operator for the armored ambulance (an *SPW* modified for medical

56. Author's Note: Firsthand account by Mühlenkamp.

57. Author's Note: B. H. Liddell Hart, *Geschichte des Zweiten Weltkriegs*, vol. I, 323. Translator's Note: This quotation, as well as all others originally published in English, has been reverse-translated from the German and may not match word-for-word with the original English version.

purposes); one driver for the wheeled ambulance; three drivers for the motorcycles with sidecars; one driver and one assistant driver for the medical equipment truck (3-ton).

The noncommissioned officers and enlisted men were logistically assigned to the headquarters company; for disciplinary purposes, they were assigned to the battalion surgeon.

The doctors reported to the battalion commander for disciplinary purposes.

Each company had an authorization for one medical noncommissioned officer and three stretcher bearers, who were equipped with motorcycles with sidecars.

When motor marching, the battalion surgeon rode on the *Sd.Kfz. 15* along with the senior medical orderly. They were part of the battle staff of the commander. The assistant battalion surgeon rode at the end of the last tank company in either the armored ambulance or in a motorcycle with sidecar.

During operations, the battalion surgeon participated in the orders conference with the battalion commander and the company commanders, receiving directives or orders from him concerning medical affairs. In addition, he also was informed of the division surgeon's planned employment and location of medical clearing facilities.

During engagements, the battalion surgeon rode in the armored ambulance, whose crew was reinforced by the medical NCO of the headquarters company. Depending on the situation, either behind the second or third wave. He had radio contact with the both the commander's tank and that of the adjutant.

Whenever a medical clearing facility was established, the assistant battalion surgeon's section with the headquarters company's medical NCO and the motorcycles with sidecars were brought forward.

During the advance of the armored battle group from Rostow into the Caucasus, the battalion surgeon was designated as the senior medical officer of the battle group, and the respective battalion and company medical personnel reported to me tactically. That attachment relationship was not rescinded, as far as I can remember, until after the capture of Chadishenskaja.

During a rapid advance, temporary medical clearing facilities were established in leapfrog fashion. The medical care of the armored group did not experience any problems during the advance into the Caucasus. The situation was more difficult along the Terek and not only because of the large numbers of casualties taken on the first day of the attack. Transportation means available to the battalion for the evacuation of wounded were often insufficient. The rapidly changing battlefield situation did not allow the establishment of a medical clearing facility until two days later. There was also the sudden appearance of jaundice, which had to be treated in the field, which was different than previous guidelines. In order to make the order of the division surgeon happen, I had to establish a field treatment facility on the left bank of the Terek in a school. I cared for up to 50 patients at a time there.

Since my assistant surgeon, *SS-Obersturmführer Dr.* Wittmann, had become unavailable, I had to commute every second day between my medical clearing facility in the *balka* below Malgobek and the other facility for the sick, which was run in an exemplary fashion by my senior medical orderly, *SS-Hauptscharführer* Bewen. This was done in order to have the more-or-less convalesced soldiers returned to the front as soon as possible. It was an unsatisfactory situation, both from a medical and from a tactical perspective.

ALAGIR—ORDSHONIKIDSE

The break in the fighting that settled in on both sides was based on the lack of available forces for the immediate continuation of operations (for the Germans) and the necessity for withdrawing the forces that had been earmarked for an attack in order to counter the threatening situation that had developed in the area around Ordshonikidse (for the Soviets).

Since *SS-Panzer-Abteilung 5* would soon be involved in the latter events, some background information is provided.

During the days of fighting for Ssagopschin and Malgobek, the *III. Panzer-Korps* succeeded in heading south and reaching the area around Elchotowo on the east bank of the Terek with the *13. Panzer-Division* and the locality of Werch-Kurp, some 7.5 kilometers south of Nish-Kurp, with the *370. Infanterie-Division.* In the face of increasing resistance on the part of the Soviets there, the *1. Panzer-Armee* regrouped. The *III. Panzer-Korps* received the mission of defeating the enemy forces in and east of Naltschik after it was relieved in the areas where it had previously advanced.[58]

The localities of Malgobek and Naltschik were roughly even with one another, with Malgobek some 50 kilometers east of the Terek and Naltschik some 35 kilometers to the west. The attack sector of the *III. Panzer-Korps* was similar to that of the *LII. Armee-Korps* on the western side of the Terek. The terrain is broken up by small rivers and creeks that flow into the river

58. Author's Note: von Mackensen, *Vom Bug zum Kaukasus,* Vowinckel Verlag: 1967.

from the northeastern slopes of the Caucasus, which parallel the river about 50 kilometers away. Those water courses flow into the Terek from the northeast.

The attack that was launched on 25 October went unexpectedly well. By 31 October, the *III. Panzer-Korps* headed east to attack from an area that was already some 40 kilometers southeast of Naltschik. On 1 November, the *23. Panzer-Division,* also attached to the corps, reached Alagir, the starting point for the Ossetian Military Road, and the *13. Panzer-Division* was in an area some 15 kilometers west of Ordshonikidse. From there, it was already in a position to threaten the Grusianian Military Road, which was so vital for the Soviets. While the *23. Panzer-Division* assumed a flank guard mission along the Fiag-Don Creek to protect the *13. Panzer-Division,* the latter reached the western outskirts of Ordshonikidse.

That development of the situation forced the Soviets to regroup in the Malgobek area. The formations that were freed up as a result, then attacked the thin rearward lines of communication of the *13. Panzer-Division* from both the north and the south to the west of Ordshonikidse. The only supply route for the division, running from Alagir to Ordshonikidse, was periodically under observed Soviet artillery fire. On 6 November, two Soviet rifle corps, one attacking from the north and the other from the south, succeeded in cutting the lines of communication.

This situation, which was becoming ever more critical for the *13. Panzer-Division,* caused the expedited relief of *SS-Division "Wiking"* in the Malgobek area. The division conducted forced marches into the sector west of Ordshonikidse.

While the first infantry battalion in, the 2nd Battalion of the *"Nordland"* Regiment, was unable to change the situation between 6 and 10 November, *SS-Panzer-Abteilung 5,* which had covered 150 kilometers in forced marches through Prochladny, the western bank of the Terek and Alagir, succeeded in establishing and holding a blocking position along the Mairamadag, south of the Alagir-Ordshonikidse road and the Fiag-Don Creek. In that, it was helped by other infantry elements of the division.

On 9 November, the *13. Panzer-Division* had to pull back its main battle line to the eastern edge of Gisel, some 7 kilometers west of Ordshonikidse. The next day, it moved back in the direction of Nischny-Ssaniba. During the night of 10–11 November, it succeeded in passing through the firm lines of *SS-Division "Wiking"* and breaking through to the west.

The nature of the difficult fighting against a vastly superior enemy at the foot of the Caucasus, under the Kasbek, which was glittering in snow and ice, is confirmed by figures supplied by the *III. Panzer-Korps.* During the operations conducted from 25 October to 12 November, the three divisions attached to the corps had made contact with 30 enemy formations. Just the *13. Panzer-Division* alone had to contend with 14 formations in its thrust on Ordshonikidse (2 rifle divisions, 8 rifle brigades and 4 tank brigades). The corps took 16,000 prisoners, knocked out 188 tanks and 4 armored trains and captured 249 artillery pieces.

The losses of the *III. Panzer-Korps* "consisted of 1,257 (63) killed, 273 (2) missing and 5,008 (165) wounded during the operations conducted from 19 October to 12 November 1942."[59]

The formations of *SS-Division "Wiking"* arrived in their new area of operations east of Alagir in the order by which they had been relieved in the Malgobek area of operations. The command post of the armored group was initially at Ardon, then Kadgoron.

✠

On 9 November, the division was redesignated from *SS-Division "Wiking"* to *SS-Panzer-Grenadier-Division "Wiking."*[60] As the elements of the division arrived in the new area of operations, they were initially attached to the *23. Panzer-Division.* This included the tank battalion. The greatly weakened formations of the *23. Panzer-Division* had only been able to fend off the increasingly stronger attacks of the Soviets by committing itself to the utmost.

On 13 November, an enemy attack against the center sector of the division's frontage was turned back. On 14 November, the enemy repeated his efforts and succeeded in penetrating the German lines between the villages of Raswet and Nart, on both sides of the Fiag-Don Creek. The tank battalion was able to seal off the penetration after it was called in, inflicting heavy casualties on the enemy. On 16 November, the enemy returned to his original line of departure in the face of the increasing pressure exerted by the German countermeasures.

In some places, the defensive fighting conducted by the tank battalion took place on terrain that was ill suited for armored vehicles. An account written by an SS war correspondent, Karl-Heinz Eckert, provides a lively account of the fighting at the time:

> The SS tank battalion received the following mission: The enemy had broken through our main line of resistance around the village of Nart with strong forces, including tanks, antitank guns and antiaircraft weaponry. The tank battalion was directed to restore the main line of

---

59. Author's Note: von Mackensen. The numbers listed in parentheses are for officers.

60. Author's Note: *Europäische Freiwillige,* Munin Verlag: 1968, 173.

resistance with two companies. To that end, they moved out from the south, not far from the village of Raswet, where the enemy was also attempting to enter. The tank's mission was to support the infantry, about a battalion strong. The tanks from *Kampfgruppe I* would also be attacking from the left so as to link up with the SS tanks later.

The two companies moved out from their assembly areas in the morning, around 1000 hours. They encountered very unfavorable terrain, which offered the enemy every opportunity for defense and also forced the tanks to run up against him on the forward slope like targets in a shooting gallery. They were unable to engage the enemy tanks with even the slightest prospect of success. The enemy was well aware of his advantage and had occupied very good positions with his heavy tanks.

The commander initially ordered a reinforced platoon to perform flank security along the northern edge of the village of Raswet, off to the right. Enemy armored efforts to break through there were to be spoiled. A motorcycle messenger guided E's platoon[61] into its positions. The way there could be observed by the enemy, who attempted to turn back the tanks with heavy-caliber artillery and a complete salvo from Stalin organs. The motorcycle messenger received some shrapnel to his vehicle, but there was no other damage.

The tanks moved into Raswet and soon reported they were being extensively engaged by antitank guns, antiaircraft weaponry and artillery and had to constantly change position to avoid becoming casualties. A short while later, E's platoon reported 10 enemy tanks.

The village of Raswet was on the west side of a creek, which flowed north and then turned somewhat west halfway to the village of Nart, where the enemy tanks were located. It was there that the enemy had succeeded in breaking through.

Some of the enemy were on the near side of the creek in a field of grain in a small depression, which offered some concealment. The other tanks were positioned in the village of Nart in a reverse-slope position. Some of them were in a rock quarry. Consequently, all of them had relatively good cover.

The friendly tanks were positioned on a slight downward slope on an almost completely flat plain. They were widely dispersed among underbrush composed of oak. On the right was the 3rd Company;

---

61. Translator's Note: For security reasons, even the names of the leaders were frequently not identified, let alone the formations involved.

the 2nd on the left. The infantry was to the left and in the depression below; it had been directed to attack on the left.

Every movement of the tanks was countered by the enemy with heavy-caliber artillery. And so the tanks were positioned facing one another; both sides ready to advance, both sides waiting for the other side to be the first to advance from his positions and run ahead of his own artillery. A direct attack by the German tanks could only mean extremely heavy casualties. By evening, this was the situation: Approximately 26 enemy tanks, effectively supported by antitank guns and antiaircraft weaponry, were positioned across from the German ones.

At first light the following morning, the artillery duels started. The clouds were low in the sky; the visibility was occasionally very poor. Occasionally, something could be seen farther to the east: An enemy armored train was puffing along across the horizon with a white trail of smoke some 12 to 15 kilometers away.

In the meantime, the enemy tanks had grown to 30 in number. The friendly tanks from *Kampfgruppe I* advanced from the northwest to the SS tanks and inserted themselves into the lines to the left. They also dispersed widely. Camouflaged with oak branches, they advanced to the edge of the vegetation.

Both of the commanders discussed the situation. A direct attack by the tanks still meant the taking of senseless casualties. It was likewise impossible to bypass, due to the terrain. Therefore, the effort was made to knock the enemy out of his positions in some fashion by means of concentrated artillery. In order to increase the effect of the artillery, all of the tanks would advance as fast as lightning under its cover and then contribute to the massed fires with their own main guns.

What followed was a bitter exchange of fire, in which the enemy antitank and antiaircraft guns also participated. The reports of the tank main guns crashed loud and clear among the duller thumps of the artillery. Tracers flitted across to the enemy and back again. They hit the tanks, ricocheted off the armor and rose skyward, visible until the tracer element burned out.

A correspondent with a movie camera climbed up on one of the tanks. When the tank rolled over a section of the enemy's trenches, the correspondent, who was a battle-seasoned *Scharführer* of the infantry, who had participated in all of the campaigns of the war, discovered numerous Bolshevists in it, who had wanted to let the tank overrun them, while they were pressed to the ground. Two hand grenades got them moving again; they ran towards the end of the trench. The tank commander, who had been alerted by the crashing of the two hand grenades, traversed the tank turret a bit and high-explosive rounds swept over the tightly knotted Russians. The tanks then disengaged from the enemy and returned to their lines of departure.

E's platoon reported that the cat-and-mouse game with the enemy's defensive weapons had picked up speed. One man was wounded under the eye, but he remained in his tank. At 3 o'clock, it started to turn dark, eliminating all visibility. A few rounds continued to be exchanged. The artillery duel with heavy calibers recommenced like when a fire that is about to go out suddenly flares up again. It eventually petered out in the darkness.

Then it was a matter of waiting: Had the enemy become worn down? Was he undertaking some sort of a change of position during the night? That night, an enemy patrol was hunted down in the vicinity of our tanks. At 3 in the morning—half an hour before it started to dawn—the counterbattery fires recommenced, initially with individual shells and then becoming ever more intense.

We were able to determine that the enemy tanks had pulled back somewhat and that there were mines in front of our own positions. Because the enemy tanks had pulled back, there was an opportunity for our tanks to advance directly against the enemy positions. There was a strong artillery preparation before the attack. In the smoke of the exploding shells, the tanks pushed their way forward. Observed from the turrets of the command tanks of the two commanders, this is how the attack played out:

The 3rd Company, given the codename of "B," reported via radio at 0835 hours, about five minutes before the start of the attack, that the German mortars had targeted the enemy well and requested a second salvo.

0837 hours: "B" received strong tank, antitank and antiaircraft fires from the right.

0838 hours: "W," the 2nd Company, which was advancing ahead of "B" on the left, reported it had reached the rock quarry and that a platoon was being pushed forward on the right.

0839 hours: "W" reported: 1 T-34 set alight. "W" requested artillery fire on the enemy batteries that were engaging the company from the flank.

0850 hours: "W" reported: Enemy tanks had pulled back across the creek and formed a strong position on the far side. Requested artillery on the village of Nart, since we were being engaged over open sights from there.

0900 hours: "W" reported: Friendly infantry was advancing from the left to the right and establishing contact with us. Question by the commander ("V") to "W": Where exactly do you want the artillery fire? On the assembled tanks to the right or on position in the village further to the left? "W" to "V": Please fire on the enemy tanks.

0920 hours: "V" to "E":[62] What's your situation? "E" to "V": Supporting the attack to the north. Receiving strong artillery and antiaircraft fire.

0930 hours: "E" to "V": Enemy infantry has entered the village. Holding Raswet together with friendly infantry.

0945 hours: "V" to the antitank forces: Antitank forces move up to my location. Commander report to the command post.

1000 hours: "W" to "V": Urgently request strong artillery fire on the tanks. Tanks are located a thumb's width left of the command post in the white houses.

1010 hours: "B" to "W": Watch out! Enemy tanks have launched an immediate counterattack on the left.

1020 hours: "W" to "V": Enemy attacking right wing with 12 tanks. Artillery fire requested on the northern edge of Raswet. Order to the antitank forces: Antitank elements move forward another 300 meters. Order to the artillery: Concentrated fire on the indicated target.

1022 hours: "W" to "V": Enemy tanks moving left to right and are attempting to get back to the rock quarry.

1023 hours: "E" was attacked from behind by enemy tanks.

1024 hours: Order to the artillery: Increase the rate of fire!

1025 hours: To the artillery: Fire on the right flank. Order to "W" and "B": Remain in the reverse-slope position and allow the enemy to approach!

1026 hours: Order to the tanks still in the attack position: Immediately move up to the right flank and assume flank security!

1030 hours: "B" to "V": Urgently request artillery fire on the depression in front of me.

1041 hours: "W" to "V": Second wave of enemy tanks—10 enemy tanks identified so far—advancing out of the grain field. "E" to "V": Platoon leader wounded. (Wound) Being dressed; remaining with platoon.

---

62. Translator's Note: The correspondent does not indicate who "E" is in this exchange, although it would logically be the platoon leader previously referenced.

The enemy artillery fires were almost as intense as the friendly ones. A friendly tank, which had to pull back to repair some minor battle damage, carried along three wounded infantry with it. Among the rolling artillery fires was the tack-tack-tack of numerous machine guns. The artillery observers directed the battery fires from the command tank from the Army. Stalin organs were firing full salvoes and were putting down thick curtains of dirt and dust. Friendly mortar fire was replying from two sides.

1110 hours: "W" to "B": Pull up further to the right! An enemy tank is attempting to swing out to the right and attack you in the flank.

1113 hours: "W" to "V": Heavy enemy infantry movement in the bottom land in front of me. Infantry has antitank guns with it.

An Army tank came back and had a wounded tank crew on it. It stopped right next to the medical armored vehicle. The wounded were placed in a small depression; the tank pulled in front to act as cover against shrapnel. The surgeon and the medical orderlies helped the wounded. Dressings were applied; wound tags for the personnel were filled out.

1130 hours: "W" to "V": Enemy tanks are crossing the creek to launch another attack.

1131 hours: "V" to "W": How effective was the friendly artillery fire?

1132 hours: "B" to "V": Four enemy tanks advancing directly on the rock quarry and have at least a battalion of infantry with them. Place friendly artillery fire around the area of the fire.

1137 hours: "W" to "V": Direction of fire good. Drop somewhat; enemy has advanced some.

1139 hours: Artillery right on target. Fire for effect. "E" to "V": Enemy infantry moving out of the right part of Nart to attack. Approximately two companies. "B" to "V": 4 enemy tanks, T-34's, coming from the same direction.

1151 hours: "E" to "V": Enemy attack on the northern part of Raswet turned back. Tank and friendly infantry back in the old positions.

1157 hours: "W" and "B" to "V": Enemy attack halted. Infantry returning to the old main line of resistance.

1158 hours: report to the division: Old main line of resistance restored. Recommendation: Insert infantry between the lead tank elements and emplace mines in front of the main line of resistance.

For the time being, the mission of the tank battalion had been accomplished. The artillery fire continued with the same intensity on both sides. The tanks and antitank elements remained widely dispersed along a defensive frontage, ready for anything. Late in the afternoon, the enemy attempted to break through one more time with his tanks. After a short, extremely intense firefight, that attack was also beaten back. Two additional enemy tanks burnt out; five others had been immobilized or rendered combat-ineffective. A sixth one was probably rendered the same. The antitank elements reported the complete destruction of a tank and one combat ineffective tank. Unfortunately, they also had a complete write-off of their own to report.

On 19 November, the division ended its attachment relationship to the *23. Panzer-Division.* The Army division was withdrawn from the front to be sent to Stalingrad to participate in the upcoming relief effort. The *"Wiking"* Division, which had all of its subordinate elements by then, was attached to the *III. Panzer-Korps* for further operations. It was placed on the right side of the corps. During the last weeks of November and especially during the first two weeks of December, the Soviets concentrated their efforts against the deep southern flank of the division, continuously attempting to envelop farther to the west by coming out of the mountain valleys and encircling German positions along the Terek front. All of those efforts were in vain. On 23 December, the *1. Panzer-Armee* decided to pull back the German "toehold" outside of Ordshonikidse to shorten the front to a line running Durdur-Elchotowo. By doing so, the division was freed up for other operations.

In all, the main line of resistance was pulled back some 25 kilometers. During the process, *SS-Panzer-Abteilung 5* disengaged from the enemy and moved back some 60 kilometers to the northwest into the area around Doschukino, a village on the Naltschik-Prochladny rail line, where it bivouacked.

The rearward movements brought rearguard actions with them, however. On 24 December, two battalion tanks were lost. On 25 December, the battalion scored its last great success in that sector. Mühlenkamp later recalled:

> I remember that it was an icy cold winter's night with a cloudless sky filled with stars. We made good progress and were able to evacuate all of our equipment. The division had prepared everything for us.

During the night, we encountered individual Russian patrols and got involved in smaller engagements in a variety of ways.

During some firefights, the place where we were celebrating Christmas was shot to pieces. Even then, however, we were able to wind up on top.

On the first day of Christmas, we reached a sector of the terrain where we had to stay in the open. The first Russian fighting vehicles appeared. In accordance with tried and true tactics, we allowed the vehicles to approach. On the first day of Christmas 1942, we set 22 T-34's alight.

That final and successful act of the play, which was also undoubtedly very impressive for the Soviets, marked almost five months to the day since the battalion had attacked across the Don to the south. Of the nearly 1,100 kilometers it had moved in advancing as far as the foot of the Kasbek, the second-highest peak in the Caucasus, almost 900 had been under combat conditions.

The continuously worsening situation in the area around Stalingrad, which threatened the northeastern flank of the German thrust into the Caucasus, forced the operation to be called off. The division was pulled out of the line and moved to the threatened sector of the front to help prevent an even worse catastrophe for the German forces pulling back out of the Caucasus.

✠

There was no longer any doubt that the Caucasus offensive, which had yielded such impressive successes, had to be characterized as a failure with the start of the events in December. The tables started to be turned, and the German forces in the field were pressed hard.

Since much of what developed at the time remained incomprehensible to the men of the tank battalion—what actually happened is partly contentious even today—an effort will be made at this point to contribute to an understanding and shed some light on questions that remained unanswered by introducing the critical commentary of Soviet Army General S. M. Shtemenko in his book *The Soviet General Staff at War, 1941–1945.*

To begin with, Shtemenko confirms the Soviet intention to evacuate the city of Rostow in July 1942:

> In order to avoid encirclement, the Southern Front was directed by the Supreme headquarters to evacuate Rostow and move across the Don. On 25 July, the forces were on the east bank of the river.[63]

A second matter of special importance for understanding the campaign in the Caucasus—the situation in the Trans-Caucasus before and during the German offensive—is discussed at great length in Shtemenko's book. The German plan to capture the Trans-Caucasus, which is often described as fanciful and utopian at best, is considered by Shtemenko as worthy of discussion. In analyzing the military situation, he came to the following conclusion:

> Things had gone comparatively well, by comparison [meaning the Soviet march into Iran]. Turkey was another matter, however. In the middle of 1942, no one could guarantee that it would not declare its allegiance to the German side. There was a reason why there were 26 Turkish divisions massed along the Turkish-Soviet border.

In further discussion, Shtemenko makes a number of interesting observations. Especially interesting are the dates:

> The Trans-Caucasian Front, which had been formed in 1941, had originally consisted of the 45th and 46th Armies and the forces stationed in Iran. In June, it was reinforced by the 44th Army. . . . The Trans-Caucasus was also covered by the forces of the North Caucasian Front. But these forces were apparently insufficient. At the behest of the General Staff, an expedited transfer of forces from central Asia and other areas was initiated. . . . On 23 June, the military council of the Trans-Caucasian Front briefed Moscow on a revised plan for the defense of the Trans-Caucasus. The plan brought all of the deficiencies into even more relief. The lack of forces had, of course, influenced their commitment. Quite properly, the area around Baku was reinforced by the moving of the 44th Army to the Terek; however, that left almost all of the main part of the Caucasus uncovered by the command . . .

63. Author's Note: Shtemenko, 57. The remaining quotes are also from Shtemenko. Translator's Note: The reader is again reminded that this is a reverse translation, having been translated from the original Russian into English, then into German, and then (for this book) back into English.

Even before a German soldier had moved out to attack from his winter positions of 1941–42, extensive defensive plans and preparations were being made in an area some 1,000 kilometers farther south and southeast against an enemy who still had not tipped his hand regarding his attack intentions.

Directive No. 41 of 5 April 1942 is available as an historical document. The German intention of crossing the Caucasus is contained in it in General Point I. The Soviet High Command must have had access to information concerning the contents of this directive and which caused the initiation of defensive preparations outlined by Shtemenko. Both of those facts cast doubt on the veracity of the statements of the former chief of staff of the Army, *Generaloberst* Halder. In his book, *Hitler als Feldherr (Hitler as Commander-in-Chief)*, he wrote:

> The fixed notion that the Russian resistance had finally been broken lulled Hitler during the ongoing operation to withdraw the majority of the armored formations of the *6. Armee*, which were especially necessary at the moment against the increasing resistance west of Stalingrad, and send them south across the Don and give the forces concentrated there a new mission: Take the Caucasus and advance to a line running Batum-Baku.
>
> That was something completely new: Instead of a unified operation directed east with a main effort against Stalingrad, which only needed to be covered from the south, two divergent operations emerged . . .

It strains credulity for the impartial observer to believe that the former chief of staff of the General Staff was not aware of Directive No. 41 of April 1942—a document he probably had a hand in preparing—in July 1942. Halder's reference to a "fixed notion" of broken Soviet resistance was most likely Halder's opinion, as has been documented in the daily logs of the German Army High Command. Similar sentiments can be found in the memoirs of *Generaloberst* Rendulic in his book *Soldat in stürzenden Reichen (Soldier in Collapsing Regimes)*:[64]

> We were filled with resentment and bitterness by the fact that no measures had been taken for the winter. The reason was the incorrect assessment of the situation by the chief of staff of the Army, *Generaloberst* Halder. In an entry in the daily logs of the Army High Command in July 1941, he stated that it was increasingly being

64. Author's Note: Rendulic, *Soldat in stürzenden Reichen*, Damm Verlag: Munich, 1965, 278.

shown that his prediction of the war being over in several months was correct. . . . When I read the assessment of the chances for success of the war against Russia in Landsberg in 1948 in a photocopy of the daily logs, it was like a revelation to me.

In the same book:

That no relief was forthcoming (filling the divisions with men, weapons and equipment) was due, among other things, to the recent and grotesque incorrect assessment of the situation by the chief of staff, *Generaloberst* Halder. In the daily logs of the German Armed Forces High Command of 19 April 1942 is written: "During the situation briefing, the chief of staff of the Army concluded from the many enemy formations that had appeared on the Eastern front since November 1941 that the Russians had made extraordinary efforts and had already used up a considerable portion of their available forces.

Shtemenko provides details of the defensive measures that were initiated in the Caucasus that started as early as August 1942. At that point, not a single German soldier had reached the Terek. It was more than four weeks later before *SS-Panzer-Abteilung 5* was moved from the Western Caucasus into the area along the Terek. To cover the main portion of the Caucasus, which had been stripped naked of forces, the X and XI Guards Infantry Corps were sent there in August, in addition to 11 separate infantry brigades.

To defend the Urukh and Terek Rivers, the "Northern Group" was formed. That was composed of the 9th Army, which also incorporated elements of the 44th Army and the 37th Army, which had pulled back from the Donez and Don areas. The group was entrusted with the defense of Baku and the Georgian Military Road. Personally directed by Stalin, Shtemenko was dispatched to the Caucasus on 21 August 1942 to coordinate and support the defensive measures. He wrote the following about an emergency program initiated on 24 August:

All of the forces that had pulled back in the north in good order were employed along the Terek. . . . On 28 August, the first steps were taken in the Baku sector to establish the 58th Army. A mixed cavalry corps was assembled in the area around Zizlyar. After a thorough study of the situation, it was decided to form three operational centers: Baku, Grossny and Wladikawkas. An entire infantry division was employed to defend the Georgian Military Road. Its main forces blocked the entrance to Ordshonikidse. Another division was ordered to the same place from the area around Gori . . .

Shtemenko describes the consistency with which the Soviets applied their defensive measures:

The Baku sector brought us a number of difficulties. During an inspection trip, we discovered that the construction of defensive lines was only progressing slowly. It was apparent there was a lack of work forces. On 16 September, based on the recommendation of the military, the defensive committee enacted a special resolution to mobilize 90,000 local workers for the daily construction of defensive facilities in the areas of Mackhachkala, Derbent and Baku. Based on that, the work proceeded at great speed. Tank ditches and traps were dug and tank obstacles emplaced, day and night. To complement that, other measures were taken by the Supreme Headquarters on 29 September to increase the defensive capability; of decisive importance was the transfer of 100 tanks into the area . . .

Once these facts are known, it is no wonder that the men of the tank battalion and, indeed, all of the forces employed there, saw such a completely different military situation once they arrived in the Terek area.

The framework for the fighting that awaited the battalion once it was moved from the Caucasus to the area southwest of Stalingrad at the turn of 1942–43 is best shown in a telephone conversation that Shtemenko had with Stalin at 1330 hours on 4 January 1943. Stalin gave him the following directive:

1. The enemy is pulling back from the Northern Caucasus, since he is burning his depots and destroying the roads. Maslennikow's Northern Group is to be reorganized as a reserve group with the mission of initiating a cautious pursuit. It is not to our advantage to throw the enemy out of the Northern Caucasus. We'll get more out of it by fixing him there and encircling him by an advance by our Black Sea Group. To that end, the main effort of the operations of the Trans-Caucasian Front is to be shifted to the area of the Black Sea Group, a matter that neither Maslennikow nor Petrow are clear about . . .

2. . . . the most important mission of the Black Sea Group is to reach Tichorezkaja, thus frustrating the enemy in getting his materiel out to the west. [Author's Note: Tichorezkaja is an important rail hub 150 kilometers south of Rostow.] To that end, you will be supported by the 51st Army and, possibly, the 28th Army [out of the area southeast of Stalingrad]. Your second and main mission is to move a strong force from the Black Sea, occupy Bataisk and Asow and break through to Rostow from the east, thus encircling the enemy group in the Northern Caucasus with the objective of either capturing it or destroying it.
3. Order Petrow to start the offensive in a timely manner without losing an hour of time and without waiting for the arrival of all of his reserves. Petrow has been operating defensively the entire time and has no experience in conducting offensive operations. Make it clear to him that he must act in the spirit of the offense . . . that he has to exploit every day, every hour . . .

It was into those offensive movements of the Soviets, which had already pushed away the Romanian field army that was positioned south of Stalingrad to cover the German southern flank, that the formations of the division were committed. The railheads for the tank battalion were identified along the Tichorezkaja-Stalingrad rail line, some 200 to 250 kilometers southwest of the city on the Volga.

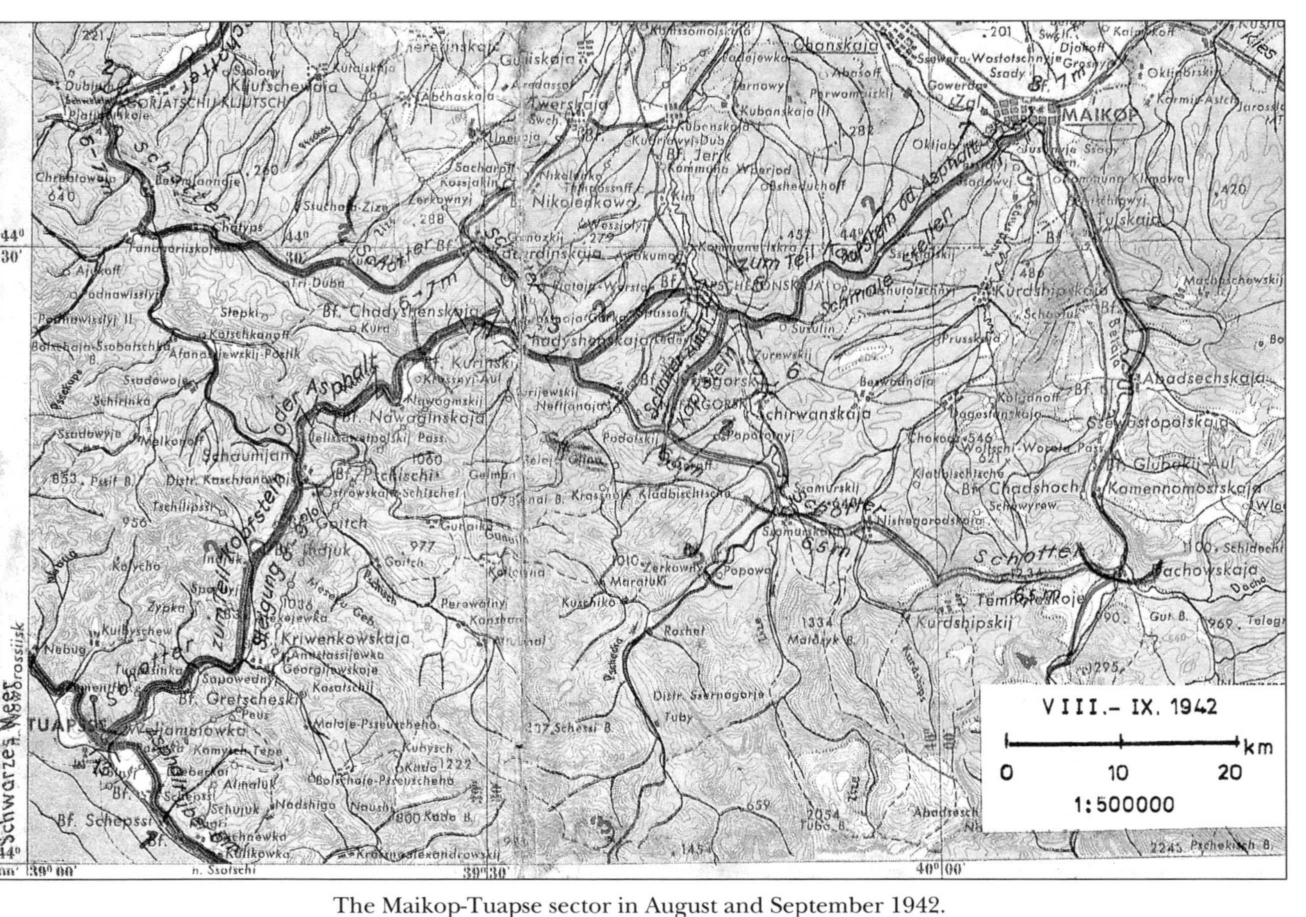

The Maikop-Tuapse sector in August and September 1942.

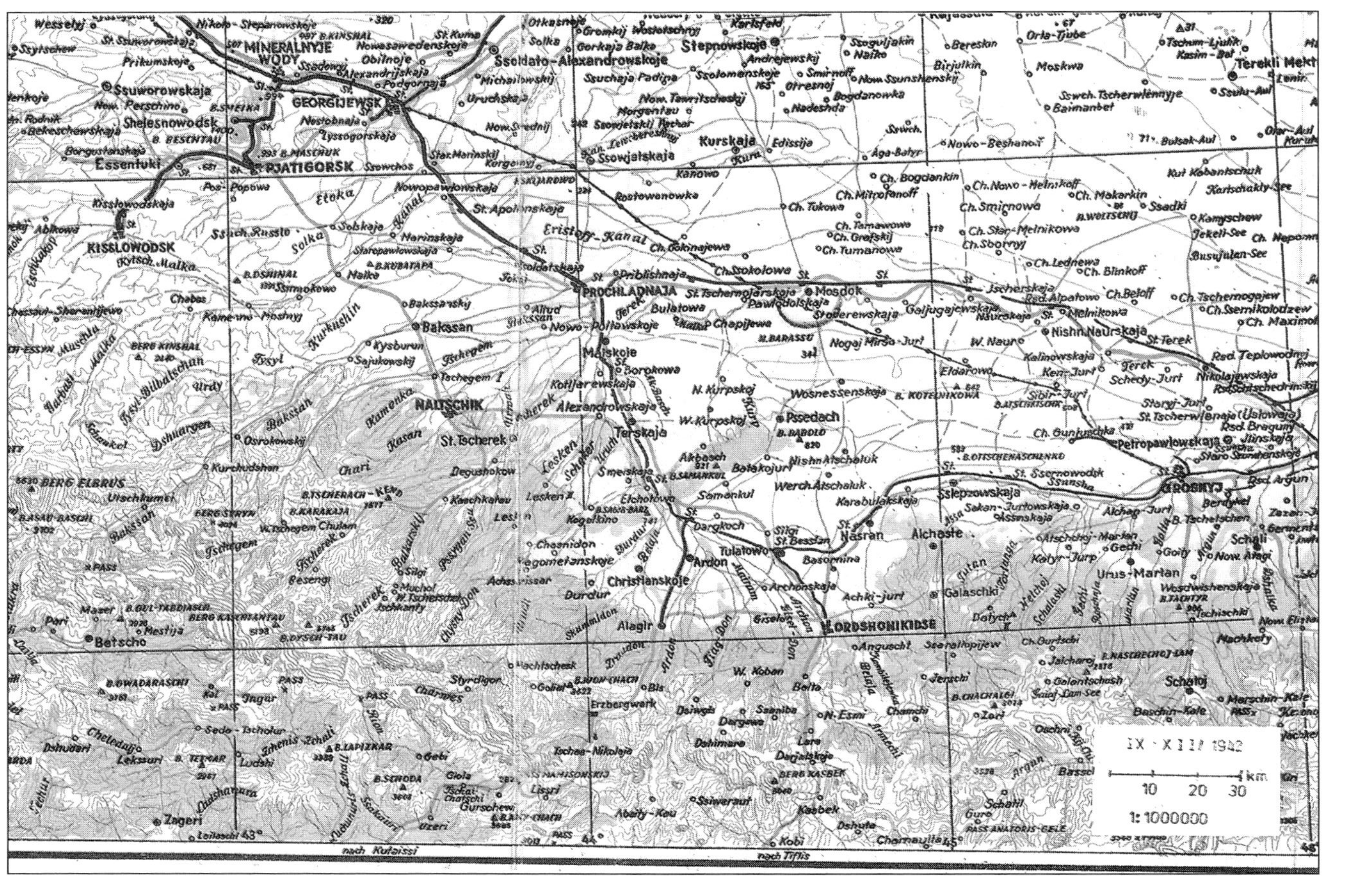

The Naltschik-Ordshonikidse-Grossnyj sector.

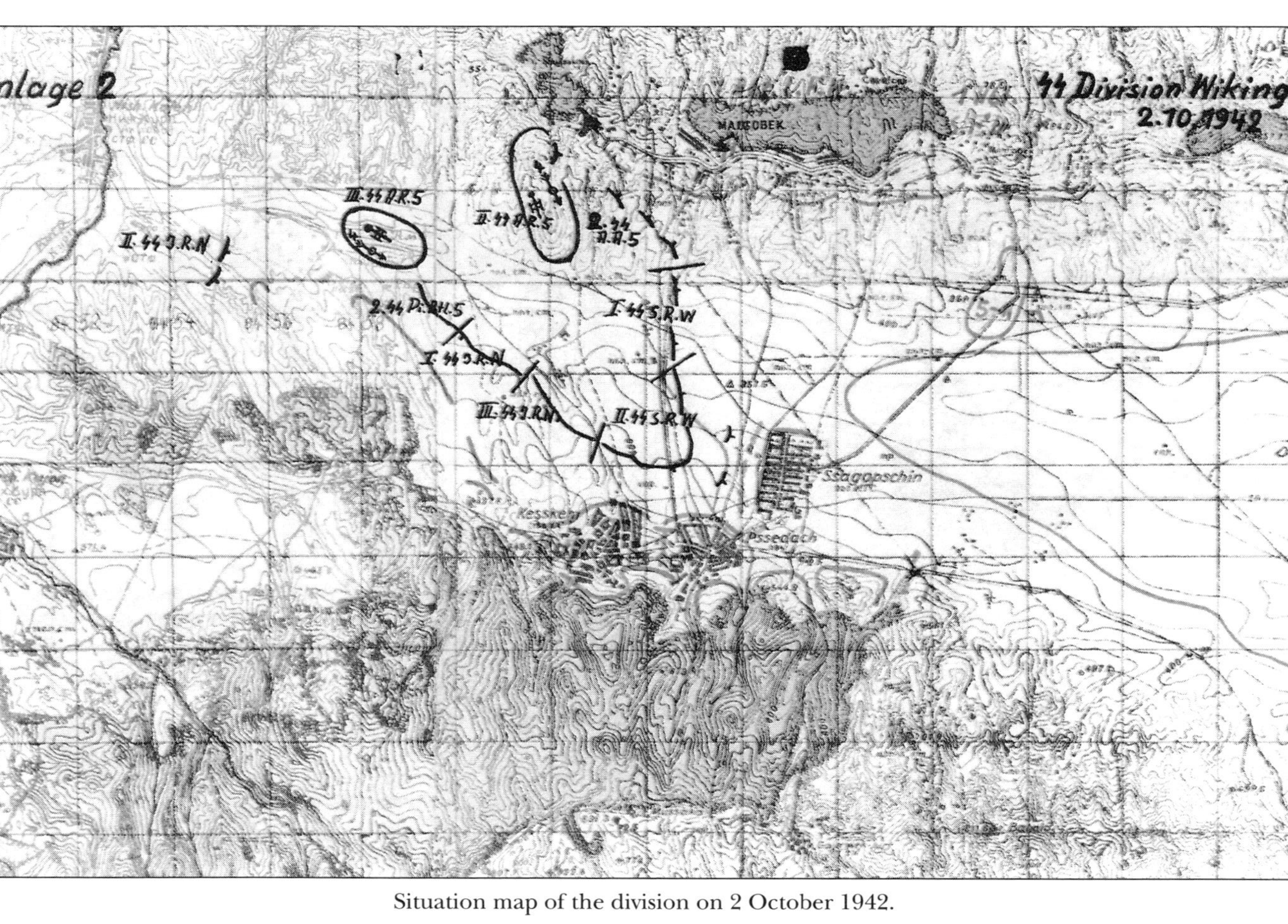

Situation map of the division on 2 October 1942.

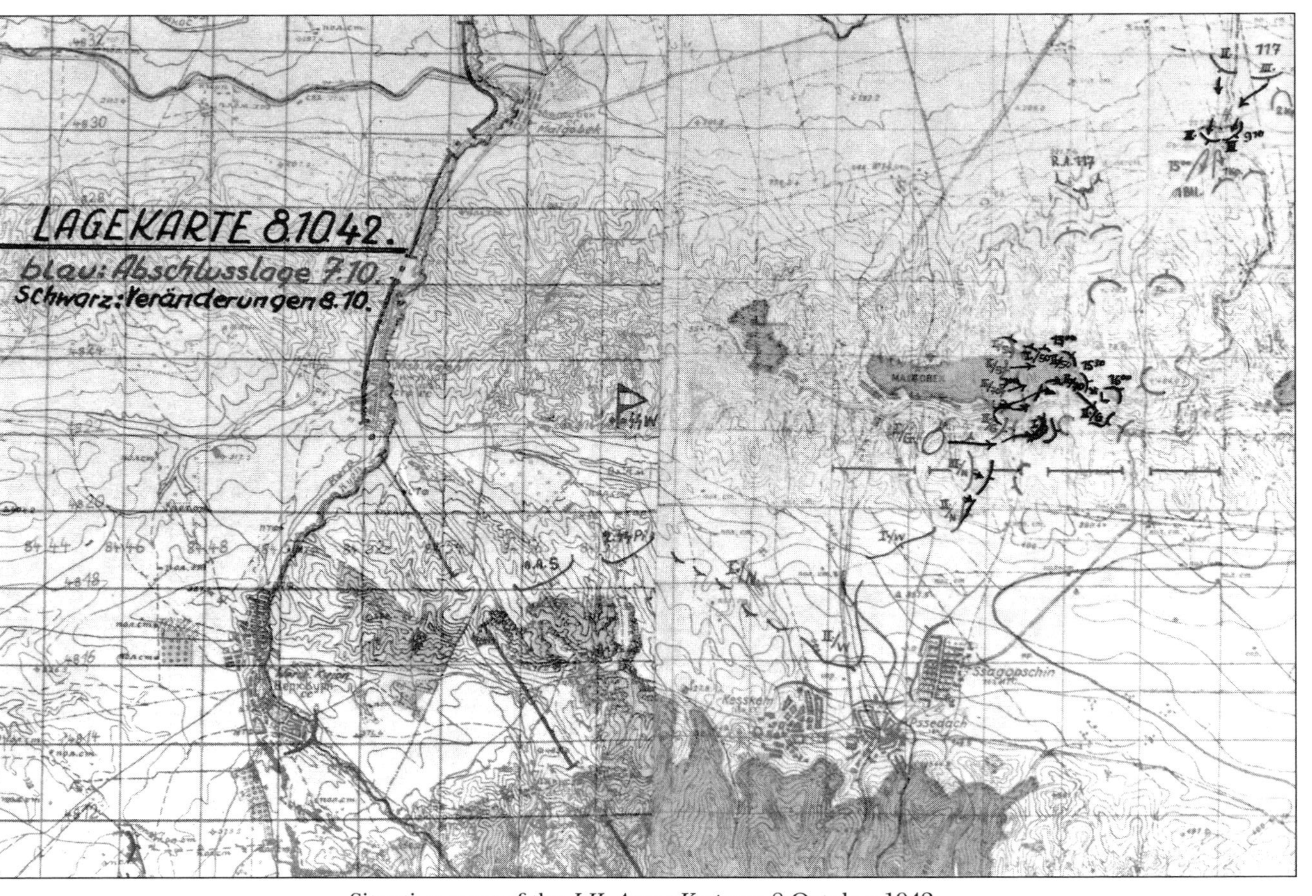

Situation map of the *LII. Armee-Korps* on 8 October 1942.

CHAPTER 3

Retreat and Defense between the Manytsch and the Don

As indicated in the previous chapter, the tank battalion was moved to railheads on the Tichorezkaja-Stalingrad rail line as part of the overall effort to stabilize the situation around Stalingrad. The battalion started rail operations on 28 December in Doschukino. *SS-Hauptsturmführer* Schneider, assigned to the headquarters of the tank battalion, has provided insight into the operations of the time, starting on 29 December:

> As a newly promoted *Hauptmann*[1] in the headquarters, I received the mission to go to Manskoje with the battle staff and load on the trains there with elements of the 3rd Company . . . we headed out at 0900 hours . . . The movement was delayed in Manskoje, because we were also supposed to take along two tanks from the maintenance facility. Everything was finally ready at 1700 hours. We moved out at a snail's pace towards the north.
>
> Of course, once again, our rail car was not heated. As a result, we spent the first part of the night in the "ice box." Finally, an *Unterscharführer* was able to locate a heater hose. That was the reason it had not become warm. The things were unbelievably scarce. And then if you could find one, it was unquestionably damaged. *Untersturmführer* Mittelbacher became our salvation in the sense that he crept over to another transport train in one of the larger train stations and, risking his life, dismounted a heater hose. It was clear that every transport was guarded, and who was going to allow someone to steal a heater hose in the winter without further consequences? Well, we were happy about the successful escapade, since it meant we didn't need to freeze any longer . . . As a result, those in the rail car

1. Translator's Note: For some reason, he refers to his rank using the Army equivalent.

slept quite well. The fact that our ribs were sore the next morning had nothing to do with the heater hose.[2]

On 30 December, the train reached Newinnowskaja at 1200 hours, after being routed through Mineralnyje-Wody. Schneider continues:

> The steppes were bleak. Their color a dirty yellow. There was no tree to be seen, near or far. You could only see the recurring slightly rolling hills. At 1700 hours we were all together on the rail line, waiting for a signal, when a few Russian bombers attempted to get us. The gentlemen were unable to get either the bridge over the Kuban in front of us, the rail station behind us or the track itself . . .
>
> In Tichorezkaja, on 31 December, we turned off from the line towards Rostow, and the train steamed to the north in the direction of Ssalsk.
>
> New Year's was celebrated on the train with a few glasses of mulled wine and grog.
>
> All of a sudden, there was a jerk and the train stopped. Outside, German and Russian railway employees shouted past one another . . . I swung myself out of the rail car and saw that there wasn't anything special happening to cause the shouting of the railway employees. But it was also clear to me that we were not alone. There were other transport trains to the left and right. From the railhead commander, I discovered that we were to detrain there.
>
> The village was called Proletarskaja and was along the Manytsch, the official border between Europe and Asia.
>
> As I stumbled my way back to my rail car, pyrotechnics suddenly climbed into the nighttime skies above the village: "Request for final protective fires" . . . "Enemy attacking" . . . "Our location." Soon thereafter, there was some wild rifle and machine-gun fire, with antitank guns joining in occasionally. All of the standard light signals used by the German Army rose into the dark night, again and again.
>
> Initially, I was somewhat perplexed. After all, if everything the signals were saying is true, then the Russians must be really attacking the city we had just reached with a vengeance. Such a possibility had been one of the unpleasant rumors that had circulated recently during our movement.
>
> There was no official source for information concerning the situation. I was just about to take security measures when I was informed that the wild gunfire was the New Year's fires from the

2. Author's Note: This passage and the ones that follow are from Schneider's diaries.

> *"Germania"* Regiment, which had just detrained ahead of us. And so we greeted the New Year of 1943 with a less-than-serious incident . . .

After almost 60 hours of being on the rails, the tank battalion had covered the 600 kilometers, which separated the Caucasian area of operations from the new one southwest of Stalingrad, at an average speed of 10 kilometers an hour.

The battle staff of the battalion and the 3rd Company were able to secure quarters in the overcrowded village of Proletarskaja, whose streets were jammed with vehicle columns.

The 1st and 2nd Companies, as well as the battalion command post, were in Kuberle, a village about 50 kilometers northeast of Proletarskaja. The division command post was also there, as well as the command post of the *LVII. Panzer-Korps*, to which the division had been allocated. The elements that had detrained in Proletarskaja moved to Kuberle on the morning of 3 January. Schneider:

> Along the road leading to the front, we were met again and again by innumerable columns coming our way. You almost feel abandoned when you head towards the enemy all by yourself. After the traffic on the road had died down, you could see what sorts of things had been abandoned along the side of the road. Valuable vehicles and special-purpose vehicles were simply left behind due to the smallest of problems that could have easily been fixed. They often had important and valuable cargoes.

By 4 January, elements of the tank battalion were conducting operations, albeit under conditions far different than they had previously experienced. Schneider:

> The battalion marched with its 2nd and 3rd Companies into the center of the division sector and bivouacked in a collective farm in the middle of the steppe. The quarters were miserable. We stayed in old stalls that were half falling apart. There was just enough room for one company. The quarters question was soon resolved by the highest levels of command, inasmuch as one company after the other was committed . . .

✠

At this point, an outline will be provided of the operational and tactical framework of the fighting that the battalion found itself involved in as part of the division, especially since the sector was so very different from the previous area of operation of the formation.

On 23 December 1942, approximately 10 days before the tank battalion arrived in sector, the *6. Panzer-Division* was involved in a relief attack in the direction of Stalingrad and had reached the Mischkowa River, recording good progress. It closed to within 48 kilometers of the beleaguered city. The *6. Armee* was supposed to launch its own attack to link up with the relief forces, theoretically further narrowing the gap to some 33 kilometers. On orders of *Generalfeldmarschall* von Manstein, it was pulled out of the line and from the command and control of the *LVII. Panzer-Korps* and moved to a sector more than 100 kilometers away. At the time, the *6. Panzer-Division* had been badly weakened, but it was still the strongest Army armored division.

> [*Generalleutnant*] Raus, the commander of the brave *6. Panzer-Division* . . . confessed that he had pangs of conscience for weeks on end, because he obeyed the order to move instead of acting against the orders and breaking through to Stalingrad and linking up with Paulus.[3]

The reorganization of the *4. Panzer-Armee* that had been ordered by von Manstein decisively weakened it. For all practical purposes, it only had the *LVII. Panzer-Korps,* which had two weak armored divisions, the *17. Panzer-Division* and the *23. Panzer-Division,* attached to it. Effective the middle of January, the *16. Infanterie-Division (mot)* joined the corps, but the three divisions were not equal to the task of holding back the onslaught of the Soviet 51st Army and 2nd Guards Army, which together had one tank corps, three mechanized corps, three rifle divisions and a cavalry corps.[4] In the last days of December and the first part of January, the field army was pushed back some 150 kilometers to an area east of Simowniki, approximately 75 kilometers northeast of Proletarskaj on the Manytsch.

As January wore on, the two aforementioned Soviet field armies were joined by a third, the 28th Army, in the Elista area. The Romanian 4th Army, which had been directed to cover the right flank of the *4. Panzer-Armee*—thus also covering the right flank of *Heeresgruppe Don*—pulled back in an ill-disciplined manner, in some cases without weapons, in individual small elements, sometimes in uniform, sometimes in civilian clothes.

---

3. Author's Note: Lenz.

4. Author's Note: Erich von Manstein, *Verlorene Siege,* Athenäum Verlag: 1955, 372.

The method of fighting was determined by the German inferiority in numbers, the steppe-like character of the terrain and the time of year. The wintery cold forced the combatants into the villages of the steppe. There was no cohesive front. Snowstorms and sheets of ice made movements difficult to a degree not previously known.

The operational objective of the enemy was to destroy the German forces between the Don and the Caucasus, as has already been indicated in Stalin's directive of 4 January. The operational objective of *Heeresgruppe Don* was to successfully defend against the Soviet attacks so as to keep the area around Rostow open for the German formations pulling back out of the Caucasus.

SIMOWNIKI

> As a result, the battalion was employed carved up in companies. A company wherever it threatened to become hot.
>
> The battalion commander no longer had any direct influence on his company commanders, since they often had to make decisions on their own that were born of the momentary circumstance.
>
> And frequently the infantry commander was constantly in the ears of an oft-plagued commander: He should do this or that. As a result, it was easy to get in the dangerous position of serving two masters, his battalion commander or the infantry commander.
>
> That nothing good came of that was clear. You frequently had to employ the entire force of your personality to ensure that your tanks remained firmly under your control. Otherwise, it could happen that the infantryman tried to take on the job of being a tanker as a secondary profession. And that was the worst possible thing: Bungling in warfare is paid for in blood.

This complaint concerns a problem whose beginnings can be traced this period of transition for the German military from the offensive to the strategic defensive. This transition—a changeover to the defensive, which characterized the German conduct of operations until the end of the war—was forced by the confluence of extremely different factors. As a consequence, the aforementioned complaint about the employment and use of the armored force came about. The punch of a massed employment of armor, which simultaneously offered the individual tank a high degree of security on the battlefield, was broken apart in a series of individual actions of far less combat power that also revealed the relative defenselessness of an individual tank on the field of battle.

As the infantryman became increasingly accustomed to the perceived protection, there also grew a corresponding dependency in crisis situations. He was also missing heavy armor-defeating weaponry that allowed determined self-defense. That these problems came about was also due, in the end, to the fact that many of the leaders to whom the tankers reported had matured militarily within the confines of infantry thinking and principles of leadership.

The war had advanced technical progress without having a simultaneous rapid growth in the training of future generations of troop commanders and general staff officers. Until the beginning of the war, the military academies of the Army used a modified version of an infantry battalion from the First World War as their focus; it was only during the course of the Second World War that the general staff officer candidates started to transition to models of commanding and controlling motorized formations. This is not an effort to find guilt; rather, it simply shows a symptom that appears unique to transitional phases of that type, where there are revolutionary changes in military technology and leadership. It cannot be forgotten that the three armored divisions on active duty at the start of the war were increased eightfold by the beginning of 1943, a span of only three years.

That afternoon, the commander of the tank battalion was at the command post of the *"Westland"* Regiment in Simowniki. On 1 January, the regimental headquarters and the 1st Battalion had become engaged in intense close combat with Soviet T-34's and infantry while detraining. While the *LVII. Panzer-Korps* believed that Simowniki was still firmly in German hands, the 1st Battalion of *SS-Sturmbannführer* Ziemssen turned back the Soviets during the night of detraining, eliminated a few Soviet tanks, dug in along the edge of the village and defended. The corps had prepared to pull back, since it had not been certain that Simowniki could be held. The following entries were made in the corps' daily logs for 1 January:

> At 1200 hours, *Grenadier-Regiment 156*[5] received orders to move back behind the Kuberle, northwest of Simowniki. The village of Simowniki

5. Author's Note: This regiment was part of the *16. Infanterie-Division (mot).* That division, along with the *17. Panzer-Division* and the *23. Panzer-Division,* had been ordered by the corps to move behind the Kuberle on either side of Simowniki.

was to be avoided, since it was under enemy fire. The newly attached *SS-Grenadier-Regiment Westland*, employed to protect Simowniki from the enemy advancing from the east, reported six enemy tanks and one battalion of infantry attacking at 0845 hours in the northeastern corner of Simowniki, where they had temporarily penetrated into the locality. The regiment turned back all further attacks and believed it would be able to hold Simowniki during the day as well.

At 1220 hours, the Chief [of Staff] of the field army reported that the holding of Simowniki appeared questionable and that the destruction of all stores and the demolition of the railway was to be directed.

1700 hours: Main body of the *23. Panzer-Division* prepared to defend in its new sector southwest of the Kuberle. Reconnaissance to the east and southeast as far as the Manytsch.

On the next day, 2 January 1943, the daily logs recorded:

Westland turned back the attack on Simowniki.
1055 hours: *SS-Regiment Westland* defended Simowniki magnificently; despite that, the attacks are increasing in intensity.
1425 hours: One battalion of *Germania* sent to Simowniki to reinforce.
Wiking tank battalion on forced march from Ssalsk to Simowniki.
2105 hours: The enemy forces outside of Simowniki consist primarily of motorized and armored formations.

Entries from 6 January:

Strong enemy pressure at and north of Simowniki.
1230 hours: Enemy moved out against Simowniki at 1130 hours with 4 tanks and 300 men. He was turned back in bitter close-in fighting.

The *"Westland"* Regiment held Simowniki for seven days. The value of those seven days cannot be measured highly enough in the race against time for holding open the area from Bataisk to Rostow for the withdrawal of the German formations across the Don. Unfortunately, the regiment had not been able to prevent the panicky flight from Simowniki prior to its arrival. According to Schneider:

47,000 new sets of winter uniforms burned. Brand-new tanks and vehicles from a depot in the homeland, which were supposed to have been issued to the forces in the field, were simply set alight. Vehicles, which were there for repair of minor damage, were also treated the same way.

On 5 January, the battalion's 2nd Company was located in Nowy Gascun, northwest of Simowniki, where it was attached to Scheibe's battalion of the *"Germania"* Regiment. An advance by that company during the afternoon scattered enemy concentrations to the northeast of Stojanowski. Stojanowski proper, which was defended by *SS-Obersturmführer* Heder and his men of the 3rd Company of the divisional engineers, was taken the next day by an enemy force of 16 tanks and strong ground elements. According to the corps' daily logs:

> The village was lost at considerable cost to friendly personnel and materiel in the face of the superior forces; the steep banks of the Kuberle prevented a further advance of the enemy to the west.

On 7 January, the Russians reinforced their elements at Stojanowski. They exploited the strong pressure on the northern flank of the *LVII. Panzer-Korps*, to push forces forward between the Ssal and the Don. At first light, *SS-Hauptsturmführer* Schneider was on his way to Nowy Gaschun with an important order:

> The move through the steppe that spread out into the darkness had something eerie about it. Moreover, it was not simple to orient yourself. After all, there wasn't a single reference point in the form of a tree, a patch of woods, a defile or something similar. At the same time, I can also confirm from personal experience that you see damned little from a tank at night.
>
> I worked my way towards Nowy Gaschun, moving by way of Amta. When the silhouette of a collective farm arose in front of me, I fired white signal flares. It would not have been the first time I received fire from friendly antitank guns. The fact that I was approaching from the rear, that is, from our own rear area, offered no protection from being engaged by your own weapons. That had to do with the way the front was organized. There was no interconnected system of trenches. In point of fact, only the built-up areas were occupied by us. They were built up into strongpoints that could defend to all sides. It was entirely possible for the Russians to sneak between two localities, hit the garrison from the rear, where it felt more secure, and easily destroy it.

✠

On 7 January, the 2nd Company of the battalion took up quarters in the clay-hut village of Kowalewski on the extreme left wing of the division. In the process, it made no serious contact with the enemy. At 1200 hours that same day, the battalion received orders that it was to serve as the division's rearguard that night. The division had been ordered to withdraw.

The 1st Company was in an all-round defensive position—known as a hedgehog—south of the road bridge at Simowniki. Its 1st Platoon was west of the Simowniki-Kuberle road, while its 3rd Platoon was east of it. The 2nd Platoon was positioned farther east along the railway bridge. The 2nd Company was retrieved and both it and the 3rd Company, as well as the battalion headquarters, were positioned west of the road to Kuberle. Schneider:

> We waited, freezing, until the last elements of *Westland* were past us. Railway engineers blew up the railway bridge. Soon, the last grenadiers had gone by. We then had to wait another half hour. But that time passed as well. After we turned around for a final look at Simowniki, which was burning, we took our leave as well and followed the grenadiers west.
>
> A snowstorm soon arose, which made visibility even worse. On top of that, there was the ice on the road, which caused first one, then the other, tank to slide off to either the right or the left. In the process, the tracks were thrown. Mounting the piles of iron was a sweet piece of work, given the cold and the visibility conditions. As a result, the battalion was split apart, which caused a shiver to go down your spine. The question frequently arose: What would happen if the Russians should suddenly pursue with a few T-34's?

Early on the morning of 8 January, around 0600 hours, the tank battalion reached Kuberle, about 25 kilometers southwest of Simowniki, on the Tichorezkaja-Stalingrad rail line. The battalion labored eight hours to cover those 25 kilometers.

There was no rest for the tired tankers. It was reported that the Soviets were in Orlowskaja, some 20 kilometers to the southwest, in the rear of the battalion. That would mean that the only supply route and railway line had been lost. The 2nd Company was immediately dispatched as a fire brigade. Towards noon, the division ordered the entire battalion there. When it arrived, however, the situation had already been cleared up. Schneider:

> A Russian infantry regiment had suddenly appeared from the east and, exploiting the surprise, entered Orlowskaja, which was only weakly screened. It was able to take half. The engineer battalion, which had been held in reserve by the division, ejected the Russians, supported by a couple of tanks and self-propelled guns, which had been on their way from the maintenance facility back to the battalion. As the fighting reached its high point, Flügel's [2nd] company arrived and turned the Russian retreat into a catastrophe. The maintenance facility counted 700 dead Russians. The Russian regiment was completely wiped out.

The daily logs of the *LVII. Panzer-Korps* record the following on 8 January 1943:

> 0745 hours: The operations officer of the *Wiking* Division telephonically informed the corps that the division had employed its engineer battalion, supported by six tanks, to clean up the situation in Orlowskaja.
>
> 1600 hours: Orlowskaja has been retaken by the engineers and tanks of the SS, with the enemy suffering heavy losses (three battalions destroyed).

While the tank battalion was still in the process of establishing itself in Orlowskaja, it was immediately ordered back to Kuberle. It rolled back in a pitch-dark night; it moved under blackout conditions, since enemy nuisance bombers were attempting to track it. In contrast, some of the Soviet formations moved freely with lights turned on. Once the battalion arrived in Kuberle, another order summoned it to the division's left wing, where a Soviet attack was expected. The tankers spent their fifth night aboard their vehicles on the way to Nowo-Lodin, a few kilometers northeast of Kuberle. Local penetrations were cleaned up there. The 2nd Company eliminated Soviet forces equivalent to almost a battalion:

> A tank company was committed against enemy forces that advanced to the west across the Kuberle as far as the area northeast of Trudowoj. It wiped out most of the enemy forces; the rest escaped to the east.[6]

The battalion command post, located in a collective farm, came under mortar fire. The Soviets even started firing into the collective farm with

6. Author's Note: Daily logs of the *LVII. Panzer-Korps.*

antitank weaponry from the high ground of the creek, which emptied into the Ssal farther to the north.

At 1700 hours on 10 January, orders were received to continue the withdrawal. The fact that they were to continue west came as a surprise to all. The tank battalion covered the disengagement of the *"Westland"* Regiment from the enemy. After the last truck from the infantry battalion had passed, the tank battalion waited another two hours. Schneider:

> During that time, Ivan fired like crazy into the collective farm. A patrol had to be fended off. Finally, we were allowed to scram. Once again, it was damned dark. The eyes of the drivers were inflamed; they could barely see anything. The tank commanders sat up front on the tanks and guided the drivers by means of hand and arm signals.
>
> After everything started moving along, an obstacle surfaced in front of us in the form of an embankment, which we were unable to move across, since the driving surface was too narrow and, on top of that, it was icy. The danger of sliding off was too great. After many attempts, we gave up on [crossing] the embankment.
>
> But how were we then to proceed? The Russians were behind us, and we were all by ourselves. We scouted for a bypass, which was soon found. Nonetheless, it still placed monstrous demands on the drivers. It was a real roller-coaster ride. One tank after the other was passed through a snarl of cliffs and slippery stretches of ice to the other side. In the morning, at 0600 hours, we landed in Kamenno-Balkoff.

Kamenno-Balkoff was northwest of the road from Kuberle, west of Orlowskaja and some 15 kilometers southwest of Kuberle. The headquarters of the *"Nordland"* Regiment was there, along with one of its battalions, which was defending the locality. The tankers were able to get a few hours of sleep. Following that, the tanks were in urgent need of maintenance and care.

The first few days of 1943 had brought the battalion a number of new discoveries and surprises in the conduct of warfare during the winter in the steppes. Kamenno-Balkoff would bring some more. Once again, we hear from Schneider:

> About three in the morning, I woke up from a restless sleep by the sounds of gunfire. At first, I thought I was dreaming. The sounds of rifle firing increased, and I had the impression in the room I was in that they were damned close. I dressed quickly and reached for my pistol. I let everything else lie there for the time being. When I stepped out of the house, rounds were whipping down the street.

A house was burning at the entrance to the village; next to it, the wonderful radio vehicle was in bright flames. While I ran quickly to the battalion command post, an antitank gun raced past me towards the road leading out of the village.

At the battalion headquarters, they already knew the Russians were in the village. The commander ordered the headquarters staff to set up an all-round defense, while I accompanied him to the location of the 2nd Company. On the way there, mummy-like figures scurried through the yards. You didn't know whether they were friend or foe. The gentlemen of the 2nd Company had to been woken up. Their surprise about the situation was no small matter. Russians in the village—thanks! The 2nd Company got ready immediately and set up a blocking position at the edge of the village. On the way back to the command post, I had an exciting experience. As I stuck my head around the corner of a house, there was . . . a Russian on the other side. With a jerk, I pulled back. The Russian did likewise. I took a detour with the commander, so we got back to the command post in one piece without having to stick our noses in the dirt a single time.

An antitank gun was positioned at the edge of the village and was firing like crazy, while the rifle rounds of the Bolshevists were whipping down the street. At first light, *Untersturmführer* Büscher launched an immediate counterattack with three *Panzer IV's*, whereby three antitank guns, a field mess and one T-34 were destroyed, without counting the many dead and prisoners.

SS-Untersturmführer Hein, the leader of the battalion's reconnaissance platoon, has also provided a firsthand account of the turbulent events of 11–12 January:

We were told to retreat, and we—that is, the light platoon with only three *Panzer II's* left—were to form the rearguard. There was a cutting cold wind, and the road to Stalingrad with its deep drainage ditches—it had been constructed by the *Organization Todt*[7]—was under a light blanket of snow that was covering a sheet of ice.

Behind us was no-man's-land, and the individual signal flares of the enemy reinforced the eerie picture of the bleak nighttime sky.

We waited tensely for radio reports in the combat vehicle. The young driver, *Rottenführer* Rötzer, chewed on a crust of bread that

7. Translator's Note: A paramilitary organization that was entrusted with infrastructure maintenance, repair and construction in the rear area.

had been frozen ice hard. Lice were marching along the collar of his uniform.

Damn! . . . The tank spun around and slid leisurely into the ditch. Cause: Left track broke! Nothing in front of us, nothing to the rear of us . . . get out of the tank all the faster. It was snowing without a break. We looked for and found the track with sticks. We pulled our tank out of the ditch with the two other ones and repaired the damage with clammy fingers, all the while attentively screening to our rear. The sounds of Russians in the distance got us well motivated.

Towards midnight, we went through the outpost line of the *"Nordland"* Regiment, talked to the platoon leader for a little while and saw his men squatting in their holes, sleepy-eyed and exhausted. Rendered a short report to the battalion headquarters and we were able to get two Russian huts at the edge of the village to sleep in. It was comfortably warm, and the persons who dwelled there were friendly.

The radio operator took over the exterior guard duties and Rötzer made himself comfortable next to the oven. I found a "Stalin" bed to sleep in. A Hindenburg light[8] flickered wanly and provided us with some sense of security.

Early in the morning, at 0500 hours, I was shaken awake by a messenger from the battalion headquarters. There was no mistaking it: Alert! He had barely given me his message when a burst from a submachine gun went through the window, and the messenger collapsed on me, dead. In less than a second, the light was swept from the table and we were flat on the floor. Soon there were several Russians in the room: *Ruki Werch!*—Hands up! Initially, we were frozen in place. Young Rötzer's entire body started shaking and—God knows!—the entire situation was damned precarious.

In the meantime—all of this happening in a matter of minutes—Russian and German commands were being shouted outside. A burst from a *MG 42* smashed against the walls of the house, and ricochets rocketed through the shot-out window. A quick decision: My Belgian FN pistol out of the holster on my rear, unload a full magazine in the direction of the flustered Russians and then Rötzer and I zigzag through the enemy—cut and run!

Rötzer was grazed, but we managed to get out. Teeth chattering and bathed in sweat, we reached an empty hut and took two Russian steppe jackets and felt boots.

8. Translator's Note: Soldier jargon for army-procured candle holders.

In the meantime, the village had become a witch's cauldron. The *"Nordland"* outposts received us in our Russian garb with rifle fire. Despite all that, we got through and reached *Untersturmführer* Büscher in his *Panzer IV.*

We talked it over quickly—we had to get our armored vehicles back—and the immediate counterattack was launched. The roadside ditches were rolled up until we reached out huts. In the meantime, the Russians had barricaded themselves there. Many dead were left lying there; the remainder surrendered.

We loosened up the frozen hatches of our vehicles with blow torches, recovered our dead messenger comrade and received new orders from the commander's headquarters.

What had happened that night? Schneider fills in the details:

Russian reconnaissance had reported that Kamenno-Balkoff was clear of the enemy. At that point, the Soviet 17th Infantry Brigade had received orders to occupy the village that same night. The 1st Battalion marched right through us into the village, barely disrupted. Only a few rifles put up resistance. One antitank gun put up a terrific defense. It was primarily due to it that the matter did not turn out even worse. The 2nd Battalion of the Russians, which was following closely behind, entered a *balka,* which ran north of [the village], when it heard the firefight. The 3rd Battalion rested on the road, about 2 kilometers outside of the locality, since the leader of that group thought the firefight sounded strange.

The first two battalions were wiped out by the immediate counterattack of the tanks. In addition to suffering many dead, 125 prisoners were taken, most of them slant-eyed Turkestanis.

The brigade consisted of three battalions, one mortar battery and an antitank-gun company. The companies numbered only some 100 men each, not much for the Russians.

At noon on 12 January, the large enemy forces attacked Orlowskaja, which was defended by the *"Westland"* Regiment. A tank company was sent there to support the defensive effort. That afternoon, the operations officer of the division reported that the situation at Orlowskaja has stabilized; the Russians have been thrown back up to 5 kilometers north of the locality. During the fighting for the locality, the commander of *Grenadier-Regiment Westland*, Knight's Cross recipient *SS-Obersturmbannführer* Polewacz, was killed in action.[9]

On the afternoon of the following day, 13 January, the tank battalion again assumed the role of rearguard. The move-out time of 1700 hours had to be delayed, since two tanks in Flügel's company had frozen front differentials that first had to be thawed out. The battalion then moved out, with the non-operational tanks being towed. Even the command tank of the commander towed a *Panzer IV*. Schneider continues his narrative:

> And so we trotted on out of there—a battered group. There was a small *balka* to be crossed behind the village that held us up for hours. The route was as smooth as a skating rink from the wheeled vehicles. Our vehicles did not have ice cleats and were barely able to climb the hill under their own power.
>
> Taking a running start, *Jumbo*, the commander's tank, almost got the *Panzer IV* to the top. It was tried over and over again. But it could not be done. The commander was on the edge of despair and angry. He mounted a self-propelled carriage and tried to find a bypass himself.
>
> In the meantime, I had *Jumbo* approach the hill in such a manner that it was on less chewed-up ground and also had the tow cables lengthened by the addition of more cables. It was *Jumbo's* turn to show what he could do. And, would you believe it, he pulled the old cart over the mountain. The path was clear again.
>
> But no more tanks made it up that spot. All of them slid off and into the *balka*. The battalion commander ordered Flügel to have his company find a bypass and to move out immediately. The battle staff took off and Flügel took another route.
>
> When we moved through a small *balka*, *Jumbo* was hit by the towed tank. Around 020 hours, we broke off the march and slept in a farmer's house in Grekow, 25 men to a room. We lay next to one another like sardines in a can.

9. Author's Note: Daily logs of the *LVII. Panzer-Korps*.

At the same time, the efforts by Flügel's 2nd Company to find a bypass went bad. Flügel's tank slid into a *balka* as a result of the already poor visibility that was worsened by snowfall. With him was also the tank he was towing. Flügel, who had been standing on his tank, went down with it and suffered a fractured skull and concussion. *SS-Obersturmführer* Uhden suffered the same fate.

The two tanks caught on fire and burned out. A third tank, which had also slid off the road, had to be destroyed by an antitank mine. The loss of three *Panzer III's* that night—none due to direct enemy action—was a severe blow.

✠

The battalion reached Beketny, a settlement previously populated by ethnic Germans. Its people had been forced out and the houses had all been destroyed, with the exception of a few. The battalion was no longer on the railway line or the major Proletarskaja-Kuberle road. Instead, it was between the two aforementioned towns, 25 kilometers northwest of the two major routes.

The 3rd Company was employed against Krassnaja-Stannja on the afternoon of 14 January. That evening, the entire battalion was alerted and ordered to moved to Proletarskaja immediately. It was believed that Soviet forces had infiltrated in the sector of the *23. Panzer-Division* east of the town and were approaching it.

The tank battalion arrived there around midnight. Reconnaissance initiated at first light could find no enemy. At noon on 15 January, however, strong enemy armored forces were reported in front of the *23. Panzer-Division.* The tank battalion was committed against those forces, which turned out to be only a few companies of infantry and four tanks. The battalion relieved the hard-pressed town and discovered that there were more friendly tanks and self-propelled guns there than it had itself. In general, however, the forces, especially the infantry and grenadiers, were stretched to the breaking point.

✠

Starting on 16 January, the German bridgehead on the east bank of the Manytsch at Proletarskaja was only being held by the *"Wiking"* Division. The tank battalion had detrained at that spot 16 days earlier. *SS-Untersturmführer* Schumacher engaged Russian infantry with his five tanks in the sector in front of the *"Germania"* Regiment on the eastern edge of the city:

> The enemy has advanced from the east into the brickworks to the east of Proletarskaja. Proletarskaja is under heavy fire. An immediate friendly counterattack, supported by tanks, threw the enemy out of the area around the brickworks back to the east.[10]

The severe, ongoing cold, the street covered in snow in places and the violent snowstorms made movements difficult.

Five tanks were sent to Stalinskij-Put, a few kilometers outside of Proletarskaja, because the enemy had crossed the Manytsch there and was threatening the division's engineer battalion. Ten battalion tanks were employed at the time—all that the battalion had operational. The next day, *SS-Untersturmführer* Büscher and his tanks, together with the engineers, had their hands full dealing with the enemy, who attacked Stalinskij-Put until the evening hours. The tanks and the engineers emerged victorious, although one tank was disabled by battle damage to its turret.

Around 1500 hours on 19 January, orders reached the battalion to once again cover the division as its rearguard when it started to pull back when it turned dark. A new line of resistance behind the Manytsch was to be occupied.

That presented the tank battalion with a dilemma that could barely be solved. The large number of tanks that were in the maintenance facility for repair could barely be moved with the amount of trailers and prime movers on hand. Both the enemy and overuse over the last several weeks had made their numbers grow unusually high. The trains and the rear-area services also had their unique problems during that period of ever-increasing withdrawals.

The trains personnel tried to make the best out of a bad situation. The region was full of collective farms and showcase croplands. Thousands of tons of grain and poultry had to be left behind. Inventive soldiers mounted makeshift pig stalls on the backs of ammunition and other trains vehicles. Up until the summer of 1943, ham was available as a staple of troop rations.

During those days in the middle of January 1943, a race against time started. Who would reach Bataisk and the bridges over the Don at Rostow first?

---

10. Author's Note: Daily logs of the *LVII. Panzer-Korps.*

Would it be the German forces in the Caucasus flowing back in an orderly fashion to the north and northwest? Or would it be the Soviets who were constantly being reinforced against an area that was growing ever smaller? On 11 January, the Soviet 46th and 18th Armies moved out of the western Caucasus towards the north. On 16 January, the two field armies were joined by the 56th and 47th Armies advancing to the northwest in the direction of the Taman Peninsula. To these forces were added the Soviet 2nd Guards Army and the 51st and 28th Armies exerting pressure from the area southwest of Stalingrad. Seven Soviet field armies had been employed against the *1. Panzer-Armee,* the *17. Armee* and the *LVII. Panzer-Korps* in an effort to encircle and destroy them.

The ever-worsening situation, coupled with the increasingly chaotic traffic situation in the area growing smaller south of Rostow, also had a disadvantageous effect on command and control as well as communications. For instance, *SS-Panzer-Abteilung 5,* which was ready to move, waited in vain to establish contact with the final elements disengaging from the enemy at 1800 hours on 19 January. Efforts on the part of the battalion to establish contact determined that there were no more friendly forces in front of them; in Proletarskaja, the few remaining railway men, who were busy with blowing up the train station, confirmed that the infantry were gone. After establishing direct contact with the division, the battalion evacuated Proletarskaja. According to Schneider: "The engineers, who were always the last to go with us, blew up the bridges and the causeways over the Manytsch."

SSALSK—GIGANT

When the battalion reached its march objective of Jekaterinonko at 2400 hours, the village was being contested. That meant that strong Soviet forces were already operating to the rear of the German rearguard.

The following morning, one platoon from the 1st Company, together with the 10th Company of the *"Nordland"* Regiment, cleared the eastern part of the village. In all, 70 prisoners were taken and 100 Soviet dead counted.

At first light on 21 January, the battalion fought along the rail line in Schablijewka, some 4 kilometers distant. While the forces in contact with the enemy at the front pulled back in a disciplined and deliberate manner, the confusion grew among the elements in the rear, where the area had been far removed from the front only the previous day. Hospitals and supply dumps were no longer being evacuated in an orderly fashion. Plunder on the part of the civilian populace increased. According to Schneider:

Whereas the Russians had always appeared on our right flank previously, a report came in at 0900 hours that the enemy was attacking the village of Buddenowo on our left flank. The tanks were unable to offer immediate help, since the bridge leading there had been blown up prematurely. Unfortunately, the ice could not support the tanks. As a result, the tanks had to take a time-consuming detour. On the way there, a vehicle from the 1st Company received a direct hit from a 7.62-centimeter gun.

Büscher attacked the enemy around 1300 hours. In the process, he lost a vehicle, which had to be blown up. One enemy tank was knocked out.

Despite all of our efforts, the situation became increasingly worse. Around 1400 hours, orders arrived to pull back. The battalion was the rearguard again.

Ssalsk, a few kilometers away, had already been burning for hours. Our companies formed convoys so that the immobilized tanks could be towed along. We were the last to fight our way though a burning Ssalsk and headed in the direction of Rostow, our next objective, by way of Gigant.

We arrived there [Gigant] during the night of 21–22 January. The Bolshevist planned economy was on display everywhere. The populace lived in finished rooms and you could see by the personal items and furnishing that confirmed that the comrades of Gigant were way ahead of their brothers on the steppes and in the innumerable villages.

That afternoon, the Russians attacked Gigant from the north with six tanks and infantry mounted on eight trucks. Friendly infantry destroyed two enemy tanks.

That afternoon, we were already pulling back to Zelina.

Around 0930 hours on 23 January, Ivan was already there. Despite that, breakfast, which included three eggs from the model farm in Gigant, was very good. Up to that point, we did not see anything of the reported masses of infantry and six tanks.

At 1300 hours, however, he started charging along the railway line, 200–300 men. Büscher, who had gone into position along the edge of the locality with his *Panzer IV's*, reported two tanks. The Russians were soon placing horrific mortar and artillery fire in the vicinity of the command post. The commander ordered a change of position to the west side of the village. By evening, the Russians had completely bypassed the village. Orders soon arrived that the forces in Zelina were to immediately pull back to Jegorlykskaja.

JEGORLYKSKAJA—ROSTOW

Schneider's narrative continues:

> We left burning Zelina with mixed feelings, since 5 tanks and 200 men were reported as approaching Jegorlykskaja as early as 1500 hours. Would the Russians finally succeed in grabbing us? They certainly had the opportunity over the last few days.
>
> On the way from Zelina to Jegorlykskaja, we had to destroy a cotton storage facility and thousands of skins. Forty heavy *Stuka* bombs had to be blown up at an airfield.
>
> As was to be expected, the Russians gave us a hearty welcome when we arrived at Jegorlykskaja. They had almost gotten us. But only almost. During the first few hours of 24 January, we entered the city[11] as the last ones in. For the most part, the tanks were positioned outside of the locality, since a stoppage along the road made it impossible to get any farther.
>
> All of a sudden, there was rapid fire in our direction from an estimated 10 main guns. The tracer ammunition painted colorful streams in the night. In the wild firing, you could barely hear yourself think.
>
> The night was pitch black. When the firefight started, it succeeded in clearing out the traffic jam, and the vehicles raced into the city. It was madness there. In the darkness, the companies and battalions got all mixed together, with the result that no one could find his unit. The clever ones, who were playing it safe, proceeded almost as far as the next locality. The tanks, on the other hand, set up on the edge of the city and oriented towards the direction of the firing. So as not to betray our positions, we did not fire a shot. Since as it was dark, we wouldn't have hit anything anyway.
>
> The Russians continued to fire blind into the village and along the road. Since there was nothing to be seen of friendly infantry, the commander decided to look for the command post for *"Westland"* and establish contact. I accompanied him. The commander moved through the yards in his command-and-control tank. The adjutant and I worked our way with some effort through the vegetation and guided the commander's driver. We finally got there. *Sturmbannführer* Reichel, the new commander, was sitting calmly in his quarters and

11. Translator's Note: Schneider seems to refer to the various built-up areas in rather arbitrary terms—for instance, calling Jegorlykskaja a locality, a village and a city. In all likelihood, it was a village.

adamantly asserted that his grenadiers were at the edge of the village, screening.

The defenses of the locality were reorganized based on the recommendation of the [tank battalion] commander. At the same time, it was promised that our tanks would destroy Ivan's tanks in the morning.

Following that, the commander summoned his company commanders. In an abandoned house, we determined how the [enemy] tanks were to be dispatched. The first thing to be done was to establish contact with the grenadiers at the edge of the village; they were to tell the company commanders where the enemy tanks were located. The company commanders were then to find the best position for their companies. Following that, the companies were to occupy those positions while it was still dark, allowing the enemy to approach the well-camouflaged tanks in the morning.

When the commander's conference was almost over, we suddenly heard a series of hand grenades. The commander cautioned everyone to remain calm, and we did not assign any further meaning to the incident.

When we went back into the road, there was a *Panzer IV* in front of the door. When asked why the vehicle was there and instead of at the entrance to the locality, the commander reported the following:

> Since his main gun was damaged, he received permission from his commander to move back to fix the damage. After a short inspection, it was determined that the damage could not be repaired without assistance. The crew had thereupon remounted the tank and dozed a bit. They suddenly heard the sound of tracks in front of their own vehicle. Moreover, it sounded as though someone were scratching at the outside of their vehicle. He, the tank commander, opened his hatch to see who was making the noise. He then heard the sounds of Russian. Shocked wide awake, he also saw the outlines of a Mark III right in front of his crate.
>
> The Russians assumed they had a damaged vehicle on their hands and then attempted to attach a tow cable to take the vehicle. The tank commander lost his patience and tossed a few hand grenades among the throng. At that point, the enemy recognized his mistake and attempted to get out of there. In the process, he moved the wrong way got stuck in the ooze of the

roadside ditch. Unfortunately, the Russians could not be given something to remember the Germans by, since the [German] main gun was defective.

As expected, the Russians attacked at first light. All of the attacking tanks were knocked out, as if that's the way it had been written into the program for the day. The battalion was able to rack up 13 "kills." It is interesting to note that there were many Mark III's among the vehicles knocked out. After that working-over, the Russians had enough for the day!

The entire battalion was involved in that success. While the *"Westland"* Regiment covered the southern and southeastern edges of Jegorlykskaja—focusing on the roads to Ssalsk and Belaja—the 2nd and 3rd Companies of the tank battalion awaited the enemy at the east side of the village, to the west of the road leading to Belaja Glina. The 1st Company was positioned north of the road leading to Ssalsk.

The Soviets attacked with five tanks to the north of the road and with six tanks at the forks in the road along the Jegorlykskaja-Ssalsk and Jegorlykskaja–Belaja Glina roads. In addition, two tanks attacked west of the Jegorlykskaja–Belaja Glina road.

After all of the enemy tanks had been destroyed, it remained quiet in Jegorlykskaja for the rest of 24 January. The onset of rainy weather after the very cold and occasionally clear days transformed the roads into sheets of ice or bottomless seas of mud. In addition, the calm was deceptive. The daily logs of the *LVII. Panzer-Korps* recorded:

The enemy is attacking Tagonrogskij with vastly superior infantry forces and has entered Balabanoff with approximately 500 men. Elements of the *II./Germania* and assault guns employed against Balabanoff.

The situation north of Jegorlykskaja has turned sharply critical. An enemy armored advance headed west, south of Tagonrogskij, with approximately 20 tanks and pushed back the reconnaissance battalion positioned at Sowch Jegorlykskaja and is blocking the main supply route.

Schneider's narrative:

The enemy was not concerned about the force in Jegorlykskaja. Instead, he was pushing tank after tank north of Jegorlykskaja in a

> generally westward direction. The meaning of that was clear to all of us. If the Russians were attempting to achieve what had been their objective for some weeks now—that is, the encirclement of the *"Wiking"* Division—then they had not picked a bad time. Almost all of the division was in [Jegorlykskaja].
>
> Around 1530 hours, the situation got worse. Nine enemy tanks blocked the main supply route. It appeared that the trap had been sprung. The only thing the enemy did not do was attack. Perhaps he had too few infantry forces. In any event, he remained passive. That was what saved us. Around 1530 hours, the battalion rolled out once again as the "last one" of the division out of Jegorlykskaja. Direction: Metschetinskaja. The movement was unpleasant inasmuch as we had to fight our way through the steppe. It was pitch black and damned cold. Pity the vehicles that hung back and got stuck in the steppe without compass and map. We arrived in Metschetinskaja just after midnight, where a regiment had already established a passage point.

If there had still been a semblance of a front line up to that point, friend and foe increasingly intermeshed with one another in the areas each other occupied. After two unsuccessful attacks on Metschetinskaja—one at first light and another at 0800 hours on 27 January—the enemy simply stopped the effort and then attempted to push his forces through to the west between the villages. The two attacks on Metschetinskaja had been turned back with the help of heavy bomber support and artillery.

Characteristic for the crossing of the open steppe areas between the villages was a widely dispersed organization of the formations. They "weaseled" with 100-meter intervals between men in small sections of 30 to 40 men, thus reducing the effectiveness of enemy aerial attacks, artillery and machine guns.

While it was quiet in Metschetinskaja the next two days, the tankers of the division were tossed back and forth to threatened sectors of the division. The *"Westland"* Regiment was still positioned at Leninka and Kalmikoff, some 15 kilometers west of Jegorlykskaja; the reconnaissance battalion was halfway between Jegorlykskaja and Metschetinskaja; and the *"Nordland"* Regiment covered the area west of the Metschetinskaja-Rostow supply route.

On 26 January, *Untersturmführer* Schumacher and his tankers gave some breathing room to the 1st Battalion of the *"Germania"* Regiment, which had been threatened with encirclement some 12 kilometers to the southeast in Krassnoarmeiskij. On his return the next morning, Schumacher and his men destroyed 10 7.62-centimeter guns and 9 heavy machine guns when they passed through a Soviet force attacking Metschetinskaja. Some 200 Soviets were also killed.

SS-Untersturmführer Büscher was knocked out while engaging two T-34's east of Metschetinskaja and was killed. *SS-Obersturmführer* Grathwol was knocked out. Besides those two tanks, the battalion lost an additional two on 28 January. One vehicle from the 1st Company slid into an iced-over *balka*; another one burned out on the way to the maintenance facility.

On 29 January, a flank attack launched by the *11. Panzer-Division* on the village of Kammenyj, which was held by strong forces, provided relief to the *"Wiking"* Division. As it appeared that success was assured—46 antitank guns had been knocked out—the battle group from the *11. Panzer-Division* received other instructions and was employed elsewhere. Consequently, the enemy held on to Kammenyj.

On that day, *SS-Panzer-Abteilung 5* boasted the strength of a weak tank company. On 30 January, it "snuck" through on a circuitous route some 20 kilometers to the north to the village of Kagalnitzkaja, the new main line of resistance. It was relatively calm there until 2 February, when the battalion was ordered to Swoy-Trud at 1200 hours. The division command post was located in Swoy-Trud, some 16 kilometers northwest of Kagalnitzkaja and about 30 kilometers south of Bataisk on the Don.

While moving out of Kagalnitzkaja, the tanks received heavy fire from antitank guns, tanks and mortars at the northwestern edge of the village. At the same time, field ambulances were crossing the icy slope, which could be seen by the enemy. They were evacuating the main clearing station that had supported the main line of resistance in that sector. The unfortunate wounded and the defenseless drivers of those vehicles—as were the drivers of all of the supply vehicles—were subjected to scarcely imaginable stress during those weeks.

The battalion reached Swoy-Trud at 1500 hours. The report that 30 tanks were about to attack proved to be a false alarm, however.

On 4 February, the battalion, which had been reinforced with assault guns, was employed on the left wing of the division in the sector of the *"Nordland"* Regiment. The regiment had been affected by operations in the sector of the friendly division to the left, which necessitated an immediate counterattack. The battalion moved out in icy cold at 0400 hours and cleaned up the situation, knocking out four enemy tanks in the process. Despite that, the regiment was pushed back during the course of the day.

At 1530 hours, orders arrived for the withdrawal to Rostow, which was intended to be the final withdrawal. Schneider continues his narrative:

Since it started to turn dark as we moved out, we took efforts to get as many kilometers as possible behind us while there was still some light. As usual, difficulties arose in the form of *balkas*, which had been transformed completely into sheets of ice by wheeled vehicles. We were always held up for hours at those places, since every tank had to make three or four running starts before it was over the top. Of course, it was also not like there was an unlimited amount of time available. After all, we were the last ones, and the Russians also wanted to get to Rostow.

The panorama offered by the villages burning around us was a luridly beautiful background to look at. We felt our way towards Bataisk. The roads were clogged up outside the village. On top of that, there was a wind sweeping around your ears. Although they were protected against the cold, it was still -31 degrees Fahrenheit. As a result, the commander decided around midnight to bivouac in Bataisk so as to give his tired crews a bit of sleep.

The little burg was full of forces that had been directed to defend it to the very end. With up to 30 men to a room—jammed in like sardines—we slept for three hours.

As we assembled, it was still pitch black. The snowstorm was still howling. The movement in the direction of Rostow appeared to be going smoothly, but then, all of a sudden, there was a stop. Just outside of the bridge over the Don—2 kilometers in length—we were told to halt. In front of us, a vehicle had careened down the embankment. Our engineers attempted to save what could be saved. It was a field mess, after all. As a result, we had halted in the icy cold and in an icy storm at the worst place—on an embankment, where we were exposed to the storm without any protection at all. I dismounted my tank; in the wintertime, it was like a refrigerator. I warmed myself on the exhaust pipes of the engineer truck in front of me.

We rolled into Rostow around 1000 hours. Even there it did not go without a hitch. The streets were incredibly packed. Up to four columns of vehicles of all types were next to one another. Every convoy commander was trying to get himself and his convoy out of there, pushing aside the others in the process . . . We fought our way through Rostow, so as to enjoy a few days of rest in one of its suburbs and restore the tanks that had been so badly mistreated mechanically.

✠

Some 6 months and 8 days ago, *SS-Panzer-Abteilung 5* had crossed the same spot along the Don to commence its attack south. Some after-the-fact critics of operations in the Caucasus speak in a practically mocking tone about the operations, which they say were pre-ordained to failure and which could have only sprung from an unbridled fantasy.

The viewpoint taken by the Soviet High Command—as reflected by Shtemenko—has already been covered. Von Tippelskirch also addressed the prospects of that last expansive German offensive in World War II in his history of the conflict:[12]

> As late as August 1942, the English considered it possible that Hitler would cross the Caucasus and conduct a large-scale offensive in the Middle East. They considered the Germans and the Italians to be strong enough with their armored field army in Africa to advance across the Nile and the Suez and on into Palestine, to strike into Syria with an invasion army starting from the Dodecanese and Crete and advance as far as into Persia with the field armies of the Eastern Front . . .

That offensive had failed. *SS-Panzer-Abteilung 5* crossed the Don at the start and at the end of that operation. For more than two and one half months, it was the spearhead of the attack; for five weeks, it frequently served, along with others, as the division's rearguard during the withdrawal. The unfortunate outcome of the operation for Germany also signaled a change in the course of the war.

The enemy's operational objective—the interdiction of the rearward lines of communications of the German forces south of the Don and their subsequent encirclement and elimination—had also not been realized.

In a special directive from the Supreme Command of the Soviet Southern Front issued on 23 January 1943, the decisive role that the encirclement of the enemy forces in the Northern Caucasus played was pointed out:

> The taking of Bataisk by our armed forces has a great historical meaning. If Bataisk is taken, we will cut off the enemy field armies in the Northern Caucasus and prevent 24 German and Romanian divisions from appearing in Rostow and Taganrog and along the flood plain of the Don. The enemy in the Northern Caucasus must be encircled and destroyed just as he has been encircled in Stalingrad and is in the process of being destroyed . . . [13]

12. Author's Note: von Tippelskirch, 267.

13. Author's Note: Shtemenko, 80.

Among those who thwarted the numerically vastly superior Soviets, who were personally spurred on by Stalin on several occasions, were the tankers of *SS-Panzer-Abteilung 5*. Their losses in dead and wounded men, noncommissioned officers and officers after nearly seven months of unbroken combat were considerable. Of the three company commanders who had set out with the newly formed battalion at the start of the campaign in June 1942, two were dead and one was wounded. Among the platoon leaders, the losses were also high. The 1st Company had lost all of its platoon leaders; the 2nd and 3rd Companies had lost most of them.

The trust that had been placed in the battalion had been justified.

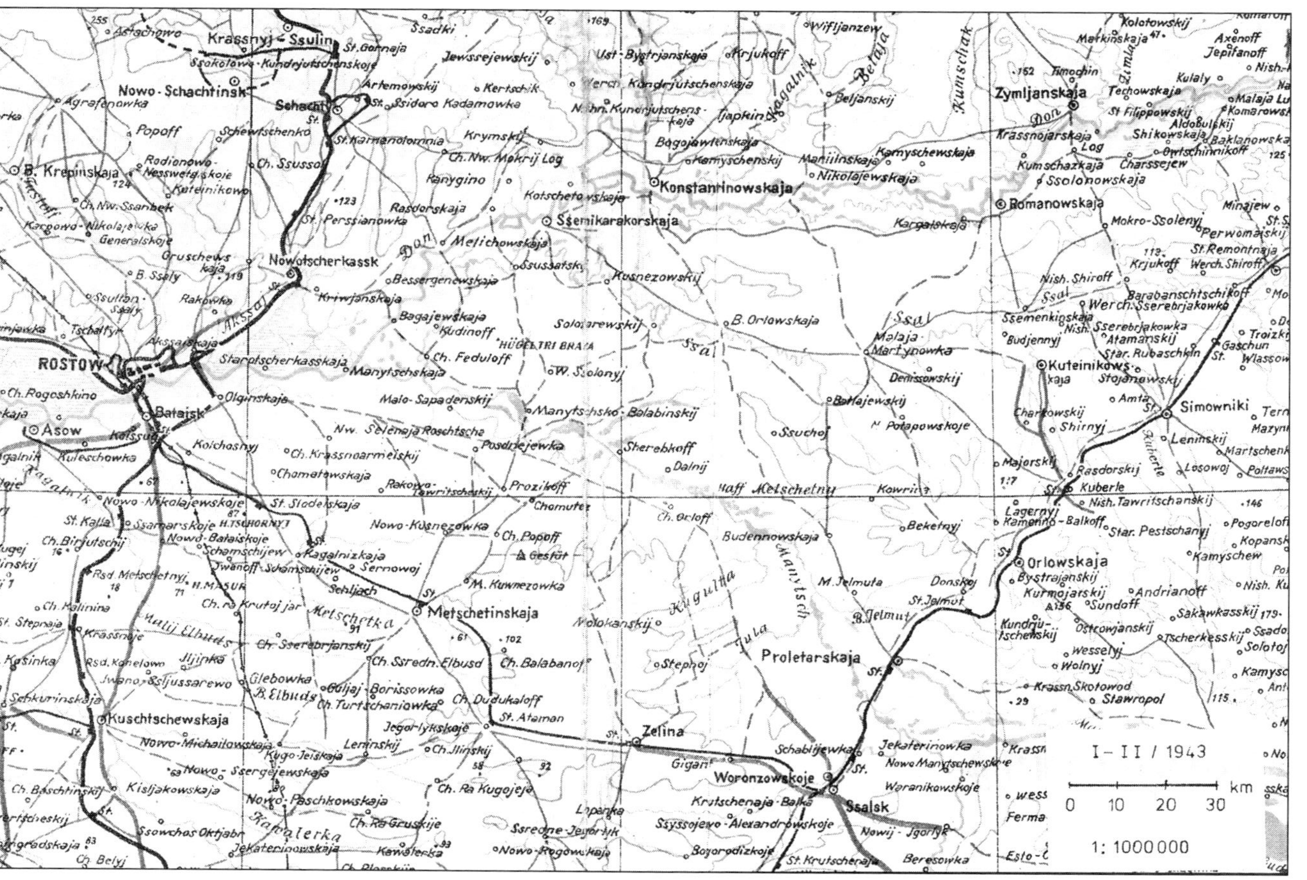

The Simowniki-Rostow sector.

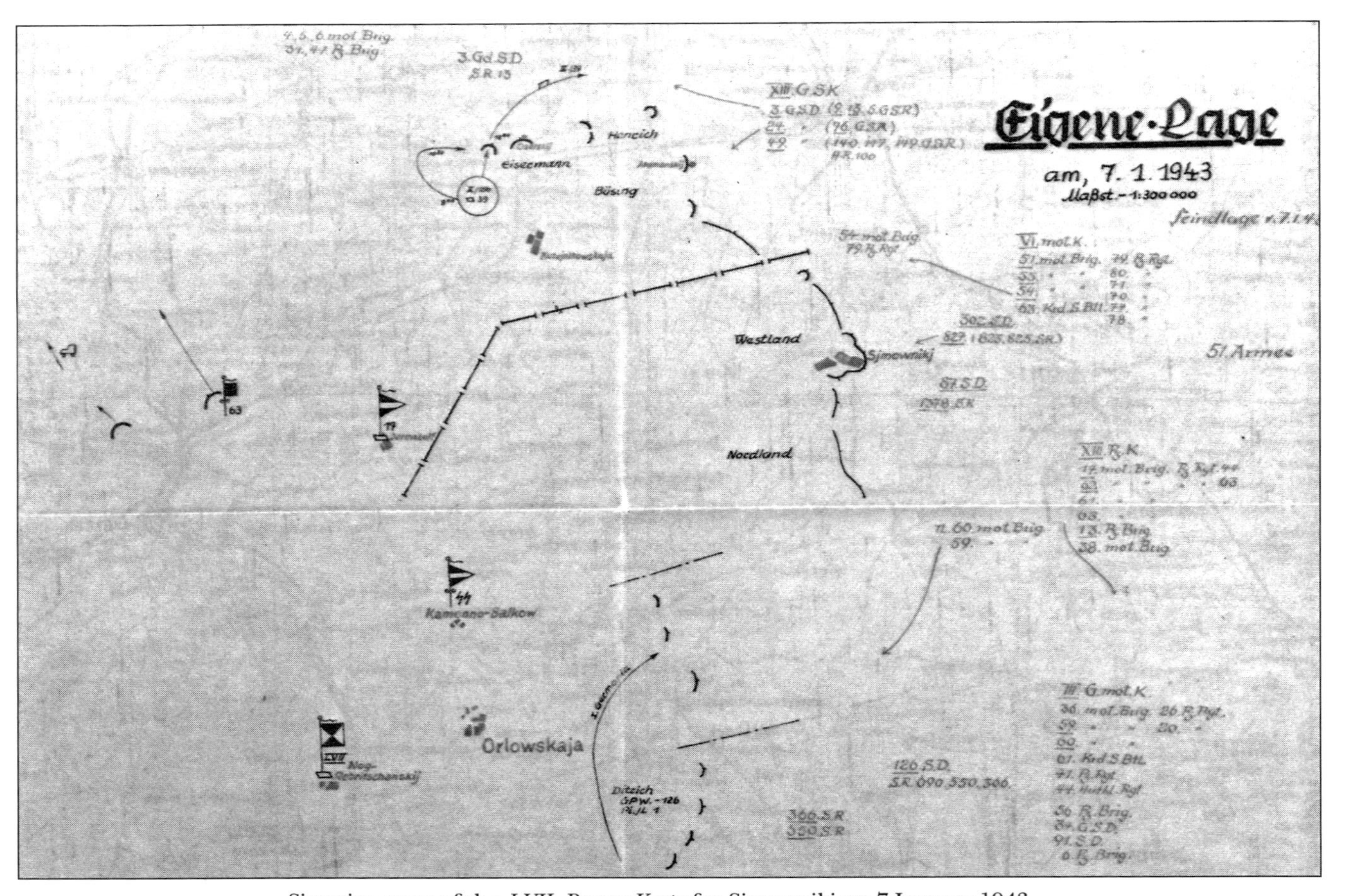

Situation map of the *LVII. Panzer-Korps* for Simowniki on 7 January 1943.

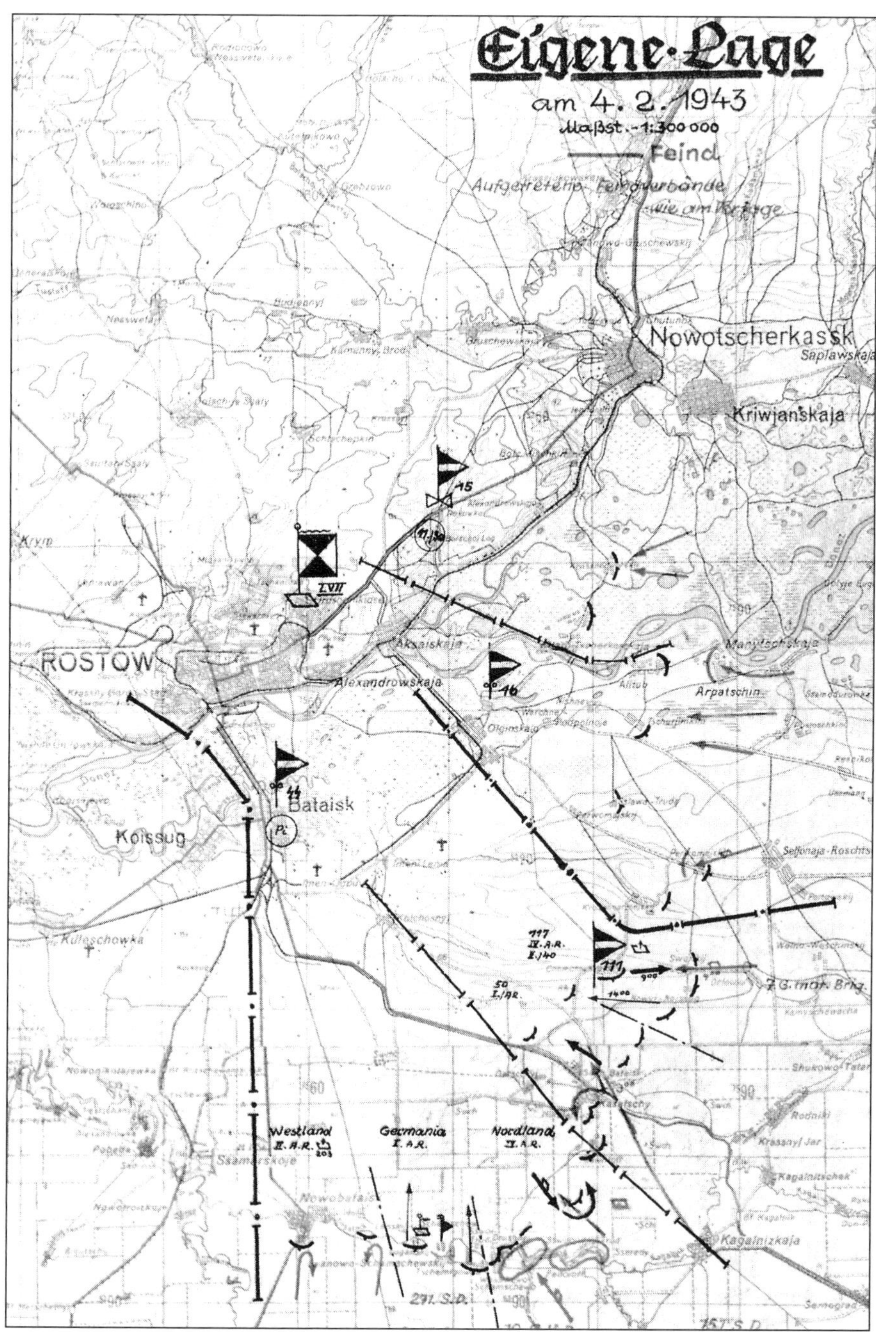

Situation map of the *LVII. Panzer-Korps* for the Don bridgehead at Rostow-Bataisk on 4 February 1943.

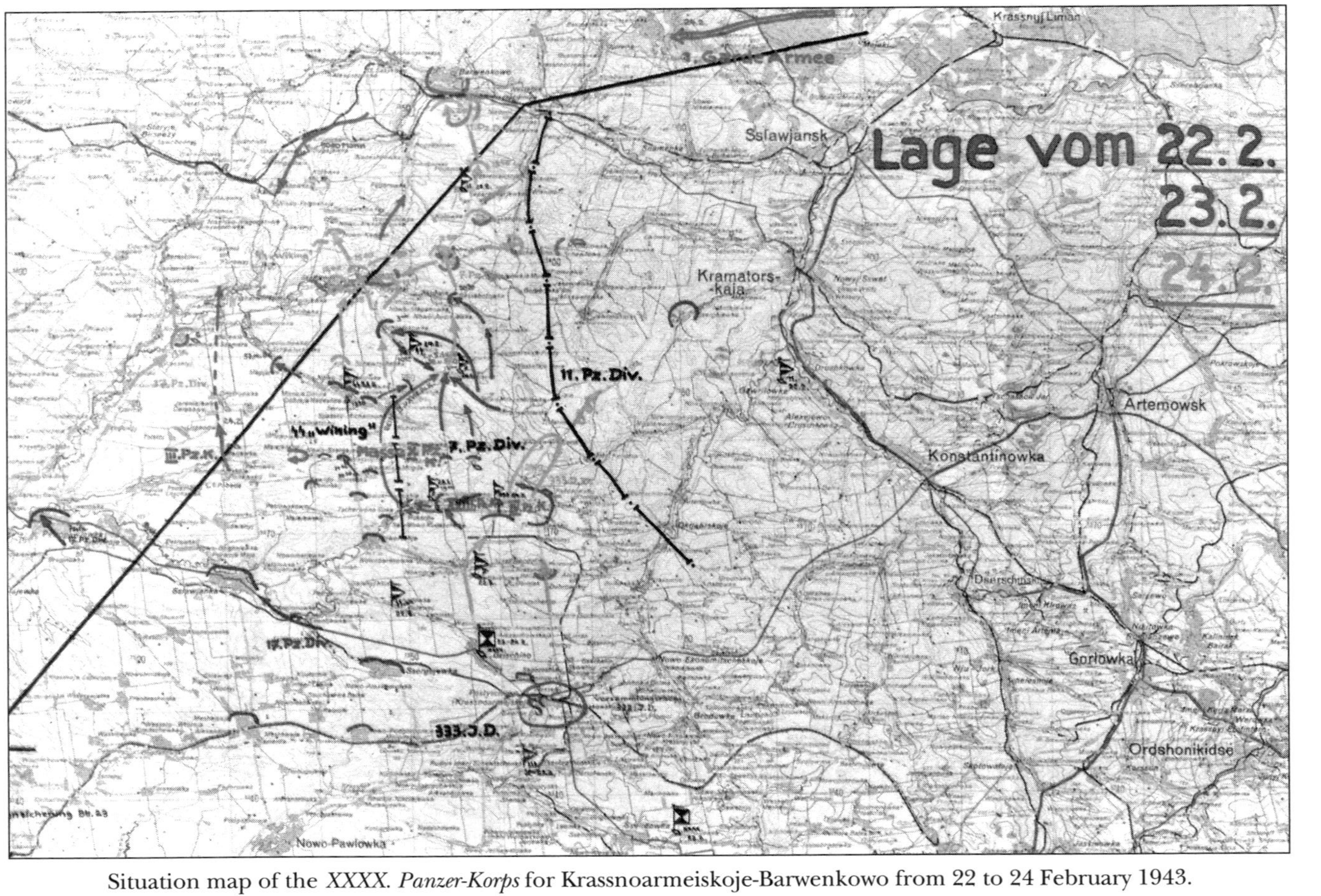

Situation map of the *XXXX. Panzer-Korps* for Krassnoarmeiskoje-Barwenkowo from 22 to 24 February 1943.

September 1942: Marching into an assembly area.

25 September 1942, south bank of the Terek and equipped for the plague of mosquitoes: (left to right) *SS-Untersturmführer* Hübner, *SS-Obersturmführer* Klapdor and *SS-Untersturmführer* Kolodzi.

The engineer bridge over the Terek at Chamidija in September 1942.

A folk dance is performed by members of the Caucasian militia.

The family of our host.

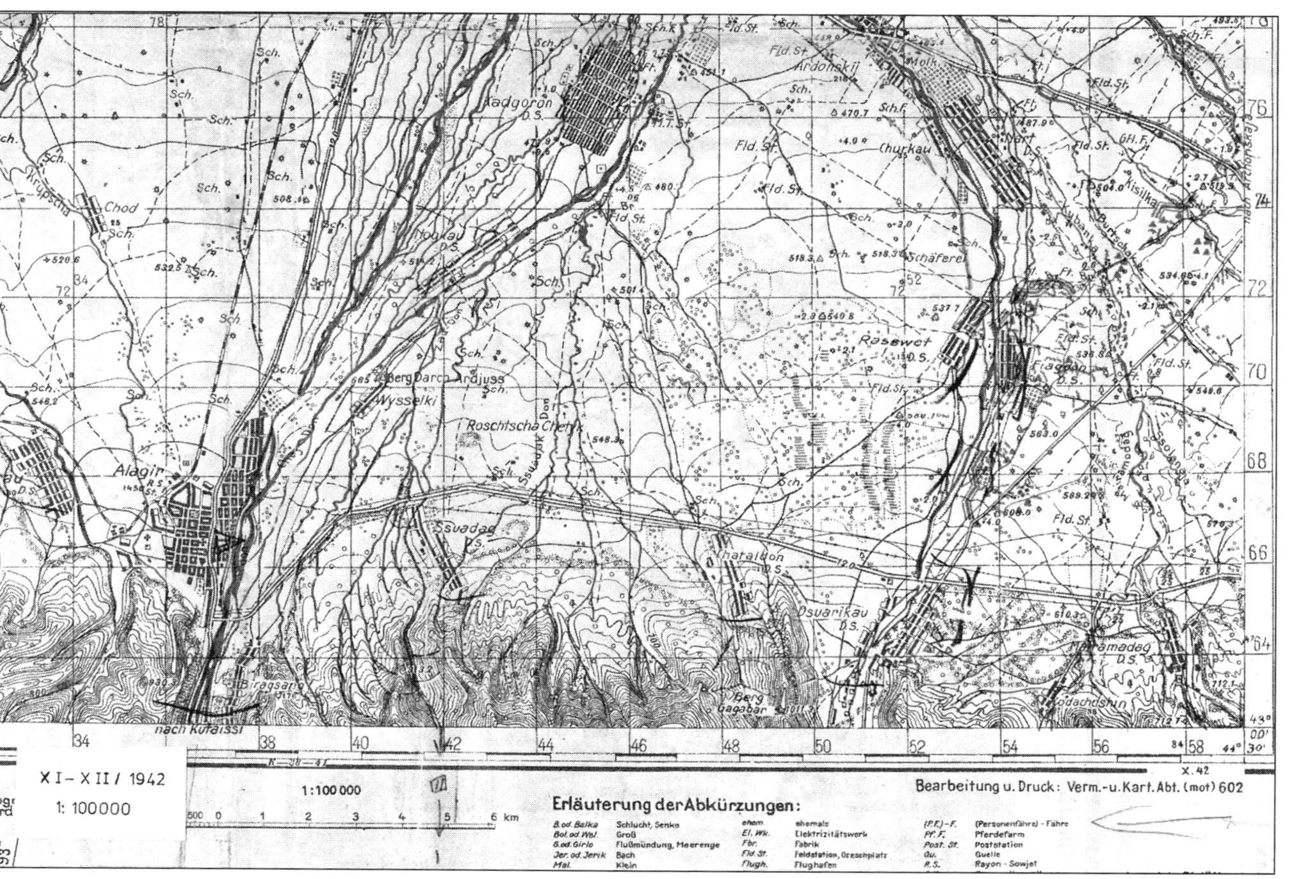

Alagir sector (west of Ordshonikidse).

25 September 1942, along the Terek: *SS-Obersturmführer* Klapdor with the men of the 2nd Platoon of the 1st Company. While Klapdor retains the traditional black tanker garb, his men have been issued the very rare mouse-gray denim version of the tanker outfit.

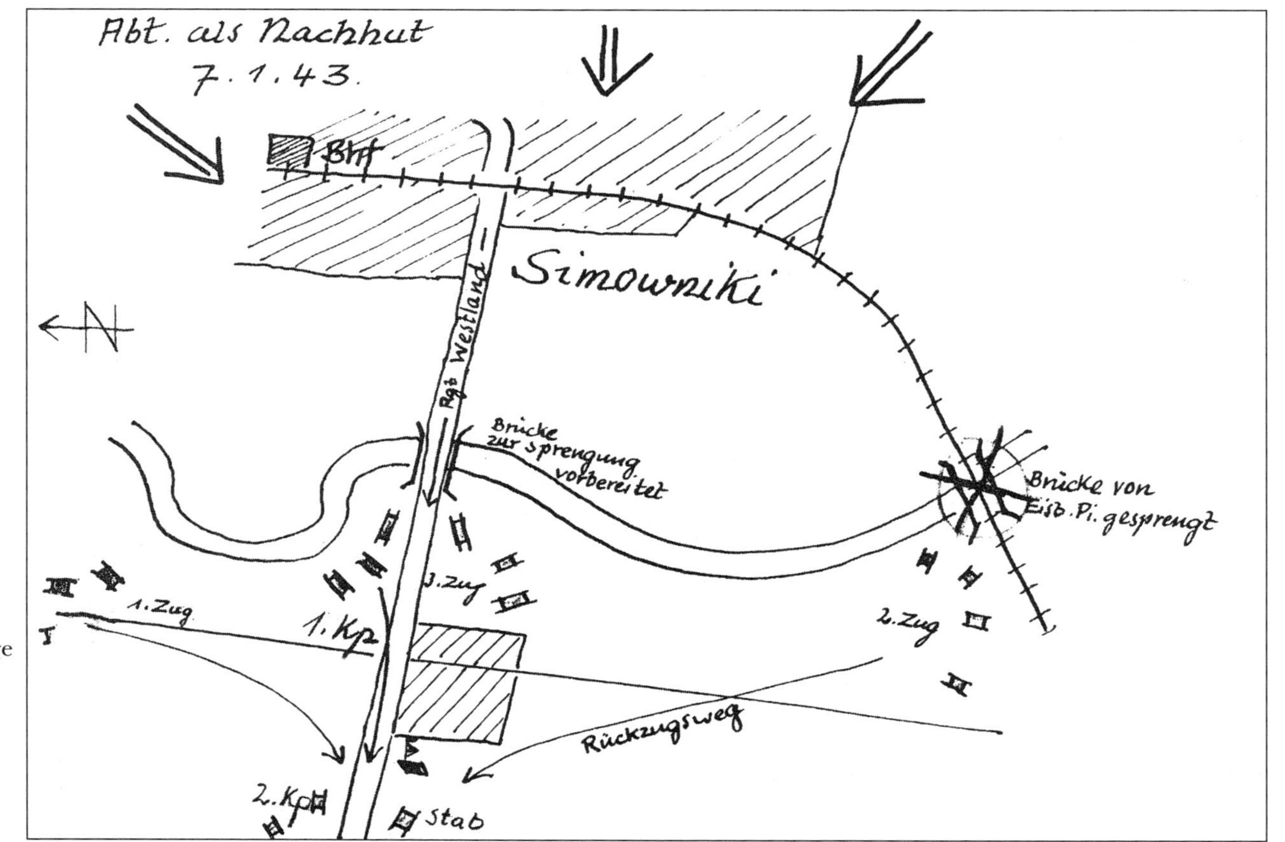

Simowniki on 1 July 1943, battalion as rearguard
Bhf = Train station
Brücke zur . . .: Bridge prepared for demolition
Brücke von . . . :Bridge blown up by railway engineers
Rückzugsweg: Withdrawal route
Stab: Headquarters

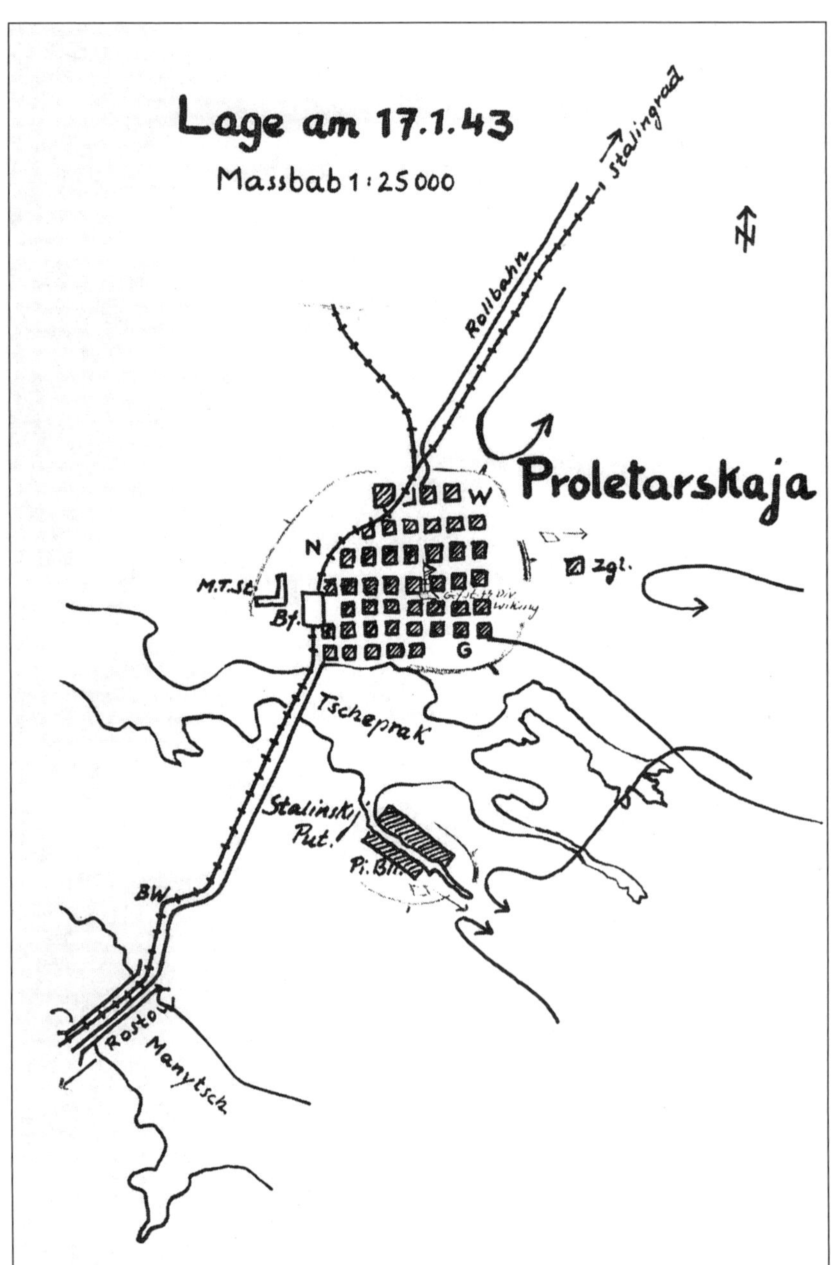

Situation around Proletarskaja on 17 January 1943.

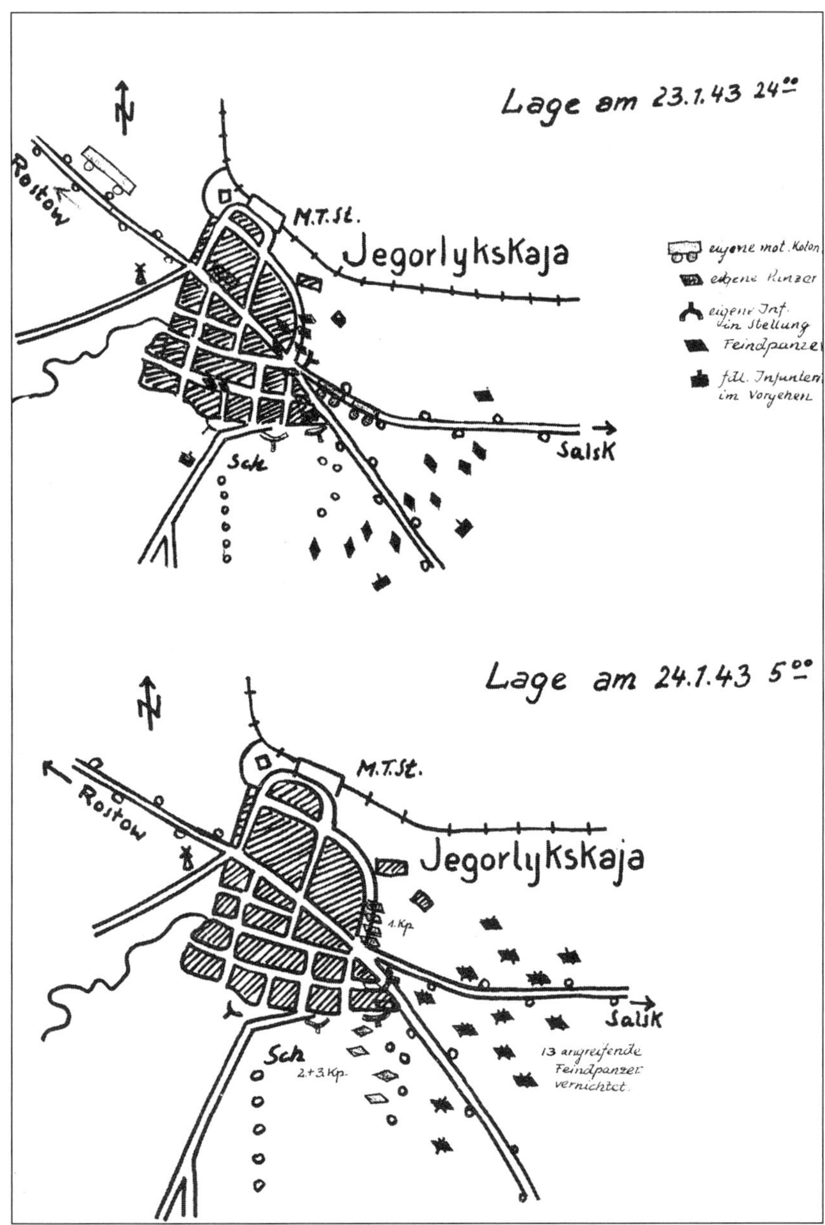

Situation around Jegorlykskaja on 23 and 24 January 1943.
Eigene mot. . . .: Friendly motorized columns
Eigene Panzer: Friendly armor
eigene Inf. In . . .: Friendly infantry in position
Feindpanzer: Enemy armor
Fdl Infanterie . . .: Enemy infantry advancing
13 angreifende . . .:13 attacking enemy tanks destroyed

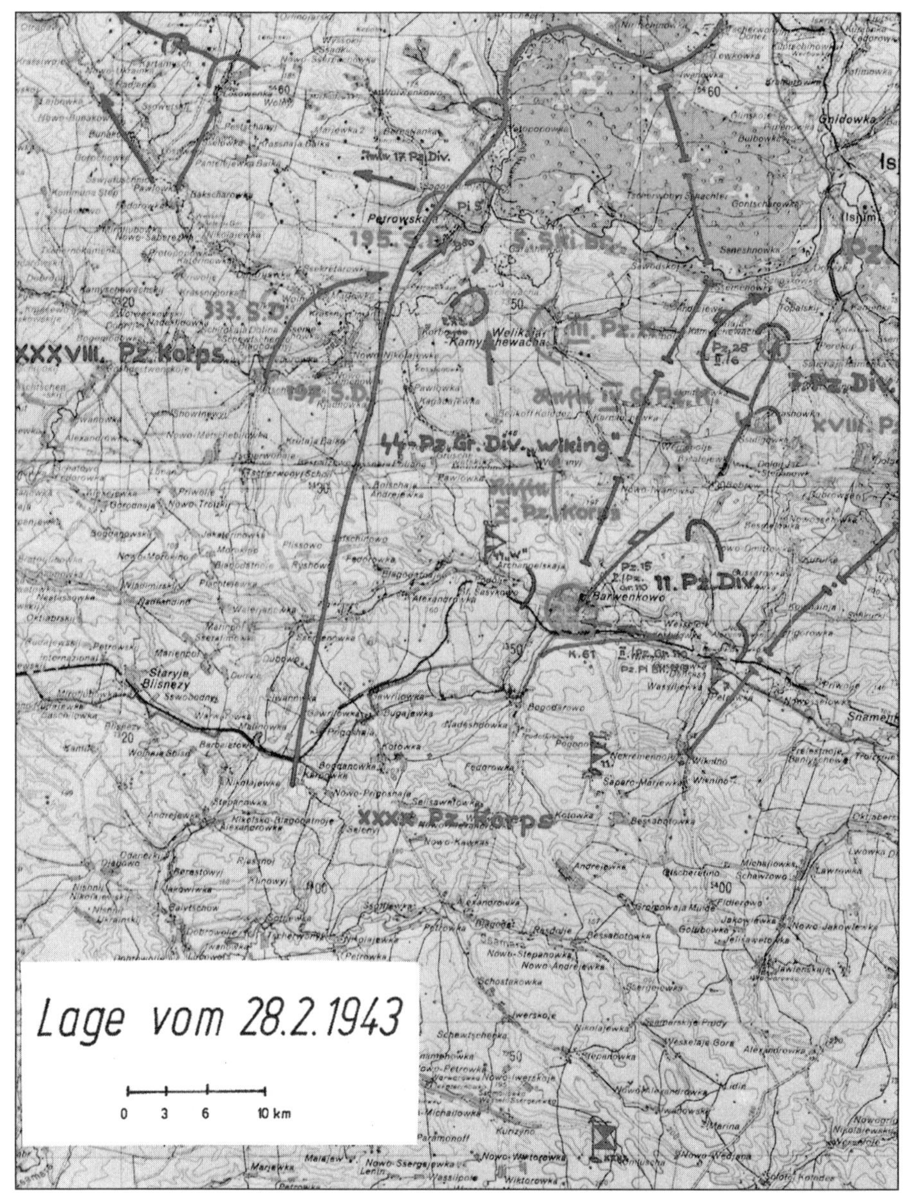

Situation on 28 February 1943.

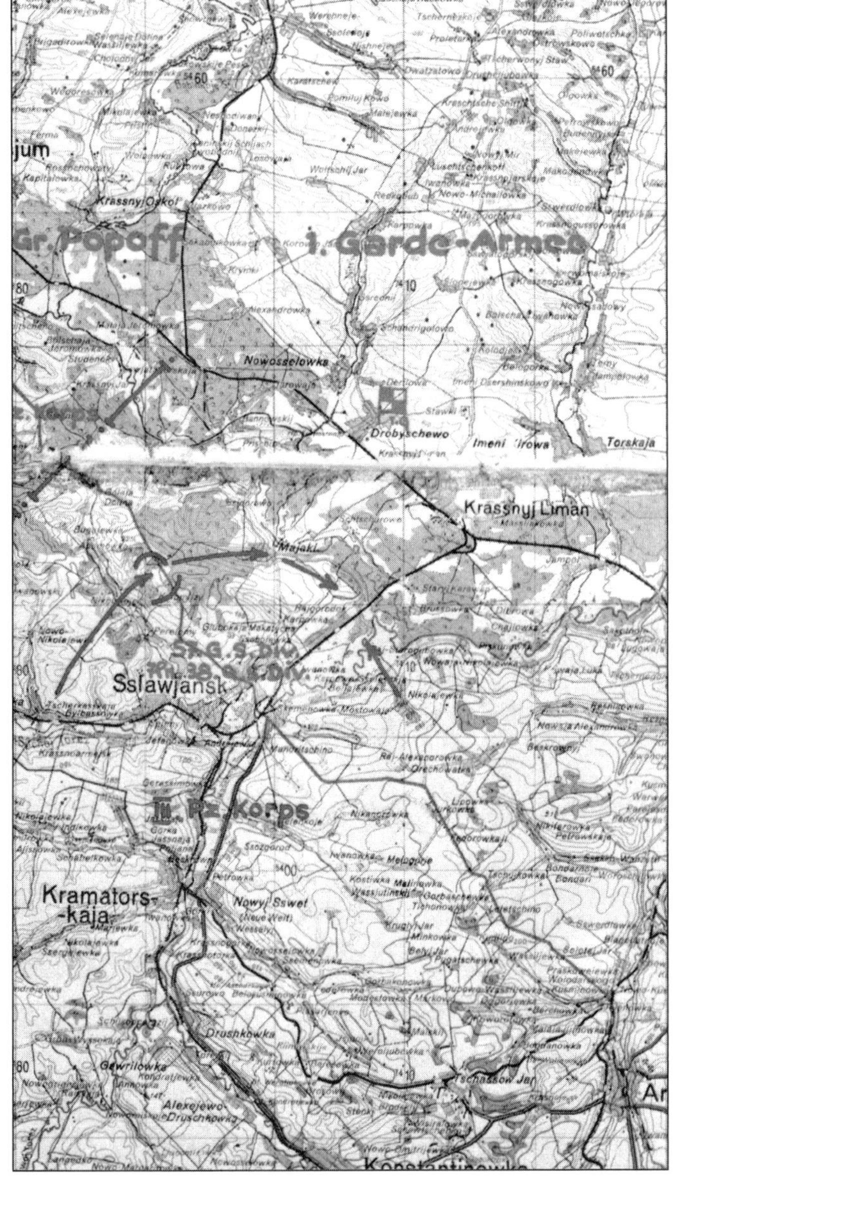

Gr. Popoff
1. Garde-Armee
Nowosselowka
Drobyschewo
Krassnyj Liman
Majaki
Sslawjansk
III. Pz.Korps
Kramators-
-kaja
Drushkowka
Konstantinowka

Situation in the division sector at 0800 hours on 27 January 1943.
Divisionsgrenze: Divisional boundary
Eigene Stellungen: friendly positions
Vorrückende Feindkräfte: Advancing enemy forces
Feindpanzer: Enemy armor
Maßstab: Scale

CHAPTER 4

Defensive Operations between the Donez and the Dnjepr

The crossing of the banks of the river by the tank battalion did not signal an end to operations that had gone on without a break for weeks and the initiation of the vitally necessary reconstitution of the battalion's elements. The bridgehead over the Don at Rostow was held open until the beginning of February by dint of extraordinary efforts. The tank battalion, as part of the division, formed the immediate reserve of the field army, along with all of the other available combat-capable elements of the *1. Panzer-Armee* and the *4. Panzer-Armee,* as they filtered back. It was not possible to rule out a second, even greater catastrophe after the loss of the *6. Armee* at Stalingrad as the fighting and events in the Don and Donez areas seemed to reach their climax.

The course of the fighting up to that point had been dictated by the Soviet operational intention of enveloping and destroying the southern wing of the German forces on the Eastern Front. In order to provide a better understanding of the individual actions of the battalion and the division, let us review the framework of events from both the German and Soviet viewpoint.

✠

The Soviet operations that had commenced on 16 December 1942 in the Great Bend of the Don against the forces of *Heeresgruppe B* had led to a breakthrough in the areas of operations of the Italian *8. Armee* and to the pulling back of the newly formed *Armee-Abteilung Fretter-Pico*[1] and *Armee-Abteilung Hollidt* in a general line running from the mouth of the Donez–Donez Bend as far as the Donez Knee, west of Kamensk-Schactinskij. As a result of the Soviet operations, the German front lines had moved another 150 kilometers to the west from Stalingrad. In the middle of January 1943, this front ran some 500 kilometers.

1. Translator's Note: Army Detachment. An army detachment was created when the available forces were greater than a corps but less than a field army group. In both instances here, they are named after their commanders.

The forces of *Heeresgruppe B* joined the army detachments of Hollidt and Fretter-Pico to the north. Along the field army group's front lines, the forces were distributed from south to north as follows: Italian 8th Army—an Italian alpine corps—Hungarian 2nd Army—*2. Armee.*

Four weeks after the start of the Soviet offensive, on 14 January 1943, the front south and west of Woronesch started to become fluid when the Hungarian 2nd Army and the Italian 8th Army unexpectedly and totally collapsed. As a result of the collapse of these field armies, the start of the new Soviet offensive began to look very similar to the one that had encircled the *6. Armee* at Stalingrad. The tragedy at Stalingrad had also started with the collapse of allied field armies—the Romanian 3rd and 4th Armies. Von Manstein wrote about the effect of the collapse in his summary of the events along the southern front in the winter of 1942–43 in *Verlorene Siege*:[2]

> Above and beyond that, the Soviets had swept away four allied field armies from the battlefield that were fighting on the German side. Many brave men, who were also present in those armies, had been killed . . . the remnants of those field armies had dissolved and had to be written off, sooner or later . . .

Shtemenko makes the following observation in this connection:

> The start of the operations was planned for 15 January. In actual fact, they started earlier. Reconnaissance-in-force was conducted along the main avenues of advance two days earlier. In the sector of the 40th Army, it was conducted so energetically that the enemy was ejected from his positions and began to pull back. The field army headquarters took notice of that and began to immediately attack with its main forces, which penetrated up to 7 kilometers deep by the end of the day. The attack was continued the following morning, and the situation developed very favorably for us. Even before the week was up, the main forces of the enemy had been split and encircled in two areas, in the areas around Rossosch and Alexejewka. The Soviet forces increased the tempo of operations in which the gave the enemy no time to regroup. By 25 January, 15 enemy divisions had ceased to exist, and 6 had suffered overwhelming setbacks . . .

---

2. Author's Note: von Manstein, *Verlorene Siege*, Athenäum Verlag: 1955, no page given. Translator's Note: Printed in English as *Lost Victories*, the text translations given here are based solely on the original German text and may, therefore, vary from the corresponding passage in the English edition.

Shtemenko comments on the selection of that particular sector of the front and its operational plan:

> The plan was extremely bold and intended to go around and encircle the main forces of the Hungarian 2nd Army in the areas of Ostrogosch, Alexejewka and Rossosch. The area around Kantemirowka, where the defensive positions had not been reestablished since our last offensive, were selected as the weak point of the enemy's defenses. The 3rd Tank Army delivered its blow there, while the 40th Army attacked south of Woronesch . . .

As a result of the total collapse of the Hungarian 2nd Army and the Italian 8th Army, which had not been expected even by the Soviets, fighting developed along the southern flank of the *2. Armee* during the last days of January with the result that it also had to pull back to the west. After crossing the Oskol, the divisions of the Soviet 40th and 60th Armies entered undefended areas and reached Bjelgorod and Kursk on 9 February.

A further consequence of the collapse of the Italian 8th Army was a strong thrust by the Soviets in the direction of Isjum during the first of February, which then threatened the northern flank of the Donez Position, which had held up to that point. After the loss of Isjum, an ever-widening gap was created between the *1. Panzer-Armee,* which formed the wing of the defense extending to the west through Slawiansk and *Armeegruppe Kempf,* which was in the process of being formed and was simultaneously pulling back to the west. It was a gap that could not be closed.

The divisions of the two Soviet field armies streamed west and southwest through that gap, which was up to 350 kilometers wide at one point, heading for the crossings over the Dnjepr and the second capital of the Ukraine, Kharkov, which is 80 kilometers south of Bjelgorod. The forces ratios between *Heeresgruppe Don* and *Heeresgruppe B* and the enemy were on the order of 8:1 in favor of the latter.

Von Manstein on the German defensive forces at the beginning of February 1943: "With the exception of the 1st Division of the *SS-Panzer-Korps,* which had arrived in Kharkov in the meantime, there were only remnants of forces facing the enemy in the entire area of operations of *Heeresgruppe B.*"[3]

The practically simultaneous operations of the Soviet Southwest Front across the Donez in the first part of February, which endangered both wings

3. Author's Note: von Manstein, 433 for this quote and 442 for the subsequent one. Translator's Note: von Manstein is referring to *SS-Panzer-Grenadier-Division "Leibstandarte SS Adolf Hitler."* The other two divisions of the all-SS corps were *SS-Panzer-Grenadier-Division "Das Reich"* and *SS-Panzer-Grenadier-Division "Totenkopf."*

of the *1. Panzer-Armee*, demanded decisions of far-reaching importance. After the evacuation of Bataisk on 7 February, the *4. Panzer-Armee* was moved to the extreme western wing of *Heeresgruppe Don*.

On 6 February, *Armeeabteilung Hollidt* was directed back to give up the eastern area of the Donez and move into the Mius Position, a repositioning that was carried out by 17 February.

On 9 February, the headquarters of *Heeresgruppe B* and the Italian 8th Army were pulled out of the line. *Armeegruppe Lanz* was formed to replace the latter. The frontage of *Heeresgruppe B* was assumed by *Heeresgruppe Don*, which had been formed by the redesignation of the former *Heeresgruppe Süd*.

✠

While all this was going on, *Heeresgruppe Don* and Hitler were wrestling with the decision to evacuate the Donez Basin. Von Manstein described those arguments in detail in his memoirs. In a nutshell, he considered the immediate evacuation of that area as necessary in order to form reserves and shorten the front. Hitler's objections—the importance of the region for the war economy and the importance of the railway termini for the supplying of the Soviet forces—dampened von Manstein's arguments. Von Manstein admitted that the Soviets were having problems with logistics, but he also stated:

> On the other hand, in the age of motorized vehicles, the distances from the enemy's railway termini to the coast of the Asovian Sea or into the lower Dnjepr were not so far as to cause a failure of the execution of the feared operations to pinch off the German southern wing.

Shtemenko provides the viewpoint of the Soviet General Staff when faced with the same problem before the commencement of operations in the same sector of the front on 14 January:

> The development of the operations along the Woronesch, Southwestern and Southern Fronts was made difficult through logistical problems. The supplying of those fronts was along the same routes that were being used during the preparation period prior to the counteroffensive at Stalingrad. In the meantime, the forces had advanced far to the west and had distanced themselves from the railway lines running off to the sides by distances of 250, 300 and even 350 kilometers. We were frustrated in those efforts to supply the

> forces along the Stalingrad-Kamensk rail line and all the way through the Donez Basin by the encircled field army of Paulus, which was positioned on both sides of that line at Stalingrad.
>
> The Woronesch-Millerowo line [running north-south] would have been suitable for that purpose, but the Liski-Kantemirowka sector was still in enemy hands. In the General Staff, we arrived more and more at the conclusion that no new wide-ranging offensive operations could be conducted before we were in possession of this railway.

The blockage of the most important logistical route to the west by the *6. Armee* encircled in Stalingrad, as highlighted by Shtemenko, justifies the question as to what would have happened if the *6. Armee* had capitulated by the end of December 1942, in other words, at a time when the German field armies south of the Don were still operating in the valleys of the Caucasus. The fate of the German southern wing would have most certainly been different.

Shtemenko provides yet another indicator of the importance of the railway lines for logistics in his critical analysis of the reasons for the operational failure of the Southwestern Front in February and March 1943:

> The forces of the Southwestern Front were not in a position to conduct an enveloping operation that had as its objective the encirclement of enemy forces that were even stronger than the ones at Stalingrad. Moreover, the enemy was getting closer to his logistics bases, while the Southwestern front was getting ever farther from its. The distance between the forces in the field and the nearest railway station in some cases was more than 300 kilometers.
>
> Classes of supply had to be brought up on the roads, and the trucks were too few in number and worn out. There were only 1,300 trucks and 380 fuel tankers available in the area of operations. They were only capable of hauling 900 tons of petroleum, instead of the 2,000 tons that the field army needed . . .

The commander in chief of the Soviet 40th Army, Marshall Moskalenko, has confirmed what Shtemenko has written, adding the following concerning the supply difficulties of his forces fighting northwest of Kharkov in the second half of February:

> Bringing up the rear-area services and the replenishment of rations, horse feed, ammunition and fuel stockpiles became ever more complicated. The rear-area services of the field army were located at

> the Waluiki rail station, already more than 300 kilometers away from us. There were not enough vehicles for transporting [the materiel] such a distance. The farther our forces advanced west, the worse their resupply became. We were lacking everything.[4]

The importance of the Donez area is emphasized by Shtemenko in his description of the Soviet objectives for the operations conducted in February:

> The intention was to exploit the unexpected weakness of the enemy in the line running Kastornoye-Starobielsk and quickly gain possession of Kursk, Bjelgorod and Kharkov and, moreover, possess the coal regions of the Donez, which the country needed so badly.

The reasons for the apparent differences of opinion by the various leaders on both sides concerning the operational aspects is confirmed by the course of the fighting. On the one hand, von Manstein was able to create the necessary prerequisites for his "backhand blow" at Kharkov due to the timely evacuation of the Donez area. On the other hand, Shtemenko confirms—in contrast to von Manstein—the considerable importance of the railway lines and stations. He blamed the lack of success for the initially successful Soviet operations in February 1943 due to the shortage of that infrastructure, among other things.

> The terrific results of the operations around Ostrogosch-Rossosch unleashed a chain reaction of events that could not have been predicted in detail in advance.

These operations were initiated, indeed provoked, by the unexpected collapse of the Hungarian and Italian field armies. The Hungarian 2nd Army had been turned out of its positions two days prior to the planned start of the Soviet offensive. Ten days later, it and the Italian 8th Army ceased to exist as field armies.

As early as 19 January, Vatutin, the commander in chief of the Southwestern Front, received permission from the Supreme Command to execute Operation "Jump," the offensive planned to eliminate the German southern wing. According to Shtemenko, the operational objectives were as follows:

---

4. Author's Note: Moskalenko, *In der Südwestrichtung*, 492.

> The field armies of the Southwestern Front were to conduct their main effort from the line running Pokrowskaja-Starobielsk to a line running Kramatorskaja-Artemowsk and then in the direction of Stalino, Voluowacha and Pariupol so as to cut off the entire enemy force in the area of the flood plain of the Don and in the area around Rostow, encircle it and then destroy it. They were to prevent any breakout to the west and the evacuation of materiel . . . one assumed that the area around Mariupol would be reached by the seventh day of the offensive. At the same time, the main crossing points over the Dnjepr were to be secured. The operation was to be conducted in coordination with the Southern Front, which had been directed to advance along the coast of the Asovian Sea.

A mobile group under Lieutenant General M. M. Popoff was entrusted with the deep breakthrough to Mariupol. The group of forces consisted of four tank corps—the III and IV Guards Tank Corps and the X and XVIII Tank Corps—and three infantry divisions—the 57th Guards Infantry Division and the 38th and 52nd Infantry Divisions. In all, he had some 180 tanks at his disposal.

KRASSNOARMEJSKOJE

On 29 January, the Popoff Group initiated operations. Contrary to Soviet expectations, it did not reach Mariupol after seven days. After 14 days, that is, on 11 February, it had only reached the railway and roadway hub of Krassnoarmejskoje, 130 kilometers north of Mariupol. The formations of *SS-Panzer-Grenadier-Division "Wiking"* reached the north bank of the Don on 5 and 6 February. New operations were awaiting the few operational tanks of the battalion.

After crossing the Don on the night of 4–5 February, the battalion mistakenly believed it was in for a few days of rest and maintenance. According to Schneider:

> In Rostow proper things were topsy-turvy. The *Landser*[5] grabbed whatever they needed from the large uniform and rations depots. Soon, there were civilians among them and took the best of what was there. A typical picture of a retreat.
>
> Every day, the Russians bombed the city, especially at night. During the night, there was firing from armed civilians . . . there was

5. Translator's Note: *Landser* was the term applied to the common soldier of the German army, much like "Tommy" in the British forces or "GI" in the U.S. Army.

> feverish work at the main train station to get important goods and, above all, rolling stock and locomotives to safety.

As a result, the thoughts of rest and maintenance proved illusory. At 0630 hours, the following day—6 February—the battalion found itself on the move to Ssambek, 50 kilometers to the west. Schneider:

> The roads leading out of the city were completely plugged up, once again . . . I had to fight to get out of Rostow. It was the same picture as the previous day. One column next to the other attempted to leave the threatened city as quick as humanly possible. The drivers cursed one another; officers were not much better, with no courtesy being shown. In the meantime, a horse-drawn battery with right-of-way turned onto the road past the cordon the military police had established.

Towards 2100 hours, nearly 15 hours later, Ssambek was reached. The following Sunday was a day of rest and, on 8 February, the battalion took up quarters in Taganrog, about 10 kilometers away. It offered good quarters and some diversions. The maintenance platoon worked feverishly on the maintenance and repair of tanks and vehicles. Schneider:

> The recovery platoon continuously went to Rostow and fetched one pile of junk after the other. It was tiresome work and offered little recognition for the self-sacrifice. The 18-ton prime movers were on the go day and night.

The operations and success of a tank battalion are directly related to the performance and devotion to duty of its maintenance services. The relationship of the technical personnel of the maintenance platoon, who had been professionally trained at Daimler Benz and Maybach, to the fighting elements of the battalion is perhaps best summed up by the firsthand account provided by its platoon leader, *SS-Untersturmführer* Weise, who comments on the activities of the platoon since its commitment in the summer of 1942:

> We were full of confidence during the first big operation, the breakthrough to Rostow. A few vehicles were lost to major battle damage from mines—torn-open, penetrated hulls and damage to the running gear. In a few days, we repaired the tanks in peach orchards on the banks of the Don and led them back to combat, following the tactical signposts and led there by the battalion by means of our radio

communications center. Great demands were placed on the running gear and engines on the way through the steppe and the Caucasus; mechanical damage surfaced. But regardless of where we went and took up quarters—whether in the woods, an orchard, a collective farm, a factory or under the open sky—we were always ready to go to work.

The sands of the steppe, the dust and the blazing sun all ate at the cylinder walls and pistons of our engines, and a few of them had to be swapped out. Soon, the supply routes were too long, and the engines had to be outfitted with new cylinder linings pistons—accompanied by the work associated with that—by the maintenance sections. In the process, our equipment on our maintenance vehicle was tested to the utmost. We did everything—from the smallest special-purpose bolt to the balancing of crankshafts. When we forded the Terek, the water was too deep for some of the tanks. They were filled with water. As was often the case in the main line of resistance and in minefields, the recovery section was employed with its large prime movers. In the oil region around Malgobek, a lot had to be done. In the face of extremely intense resistance on the part of the enemy, 22 tanks were battle damaged in a short span of time. Most of them were reported as total losses. But when we left the area where we had conducted repairs and moved on, there were only three totally burned out tanks left behind.

. . . Faced with snow and icy cold, the utmost was demanded of man and machine in the new area of operations as we moved towards Stalingrad. We were still going with the first tanks we had received.

By then, we were familiar with every bolt, part and line . . . nothing could shock us at that point. Every type of work was conducted: Transmissions taken apart and repaired; turrets and main guns exchanged; additional armor and safety devices installed; changing a tank engine in 24 hours; transmissions in two days; differentials, main gun and radio problems in a matter of hours; the same for more minor running gear damage.

Another source of worry were the innumerable truck and staff car repairs. Even jammed rounds were shot out of dismounted barrels; the tubes remounted. Nobody would have thought it possible.

The goal of all those efforts in Taganrog was the reinforcement of the single operational group of the battalion. Not even a company in strength, it was led by *SS-Obersturmführer* Grathwol. The vehicles recovered by the maintenance personnel were loaded on rail cars on the evening of 13 February, moving out that same evening. Even the non-combat-capable vehicles of the battalion headed out on that day for Amwrosiewka, about 80 kilometers to the north, moving through Pokrowskaja and Uspenskaja. The area and the names of the villages were familiar to the "Vikings," since they had fought there during the harsh winter of 1941–42.

Three days later, the non-combat-capable elements were moved to Stalino, another 50 kilometers to the northwest. Stalino remained the main base for the battalion until about the middle of March. The operational element—*Gruppe Grathwol*—was involved in hard fighting in the Krassnoarmejskoje area, a road and railway hub about 60 kilometers northwest of Stalino, supporting the division.

✠

On 8 February, the same day the tank battalion reached Taganrog, the lead elements of the division were at Amwrosiewka on their way north. They reached Stalino on 10 February, where the headquarters of *Heeresgruppe Don* was also located at the time. At 1515 hours on that day, the division received orders that it was

> attached to the *XXXX. Panzer-Korps* effective 1800 hours and is to move through Konstantinowka in such a manner that it arrives west of Kriwoy Torez on 12 February, at the latest.[6]

At 2200 hours, the corps informed the field army of the mission it had for the division:

> *SS-Panzer-Grenadier-Division Wiking* reaches the area east of Ssergejewka by means of a night march and moves out from there in the morning along both sides of the road leading to Kramatorskaja.
> Attack objective: West bank of Kriwoy Torez.
> Enemy situation: III Tank Corps is pulled out of Kramatorskaja for other commitment, while the IV Guards Tank Corps is to hold Kramatorskaja under all circumstances. The remaining mobile formations of Group Popoff (X and XVIII Tank Corps) continue to form a main effort on both sides of the Bachmut.

6. Author's Note: This quote and the following two are from the daily logs and annexes of the *XXXX. Panzer-Korps.*

At 0400 hours on 11 February, the following order from the *XXX. Panzer-Korps*, sent telegraphically, reached the division:

1. Strong enemy armor forces advancing southwest along the Kramatorskaja-Ssergejewka-Grischino road. Lead elements in Alexandrowka at 0100 hours.
2. *SS-Panzer-Grenadier-Division Wiking* moves out immediately and reaches Krassnoarmejskoje with all of its elements by the shortest route possible. Do not wait to assemble ahead of time. Reaching Krassnoarmejskoje is of decisive importance.
3. Roads:
   a) Artemowsk–Konstantinowka–Nowo Ekonomitschewskoje.
   b) Stalino-Ismailowka-Galjuznowka-Sselidowka-Otradnyj.
4. Officers from the *1. Panzer-Armee* are available in Gorlowka for alerting and guiding the division. Request them from the Operations Section of the field army.

The advance guard of the division, the *"Nordland"* Regiment, fought its way towards the city from the south. Moving out to the flanks, the *"Westland"* Regiment (east) and the *"Germania"* Regiment (west) encountered strong armored forces. Thanks to the divisional artillery, using considerable amounts of munitions, and the initially available eight tanks, the enemy was deceived into thinking a considerably stronger force was attacking.

The intent was to stop the lead elements of the Popoff Group, which had penetrated into the road and traffic hub that was so vital for the supplying of the Don-Mius front, and then throw them back. The Popoff Group had covered some 100 kilometers in a 10-day advance south from Isjum. It was in the process of attempting to envelop the left wing of the *1. Panzer-Armee* south of Slawiansk.

In between the forces of the Popoff Group and the elements of the *XXXX. Panzer-Korps*, which were protecting the left wing of the *1. Panzer-Armee*, was the Kriwoy-Torez, a south-to-north tributary of the Don, which originated about 10 kilometers east of Krassnoarmejskoje. The effort to envelop the Soviet forces, which was initially the German intent, collapsed after the terrain west of the river was reconnoitered. According to von Manstein, the reconnaissance had revealed

> that an advance by friendly armored formations in the terrain west of the Kriwoy-Torez to envelop the enemy was supposedly not possible. The terrain, which was broken up by deeply cut defiles, was so snowed over that the employment of friendly armor forces would not

be possible . . . For his part, however, the enemy advanced as far as Grischino across the allegedly impassable terrain west of the Kriwoy Torez during the night of 10–11 February with strong armored forces.[7]

Of course, the ruthless employment of forces by the Soviet leadership on the Eastern Front is well known. Shtemenko characterized the winter of 1942–43 in the following terms:

The winter of 1943 was exceptionally cold, with strong storms and heavy snowfalls. But this was the second winter of the war, and no one paid attention to the weather conditions.

Early on the morning of 12 February,

Wiking moved out to attack Krassnoarmejskoje again and, in the face of tough resistance by armored forces (including a lot of antiaircraft weaponry and antitank guns), penetrated about 1 kilometer into the city at 1130 hours with the group (*Westland*) advancing from Rownyj.

The lead attack elements of the southern group (*Nordland*) entered Nowo Alexandrow and was positioned with elements just south of Wosdweshenskij.

The regiment employed against Grischino (*Germania*) mounted up at Kotlina due to the poor road conditions and turned towards Molodezkij, so as to then attempt to envelop via Ssergejewka.[8]

The enveloped enemy put up bitter resistance. After six days, on 18 February, the forces in Krassnoarmejskoje and Grischino were eliminated. Elements were able to escape to the north:

The civilian populace participated heavily on the side of the Russians during the fighting for Krassnoarmejskoje . . .

After the conclusion of the fighting in the Krassnoarmejskoje area, assorted enemy orders were captured. Of note was the report of the commander of the IV Guards Tank Corps to the Commander-in-Chief of the Popoff Group, in which the fighting on 18 February in Krassnoarmejskoje was described . . .

---

7. Author's Note: von Manstein, 447.

8. Author's Note: This entry and the next are from the daily logs of the *XXX. Panzer-Korps.*

> In addition, the [commanding general] reported that the fighting in Krassnoarmejskoje had cost many casualties and a great deal of materiel.
>
> It was literally stated that practically nothing was left of the 14th Guards Tank Brigade or the 3rd Guards Rifle brigade.
>
> In addition, it should be further noted that the assistance of the X Tank Corps was insufficient, inasmuch as it had not received the promised logistical support.[9]

The importance of the breakthrough of the Popoff Group to Krassnoarmejskoje—both in the estimate of the situation by the Soviets and the ultimate halting of the Soviet forces by the *"Wiking"* Division for the Germans—can be gleaned from the following passage by Shtemenko:

> His reports [Vatutin's] to the General Headquarters were still infused with optimism, which was fueled by the breakthrough of the tanks to Krassnoarmejskoje. Vatutin believed that all of the enemy's resistance would soon be broken.

The German will to resist not only did not collapse, its intentions would soon be revealed in a counteroffensive from the south and the southwest that was being prepared by *Heeresgruppe Süd*. In a time-phased operation, the *4. Panzer-Armee* and the *1. Panzer-Armee* moved out to attack on 18 and 19 February. The Popoff Group, which was directly hit by the offensive of the *1. Panzer-Armee* and indirectly struck by that of the *4. Panzer-Armee*, adopted a barely comprehensible passivity during those days. At the same time, the lead tank elements of the Woronesch Front was positioned at the crossings over the Dnjepr at Dnjepropetrowsk and Saporoshe. Shtemenko explains the passivity from the standpoint of a leading member of the Soviet General Staff and attributes it to deficient planning and the unsolvable supply problems for the operation at the time. Even though the shortcomings of the operation were known in advance, it was ordered anyway due to a complete misreading of the German intentions:

> The defensive intentions of *Heeresgruppe Don* were not identified in time. The movements of enemy columns while they were being

9. Translator's Note: In this instance, the word *Nachschub* was used, which is translated in its normal logistical sense; however, it could also be used to refer to reinforcements, and it is not clear from the passage whether that might have been meant, although from the previous context (Shtemenko), it most likely refers to the Soviets being unable to match supply with demand.

> reconstituted was considered to be a continuation of the headlong flight, the attempt to avoid fighting in the flood plains of the Don and the effort to reach the western banks of the Dnjepr as soon as possible. The high command of the Southwestern Front held on to that misinterpretation, even though the facts, which should have made it take notice, were already visible.

Marshall Moskalenko offered his insight into the attitude of the Woronesch Front:[10]

> Even as the enemy increased his pressure from the south and southwest, the front headquarters continued to believe that he was pulling his forces back across the Dnjepr to the west and northwest of Kharkov. At least that was what was to be gotten from the directive of 26 February, which called for the 40th Army to advance as far as possible to the west and take Sumy, followed by Poltawa.

The argument that the "Nazi forces were in headlong retreat" was not revised on 21 February, even though, according to Shtemenko,

> it was certain that several SS divisions had moved out to counterattack. The directives sent to M. M. Popoff, the commander of the mobile group, stated unequivocally: "The situation that had arisen as a result of the enemy's intention to pull all of his forces back across the Dnjepr demands decisive action."

On that same 21 February, the division received orders from the *XXXX. Panzer-Korps* at 2035 hours:

> Enemy moving back towards the Geiluschka sector, battered. The *11. Panzer-Division* advances on 22 February from Nowo Alexandrowka to Stepanowka.
>
> *SS-Panzer-Grenadier-Division Wiking* is to continue to advance through Kriworoschja to Nowo Petrowka—without halting and without waiting for forces of the division to be concentrated—and block the Geiluschka sector. The *Germania* Regiment is returned from attachment. Forces still in Krassnoarmejskoje are to be moved out in an expedited fashion.

---

10. Author's Note: Moskalenko, 493.

By noon of 22 February, the division had taken Jekaterinowka, Wawarowka and Nowo Petrowka. At 2035 hours on 23 February, the division was telegraphed new orders from the commanding general:

> *SS-Panzer-Grenadier-Division Wiking* advances on Iwerskoje to establish contact with the *11. Panzer-Division* and, for the time being, prevents the enemy from breaking out to the west along a line running Iwerskoje-Jekaterinowka-Kriworostoje. Next objective: Alexandrowka on the Ssamara.

This was followed by further orders from the corps: "immediately advance on Stepanowka with strong forces."

On 24 February, the remnants of the battered Popoff Group continued to attempt to escape to the north in front of the *7. Panzer-Division* and the *11. Panzer-Division*. The corps daily logs described the action:

> What is new is the fact that the *III. Panzer-Korps*, on the west flank of the corps, has also received orders to march north. That means that the enemy has finally given up his intention of blocking a perceived German retreat to the west and is attempting to save strong elements of his beaten field army by heading north.

On 25 February, the division took Bogdanowka and occupied Gawrilowka early in the afternoon with its advance guard, after Alexandrowka and Ssofiewka had been taken the previous day. The mission for the pursuit of the enemy:

> *SS-Division Wiking* sets up a blocking position, oriented to the west and northwest, advances with a strong battle group as far as the Donez east of Petrowskaja and holds the crossing point there open.

By the evening of 27 February, Archangelskaja was taken in hard fighting. Of the 14 enemy tanks there, 6 were knocked out. Gruschewacha was in German hands. On 28 February, the division submitted the following daily report to the corps: "*SS-Panzer-Grenadier-Division Wiking* [has taken] the bridge over the Bereka north of Gruschewacha intact and is securing. Bridge over the Donez at Petrowskaja destroyed."

✠

In addition to its success barely four weeks previously—holding open the crossings over the Don at Rostow for the pulling back of the formations of the *1. Panzer-Armee* and the *4. Panzer-Armee*—the division could add another: At that decisive juncture as part of the *1. Panzer-Armee*, it contributed in thwarting the efforts of the enemy to envelop and destroy the southern wing and helped firm up the Donez Front.

This achievement, in which the tank battalion participated with only the equivalent of a single company, was praised in a division order-of-the-day. Von Manstein also found words of praise in his memoirs. To the amazement of some readers, he then added the following:

> Looking aside from the fact that it had been considerably weakened during the previous fighting, it suffered from a decisive lack of leaders. The division was composed of SS volunteers from Baltic and Nordic countries. Its losses had been so great that, for a while, there were not enough officers with the corresponding language skills available. That the combat power suffered within the force, which was in and of itself good, was understandable.[11]

That claim, which was not supported by any details, needs commentary for two reasons. The claim concerning the composition of the division can only rest upon false information having been supplied to von Manstein. The designations of the grenadier regiment point to their composition: *Germania, Westland* and *Nordland.* The *"Germania"* Regiment had been composed of native Germans even before the war started. The remaining two regiments took their volunteers from the respective cardinal directions of their designations. The framework of the latter two regiments was a strong contingent of Germans among all ranks. The German element predominated among the division troops as well.

It is not known where von Manstein based his claim about language difficulties causing a reduction of combat power within the division. Without wanting to fundamentally discount the possibility of individual cases—see the section on the Estonian volunteer battalion—still-living members of the division have a hard time understanding a generalization such as this. Moreover, may it be permitted to the author to say that he was a unit commander within the reconnaissance battalion, in the *"Nordland"* Regiment and in the tank regiment of the division, where he had the opportunity to lead Dutch, Flemish, Danish and Norwegian soldiers, and that he never had at any time language issues, not least of all thanks to the fact that the languages are related and to the language abilities of the volunteers.

---

11. Author's Note: von Manstein, 449.

It is possible that von Manstein had his doubts on the leadership qualities of the officers of the *Waffen-SS*. In the daily logs of *Armeegruppe Kempf* on 19 February, there is an entry for 1035 hours, which occurs at about the same time as events within the division:

> The chief of staff of the *SS-Panzer-Korps* reported that he considered the sending of general-staff officers as liaison officers to the SS command centers as a lack of confidence *vis-a-vis* his own general-staff officers.[12]

Another indicator of the lack of confidence in the leadership abilities of the headquarters of the *SS-Panzer-Korps* is given in the same set of daily logs for 16 February at 1050 hours, wherein von Manstein stated: "Once again, the question should be addressed as to whether the *SS* corps headquarters of Hausser should move out of the picture and the divisions be directly attached."

This is the same *SS-Obergruppenführer* Hausser who had evacuated Kharkov on 15 February 1943 in contravention of repeated *Führer* orders and those of the intervening commands. Four weeks later, he would take back that city with his reorganized divisions.

The divisions that had been freed up as a result of the evacuation were the prerequisite "for the expansive and well-conceived operations plan of Manstein," as Hausser later wrote concerning what happened. He asked the question: "How else could Manstein have conducted his offensive to the north between the Don and the Dnjepr?"[13]

KAMYSCHEWACHA—MICHAILOWKA

Let us return to the main body of the tank battalion at Stalino. It was there that the maintenance platoon worked feverishly to repair and return operational armored and wheeled vehicles to the battalion.

The battalion proper underwent a massive organizational change during this period. Almost one year after the establishment of the battalion, the directive was issued to establish a second battalion for the division and a corresponding regimental headquarters. The battalion commander, *SS-Obersturmbannführer* Mühlenkamp, was entrusted with the mission. Assuming

12. Author's Note: This quote and the next are from *Befehl des Gewissens*: Munin Verlag, 1976. Translator's Note: Normally, liaison officers exchanged between and among headquarters were not general-staff officers.

13. Author's Note: Paul Hausser, *Waffen-SS im Einsatz*, 1st edition, Plesse Verlag: 1953, 100.

command of the 1st Battalion of the soon to be regiment was *SS-Sturmbannführer* Köller.

The change of command ceremony took place on 28 February. The detailing of numerous experienced personnel to form the cadre and framework for the new battalion and regimental headquarters was a palpable loss to the 1st Battalion, which had already been weakened.

On 4 March, the repaired tanks and vehicles were sent forward to *Gruppe Grathwol* at Kamyschewacha. That entailed crossing 150 kilometers of muddy road. As a result of melting snow, every kilometer was a struggle.

The back-and-forth traffic between the combat elements of the battalion and the supply elements lasted until 14 March. The Red Air Force seemed to accompany the convoys, and the battalion adjutant, *SS-Obersturmführer* Birnschein, fell victim to one such attack. He convalesced from his shoulder wound at the military hospital in Stalino.

On 15 March, the disparate elements of the 1st Battalion were reunited in an area west of Isjum on the southern banks of the Donez.

The battalion command post was located in Kamyschewacha; the rear-area services were at Podolje.

The front was quiet the next several weeks. The men of the battalion used all means at their disposal to restore its combat capabilities. Even the trains elements conducted combat training.

The secret wish that the division and, by extension, the battalion, would be pulled out of the line, did not materialize. The dream of leave in the homeland remained just that—a dream. On 1 April, it was decided that the division would undergo a battlefield reconstitution.

During a commander's call in Kamyschewacha, Schneider noted

> . . . the battalion experienced a rebirth. The companies were issued new tanks. It should be noted, however, that it was not with the materiel that we would have wanted. Typical: The last few tanks were retreads.

The 1st Company received 13 tanks: 7 *Panzer III's* (5-centimeter long), 4 *Panzer IV's* (short) and 2 *Panzer IV's* (long). The composition of the remaining companies at the time remains unknown.

✠

On 5 April, the division started moving to the reconstitution area designated for it at Losowaja, some 60 kilometers southwest of Kamyschewacha, on Main Supply Route IV from Dnjepropetrowsk to Slawiansk. Due to the extraordinarily cramped situation as the result of the occupation of the area by rear-area entities, the battalion moved to the villages of Michailowka-Ssossipatrowka on 10 April.

Schneider writes about the reconstitution and its beginnings:

> It was a typical Ukrainian village, and it did not make a good impression in light of the terrible weather. As it later turned out, however, we enjoyed ourselves in its clay huts, since we did not want to leave. I had the tracked section with me again; the dance could start. The guidelines for the training were already there. Those warriors—oh, so very old!—would make faces if we tried to get them fired up.
>
> The company industriously set up its quarters. Tanks were camouflaged; fuel dump and a maintenance facility for the maintenance section established. The procurement officer set about looking for an oven and a cellar, where the easily spoiled food items could be stored.
>
> The first sergeant established a work detail that was already busy trying to build a sauna. Others were taking pains to organize a classroom, and a sandtable sprung up nearby.
>
> I sat together with my platoon leaders to put together the new tank crews. Things were hopping like an anthill.

On 20 April—the *Führer's* birthday—the commander gave a training holiday. Appropriate talents in the companies arranged for the culinary treats of the day. Fiebelkorn, a master confectioner, and the cook of the 2nd Company impressed us, as always, with his artistry. The dining facility of the battalion headquarters in Michailowka was transformed in a few days by the artists of the maintenance platoon by the outfitting of wall lamps made out of wrought iron and brass shell casings. The candlelight created a fitting atmosphere. Five days later, Easter offered another opportunity to forget the war. The ability to improvise, the mental alacrity and the imagination of the German soldier are recorded by Schneider:

> In the afternoon, at 1600 hours, the company social gathering started. Tables and chairs had been set up in a rectangle in the dewy green of a meadow. A living curtain, formed from a wild hedge, provided the background. Our master confectioner, Fiebelkorn, had not held back in his artistry. As a result, three different types of cakes could be presented to the men, with a decent cup of real coffee as well. Moods were elevated by humorous skits and portrayals. Following that, there were games such as sack races, egg races, knight fighting

and similar things, which the commander and his platoon leaders also participated in. For refreshments, various sorts of *Schnaps* were served.

In the meantime, a large percentage of the local populace also joined us. Spurred on by our *Landser* songs, a few *Barischnas*[14] offered a few Russian folk tunes and dances and gave it their best. The *Starost,*[15] who sat next to me . . . felt the need to dance. But just for a short time. The Schnapps, which he took a great liking to, soon made him incapable of moving. The highly successful afternoon gathering was closed off with a hearty evening meal and a song, both in the presence of the commander.

PETROWKA—IWANOWSKI

The first phase of the battlefield reconstitution of the newly redesignated 1st Battalion was completed on 10 May 1943 in the Michailowka-Ssossipatrowka area. The 1st Company was attached to the *"Germania"* Regiment, along with a company of engineers, to serve as the ready reserve for the corps behind the front lines of the *46. Infanterie-Division* in the Petrowka area. Three days later, on 13 May, the rest of the battalion followed. On 14 May, the ready reserves were pushed further forward in the direction of the front. The 1st Company took up quarters in Iwanowski, a village consisting of two rows of houses. It was already overfilled with refugees from the villages along the Donez. The civilians welcomed the quartering parties, since it meant a degree of security from the annoying partisan ambushes.

In a short period of time, Iwanowski, "The Home Base of the 1st Company," underwent the transformation that had occurred at Ssossipatrowka a few weeks earlier. Training proceeded in a deliberate manner. Opportunities for sports and available free time were created with a sheer inexhaustible supply of talent. An athletic field was set up in a few days out of nothing. It was encircled by a 400-meter track. There was nothing lacking in an obstacle course, either: water ditch; crawling obstacle; swinging beams; hurdles; and an escalading wall. There were pits for broad- and high jumps. There was even a flag pole. To bring about bathing opportunities, we went back to the proven method of using fuel canisters—cleaned out, of course, and containing water—which was then sprayed out by means of fuel pumps.

The high point of those efforts was the sports fest of Iwanowski, which was followed by a victory celebration that remained unforgettable for all those who attended. Fiebelkorn won the most sought-after prize: home leave and an immediately available ticket.

---

14. Translator's Note: A young woman or girl.

15. Translator's Note: A village elder.

The enemy granted the battalion six weeks to restore its combat capabilities. Starting on 1 July, it was prepared to move again.

BEREKA—KHARKOV AREA—BEREKA

On 5 July, the battalion rolled in the direction of Krutaja-Balka, moving via Barwenkowo and Bol. Andrejewka. In addition to the *"Wiking"* Division, an Army armored division also rolled north. So as to avoid enemy reconnaissance, the rail movements were ended each time at 0300 hours.

The interlude as a ready reserve behind the Bereka ended on 10 July. The battalion then headed in the direction of Kharkov. The battalion marched from Komarowka, a suburb of Kharkov, to Woroschilowsk, some 50 kilometers to its north, during the night of 12–13 July. Nothing happened with regard to the assumed participation of the division within the framework of Operation "Citadel" along the Kursk salient. After waiting two days in Woroschilowsk, the moved out again during the night of 15–16 July. Instead of heading north, however, it went back south to the already familiar area behind the Bereka. All of the movements were tied into the major fighting at Kursk, even though the division was not directly involved.

After a break of three months, there had been new operational-level movements in the southern part of the Eastern Front. The last great offensive operation conducted by the Germans—Operation "Citadel"—had just failed. The offensive had started on 5 July against the Soviet forces concentrated in the salient that jutted westward from the Kursk area by launching pincer attacks against the salient's base from both the north and south. The objective of the operation had been to regain operational freedom of movement and initiative. The Germans had concentrated large numbers of forces for the operation. In the north, there was the *9. Armee* of *Generaloberst* Model, which was comprised of five armored, one mechanized infantry and seven infantry divisions. *Armee-Abteilung Kempf* and the *4. Panzer-Armee* in the south had 11 armored and 7 infantry divisions.

The *9. Armee* attacked along a frontage of 90 kilometers in the north. It "got bogged down after initial success in the first few days of the attack, after it had broken through to a maximum depth of 15 kilometers along the enemy front."[16]

The two field armies attacking in the south penetrated as far as 35 kilometers into the Soviet defensive network. There were more than 100 kilometers between the spearheads of the two attacking forces when the *9. Armee* had to call off its efforts on 12 July, nine days after the start of the

---

16. Author's Note: von Tippelskirch, 330.

offensive. The two forces in the south called off their efforts five days later, on 17 July.

The failure of the operation represented the ultimate turning point in the eastern theater of war. It was a straight path from there to the conquering of Berlin.

SSREDNIJ—GOLAJA DOLINA

The men of the 1st Battalion of the regiment could not see the purpose of the many marches of the previous few days. When they marched back to the south from Bereka along Tank Trail "East" during the night of 16–17 July, "they racked their brains and could not find an explanation for why they were returning to their former holes."[17]

But when they were ordered to Kamyschewacha on the evening of 17 July, things were clarified. The Soviets had crossed the Donez to the north of the village with strong forces and had started to attack. The fighting that followed for the next few weeks and months was dictated by the Soviet counteroffensive. Kamyschewacha was reached after a night march; it was filled up with trains elements and corps troops.

The next morning, 18 July, the 1st and 3rd Companies of the battalion, which had been attached in support of *Kampfgruppe Dorr* of the *"Germania"* Regiment, attacked with the battle group to block a Soviet penetration north of Barabaschewka. The clearing of the terrain succeeded on the first try, advancing as far as the southern outskirts of Ssrednij. The next attack objectives were Mal. and Bol. Garaschewka. While masses of fleeing Soviets on Hill 123.1 offered the tanks welcome targets, the tanks themselves were covered by Soviet 18.2-centimeter artillery once they reached the forward slope. A deep and broken-up *balka,* 1 kilometer in front of the palpably close objective of Garaschewka, seemed to be impassable for both the tanks and the infantry. The battle group commander was wounded for the ninth time. All of a sudden, bright flames arose from tank 113, and the crew bailed out.

The tanks were able to stop taking direct fire by backing up to the reverse slope and finding concealed positions behind a hedge.

A second attack conducted in the afternoon also failed along the deep defile. The effort to completely clear out the village of Ssrednij, which had been left up to *Kampfgruppe Sitter,* likewise failed that evening, although the battle group held on to its positions in the village. Neither the attack of the 1st Company from the west or the 3rd Company from the south, during which two tanks were lost, brought any success.

---

17. Author's Note: Direct quotes and input for the narrative for this section are from the Schneider diaries.

At first light on 19 July, the tanks of the 1st Company attacked Ssrednij again. The Soviets, who had infiltrated into a fruit orchard to the south of the village during the night, made life difficult for the tank crews with their antitank rifles.

A radioed warning from the battalion caused the 1st Company to break off combat and seek covered positions in a hedgerow. A large-scale Soviet attack on Ssrednij was planned for 0815 hours, it had been reported. Right on time, seven T-34's raced through the village. Three of them, to the rear of the men of the 1st Company, who were waiting in ambush, were knocked out and set alight. The remaining four tanks, which had become more careful and moved indecisively among the houses of the village, also fell victim to friendly tanks that cleverly snuck up on them.

Despite the onset of heavy artillery fires on Ssrednij and constant Soviet attacks, *Kampfgruppe Sitter*, which had had its companies reduced to between 10 and 20 men, continued to hold the village. Another company from the *"Germania"* Regiment arrived to provide reinforcement.

The tanks of the 1st Company pulled back about 500 meters to escape the increasingly intense artillery fire. To help provide security, two tanks under the command of *SS-Untersturmführer* Senghas, remained behind in the village. They held out in their positions there during the afternoon hours.

The commander of the assault-gun company, which was sent forward to assist *Kampfgruppe Sitter*, was killed by the murderous artillery fire on his way to the command post. The commander of the tank battalion's 1st Company was able to observe a Soviet attack through binoculars in the sector to the right. Soldiers of one of the division's foreign volunteers battalions, *SS-Freiwilligen-Bataillon Narwa*,[18] were able to stop a breakthrough by nearly 100 Soviet armored vehicles.

A relief effort to be launched the following night with two tank companies, the assault-gun company and the engineer battalion was also a failure. The lack of success can be attributed to difficulties in orienting on the terrain, unclear command-and-control relationships and inadequate communications among the units and formations involved.

On 20 July, the 1st Company of the battalion, which was screening south of Ssrednij, was relieved by the 3rd Company at 1000 hours. The 1st Company remained attached to the *"Germania"* Regiment and moved to the village of Broschowka by way of Kamyschewacha and Dimitrijewka. The next 10 days

18. Translator's Note: SS Volunteer Battalion "Narva" was composed of volunteers from Estonia. It was formed to replace the Finns, who had returned to Finland after their tour of duty was up and the Finnish government opted not to allow them to remain on the Eastern Front. The Estonians fought bravely and eventually formed the nucleus of an entire SS division that had Estonian volunteers as its predominant nationality—the *20. Waffen-Grenadier-Division der SS*.

there were spent in the patch of woods to the south of that village cleaning and maintaining the vehicles and weapons. During the early-morning hours of 3 August, the *I./SS-Panzer-Regiment 5* marched back to the northwest in the direction of the area around Bereka. The back-and-forth movements of the previous few weeks had almost become a habit.

A strong Soviet advance to the south of Isjum on Golaja-Dolina had resulted in a penetration that was 12 kilometers wide and 10 kilometers deep. That meant that the tank battalion had to turn around again to restore the situation in the threatened area. The 1st Company was reattached to the *"Germania"* Regiment, which had been entrusted with cleaning up the penetration. From the regimental command post in the patch of woods 1 kilometer west of Krassnopolje, the company reached the command post of the 2nd Battalion of *Panzer-Regiment 39*, the tank regiment of the *17. Panzer-Division*, at its command post in Golaja-Dolina around 1600 hours. The Army tank battalion had been directed to support the *SS* mechanized infantry regiment, and the two tank elements combined forces. In addition, mechanized infantry elements from the *17. Panzer-Division* were also in support. The Army tank battalion had already boldly attacked the Soviets and knocked out 23 of their tanks—T-34's and KV-I's. Just before the *1./SS-Panzer-Regiment 5* received its attack orders at the southeastern portion of Golaja-Dolina, it lost a *Panzer IV* to a T-34. It burned out completely.

SS-Hauptsturmführer Schneider, the commander of the 1st Company, attacked a short while later with three tanks from his company. The Soviets, who had initially taken up the fight with antitank rifles, started to run. Senghas knocked out a British Lend-Lease Mark III, and the company, joined by an infantry battalion from the *17. Panzer-Division*, which had been threatend by the tank attack, reached the Golaja-Dolina–Slawiansk road, blocking it. An attack that was launched later that day towards the fruit orchard 1.5 kilometers east of Golaja-Dolina was eventually broken off due to darkness. At first light on 4 August, the orders conference for the continuation of the attack took place with the commanding general, Heinrici,[19] and the division commander, *SS-Brigadeführer* Gille. Let us continue with the reworked diary entries of Schneider to get some flavor for the fighting at this time and place:

> The tanks positioned themselves, unnoticed, in a broad *balka*. It was terrific attack weather. We moved out right on time. The high ground was taken at speed, without the Russians even having time to notice what was happening. When we were topside, however, and were

19. Translator's Note: Unless Klapdor has the name completely wrong, he should have "commander in chief," since *Generaloberst* Gotthard Heinrici was already a field-army commander at this time (*4. Armee*).

getting to go into the valley towards the fruit orchard, we received intense fire from artillery, antitank guns and tanks. Senghas's tank was knocked out, with another one immediately following. The latter burnt out. It was Rempi's crate. There were wounded in both instances. As a result, we spent all of the day in glaring heat screening behind Hill 199.5. At 1500 hours, there was suddenly a commander's call. New orders:

The fruit orchard was to be taken. The reinforced battalion was to attack after an artillery preparation with mounted infantry from the 2nd Battalion of *Germania.* At the same time, the division reconnaissance battalion was to move out from the north. Attack start: 1600 hours.

Since time was of the essence, the preparations were made with too much haste. The infantry were jumping around, trying to find their units. Other jumped up hastily on the tanks, which were already moving. As the clock struck 1600 hours, we were moving over the top of the hill.

We then received fire, the likes of which I had never experienced before. A wall of fire appeared in front of me. Fountains of dirt, with flashes from the exploding munitions in between. I was moving with my company on the left wing and saw two, then three, then four and finally five tanks blazing in front of us. And in between there was the whooshing of the shells, not to mention the antitank-guns that were taking us in their sights.

We covered 500 meters in that inferno. I had just reached the first few fruit trees, when the commander radioed us to return to our lines of departure.

I counted the heads of my men and found out that another two vehicles had been lost—total write-off's. Two additional vehicles were slightly damaged were out of the question for immediate employment. And so I set up on the reverse slope in order to repel any possible immediate counterattacks—with a whopping three vehicles with 5-centimeter main guns. The gentlemen from the Army were still disorganized; they were still reassembling.

The poor grenadiers took bad losses. Mounted on the tanks, they were exposed to shrapnel without any defense.

In his original diaries, Schneider went on to discuss the coordination between the tanks and the infantry in general and the sinking combat morale of the infantry. His tanks were split up and posted behind their positions. Schneider then went on to write:

> The end effect of the attack on the fruit orchard was the equivalent of nothing. It cost a lot of people and materiel. That could have been avoided. *Brigadeführer* Gille, when he submitted his final report by telephone to the commanding general, Heinrici, did not hesitate to say he was not interested in ever working together with the *Herr General* again. I should add that the idea for that idiotic attack came from the commanding general and that Gille, along with all of the various other [subordinate] commanders was against it.
>
> During the night, the *Germania* Regiment and my company were pulled out of the line and returned to the command and control of the division.

The regiment and the company returned to the Bereka area on 6 August, where the tank company was given two days for maintenance and rest as part of the battalion.

With that, the 1st Battalion of the tank regiment had finished its operations as a "fire brigade" as part of the division along a frontage of some 200 kilometers southeast of Kharkov—at least in that sector of the front. In the coming weeks, the battalion would continue to function as a "fire brigade" northwest of Kharkov, as the German forces moved back to the Dnjepr Line.

KLENOWOJE—KRYSSINO—KADNIZA

There were rumors that trouble was brewing in the Kharkov area and the rumor was fed by the fact that the tank battalion had to leave the main road when it was marching north to allow *SS-Panzer-Grenadier-Division "Totenkopf"* and *SS-Panzer-Grenadier-Division "Das Reich"* right-of-way on their march north. According to Schneider:

> On 11 August, we rolled in the direction of Kharkov. There was traffic on the road like on the *Kurfürstendamm.*[20] The closer you got to the city, the crazier the traffic on the road. The *Luftwaffe* [ground personnel] and the agricultural managers[21] were in a hurry to leave the city . . .
>
> It was strange to see an unending column of vehicles composed of military personnel of all branches waltzing past you in an effort to get to safety.
>
> Heading in the other direction was a very thin membrane trying to hold up the Russians.

---

20. Translator's Note: The street with the main shopping district in Berlin.

21. Translator's Note: German agricultural overseers, who had been employed to raise crop productions in the conquered territories.

> We passed Kharkov for a second time. In the city, they were still in the process of loading up all industrial infrastructure on trains. That meant the situation was pretty rotten.

The division reached the area northwest of Kharkov on 12 August. Strong enemy forces, bent on enveloping the city, were advancing north of it in the general direction of a line running Olschany-Kryssino.

> The main forces of the *Wiking* Division reached Olschany on 12 August in order to relieve the elements of [*SS-Panzer-Grenadier-Division*] *"Das Reich"* that were screening there for employment elsewhere. [The *"Wiking"* elements] had orders to establish defensive positions on the Ridgeline 202.4 north of Kryssino, where outposts of . . . *"Das Reich"* were still screening.
>
> But the [Soviet] advance guards were also trying to get to the ridgeline.
>
> *"Wiking"* employed its tank battalion on a wide front to attack the middle of the ridgeline . . . [22]

For the first time in that round of defensive fighting, an attack was ordered conducted at battalion level. The 1st Company was to advance on the left, the 3rd Company in the middle and the 2nd Company on the right. A battery of assault guns was to follow the 3rd Company. The assembly area was in the "Egg Woods," north of Kadniza, and the formation moved out at 0800 hours.

The first attack objective, Hill 209.5, was crossed by the tanks, which were spread out for the attack across 1.5 kilometers of steppe. They then advanced as far as Hill 202.4, which would assume critical importance over the next few days in that sector of the front. The command tank of the 1st Company was hit and burned out.

On the next day, the battalion was ordered to attack the village of Klenowoje, about 1.5 kilometers away. It was to be taken along with the 2nd Battalion of the *"Germania"* Regiment. Schneider:

> From the very first day of the attack, it was known that the city was heavily occupied by the Russians. The 2nd Company had lost a vehicle there as the result of flanking fires. It burnt out, and the poet Kurt

22. Author's Note: Straßner, no page listed.

Eggers[23] died a soldier's death there. An eyewitness confirmed the enemy report.

Around 1400 hours, the battalion moved out with the 2nd Battalion of *Germania* to attack. The attack had already bogged down by the time it was in the cornfield 1 kilometer outside of the village. Since the tanks were absolutely unable to identify any targets and were exposed to murderous defensive fires the entire time, they turned around.

After another comprehensive commander's conference, the battalion moved out again at 1600 hours. The 3rd Company screened off to the west of the southern edge of Klenowoje towards reported armored forces. I moved with the 1st Company on the left; the assault guns were in the middle. On the right, there was Beck with his 2nd Company. The [infantry] battalion moved with us. Battalion is saying a bit much, since the companies only had 25 men each. With a certain amount of grim fury in our bellies, we worked our way forward through the cornfield. The Russians were firing like crazy again. But this time we needed to do it. It was my misfortune that there was a deep *balka* in my attack sector. I held a course more for the center and moved along the *balka* in an effort to find a bypass or a bridge.

I reached the first houses with the assault guns. The Russians then started to fire with increased fury from the opposite slope. The assault guns moved back because of the fire. Since I was powerless all by myself, I initially pulled out of the line of sight of the enemy by seeking concealment behind a house. I had barely reached that spot, when a man from the assault-gun battery came jumping up to me and asked for assistance in towing out his vehicle. So . . . out again into the fire to recover the vehicle, which had driven into the middle of a manure pile. The men worked feverishly to attach the tow cable. When everything was ready, we gave it a jerk and the crate was freed up again. I was unable to find a crossing point. There was nothing

23. Translator's Note: Eggers was a National Socialist literary figure, who was the editor-in-chief of the SS house magazine, *Das schwarze Korps (The Black Corps)*, and also went to the front in the guise of a war correspondent for the *Waffen-SS*. After his death on the battlefield, the *SS-Kriegsberichter-Abteilung* (SS War Correspondent Battalion) was redesignated as *SS-Standarte Kurt Eggers* and the members of the formation wore a cuff title with the deceased's name. A *Standarte* was ostensibly a regimentally sized formation, although there were nowhere near the number of war correspondents that a "regiment" would imply, at least all gathered in one location. It had cells throughout occupied Europe and included a number of foreign nationals, including U.S., New Zealand and British citizens, among its ranks. It also supplied war correspondent platoons to all of the major *Waffen-SS* field formations.

> to be seen of my company, either. Since I was all by myself up front and was also unable to discover any infantry, I moved back along the *balka*. All of a sudden, I saw tank tracks. That meant that my guys had gone behind me through the *balka*. Time to get moving and follow them!
>
> It was like a roller coaster. It went down, steeply, 10 meters. The engine, in first gear, started to howl. I had barely reached the bottom and wanted to climb up the other side when my sled spit a few times and then had nothing else to say. All of the efforts on the part of the driver to get the engine turned over were in vain. Great!
>
> The Russians were hopping around on a bridge about 500 meters away. An antitank gun was constantly firing down the *balka*, and I was in a mousetrap—immobile. A terrific situation. I cussed and cursed. But the engine did not stir. Gradually, the whole crew started to sweat. After 15 minutes, the overheated engine finally came to life. The radiator water measured 230 degrees Fahrenheit.
>
> Slowly, like a snail, my vehicle climbed up the slope in front of us. I had barely arrived at the top when I saw my company in firing order and things were banging all around it. Enemy artillery was impacting in between. What a sight! There was a fruit orchard to the right of me; the 2nd Company was fighting on the extreme edge of the city. There was nothing to be seen of our friends, the grenadiers, far and wide.
>
> I decided against moving into the locality without an infantry escort. To continue remaining where we were was nonsense, since we had not reached the actual attack objective, that is, the village . . .

As it turned dark, the tanks pulled back, initially screening at Hill 209.5. They then rolled back to Maximowka to refuel, rearm, take care of minor problems and sleep.

The attack by the 2nd Battalion of the *"Germania"* Regiment had failed, since its commander, *SS-Hauptsturmführer* Juchem, went missing in action at the start of the attack and the necessary leadership was missing.

By the following morning (14 August), Hill 202.4 was lost and in Soviet hands. The 1st Company of the tank battalion was given the mission of taking back the hill, in conjunction with Schreiber's company from the *"Germania"* Regiment. Schneider:

> At the northern edge of the woods north of Kryssino, I found a small bunch of infantry. Among them was also *Hauptsturmführer* Schreiber, the commander of the sector. All of the officers of his battalion, with

the exception of his adjutant, *Obersturmführer* Friedrich, had been taken out of action. The battalion only had a trench strength of only about 60 men.

After discussing the situation briefly, we moved out. With the support of the tanks, we succeeded in taking back the hill. Sixty men had the responsibility of covering a sector that was 2½ kilometers wide. That was our front. But the great thing was that I did not find a single man who had given up the fight in any kind of manner . . .

The ceaseless defensive fighting northwest of Kharkov in August 1943, which fixed the division in the area around Maximowka-Klenewoje, were designed by the Soviets to provide flank security on the south for their main forces advancing westward farther to the north. The Soviet attacks were relentless and, in some cases, conducted with strong forces, especially artillery. Early on the morning of 15 August, the Soviets attacked from out of Klenowoje against Hill 209.5 with strong infantry elements. Hill 228.1 was also hotly contested. The 1st Company of the tank battalion was once again dispatched to a threatened sector. Schneider:

I identified the enemy in the small saddle between the hilltops. The Russians were advancing against our weak outposts in battalion strength. I was really happy that they were doing that, since I was right on their right flank. Fortunately for us, I was unable to identify any Russian tanks. So . . . let's go! I had the company disperse and grabbed Ivan by surprise in his flank. In some places, the Russians skedaddled back to Klenowoje. Our main guns provided the final blessing. The northern slope of the attack hill was soon swept clean. In the heat of battle, we had not noticed that the Russians were covering us with artillery. We turned towards the north and wound up in the Tarowka collective farm. I established contact with Heder's company there; he was in charge of that sector.

Thing's didn't look good at his location, either; the company was more like a platoon in strength. He had mostly Estonians, who had not mastered German. It was understandable how difficulties in command & control increased, especially whenever things started to get hot.

In the company command post, I also met the commander of the 2nd Company, *Obersturmführer* Multhoff. His company was screening out behind the main line of resistance . . .

As it started to turn dark that night, the Soviets attacked Hill 202.4 with tanks, following a strong artillery preparation. They took the hill.

The 1st and 3rd Companies, together with the 2nd Battalion of the *"Germania"* Regiment, were ordered to take back the hill in a nighttime immediate counterattack. Details were carefully planned and discussed. Schneider:

> . . . after the smoke had cleared away from the salvoes of the friendly artillery, we moved out right at 1300 hours.
>
> We moved to just before the hill without firing. I had reserved the right to open fire. But when my vehicle, which was moving in the middle towards the hill, started firing, all hell broke loose. The colored pearl-white streams from the tracer ammunition, mixed in with the flashes from the armor-piercing rounds and the impacts and reports of the high-explosive rounds, presented a wonderful picture. The Russians cleared out in that inferno, as if the devil incarnate were on their tails. As we later discovered during the day, they had left behind rifles and pieces of equipment in great numbers. We advanced far behind the objective and into no-man's-land. But there were no [enemy] tanks to be seen. Apparently, they had been withdrawn after they had scored their success.
>
> I had the company continue to screen until the grenadiers had re-established themselves in their holes. Then we moved back to the reverse slope.
>
> Schreiber and even Schumacher were excited about the success. The infantry had not suffered a single loss.

The game was repeated on 16 August. The German grenadiers were ejected from Hill 202.4 again. The 1st and 3rd Companies of the tank battalion took it back and brought a company of engineers forward to reinforce the 2nd Battalion of *"Germania."* As was often the case, the pulling back of the tanks afterwards was misconstrued. The engineers wanted to go back with the tanks. In the end, however, Schneider reports that it was possible "to force them to act reasonably."

The front lines were thinly held. An armored patrol determined that there was a gap of some 1.5 kilometers at the boundary with the engineer company. It was an extraordinarily unpleasant situation, especially with such a diligent enemy.

After a quiet 17 August, the tankers were awakened on the morning of 18 August with continuous barrage fire. The Soviets attacked Hill 209.5, the Tarowka collective farm and Hill 228.1 with strong infantry and armored elements. The tank battalion ordered its elements to immediately move in the direction of Hill 209.5. Schneider:

> I moved between the center and western patches of woods to the north of Maximowka and positioned myself on the northern edge of the center patch of woods. Russian infantry was working its way forward directly towards my location. And it wasn't just a small amount that was coming.
>
> I attacked with the four crates I had. They pulled back to the south. But our machine guns had their effect. Often, three puttered, sometimes all four at once. Since we had created some breathing room and had a field of view to the right, we could see how four . . . five . . . no, six T-34's and an assault gun had approached in a column just north of Hill 209.5. Unfortunately, we only had one *Panzer IV* with the good 7.5-centimeter main gun.[24] It was possible to rip open all of the rascals, however, since their turrets were all pointed south. By the time they would identify us, they'd all be burning and smoldering. So Senghas fired at the brothers. The second round was a hit, and the Russian tank started to develop smoke soon thereafter. Senghas immediately shifted targets, and the second one was ablaze after a few rounds. The first tank that had been hit was also consumed by flames when it started to back up.
>
> Unfortunately, Zäh and I were unable to participate in the engagement with the 5-centimeter vehicles, since our main guns would not reach that far. We limited ourselves to keeping the Russian infantry off of Senghas' back. We were unable to prevent a Russian antitank gun from setting the successful tank alight. Too bad, since Senghas was doing such a bang-up job. The last 7.5-centimeter vehicle of the company burned out with his tank.
>
> On top of everything else, however, Senghas was wounded pretty badly. He left the engagement with shot-shattered upper arm. It was only with great difficulty that the knocked-out crew could be evacuated and brought to safety. At that point, I was pulling security on the northern-most corner of the center patch of woods. I could no longer operate offensively with the crates . . .

While the "stockpiled" 1st Company defended and screened, the 7.5-centimeter *Panzer IV's* of the 3rd Company attacked the masses of Soviet infantry and tanks attacking approximately 3 kilometers farther east. It was a major day of fighting in which the Soviets strove to advance beyond their

24. Editor's Note: The author is referring to the high-velocity L/48 main gun.

previous efforts in taking Hills 209.5 and 228.1 and reach the rail line and roadway at Maximowka. On 18 August, the enemy attempted a decisive win in that area with more than 100 tanks, which represented the employment of two tank corps. Gustav Waber, who was assigned to the 3rd Company at the time, has provided a first-hand account:

> We were positioned with our tanks in the village of Maximowka in a valley. Up higher, on a rise, we saw a collective farm, most likely a former country estate. At that point, the hilltop made a bend. As a result, the collective farm occupied a dominant position. Our infantry held the ridgeline and spit generously in the soup of the Russians up front in the valley. It should be mentioned that our infantry was distributed thinly, however, since the division had a sector of 15 kilometers to hold at the time and had been badly battered in that fall of 1943 when it came to infantry. On that morning, around 0400 hours, the Russians started with an insane barrage fire. He fired at our position with every heavy weapon he had. We were lying on straw under our tank. Exactly two hours later, the artillery fires stopped. It was as quiet as a cemetery. We quickly prepared our tank for combat, since things could start up at any moment.
>
> We had scarcely mounted our tank when, lo and behold, we started to hear the sound of the *MG 42's* of our infantry on the hill. It was an hour, however, before we were told to move out. Since the Russian infantry was unable to take the hill, they had called up tanks, trying to break through with all means at their disposal.
>
> We quickly moved up the hill. On the way there, we encountered the surgeon in his ambulance. When he was asked what it was like in the collective farm, he only laughed. There were five men up there. Each had an *MG 42* and a mountain of ammunition. The barrage fire hadn't done anything to them; they had just finished turning back their ninth large-scale attack in two days. I started to well up. Five men were holding an estate, and there had been mountains of corpses lying in front of them for days. They had to have nerves of steel.
>
> When we reached the hilltop and looked down into the valley, our hair stood on end. It was swarming with enemy tanks. When the first T-34's had approached close enough, we greeted them with our long 7.5-centimeter main guns. Although we scored hit after hit, we were not able to take on all of that onslaught.
>
> Individual T-34's were already infiltrating and attempting to effect the breakthrough. Then, in our hour of need, three *Tiger* tanks came

to our help from a neighboring Army unit. During their approach they started to sweep away the T-34's that had broken through with their long 8.8-centimeter main guns. We immediately felt some relief. Then we worked together. The area looked like some industrial park. There were burnt-out T-34's everywhere. It was not until it was dark that the tank engagement was over.

When we heard the results, we were jubilant. We had knocked out 84 T-34's in conjunction with the *Tigers*. Our victory was even announced in the Armed Forces Daily Report. Friendly losses were minimal.

The next morning, the Russians tried once again. When the fog started to lift, we knocked out a number of T-34's. When we continued to knock them out, they pulled their tanks back at 0900 hours. Two days later, they broke through further to the right of us. I will always remember that tank engagement and those five European men of the *SS* in that collective farm . . .

A telegraph from the operations section of the headquarters of the *8. Armee* praised the performance of the forces on that hill:

Over the last few days, the corps has added two great successes to its credit:

1. The defensive victory of *SS-Panzer-Grenadier-Division Wiking*, which knocked out a total of 84 tanks after the employment of the *Tiger* battalion.
2. The bold advance of *SS-Panzer-Grenadier-Division Totenkopf* across the Merla.

My thanks and recognition to the leadership and the forces in the field.

/signed/ Wöhler

I am happy to be able to transmit the attached letter of recognition from the Commander-in-Chief of the *8. Armee* to the attached divisions and corps troops.

/signed/ Breith

General der Panzertruppen and Commanding General of the *III. Panzer-Korps*[25]

25. Author's Note: *Europäische Freiwillige.* Munin Verlag: 1968.

During the ceaseless fighting, during which the enemy attempted to gain access to Kharkov by enveloping it from the northwest and west, the *I./SS-Panzer-Regiment 5* was the backbone of the division. It held a sector nearly 22 kilometers wide with combat strengths that decreased on a daily basis. It was a sector that could not be occupied continuously, either along the front or in depth to the rear. Nor could it be held even at the points felt to be the most threatened. It was one of the incalculable aspects of warfare that the gaps in the front that naturally arose remained hidden to the enemy and did not lead to a catastrophe.

The front lines of the division ran from east to west, somewhat north of the villages of Olschany-Sinkowsky-Kadniza-Maximowka-Krissyno. After screening a gap in the front to the west of Hill 209.5 for several days, the 1st Company of the tank battalion received the mission to relieve the 2nd Company east of Kadniza, where it had also been screening a gap in the lines of several kilometers. That gap, between *SS-Freiwilligen-Bataillon Narwa* in Kadniza and the *"Westland"* Regiment in Sinkowsky had been caused by the reduction and shifting of the front of one of the battalions of the *"Germania"* Regiment to the west by the Soviets, who were assaulting in that area as well. The battalion commander, in addition to other officers, had been killed. The trench strength of the battalion was around 70 men.

As the friendly forces on the left, *SS-Freiwilligen-Bataillon Narwa* held a sector of approximately 3 kilometers with 120 men. Soviets had already infiltrated into the village of Kadniza, which meant that they were to the rear of the Estonians. An armored patrol conducted by Lohmüller and Dienersberger of the 1st Company was greeted in the village by the enemy with handheld antitank weaponry. The wounded being evacuated, as well as messengers and ammunition bearers, were also being engaged from the village.

But even the powers of the Soviets were not limitless. They remained quiet on 20 August.

The next day, the 1st Company was dispatched to Sinkowsky, the command post of *"Westland,"* on the right wing of the division. They had barely arrived at 1600 hours, when it was sent back to the left wing of the regiment. *SS-Obersturmführer* Multhoff, the commander of the 2nd Company, briefed the 1st Company with his accustomed self-confidence. That morning, his company had practically wiped out a strong Soviet assault detachment of company size in the gap between the Estonians and *"Westland."* At the moment, the Soviets were attacking the left wing of *"Westland"* and not, as one would have expected, into the gap that started a few hundred meters further to the left.

Two Soviet tanks were knocked out. The attack was turned back. On 23 August, the enemy did not attack. That evening, at 1900 hours, the 1st

Company was sent to Olschany and the command post of the friendly forces on the right, the 2nd Battalion of *SS-Panzer-Grenadier-Regiment "Deutschland"* of *SS-Panzer-Grenadier-Division "Das Reich."* Schneider provides perspective on the uncertainty on one side and the necessary decisiveness on the other when he and his company reached Olschany:

> I arrived in Olschany at night. The city looked dead. No civilian to be seen, but no soldier, either. In the direction of the enemy, not too far away at all, an occasional round impacted. MG fire also interrupted the stillness occasionally. If our hearing wasn't deceiving us, it was not too far to the front lines.
>
> I made a great effort to find some sort of markings leading us to Bissinger's command post. But it was not to be found. Making a snap decision, I had an all-round defense set up along the road. I set up guard posts and had the company rest. At least we could get a few hours of sleep by doing that . . .

On the two days that followed, 24 and 25 August, there was relative quiet. Steinkohl and Lohmüller, two tank commanders, received special praise from the commander of *"Westland"* for cleaning up a Soviet penetration.

✠

The uninterrupted defensive fighting of the division from 12 to 25 August was capped on the night of 25–26 August by a movement to the rear that did not end until the crossing of the Dnjepr at the end of September. The division moved back as part of the *8. Armee*, as *Armeegruppe Kempf* had been redesignated. The withdrawal of the field army was precipitated by the operational-level breakthrough of strong Soviet forces in the sector of the *2. Armee* on the right wing of *Heeresgruppe Mitte.* The Soviets were aiming for the upper course of the Dnjepr.

At the same time, the Soviet Southern, Southwestern, Steppe and Woronesch Fronts had also initiated decisive offensive operations at the beginning of August. Those efforts led to success on both sides of Isjum, caused the Mius Position to be lost, followed by Taganrog on 29 August, and saw the Soviet field armies reach the Dnjepr four weeks later.

✠

The general line of withdrawal for the division was initially the Kharkov-Poltawa rail line, followed by an almost oblique movement in the direction of the Dnjepr in the area of Tscherkassy.

During the night of 25–26 August, the withdrawal movements started for the 1st and 3rd Companies, together with the 2nd Battalion of the *"Westland"* Regiment, ending in the Wjasowy area, south of Olschany. For the first time, the Red Air Force also bombed. It lit up the target areas, striking at night, as well.

While the friendly forces to the right, the *3. Panzer-Division*, continued to pull back, the 2nd Battalion of *"Westland"* and the 1st Company held off the hard-pressing Soviets. The 1st Company of *SS-Untersturmführer* Moritz knocked out three tanks that day.

During the afternoon of the following day, the enemy broke through between the 2nd Battalion of *"Westland"* and the 2nd Battalion of *"Germania."* By the time it turned dark, the *"Westland"* Regiment, supported by the 1st and 2nd Companies, sealed off the enemy penetration. The 28th of August was marked by renewed withdrawals. According to Schneider: "Even the simple foot soldier wants to know where it's all heading." On 29 August, Schneider entered the following:

> We moved out at 0030 hours. The company had the mission of covering the *Westland* Regiment during its withdrawal on the right wing of the division. The withdrawal transpired without enemy interference. The Russians dropped bombs at night, illuminating the terrain as bright as day by means of new illumination rockets, lighting up the withdrawal route as well as the village along it. As always, the casualties in comparison to the effort expended were nothing.
>
> The regiment rolled past us to the rear around 0200 hours. We were all alone at that point. In order to create the time needed by the division to establish its new defensive positions and occupy them, the tank battalion occupied the 30-kilometer-long frontage of the division by means of strongpoints in no-man's-land.

During the course of the next day, the enemy, who was pursuing with tanks and infantry, was turned back. Four enemy tanks were knocked out, and the enemy left 100 dead on the battlefield. The tank battalion quartered in Buski. The grenadiers occupied their positions.

The spirit of the tankers remained unbroken, their devotion to duty unflinching. There was no unnecessary loss of valuable materiel and equipment. Gustav Waber of the 3rd Company provides firsthand information:

It went without saying that the units of a front-line sector supported one another whenever things were hot. For instance, one day, three *Panzer IV's* of the company received orders to support a neighboring infantry company of the Army that was facing an imminent attack. We immediately raced off, and we had barely reported in when the whole affair got underway. By the afternoon, the charging of the Russians, which resulted in the slaughter of their people, was over, and out patrols reported fortifications being dug on the other side. Since that meant that a break in the action would probably set in, we set off for home, tired and low on ammunition.

Not perceiving anything out of the ordinary, we moved along the edge of a valley, right up next to the steep slope. There was a meadow around us, green and filled with flowers. All of a sudden, the lead tank—our tank—sank and the tracks were soon churning without effect in the soft marshland ground. We had bottomed out. We quickly warned our other comrades. We then look at the damage. A horrible mess! Who would have thought . . . just 5 kilometers to go!?

We immediately tried to free ourselves up. The two other tanks positioned them self across the front of us and attempted to pull us out. The cables grew taut to the breaking point. We didn't budge from the spot.

We then carted large rocks out of the slope and placed them in front of the tracks. All of a sudden, a wild firefight started up. Our loader went to a nearby rise in the ground to check things out. He came back, breathless: "The Russians are attacking to the left of us in the sector of another Army infantry company. Due to a lack of ammunition, they are pulling back two hills."

Even though we redoubled our efforts, we could not get out. The tracks dragged the rocks under the tank, but we continued to be frozen to the ground. Our infantry started to come past us. We asked them to hold the hill to the left of us until we could get free. They told us we needed to get out of there. We were already in no-man's-land and would soon be in the middle of the Russian infantry.

What were we to do? Blow up the tank? No! We would not do that unless it was absolutely necessary.

When the infantry left us their last crates of ammo, we felt better. We quickly traversed all of the turrets towards the left hill, where the Russians would have to appear in a few minutes.

And then nothing but rocks—as fast as our practically bursting lungs could move them. We worked feverishly, doggedly. At that point, we had a mountain of rocks in front of our tank. Our comrades began to pull again, while our tracks slowly swallowed the stones, one by one.

Suddenly, there was a slight movement forward. We slowly began to lift up. Hurrah! At the last possible moment! At that point hang hard left and slowly, very slowly approach the slope and get away from the marshy spot. Soon we were moving under our own power.

Just as we were undoing the cables, we heard the hundredfold hoarse *Urräh* of the Russians. Immediately following that, the first bullets began whizzing past our heads. But we were out of the marsh by then and were returning fire until the infantry had collected itself, grabbed ammunition and had gone into position on the hill on the right. When the Russian attack then collapsed in the face of the combined fires, we moved back to our company, where we were finally able to get ammunition for ourselves.

✠

On 30 August, the 1st Company was on the extreme west wing of the division in the sector of the Estonians, who were under the command of *SS-Hauptsturmführer* Grafhorst. The company was in Woitenkoff. Of particular concern to us there was the boundary between the divisions. On 31 August, the company rolled to the middle of the divisional sector around the Tetschjutschina *balka*, where it established contact with Oeck's 3rd Battalion of the *"Westland"* Regiment. The route there led across a railway line. Schneider:

I was not yet at the aforementioned crossing point, when I was presented with a fantastic scene. Shells were impacting on and in the vicinity of the route leading forward. In and of itself, that was not too bad. What was worse was the fact that antitank guns, limbered to their tracked prime movers, and an entire battery were scrambling rearward. Among them were a few infantry jumping along behind, taking cover whenever artillery impacted.

I had my company halt, so that I could study the map without disturbances. I had not seen anything like that before and found a possible explanation in the possibility that I had gotten lost. But everything checked out. I had to cross over the rail line to get to Oeck. But why were our own troops pulling back?

Making a snap decision, I left my unit behind and had a vehicle monitor the radio, so that I had the boys on a leash. Behind the railway crossing, you could more or less see what was happening. Summed up: It was a free-for-all. According to the grenadiers standing around me, there were no more German soldiers in the village in front of me that had the strange name. That meant that Oeck was no longer to be found there, either.

Since the situation demanded fast action, I also didn't need the good man. According to the O4,[26] *Obersturmführer* Kaufmann, the Russians had broken through with strong infantry forces and had taken the locality. You could see new hordes of Russians moving towards the village from our location. To the right, there was no longer any contact [with friendly forces].

I immediately had my company come forward and deploy from the march. The attack formation formed up in the blink of an eye. A little verbal shorthand, and my 12 vehicles were soon rushing towards the Russian-occupied village. Just outside of the village, I had the entire company fire. A few of the huts went up in flames. And then we moved on. Attack objective: Northern edge of the village.

It made your heart glad to see the company racing ahead. I saw my long-time tank commanders, who had proven themselves in incomparable ways in many engagements, grinning when we fired the salvo and then saw its effect. In a competitive mindset concerning mastering the situation, each of them was eager to be the first one into the village. That explained the outrageous tempo that each of the tank commanders had ordered to his driver.

The bunch took off like on a crazy hunt. I was on the right wing. From there, I was able to recognize a *balka* with fairly deep and steep walls. Without wasting any time, however, the vehicles set about trying to overcome the trench. And would you look at that . . . the first few were already pushing their way into the village.

From my position, with the turret at 3 o'clock, I suddenly saw a lot of Russians, who were moving from the railway track towards the village. While I was still engaging them, the main body of the company bolted into the village. There were many dead among the Russians. When I rolled on in, there were already elements of the grenadiers from *Germania* there, and we were able to transfer 60 prisoners to the infantry. In addition to leaving about 100 dead behind, the enemy also left behind 10 antitank rifles, 7 heavy machine guns and 12 light machine guns. In addition, there were a lot of small arms. Together with the grenadiers, I then took Hill 203.4, which was north of the locality.

26. Translator's Note: One of the two authorized assistant operations officers of the division.

✠

The attentiveness of the attacker is always focused on the boundaries between troop units of the defender. It was not uncommon to find weak zones among the defenses that led all the way into the depths of the main battle area. Sometimes, it was a case of the two units bordering one another placing too much trust in the defensive efforts of the other. Sometimes it was the result of unclear command-and-control relationships that left necessary measures undone.

✠

While it was the 1st Company of the tank battalion that was able to intervene in the middle of the division sector on 31 August, it was the 4th Company, which was equipped with assault guns, that saved the day on the right wing. It was there along the boundary with the friendly forces to the right, the *3. Panzer-Division,* that the enemy had penetrated with strong armored forces that same day. To seal off the enemy penetration, the 4th Company was attached to the *"Germania"* Regiment during the night of 31 August–1 September.

The 4th Company also had an acting commander for its new mission, *SS-Untersturmführer* Hein, since the commander, *SS-Obersturmführer* Jessen, had been wounded the previous day. The combat capabilities of the company were reduced by the fact that the radio sets were in desperate need of maintenance, repair and overhaul. Hein has provided a firsthand account:

> But I rumbled through the night to the designated place, reported to the commander and set up an all-round defense to allow the company a short sleep to recover.
>
> The morning fog had just lifted, when we heard confirmation of the bad news of a Russian armored breakthrough along the boundary to the *3. Panzer-Division.* Immediate actions was required. We moved along the rail line to Poltawa in vegetated terrain that resembled a dolmen.[27] It was marked on the map as "Gruschki's Grave." We set up an ambush position. There was nothing to be seen of friendly forces far and wide. The hills in front of us gave us the direction in the eerie morning twilight from which the enemy had to come.
>
> The engines had been turned off. As a result, we could hear the roaring sounds of a large armored formation that was approaching

27. Translator's Note: A dolmen is a type of single-chamber megalithic tomb, usually consisting of three or more upright stones supporting a large flat horizontal capstone (table). (en.wikipedia.org/wiki/Dolmen)

thundering over towards us. After a few minutes, we saw about 40 tanks with infantry mounted like grapes pressing towards us over the hills. They were already deployed for contact. "12 o'clock . . . 1,000 meters . . . armor-piercing . . . fire!" The gunner and the loader reacted as fast as lightning. Four rounds . . . four hits . . . four burning tanks. The Red Army men jumped off in a panic. All of that took place before our eyes in a matter of seconds. I could not measure the time, the situation was so tense. Eleven burning T-34's and four immobilized tanks blocked the Russian attack. Moving in reverse, they backed up as fast as lightning over the hill. My men jumped out of their turrets, yelling with excitement about their success. But they already had an inkling that the next attack would come out of the depressions to either side of the hill. We quickly assigned targets. The missing radio communications were replaced by hand & arm signals. The enemy's next attack—the effort to envelop—had already started. It went without a hitch, just like on a sandtable exercise. The enemy was turned back again. Two T-34's were left behind, burning, while two others were immobilized. A KV-II rolled past us at speed with its 52 tons. "Turn around . . . move out!" We followed him with one of the assault guns. Distance: 250 meters. Fire . . . target hit . . . ricochet! The macabre game was repeated four times. Then: "Hurrah!" The Russians bailed out, and the KV-II belonged to us. We pressed forward to it. The Russians then mounted up again quickly. "Turret . . . 6'oclock!" We were ready to fire again. But the Russian started to turn away slowly, exposing his side to us. One round—it was burning. But that was our last armor-piercing round . . .

No radio contact with the battalion; all rounds expended. As a result—it was about 1100 hours by then—we were chased like rabbits by 20 enemy tanks, but we were able to reach the protection of the railway embankment without sustaining any losses. We were greeted there by the 3rd Company, which was rolling up in our hour of need. It took the enemy off our hands. Reported to the battalion. Quick repairs to our guns; set up the radios again. During the evening hours, we rolled away towards our new position, 2 kilometers south of our previous engagement area. Nothing happened that night. We set up an all-round defense. The vehicles were well camouflaged. A bit of sleep did us good. At first light we identified the enemy, who had camouflaged himself with heaps of straw. He was spread out in our old position, ready.

Radio to the battalion to request reinforcements. That enemy force could be taken. To realize that opportunity was the wish of everyone. We were itching to take action. The wounded commander of the assault-gun battery of *"Das Reich"* reported to my location. We set about wargaming the options.

We climbed the tower of the railway station with all of the tank and assault gun commanders—nine combat vehicles in all. An artillery observer joined us. The targets were quickly identified and divided among seven tank and assault gun commanders. Two remained in reserve. The artillery observer wanted to fire smoke.

At 1100 hours, our vehicles rolled out to attack. Using the concealment offered by the smoke, we reached the designated firing position, 500 meters in front of the enemy. "Fire!" Nine enemy tanks were immediately set ablaze. Four T-34's attempted to flee and were taken out from the rear. Moving on a zigzag course, a couple of armored cars disappeared behind the protection of the hill. It was like target practice; we rolled up a trench line of the Soviets, where the escort infantry had hunkered down.

The path was then clear for the planned counterattack of the *"Der Führer"* Regiment,[28] which was scheduled for that afternoon. We held on to "Gruschki's Grave" that long.[29]

In a certificate of recognition dated 7 November 1943, the Supreme Commander in Chief and *Führer* of the *Reich* praised the achievements of *SS-Untersturmführer* Hein on that day.

✠

The attack by the *"Der Führer"* Regiment, supported by the *Panther* battalion of *SS-Panzer-Regiment 2*, was delayed; towards evening, it received effective support from *Stukas*. Despite all that, the hill near "Gruschki's Grave" had to be evacuated the following night. The *Panther* battalion set up quarters a good kilometer from the village of Tetschjutschina-Balka.

An effort to establish contact early in the morning of 2 September, around 0700 hours, by the tanks of the 1st Company with the *Panthers* screening outside did not end well. Three of the tanks of the 1st Company were knocked out at the edges of the village by the *Panthers* in a friendly fire incident that was understandable given the fluid nature of the front. Among the badly wounded was *SS-Hauptsturmführer* Schneider, whose first-hand accounts by

28. Translator's Note: Another mechanized infantry regiment of *SS-Panzer-Grenadier-Division "Das Reich."*

29. Author's Note: *Europäische Freiwillige*, 218.

means of diary entries end at this point. His gunner, Abraham, was mortally wounded.

In the weeks that followed, the tank battalion took ever greater leaps to the rear as part of the division. By 7 September, a line running Walki-Tschutowo-Poltawa, about 40 kilometers to the west, was reached. As was the case previously, the enemy was turned back in hard fighting, although the commander of the 2nd Company, *SS-Obersturmführer* Multhoff, was badly wounded at Walki during the course of the fighting.

On 19 September, new, bitter fighting erupted in the newly reached lines running Choral-Lubny, about 140 kilometers to the northwest, during which massed enemy forces were once again unable to score a decisive success.

Although they had to pull back again and again, the tank companies contributed decisively in helping to plug gaps in the front and winning the necessary time for the rearward flow of the formations towards the Dnjepr crossings.

THE DNJEPR CROSSING

The overwhelming personnel and materiel superiority of the enemy, which von Manstein had labeled as 8:1 in the enemy's favor as early as the spring of 1943, had grown yet again and had received an additional dimension through the use of massive amounts of airpower. Soviet airborne forces from several brigades jumped behind the German defenses along the Dnjepr on 24 and 25 September. They landed in the Kanew area, north of Tscherkassy. The tactical objective for the airborne forces was to establish bridgeheads along the west bank of the Dnjepr before the Germans had a chance to establish themselves in suitable positions along the natural water obstacle.

At the same time, the tank companies of the battalion were fighting their way back to Tscherkassy by way of Irklejew. They crossed the river there on 27 September. On that very same day two years previously, the reconnaissance battalion of the division, reinforced by the motorcycle infantry companies of the three infantry regiments, had crossed the mighty river 100 kilometers further south at Krementschug in an effort to open the bridgehead at Dnjepropetrowsk from the east.

The men of the division were faced with eliminating the Soviet paratroopers from the positions that had been designated for them and attacking, reducing and eliminating Soviet bridgeheads on the west bank of the river in bitter fighting. To the disappointment of the forces in the field, the Dnjepr did not prove to be the long-desired barrier that would offer breathing room behind it. The forces found only partially completed field fortifications, if they found any field fortifications at all.

One of the main reasons for that was the fact that the field armies of *Heeresgruppe Süd* were forced to use the few large-scale crossing point options to be found at Saporoshe, Dnjepropetrowsk, Krementschug, Tscherkassy and Kiev. The canalization of the movements had led to a major loss of time. As a consequence, the enemy had already established bridgeheads on the west bank between the German crossing points and before the defenders could reach the positions designated for them.

✠

The disappointment regarding the status of the defensive preparations along that naturally strong river barrier was great. The question of why there were only five crossing points for the field armies of *Heeresgruppe Süd* has no satisfactory answer. Not only did the use of the five crossing points cost a lot of time, it also cost a lot of time for the forces to then occupy 700 kilometers of river front.

In the bridgehead the Soviets had already established between Dnjepropetrowsk and Krementschug, new forces were already being ushered across to expand the bridgehead, both in depth and breadth.

With regard to the Soviet bridgehead north of Kanew, von Manstein has written: "He had several airborne brigades jump south of the river and crammed eight rifle divisions and one tank corps into the narrow strip of land within a short period."

Von Manstein does not answer the question as to why the German infantry divisions did not cross the river by means of ferries, footbridges and military bridges, all the while employing the help of the many small islands present.

The men of the "*Wiking*" Division remembered the footbridge in Dnjepropetrowsk that had been used two years previously when crossing the river to the east. Even though it was under artillery fire, it enabled contact between the two banks of the river and allowed the bridgehead to be resupplied.

Soviet Marshall Koniev has written about the crossing of the Dnjepr by his formations:

> When we started to force the Dnjepr, we knew that the enemy was leading his forces in the Ukraine east of the river to the crossing points at Krementschug and Dnjepropetrowsk. By 25 September, there were 14 infantry divisions and 2 armored divisions of the *8. Armee* and the *1. Panzer-Armee* there. That meant he had devoted most of his attention to the Krementschug sector. He was expecting that we would cross the river there and prepared accordingly. We took

> under consideration the fact that the enemy had not yet established a firm defense between Krementschug and Dnjepropetrowsk, which was why he was concentrating his main efforts there. We wanted to conduct the main effort there.[30]

Koniev discovered that the stores of pontoons had not been brought up in time despite all efforts to that end and continues in his writings:

> That rendered the operational planning of the front—forcing the Dnjepr from the march—null and void. Our forces crossed the river along a broad front, destroyed the enemy's defensive networks and delivered him a devastating defeat.

30. Author's Note: Koniev, *Aufzeichnungen eines Frontoberbefehlshabers,* Militärverlag der Deutschen Demokratischen Republik. Berlin: 1978.

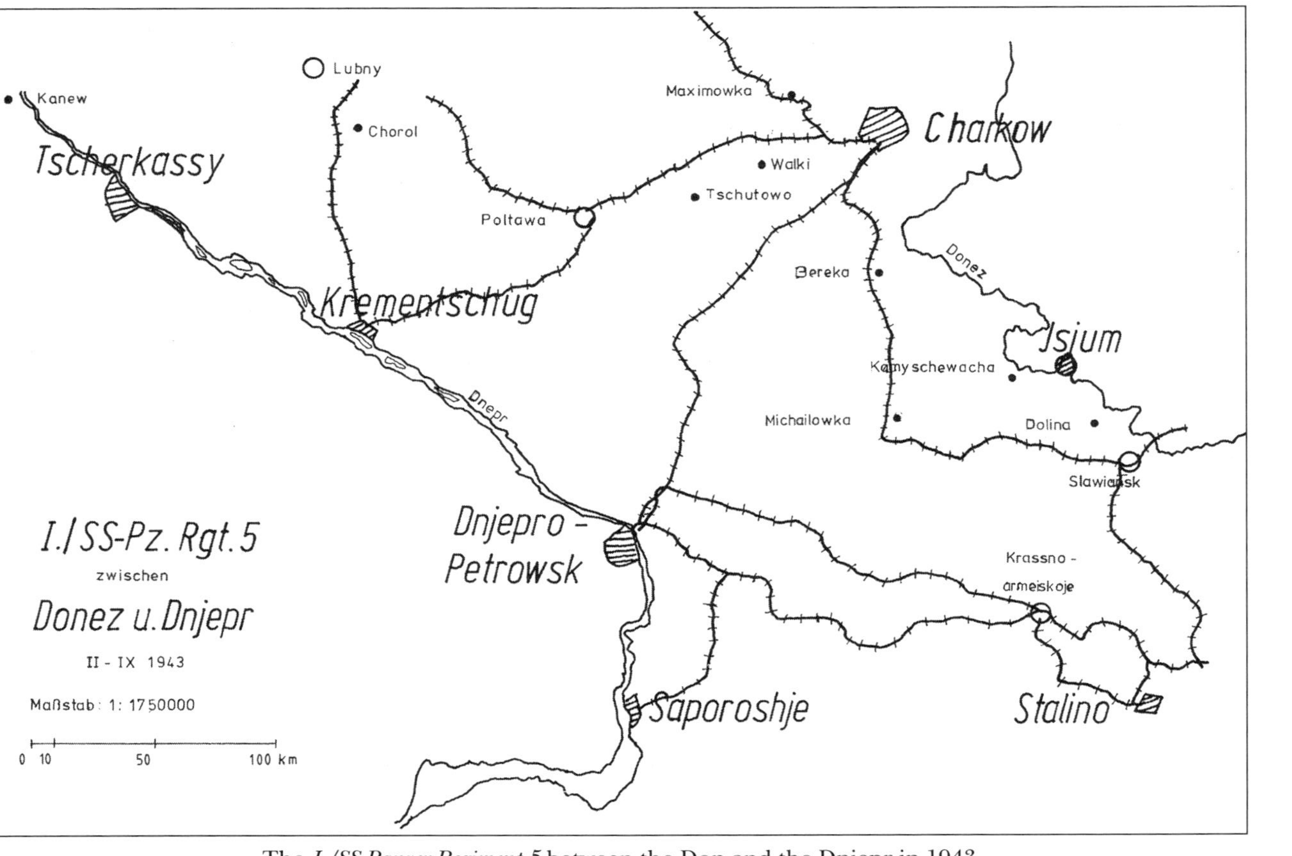

The *I./SS-Panzer-Regiment 5* between the Don and the Dnjepr in 1943.

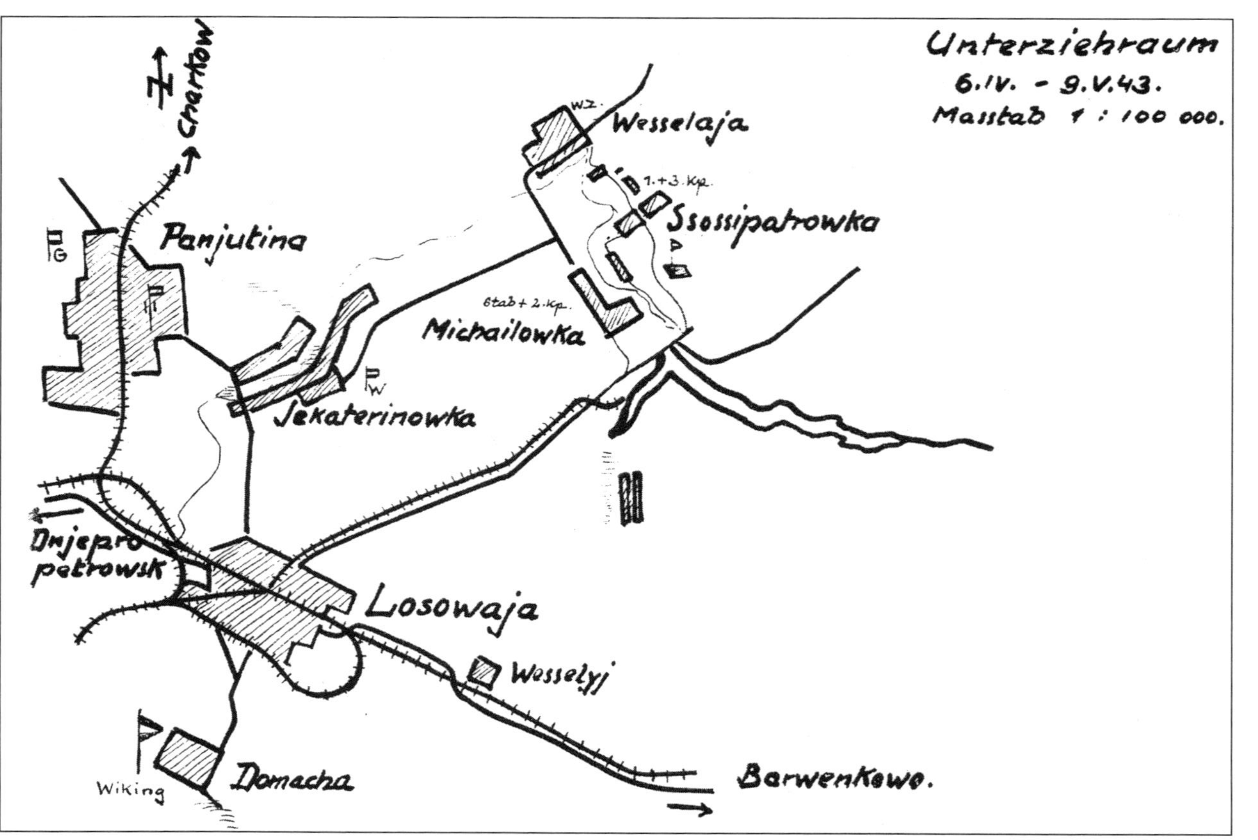

Billeting area around Losowaja from 6 April to 9 June 1943.

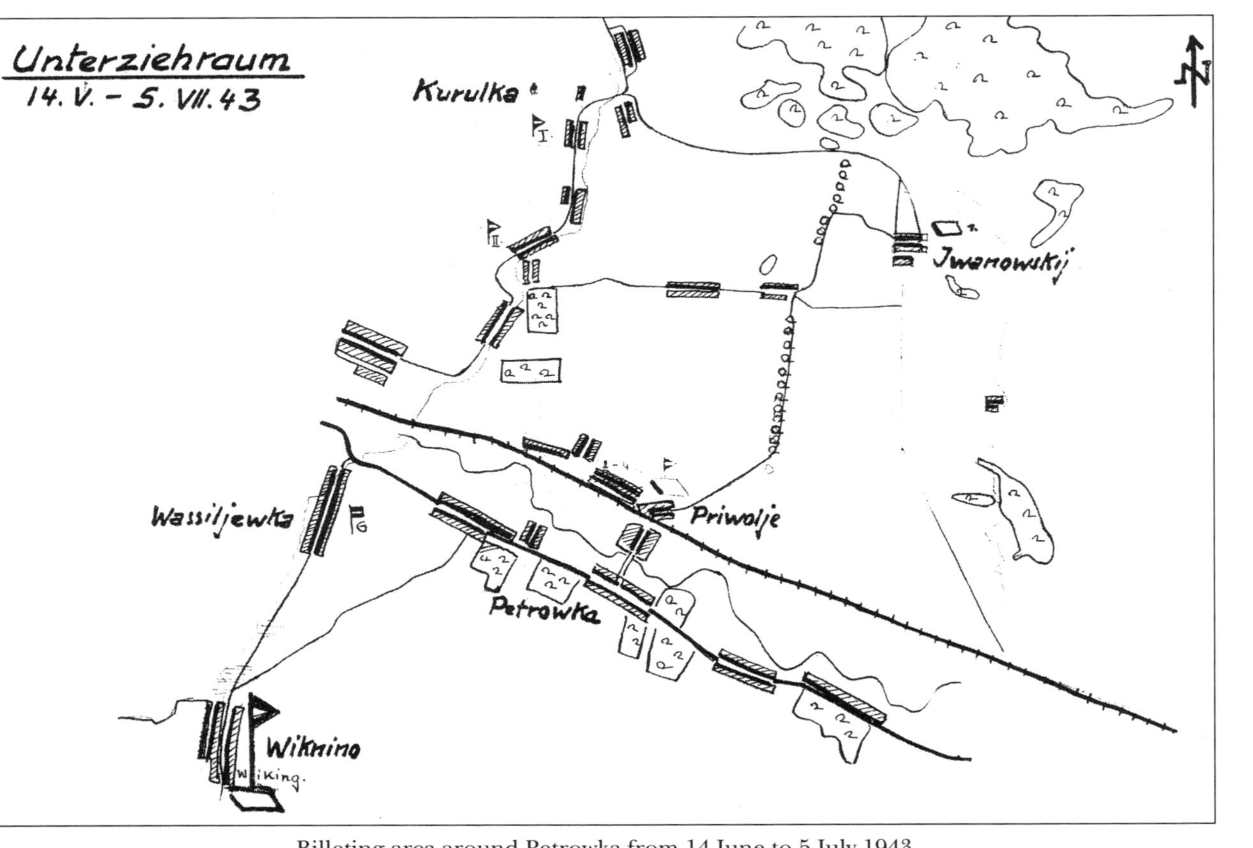

Billeting area around Petrowka from 14 June to 5 July 1943.

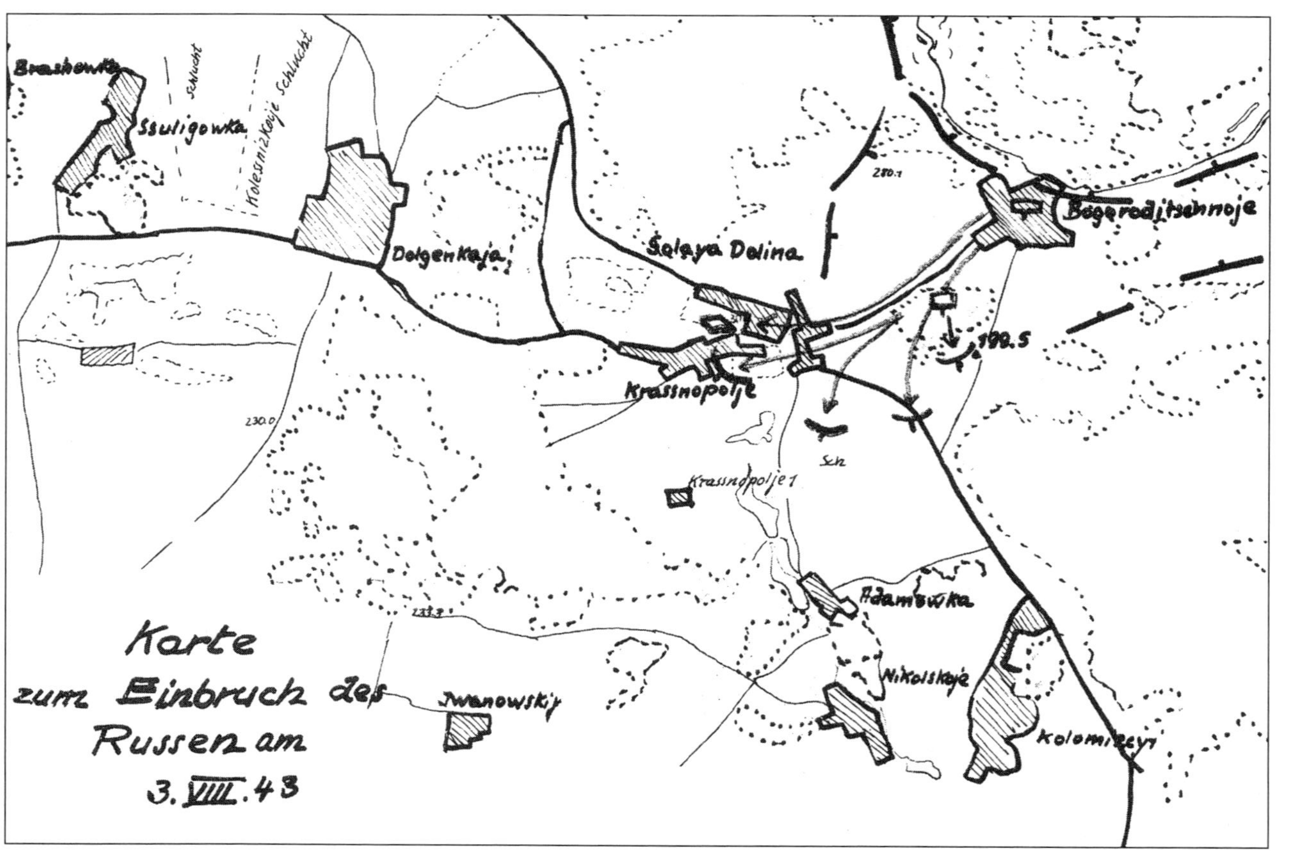

Penetration of the Soviets on 3 August 1943 along the Donez at Golaja-Dolina.

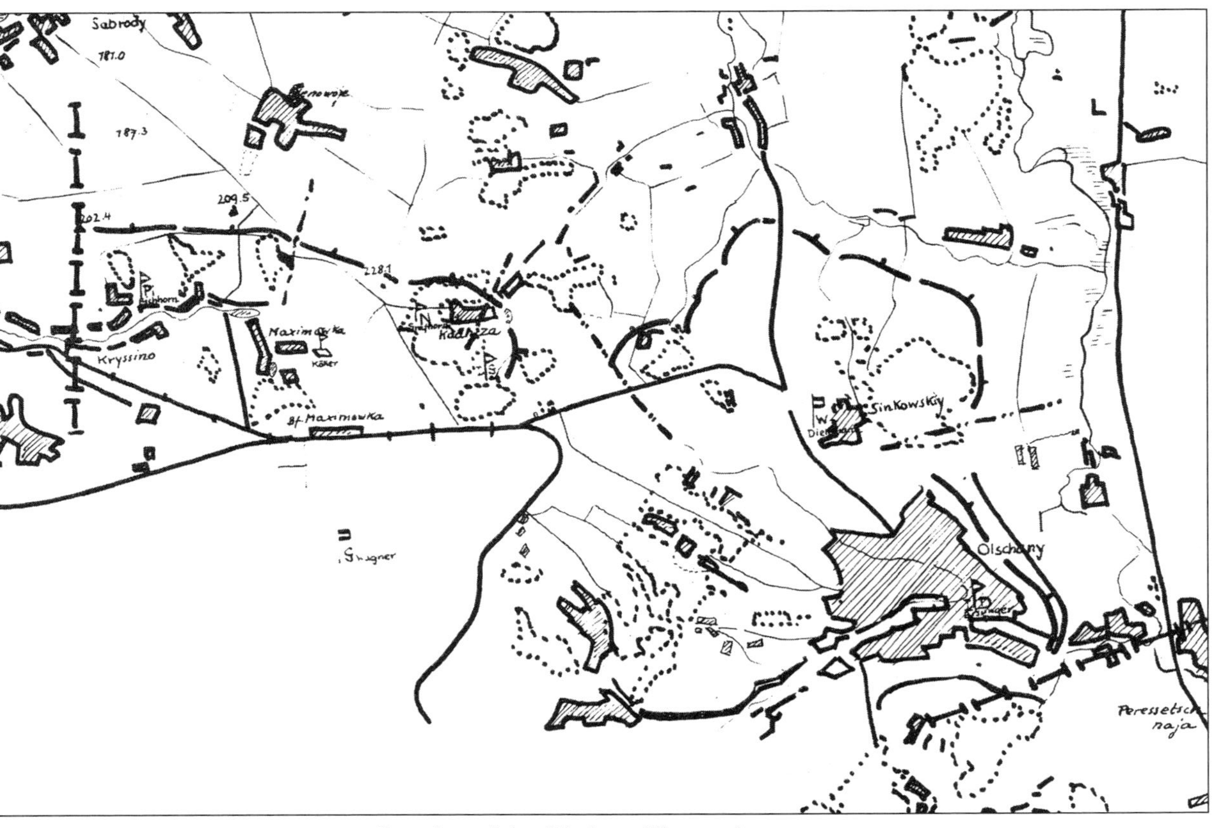

Overview of the Olschany-Klenowoje sector.

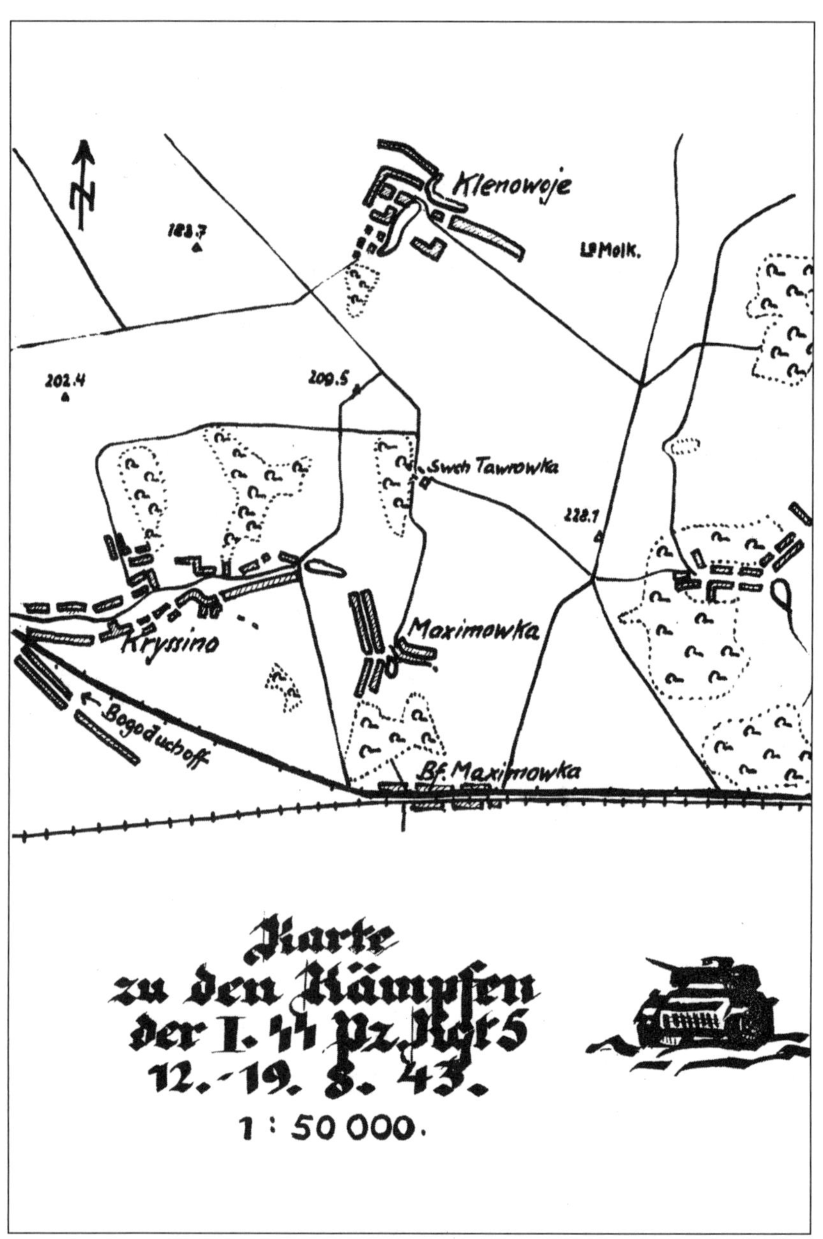

The fighting of the 1st Battalion of *SS-Panzer-Regiment 5* from 12 to 19 August 1943 in the Maximowka-Klenowoje sector.

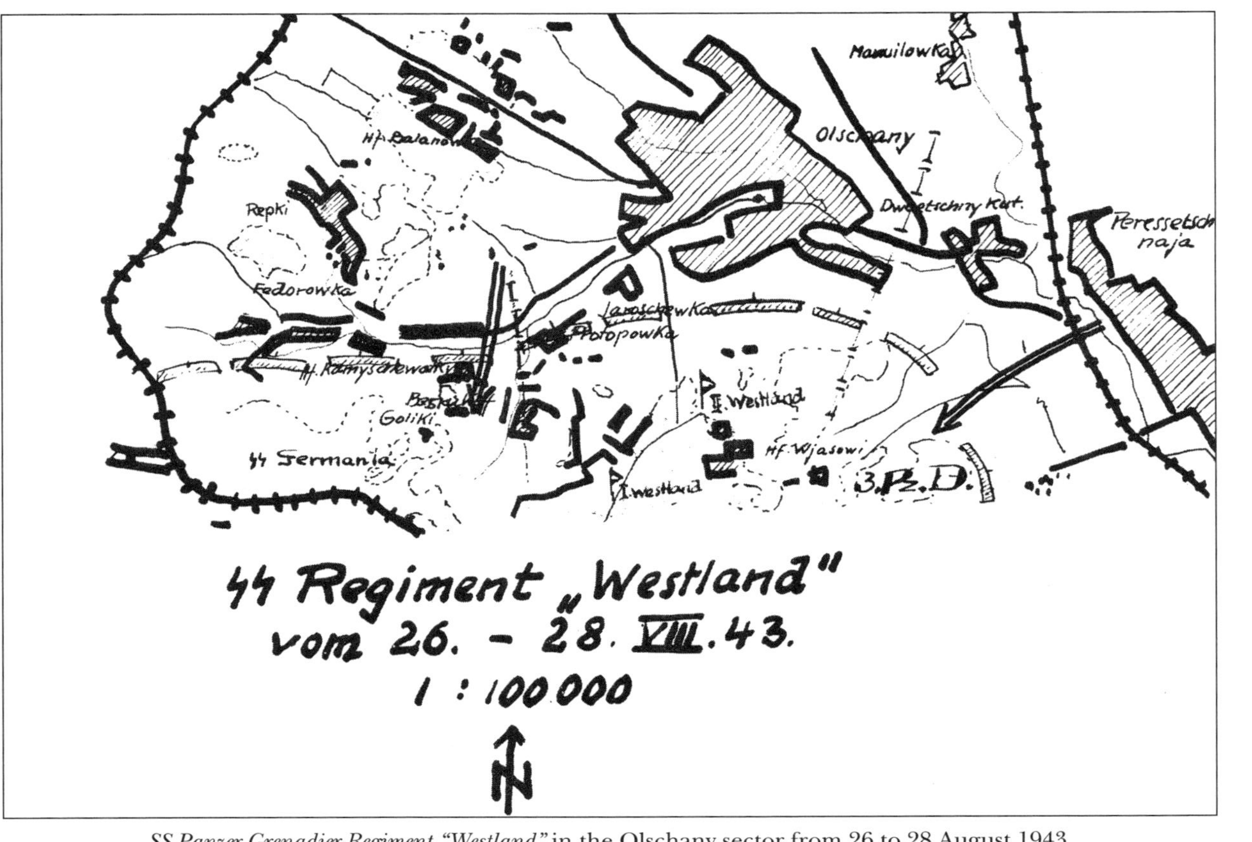

SS-Panzer-Grenadier-Regiment "Westland" in the Olschany sector from 26 to 28 August 1943.

April 1943, Ssossipatrowka: *SS-Hauptsturmführer* Schneider speaks at a 1st Company party.

After the fighting at Ssrednyj on 18 July 1943: (from left to right) *SS-Sturmmann* Stücklschweiger, *SS-Unterscharführer* Putensen (wounded), *SS-Untersturmführer* Senghas (on the *Panzer III*) and *SS-Oberscharführer* Rulf. This tank was part of the 1st Company.

Villagers at market in Karlovac in Croatia in September 1943.

A farmer in traditional garb at market in Croatia.

In the summer of 1943 between the Dnjepr and the Donez: *SS-Hauptsturmführer* Schneider awards men of the 1st Company with the Iron Cross, 2nd Class.

Budapest in 1939, looking from the Danube towards Parliament and the west bank of the river, with the *Burgberg* ("fortress hill").

CHAPTER 5:

In the Pocket Battles between the Dnjepr and the Bug, out of the Dnjepr Line and into the Tscherkassy Pocket

The Dnjepr between Moschny and the southern outskirts of Kanew was the forward line of defense that the division had been assigned. The division was unable to occupy it, as had been anticipated. Instead, the terrain had to be taken. The division command post was located in Goroditsche, 48 kilometers southwest of Tscherkassy.

The Soviet paratroopers and the small bridgeheads brought their share of casualty-intensive fighting. Although enemy groups in the Irdyn Marshes, to the west and southwest of Tscherkassy, could be reduced, they could not be eliminated. The marshes hid the enemy and sheltered him from the attacker. The fighting was characterized by ambushes and snipers.

SS-Untersturmführer Ploen was a platoon leader in the battalion's 4th Company. In November, the company was located in Beloserje, 9 kilometers west of Tscherkassy, under the command of *SS-Obersturmführer* Jessen. There were marshes between it and the city of Tscherkassy. Ploen, who was badly wounded on 17 November, has provided the following information of the type of fighting encountered in the region:

> Upon request, the guns moved to the main line of resistance. On 13–14 November, three assault guns reconnoitered in the Swidowok sector. *Unterscharführer* Trodler dismounted to check on something on his vehicle and was shot in the head. Together with *Hauptscharführer* Hackfort, we attempted to recover Trodler. In the process, Hackfort was badly wounded by sniper fire. We succeeded in recovering both

comrades. Both of them succumbed to their wounds a few hours later, however.

The tank battalion supported the *"Westland"* Regiment and *Grenadier-Regiment 164* of the *57. Infanterie-Division* in attacking the Soviet forces positioned on the so-called "Foxtail Island." *SS-Obersturmführer* Hein provides a first-hand look at the "jungle fighting" that resulted in heavy casualties:

> At the edge of the wooded area east of Tscherkassy, which was occupied by partisans and regular Russian forces, the Dnjepr divided itself by means of a long, extended island, which was, once again, divided by a long and extended sandbank. With its vegetation reminiscent of a primeval forest, it created the impression of an utterly impossible area for fighting. The island was intended to serve as the springboard for the Russians to get to the west bank. And the enemy had a habit of making the impossible possible. Enemy combat engineers, working many a night, had constructed a bridge below the water surface from the east bank to the island.
>
> On 7 October 1943, the security forces of the division were surprised by antitank-gun and mortar fire, as well as snipers, blocking the riverbank road to Moschny.
>
> In an operation entailing a number of casualties, without an inkling of the strength of the enemy on the island, the *II./Westland* succeeded in getting a foothold on the tip of the island and initially throwing the Russians back across the sandbank. Strong enemy forces then pushed our grenadiers back during the morning twilight. The situation became extraordinarily serious for our soldiers. A mortar crew that had been overrun by the enemy was found massacred during a failed immediate counterattack. The combat situation caused the division to consider the use of tanks.
>
> Only three *Panzer III's* with elevated exhaust stacks were available. The crews—Hein, Bock and Schnell—were selected, and a ford site was reconnoitered in the raging torrent during the night of 8 October. *Oberscharführer* Bock moved ahead with a long stick. The hulls of the vehicles sloshed full of water. The risky undertaking succeeded during the final hours of the night. The enemy did not appear to have taken notice of the undertaking, since barely a single round disturbed the operations by the submarine tanks. There was a short discussion of the situation with the commander of the *III./Westland*, and the attack was scheduled for seven in the morning.

> Our artillery fired smoke so as to cover the gap, which could be observed. Trying to avoid too much battle noise, we crossed a slope that was more like a wall and landed in the middle of the enemy. Antitank guns were overrun, with the tracks crunching as steel collided with steel. The main guns and machine guns were giving it everything they had. With the exception of a few practically screamed commands, the crews remained at their stations, as if strapped down. The combat vehicles were rocked back and forth by the impossible ground conditions; the expressions on the men's faces frozen, with sweat pouring out of every pore. A few of the crew may have whispered to themselves: "Tracks don't break . . . tracks don't break!" The Russians were completely taken by surprise. They ran back, panicky, between the tanks. Whoever was unable to escape and who dodges a bullet was taken into captivity. By our actions, the tip of the island had been taken.

While the enemy was relatively quiet over the next few weeks along the Dnjepr north of Tscherkassy, he moved out with his massed field armies on an offensive from the bridgehead between Krementschug and Dnjepropetrowsk and in the north on both sides of Kiev. By 10 November, the Soviets succeeded in ripping open the German front along the Dnjepr between Krementschug and Dnjepropetrowsk for a distance of 150 kilometers. He was able to drive a deep wedge between the *1. Panzer-Armee* on the lower course of the Dnjepr and the *8. Armee.* In the north, the enemy succeeded in enveloping Kiev on both sides and causing it to fall on 6 November. The Soviets then thrust immediately to the west and reached Shitomir and Fastow by 11 November, some 130 kilometers west of Kiev. The enemy was then brought to a standstill and even pushed back a bit, but the over-all situation had changed dramatically for the Germans.

Following Soviet attacks in the middle of December out of their bridgeheads south of Krementschug and at Tscherkassy, whereby the city of Tscherkassy also fell, they launched a large-scale offensive from out of the Kiev area during the last few days of December. They drove a wedge 300 kilometers wide between *Heeresgruppe Süd* and *Heeresgruppe Mitte* and advanced far to the west. By the middle of January 1944, Soviet forces that had pivoted south had reached a line running Berditschew–Bjelaja Zerkow.

The formations of the 2nd Ukrainian front, which were attacking from the east out of the Krementschug area, reached the city of Kirowograd on 9 January 1944, 100 kilometers south of Tscherkassy. On 28 January 1944, the lead Soviet spearheads of the gigantic pincers movement—heading from Bjelaja Zerkow in the north and from Kirowograd in the south—established contact at Swenigorodka, some 25 kilometers southwest of Tscherkassy on 28 January 1944. The divisions of the *XI. Armee-Korps* and the *XXXXII. Armee-Korps*, including the *"Wiking"* Division, were encircled.

THE TSCHERKASSY POCKET

In the 20 days that followed in the Tscherkassy Pocket, the 10 divisions proved their steadfastness in the face of deceptive enemy propaganda, proved their bravery against the suffocating superiority by the seven Soviet field armies participating in the encirclement and proved the exemplary leadership of the responsible officers.

For "Vikings" of long standing in the division, the names of the local villages—names such Taraschta, Boguslaw and Smela—conjured up memories of hard fighting two years previously. Back then it had also been a matter of standing fast in the face of powerful blows and pressure from enemy formations coming from the Tscherkassy area. The situation was the same; the roles had been reversed. The area of the German forces encircled to the west of the city was growing ever smaller. The relief efforts from the outside, those of the *XXXXVII. Panzer-Korps* and the *III. Panzer-Korps*, failed. Hein provides the reader with dramatic insight into the events of the final days of January 1944:

> 26 January 1044: Tank battalion occupies a staging area for defending against enemy attacks in Budki-Rotmistrowka and screens in the direction of Smela. Attacks successfully repulsed. Battalion still has around 25 *Panzer IV's*.
>
> 27 January 1944, 0500 hours: The enemy succeeded in breaking through with strong infantry forces just east of Rotmistrowka.
>
> 0700 hours: In a counterattack, the enemy forces that penetrated were enveloped by the 2nd and 3rd Companies out in an open field of snow and totally eliminated. A battery from the artillery regiment supported, firing over open sights.
>
> 1200 hours: Battalion screening with all combat vehicles on the edge of Budki.

On 28 January, Hein personally received the mission from the division commander to clean up the situation at Olschany with four assault guns and screen there. Hein:

> 28 January 1944, 1800 hours: Arrival at Olschany. Strong enemy forces, supported by artillery. Self-propelled guns already at the northern outskirts. The liaison officer for the division support command led

me through the village to the command post, and I was briefed on the situation: Friendly logistics forces had established weak security at the edge of the village with nothing but infantry weapons and were being heavily pressured. The enemy had already established himself in the first few houses [of the village].

1900 hours: Counterattack with four assault guns (no radio contact due to the loss of the equipment). Enemy was ejected and had to pull back behind the hill, suffering heavy casualties. 5 self-propelled guns knocked out. Friendly losses: 1 assault gun.

29 January 1944, 0200 hours: Advance with two guns on Kirillowka. Brought back all of the fuel stockpiles there to Olschany.

Effective 0900 hours: Repeated attacks by the enemy against the northern and eastern edges of Olschany. Small penetrations were immediately cleaned up. Defensive effort is now organized clearly. Motor pool has been mostly moved to Goroditsche.

2200 hours: Enemy penetration at the northern edge is cleaned up by close-in fighting. Division has been repeated requested for reinforcements.

30 January 1944, 0600 hours: In a counterattack, the enemy was thrown back across the hill in the direction of Pidynowka. The enemy is shifting forces to the west.

0800 hours: The enemy attacked by surprise from out of the west with tanks in support. A strong enemy antitank-gun belt covered the forces from the rear. Defensive positions established with two assault guns along the road, and the attack was turned back at the last moment.

1500 hours: 1 assault gun with damage to the steering brakes.

Arrival of one company from the *"Narwa"* Battalion. Counterattack planned with the company commander and conducted by surprise through a depression in the direction of Juckowa and against Tolstaja. Enemy in a panic. The entire antitank-gun belt (around 15) rolled up.

Three enemy tanks eliminated and 250 prisoners taken.

1700 hours: Positions withdrawn to the old hill, since not enough forces for manning a forward outpost.

Encirclement of Olschany and the division of the pocket along the Olschany-Goroditsche road prevented.

Those decisive actions on the part of Hein resulted in his being awarded the Knight's Cross to the Iron Cross on 4 May 1944.[1]

✠

After being encircled for 10 days, the pocket was reduced in half from its original 60 kilometer diameter after the Dnjepr line was finally evacuated on 8 February. In addition to the weather conditions, the shallowness of the pocket made movements increasingly difficult. The enemy's pressure grew accordingly.

✠

Starting on 7 February, all of the measures taken in the pocket were conducted with an eye towards the intended breakout effort, which was to be accompanied by a relief effort from the outside.

Orders arrived at the command post of the tank battalion in Waljawskije at 0830 hours on 9 February to move all of its tanks and assault guns to Korsun. The tracked vehicles were there by 1400 hours; the wheeled vehicles arrived in the evening.

On the next day, feverish efforts were undertaken to prepare the vehicles operationally. In order to consolidate all excess personnel, all of the tank crews that no longer had any tanks were formed into an infantry company of four platoons, along with truck drivers and other men of the trains. The acting commander of the *ad hoc* unit was *SS-Hauptsturmführer* Wittmann.

The "infantry" company had a combat strength of four officers and 220 enlisted personnel. It was employed on 11 February against enemy forces at the Korsun train station. Each of the platoons had three machine guns above and beyond the small arms and hand grenades it had received. During the night of 11/12 February, the company closed a gap at Arbusino, about 1 kilometer east of Korsun. At the same time, it established contact with an Army unit.

Until the evening of 13 February, the "infantry" company of the battalion conducted defensive operations and launched immediate counterattacks against attacking company-sized enemy forces. The unit helped prevent the forward elements form being cut off. While that was happening, the operational tanks were sent to Jablonowka, about 4 kilometers west of Korsun, under the command of *SS-Untersturmführer* Schumacher.

1. Translator's Note: According to Scherzer, however, he was the commander of the 2nd Company of the 1st Battalion at the time. (Veit Scherzer, *Ritterkreuzträger, 1939-1945*, Scherzers-Miliaire-Verlag: Ranis, 2005, 350.)

The battle staff of the battalion had already been summoned to the command post of the *XXXXII. Armee-Korps* in Jablonowka the previous day.

An impressive indicator of the extraordinary difficulties was noted by von Manstein in his memoirs, when he described the effect of the dominant weather conditions of the time. For the forces in Tscherkassy, that was in addition to the difficulties of moving in the reduced pocket, which was also subjected to the strong pressure being exerted by the enemy. Von Manstein:

> I attempted to get to the front lines of the assault groups on two occasions. I got hopelessly stuck each time in the snow or the mud. The weather changed daily between snowstorms and thaws.[2]

✠

In order to establish good jumping-off positions for breaking through the Soviet encirclement, the senior commander in the pocket, the Commanding General of the *XI. Armee-Korps, General der Infanterie* Stemmermann, attempted to push the southwestern tip of the pocket further in the direction of Schanderowka, since it was already pointing in that direction. From there, the lead elements of the assault detachments of the breakout forces would only have another 13 kilometers to advance to link up with the lead elements of the *III. Panzer-Korps.* The pressure to get to Schanderowka and the movements of the forces involved were expedited, since it could not be ruled out that the lead elements of the relief forces might be pushed back to the southwest themselves by the intensifying Soviet attacks.

During the night of 11–12 February, the tank battalion moved forward into the area around the Sawdski brickworks and then reached Nowo Buda, about 3 kilometers south of Schanderowka, around 0900 hours that morning. It established contact there with the local-area commander, *Major* Brese.

The lingering thaw made movements across the terrain, which could be observed by the enemy, very difficult. An assault gun was knocked out. The tanks screened towards the northwest from the Nowo Buda–Schanderowka road. They were refueled with captured fuel.

Enemy tanks that had penetrated through the German lines in the Nowo-Buda area lent an additional air of uncertainty. The enemy was also exerting pressure from the northwest.

On 13 February, *SS-Untersturmführer* Schumacher ejected the Soviets from the eastern portion of Nowo-Buda with two tanks. The enemy had succeeded in making several small penetrations there with two battalions.

---

2. Author's Note: von Manstein, 585.

On 14 February, the Soviets launched another attack, this time with 11 tanks. Schumacher advanced with two tanks into the southern portion of the village, which had been reoccupied by the enemy. One of his tanks was hit by an antitank gun and damaged.

Schumacher then proceeded to knock out seven enemy tanks with his own tank. He expended all of his armor-piercing rounds; with his remaining high-explosive rounds, he forced the crews of three more tanks to abandon their vehicles. When a second tank came to the aid of Schumacher, the three abandoned tanks were set ablaze. Then a fourth one was set alight, when it attempted to approach Schumacher from the rear.

On the same day, however, four friendly tanks, including the one of *SS-Oberscharführer* Fiebelkorn, were knocked out while screening. Another battle group under the command of *SS-Oberscharführer* Schweiss knocked out four enemy tanks in the Komarowka area, 3 kilometers west of Nowo-Buda.

Despite taking extraordinary losses, the Soviets continued their heavy attacks on Nowo-Buda the next day. At 1545 hours, they once again assaulted the southern portion of the village. Once again, Schumacher made a name for himself by knocking out two enemy tanks with his *Panzer III.*

The tanker "infantry" company of *SS-Hauptsturmführer* Wittmann, which had been defending in the area around Arbusino, pulled back as ordered during the night of 13–14 February to positions on the high ground west of Korsun. The pursuing enemy was pushed back in some areas by means of immediate counterattacks. At 2200 hours, Wittmann's men pulled back again and reached Schanderowka on 15 February, in accordance with their orders.

On 16 February, the enemy renewed his attacks on Nowo-Buda with reinforced forces. The enemy attacks led to the loss of the southern portion of the village at first light. The 1st Battalion of the *"Germania"* Regiment, which was reinforced with two tanks, held its positions, however.

At 1500 hours, the liaison officer of the *"Germania"* Regiment brought the tank battalion the order to break out. It stated that the battalion was to disengage from the enemy at 1900 hours and move to Schanderowka. It would receive further orders from the division there.

After the battalion commander returned from the division headquarters—he had gone to Schanderowka at 1700 hours with his adjutant—he issued the following order:

> The tank battalion immediately moves to the western portion of Schanderowka after the return of the battle group from Nowo-Buda and immediately prepares to break out from there.

> All armored elements move out at 1920 hours, organized as follows: 1 Command Tank; 2 *Panzer IV's*; 4 *Panzer III's*; 6 assault guns; the wheeled elements immediately follow the armored elements.[3]

The movements of the troop elements into the designated areas were made very difficult by the prevailing bad weather conditions, but they were made decisively difficult by the fact that some 50,000 encircled men had been pressed into an area roughly 7x8 kilometers.

At 2100 hours, the battalion arrived at the western edge of Schanderowka. The first tank in the march order, the command tank, broke through the bridge that led over the creek there. It took hours before the bridge was repaired enough that the individual tanks could cross, assisted by an 18-ton prime mover. The last tank crossed the bridge at 0145 hours on 17 February.

The tanker "infantry" company was given the mission of screening the flanks of the breakthrough group west of the village.

Half an hour remained after the successful occupation of the staging area and the scheduled start of the attack. Everyone was acutely aware of what was at stake. The hope that relief forces on the outside would move towards the breakout point helped encourage the soldiers. On that 13 February, the chief of staff of the *8. Armee*, *General* Speidel, radioed the pocket commander, *General* Stemmermann: "Breith with forward-most elements at Lißjanka. Vormann advancing from the bridgehead at Jerki in the direction of Swenigorodka. What is the situation there? Best wishes for success!"[4]

Two days before the planned breakout, on 15 February, the *8. Armee* sent the following message: "Capabilities of the *III. Panzer-Korps* restricted. *Gruppe Stemmermann* must break through at Dshurshenzy and reach Hill 239 with its own forces. Establish contact there with the *III. Panzer-Korps*."

At 1500 hours on 16 February, 11 hours before the start of the attack, von Manstein radioed Stemmermann: "Watch word: Freedom. Objective: Lißjanka."

Approximately 13 kilometers separated the breakout group and the hills at Dshurshenzy, where the lead elements of the *III. Panzer-Korps* awaited it. The daily logs of the battalion portrayed the breakout attempt thusly:

> At 0210 hours, the battalion moved out to conduct the ordered breakthrough. Route in very bad condition. Initial enemy resistance southwest of Chilki. The last remaining wheeled vehicles of the battalion were blown up there, since it was no longer possible for them

3. Author's Note: Daily logs of the *I./SS-Panzer-Regiment 5*.

4. Author's Note: This quotation and the next two are from *Europäische Freiwillige*, 240–43

to move any farther (deep depressions, mud). Enemy tanks moved out from Komarowka and attempted to prevent the breakthrough by means of heavy fire.

Untersturmführer Schumacher was committed south of Chilki with all of the available vehicles to eliminate the [enemy] tanks appeared there from Komarowka. Two tanks were eliminated. The command tank had to be blown up because of differential and track problems.

The commander and the adjutant switched over to *Untersturmführer* Schumacher's tank. *Untersturmführer* Schumacher assumed command of the remaining tanks.

The commander and adjutant attempted to hold together the men of the battalion, which was not possible due to the over-all murky situation. The commander then mounted an 18-ton prime mover, since it was the only vehicle capable of moving forward in that terrain.

Enemy tanks arrived, moving from north to south, and engaged the tanks advancing southwest in the direction of Lißjanka, along with the other vehicles that had made it that far, with machine guns and main guns.

At the patch of woods east of Dshurshenzy, where the prime mover had to cross an open area, it was engaged by enemy tanks. The prime mover received a direct hit right behind the driver's seat. The commander, *Sturmbannführer* Köller, met a soldier's end.

Enemy tanks appeared once more at the western tip of the woods, approaching from Dshurshenzy. The high ground at the tip of the woods could not be crossed by the tanks. As a result, they had to be blown up.

The men of the battalion fought their way through individually. Towards evening, the majority of the battalion arrived in Lißjanka. The adjutant was wounded during the breakout attempt.[5]

The sober language of the daily logs allow the reader to somewhat imagine the difficulty of what was experienced and also the scope of the tragedy that unfolded. The following first-hand accounts are well suited to allow even those unfamiliar with war to picture the events of that day.

During the intense tank engagements for Nowo-Buda, *SS-Oberscharführer* Fiebelkorn was knocked out in his tank (112):

While bailing out, all of the members of the crew were wounded. Fiebelkorn, who was the last to leave the vehicle, also broke his foot

5. Author's Note: Daily logs of the *I./SS-Panzer-Regiment 5*.

when jumping off the tank. The battalion worked its way to the battalion command post and was moved that evening on supply vehicles to the battalion surgeon's location.

Since none of the clearing stations were accepting any more wounded, all of the company's wounded remained at the battalion location. Every unit was obligated to get its own wounded out of the pocket.

After the tanks and the infantry moved out, an 18-ton prime mover, with three machine-gun crews on board to provide security for the wounded, moved slowly behind the fighting elements. It was followed by two prime movers with wounded aboard and the trains elements.

After moving about 7 kilometers, the prime mover, which had the commander and *Oberscharführer* Fiebelkorn aboard, received two hits on the right front side. The commander was killed, and the wounded, for the most part, were wounded again. When the [enemy] fire abated, the wounded were transferred to *Panje* carts and the march was continued. The first patch of woods southeast of Dshurshenzy was reached. When the lead tank elements approached the edge of the woods, they suddenly received heavy flanking fires from 14 T-34's on the hill. During the tank engagement that ensued, the enemy tanks pulled back.

Fiebelkorn took cover in that patch of woods. I then got him a [horse-drawn] vehicle with a driver and four horses and told Fiebelkorn to work his way out. I told him that we would soon be at the objective.

After I had secured the team for him, he rode on it about 1 kilometer further. The coach driver then simply halted and tried to get through the heavy defensive fires on his own. Fiebelkorn called for help and was lifted from the wagon by a *Sturmbannführer* he did not recognize. Right after he had been lifted off, the wagon was hit and was blown apart.

Fiebelkorn crawled into a foxhole, remaining there by himself for hours. He asked comrades passing by to take him along. No one was in the position to take him. As it turned dark, Fiebelkorn worked his way forward and encountered two other wounded soldiers, whom he helped along.

During the morning hours of 18 February, Fiebelkorn noticed that he had gone the wrong way and was in an enemy position. Since there were heavy snow squalls and the men were of the opinion that they could not be seen, they dug themselves into the snow, intending to wait until it turned dark again.

> When the time arrived that they could head out again, Fiebelkorn gave words of encouragement to the two others and they crawled forward. A short while later, one of the two soldiers died. A few minutes later, the other one also passed on.
>
> Fiebelkorn then crawled on by himself and reached a German outpost, using the last remaining strength he had.
>
> In addition to the wounds he had suffered, he also had frostbite on both feet, both hands and his right knee.
>
> After reaching the outpost position, Fiebelkorn lost consciousness and did not wake up until he was being unloaded from a transport aircraft.
>
> When I visited, he said to me that he had only been able to bear the efforts he had made as a result of his stubbornness and his firm resolve to keep his family intact. Taking consideration of his wife, who was bearing their second child at the time, he only told her that he had made it out of the pocket intact and had only been wounded in the right hand.[6]

Hans Lehni, a tanker turned "infantryman" also recalls the event of 17 February in his firsthand account:

> Elements of the 2nd Tank Company were in position on a ridgeline, adjacent to Stobes' tank battalion. The position was directed to be held until 2400 hours.
>
> It was the middle of the night when the Russians suddenly attacked. Based on the [loudness of the] *Urräh!*, there appeared to be a lot of them . . . supported by a few tanks. Using the machine gun we had dismounted from our destroyed tank, we let loose into the middle of them.
>
> Then the *Urräh!* was right behind us. The Russians were at the location of the headquarters, where their main thrust had broken through.
>
> Our mission had been accomplished, since it was 2400 hours. We pulled back into a valley, where soldiers from all braches were assembling.
>
> Suddenly there was a shout: "Volunteers needed!" It had been directed that the Russians were to be ejected from the hill. I volunteered. The hill was retaken with a great deal of élan.
>
> Once we returned back into the valley, the soldiers were gone. You could follow their paths in the snow, seeing where they had

6. Author's Note: *Europäische Freiwillige*, 257–61.

congregated or taken off. That's how I got to a hill, where I stayed for a while. By then, it had turned to daylight. But then I heard the sounds of an engine on the ridgeline behind me. It did not sound like Russian tanks, however. An 18-ton prime mover appeared over the top of the hill. Since I knew there were no more vehicles, I did not know what was happening. The machine came closer. With my submachine gun at the ready, I approached it. There was nothing but soldiers on the prime mover, mostly wounded. I jumped up next to the driver. We had hardly gone 200 meters, when I shouted: "Russian tanks on the opposite slope!"

There were about 10 to 15 of them. Two of them had already stopped. I yelled to *Sturmbannführer* Köller, who was sitting next to the driver: "Watch out . . . they've seen us!" I jumped off. I immediately distanced myself from the prime mover, which had stopped. It was soon hit in the middle of the driver's compartment.

Since the prime mover moved out down the slope—which I could follow for a while—I assumed that not a lot had happened. I decided to take off and follow the tracks of comrades who had preceded me. The tank battalion commander, *Sturmbannführer* Köller, was killed there.

SS-Obersturmführer Frels corroborates Lehni's account:

During the breakout from Tscherkassy, the 18-ton prime mover of *Sturmbannführer* Köller caught up to me after my *Kfz. 15*, which was also carrying the battalion surgeon, was no longer operational after being hit by a 7.6-centimeter gun. Köller stopped and took me and others aboard. I remember the events exactly. On the bench seat in the driver's compartment were, from left to right, the driver, *Sturmbannführer* Köller, I and someone else to my right.

A little but later, while crossing a hill, the prime mover received a 7.6-centimeter hit to the left front. The engine still ran, but the steering and the wheels were gone. Köller received several bits of shrapnel, which immediately caused his death.

We jumped off the vehicle to the right, but the driver let the vehicle continue to move into the valley. Everyone got away alive. In the valley, at the edge of some woods, the corpse was covered with branches, since there was no other conceivable way to bury him due to the fire from the Russian tanks. Death was confirmed by a surgeon, whose name I cannot remember.

Obersturmführer Hein, who was not able to fight in a tank due to a wound, was put in charge of the battalion's rearguard:

> 15 February 1944: Orders conference for the breakout: I was given the signals section and the prime movers, since I was not capable of being in a tank. Move-out time was established at 0000 hours on 17 February for the rearguard.
>
> 16 February 1944: Tough waiting it out! Heavy fire all day long. Effort to funnel around six tanks over an emergency bridge failed. Engineer battalion commenced repair of the bridge. The start of the attack for the tanks delayed by about three hours.
>
> 17 February 1944, 0500 hours: Greatly delayed move out for the radio vehicles and the prime movers.
>
> 0530 hours: Flank attack from the southeast by about 20 T-34's. Vehicle section separated. My radio vehicle was hit; I reached a swell in the ground on the run.
>
> 0700 hours: Small patch of woods in the vicinity of Komarowka offered the first opportunity for cover. Enemy attacked from the northeast with T-34's; positioned in front of the patch of woods. Prisoners that had been brought along armed themselves and created a murky situation.
>
> 0900 hours: In the woods was the last friendly *Panzer III,* with a short main gun.[7] Crew killed. The vehicle was manned by me. An Army *Oberst* took charge, and the enemy pulled back about 100 meters after being engaged.
>
> 1000 hours: Break out from the patch of woods. The *Panzer III* only made it about 100 meters, since it had radiator damage. Under heavy fire, including antiaircraft weaponry, we reached a defile (*balka*) south of Hill 239. An artillery battalion was pushing guns into the defile.
>
> 1200 hours: Enemy blocked the exit point with about 10 T-34's. Deserters were mowed down by machine guns on the T-34's.
>
> 1300 hours: Breakout from the defile by attacking the tanks frontally. They pulled off to the side. Heavy casualties.
>
> 1400 hours: Small patch of woods in front of Hill 222.5 reached. Complete exhaustion. Appeared unlikely that we could get any further. Breakout attempts were withering in the enemy's fires. Wounded were overrun by tanks. Hid in the woods until dark.
>
> 2100 hours: Patrol led by officers reconnoitered a route through the moors.

7. Translator's Note: This would have been a 3.7-centimeter main gun, which was hopelessly outgunned by the opposing T-34's.

2300 hours: Any weapons or pieces of equipment that made a lot of noise were discarded. Enemy positions were bypassed in silence in single file, each man holding on to the man ahead of him.

18 February 1944, 0300 hours: The Gnoloi-Tikisch River was reached without incident. Crossing possible over dead horses and *panje* carts.

0330 hours: Challenge issued by an outpost from the *1. Panzer-Division*: "Freedom!"

✠

The Tscherkassy Pocket never turned into another Stalingrad. The forces in the field and their leaders resisted the promises made by the Soviet leadership on flyers and bills and the German generals who had joined the Soviet side. They did not give up hope on the hill at Dshurshenzy, when they ran into the fires of Soviet tanks instead of the passage points of the *III. Panzer-Korps*, as the radio message from the Chief-of-Staff of the *8. Armee* had led them to expect. The decisive event of 17 and 18 February was the breaking through of the inner and outer encirclements by decisive leadership in the pocket that was prepared to do anything and an extremely capable and brave force in the field. Of the approximately 56,000 soldiers, who had been encircled at the end of January, some 30,000 made the breakthrough to friendly lines. Some 3,000 wounded were flown out of the pocket.

In the map book *Der Kessel von Tscherkassy* (*The Tscherkassy Pocket*), published by the Munin Publishing House, one can find a summary of the events of 17 February written in matter-of-fact language by the division commander at the time, *SS-Gruppenführer* Gille:

> In the morning, at 0430 hours, the [German] attack in front of Hill 239, which was to have been the passage point with the relief forces, bogged down in the face of heavy enemy defensive fires. The enemy had established a strong defense there with thanks. Getting though had no prospect of success, since the [German] heavy weapons had not been brought along due to the unfavorable terrain.
>
> Swinging far out to the east, the leadership of the attack spearhead then found a way that offered less resistance. But there were also difficulties there, as well. The Gniloi-Tikisch, a river that was in flood stage and still had ice, had to be swum across in icy cold conditions and ever-increasing enemy fires. Unfortunately, for many soldiers, who had seen deliverance in front of them, it was to become their grave. On the far bank, they then had to continue on in icy cold

with completely drenched clothing. At the time of the crossing, the clothing became frozen, with the result that it was difficult to move arms or legs. The enemy artillery and tank fire grew in intensity, and the way to the friendly lines seemed endlessly long.

The torrent of soldiers who followed the path cleared by the attack spearheads resembled a giant snake. Wherever the enemy tried to hold them up, they eluded them to the side or battered down the obstacle so as to then continue their journey. The men of the pocket fought the entire day to get to their own lines, which had only advanced as far as Lißjanka, a few kilometers southwest of the arranged passage point. The final rearguards did not reach the friendly passage points until the night of 18 February.

Although most of the materiel had been lost, the majority of the personnel could be saved.

The fighting at Tscherkassy signaled an end to almost a full year of uninterrupted, difficult fighting by the division and its tank battalion. The performance of the division and its personnel in the retreat conducted in the Donez Bend and the subsequent withdrawals to the Dnjepr and the western Ukraine will likely remain the standard by which such operations can be judged.

The commander in chief of the Soviet forces at the encirclement, the previously quoted Marshal Koniev, claimed in his memoirs that he had spoken several times on 17 February with the commanders of various divisions "who had stood at the outer front along the banks of the Gorny Tikitsch. They reported that not a single German soldier had made it through their positions . . . "[8] In the same connection, Koniev wrote about the telephone reports of his various field army commanders in chief: "They stated not a single German had made it through either the inner or the outer front." After making that claim, astounding in and of itself, Koniev continued:

> The SS General Gille, about whom the Goebbels propaganda later made a big show, had probably taken off earlier in an aircraft or had slipped through the lines in civilian clothing. I consider it out of the question that he broke through our lines in a tank or in some other kind of vehicle.

8. Author's Note: Koniev, 134–35.

RECONSTITUTION OF THE *I./SS-PANZER-REGIMENT 5*

Hein continues with his observations:

> An empty school was marked with a directional sign—*G* (for Gille)—as the collection point.
>
> Apathetic and yet happy with regard to the successful breakout, the men sat on the sandy soil. Gradually, familiar faces began to appear. The men were happy to see one another. *Unterscharführer* Schweichler entered through the door. He was the gunner on the commander's tank. The dismounted machine gun was across his shoulder; belts of ammunition were slung over his shoulders.
>
> He saw me, set the machine gun on the ground and reported in his East Prussian dialect: "*Obersturmführer, Unterscharführer* Schweichler reports from the pocket."
>
> "Schweichler, how in the world did you get through?"
>
> "*Obersturmführer*, the worst was not being able to shit for 24 hours. Request permission to leave to do the same."
>
> An *Oberleutnant* from the Army next to me: "I'm envious that you have these types of men!"

✠

The battalion initially assembled at Bushanka, some 5 kilometers behind the front lines. During the next two days, it was in Risino, approximately 18 kilometers southwest of Lißjanka. The division also assembled there. On 21 February, the battalion moved to Dsengolowka, 35 kilometers southwest of Lißjanka, along the east-west rail line running from Schpola to Uman. There, some 20 kilometers northeast of Uman, the exhausted men were far enough removed from the fighting.

✠

The battlefield reconstitution area of the division was the General Government of Poland. On 25 February, the battalion moved by rail to Lublin, where it arrived at 0100 hours on 1 March. On 2 March, the men underwent delousing. At 1800 hours on the same day, the rail journey continued to Tomaszow. The military facilities there were occupied on 3 March, starting at 1300 hours. The battle staff set up operations in the school, and the maintenance platoon took up quarters in the enlisted club.

The next few days were filled with reorganizing the units and assignment of personnel duty positions. The 13th of March turned out to be a major disappointment, inasmuch as the eagerly anticipated home leaves were cancelled by virtue of a general rescission of leave. Only the Germanic volunteers and the wounded were allowed to depart.

Starting at 1540 hours on 18 March, the battalion was moved again. It was sent to Cholm, where the units arrived during the course of the night of 19 March. At 0600 hours, the military facilities on the west side of the city were occupied. Starting at 1100 hours, Along with the respective crews, *SS-Obersturmführer* Jessen, who had since convalesced and returned to his unit, received 17 assault guns at the Cholm train station. The march unit immediately headed in the direction of Kowel, where it was to transfer the vehicles to an Army unit that was also headed there.

✠

In the meantime, the command of the battalion had passed to *SS-Sturmbannführer* Kümmel. From his comprehensive report of 19 March, we can gather the following information concerning the losses of the battalion at the Tscherkassy Pocket:

> The losses in the pocket were relatively high. Up to now,
> 22 dead,
> 81 wounded (hospitalized),
> 65 wounded (remaining with the unit),
> 63 missing-in-action,
> 49 sick personnel and
> 2 killed in accidents
> have been identified. I am assuming that a larger portion of the missing-in-action, of whom we still have not had any information, will still arrive or be found in hospitals.

Among the dead were the commander of the battalion, *SS-Sturmbannführer* Köller, and the commander of the 1st Company, *SS-Obersturmführer* Moritz. Among the missing was *SS-Obersturmführer* Stadler.

Counted among the wounded were *SS-Hauptsturmführer* Soboto, *SS-Obersturmführer* von Unruh and the battalion adjutant, *SS-Obersturmführer* Wolf, who had been hospitalized in Lublin with shrapnel wounds to his back.

The reconstitution of the battalion proceeded with the following new company commanders:

- 1st Company: *SS-Obersturmführer* Brand
- 2nd Company: *SS-Obersturmführer* Hein
- 3rd Company: *SS-Obersturmführer* Schumacher and

- 4th Company: *SS-Obersturmführer* Jessen.

The training company was commanded by *SS-Obersturmführer* Mittelbacher, who was also designated to be the battalion adjutant.

✠

What especially stood out was the large loss of noncommissioned officers with specialties and, most painful of all, the loss of four *Stabsscharführer*[9]—the "mothers of the companies." In addition, there were shortages of everything: From vehicles as means of movement and field telephones cable for communications to the most elementary consumables, such as toothbrushes, razors and toilet articles of all kinds.

To reestablish the battalion as a tank formation, 22 *Panzer IV's* were earmarked for delivery. Assembling the necessary crews proved to be difficult. The most primitive of requirements for repairing armored vehicles were also missing.

✠

In accordance with a telegraph originating form the Army High Command and routed through the division's logistics section, a detail was sent under the command of *SS-Obersturmführer* Brand at 1400 hours on 23 March to the Army Materiel Command at Madgeburg-Königsborn.

✠

During that phase of the reconstitution of the battalion in Cholm, an advance party from the newly formed regimental headquarters arrived on 21 March. Together with the recently formed 2nd Battalion, the regimental headquarters was on its way to Cholm, where the entire regiment was to be in one place together for the first time.

The fighting that had characterized the winter battles of 1943–44 that were starting to wind down in March had seen the German field army in the East lose the Dnjepr Line and portions of the western Ukraine. The Red Army had taken back most of its lost territories and was preparing, for its part, an attack on the outer limits of the *Reich* or the zone of interest of the *Reich* at its eastern frontiers.

---

9. Translator's Note: The *Stabsscharführer* was not technically a rank but a duty-position description. It was the equivalent of the U.S. first sergeant or the sergeant major in the British Army.

It was an urgent matter to restore the operational capabilities of the formations that had escaped from the Tscherkassy Pocket, most of which had lost their weapons and equipment. Correspondingly, the 1st Battalion intensified its reorganizational efforts with regard to personnel, the training of technical specialists, such as tank drivers and radio operators, and the reequipping with weapons, vehicles and equipment, as much as was within the realm of possibilities.

The division had been redesignated as the *5. SS-Panzer-Division "Wiking"* on 22 October 1943, but the change was nominal inasmuch as little was seen in the field to reflect the upgrading to an armored division. The core of an armored division, its tank regiment, had been in existence since March 1943 with the establishment of a second battalion, but it had not become available for operational deployment until the following year. The reader is reminded that the original commander of the 1st Battalion, *SS-Sturmbannführer* Mühlenkamp, had been reassigned in order to form the 2nd Battalion and the regimental headquarters.

ESTABLISHMENT OF THE *II./SS-PANZER-REGIMENT 5*

The location for the establishment of the 2nd Battalion was the Altneuhaus Training Area, located along the southern part of the larger Grafenwöhr Training Area in the Upper Pfalz. Located near the village of Vilseck, the reservation offered good and modern accommodations in thinned-out stands of pine and spruce trees. Moreover, there were good opportunities for gunnery and combat training.

The filling of the personnel slots for the four line companies was completed by the end of May 1943. The backbone of the battalion consisted of noncommissioned officers and technical specialists levied from the 1st Battalion, who were the guarantors of successful specialist training. For obvious reasons, this training needed to be conducted under compelling time restraints.

With regards to origins, most of the battalion was composed of ethnic Germans, although there were also Flemish, Dutch, Norwegians and Saxons from Transylvania. The battalion commander was a former battalion commander from the *"Germania"* Regiment, *SS-Sturmbannführer* Scheibe. The battalion adjutant was *SS-Obersturmführer* Förster and the administrative officer was *SS-Obersturmführer* Paschke.[10] The battalion surgeon was *SS-Obersturmführer* Wiesenberger. In command of the line companies were:

10. Translator's Note: The designation of an administrative officer—an IVa in accordance with typical German staff abbreviations and used in the original German—must be considered unusual, since this specific function was generally only found at division level. Perhaps it is the author's way of designating the functions of an otherwise unassigned officer.

- 5th Company: *SS-Hauptsturmführer* Klapdor
- 6th Company: *SS-Obersturmführer* Dedelow
- 7th Company: *SS-Hauptsturmführer*
- 8th Company: *SS-Obersturmführer* Nicolussi-Leck

A few *Panzer III's* and *Panzer IV's* were on hand for training purposes.

The organizational efforts and the training were under the direct influence of the regimental commander. He and his headquarters were also quartered in Altneuhaus. Mühlenkamp's adjutant was *SS-Hauptsturmführer* Zimmermann and his administrative officer was *SS-Hauptsturmführer* Hagen. The regimental engineer[11] was *SS-Hauptsturmführer* Sobota.

Vilseck and the surrounding area allowed many of the men to have their wives present for the summer months, if only for a limited time of unpredictable length. At the same time, this allowed some of the women the opportunity to escape, for a short period, the growing bombing terror of the Western Allies on the large cities.

In order to attend to their loved ones, some soldiers were granted emergency leave to go to Hamburg. Upon their return, they reported their horrific impressions of the results of the bombing raids on the million-plus city at the end of July and the beginning of August 1943. In four nighttime raids and three daytime ones, some 3,500 bombers had dropped 9,000 tons of bombs on the densely populated residential areas of the city.[12]

The burning funeral pyres along the inner-city waterways, the mountains of corpses along the cordoned-off city blocks and the desperate search by those who escaped to find next-of-kin under the rubble and at collection points showed the men another dimension of the war, a perversion of it, actually, and a hitherto unknown barbarism.

✠

The battalion was also deeply affected by a different, politically related event during those summer months. An *SS-Oberscharführer* assigned to the 5th Company, the Crown Prince of Mecklenburg, was released from duty at his own request as a liaison officer between the Danish royal house and the German government, even though he was related to the Danish royal family. The willingness of the crown prince to serve his country as a noncommissioned officer in the *Waffen-SS* earned a great deal of respect.

11. Translator's Note: There is no equivalent position in the U.S. Army, since the battalion or regimental engineer was expected to not only oversee the maintenance operations of the respective formation—the battalion maintenance officer in the U.S. Army—but also to advise the commander on "true" engineering functions, such as courses of action in overcoming natural and manmade obstacles.

12. Author's Note: *Bilanz des Zweiten Weltkriegs*, Stalling Verlag, 1953, 167.

✠

The prevailing morale of the forces in that fourth year of war and third year of conflict between Germany and the Soviet Union may be demonstrated, perhaps, by means of a different, military-related example. A tank battalion of the Army, which was also being established at the Grafenwöhr Training Area at the same time, was issued the *Panzer V*, more familiarly known as the *Panther*, out of turn and ahead of the battalion at the beginning of July. It was said that the battalion was going to be sent to reinforce the heavy fighting in the Kursk sector. The personnel of the 2nd Battalion felt both jealous and affronted. The decisive importance of the major battle in the Kursk salient was not known at the time. From the standpoint of the common German soldier, the offensive had been launched as a preventative measure to beat the Soviets to the punch before they concluded their build-up and offensive. By doing so, the punch would be taken out of the expected major Soviet offensive.

Regardless of the feelings of the men, the status of training of the newly formed battalion did not justify its commitment at the front at that point. For instance, the noncommissioned officer training company of *SS-Obersturmführer* Nicolussi-Leck had just started its program of instruction. The latter officer not only contributed to the training of the battalion by turning out future tank commanders, but he also contributed significantly to its morale during off-duty hours by providing several barrels of wine from his South Tyrolean home town of Bozen.

The nearby and surrounding areas and the hospitality of the locals, whose harvests were supported as much as possible, offered a lot of incentive to forget the actual war. In August 1943, however, the training time in Germany was over. The 2nd Battalion was rail loaded to Karlovac (German: Karlstadt) in Croatia. At the same time, the *III. (germanisches) SS-Panzer-Korps*, under the command of *SS-Obergruppenführer* Steiner and also being formed in the Grafenwöhr and Bayreuth area, was moved to Zagreb (German: Agram). In order to make maximum use of the training opportunities at Altneuhaus, the 2nd Noncommissioned Officer training Company of *SS-Hauptsturmführer* Klapdor remained behind. The platoon leaders were *SS-Untersturmführer* Wilde, *SS-Oberscharführer* Schicker and *SS-Oberscharführer* Weißschuh. In addition, there was also the senior communications specialist, *SS-Unterscharführer* Koopmann.

On Wednesday, 6 October 1943, the 2nd Company also departed Altneuhaus, reaching Graz in Austria in foggy, rainy weather by way of Weiden, Regensburg and Salzburg. After a day there, it continued on through the Steiermark region, passed by Marburg and spent another day at Anderburg.

Finally, during the evening of 13 October, it arrived in Karlovac, after needing an entire day to cover the 60 kilometers from Agram to the final destination.

Karlovac was a medium-sized city. On the far side of the 80-meter-wide Korana, which had an impressive waterfall, were flatlands that eventually rose again into wooded hills. The city looked Austrian in the way it was laid out and in its architecture. We could see German names at the cemetery.

The impression the city left on us can be gleaned from excerpts from two letters the author wrote on 16 and 23 October:

> If we didn't have to build defenses and everything in the city were not so enormously expensive, we could think about anything at all, except the war. Although there were all sorts of bandits[13] in this country, they haven't bothered us yet. Without those things, the country could be considered a small paradise. Today, but especially on market days, it's a riot of color. The farmers come into the city; the women wear their colorful, pretty peasant costumes with the red and white hose, the thick white pleated skirts and the colored bodices. On top of that, jewelry of all colors and shapes. Basically, they carry everything on their heads, whether gourds, baskets, water vessels, etc. with amazing grace . . . (16 October)
>
> The evening and the nights are somewhat unusual. That is, the city remains illuminated. At least that means you can't get lost. Around 1900 hours, everybody's on the main avenue. It's a short promenade, packed with people. Around 2100 hours, everyone disappears in the blink of an eye . . . (23 October)

The battalion's quarters were good. The battalion command post was located in the "Korana" Hotel and along the river. Elements of the regimental staff were in the Central Hotel, with the officer's club being there as well. The old hands from Russia knew how to enjoy their good fortune. We lived as if on an island.

The Croatian state was a unique construct. It had all of the governmental and other agencies; it even had borders on the map. But it was not in a position to exert its influence in the interior, let alone play a role in external affairs.

That was where the 2nd Battalion came in. Instead of the necessary tank training, security duties awaited it. The loss of Italy from the Axis alliance meant that the Italian forces stationed in the Balkans also had to be disarmed. The 2nd Battalion encountered rail transports of disarmed Italian soldiers heading north as it made its way south. At the same time, the negotiations

13. Translator's Note: The Germans usually referred to the partisans as gangs, bandits or terrorists.

being conducted between the Italians and Tito's forces came to a halt. Tito's partisans were operating pretty much in the open.

The Croatia militia, the *Ustascha,* was friendly to us tankers, but it carried little weight militarily. As a result, the outskirts of Karlovac were continuously safeguarded by the companies of the battalion in field positions. All entrances to the city were controlled. The woods started on the far side of the outpost lines, which meant that that was where the operational zone of the partisans started.

The major lines of communication and the railway lines between the larger localities, which were guarded in a similar fashion, were controlled and kept open by means of combat patrols or armored trains. Empty freight cars were placed in front of the locomotives to keep losses down in the event of demolitions.

Of course, all of those measures could not prevent communications between the partisans in the city and those outside because of the well-known good nature of the Germans. A example regarding the fate of efforts on the part of the senior German command to reduce the increasing partisan activities to a minimum is illustrated by the following incident: The German leadership had decided to conduct a large-scale operation to contain partisan activity. On the occasion of the arrival of the headquarters of a division earmarked to conduct that operation, the local officials invited the arriving headquarters to an evening social. The commander of the 2nd Battalion, along with the commander of the 5th Company, were also invited. As the evening wore on, the mood got livelier and less inhibited. The division commander was the object of a toast. A high official of the Croatian civilian administration proposed to address him on familiar terms[14] and climbed up on a chair. The operations officer of the commander felt uneasy about the entire situation and took pains to shift his commander's attention elsewhere.

Late in the evening, the Croatian official, who had withdrawn from the others into a darker corner of the house, was observed writing some notes. That observation was discussed with the operations officer and *SS-Sturmbannführer* Scheibe. It was decided to invite everyone into the tank battalion's officer's club so as to then somehow gain access to the notes.

Everything was arranged, but the plan did not succeed. The Croatian official never went to the club. By chance, however, he was identified in his vehicle by outposts on one of the roads leading back into the city. That meant he was outside the city limits. The German command authorities were powerless to do anything since it would have meant interfering in the affairs of an allied state.

---

14. Translator's Note: The Croatian suggested using the informal and familial *du* for the second-person singular in lieu of the usual *Sie* in such situations.

The formations of the division employed against the partisans hit thin air when they started their operations. They suffered some casualties as the result of ambushes, and the entire operation went up in smoke without achieving any effects.

No tank training could be conducted on a large-scale basis until December 1943. With the exception of taking a few test runs on the Korsana in the recently arrived *Schwimmwagen,*[15] all of the training was infantry-based. Anti-partisan directives were discussed and memorized. Fighting methods against enemy commando forces with weapons hidden on their bodies were practiced, based on lessons learned from English commando operations in France and Norway.

On 12 December, an advance party, consisting of *SS-Hauptsturmführer* Klapdor, *SS-Obersturmführer* Paschke and *SS-Untersturmführer* Steiner, was sent to Falaise in Normandy to prepare for quartering the 2nd Battalion there.

With the support of the military authorities in Caen and the elements of the *10. SS-Panzer-Division "Frundsberg,"* which was stationed in the same area, quarters were taken and prepared. The first two *Panthers* were sent to Falaise for issuance to the battalion. A few days later, the advance party celebrated Christmas there as well.

A telegraph received on 26 December may serve as an example of the increasing uncertainty that was already occurring in 1943 regarding planning and the quick changing of decisions that had been made: The advance party was summoned to Erlangen[16] from Falaise, which was the new location of the 2nd Battalion.

In January 1944, approximately 30 *Panthers* were sent to Erlangen for the battalion. The first loss suffered by the battalion on the *Panther* was when a *Ju 87* had to make an emergency landing and grazed the turret of one of the tanks.

15. Translator's Note: The amphibious version of the *Kübelwagen.*

16. Translator's Note: The military facilities at Erlangen were the site of an Army school for new-equipment training on the *Panther.*

On 24 January, the former commander of the 5th Company, *SS-Hauptsturmführer* Klapdor, was given acting command of the 2nd Battalion. On 6 February, the battalion left Erlangen by rail and moved to the French training area at Mailly le Camp by way of Bamberg, Aschaffenburg, Saarburg and Elfrigen, arriving there on 8 February. It was there that the battalion was intended to receive its final polishing. The training area, which is located between Chalons sur Marne and Troyes, offered adequate opportunities for gunnery and formation training.

The training of the battalion was supported and monitored by a headquarters training element of the Army, which was stationed about 80 kilometers away in Reims. The tank training and support element also oversaw the activities of the tank regiment of the *10. SS-Panzer-Division "Frundsberg"* and a tank battalion of the Army. For preparing the formation for operations in the East, Mailly le Camp was ideal: muddy and seemingly bottomless during rainy weather and dry and dusty otherwise.

The streams of bombers of the British and American air forces passed overhead daily. The number of bombers and their escorts, showing their condensation trails almost in defiance, seemed endless. With heavy hearts, the tankers saw them fly in the direction of Germany.

It later turned out to have been prudent to evacuate the barracks on the training area as a precautionary measure, since it also became the target of a raid. No casualties were suffered.

On 14 February, the training status of the battalion found its recognition in words of recognition from the General Inspector of Armored Forces, *Generaloberst* Guderian. The tankers were filled with certain pride in hearing Guderian praise the spirit and foundations of the *Waffen-SS* while addressing the officers of the Army battalion that was being inspected.

✠

A few days prior to the movement back to the Eastern Front, on 12 March, the men of the battalion, most of whom were combat veterans, visited the fortresses and cemeteries of Verdun, only about 100 kilometers east of the training area. They were familiar with war; they did not yearn for it. Despite all of that, they found themselves in a situation that forced them to enter battle at the cost of their own lives for the justified and essential self-interests of their nation, just like the countless and unnamed soldiers under the white crosses, in the filled in trenches and in the damp casemates.

✠

On 18 March, the training period for the battalion at Mailly le Camp was over. The march orders did not specify a destination. The tracked vehicles quickly loaded the trains without incident on the newly built end ramps. While the loading was going on, the *Flak* succeeded in bringing down one of the silvery four-engined bombers from the mighty stream over the training area.

The battalion reached southern German territory on expedited rail transport. Contrary to expectations, however, the battalion had not been earmarked for employment in the southeast. It was diverted to Poland and into the area around Cholm. The regimental and battalion commanders, who had initially traveled to Vienna, arrived there around 1600 hours on 24 March.

The skies were thick with clouds. As was the case every year, winter in the east ended with a period of thaws and mud. The city of Cholm was characterized by its location near the frontiers of Poland and the Soviet Union.

The battalion was put up in military facilities on the outskirts of the city. The streets and roads in and around the city were worn out and in bad shape, in some cases seemingly without foundation. March exercises in the vicinity made it clear down to the last man that he was back in the East again.

The remaining 42 *Panthers* were released for issue[17] and the main guns calibrated, but not without some difficulty. There were still civilian authorities in the city, a fact driven home by the fact that requests had to be submitted—within the necessary time period!—to block off certain areas for the necessary calibration of the main guns.

✠

For the old hands among the "Vikings," the return to the East dredged up memories of the time just prior to the start of the fighting against the Soviet Union in June 1941. At that time, they were positioned just a few kilometers south of this city as part of an apparently invincible field army. They marched to the southeast, by way of Rawa Ruska and Lemberg, the capital of Galicia. The field army fought its way forward across the seemingly endless expanse of the Soviet Union as far as the mountains of the Caucasus only, three years later, to return to the original line of departure to defend the frontiers of the *Reich* against an enemy who appeared to be impervious to misfortune and defeats.

17. Author's Note: According to the General Inspectorate for Armored Forces (*RH 10/20*), 42 tanks were en route on 25 March. The force-structure branch of the Army General Staff had taken 41 *Panthers* from the *2. SS-Panzer-Division "Das Reich"* and given them to the *5. SS-Panzer-Division "Wiking."* (Information received from the German Federal Archives on 4 August 1979.)

✠

Although the entire regiment was located in the Cholm area in that March of 1944, the two battalions were not yet a tactically cohesive unit. The 1st Battalion continued its personnel reconstitution and received new vehicles, weapons and equipment. *SS-Obersturmbannführer* Pätsch assumed command of the 2nd Battalion from *SS-Hauptsturmführer* Klapdor, who was sent to attend general-staff training. The 2nd Battalion was staring its first operational employment in the Kowel area in the eye.

KOWEL: DEVELOPMENT OF THE SITUATION AND ENCIRCLEMENT OF THE CITY

The western Ukrainian city of Kowel is located 85 kilometers east of Cholm and 60 kilometers east of the Bug, the former Polish-Soviet frontier. It is located along the rail line running Warsaw-Lublin-Cholm-Rowno, as well as being a point of intersection for the rail lines running northwest towards Brest Litowsk and southwest to Lemberg, about 280 kilometers away by means of Sokal.

The improved road leading from Rowno to Brest Litowsk touched Kowel at the halfway mark. In some areas, the rail lines and the roads around the city, which was surrounded by marshland, were elevated on bridges and other manmade artifacts. The Turja, which flows through the western part of the city, is up to 200 meters wide in some places. The city is about 4 to 5 kilometers across.

The importance of the city as a transportation hub is underscored by its location along the Turja. That river is the western-most one of the seven larger tributaries that flow towards the Pripjet from the south. Along with the same number of tributaries flowing in from the north, the Pripjet forms a river system of approximately 800 kilometers in length. The marshes of the same name abut the river, going from west to east, in the area between the Bug and the Dnjepr. The Pripet flows into the Dnjepr about 80 kilometers north of Kiev. The marshes are about 500 kilometers wide from east to west and about 200 kilometers long from north to south and form a considerable barrier to military operations.

It is terrain suited to partisan operations on the one hand and security forces without heavy weapons and vehicles on the other.

The road and rail connections between Kowel and Brest Litowsk form the western boundary for the marshland. For planning and executing military operations, that fact means that the possession of both areas is a prerequisite for resuming cohesive operations west of the marshland in attacking to the west. Up to that point, operations were forced to be conducted in an uncoordinated manner on both sides of the marshland.

In the First World War, Kowel formed a linchpin of the front in the summer of 1916 when Brussilow launched his general offensive. Kowel was successfully defended by the Austrian general, von Linsingen, against Russian Guards forces from 28 July to 4 November of that year.

For the defender, the possession of both cities is of decisive importance for a sustainable defense. The cities allow the defender the means to move operationally close to the front. Movement options that the attacker also needs desperately.

A short review of the development of operations in the southern and center sectors of the eastern front in the spring of 1944 illustrates the aforementioned.

✠

Attacks by the 1st Ukrainian Front, the northern-most of three "Ukrainian" field armies, broke open the front of *Heeresgruppe Süd* at the beginning of March 1944 at several places. In some cases, the penetrations were deep. The attacks that were conducted almost directly south reached the Tarnopol-Proskirow rail line.

Prior to renewing his offensive thrusts on 21 March, the Commander-in-Chief of the field army, Marshal Zhukov, conducted local attacks to protect his northern flank. Those attacks succeeded in advancing the Soviet forces to a line running Kremenecz-Dubno-Kowel. Moving along the southern side of the Pripet Marshes, his forces were protected to the north. The main offensive to the south that was launched on 21 March led to a breakthrough in the sector of the *4. Panzer-Armee* and, as a direct consequence, to the envelopment and encirclement of the *1. Panzer-Armee* in the Kamenecz-Podolsk area on 24 March.

The *4. Panzer-Armee* held a line along its northern wing—in some cases not even continuous—that ran north of Tarnopol-Brody-Luzk as far as Kowel. In the middle of April, the *1. Panzer-Armee*, with the help of the *II. SS-Panzer-Korps* and its two divisions, the *9. SS-Panzer-Division "Hohenstaufen"* and the *10. SS-Panzer-Division "Frundsberg,"* which had been brought in from France, succeeded in fighting its way free in the Buczacz area. The continued advance west of the 1st Ukrainian front by the end of March—its forward forces were more than 350 kilometers west of the Dnjepr on both sides of Kiev—had direct consequences for *Heeresgruppe Mitte*. As a result of the Soviet advance south of the Pripet Marshes, the southern wing of the field-army group, which was north of the marshes, had also been extended by some 350 kilometers.

Direct contact between the *2. Armee*, which was covering the field-army group's southern flank, and the *4. Panzer-Armee* to the south, which had been pushed back due to its reverses, had been lost north of Kiev on 12 November 1943 and never restored. The screening of the gap and, by extension, the southern flank of *Heeresgruppe Mitte*, fell to mobile formations and elements of the Hungarian Army. Based on an agreement with the Hungarian government, however, the sovereign forces of that country could only be employed against partisans, since they were considered to be insufficiently equipped to take on Soviet forces directly. Correspondingly, the security forces south of the Pripet Marshes continuously pulled back in the course of the fighting there.

After the successful encirclement of Kowel in the middle of March—a consequence of the aforementioned local attacks conducted by the 1st Ukrainian Front to protect its flanks and Soviet movements from the area around Kiev through Sarny, which hinted at offensive preparations towards the northwest in the direction of Brest Litowsk—the *2. Armee* moved its main defensive effort to its west wing. It took measures to secure the area around Brest Litowsk, to relieve Kowel and re-establish direct contact with the *4. Panzer-Armee* and, by extension, *Heeresgruppe Süd*.

✠

Kowel had been encircled since the middle of March. The German high command had declared the city to be a *fester Platz*[18] and initiated measures to relieve it. The value of these *feste Plätze* for the defensive effort varied, and not only among members of the senior command. Many frontline commanders did not consider them as decisively important. According to von Tippelskirch, who is not only quoted and referenced to a large extent in this work but was also a frontline commander-in-chief:

> Unfortunately, Hitler found a strong advocate for his demands [for *feste Plätze*] in the Commander-in-Chief of *Heeresgruppe Mitte*, *Feldmarschall* Busch, who replied to all of the misgivings of his field army commanders—especially forcefully advanced by the Commander-in-Chief of the *3. Panzer-Armee*, *Generaloberst* Reinhardt—

18. Translator's Note: A concept akin to the U.S. Army's use of the term "strongpoint," in which a terrain feature is strongly fortified into an all-round defensive bulwark. Towards the end of the war, Hitler designated a number of German cities to be *feste Plätze*, but these were often nominal strongpoints only, which acquired "strongpoint" status by dint of the enormous expenditure of blood. In this case, however, Kowel's status as a *fester Platz* had some merit, even though the actual resources within the encircled city were relatively meager, as the reader will soon discover.

> that the *feste Plätze* would tie up such strong enemy forces when they were encircled that the lack of those same forces outside of the *feste Plätze* would only play a secondary role.[19]

With regard to Kowel, however, he writes: "In the case of important railway hubs, however, a holding [of them] may have been justified."

By the second half of February 1944, the pressure exerted by the partisans on the city was becoming more palpable. In the daily report submitted by the head of the partisan groups on 25 February, strong partisan pressure from the woods on both sides of the Stochod against the Kowel—Rokitno—Kiev rail line at Poworsk, some 35 kilometers east of Kowel, was reported. *SS-Kavallerie-Regiment 17*[20] was assembled about 20 kilometers to the northeast of the city to push back the enemy forces at Krzeczewicze. The after-action report later went on to say that there were no forces available to defend the city proper.

In order to counter the increasing threat to the city at the beginning of March by reinforced partisan activity coupled with the westward movement of regular Soviet forces, the German high command ordered that the *"Wiking"* Division, still in the process of reforming itself in the Lublin—Cholm area, move to Kowel. There was not enough time to execute the directive, however.

The trench strengths of the forces in Kowel, before the encirclement (15 March) and after the relief (15 April), were as follows:[21]

1st Group: *Oberst* von Bissing with consolidated companies

Formation	15 March	15 April
Bataillon von Stock	431	90
Bataillon Fester	397	79
SS-Kavallerie-Regiment 17	877	355
Landesschützen-Bataillon 637[a]	246	110
Landesschützen-Bataillon 476	263	129

19. Author's Note: von Tippelskirch, 389.

20. Translator's Note: The 17th SS Cavalry Regiment was an actual horse-mounted formation and was one of the four line regiments of the *8. SS-Kavallerie-Division "Florian Geyer,"* which was wiped out in the defense of Budapest at the end of the war.

21. Author's Note: Annexes to the daily logs of the *2. Armee.*

2nd Group: *Oberstleutnant der Schutzpolizei* Golz[22]

Formation/Unit	15 March	15 April
Pionier-Bataillon 662	150	93
I./Sicherungs-Regiment 177[b]	294	99
II./SS-Polizei-Regiment 17	304	102
3./Pionier-Bataillon 50 and elements of *Eisenbahn-Bau-Pionier-Regiment 5*[c]	382	266
Bataillon Tenner	267	72
1./Artillerie-Abteilung 426 minus 1 battery		
1./Flak-Abteilung 854 minus 2 batteries		
Eisenbahnpanzerzug 10[d]	60	22

Notes to Tables:
a. Translator's Note: A *Landesschützen-Bataillon* was a rear-area security detachment not intended for front-line service, since it had virtually no heavy weapons and was composed of personnel who generally did not meet the prerequisites for front-line service (older than 35 and younger than 45). In effect, they were militia forces.
b. Translator's Note: A *Sicherungs-Regiment* or *Bataillon* was a formation intended for security duties, such as the guarding of depots or the escorting of convoys. It also did not have any heavy weapons and was not intended for front-line fighting. It was a regular part of the Army, however.
c. Translator's Note: 5th Railway Construction Regiment.
d. Translator's Note: Armored Train No. 10. Both sides employed armored trains during the fighting in the East, which had assigned crews and, frequently, a fixed configuration.

22. Translator's Note: The *Schutzpolizei* was the uniformed civil police in the *Reich*, albeit organized in paramilitary fashion and organized in formations up to a regiment in strength.

THE RELIEF OF "FORTRESS KOWEL"

On 16 March, *SS-Gruppenführer* Gille and his assistant operations officer, *SS-Hauptsturmführer* Westphal, landed around noon in a *Fieseler Storch*[23] at Kowel.

The formations of the division, which had set out for Kowel the same day by rail, were unable to make the city in time, since the Soviets had already closed their ring. Westphal provides some first-hand information:

> As it turned evening we slowly grew accustomed to the fact that we were sitting in a city that was slowly but surely being encircled by the enemy on all sides. Even the reports from the units employed in Kowel showed that the Russians were advancing on all sides.
>
> Four Soviet rifle divisions, namely the 76th, the 143rd, the 184th and the 320th, had been identified. *Germania* and *Westland* attempted an attack the next day as well to break through to Kowel. But the enemy had grown to be too strong.

The scope of the critical situation around and in Kowel on 16 March and the days that followed is reflected in the concise report of the commander of the divisional artillery, *SS-Standartenführer* Richter. He had been given the mission of coordinating the movements and operations of the division's formation outside of Kowel:

> As the senior commander, I was given the mission of forming a *Kampfgruppe* out of the [formations] that were in the Zamosz area, advancing in the direction of Kowel by rail, moving from Zamosz via Wlodzimiercz, and clearing a way into the city. At the same time, a unit from the *Germania* Regiment was employed against Kowel from the west. It had to leave the train between Maciejow and Kowel when the locomotive was hit and placed out of commission, taking casualties and fighting its way back to the west. Based on that event, I was relieved of the order that had been issued to me at the last moment. Relief of the city from the west was directed.
>
> The change turned out to be the proper one, since movement was then being conducted along the main rail line running from Lublin to Kowel, which was necessary for logistics . . .
>
> Taking two officers and two enlisted men, I set out to accomplish my mission without a vehicle and without communications means. The

---

23. Translator's Note: The *Feisler Fi 156* "Stork" was a light, all-purpose single-engine utility aircraft that was used throughout the war. It had exceptional short take-off and landing capabilities.

rail station at Cholm was not up to the task of handling the additional crush of transport trains. And it took hours before I was able to take off in the direction of Kowel with the first transport. As a result of the threatening situation east of the Bug, partisan activity between the Bug and Kowel had come back to life and endangered the rail line and the bridge over the Bug. The necessary measures needed for security of the transports therefore delayed their departure. When the first trains unloaded in Luboml and security was established north and south of the rail line by units of the artillery regiment, the tempo changed. In spite of the aerial attacks that immediately commenced, the offloading was conducted at a rapid pace. The 3rd Battalion of *Germania* was sent to me as the only combat-capable formation. It had been recently established as an *SPW* battalion.[24] During the first few days, the important locality of Maciejow, which had already been occupied by the enemy, could be retaken with the latter battalion as the result of a bold assault. Screening to the east could be conducted.

As more units arrived, terrain was taken to the east, south and north. Repeated attacks on the rail station at Maciejow and the security elements to the north were turned back. Unfortunately, the commander of the 7th Battery [of the regiment], *Obersturmführer* Sommer, was killed.[25]

The ability to screen the corridor [leading to Kowel] enabled the repair of the rail line, with the result that the *131. Infanterie-Division*, which had been brought forward in support, could be detrained at the Maciejow rail station. The division was only marginally disturbed by the aerial attacks that started up. It was not until this division was employed that a proper front could be established and the logistical support of *Kampfgruppe Richter*, which had been attached to the [Army] division, be assured.

Artillery pieces and other heavy and light weapons, as well as vehicles and signals equipment, also gradually began to arrive from Lublin, with the result that our combat power constantly increased. However, we did not have the tanks needed for an advance on Kowel.

Even though the defenders of Kowel, which had been cut off from any friendly contact on the ground, could be supplied from the air, the worsening

24. Author's Note: According to the annexes to the daily logs of the *2. Armee*, the battalion still did not have any *SPW's* or motorized vehicles.

25. Author's Note: The artillery regiment's personnel were employed as infantry.

situation demanded immediate help and relief. Every casualty weakened the already small number of defenders, who had already been pushed back to the outskirts of the city and were fighting in the suburbs in some places.

The *II./SS-Panzer-Regiment 5*, which was unloading in Cholm through 24 March, received orders on 26 March to relieve the *fester Platz* of Kowel. In response to a pressing message from *SS-Gruppenführer* Gille the previous day, the headquarters of the *4. Panzer-Armee* responded: "*Panzer-Abteilung Wiking* only operational with one company. Permission to use that company, as you have recommended, has been requested up the chain of command."[26]

The first train departed Cholm at 0030 hours on 27 March. The insufficient capacity of the rail station, coupled with the lack of an end ramp, caused disadvantageous delays. The situation of the encircled men had dramatically worsened in the previous few days: "Large-scale attack starting at 0400 hours with at least 10 batteries, tanks and mounted infantry, supported from the air."[27] The number of wounded jumped to 750. On 21 March, Gille urgently requested fighter cover to protect against the constant low-level aerial attacks. At 1315 hours, the headquarters of the *4. Panzer-Armee* answered: "Fighter cover not possible at present due to too little range and muddy fields."

Five hours later, Gille radioed again: "Heavy losses and much damage to the city as the result of constant low-level aerial attacks, a total of 12 runs. Armored Train No. 10 destroyed as a result of a direct hit. In all, 900 wounded."

On the following day, 10 enemy tanks penetrated into the middle of the city. Five of them were destroyed in close-in fighting; one was destroyed by *Flak*. Aerial resupply was conducted, but no air cover was provided.

On 27 March, the main line of resistance in the northern part of the city had to be pulled back 600 meters. Starting at 0200 hours, the Soviets attacked with strong forces supported by tanks along the south and the east as well. The main line of resistance on the east side had to be pulled back 500 meters. Gille radioed:

> Artillery ammunition almost expended; constant low-level aerial attacks.
>
> 28 March: Situation serious; artillery ammunition expended. Urgently request resupply with light field howitzer ammunition.

---

26. Author's Note: Annexes to the daily logs of the *2. Armee*.

27. Author's Note: Annexes to the daily logs of the *2. Armee*. Radio message form Gille at 0545 hours. The following quoted passages are also all from the daily logs of the *2. Armee*.

A little more than 24 hours later: "Heavy fighting to the south and east; heavy casualties."

During the night of 29–30 March, the hard-pressed encircled men requested the following at 0130 hours:

> *Kampfgruppe Gille* must insist on a breakout on 30 March, since the enemy is at the railway facilities and, as a result, dominates the aerial resupply with direct fires and there are no more forces available for an immediate counterattack.

After the arrival of the 2nd Battalion's 8th Company in Maciejow at 0530 hours on 27 March, the regimental commander, *SS-Obersturmbannführer* Mühlenkamp, established contact with *SS-Standartenführer* Richter, the division's battle group commander, and with the *131. Infanterie-Division.*

The most pressing need was to expand the area available to prepare for the attack to the east and, initially, to the southeast of Maciejow. That would mitigate the pressure of the enemy on the rail line and the road from Maciejow to Kowel.

At 1330 hours, the 8th Company attacked the enemy 500 meters north of Targowiscze, some 7 kilometers southeast of Maciejow. The enemy fled. He evacuated Targowiscze with approximately three companies and pulled further back to the southeast. As a result of the simultaneous withdrawal of a 7.62-centimeter battery, direct enemy influence on the rail line was eliminated.

On 28 March, the 8th Company was pushed forward to Tupaly, about 8 kilometers east of Maciejow. After it arrived there at 1500 hours, it was attached to the *131. Infanterie-Division.*

It was there that both Mühlenkamp and Richter established contact with the commanders of the *Westland* Regiment and *Artillerie-Regiment 131*, the divisional artillery of the Army infantry division. Terrain reconnaissance with *SS-Sturmbannführer* Dorr, the regimental commander, and *SS-Sturmbannführer* Hack, the commander of the *"Germania"* Regiment's 3rd Battalion, was followed by a conference with the commander of *Grenadier-Regiment 434*, *Oberst* Naber, at 1900 hours. In acknowledgement of the pressing radio traffic from *SS-Gruppenführer* Gille and the need for speed, the 8th Company was moved forward from Tupaly to Stare-Koszary, another 5 kilometers east.

The 8th Company positioned itself at the crossroads at the southeastern corner of Stare-Koszary, prepared to attack Czercasy, about 4 kilometers to the northeast. Infantry from *Grenadier-Regiment 434* were mounted on the rear decks of the tanks. The friendly forces to the right was the 3rd Battalion of *"Germania."* On the left was *Grenadier-Regiment 434*. Czercasy was north of the Maciejow-Kowel rail line, was protected on three sides by marshland and could only be attacked from the west or southwest.

The attack, which was scheduled to begin at 1100 hours, did not start until noon. Two and one-half hours later, the commander of the 8th Company, *SS-Obersturmführer* Nicolussi-Leck, reported:

> Company on the hill 600 meters west of Czercasy. Positions broken through and penetrated. Infantry being engaged. Heavy snowfall hindering visibility. When snowstorm over, I'll continue to advance. Request doctor for the wounded.[28]

Late in the afternoon, *Grenadier-Regiment 434* was at the same location to the left of the tanks with several of its companies. The grenadiers of the *"Germania"* regiment were held up, however.

Since the terrain north and east of Czercasy was judged to be marshy and could not be observed as a result of the snowfall, Mühlenkamp ordered Nicolussi-Leck's company to attack and take the village itself, orienting in its defense to the north, east and south. Ten minutes later, at 1715 hours, the 8th Company reported:

> Czercasy being cleared by friendly infantry; eight tanks operational; eight tanks disabled. Located in the area south of the rail line. Infantry south of the rail line not on line with me.

SS-Gruppenführer Gille was informed by radio about the situation. Before the 8th Company went on radio silence for the night, it submitted a report at 1900 hours concerning the events of the day: "Captured or destroyed were 7 7.62-centimeter antitank guns, 4 artillery pieces of 7.62-centimeter caliber, 200 to 300 dead and prisoners. Machine guns and other weapons still not determined." The 8th Company itself suffered the loss of one platoon leader (killed in action) and three wounded.

BREAKTHROUGH OF THE *8./SS-PANZER-REGIMENT 5* TO KOWEL

Based on the terrain conditions and the enemy resistance, the regiment decided not to continue the attack on 30 March. The intended radio order read:

---

28. Author's Note: *Chronik Pz.Rgt. 5.* The next few quotations are also from the same source.

> No operations on 30 March. Company is designated the division reserve and moved to Stare-Koszary at first light. Mounted assault detachments are to be released to their units.

The radio traffic could not be relayed directly to the 8th Company, since it would not turn on its radios to reception until 0400 hours. It also proved impossible to reach *Grenadier-Regiment 434.*

From *SS-Oberstürmführer* Hein, who had been dispatched to Stare- Koszary with a 1-ton prime mover and a Model 5 radio set, the regiment discovered at 0510 hours that the 8th Company, along with the original mounted infantry, had moved out on its own initiative along the rail line to Kowel to continue the attack. As of 0510 hours, it was 2 kilometers west of the outskirts of Kowel. At 0530 hours, Nicolussi-Leck made the following assessment of the situation:

> Have 9 tanks forward, 2 of which have been disabled due to mines. Rest of the tanks are along the railway embankment. The accompanying infantry, approximately a battalion, has formed a bridgehead in front of the tanks. Minesweeping cannot be conducted, since there are no engineers with us. The gap between the tank company and the regiment is being screened by [the Army] through Czercasy to the north. To the south, Hack's unit is hanging far back. The wooded terrain is clear of the enemy. Hack's unit would advance quickly [there]. Enemy resistance completely broken. There are very good prospects for getting through. If the bridge is blown, engineers up front. Embankment is also suitable for heavy vehicles.

From that point forward, the regiment no longer had any contact with the young officer. The *Chronik Pz. Rgt. 5* then states: "Around 1000 hours, the *131. Infanterie-Division* reported that the tank company and its escorting infantry arrived in Kowel at 0905 hours."

The advance of the 3rd Battalion of the *"Germania"* Regiment south of the rail line was made difficult by the extensive woods. The woods paralleled the rail lines in distances ranging from 500 to 1,000 meters until they reached a point about 2 or 3 kilometers west of the city, where they extended all the way to the rail line embankment and then crossed over to the northern side. From that point forward, the rail line advanced through open marshland.

✠

SS-Obersturmführer Nicolussi-Leck has provided a firsthand account of his decision to break through to the encircled city during the early morning of 30 March:

> At 0300 hours on 30 March 1944, I had nine operational tanks available. I moved out at 0400 hours in column along the railway embankment, then deploying on the right in the direction of the woods.
>
> We received fire from two enemy tanks in the woods to the right of the railway embankment 2 kilometers east of Czercasy. After eliminating them, 2 [friendly] tanks were lost to mines while advancing in the vicinity of the Czercasy rail station.
>
> The infantry, which had remained behind during the firefight, reached the lead elements of the tanks and provided a veil of security to their front, which included the rail facilities, the woods to the east and the ammunition dump to the right of the railroad. Enemy resistance was extremely slight.
>
> At 0600 hours, the mine obstacles had been cleared by assault engineers. *Hauptmann* Bolm told me that he had received orders not to advance any farther. I told him I could no longer stop and moved out right away with the accompany assault troops. I ordered the two immobilized tanks under the command of *SS-Oberscharführer* Faas to prepare for maintenance teams and defend the strongpoint of Czercasy at the same time, thus keeping the rail line open for the tanks to follow. To that end, *Hauptmann* Bolm provided a squad of infantry to provide close-in security for the [immobilized] tanks.
>
> When my lead tanks were 2 kilometers west of Kowel, I received the following radio message: "Order from the battalion commander: The tanks are to halt." That report was called out by a messenger from *Hauptmann* Bolm to the trail tank and then forwarded to me via radio. Since my lead tanks were already engaged in combat with enemy infantry and tank hunter/killer teams, which were blocking the northwestern exits of the city, and, a short while later, an intense firefight developed with 10 to 12 antitank guns and artillery pieces from the general line running Kowel to Moszczona, it was not possible for me to halt and I therefore left *Hauptmann* Bolm's message unanswered. Moreover, I was under no command & control relationship with him. A heavy snowfall temporarily eliminated the threat from the left flank and, at the same time, all of the blocking positions that were in front of Stecker's strongpoint [defending the city] were rolled up. In all of this, the accompanying assault troops performed magnificently. We

> no longer had any contact with *Hauptmann* Bolm's infantry. Around 0730 hours, we reached the curve in the rail line and established contact with *Hauptmann* Stecker.
>
> After completing some special requests from the defending forces with regard to combating the enemy in the northwestern portion of the city, I moved to Gille's command post with my seven tanks and reported to [him] at 0815 hours.

The seven *Panthers* represented a significant increase in combat capabilities and reinvigoration for the defenders, who were steadily growing weaker. The ring around the city had been penetrated but not rolled up. After Nicolussi-Leck's small battle group had punched its way through, the ring closed up again.

Later on, the plucky Tyrolean German would receive the Knight's Cross to the Iron Cross for his feat of arms (9 April 1944)

FINAL RELIEF OF THE CITY

The two tanks that had to be left behind at the Czercasy rail station drew the attention of the enemy. It was there, some 1,500meters in front of the main line of resistance, that the two *Panthers* and 12 grenadiers under the command of *SS-Oberscharführer* Faas had to fend off enemy attacks from the northeast in the afternoon. Four tanks under *SS-Unterscharführer* Kasper that had remained behind the previous day and were located south of Czercasy supported Faas and his men.

During the night, *SS-Hauptsturmführer* Treuker's 11th Company from the *"Germania"* Regiment succeeded in advancing through the enemy and reinforcing Faas' group. The enemy resumed his attacks the following morning and inserted himself in company strength between the "tank island" and the main line of resistance. It proved impossible for the Germans to prevent the railway embankment from being mined again.

The stranded tanks were attached to the 3rd Battalion of *"Germania,"* which was entrusted with providing their security and logistical needs. Despite the command-and-control relationship, the small group of reinforced defenders was pretty much on its own. Late in the afternoon, the situation turned critical as a result of the dwindling supplies of ammunition. It was not possible to resupply the group from the air.

Two tanks from Kasper's group that had managed to make themselves mobile again pulled back in accordance with orders when it turned dark in an effort to return to the main line of resistance. Half way to their goal, they were knocked out by enemy antitank guns in the woods.

By then, the enemy strength between Faas' group and the main lines had grown so strong that an attack by a ski battalion from *Jäger-Brigade 1* that was set for 2200 hours bogged down south of Czercasy. The two *panje* carts loaded with infantry munitions never reached the encircled group.

During the night, the Soviet infantry pushed up to within 200 meters of Faas' position, while the enemy's heavy weapons started registering their fires. One of the tanks on the railway embankment was set alight.

Late in the morning of 1 April, the encircled men requested ammunition, medical supplies and rations. *SS-Hauptsturmführer* Treuker reported at 1445 hours:

> Strongpoint reduced to extremely narrow area. Pressed hard from the west and the south. Can only hold out a few more hours. Request barrage fire 500 meters more to the east up to that point.

Mühlenkamp and the operations officer of the *131. Infanterie-Division* both came to the conclusion that neither the disabled tanks could be recovered nor the isolated position be held any longer. Orders were issued: "Blow up the remaining tanks. Fight your way through to Kowel!"

Treuker, however, decided to try to break out to the west to reach the main line of resistance. Although he was wounded, both his 11th Company and Faas' tankers reached the lines.

One day after the successful breakthrough to Kowel by the 8th Company, the tanks of the 7th Company were unloaded at 1100 hours of 31 March in Maciejow. One hour later, one of the company's platoons was engaged in defending against an attack in the area around Perewisy, 4 kilometers east of Maciejow and north of the rail line. Around 1700 hours, the enemy was turned back, with the result that the company was able to assemble that night in the Tupaly area before being pushed forward to Stare-Koszary.

The sounds of heavy fighting from the direction of Czercasy and the report of *Grenadier-Regiment 434* that the enemy had broken through there and retaken the village made it necessary to commit the 7th Company. Preceded by *Stuka* support, the company moved out at 0530 to conduct an immediate counterattack, along with *Hauptmann* Eppinghaus's grenadier battalion. At 0710 hours, *SS-Obersturmführer* Schneider was able to report:

> Strong flanking by antitank guns from the south. 6 tanks bogged down in the marshes; 2 tanks lost to mines; 2 lost due to damage to the main guns (from enemy fire); 2 tanks have established contact with the *I./Grenadier-Regiment 434*. 3 tanks still operational and positioned under cover.

The five tanks that were still operational, along with the grenadiers and the ski battalion, attacked again at 0745 hours. The enemy off to the right flank was kept low by means of artillery and airpower. Five hours later, the enemy was finally ejected for good and Czercasy, effectively supported by the tanks of *SS-Untersturmführer* Sticker, retaken.

Late that evening, the 7th Company, which had been ordered back to a patch of woods 2 kilometers east of Tupaly, only had two operational tanks left. Most of the tanks had been left immobilized in the middle of the attack sector. The maintenance services were working feverishly.

✠

The defenders of Kowel had been holding out for 17 days in their positions on the outskirts of the city against the pressure of an increasingly stronger enemy force. For six days, the relief forces had been trying to break open an entrance to Kowel from the west, initially with the 8th Company and, just two days earlier, the 7th Company of the tank regiment.

On 2 April, the force ratios changed dramatically in favor of the relief forces. The previous evening, the commander of the 2nd Battalion, *SS-Sturmbannführer* Paetsch, arrived around 1900 hours in Maciejow. The remaining units of the battalion arrived the following day: 0630 hours for the 5th Company; 1130 hours for the Headquarters Company; and 1540 hours for the 6th Company. With them came an additional 28 *Panthers*, substantially increasing the available combat power.

The 2nd Battalion, minus its 8th Company, assembled in the woods 2 kilometers southeast of Tupaly.

✠

After the combat zone of Kowel was allocated to *Heeresgruppe Mitte* as part of its sector, the *LVI. Panzer-Korps* was directed to participate in the relief of the city. With its *4. Panzer-Division* and *5. Panzer-Division*, it approached the city from the northwest. The advance guard of the *5. Panzer-Division* reached Smidyn, 10 kilometers northeast of Maciejow, on 2 April; the advance guard of the *4. Panzer-Division* reached Stare-Koszary on 3 April.

Since the attack preparations of the *4. Panzer-Division* were delayed by 24 hours, the *II./SS-Panzer-Regiment 5* supported the *5. Panzer-Division* in its attack on Krühel on 3 April. To that end, the tanks of the 6th Company were positioned on the southern edge of Krasnoduby on Hill 196.1, approximately 1.5 kilometers north of the rail line between Tupaly and Stare-Koszary.

The attack by the grenadiers of the *5. Panzer-Division* on Krühel was not successful. At 1345 hours, the 6th Company reported: "Nothing seen regarding a friendly infantry attack. Receiving occasional fire from the village by enemy infantry."

At 1740 hours, the company was pulled back to its quartering area east of Tupaly.

The night of 3–4 April saw little sleep. The clocks were reset to summer time. The attack forces occupied their staging areas. At 0315 hours, an artillery preparation commenced. Two hours later, at first light, the tanks attached in support of the attacking infantry moved out.

At 0513 hours, the 6th Company was 500 meters south of Krasnoduby in the positions it had occupied the previous day, facing the same enemy forces in and east of Krühel. The 5th Company was on the southern outskirts of Stare-Koszary in support of the 2nd Battalion of *"Germania"* against the wooded high ground 2.5 kilometers to the southeast. The 7th Company was in the woods 2.5 kilometers southeast of Tupaly behind *Grenadier-Regiment 431.* The mission of the 7th Company: After the reinforced *Ski-Jäger-Regiment 2,* the 2nd Battalion of *"Westland"* and the 3rd Battalion of *"Germania"* reached their attack objectives to the southeast, the 7th Company was to attack Kalinowka, approximately 3 kilometers south-southeast of Stare-Koszary, and the cemeteries further to the south. The tank attack was intended to bring relief to the friendly forces to the left advancing along the wooded high ground southeast of Stare-Koszary, which included the 5th Company.

Ninety minutes after the start of the attack, at 0640 hours, the 5th Company was 1.2 kilometers southeast of Stare-Koszary with two of its platoons and had broken through the enemy positions in front of the woods. The friendly infantry was in the process of moving from those positions and into the woods. An hour later, the 6th Company, which was supporting the advance of the *4. Panzer-Division* north of the rail line, reported that Krühel had been taken. The woods and the solid ground north of Stare-Koszary—the first attack objective of the *4. Panzer-Division*—were also reached at that time, according to a report submitted by *Grenadier-Regiment 434.* The possession of the solid ground was a pre-requisite for the attack to follow on Moszczona, where it was possible for mechanized forces to then bypass the marshland west of Kowel from the north.

The attacks against the enemy's positions along the high ground and in the woods southeast of Stare-Koszary has a less auspicious outcome. At 0850 hours, the attacks of the 2nd Battalion of *"Westland"* and the 3rd Battalion of *"Germania"* bogged down in front of the woods. Enemy immediate counterattacks were turned back. The Soviets were defending stubbornly from the woods, where extensive field fortifications had been constructed about 50 meters within the woodline.

Although the northern attack group, with the 5th Company in support, was able to advance to within 400 meters of the woods on both sides of the Stare-Koszary–Kowel road, the open position from there to the woodline could not be crossed in the face of eight identified enemy antitank guns firing from concealed positions in the woods. Through the early afternoon, the enemy antitank guns fired at a tank that had been immobilized by a mine and damaged two more with hits to the turret and running gear. The company was basically pinned down in the positions it had reached. It was not possible to launch a concentrated attack with all of the assault guns and tanks against the northern tip of the woods, where portions of the assault battalion had been able to penetrate, since the enemy would then reoccupy the important hilltop positions.

It was not until a *Stuka* run at 1435 hours that the concentrated forces were successful in penetrating into the northern portion of the woods. It was not possible to roll up the enemy positions from north to south, however.

When asked whether he could disengage from the enemy, an *SS-Obersturmführer* answered negatively at 1545 hours. He reported to the regiment: "The company cannot be pulled back until it turns dark, since it is being engaged by snipers and machine guns. Evacuation of the tanks and the wounded only possible when dark."

The tank companies of the regiment that were available for other commitment on the afternoon of 4 April—the 6th and 7th Companies—received orders from the regimental commander at 1625 hours:

> The regiment follows behind the *4. Panzer-Division* and reached Moszczona. The 5th Company remains with the *131. Infanterie-Division* and will follow later. The supply services of the regiment remain until further orders in Maciejow, Tupaly and Stare-Koszary.

The *LVI. Panzer-Korps* slowly started to gain ground with the *4. Panzer-Division* on the left and the *5. Panzer-Division* on the right. It sent the following message to the encircled defenders of Kowel at 0930 hours: "We have initiated the decisive thrust on Kowel." To get there, it had to defeat four enemy divisions, some complete and other represented only by subordinate formations. To the east and south of the city, there were an additional three divisions.

In the face of strong resistance, the *4. Panzer-Division,* under the command of *Generalleutnant* von Saucken, took Moszczona around noon. It then advanced on Dubowa, where it became engaged in a large armored engagement to the west of that village in the afternoon. The movements of the division were considerably disrupted by the enemy forces in the Czercasy cemetery and by flanking fires received from the patch of woods north of the rail line to the east of the village. The attacks of the *131. Infanterie-Division* against both areas were not successful.

By the evening of 4 April, however, the *4. Panzer-Division* was able to break through the tank obstacles and cross the rail line west of Dubowa.

Following the *4. Panzer-Division,* the *II./SS-Panzer-Regiment 5* reached Moszczona at 1745 hours. It then joined in the fighting along the route leading to the southeast in the direction of Kowel. In the face of light resistance, it reached the bend in the road some 2 kilometers southeast of Moszczona.

At first light, which was at 0315 hours, the 1st Battalion of *"Germania,"* which had been pushed forward, attacked farther to the southeast, while the 6th Company screened to the east and northeast and the 7th Company to the northeast and north. The regimental commander and his liaison officer moved with the 2nd Battalion in their command tanks. Without encountering enemy resistance, the battalion reached the railway crossing 2.5 kilometers northwest of Kowel, where the forward positions of the encircled forces finally received the long-for reinforcement against the enemy forces after weeks of anticipation. As early as the previous evening, at 2330 hours, initial contact had been made. The local area commander in Kowel, *SS-Gruppenführer* Gille, had his headquarters radio the *2. Armee*: "One battalion of *SS-Germania* and the commander of *SS-Panzer-Regiment 5* have arrived at the forward strongpoint at the rail crossing west of Kowel."

In the effort of the two tanks to continue in the direction of the city the commander's tank rolled over a mine. After the immobilized tanks was safeguarded by infantry, the commander returned to the location of the headquarters of the 2nd Battalion in Moszczona.

Attached to the *4. Panzer-Division,* the 6th Company had been advancing rapidly to the southeast ever since 0530 hours. The 7th Company advanced east in support of *Panzergrenadier-Regiment 12* of the *4. Panzer-Division.* The 6th Company crossed the Dubowa-Kowel road leading into Kowel from the north, eliminated an enemy battery and was at the cemetery on the northeast outskirts of Kowel at 1230 hours. It then screened from that position, orienting to the east and north.

The 7th Company, continuing its attack east with *Panzergrenadier-Regiment 12,* swung south, using the embankment, and attacked Dubowa by crossing the high ground outside of the village to the south. After eliminating heavy concentrations of antitank guns and artillery, Dubowa fell later that morning. At 0750 hours, Gille received the following radio traffic from the *LVI. Panzer-Korps*: The *4. Panzer-Division* along the Moszczona-Kowel road and in Dubowa; will penetrate. What is the enemy situation on the northern and western outskirts? If possible, support the attack."[29]

But Gille's forces were insufficient to accommodate the request. At 1315 hours, he relayed a message to the *4. Panzer-Division* through the *131. Infanterie-Division*: "North and west front of Kowel: Weak outposts composed of militia, police, railway construction workers and alert units."

With its left flank being covered by the *5. Panzer-Division*, the *4. Panzer-Division* moved out with its main effort—*Panzergrenadier-Regiment 12* supported by the tanks of the *II./SS-Panzer-Regiment 5*—to the south and broke the final enemy resistance to the north of the city.

At 1400 hours, the corps radioed the *2. Armee*: "*4. Panzer-Division* penetrated into Kowel from Dubowa on the main route. Contact established."

The enemy, who was numerically quite superior, had been deprived of the already palpable fruit of his three weeks of efforts—despite extremely hard resistance and despite the extremely unfavorable terrain for the attacker. For the time being, the operationally important railway hub of Kowel was to remain in German hands. Because of that, the Soviet preparations for the offensive to take Brest Litowsk were thwarted.

The assistant operations officer of the division, *SS-Hauptsturmführer* Westphal, provides a view of the situation during the final days for those encircled in the city:

> The defensive ring around Kowel that was occupied by us had been increasingly reduced by the attacks of the overwhelming enemy forces. Our command post was so close to the forward lines that it could be reached by rifle fire. The number of wounded was large and their quartering brought with it special difficulties, since hardly any of the houses had basements. Medial attention was also difficult, since there were not enough doctors, medical supplies and medicines on hand. One doctor had even been flown in in a glider. The garrison was barely sufficient to man the defensive ring. The companies consisted of only a handful of soldiers. Enemy tanks succeeded again and again

29. Author's Note: This quote the next two are from the annexes to the daily logs of the *2. Armee*.

in penetrating into the city. The brave defenders knew enough to keep the Russian infantry from following.

There were tanks in front of the command post an hour ago, until one of them was knocked out with a *Panzerfaust*[30] and the other pulled back. Another enemy tank ran off a bridge in the city and into the creek; the crew was taken prisoner.

On our maps, we marked the tips of the attack force that was advancing on Kowel from the west. After all, we could calculate when the forces in Kowel would no longer be able to hold out as a result of the heavy losses sustained during the continuous enemy attacks. But no one lost faith; everyone counted on being relieved.[31]

EXPANSION OF THE CORRIDOR

After the successful breakthrough, all efforts turned towards expanding the narrow corridor to the east and the west and pushing back the enemy forces from the city outskirts.

On that same day, the 6th Company was attached to the 1st Battalion of *"Germania,"* which was given the mission of attacking from east to west along the Kowel–Stare-Koszary rail line to establish contact with the *131. Infanterie-Division.* The attack met with no success, however.

On the evening of 2 April, the *131. Infanterie-Division* reported through the chain of command: "Advance of *SS-Germania* with *Panther* support from the railway crossing to the west bogged down in enemy antitank gun and infantry fire from the eastern edge of the large woods."[32]

The enemy forces in the Czercasy Woods also did not pull back, even though "approximately 50 enemy antitank guns were destroyed by assault guns, *Panthers* and heavy weapons."

The attacks conducted the next day from the west, south and southeast against the bitterly defending enemy also remained without success. On the other hand, the *VIII. Armee-Korps* succeeded "in establishing contact between the *131. Infanterie-Division* and the friendly strongpoint on the railway crossing west of Kowel by means of attacks from the east and west."

On the evening of 5 April, the *VIII. Armee-Korps* and *Kampfgruppe Gille* were temporarily subordinated to *General der Infanterie* Hossbach, forming *Gruppe Hossbach,* which also had the *LVI. Panzer-Korps. Gruppe Hossbach* was given the following orders:

---

30. Translator's Note: A handheld antitank rocket launcher with a hollow-shaped warhead. It had an effective range of about 100 meters. It was reverse-engineered by the Soviets to later produce the world-famous RPG-7.

31. Author's Note: *Europäische Freiwillige.*

32. Author's Note: This quote and the next are from the daily logs of the *2. Armee.*

> . . . to relieve Kowel for good and to hold the city, including the bend in the rail line on the eastern outskirts, as a permanent outpost in the new main line of resistance to be formed. The Turja is to be taken on both sides of Kowel. It is to be held in the north and built up into a main line of resistance all the way to the point where it flows into the Pripet.[33]

That mission defined the operations and the fighting of the 2nd Battalion of the tank regiment over the next few weeks.

The front lines were practically intermeshed at places. The enemy's pockets of resistance in the extensive marshland west of the city was peppered with antitank guns that put up a stubborn defense and also proved annoying. These are mentioned so that the reader has an appreciation for the difficulties associated with attempting to recover the regimental commander's tank, which had run over a mine on the morning of 5 April.

SS-Untersturmführer Niemann, whose *Panther* had remained there to cover the stricken tank, received hits on his hull and turret from antitank guns located 2,500 meters away. The engagement grew so intense, that a platoon from the 5th Company had to be brought forward to provide additional cover. It was not until 6 April that the command tank could be recovered under cover of darkness.

After a few days of rest, the 6th Company supported an attack of *Panzergrenadier-Regiment 33* of the *4. Panzer-Division* on 10 April. The attack gained approximately 6 kilometers of ground to the northeast, moving the front forward to a line running Bachow–Hill 179. A counterattack launched by the enemy from the north on 12 April and supported by tanks was defeated by the 6th Company, which knocked out 15 enemy tanks in the process.

After another four days of rest, the 5th and 6th Companies occupied staging areas during the night of 16–17 April in the western part of the city in order to establish a bridgehead over the western arm of the Turja. Once done, they were to take Hill 189.5, the foothills of the same high ground to

33. Author's Note: Daily logs of the *LVI. Panzer-Korps*.

the southeast and the military facilities in the southwestern portion of the city.

Pionier-Bataillon 50,[34] which inaugurated the attack at 0130 hours to clear the way, encountered extremely heavy resistance and its efforts bogged down. At 0635 hours, *Kampfgruppe Gille* radioed the *LVI. Panzer-Korps*:

> *Stuka* attack on Wolka effective. Friendly attack on the southwestern portion of Kowel against strong enemy forces bogged down. Urgently request *Stuka* attack on the southern military facilities along the Kowel-Turzysk road. Request notification of start time [of the sorties].[35]

The 6th Company looked for a crossing site over the Turja in vain until early in the morning. It was not until *Kampfgruppe Dorr* had taken Hill 189.5 by attacking along the rail line from the north at 0700 hours, that the regimental commander decided to look for crossing points further to the north.

At 0900 hours, the 6th Company was finally able to cross at a point it had reconnoitered—after the mines had been cleared and regimental combat engineers had built a corduroy road. After establishing contact with one of *Kampfgruppe Dorr's* companies, which had entered the western portion of Kowel after advancing from Hill 189.5, the 6th Company attacked south. The 5th Company, which was trailing, also immediately turned south and assisted the infantry in clearing the western portion of the city. By the early afternoon, the attack objectives had been reached. The 5th Company was positioned with its left wing in the southern military facilities, while the 6th Company was in front of it on Hill 188. The northern edge of the woods at Libliniec on the rail line had been reached.

On 18 April, the regimental headquarters and the 2nd Battalion had 48 operational tanks and 1 recovery tank (40 *Panzer V's*, 4 command tanks and 4 *Panzer IV's*). The final operation to take the west bank of the Turja to the south of Kowel by the *LVI. Panzer-Korps* was planned for 27 April. Preparations got underway.

At 0500 hours on that day, the 5th and 6th Companies, as well as the regimental and battalion headquarters, were positioned at the windmill at the southwestern corner of Kowel. Positioned to the south of the city was an armored engineer company, the regiment's 8th Company, the 2nd Company

---

34. Translator's Note: The engineer battalion had belonged to the ill-fated *22. Panzer-Division*, which was later consolidated with the *23. Panzer-Division*. The battalion was designated a general headquarters force at this point, employed at the discretion of the field army to which it was allocated at the time.

35. Author's Note: Daily logs of the *2. Armee*.

of *Panzerjäger-Abteilung 49* (*4. Panzer-Division*) and one platoon from the 1st Battalion of *Flak-Regiment 64*.

The infantry, attacking along both sides of the Kowel-Sokal-Lemberg rail line, reached the village of Lubliniec with its right-hand battalion and the woods south of Hill 189.5 with its left-hand battalion. Following that, *Major* Wuehl reported: "Village of Lubliniec firmly in our hands. Hard resistance in the woods east of the rail line."[36] At that point, the 6th Company moved out (0700 hours). It was not able to cross the railway crossing until artificial smoke was employed. All the while, it was facing heavy enemy resistance and antitank-gun fires. It was then possible for the regimental combat engineers to clear the mines under the cover of the tanks, although the continued attack of the armor was delayed until 1500 hours.

The enemy used those hours to disengage his forces employed further to the west into the woods southwest of Stare-Koszary, then allowing him to pull back to the southeast through the village of Dolhonosy, about 3 kilometers west of Lubliniec. At 1500 hours, the 6th Company crossed the marshland on both sides of the rail line that had been cleared of mines, destroyed seven antitank guns and reached Lubliniec. Turning to the east, it then took Hill 191.4, found itself in the rear of the enemy in the woods southwest of Kowel, and made it easier for the infantry to clear the same woods of the enemy.

The 5th Company was brought forward, advancing further to the southeast from Lubliniec and taking Hill 193.3. Armored reconnaissance sent forward to Horodelec (on the Turja) overran a column of 12 trucks with limbered antitank guns and blocked the crossings over the river.

The southern attack group—the 8th Company of the regiment, the antitank company from the *4. Panzer-Division* and the attached *Flak* platoon—screened the attack to the west of Lubliniec, oriented to the west and southwest.

As had been the case in the efforts in the northeastern part of the city, the attacks helped loosen the enemy's grip around Kowel in the southwest and allowed the front lines to be extended 6 kilometers to the southwest.

In addition to losing light infantry weapons, the enemy lost 3 Mark III tanks, 43 heavy antitank guns, 6 light antitank guns, 7 heavy mortars, 4 light infantry guns, 19 antitank rifles, 3 light antiaircraft guns and 28 trucks. The *LVI. Panzer-Korps* ordered the final clearing of the area around Kowel at 1225 hours on 27 April:

> The *131. Infanterie-Division* assumes command of the east attack group after direct coordination with *Gruppe Gille*. In continuing the attack, the *131. Infanterie-Division* takes Horodelec and holds it. *Gruppe Gille*

36. Author's Note: *Chronik Pz.Rgt. 5*.

> takes the Turja from the northern outskirts of Horodelec as far as Kowel. It establishes defensive positions on the west bank. The *131. Infanterie-Division* clears the rear area, especially the woods southeast of Stare-Koszary and south of Czercasy, starting today.[37]

The victory along the Turja was described in the Armed Forces Daily Bulletin of 28 April 1944:

> Formations of the Army and the *Waffen-SS*, magnificently supported by the *Luftwaffe*, broke through deeply echeloned enemy defensive positions southwest of Kowel and pushed the Soviets back to the Turja River line.

MACIEJOW—SOKOL—MACIEJOW

The regiment's 2nd Battalion occupied quarters in the Maciejow area from 9 May to 9 June. The regimental headquarters and the Headquarters Company, as well as the battalion headquarters and the 5th Company, were located in Maciejow proper. The 7th Company was in Bielicze, 2 kilometers to the north. The 6th Company was quartered in Paryduby, 5 kilometers to the northeast; the 8th Company and the battalion maintenance contact teams in Somin, 3 kilometers to the south; and the regimental engineers and the maintenance platoon in Okunin, 3 kilometers to the southwest.

Designated as the ready reserve of the *LVI. Panzer-Korps*, the units conducted reconnaissance in the sectors of the *26. Infanterie-Division*, the *4. Panzer-Division*, the *342. Infanterie-Division* and the *131. Infanterie-Division.* At the same time, the regimental headquarters coordinated with the aforementioned divisions. Almost five weeks passed without any noteworthy incidents. The valuable time was used to repair and maintain the vehicles, weapons and equipment and to perfect training and combat readiness.

On 9 June, orders arrived moving the tank regiment and the 3rd Battalion of *"Germania"* to Sokol, 90 kilometers southwest of Maciejow. The last train was unloaded there two days later. The elements were administratively attached to the *10. SS-Panzer-Division "Frundsberg"* and tactically reporting to the headquarters of the *II. SS-Panzer-Korps.* The corps headquarters was located at Zloczow.

On 12 June, *Kampfgruppe Mühlenkamp* reverted to the command and control of the *4. Panzer-Armee,* since the SS corps was moved back to Normandy. The next few days were filled with terrain and route reconnaissance in the sectors of the divisions there. There was the corresponding coordination, as

37. Author's Note: This quotation and the next one are from the annexes to the daily logs of the *LVI. Panzer-Korps.*

well as a radio exercise with all of the subordinate elements of the *4. Panzer-Division (26 June). SS-Obersturmführer* Wolf was in charge of the communications effort of the regiment for the radio exercise.

On 22 June, there was a change of command within the 2nd Battalion, with *SS-Hauptsturmführer* Reicher replaced *SS-Obersturmbannführer* Paetsch, who left to assume command of the tank regiment of the *"Frundsberg"* Division.

Starting at 0700 hours on 25 June, *Kampfgruppe Mühlenkamp* departed the sector by train to return to the area west of Kowel. It once again reported to the *LVI. Panzer-Korps*, located in Chworostow. They reasons for these movements, to include those of the *II. SS-Panzer-Korps* to the Normandy front, were important in the history of the war and perhaps need a bit of explanation.

The divisions of the corps that were sent back to Normandy on 12 June—the *10. SS-Panzer-Division "Frundsberg"* and the *9. SS-Panzer-Division "Hohenstaufen"*—had been formed in France in 1943 and 1944. They were familiar with the area west of the lower course of the Seine as a result of their training, map exercises and communications exercises. They had practiced numerous options for operations against enemy forces that might land in that area. The corps had been moved to the Eastern Front in April 1944 to assist in the relief of the encircled *1. Panzer-Armee.* After the conclusion of those operations, the corps remained in the east as a field army and field-army-group reserve force from the end of April until its movement west on 12 June into the area around Lemberg. One week after the landing of the Allies in Normandy, the corps was sent back to the area it was familiar with, although the enemy had established a firm beachhead by then. Another two weeks would pass before the corps would be committed against the Western Allies, who had already overcome any weaknesses associated with their amphibious landings. The first phase of the invasion had succeeded at the place where two strong armored divisions could have countered it instead of the two weak infantry divisions that had engaged it instead, had the corps been sent back to the area on both sides of the Orne after the fighting in Galicia to relieve the *1. Panzer-Armee.*

The reason for the concentration of armored forces in the area northeast of Lemberg, in addition to the original movement of the *II. SS-Panzer-Korps,* was the expectation of a large-scale Soviet offensive against the northern wing of *Heeresgruppe Nordukraine.*[38] That accounts for the movement of *Kampfgruppe Mühlenkamp* into the Sokol area in the middle of June as well.

In this connection, we read the following in von Tippelskirch's book:

> But in the General Staff of the Army, the preconceived notion of an attack against *Heeresgruppe Nordukraine* had established such deep roots—bolstered by the unequivocal assessment of Model, who

38. Translator's Note: Army Group "North Ukraine."

commanded the front in Galicia—that no one deviated from it. Although the Russian build-up in the area of *Heeresgruppe Mitte* could not be denied, it was accorded only secondary importance within the framework of Russian planning.

With regard to the mistaken assessment of the German command concerning the Soviet operational intentions Shtemenko informs us that a large-scale deception effort enabled the success that was so important for the Allied war effort. He commented on the nature and scope of the deception measures, as well as their necessity and the successful element of secrecy:

> During the preparations for the operations in Belorussia, the General Staff desired that the German command be convinced that the main thrust of the Soviet armies in the summer of 1944 could be expected in the south and in the area of the Baltics.
>
> On 3 May, the commander in chief of the 3rd Ukrainian front received the following directive:
>
> In order to deceive the enemy, it is your mission to conduct a deception campaign at the operational level. Eight or nine infantry divisions, reinforced by armor and artillery, must be concentrated across the right flank of the front and beyond. The pretence of an staging area must be as realistic as possible in which the movements and the distribution of differing groups, vehicles, tanks, rifles and equipment must be visible. Antiaircraft weaponry is to go into position, wherever dummy tanks and artillery are moved, and the entire area needs to demonstrate measures of air defense preparedness by means of antiaircraft weaponry in appropriate positions and the maintaining of regular fighter patrols.
>
> The visibility and realism of the deception measures is to be monitored by means of aerial observation and aerial photography. The operational deception campaign will be conducted from 5 to 15 June.
>
> The 3rd Baltic Front received similar instructions. In that sector, the deception campaign was to be conducted east of the Chereckha.
>
> Both of the baits were immediately swallowed, and the German high command demonstrated a great deal of unrest, especially in the south. Aerial reconnaissance was increased to find out what we were doing north of Kishinew. Leaving our tank armies in the southwest sector was also a type of bluff. Enemy reconnaissance was casting a watchful eye on them and, because none of these field armies were being moved, it led to the [German] conclusion that our offensive was most likely to be expected there . . .

> Measures were taken to keep our intentions secret. Only a very small circle was directly concerned with the preparation of plans for the summer offensive taken as a whole or for the operation in Belorussia in particular. In fact, the intent was only known to five people: The deputy supreme commander in chief; the chief of the General Staff and his deputy; the chief of staff of the Operations Directorate and his deputy.
>
> All correspondence relating to it, as well as any telephone conversations or telegraphic communications, were strictly forbidden. Severe monitoring measures were instituted. Recommendations from the fronts [field armies] concerning operations were only discussed between two to three people. Usually, they were written by hand and generally personally brought over to the commanding officers. The forces in the field were instructed to perfect their defense; the front, army and division newspapers were to only publish things that dealt with the defense . . .

Apparently, the Soviets were familiar with treason as well. That aspect of the war, especially on the German side, still remains one of the most closely guarded secrets of the war, for understandable reasons. As a result of the failure to properly assess the Soviet operational intentions for the summer of 1944 and the placing of operational-level reserves behind *Heeresgruppe Nordukraine,* the landings by the Western Allies in the coastal region of Normandy were decisively benefitted and the fate of *Heeresgruppe Mitte,* which had been stripped of its reserves, was sealed during the first onslaught of the overwhelmingly superior Soviet forces at the end of June 1944.

At the same time, there is still the great admonition from Moltke:

> Just criticism does not allow the course of events after the fact or the knowledge of how things worked when available later on to form the basis of a judgment. Rather, it must ask the question: What could the leaders of these events have known at the time they acted . . . It is incomparably harder to act than it is to pass judgment later on.[39]

On 26 June, the 3rd Battalion of *"Germania,"* which was the regiment's *SPW* battalion, was positioned in the woods north of Maciejow. The elements of the tank regiment's 2nd Battalion that had already arrived were quartered in the woods south of Tupaly. Elements of the 2nd Battalion that had been held back in Sokol were only able to be loaded after the regimental commander

39. Author's Note: *Ausgewählte Werke Feldherr und Historiker,* Verlag von Rainer Hobbing, Berlin, 1925.

appealed directly to the field army. The remaining elements arrived in Maciejow on 3 July. The 3rd Battalion of *"Germania"* was then released from attachment to *Kampfgruppe Mühlenkamp* and reattached in support of the *26. Infanterie-Division* on 6 July.

On 6 July, the 2nd Battalion was positioned south of the Maciejow — Kowel rail line to the south and southeast of Stare-Koszary. It was the ready reserve. The Red Air Force bombed the southern portion of the staging area during the afternoon. At the same time, the 8th Company reported concentrations of Soviet infantry in the Dolhonosy area, which were then shelled by German artillery. At 1445 hours, 17 Soviet tanks and infantry attacked Nowe-Koszary; the force was turned back.

The enemy attacks that followed featured ever-changing main efforts, which required rapid reactions, reorganization and movement on the part of the companies of the 2nd Battalion.

Late in the afternoon, the *LVI. Panzer-Korps* ordered the immediate movement of the battalion into the Smidyn area, northwest of Maciejow. A few hours later, the companies were positioned in the woods to the southwest of the village.

The following night, the Soviets penetrated the main line of resistance at Krühel and attacked in the direction of Krasnoduby. The enemy's artillery fires increased in intensity all along the front. The 5th and 6th Companies ejected the enemy from Hill 197.2, approximately 2 kilometers north of Krühel, in the course of an immediate counterattack.

During the night of 7–8 July, the front was straightened out—it was jutting, like a wedge, to the east in the direction of Kowel—by pulling back to a general line running Smidyn-Krühel, east of Maciejow. The enemy, who was pressing his attacks in that sector, was pushed back by the tank companies, which were then positioned at Hills 206 and 220 to screen.

During the course of the flawlessly executed withdrawal movements, the 7th Company was ordered to the Smidyn Bridgehead and attached to the 3rd Battalion of the *"Germania"* Regiment. While most of the battalion quartered in the eastern part of Maciejow during the night of 8–9 July, the regiment moved its command post to Bilicze on the northern outskirts of Maciejow.

Even though the Soviet attacks along the entire front were increasing in intensity and numbers, no one was expecting the major attack that developed, which sought as its objective the taking of a bridgehead over the Bug, 15 kilometers west of Luboml, by advancing through Maciejow and Luboml with strong armored forces. The attack, which was characterized by an almost lavish commitment of materiel, tanks, aircraft and artillery in its preparation and execution, did not achieve the desired results. In coordination with the infantry elements in position, the 2nd Battalion of the regiment defeated superior numbers of enemy tank forces and decided the engagement at Maciejow in its favor during the two days that followed by selecting good defensive positions, cold-bloodedly waiting for the right moment to fire and demonstrating a critical amount of steadfastness

A participant in the fighting, *SS-Obersturmführer* Lichte, has provided a firsthand account, starting with the initial withdrawal to Maciejow:

> The enemy did not notice the withdrawal movements—at least, that's what we thought—and everything proceeded without incident during the cover of the night. At first light, the battalion staff set up operations with its three tanks and the communications section in a farmstead on the east side of Maciejow.
>
> To celebrate the successful action—it was a brilliant Sunday morning—the adjutant and the liaison officer decided to do some general personal hygiene after living in the woods without suitable sanitary facilities. A former Soviet soldier, whom we picked up somewhere and had incorporated into the ranks of the communications section, got a few buckets of water. "Ivan"—that's what everyone called him—was a jack-of-all-trades. He was an excellent cook; he was coldblooded and resourceful in finding breaks in the wires; and, when things turned hot, he always grabbed a rifle so as not to have to trade sides once again.
>
> The twin pillars of the headquarters first turned to their beards. The ritual was disturbed in a most unfriendly way by a low-level air attack that was delivered with an intensity hitherto unknown. After the roof of the house caught fire, the adjutant and the liaison officer, clothed only in swimming trunks, excused themselves to a tank dugout outside of the house door, pulling along a field telephone. After cranking it a bit, both of them determined that the wires to the companies had been cut. Since strong artillery fire had commenced in the meantime, it was clear what the culprit was. Ivan, our friend and *Hiwi,*[40] jumped out into the heavy fire to find the break.
>
> All of a sudden, the two warriors in their swimming trunks heard the sound of engines. The unforgettable liaison officer, *Untersturmführer* Jensen, who hailed from Holstein and was well known for his non-flappable nature, asked the adjutant: "What kind of idiot is driving around in this type of artillery fire?"

40. Translator's Note: *Hilfsfreiwilliger* = Volunteer. These were former Soviet soldiers who either defected to the Germans or decided to cast their lot with the German Army after being captured. The Army grew to rely on them to a great deal in the course of the war, even incorporating personnel allocations for them in tables of organization and equipment.

They lifted their noses over the edge of the dugout and saw three full-fledged T-34's only 50 meters away. The tank commanders were standing in their cupolas and observing. Thank god, it was in the wrong direction. The adjutant and the liaison officer jumped into a nearby well camouflaged *Panther* in their non-regulation uniforms and knocked out two T-34's. The [battalion] commander took on the third one at just that moment. At that short of a distance, all of the Ivans literally flew into the air.

It goes without saying that all of the companies launched[an immediate] counterattackwithoutwaitingfororders.Theengagement that developed under the leadership of the battalion commander, *Hauptsturmführer* Reichert, proved to be a high point in the history of the *Panther* battalion. First off, the T-34's that were romping around in the firing positions of the artillery were nailed. Then our own front lines were reached. The reverse-slope position that we occupied was so ideal that tactics instructors at Wünsdorf could not have invented a better one. Despite that, the enemy assaulted for two days with continuously new waves of tanks and lost a total of 99 T-34's and T-43's, without one *Panther* being a total write-off.

Whatever caused the commander on the opposite side to run into the same trap again and again and lose nearly all of his regiment in the process will always remain incomprehensible to someone who understands something about tanking.

In a summery of the fighting from 6–10 July in the area between Kowel and Maciejow, the Armed Forces Daily Report of 11 July announced:

In the area around Kowel, forces of the Army and the *Waffen-SS* have turned back the assault of 10 rifle divisions, a tank corps and two tank brigades in four days of hard defensive fighting. In the process, they inflicted considerable losses in men and materiel. During the fighting, 295 enemy armored vehicles were destroyed at the front and in the rear area by the combined effects of all weapons.

The *342. Infanterie-Division*, from the Rhine and Mosel area and under the command of *Generalmajor* Nickel, the *26. Infanterie-Division*, from the Rhine and Westphalia area and under the [acting] command of *Oberst* Frommberger, and a battle group from the *5. SS-Panzer-Division Wiking*, under the command of *SS-Standartenführer* Mühlenkamp, distinguished themselves through their exemplary bravery.

✠

The defeat of those attack groups meant the continued blocking of the important crossings over the Bug and the approaches to Brest Litowsk from the south. It thus brought about decisive relief along the southern flank of *Heeresgruppe Mitte,* which was in a desperate struggle and already in a state of dissolution in some places.

External recognition came in the form of the award of the Oakleaves to the Knight's Cross to the Iron Cross to the regimental commander, *SS-Standartenführer* Mühlenkamp, and the Knight's Cross to *SS-Oberscharführer* Fred Großrock, a platoon leader in the 6th Company. Großrock's platoon had destroyed 26 enemy tanks in the fighting.

The enemy continued his attacks, which were supported by armor and aircraft, on both sides of the railway line on the two days that followed. The 2nd Battalion, which was relieved east of Maciejow during the night of 11–12 July by *Sturmgeschütz-Brigade 600,* succeeded in knocking out an addition 18 enemy tanks in the course of immediate counterattacks between Scaino, Krühel and Krasnoduby and in restoring the situation. That was the last round of fighting on the part of the battalion west of Kowel.

At 2145 hours on 12 July, the regimental headquarters and the 2nd Battalion conducted a deliberate withdrawal to the west. They marched through Ruda, 5 kilometers west of Maciejow, and then to Borki, located east of Luboml. The 2nd Battalion was immediately loaded on trains there, while the battle staff of the regiment motor marched to Cholm. After reporting to the operations officer of the division there around 2245 hours, the battle staff then continued in the direction of Brest Litowsk, which was reached at 0700 hours on 14 July after spending a short night on the Wladwa-Brest road.

✠

The unexpected withdrawal of the regiment from the area of operations around Kowel and its shifting to the Brest Litowsk area stood in conjunction with the increasingly rapid state of catastrophe engulfing *Heeresgruppe Mitte.*

The Soviet offensive had started on 22 June. Ten days later,

> approximately 25 divisions had been eliminated or encircled; only a few of the divisions on the southern wing were still intact. Those that had escaped were barely capable of fighting . . .
>
> On 4 July, *Heeresgruppe Mitte* reported it was facing 126 rifle divisions, 17 motorized brigades, 6 cavalry divisions and 45 tank formations of brigade size along 350 kilometers of front, to which it could only counter with eight formations of division strength . . .

> On 12 July there were indicators in the sector of the *2. Armee* of Russian intentions of breaking through in the direction of Bialystok and Brest-Litowsk.[41]

The tank regiment, as well as the entire division, which was also marching into the area, was inserted into that turbulent situation after *Feldmarschall* Model, the commander of *Heeresgruppe Ukraine,* was also given simultaneous command of *Heeresgruppe Mitte* on 28 June, following the relief of the previous commander, *Feldmarschall* Busch.

At that point, the regiment was reunited with its 1st Battalion. The battalion, which had been undergoing reconstitution from April to June, was initially in Cholm and then at a training area in Dubica before returning to the Eastern Front.

RECONSTITUTION OF THE *I./SS-PANZER-REGIMENT 5* FROM APRIL TO JUNE 1944

The battlefield reconstitution of the 1st Battalion was initially conducted in Cholm under some pressure, but it was hampered by the bottlenecks that increasingly occurred in the fifth year of the war in all areas, not least of all in the training status of the replacement personnel and the quality of the equally necessary, as well as important, noncommissioned officer corps.

At the beginning of April, the training company that *SS-Obersturmführer* Mittelbacher led, was split up into the various line companies to start hands-on training. By then, 22 tanks had arrived from the Army Materiel Command in Magedeburg-Königsborn. The Headquarters Company received two tanks for training purposes, while the four line companies received five each. Other vehicles and signals equipment also arrived during the first few days of April, brought by details headed by *SS-Untersturmführer* Hohenester and *SS-Oberscharführer* Bollermann.

The increasing partisan activity made it clear that this was no peacetime training. Instead, it was training being conducted in an occupied country that could become the front lines the following morning. For instance, a *Kampfgruppe* under the command of *SS-Untersturmführer* Schumacher had to be committed on 5 April to combat a group of about 100 partisans that had appeared barely 3 kilometers northwest of Cholm.

Four members of the battalion fell victim to the increasing uncertainty on the roads on 14 April: *SS-Obersturmführer* Paschke, *SS-Obersturmführer* Müller,

41. Author's Note: von Tippelskirch, 467.

SS-Rottenführer Waldenburg and *SS-Rottenführer* Palei. Paschke was on his way back to the battalion from Berlin. The four men executed by the bandits were buried in Cholm on 16 April.

The unique atmosphere in Cholm—shifting between war and peace—was made all the clearer by many an event such as the sending of officer candidates to the homeland, theater and movie presentations in both Cholm and Lublin, concerts by the regimental band for the wounded at the military hospital and musical presentations at the movie theater.

On 20 April, the entire regiment felt gratified to learn that the Diamonds to the Knight's Cross, Oak Leaves and Swords to the Iron Cross had been awarded to Gille by the Supreme Commander in Chief. At the same time, the regimental commander, Mühlenkamp, was promoted to *SS-Standartenführer.*

On 2 May, the headquarters positions of the battalion were all filled. *SS-Obersturmführer* Wolf again assumed the mantle of battalion adjutant after returning from convalescent leave. *SS-Obersturmführer* Mittelbacher became the battalion's liaison officer.

Recognition of the accomplishments of the battalion during the difficult winter fighting was to be found in the award of the Knight's Cross to the commanders of the 2nd and 3rd Companies, *SS-Obersturmführer* Hein and *SS-Obersturmführer* Schumacher. In addition, the German Cross in Gold was awarded to *SS-Sturmbannführer* Schneider, who had been the commander of the 1st Company and had also been badly wounded in the meantime. On 19 May, the battalion changed command. *SS-Hauptsturmführer* Säumenicht assumed command from *SS-Sturmbannführer* Kümmel, who was reassigned to the divisional reconnaissance battalion. Säumenicht came from the *3. SS-Panzer-Division "Totenkopf,"* where he had been a tank company commander and recipient of the Knight's Cross.

✠

A plethora of personnel and organizational problems had to be solved in addition to the issues of training and combat readiness. In an after-action report dated 2 May, the commander of the 1st Company, *SS-Obersturmführer* Brand stated "that the majority of the noncommissioned officers still had to trained in order to be fully qualified instructors." He is clearly addressing the dilemma that by nature surfaces in a war lasting several years:

> Training suffers by the fact that the majority of the noncommissioned officers of the company are not, at the same time, fully qualified instructors themselves, since they have all been justifiably promoted more or less on the basis of their service in the field. Despite that,

> they have to become fully qualified instructors, since they are noncommissioned officers."

The 1st Company as a whole had only 5 tanks, 40 rifles, an equal number of bayonets, 21 submachine guns and 66 pistols at its disposal at the time. For fieldwork, it had 10 pick axes and 10 shovels. In Brand's same report, he complained about a lack of footgear, as well as deficient footgear. There were no shelter halves at all available.

SS-Obersturmführer Hein wrote the following concerning the training status of the 2nd Company on 21 May:

> The trench strength of the 2nd Company consists of 3 officers, 19 noncommissioned officers and 35 enlisted personnel compared to an authorized strength of 3 officers, 44 noncommissioned officers and 79 enlisted personnel.
>
> The training and the appearance, as well as the mental capabilities, of the newly assigned men are, with few exceptions, far below average.

Knowing this is necessary for forming a considered opinion of the performance of the forces during differing phases of the war. On the other hand, it was by no means the sign of beginning resignation. In the same report, Hein concludes:

> Despite all that, the over-all impression of the company is that it has what is needed for a reconstitution, especially since there is a pronounced desire to participate in upcoming operations and a general desire to perform duty.

After stressing that appropriate classes needed to be held for all of the duty positions of a tank crew—commander, gunner, loader, radio operator and driver—Hein continues in conclusion:

> Even though no substantive difficulties have surfaced after the issuance of weapons and equipment, as well as training manuals, the lack of knowledge of all ranks—especially regarding those documents—makes itself unfavorably manifest again and again as a prerequisite for tank training. In that regard, the accusation has to be leveled against the replacement detachments that they have not concerned themselves sufficiently with infantry basic training and the handling of weapons and equipment.

The debilitating effect of a war lasting for several years in the personnel, training and production areas becomes visible in these reports. The reality of a fifth year of war was an increased demand for performance while, at the same time, getting decreasing quantities of materiel assistance and an increasing diminution of the training of the replacement personnel.

However, the core of the forces in the field had not softened. It attempted to negate those difficulties by means of intensive training and the comradely integration of the "new ones." Inner drive and a fully grounded sense of military obligation—even in the face of military setbacks—could be transmitted with success.

On 4 June, the 1st Battalion received orders to move to the training area at Debica in Croatia and intensify its training there. The last of the seven transport trains arrived on 10 June. The battalion set up operations in Ring IV of the camp.

After 20 days that were set aside to establish combat preparedness, the battalion was sent by rail in four trains to the Sokol area on 1 and 2 July. It finally linked up with the division, which was the operational reserve of the *4. Panzer-Armee* at the time. The billeting areas of Torki, Pusow and Kniaze were selected because they allowed the battalion to act quickly to hold open the Tartarow-Stojanow road.

From two reports submitted on 3 and 5 July by the battalion commander, *SS-Hauptsturmführer* Säumenicht, it could be seen that:

> Despite the short duration, the rotation of the battalion to the [training area near Debica] led to a rapid increase in the training status of the battalion, especially in the area of individual and crew training, because of the favorable conditions there. Squad training can be considered as completed with the departure from the training area and the movement to the Torki area.

With regard to uniforms, the battalion was not only completely outfitted, it also had the prescribed reserves of 10 percent. The ammunition lift capacity of the trucks of the ammunition section of the battalion was 6 tons. That was only sufficient to transport 25 percent of the basic load of ammunition prescribed for the 22 *Panzer IV's* and 21 assault guns on hand. There were also only 6 tons of lift capacity for fuel as well. In order to transport a single "consumable load,"[42] which was enough fuel for the battalion to move 100 kilometers, a lift capacity of 11.2 tons was needed. The additional trucks needed had been requested but they were not expected to arrive any time soon.

There were still some bottlenecks with personnel as well. A battalion signals noncommissioned officer, talented in organizational matters, was missing, as were medium-wave radio sets and tank radio sets. An example of how sensitive a mechanized formation was in its combat readiness and quickly ordinary things seemed to come apart may be demonstrated perhaps by the following excerpt from one of Säumenicht's reports: "Sources of electricity and batteries are available in sufficient numbers, but there is no acid for putting new batteries into service."

In his summary, the commander stated:

> Furthermore, an additional period of approximately four weeks is considered necessary to bring the replacements, who are arriving in waves in the units, to a uniform level of training and allow them to assimilate into the spirit of the battalion.

The development of the situation did not allow those four weeks.

According to orders received on 4 July, the battalion was divided into a battle group, which had to be ready to be committed, and a training group. The *Kampfgruppe* was formed from the 3rd and 4th Companies and the headquarters Company and was commanded by *SS-Obersturmführer* Senghas. Of the 22 *Panzer IV's* available, the 3rd Company took 20, with two of them being converted to command tanks. The 4th Company took the 21 available assault guns. Both companies were deemed combat ready.

The 1st and 2nd Companies were sent back to the Debica training area under the command of *SS-Obersturmführer* Hein. Lacking any and all training materials, agreements were struck with the division's antitank battalion, which was also there at the time, and an assault-gun replacement detachment to take part in instructional demonstrations and exercises. At the same time that the two training companies and the regimental music were sent back to Croatia, *SS-Hauptscharführer* Krause established a collection point that gathered up materiel, equipment and uniform articles that were not urgently needed at the front. Thanks to his efforts, the battalion gained a little more lift capacity in the form of additional trucks.

Using all means of improvisation available to it, a combat-ready formation came into existence. It was loaded by rail on 10 July at Krystinopol and

42. Translator's Note: *Verbrauchssatz*. This was usually abbreviated as *VS*. 1 *VS* was the equivalent of 17.2 tons or 17,200 liters of fuel.

Sokol and detrained the next day at Luboml. The 1st Battalion then motor-marched to the patch of woods 3 kilometers southeast of Nowosiolki, about 6 kilometers south-southwest of Maciejow. Its orders read that it was to conduct terrain and route reconnaissance for operations to the east, specifically in a sector about 15 kilometers wide between Dolsk, to the southeast, and Paryduby, to the northeast of Nowosiolki. Those efforts never came to pass.

When it had arrived in the Maciejow area, the 1st Battalion was placed back under the command of its parent regiment. As has already been described, the regimental headquarters and the 2nd Battalion had been pulled out of the line in the Kowel area during the night of 12–13 July and brought back to Luboml, where it was then loaded on trains. The 1st Battalion was directed at about 1500 hours on 13 July to return to Luboml, where it was to follow the regiment on 15 July in four rail movements. The 1st Battalion was to detrain at Haynowka, a village about half way between Brest Litowsk and Bialystok, according to the rail transport officer, *SS-Obersturmführer* Niemann.

The battalion battle staff, which motor marched to the new area, arrived there around 0700 hours on 16 July. It was briefed on the situation by the regiment at its command post in Zbucz, about 10 kilometers west of Haynowka. The confusing situation and the turbulent course of events had already overridden the original orders for the 1st Battalion that had been issued on 13 July.

The never-ending task of repairing field telephone communications—a tedious, highly dangerous and most essential job. Close by is a *SdKfz. 250/3* command half-track and, in the background, two *Panzer V Panthers.*

A *Sdkfz. 165 "Hummel"* (Bumble Bee) self-propelled 15-cm howitzer on the *Panzer III/IV* chassis.

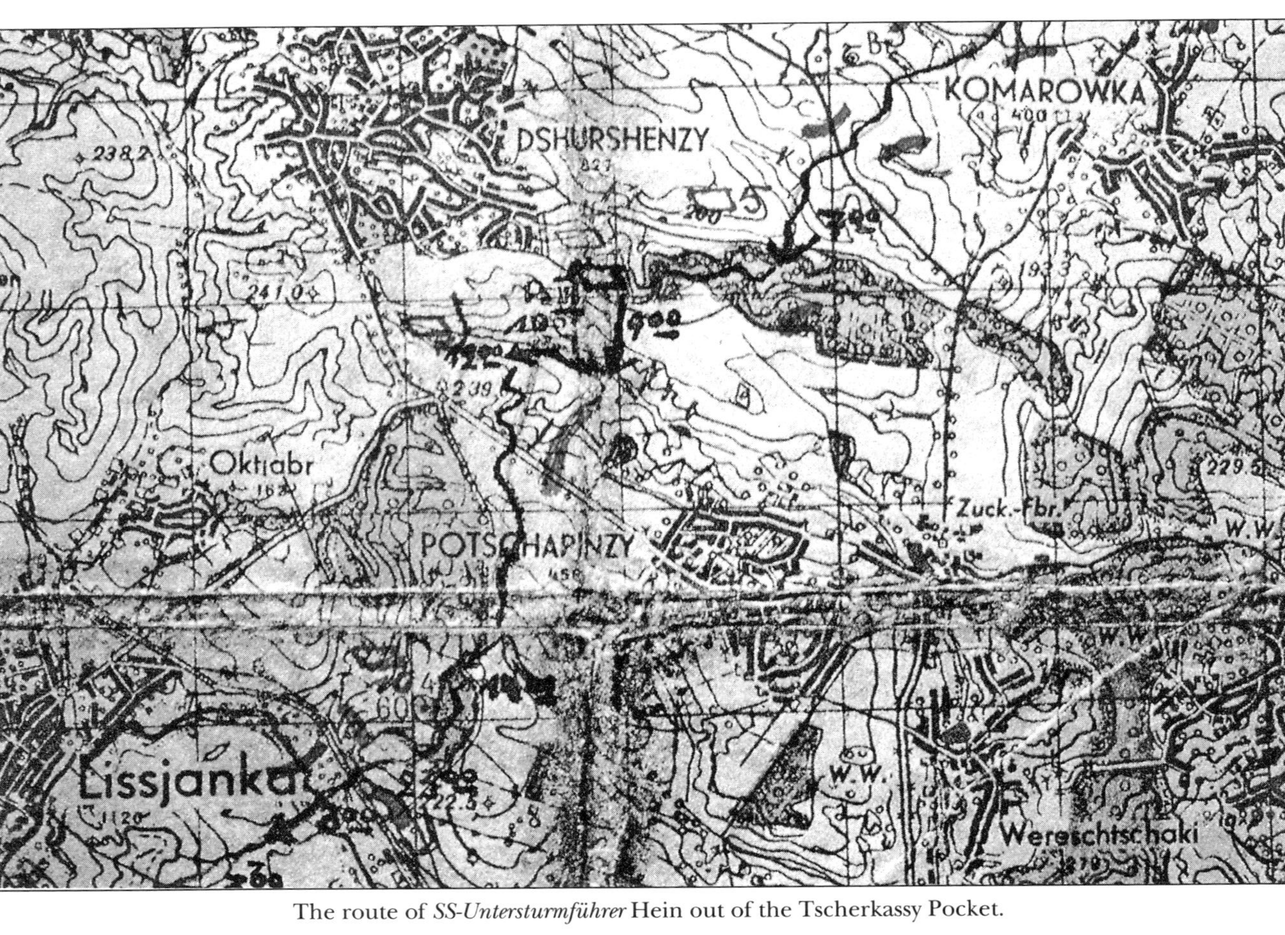

The route of *SS-Untersturmführer* Hein out of the Tscherkassy Pocket.

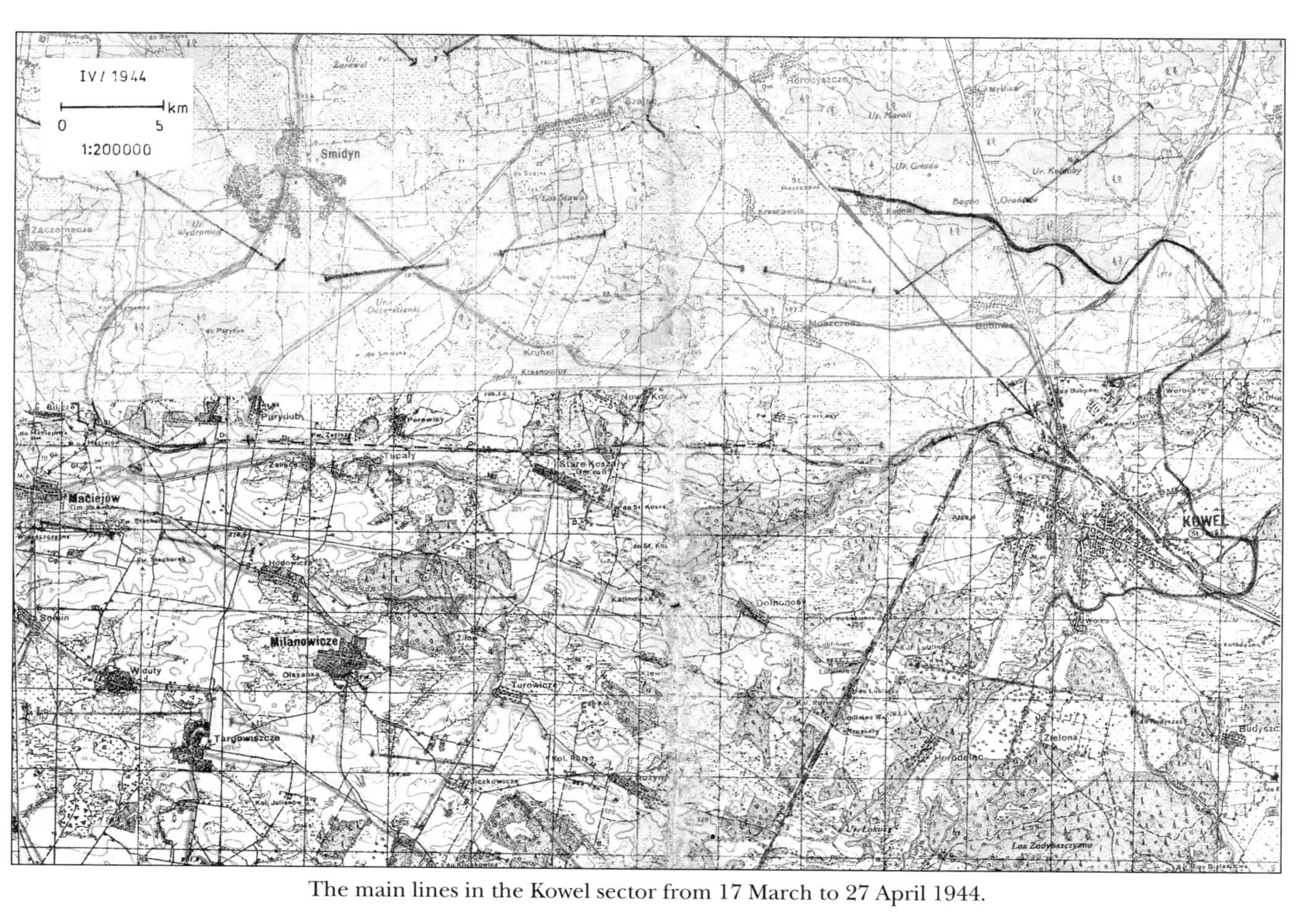

The main lines in the Kowel sector from 17 March to 27 April 1944.

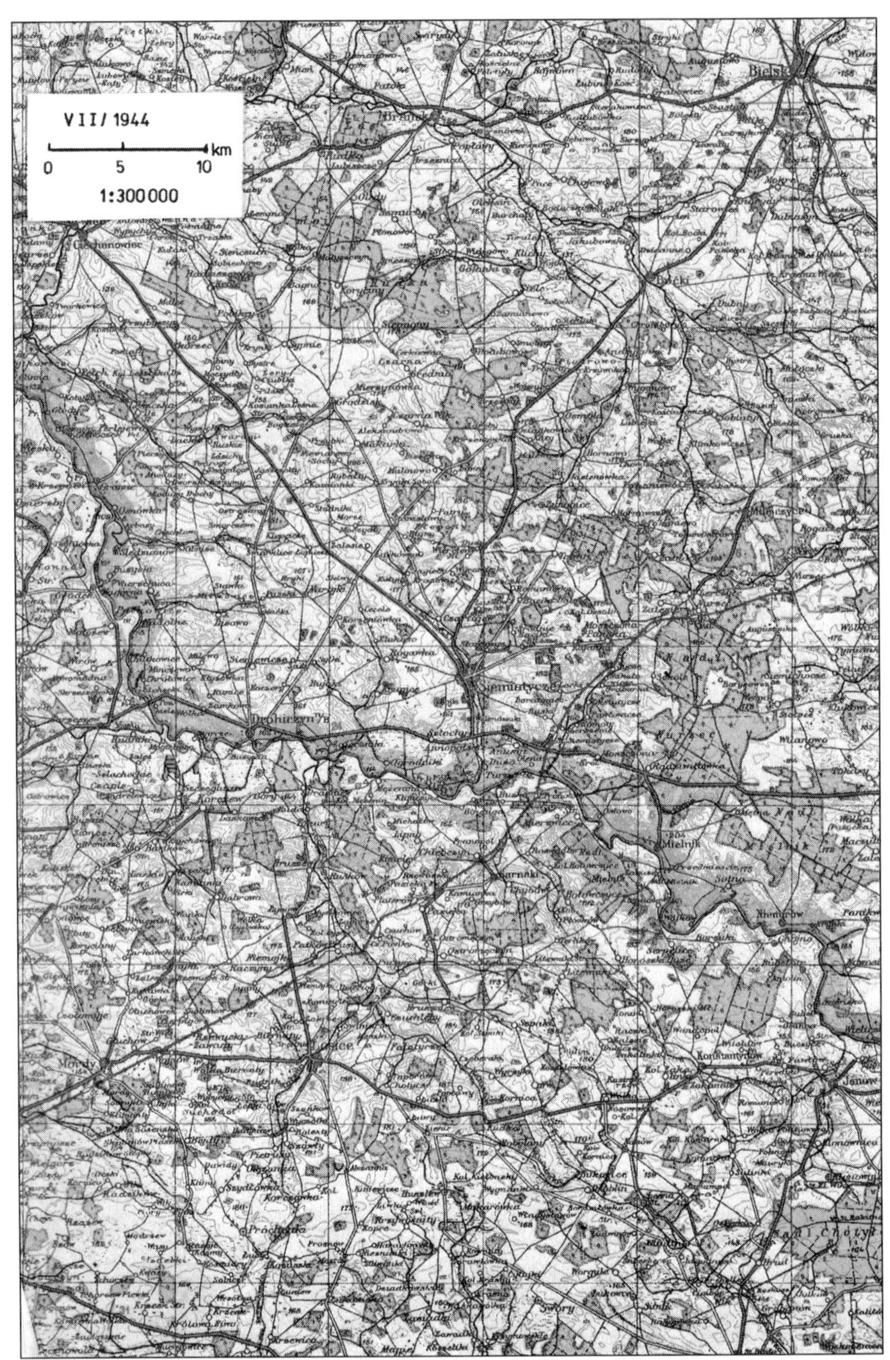

The Kaminiec Litewski–Cheremcha sector.

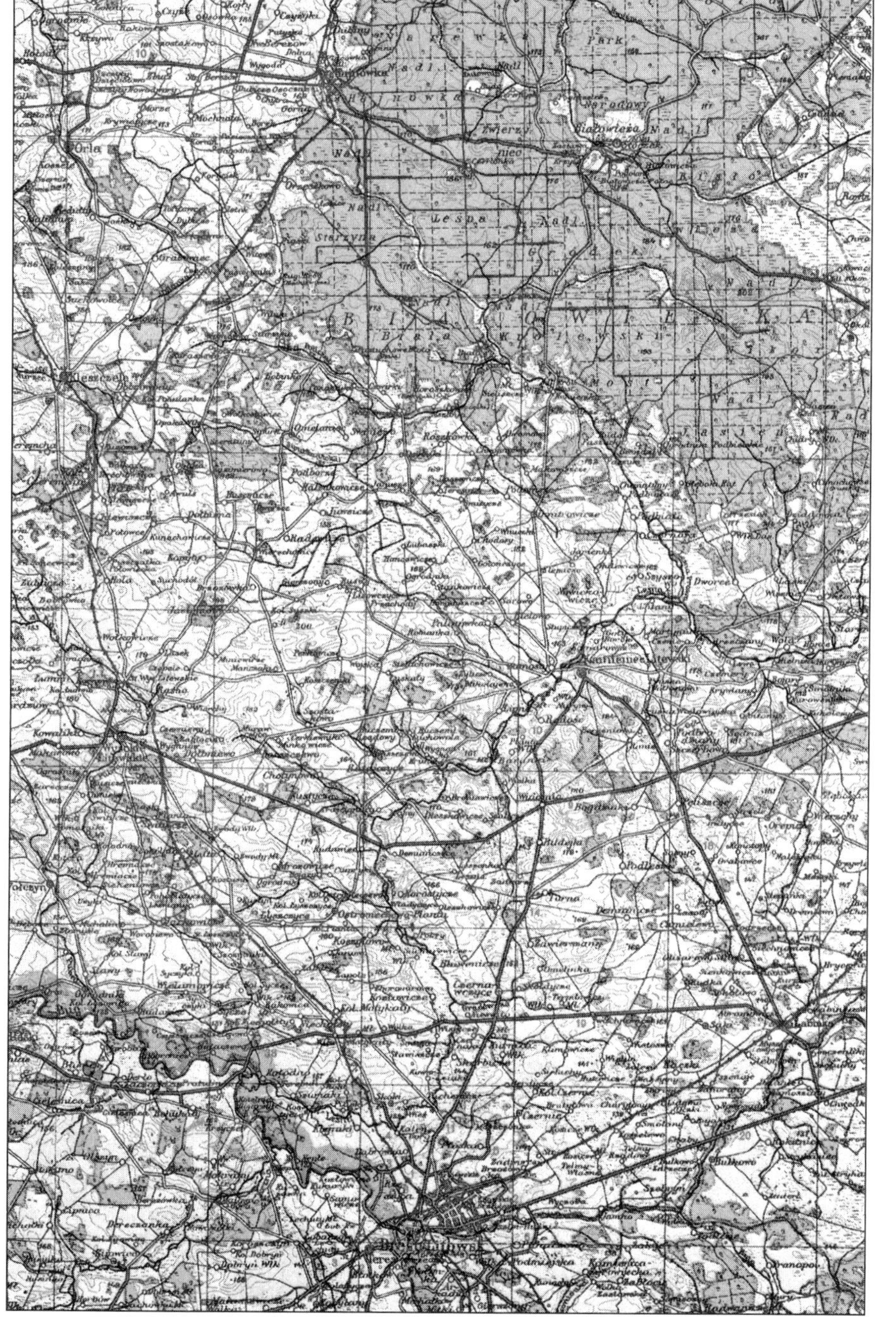

Panthers of the 5th Company prepare to advance.

Another view of *Panther* 534 accompanied by *Panzergrenadiere.*

Outside of Kowel on 3 April 1944: *SS-Sturmbannführer* Päetsch supervises the final preparations for the upcoming attack. The *Panzer* appears to be a *Panther Ausf. D* converted to a command vehicle due to the mounting of a star antenna.

5 April 1944, Kowel: Tanks of the 6th Company and the reconnaissance platoon entered the northern portion of the town.

March 1944: *SS-Untersturmführer* Renz with his reconnaissance platoon awaiting rail transport to Cholm-Kowel.

Tanks of the 5th Company in Kowel.

CHAPTER 6

Between Brest Litowsk and Warsaw

The situation, in which the armored group of the *5. SS-Panzer-Division "Wiking"* was about to be inserted to the north of Brest Litowsk and along the southern wing of *Heeresgruppe Mitte* needs to be outlined for the reader.

Ever since 22 June 1944, the front lines of *Heeresgruppe Mitte* had withdrawn some 400 kilometers west of its initial positions under the pressure of a vastly superior enemy force. The left wing and the center sector of the field-army group appeared to be dissolving as a result of deep breakthroughs, the encirclement of large formations and the continued strong enemy pressure. The situation was able to be stabilized temporarily when reinforcements were introduced and the elements lined up along the Njemen on both sides of Grodno.

Along the southern wing of *Heeresgruppe Mitte*, the *2. Armee* was still offering resistance along a cohesive front. But it was also pulling back to the west under the pressure exerted by the enemy. The losses in equipment and weapons were considerable, which the three weeks of retreating—averaging 20 kilometers a day—had caused. In some cases, companies had only one machine gun. Heavy weapons, especially tanks and antitank guns, had been lost or destroyed, for the most part. For instance, the *12. Panzer-Division* had only one operational tank on 20 July, even though it had a total of 53 crews available.[1]

✠

The ability to offer resistance and the fighting morale varied within the *2. Armee*. In some cases, the divisions were effectively destroyed; in other cases, the continued to fight even under the most difficult of conditions. In individual cases, the combat morale was forced by draconian measures. Commanders and officers of all ranks, including division commanders, were relieved. Most of them continued to fight under harsh deprivation and the hardest of conditions, carrying along the weak ones as well. *General*

1. Author's Note: All of the quotes in this section are from the daily logs and their annexes for the *2. Armee*, except where specifically identified differently.

der Kavallerie Harteneck, the commanding general of the *I. Kavallerie-Korps* reported to the commander in chief of the *2. Armee*:

> *129. Infanterie-Division* too tired. The men do not even hear impacting artillery any more. Weapons are not in order, since no cleaning materials are on hand. They no longer hold; instead, they run away.

The following day, the front collapsed in that division's sector. On 13 July, the field army reported to the field-army group: "The *129. Infanterie-Division* simply does not want to fight any more."

The chief of staff of the *LV. Armee-Korps, Oberst i.G.* Hölz, declared on 14 July: "I no longer see the possibility of conducting deliberate resistance." The corps commanding general, *General der Infanterie* Herrlein, recommend that same day: " . . . to no longer offer a delaying action. Instead, transition to a deliberate retreat."

On 19 July, the *XXIII. Armee-Korps* reported:

> There are forces in the field that have not seen a field mess for the last 6-10 days. A large portion of the men are barefoot. It is not uncommon for the men to only get two hours of sleep a day.

In some cases, the discipline in the rear areas was poor. It caused *Feldmarschall* Model to remind the senior commanders:

> Keep an eye on the tanks and the heavy antitank guns so that they do not screw around in the rear. He cited the example of Grodno, where he had been fired at by a Russian tank and, while moving through Grodno, found five heavy antitank guns, which no one employed, and everyone was fleeing from the one tank in a panic. That same day, he saw five *Tigers*, which were headed to the southwest to the rear, with supposed light battle damage.

✠

The question of command authority was the object of almost daily conflicts between those responsible at the different levels of command. It was becoming apparent that the movement rearward, which was increasingly picking up speed, was not being forced solely by the enemy:

> The decision of *General* Weidling, to pull back with his southern front, is the product of a rumor. Supposedly, the intelligence officer of the

> *12. Panzer-Division* reported to the commander of the *50. Infanterie-Division, General* von Pfuhlstein, that the *12. Panzer-Division* had been broken through and was running away.

Generalmajor von Treskow,[2] the chief of staff of the *2. Armee*, claimed that bad connections on the telephone lines caused miscommunications between him and the chief of staff of the *LV. Armee-Korps*, as well as with *General der Kavallerie* Harteneck. As a result, withdrawal movements were initiated on 18 and 19 July within the *LV. Armee-Korps*, which were not needed to the extent conducted and which also affected the friendly forces on both flanks. Because their flanks were then exposed, they also had to pull back.

Feldmarschall Model, who seemed to be everywhere at once and was firmly determined to get the situation under control, ordered the forces under his command to defend. Every withdrawal was to be reported the day prior to its execution along with the new line that was intended to be occupied. The movement was then dependant on permission being granted from the field army or the field army group.

In no uncertain terms, he laid out his requirements to the commander in chief of the *2. Armee, Generaloberst* Weiß, on 12 July: "I want to make it abundantly clear that you have no discretion at all." On another occasion, he made his intent very clear:

> The standpoint of the field army—to want to conduct the fight as a delaying action—is completely absurd. We are currently in a crisis situation that has to be mastered with all means possible. The conduct of the fighting must be geared towards causing the Russians as much damage as possible.

That same day, a few hours later, *Generalmajor* von Treskow, informed the chief of staff of the field army group, *Generalleutnant* Krebs: "The Russians cannot be held with these forces. Orders for a delaying action must be issued." Krebs responded: "When ordered to defend, 30 kilometers were covered. What's going to happen when we order a delaying action . . . You must have your orders conform to those of the Field Marshal!"

On 14 July, von Treskow attempted to force his opinion once again. He pointed out the superiority of the enemy forces, which were positioned in

---

2. Translator's Note: More commonly spelled as Tresckow. He was a leading member of the conspiracy to kill Hitler, a fact never touched upon by the author, perhaps because he assumes the average German reader would immediately make the connection, especially since there are insinuations of treachery in his handling of operations in the sector of the *2. Armee*.

front of the *2. Armee* with four field armies: "The condition of our own forces is bad. Even the condition of *Wiking* is limited."

At 1450 hours that same day, a few hours after the commander of the *5. SS-Panzer-Division "Wiking"* appeared at the field army headquarters in Bielsk, von Treskow held out no signs of hope:

> If you believe that we can hold here against the enemy onslaught with our forces then you are mistaken. No attack can be considered at all without incurring the danger that the forces in the field will be destroyed.

Once again, that evening, von Treskow once again attempted to win back some freedom of action for his field army during a joint conversation with the chief of staff of the field army group (Krebs) and the commander in chief of the *2. Armee* (Weiß). He pointed out the negative effect on the sanctity of orders in light of the current way orders were being issued and the dwindling trust of the forces in the field in their command. He repeated that the orders to defend would not be followed by most. In addition, the few valuable leaders and formations left would be destroyed. Krebs replied:

> At present it is imperative to unconditionally delay the advance of the Russians. New divisions are being brought up and, as a consequence, a defense will be possible . . . The Field Marshal is of the opinion that insufficient time will be won if the field army is given freedom of action. Moreover, even if granted, it would lead to a destruction of our own forces . . .

Once again, Krebs formulated the mission given by the Field Marshal:

> Resistance is to be conducted in such a manner that the forces are positioned in the line that has been ordered for the day. But further destroying [of forces] and encirclements are to be avoided. The field army is to report daily where it will offer resistance the following day.

The command-and-control difficulties were intensified by two additional factors: Issues with allied forces and logistical bottlenecks at the front. All the commanders at the front rejected the use of the Imperial Hungarian II Corps

(Reserve). The chief of staff of the *XXIII. Armee-Korps, Oberstleutnant* Reimpel, even requested the *2. Armee* remove the Hungarians on 14 July:

> The corps request that the Hungarian cavalry division be removed. The Hungarians are available for your use. Better no help than Hungarians. Whenever Hungarians are at the front, they draw the Russians like a magnet. If there's nothing there, then the enemy doesn't dare enter a gap.

The commanding general of the *XXIII. Armee-Korps, General der Pioniere* Tiemann, requested: "The Hungarians have blown up a bridge. Request they be removed from the area of combat operations as soon as possible."

On 19 July, *Generalmajor* von Treskow reported to the field-army group: "The Hungarians have cracked, even though some of them are good."

The chief of staff of the *XX. Armee-Korps, Oberst i.G.* Wagner, reported on 21 July:

> Giant goat screw in the neighboring sector. Russians have broken through in the sectors of the Hungarian divisions. Lead enemy elements at Stradecz, 7 kilometers south of the fortress belt [Brest Litowsk].

✠

The logistics difficulties at the front appear to have less to do with the availability of ammunition and fuel products as in the organization of their delivery. *General der Kavallerie* Harteneck reported to the field army on 20 July: "Ammunition situation is poor. We only have ammunition until noon."

The senior quartermaster for the *2. Armee* determined: "Telephoned the entire night. An ammunition train was misdirected by the movement office.[3] That is the reason."

On 21 July, he reported: "Fuel train still hasn't arrived. Have taken every last drop out of my depots. Completely sold out . . . " In his daily report, the following is to be read: "If the misdirections continue, all supply efforts are endangered."

Von Treskow noted the following for his discussion with Krebs on 12 July: "Fuel train at Baranowitsche taken away."

---

3. Author's Note: The military transportation office reported to *General der Infanterie* Gercke, who later had all of his daily logs burned. (*"Europäische Wehrkunde"*, Issue 12, Volume 29, Munich, December 1980)

On 14 July, Wagener complained: "All is not in order within the transportation command."

The deputy chief of staff for operations for the *2. Armee*: "At present, there are major difficulties with the transportation offices."

A few days previously, the commander in chief of the *2. Armee* stated: "In addition, there have been assorted glitches in railway deliveries."

It appeared that the transportation command also had difficulties of its own in coordinating measures and countermeasures to be taken in the rear area, for example in the area of demolitions. On the morning of 20 July, von Treskow briefed Weiß: "Demolitions are being conducted, in part by the transportation command." The commander in chief replied: "That was quick work. The bridge was still in order this morning; destroyed a short while later." When von Treskow reported the same thing to the chief of staff of the field army group: "That can't be true! Only the field-army group can release demolitions. The field army has to issue the demo order!"

The "disorganization" in an area that was of decisive importance for the execution of friendly movements is reflected in the following entry from the daily logs of the *2. Armee* for 22 July:

> The chief of staff of Harteneck's cavalry corps "reports that there was an engineer lieutenant at the corps headquarters who has the mission of preparing demolitions on man-made objects in the rear area and also of executing them. Thank God, he established contact with us so that we are able to prevent him from doing that for the time being."

The sector of the *2. Armee* was the designated area of operations for the *5. SS-Panzer-Division "Wiking."* On 14 July, the following orientation was sent to the division from the headquarters of the field army:

> TO: *5. SS-Panzer-Division Wiking*
> 1. *5. SS-Panzer-Division Wiking* is moved into the area of operations of the field army as the field-army group reserve.
> 2. Detraining and staging area of the division around Grodek; forward-most elements along the Swislocz.

> 3. Route for the motor march elements: Brest–Kaminiec Litewski–Bialowieza–Haynowka–Narew.
> 4. The division is to be prepared for operations to the east, northeast and southeast; conduct route reconnaissance and increase the load capacity of bridges for tanks.

The rail-loaded portion of the division took up 33 trains and was routed through Cholm-Lublin-Siedlce into the area of operations.

The motor march elements of the division, moving via Wlodawa, started to arrive into the area around Brest Litowsk by the evening of 14 July. The march discipline was very good, according to the daily report of the field army provost marshal in his daily report.

✠

At 1200 hours on the same day, the division commander reported to the headquarters of the *2. Armee* its main command post. His aide-de-camp, *SS-Untersturmführer* Lange, reported:

> Around 14 July 1944, the *5. SS-Panzer-Division Wiking*, arriving from different employment, was attached to the *2. Armee* (Sector roughly Brest Litowsk–Bialystok).
>
> As a result of the attachment, the division commander, Gille, reported to the command post of the headquarters of the *2. Armee* in the area west of Bialystok. I accompanied him.
>
> The chief of staff of the *2. Armee*, *Generalmajor* Henning von Treskow, was seen in his office. He was in the process of conducting a telephone conversation with *Heeresgruppe Mitte* and reported the capture of several localities by the enemy and the signs of dissolution and chaotic conditions among the friendly forces.
>
> While the telephone conversation was still ongoing, Gille interjected his own comments in that regard: "But, *Herr General*, that is not correct. There is no enemy there. My Vikings are marching there. We just flew over that area . . . "
>
> That was embarrassing to Treskow, and he quickly ended his telephone conversation.
>
> After briefing us for about five minutes, the chief of staff escorted my division commander to the commander in chief of the *2. Armee*, *Generaloberst* Walter Weiß.

✠

Generalleutnant Krebs informed von Treskow on the evening of 14 July about the intentions of the field-army group in using the division, which was still in bound:

> *Wiking* may not be employed piecemeal. *Wiking* must be held in reserve in case of breakthroughs. The orders of the field marshal are: Hold the Ros and, wherever there's been a penetration, hold a line about 10 kilometers behind it. It is intended to conduct counterattacks with "Totenkopf" and "Wiking;" "Totenkopf will be employed form the sector of the *4. Armee.*

Feldmarschall Model discussed the employment with the commander in chief of the *2. Armee*: "Employ the *Wiking* armored division intelligently; not in the woods. Preferably from the area around Harteneck."

At 1130 hors on 15 July, the division received the following information by telegraph from the headquarters of the *2. Armee*:

> First employment of the division most likely to destroy the enemy on the southern wing of *Gruppe Harteneck*. Establish contact with *Gruppe Harteneck* immediately in order to effect the necessary preparations.

By midday of 15 July, the command elements of the division and the regiments that had motor marched had arrived in the Bialystok area. A total of 558 vehicles had passed the route control point in Bielsk early that morning.

✠

The command post of the tank regiment was in Bialystok. The command post of the 2nd Battalion, with the Headquarters Company and the 5th and 6th Companies, which had already arrived with some of their elements, was in the woods 4 kilometers east of Bialystok.

While contact was established as directed east of Bialystok and the reconnaissance conducted, the division received a telephonic warning order at 1400 hours: "Tank division is to move forward immediately in the direction of Haynowka. Division commander immediately to the headquarters of the field army by *Storch*; trains are to be diverted accordingly."

In a telegraph message at 2050 hours, the new mission was listed under paragraph 1:

> 1. *5. SS-Panzer-Division Wiking* assembles on both sides of Haynowka in such a manner that it prevents any advance by the enemy from the

> Pouszcza Bialowieza to the west, north or south by offensive blows in an eastern, southeastern or northeastern direction. As far as possible, it is the mission of the division to stop an advance of the enemy already in the forest by committing elements of forces forward.

✠

By early morning of 16 July, two-thirds of the motor march elements had arrived in the Haymowka area after a move of 50 kilometers. Seven trains had also arrived. By 1155 hours, the division operations officer, *SS-Obersturmbannführer* Schönfelder, was already receiving new movement instructions from the chief of staff of the *2. Armee*:

> Recon a displacement to Kaminiec Litewski so as to hit the enemy there, who is advancing on Brest . . . You have to attack as soon as possible across the Lesna to the east.

When Schönfelder informed von Treskow that the divisional artillery had still not arrived, von Treskow replied: "If [the enemy] advances to Brest there is extreme danger for the *XX.* and *XXII. Armee-Korps.* You have to attack."

Four hours later, Schönfelder received the orders to move:

> Move without delay with as large a battle group as possible into the Kaminiec Litewski bridgehead. Take as strong as possible forces across to the east bank so as to be able to attack to establish contact with the northwestern wing of the *XXIII. Armee-Korps.*

At 1715 hours, *SS-Gruppenführer* Gille rebuffed the demand of the field army to leave outposts in the area around Haynowka to face potential enemy forces coming from the direction of Bialowieza, thus dividing his forces:

> We are not a division; we are a battle group. Just one third are on hand. The blow that I plan to deliver also has to have impact. To that end, I need everything that I have available . . . Tanks and mechanized infantry are currently moving out. Marching on two roads.

Six hours later, the division reported the arrival of the first elements in Kaminiec Litewski. Within the space of a little more than 30 hours, it became the third staging area for the division and was more than 100 kilometers from the first one.

Effective 2000 hours, the division was removed from its status as field army group reserve and allocated directly to the headquarters of the *2. Armee.* It found itself in the sector of the *XXIII. Armee-Korps.* At the same time, the *3. SS-Panzer-Division "Totenkopf"* was allocated to the *4. Armee* in the Grodno area.

KAMINIEC LITEWSKI

The armored group of the division, *Kampfgruppe Mühlenkamp,* consisted of the tank regiment and the 3rd Battalion of the *"Germania"* Regiment, which was equipped with *SPW's.* On the morning of 17 July, the battle group command post was located on the fork in the road on the southeastern edge of Kaminiec Litewski, where the road headed for Peliszcze in one direction and Widomla in the other.

The battle group had 20 operational *Panthers.* Later that day, another 17 *Panthers* arrived, as well as elements of the 1st Battalion, consisting of the 3rd and 4th Companies. The 3rd Company road marched in from Czeremcha, and the 4th Company, which had been diverted to Wysocki Litarski, from Wysocki. The maintenance platoon of the 1st battalion was ready for operations in the Wysocki Palace grounds.

Kaminiec Litewski is on the east bank of the Lesna. At that point, it turns from a northeasterly and easterly course to bend to the southeast and then to the south, where it then empties into the Bug northwest of Brest Litowsk. To the north is the *Puczcza Bialowieza,* a wooded area of almost primeval scope that spreads north to south for a distance of 50 kilometers. From east to west, it is almost 40 kilometers wide. The woods are crossed by one north-south road and one east-west road. For major formations, the woods were practically impassable.

Along its western boundaries, starting around the area of Haynowka, there are numerous patches of differently-sized woods, like islands, flanking the Haynowka-Czeremcha-Siedlce rail line that make the transition between the vast expanse of woods and the open area that extends to the Bug, some 50 kilometers to the southwest. The woods continue on in the same vein to the south and southwest from the southwestern edge.

The enemy was in the process of breaking through the northwest wing of the *XXIII. Armee-Korps* along both sides of the major road leading from Pruzana from the northeast to the southwest through the southern expanse of woods. The headquarters of *Heeresgruppe Mitte* made the following observation in its daily report of 16 July:

> After the enemy succeeded yesterday in the course of the fighting to push back the inner wings of the *XXIII. Armee-Korps* and *Gruppe Harteneck* to the south and the north, he is advancing today through the gap that resulted with a mechanized corps, a cavalry corps and at least three rifle divisions in the deep northwest flank of the *XXIII. Armee-Korps* to the southwest in the direction of Brest.
>
> Based on the threatening development of the situation, *SS-Panzer-Division Wiking* had to be shifted to the area east of Kaminiec Litewski—even though it had not completely assembled in the Bielsk Podlaski—Haynowka area—so as to attack east at noon on 17 July to enable the left wing of the *XXIII. Armee-Korps* to fight its way back to the line of resistance designated for tomorrow.[4]

The commander of the armored group ordered the envisioned attack. At 1100 hours, the available companies of the 2nd Battalion, the 5th and 7th Companies, moved out along the Kaminiec Litewski—Peliczcze road, along with the 3rd Battalion of *"Germania,"* and advanced as far as the crossroads north of Peliczcze. At the same time, *Kampfgruppe Hänle* of the *7. Infanterie-Division* attacked from the south to the north. Towards noon, contact was established. This meant that the lead elements of the enemy forces, which had already reached the area around Widomla, were cut off from their rearward lines of communications for the time being.

In the meantime, both companies of the 1st Battalion had also reached Kaminiec Litewski. They occupied their assembly areas: The 4th Company of *SS-Hauptsturmführer* Zimmermann to the left of the road to Widomla and the 3rd Company of *SS-Obersturmführer* Schumacher to the right of the road abutting the Lesna.

At 1500 hours, the 1st Battalion received the mission to take the hill 1 kilometer north of Widomla, working together with elements of the *"Germania"* regiment. The intent was to determine the strength and the direction of movement of enemy forces that had broken through to the west along the Sedruz-Widomla road. At 1700 hours, the 3rd Company attacked. The 4th Company covered the left flank to the southeast along the road to Widomla.

Two kilometers north of Widomla, the German attack was engaged by enemy tanks and a strong antitank-gun belt in flanking positions on both sides of the town. In exchange for destroying three antitank guns and a Sherman,

---

4. Author's Note: From the daily logs or their annexes of the *2. Armee*. As with the previous section, unless attributed otherwise, the quotations are from this source.

the 3rd Company lost four tanks, those of *SS-Obersturmführer* Schumacher, *SS-Untersturmführer* Rüger, *SS-Oberscharführer* Ruf and *SS-Unterscharführer* Elend. Three of the tanks burned out; a fourth one—vehicle 324—was recovered by *SS-Obersturmführer* Hohenester. Two of the dead that were recovered showed evidence of mutilation.

After the tanks and the *SPW's* were pulled back, the battalion commander, the battalion adjutant, the commander of the 4th Company and several noncommissioned officers and enlisted personnel were wounded by a direct hit on the bridge over the Lesna, 2 kilometers northwest of Radosz, where they were holding a situation conference.

The battalion had had little good fortune on its first day of combat operations. The first combat operation after it had been reconstituted was a reconnaissance mission that could not be accomplished. The daily logs recorded the following[5]:

> The entire operation demonstrated that a reconnaissance-in-force with tanks does not always bring success, such as that which one is accustomed to in other reconnaissance units, and further, above and beyond that, due to the uniqueness of the combat arm and its ill suitability for such missions, heavy losses must be accepted.

✠

In the sector of the 2nd Battalion, the attack of the 7th Company, whose left flank was covered by the 8th Company, led to the capture of Szczerbowo and Podbrziany, some 7 kilometers southeast of Kaminiec Litewski.

> As a result, the good opportunity southeast of the Bialowiez Forest that had been offered to the enemy for a breakthrough to Brest the previous day had been taken from him . . . The day brought the *2. Armee* a considerable defensive success. The lead elements of the attack wedge aimed for Brest have been cut off and are faced with their destruction.

✠

During the night of 17–18 July, the tank regiment regrouped. After the 4th Company was relieved by the 5th Company, the battle staff of the 1st Battalion joined the battle staff of the 2nd Battalion in the western portion

5. Author's Note: Daily logs of the *I./SS-Panzer-Regiment 1.*

of the bridgehead so as to be available to the division for missions involving the main effort.

The division's mission: Eliminate the enemy forces that had broken through and were cut off and then push the enemy back across the Lesna to the east. Even though the division only wanted to reconnoiter until such time as the artillery regiment arrived, *Generaloberst* Weiß issued orders at 0900 hours: "The division must attack today and eliminate the enemy."

During the morning hours, the maintenance platoon of the 1st Battalion reported the destruction of an enemy truck, an armored personnel carrier and an antitank gun at Rudawicze, a crossing point over the Lesna 11 kilometers west of Widomla, by *SS-Unterscharführer* Sander.

Early in the afternoon, the enemy attacked from out of the woods 2 kilometers east of Pruska Wielowieska in battalion strength, supported by 13 7.62-centimeter antitank guns. The 4th Company, under the command of *SS-Untersturmführer* Bauer, launched an immediate counterattack against Topole, along with the 1st Battalion of *"Germania,"* which had arrived in the meantime, together with the regimental headquarters company and the regimental armored engineer platoon. One antitank gun was eliminated and another one was captured.

The 7th Company was involved in fighting for Hill 178 and around Czemery, some 7.5 kilometers east of Kaminiec Litewski. The 8th Company attacked Ranie, 5 kilometers south of Kaminiec. When Czemery was recaptured, the 2nd Battalion of the tank regiment found itself along the banks of the Lesna Lewa.

That evening, the *2. Armee* entered the following in its daily logs:

> Although the attack spearheads of the IV Guards Cavalry Corps had been temporarily cut off from their rearward lines of communications, they continued to advance further today as far as the Bug to the northwest of Brest.
>
> The recently established contact between the *7. Infanterie-Division* and the *5. SS-Panzer-Division Wiking* precludes these forces from being sustained and thus create the prerequisites for their elimination.

The daily logs of the *XXIII> Armee-Korps*:

> . . . The *7. Infanterie-Division* and the *5. SS-Panzer-Division Wiking* succeeded in closing the gap southeast of Kaminiec Litewski by

> attacking from the north and south, thus cutting off the strong enemy infantry, armor and cavalry forces, which had already advanced to the west across the Bielsk-Brest railway line as far as the Bug north of Janow Podlaski, from their rearward lines of communications. Both divisions are currently attacking northeast to take the Lesna-Lewa river line and establishing contact with the *102. Infanterie-Division.*

✠

As had already been expected for some days, the Soviets then commenced an envelopment operation further to the north, forcing the withdrawal of the division from the area around Kaminiec Litewski:

> The 65th Army, which had concentrated in the wooded terrain of the *Puczcza Bialowieza,* started its operations to envelop Brest from the west today. In its avenue of advance through Kleszczele to the southwest towards the Bug, there are hardly any friendly forces facing it at present.
>
> The *XXIII. Armee-Korps* has been ordered to expeditiously pull the *5. SS-Panzer-Division Wiking* and all available forces out of the line and commit them against the deep flank of the 65th Army.

For 19 July, however, the mission of the division and especially the mission for its armored group was to stabilize the front of the *XXIII. Armee-Korps* along the Lesna. The tank regiment's 1st Battalion was pulled out of the line during the night of 18–19 July and assembled in the center of Kaminiec Litewski.

At 0915 hours, it established contact with the 1st Battalion of *"Westland"* in Klepacze, some 7 kilometers north of Kaminiec Litewski, and directed to provide it with support. Contact was also established with the blocking forces of the *35. Infanterie-Division* in Dimitrowiecze. It was in that sector, in the area around Szyszowo-Czernaki-Podbiala, that the enemy had penetrated with around 500 men and was attempting to expand his penetration to the west and southwest. That morning, the *35. Infanterie-Division* was able to take back Podbiala.

At 1600 hours, the 4th Company of the tank regiment attacked in the direction of Szyszowo, after staging in Hulewicze and advancing across Hill 156. It cleared a path into the village for the 1st Battalion of *"Westland"* by means of its fires. The tank company itself swung around the village and approached it from the north and enabled the infantry to take the village after eliminating stubbornly defending Soviet forces in the northern part of the locality. From the high ground to the north of the village, the Germans were then able to control the Lesna Prawa Creek, which flowed from the north and joined the Lesna Lewa, coming from the east, nearby. That evening, a battalion-size Soviet counterattack with heavy artillery support collapsed in the face of the fires from the company, which was equipped with assault guns.

While the 8th Company supported the elements that were encircled in Widomla on 19 July from its positions on Hill 182.5 in the vicinity of Ranie, the attack east that was supported by the 2nd Battalion of the regiment against the last enemy bridgehead over the Lesna at Podrzeczany, which had high ground in front of it, was unable to reduce the enemy presence there.

Counterattacks of battalion size conducted by the enemy against Czemery were turned back. A penetration into Topole was immediately sealed off and cleaned up. According to the *2. Armee*, the *XXIII. Armee-Korps* "finally had a cohesive front running from north to south once again."

The unimpeded advance of the 65th Army to the southwest in the direction of Bielsk demanded the immediate relief of the *"Wiking"* Division from the front. At 1800 hours, the *XXIII. Armee-Korps* received the following orders from the *2. Armee*:

1. Enemy forces of unknown strength have occupied Kleszczele after moving out of the *Puszcza Bialowieza.*
2. The *XXIII. Armee-Korps* expeditiously pulls the *5. SS-Panzer-Division "Wiking"* out of the line and advances northwest with it and [other] elements that are as strong as possible to the east of the Brest-Bialystok rail line to the northwest,[6] to defeat the enemy northeast of Kleszczele and establish contact with *Gruppe Merker* northeast of Orla.

The enemy forces northwest of Brest are to be blocked with a portion of the [available] forces and eliminated, as far as the execution of the first-named mission permits.

SS-Panzer-Regiment 5 and the three grenadier regiments of the division can certainly be considered the defiant cliff in the ocean during those weeks in terms of their resistance and efforts in the face of the massed Soviet attacks. Von Treskow had closed out his orders to the division operations officer and

6. Translator's Note: Redundancy in the original.

his assistant with the words: "Hold up the enemy! There's nothing holding in the west any longer. The path into the *Reich* stands open!"[7]

The division disengaged from the enemy slowly and inflicted heavy casualties on the enemy in the process. By then, it also had its artillery regiment and other heavy weapons, following the unloading of the last train. At 0900 hours on 20 July, the division moved out from its assembly area around Kaminiec Litewski and started to head to the northwest.

The regiment, which had its headquarters in Wojska, 12 kilometers west of Kaminiec, had pulled the 1st Battalion out of its positions north of Szyszowo during the night. The battalion remained in the western portion of Wojska until 1400 hours. It reached the woods west of Jasienowka with its Headquarters Company around 1530 hours. At the same time, the 3rd Company and the battle staff arrived at Miniwicze, 3 kilometers to the south. Even though those villages were several kilometers behind the front that was to the northwest, the uncertain situation required outposts oriented to the south as well. Late in the afternoon, the 4th Company was withdrawn from the Kaminiec Bridgehead.

✠

The 2nd Battalion was initially fighting along a sector 40 kilometers across. Launching an immediate counterattack, it hit Hill 178.4 and Czemery along the eastern edge of the Kaminiec Bridgehead to the south of the Lesna. The main body of the 2nd Battalion and the 3rd Battalion of *"Germania"* attacked to the northwest and reached Sipurka Creek. The 5th Company attacked the villages of Kalenkowiecze and Padborcze, 25 kilometers northwest of Kaminiec. The 7th Company found itself engaged in fighting 10 kilometers further to the west at Dolbizna and Chlewiczcze.

The unfavorable terrain and the practically unimpeded movement of the enemy, who had already crossed the Brest-Bialystok rail line at and north of Kleszczele and was headed southwest, caused the division to regroup and advance north from further to the southwest. It had to prevent the lead elements of the 65th Army, which were approximately corps sized, from marching any further.

On the morning of 21 July, the division moved out from the area around Wysocki Litewski to attack once again. The tank regiment, which had a total strength of 1 *Panzer IV* (long), 44 *Panthers* and 13 assault guns, crossed the Czeremcha-Brest rail line about 10 kilometers south Czeremcha of with its 1st Battalion. It moved out from Tumin, west of the rail line, and head north towards Bobrowka, paralleling the tracks. A few Soviet horse-mounted patrols

7. Author's Note: Straßner, no page cited.

were quickly driven out of Tumin. Fairly strong enemy columns continued to move unimpeded by the 1st Battalion south of the Czeremcha-Nurzec rail line, since a bridge northwest of Tumin that had collapsed prevented an immediate advance and no engineers had been attached to the battalion. An expedient crossing point demanded a number of hours. Most of the 2nd Battalion was still involved in fighting about 6 kilometers southeast of Czeremcha, The 7th Company pushed back the enemy at Dolbizna, and the 6th Company, which had been brought forward from the Kaminiec Bridgehead in the meantime, attacked in the vicinity of Awuls, to the southeast of Czeremcha.

The 8th Company and the regimental engineers swung out further to the west on the insistence of the corps and the division and attacked north against columns marching on the Wolka-Nurzec-Tymianka road.

It was not until 2000 hours that the 1st Battalion reached Bobrowka. It was able to establish contact with the 5th and 7th Companies of the 2nd Battalion of the *"Westland"* Regiment there.

✠

The *XXIII. Armee-Korps* and the headquarters of the *2. Armee* continued to press for a faster operations tempo, since the enemy was already threatening the bridge over the Bug southeast of Siemiatycze. On 22 July, the division received the following mission:

> The enemy elements that have advanced across the Brest-Bialystok rail line to the west are to be cut off from their rearward lines of communications and, as a result, restore the cohesiveness of the field army front.

At the same time, the corps provided the field army with its rationale for the "slow progress" of the division:

> *Wiking* must first create a basis for starting operations. It is intended to mass [the division] and advance north. One regiment northeast of Hola (east of the Brest-Czeremcha line); one from Bobrowka to the north; one group diverted to Nurzec . . . The *292. Infanterie-Division* has been attached to *Wiking* . . . Difficult terrain, strong enemy. Enemy is very strong in the woods. He is not observed there by aerial reconnaissance.

Shortly after it moved out, the supplying of the division became questionable, since the encircled enemy forces northwest of Brest that had not yet been eliminated had interdicted the rail line at Wysocki.

It should perhaps be mentioned at this point that *Generalmajor* von Treskow died on that 21 July 1944. According to the annexes to the daily logs of the *2. Armee* that were concerned with telephone conversations, he left the command post at 1000 hours with the intention of getting a better view of the situation by visiting the locations of the *28. Jäger-Division*, the *12. Panzer-Division* and the *LV. Armee-Korps*. At 1545 hours, *Oberst i.G.* Hölz, the chief of staff of the *LV. Armee-Korps* reported to the field army: "*General* von Treskow was killed in the woods northeast of Nowosiolki during a reconnaissance in the sector of the *28. Jäger-Division*."

Nowosiolki was about 25 kilometers east of the *LV. Armee-Korps* command post in Jurowek, north of Bialystok. According to reports submitted by the corps, there had already been fighting there during the morning hours. The wooded area to the north of the village was filled with partisans. The daily logs make no other commentary on the incident from 21 July.

CZEREMCHA

The main effort of the fighting conducted by the tank regiment the following afternoon was west of the rail line. The 2nd Battalion, which had been pulled out of the line in the areas around Awuls and Dolbizna, moved to the area west of the 1st Battalion. The 2nd Battalion, together with the 3rd Company and the 2nd Battalion of the *"Westland"* Regiment, pushed the enemy out of Zubacze back to the north in the direction of Czeremcha. The attacking elements established contact around 1700 hours just south of the railway embankment south of Czeremcha with *gepanzerte Gruppe Westphal*. The latter, which had the 8th Company of the regiment integrated into it, had likewise pushed the enemy back. In its case, the enemy fell back through Barka to the northeast, also towards Czeremcha.

Further to the west, the 6th Company, together with the regimental Headquarters Company, attacked Tymianka; the 5th Company pressed forward to the northwest in the direction of Siemichocze. By the evening, the jump-off positions for the grenadiers for the decisive attack on Czeremcha were reached, that is, the edges of the woods that ran up to 3 kilometers deep that were west and southwest of the town.

At 0700 hours on 23 July, the 3rd Company screened along the railway crossing 4 kilometers south of Czeremcha, orienting east, north and northwest.

The 4th Company marched via Barka in the direction of Borowiki. Working in conjunction with the 8th Company, the tanks eliminated the enemy's heavy weapons along the west flank of the assaulting grenadiers, enabling their penetration into the town.

At 1600 hours, the 1st Battalion was positioned north of the road leading west out of the town. The 3rd Company was not yet with it, but it was in the process of being brought forward. The battalion crossed the Kleszczele-Czeremcha road, pushed itself forward along the patch of woods between the road and the railway embankment and reached the railway embankment at Kuzowa, north of Czeremcha. After suppressing the heavy defensive fires from Kuzowa, the 4th Company moved directly south to the northern part of the train station, which had also been reached from the south by the 7th Company in the meantime. The 3rd Company also joined the fray and reached the western outskirts of the town by advancing directly to the southeast.

The tankers of the 2nd Battalion also fought with success that day. The 5th Company, deployed the farthest to the west, broke through the Soviet positions at Augustynka to the north. The 6th Company screened north from Hill 189, while reconnoitering the villages of Nurzec and Rogacze north of the railway line. The 8th Company, together with the regimental Headquarters Company, attacked Hill 181.2 northwest of Czeremcha and established contact with the *4. Panzer-Division* in Kleszczele.

The days that followed were characterized by increased efforts on the part of the Soviets to retake Czeremcha. The pressure manifested itself by the commitment of armor and fighter-bombers, which had already started to make their presence known as early as the fighting on 23 July. There was extensive mining of the streets and roads in and around Czeremcha—a hallmark of the Soviets, who seemed to undertake such mining efforts with striking rapidity whenever they pulled back—and they took their toll.

Early on the morning of 24 July, the 4th Company knocked out two T 34's and one 7.62-centimeter antitank gun just east of the railway embankment in Czeremcha. The 7th Company turned back an attack along the railway embankment and eliminated the enemy in an immediate counterattack, as he was pulling back in the direction of Chlewiszcze. The 6th and 8th Companies held on to their positions at Rogacze and Klesczele.

The over-all situation necessitated a large-scale withdrawal of the division to the west bank of the Bug, however. *Kampfgruppe Westland* was formed, consisting of the *"Westland"* Regiment, the 1st Battalion of the tank regiment and the 1st Battalion of the divisional artillery. It held the new line and enabled other formations to pass through.

As part of that operation, the 4th Company relieved the 8th Company south of Kleszczele at 2300 hours, receiving the mission to block the enemy's columns on the Kleszczele-Dasze road.

The 3rd Company was designated as a mobile reserve for the regiment. Based on an alarm issued by the commander of the 4th Company of *"Westland,"* *SS-Hauptsturmführer* Amberg, the company was alerted on 25 July. It attacked fairly strong Soviet forces that had penetrated into Czeremcha and drove them out. The enemy left 30 dead behind, as well as one artillery piece and one antitank gun. While the 3rd Company occupied outpost positions on the east side of the town, the 4th Company, in conjunction with the mechanized infantry, was succeeding in its mission, that is, blocking the enemy's columns on the Kleszczele-Dasze road.

The Soviets prepared to attack again and moved out at 1700 hours with 200 men and 12 tanks, exiting the woods west of Czeremcha and re-entering the town, after overrunning the infantry positions. The Soviet infantry were stopped by the quad *Flak* of the 1st Battalion's Headquarters Company, however. One antitank gun from the 1st Company of *"Westland"* knocked out two T-34's and five T-34's were shot to pieces and set alight by the *Panzer IV's* of the 3rd Company. The remaining five T-34's were eliminated by the 8th Company, which attacked from the south and hit the Soviet armor in the flank. *SS-Obersturmführer* Senghas, the 1st Battalion's headquarters Company commander, provided the following matter-of-fact account of the events in Czeremcha on 25 July in the after-action report rendered by the *Flak* platoon:

> In position around Czeremcha and the woods west of Czeremcha. Around 1000 hours, breakthrough of the Russians in the eastern part of Czeremcha. Decisive defensive efforts on the part of the two guns of the *Flak* platoon. Old main line of resistance re-established.
>
> Towards 1700 hours, I saw friendly infantry pull back. The sounds of fighting coming from the west out of the woods. A noncommissioned officer from the *Westland* command post reported that a quad *Flak* needed to be sent forward. The Russians were going to attack with strong forces.
>
> No. 2 gun moved to the main line of resistance and opened fire against the wood line. All of a sudden, 12 T-34's came out of the

> woods. At the same time, orders arrived for the battalion to pull both of the guns back, since the guns were defenseless against tanks. By order of the battalion commander of the 1st Battalion of *Westland*, the guns remained in position, however, and attempted to escape the tanks, some of which were moving past, by continuing evasive maneuvers by the prime movers.
>
> Two of the T-34's were knocked out by the 14th Company of *Westland*. One of the antitank guns of the 14th Company then received a direct hit and was disabled.
>
> Gun No. 1 succeeded in knocking out two 7.62-centimeter antitank guns and separating the infantry from the tanks, causing them to suffer heavy casualties. As a result, the Russians were only able to enter Czeremcha with their tanks. Later on, they lost all of their tanks when they entered the kill zone of our tanks and the 8th Company advanced with its *Panthers*. Both of the guns were pulled back , since they had accomplished their mission. One man received a stomach wound, but he remained with his gun. At night, the old positions were reoccupied.

Early in the morning of 26 July, the enemy resumed his attacks after a strong preparation consisting of antitank guns, artillery, rocket launchers and mortars. Once again, the Soviet infantry succeeded in infiltrating into Czeremcha through the increasingly thinned-out ranks holding the positions. Once again, they were destroyed, when the enemy tanks failed in their efforts against the friendly defenses.

✠

Within the 2nd Battalion on 26 July, the 7th Company continued its fight of the previous day, some 10 kilometers east of Czeremcha in the vicinity of Buszcyacze, against enemy forces pressing from the northeast. In an immediate counterattack launched north of Werpol, some 17 kilometers to the southwest of Czeremcha, the 5th Company ejected enemy forces from Hill 176. The 6th Company conducted an immediate counterattack along the Biala-Podlaska–Terespol road.

The enemy continued his persistent drive south along both the east and west flanks of the division. As part of the planned withdrawal movements to the southern banks of the Bug, the reinforced *Kampfgruppe Westphal* disengaged from its northern-most positions around Kleszczele and in Czeremcha during the night of 26–27 July.

The main body of the 1st Battalion reached the area around Tokary, about 17 kilometers south of Czeremcha, in one move. In the process, however, the 4th Company lost two assault guns in an attempt to recover a stuck assault gun south of Kleszczele (the bogged-down vehicle and one of the recovery vehicles). As a result of the time lost in the recovery effort, the company then had to fight its way through the enemy during the latter half of the night. It did not reach the area around Tokary until around 1500 hours.

At the same time, the 3rd Company relieved the 8th Company, which had been in position at Wilanowo, about 5 kilometers to the northwest. The company rejoined the 2nd Battalion and crossed the Bug to the south.

During the night of 27–28 July, the 1st Battalion moved back to the patch of woods northeast of Mackowicze. In the course of those moves, enemy air attacks made the operation difficult, especially for the 4th Company south of Tokary.

As the ready reserve in the bridgehead north of the Bug, which was about to be evacuated, the 1st Battalion reconnoitered employment options around Siemiatycze. *SS-Untersturmführer* Kampe's platoon from the 3rd Company covered the withdrawal of an infantry battalion from the *292. Infanterie-Division.* As a precautionary measure, all of the damaged tanks and assault guns were taken across the Bug by evening, and the operational elements of the 1st Battalion crossed the river at 2100 hours, heading towards the Zakalinki area.

The area of operations just northwest of Brest Litowsk, which had been designated several days previously, was no longer under consideration as the result of the rapid development of the situation. The 1st Battalion of the tank regiment was stopped during its night march after it had been detached from the rearguard. Its new march objective was no longer to the east; instead, it was to head west. The battalion initially marched to the southwest via Losice and Mordy, then turned to the northwest, moving though Paprotnia, before reaching the new billeting area at Kozuchowek, more than 90 kilometers west of Brest Litowsk.

The companies required more than 11 hours to cover the nearly 80-kilomter march. While all of the wheeled vehicles were able to cover the distance without any breakdowns the line companies only made it to Kozuchowek with anywhere from three to six combat vehicles as a result of the heavy mechanical demands of the previous few weeks. Any and all options for recovering the vehicles were used. The 29th and 30th of July were designated as maintenance and repair days for the battalion.

The garrison of Brest Litowsk, under the command of *Generalleutnant* Felzmann of the *251. Infanterie-Division*, was able to break through the enemy forces encircling the city and escape to the west. According to the daily logs of the *2. Armee*:

> During the evening of 27 July, the encirclement was complete. On 27 July, orders were issued to break out . . . 700 wounded got out. Artillery pieces, which had to be left behind, were blown up . . . Nothing was left in Brest except alcohol (in order to divert the Russians). Everything else—forts, bridges, bunkers, 70 rail cars that had been moved onto a bridge—were blown up.
>
> The *Hiwis* performed magnificently!

The operations tempo increased. At 1300 hours on 31 July, the 1st Battalion moved out to the northwest. It marched via Sokulow to the west as far as Wengrow, where it then turned south as far as Grebkow, then heading west as far as Mlencin, approximately 10 kilometers east of Stanislawow. After a march of about 60 kilometers, the 1st Battalion found itself in the new area of operations of the regiment, about 35 kilometers east of Warsaw.

DEVELOPMENT OF THE SITUATION BETWEEN THE BUG AND THE VISTULA: OVERVIEW

The large-scale withdrawal of the division from the combat area of operations east of the Bug to an area east of Warsaw was necessitated by the overall development of the situation. The enemy had succeeded in making deep breakthroughs along a wide front.

After the 1st and 4th Ukrainian Fronts initiated offensive operations in support of the Soviet main effort, they succeeded in breaking through around Brody on 16 July. The breakthrough enabled Marshal Koniev to advance his forces as far as the area north of Lemberg.

The right wing of the 1st Ukrainian Front broke through the *4. Panzer-Armee* in the vicinity of Kowel; by 22 July, it was on the west bank of the Bug outside of Cholm. After the fall of the city of Lublin on 24 July, the *4. Panzer-Armee* moved back to Krasnik and Pulawy in the direction of the Vistula. On that same 24 July, the 1st White Russian Front crossed the Bug at Wlodawa, about 60 kilometers south of Brest Litowsk, and quickly gained ground to the north and the northwest, reaching Biala and Lukow and approaching the city of Siedlce in the center of its attack wedge. Together with the threat to Warsaw that was developing, there were signs of an effort to envelop the southern wing of *Heeresgruppe Mitte.*

The operational objective of the Soviets appeared to ambitious, that is, a breakthrough between the Narew and the Vistula, northwest of Warsaw, and continuing on to the northwest so as to isolate *Heeresgruppe Nord* and elements of *Heeresgruppe Mitte* after reaching East Prussia and cutting off their rearward lines of communications.

The effort to thwart those objectives was the goal of the fighting of the next few weeks, fighting in which *SS-Panzer-Regiment 5* also played a significant role.

✠

The measures taken by the German command were marked by the *9. Armee* attempting to establish a front between Pulawy and Warsaw, neighboring the *4. Panzer-Armee,* and the *2. Armee* establishing a "southern front" from Siedlce and Biala, which had become necessary as a result of the Soviet operations. The establishment of the "southern front" served to enable the garrison of Brest Litowsk and the elements committed further south to be evacuated on 28 and 29 July, as well as to expedite the disengagement from the enemy by the *5. SS-Panzer-Division "Wiking"* and its movement back.

As a result of the inferior strength of the forces in the bridgehead southeast of Warsaw, the Soviet III Tank Corps succeeded in breaking through the west wing of the *2. Armee* and the Warsaw Bridgehead. It was possible to encircle the Soviet elements that had broken through, however, and eliminate them with heavy assistance from the *Luftwaffe.*

✠

In the hard, seesaw fighting that took place in August, the enemy did not succeed in getting the breakthrough that he strove for. Nevertheless, the 1st White Russian Front was able to push back the inner wings of the *2. Armee* and the *9. Armee* the following month. It was along the inner wing of the *2. Armee* that the division was positioned, with the *3. SS-Panzer-Division "Totenkopf"* next to it.

The tankers of the regiment fought in all cardinal directions of the compass during those months. They were able to escape all efforts to encircle them and hold out wherever they were ordered.

In their efforts to break through between the Narew and the Vistula, according to von Tippelskirch, the Soviets employed 60 to 70 rifle divisions,

10 tank and mechanized corps, 3 cavalry corps and numerous Red Air Force elements along a front about 120 kilometers wide.[8]

The superiority of the Soviets on the battlefield—in terms of both personnel and materiel—was overwhelming. Despite that, they were not able to break through the German front east and, later, north of Warsaw. Thanks to the German command efforts and the training of the forces in the field, which was still at a high standard, the fighting continued along a front that was initially oriented to the west and southwest. It then pivoted to the south and, finally, it swung 90 degrees around the pivot point of Warsaw, flanked by the Narew and the Vistula, where it again oriented east.

THE FIGHTING FOR THE BUG AND THE NAREW

The main body of the division, which had been pulled out of the line from the fighting around Czeremcha during the final weeks of July, was committed on the right wing of the *2. Armee* east of Warsaw. There was a gap between that right ring and the forces of the *9. Armee* that were manning Warsaw. It had been torn open by the advance of the Soviet III Tank Corps across a line running Kaluszin-Minsk and a breakthrough to the northwest. The leading elements of that corps were positioned around Radzymin.

Although a few bridgeheads could be established to the south at Modlin and south of Serock, the enemy was moving unimpeded. There was a danger that he would cross the Bug and the Narew to the north, then advancing to the northeast with some of his forces. The division was given the mission to attack west, cut the enemy off from his rearward lines of communications and establish contact with the forces east of Warsaw.

After the division took Stanislawow at 2000 hours on 30 July, where the enemy forces were eliminated and several armored vehicles and trucks were captured, it conducted a reconnaissance-in-force another 10 kilometers to the west the next day. It should be noted that the movements of the division were impeded by the poor state of the roads (dried out and sandy)

The 1st Battalion arrived in the area east of Stanislawow on 31 July. Upon reporting to the regimental command post on the western side of the village, he was ordered to relieve the 2nd Battalion, which was employed at Sokule, 3 kilometers to the southeast.

It was there that the 3rd Company assumed a portion of the southern front along the corridor that was being driven forward in the direction of

8. Author's Note: von Tippelskirch, 473–74.

Warsaw. The elements of the 2nd Battalion that were freed up were then available for further commitment to the west.

The 4th Company remained in the Mlencin area as the 1st Battalion's reserve; it positioned itself near the battalion command post at the crossroads to the west of the village.

✠

On the evening of 31 July, the field-army group ordered a continuation of the attack the next day:

1. The attack to close the gap east of the Warsaw bridgehead is to be carried out at first light on 1 August 1944 from Stanislawow to the west by the *IV. SS-Panzer-Korps*.[9] To that end, the headquarters of the *2. Armee* provides the *IV. SS-Panzer-Korps* with the armored group and three battalions of the *3. SS-Panzer-Division Totenkopf* the previous evening.
2. The *9. Armee* clears the Warsaw-Radzymin road by attacking from the southwest on 1 August.[10]

After the enemy had made considerable penetrations into the city of Siedlce, the *3. SS-Panzer-Division "Totenkopf"* was permitted to give up the city. On 31 July, it defended along a line running Proszew—southern outskirts of Mokobody—course of the Liviec as far as Krezesin. The *"Totenkopf"* Division had contact on its right with the *"Wiking"* engineer battalion.

During the night of 31 July/1 August, the *"Totenkopf"* Division moved forward through Mlencin and Stanislawow into the corridor being created by *"Wiking"* and relieved elements of the latter division along the southern front.

By the evening of 1 August, the main body of the *"Germania" Regiment* and the tanks of the 2nd Battalion established contact from the west with the *19. Panzer-Division* at Hill 129, north of Okuniew. Contact was maintained the following night as well.

During the course of the day, the enemy brought up new forces from the south and conducted heavy attacks south of Stanislawow, at Mlencin and southeast of Grebkow, especially during the morning.

9. Translator's Note: It was about this time that the corps structure of the German Army started to become fixed in nature rather than task-organized. To that end, the *IV. SS-Panzer-Korps* would eventually consisted of both the *5. SS-Panzer-Division "Wiking"* and the *3. SS-Panzer-Division "Totenkopf"* being permanently assigned to the corps.

10. Author's Note: Unless attributed otherwise, this and the following direct quotes come from the daily logs and their annexes of the headquarters of the *2. Armee*.

Together with the *"Westland"* Regiment and the divisional engineers, who were defending southeast of Stanislawow, the tanks of the 3rd and 4th Companies repeatedly conducted immediate counterattacks, especially at Sokule and Ludminowo, and restored the main line of resistance.

Lingering rain made movement difficult. Unimproved roads could not be negotiated by wheeled vehicles in some instances.

By the evening of 2 August, a breakthrough to Radzymin was effected by the *19. Panzer-Division* from the southwest and armored elements of the *4. Panzer-Division* from the northeast. That meant that the enemy forces that had broken through were blocked from advancing north.

On the following day, the enemy, who was suffering from a lack of fuel and had been pushed into the area in and east of Welomin, attempted to break out to the south and southeast along the northern front of the *"Wiking"* Division. The division employed a battalion of the *"Germania"* Regiment, reinforced with tanks from the 2nd Battalion, against those enemy forces north of Michalow. The unimproved roads there proved to be a challenge even for the tracked vehicles.

The final breakthrough to the west was ordered for 4 August:

> All available forces are to be concentrated along the western wing so as to offensively establish and maintain contact with the *9. Armee* by moving at 0800 hours on 4 August from the area around Michalow through Dluga Koszielna.

Despite the increasing enemy pressure along the southern front, the field army had finally established a cohesive front and also defeated the encircled enemy force.

A look at the combat strengths of the forces at the end of this round of defensive and offensive actions is instructive. On 2 August, the tank regiment reported the following vehicles operational: 8 *Panzer IV's* (long), 45 *Panzer V's* and 12 assault guns. Those numbers did not represent a complete tank battalion. On the other hand, the magnificent performance of the maintenance services in keeping that many combat vehicles operational after two weeks of extraordinary wear and tear is noteworthy.

On 29 July, the combat strength of the division was listed as 2,200 men. On 3 August, that meant that 147 men had to cover each kilometers of front.

If those numbers seem relatively "reasonable" for the *"Wiking"* Division, which was attacking, then consider that for the same time, the "defending" *"Totenkopf"* Division had only 78 men to cover the same kilometer of front.

On average, the divisions and larger formations allocated to the *2. Armee* had 115 men to cover 1 kilometers of front.[11] The frontages represented a many-fold overextension of the norm. When one considers the physical condition of the overetaxed fighting forces and their shortfalls of materiel, then what they accomplished was as amazing as it was admirable.

✠

The battle staff of the 1st Battalion moved to the middle of Stanislawow on 2 August; on 6 August, after receiving a direct hit from a rocket launcher salvo, it moved into the patch of woods 1 kilometer to the northwest. The 3rd Company joined it there, after leaving a platoon on the southern edge of Stanislawow to screen.

On 7 August, the battalion had the 4th Company move to its location from the Mlencin area, whereupon it then moved to the patch of woods northeast of Turze. From there, the 4th Company moved Paetow's platoon 2.5 kilometers to the south to the edge of Helenow on the west side of the Wyskow-Tluszcz-Minsk rail line so as to screen in the direction of Ciskowka and cover the withdrawal of the combat outposts of the 2nd Battalion of the *"Germania"* Regiment, if needed.

While conducting route reconnaissance for employment options in the sector of the *"Germania"* Regiment the following day, *SS-Untersturmführer* Schneider was badly wounded by an artillery shell. He later died of his wounds at the main clearing station at Rowne, some 15 kilometers north-northeast of Stanislawow, that afternoon. He was buried on the western outskirts of the village. The company commander of the 5th Company, *SS-Obersturmführer* Jessen, and his platoon leader, *SS-Untersturmführer* Erd, were also badly wounded by the same shell.

The 3rd Company was moved to Wolomyn along the Warsaw-Bialystok rail line, 18 kilometers northeast of Warsaw, to serve as the tank ready reserve of the corps.

As a rule during the previous fighting, the battalions of the regiment had been divided up and employed as companies in the individual sectors. That

11. Author's Note: According to the daily logs of the *2. Armee*, the field army had a total length of 266 kilometers of front (3 August), for which it had a combat strength of 30,656 men (as of 29 July).

trend continued, although the dwindling strengths of the companies often forced them to be split apart and individual platoons committed to support the sectors of the grenadiers so as to prevent local penetrations.

✠

In the meantime, the enemy forces had closed up. In expectation of the resumption of his attacks, all of the regimental trains were moved to the woods south of Krusze, approximately 10 kilometers to the northwest, during the night of 9–10 August.

A half hour after they left, the Soviets opened concentrated fire with their heavy weapons on the regiment's combat positions on both sides of Stanislawow. The attack, which was conducted with strong forces to the northeast, was able to be turned back in the sector of the 2nd Battalion of *"Germania,"* employed on the right, and the elements of the *"Totenkopf"* Division, employed along the division's right-hand boundary. On the boundary between the *"Germania"* and *"Westland"* Regiments, the enemy succeeded in breaking through at Dworzek and to the south. He was able to take the high ground at Pustelnik, to the southwest of Stanislawow. Exploiting his initial success, the enemy attacked around noon from Cisowka to the east, crossed the railway embankment at Pustelnik and infiltrated into the woods at Retkow, further to the east. Two additional enemy attempts to gain ground were thwarted in the concentrated fires of all available weapons.

The commander of the 1st Battalion of *"Germania," SS-Sturmbannführer* Müller, was able to establish a front oriented to the south and seal of the enemy penetration by swinging back his 3rd Company, employing mobile forces and committing the 4th Company of the tank regiment.

At the same time, a counterattack conducted by the 2nd Battalion of the tank regiment a few kilometers further east succeeded in ejecting the enemy from Stanislawow, who had entered the town once again. As a result, the enemy was unable to obtain his objective of the day, the Minsk-Stanislawow-Jadow road (running north-south).

✠

During the night of 11–12 August, the division disengaged from the enemy and occupied a prepared main line of resistance: rail line 4 kilometers south of Tluszcz—western edge of the patch of woods at Grabow—woods southeast of Sulejow.

In view of the development of the situation in the sector of the friendly forces to the left, the *5. Jäger-Division*, the lefthand regiment, *"Westland,"* pulled back more than 10 kilometers in a north-northeast direction, while the right wing of the *"Germania"* Regiment, serving as the pivot point, only moved slightly. The entire front of the division had previously oriented southwest; at this point, it had shifted to the southeast.

The 1st battalion, with its command post on the western edge of the woods at Grabow, was directed to support the *"Westland"* regiment, while the 2nd Battalion received the same orders for *"Germania"* on the right. In addition, the 1st Platoon of the 4th Company was also directed to support the 3rd Battalion of *"Germania."*

The withdrawal had not escaped the notice of enemy aerial reconnaissance. The Soviets followed the withdrawals with determination; by the early morning hours, the combat outposts and the forward-deployed forces had been pushed back in both regimental sectors. The regimental engineer company, which was located along the southern edge of Miendzyles, 10 kilometers to the southwest of Sulejow, was constantly being outflanked and had to pull back through Franciskowo in the direction of Mionse. An immediate counterattack conducted by the 1st Battalion of *"Germania."* With the *7./SS-Panzer-Regiment 5* in support, was able to create some breathing room for the time being.

✠

In conjunction with the 2nd Battalion of *"Germania,"* the 6th Company was able to toss the enemy back and restore the former main line of resistance. In the process, the enemy suffered high casualties and the loss of numerous antitank weapons.

✠

In the sector of the *"Westland"* Regiment, which was the main effort of the enemy that day, the Soviets succeeded in penetrating the boundary between the 1st and 2nd Battalions, after exerting increasing pressure. The penetration was sealed off and cleared by means of an immediate counterattack by the 4th Company of the 1st Battalion and the 15th Company of the *"Westland"* Regiment. The 1st Company of *"Westland"* at Kury, as well as the 4th Company at Bialki, were able to reclaim their old positions by that afternoon.

A new enemy attack in the early evening hours that was supported by increased and concentrated heavy weapons fires was able to break through the sectors of the *"Westland"* Regiment's 7th Company east of Bialki and the 5th Company southeast of Sulejow. An immediate counterattack by the *4./SS-Panzer-Regiment 5* was unable to restore the situation due to the decimated condition of the grenadier companies. Under cover of darkness, the main line of resistance was pulled back to a line running from the eastern edge of Sulejow—Hill 113—northern edge of the patch of woods 2 kilometers south of Sulejow and Bialki. During the night, the 3rd Company returned to the area of operations of the 1st Battalion of the tank regiment and reverted to its command and control.

The enemy resumed his attacks on 14 August with undiminished intensity. Although he attacked south of Mionse and Grabow, his main effort was directed against the sector of the 2nd Battalion of the *"Westland"* Regiment in the Sulejow area. After strong preparatory fires, he attacked the city from the south and southeast and also from the northeast (from Wujowka), taking the locality. An immediate counterattack was launched by *SS-Obersturmführer* Nicolussi-Leck's 8th Company, which received covering fire along the flanks by the 4th Company. Around 0800 hours, Nicolussi-Leck's men had pushed the enemy back to the center of the city and temporarily sealed off the penetration, although two *Panthers* were lost in the process. In close-in combat with Soviet tank hunter-killer teams, *SS-Unterscharführer* Abenseth of the 4th Company was killed.

Towards noon, an advance by the *3./SS-Panzer-Regiment 5* and the regiments engineers rapidly advanced through the center of the city and to the south, but it was not powerful enough to push the enemy all the way back to his lines of departure. Additional Soviet attacks up through the evening could be turned back, however.

SS-Hauptsturmführer Heder's division escort company assumed the duties of protecting the tanks of the 3rd Company that night. Defensive preparations were intensively pursued. Elements of the division's military police established new positions extending out from the division's lefthand boundary, north of Sulejow, through the edge of the woods 2 kilometers to the northwest as far as a contact point with the 1st Battalion of *"Westland."* Divisional engineers laid mines in front of and between positions.

Contrary to expectations, the enemy remained relatively quiet the next few days. It appeared that he was regrouping. A heavy infantry force, about a battalion-sized element, along with 20 T-34's and assault guns occupied the woods south and southwest of Sulejow.

Sulejow proper was evacuated by 2300 hours on 14 August by the 3rd Company and Heder's escort company. After mining the roads headed west and southwest, *SS-Obersturmführer* Schumacher's company moved to Wilczoch, 2 kilometers south of the city, where is was designated as a mobile reserve.

Small penetrations in the sectors of the 2nd and 1st Battalions of *"Germania"* were sealed off and eliminated by Olin's platoon from the 7th Company of the tank regiment and Großrock's platoon from the 6th Company.

At first light on 15 August, the enemy attacked the positions of the 2nd Battalion of *"Germania"* on the right wing of the division. Olin's platoon again came to the rescue, this time in the sector of the 6th Company of *"Germania,"* by attacking enemy infantry and 4 T-34's northwest of Mionse. At the same time, *SS-Obersturmführer* Schneider committed the remaining three tanks of his 7th Company and two tanks from the reconnaissance platoon of the 2nd Battalion against enemy forces attacking on Hill 105. Despite Schneider's efforts, he could not prevent Jasienica from falling into the hands of the enemy, who had a massive superiority in infantry. At that point, the commander of the 2nd Battalion, *SS-Hauptsturmführer* Flügel, who had preciously served as the regimental adjutant, launched an immediate counterattack against Jasienica and, benefitting from artillery support, was able to take both it and Hill 105 back.

During that fighting, Soviet forces that had broken through further to the east reached the north bank of the Cienka and penetrated into the eastern portion of Tluszcz. Thanks to an immediate counterattack under the command of the regimental adjutant, *SS-Obersturmführer* Wolf, and *SS-Obersturmführer* Bauer, the enemy was ejected.

In order to eliminate the threat to the rearward lines of communication, the 3rd Company was withdrawn from the *"Westland"* Regiment's sector and personally directed by *SS-Standartenführer* Mühlenkamp against Hill 99, about 1 kilometers south of Wilczaniec. In the course of that rapid and successful attack, during which the enemy lost 12 antitank guns and left behind 110 dead, "*Untersturmführer* Meyer, who saw action for the first time within the battalion, particularly distinguished himself though his dashing and aggressive actions."[12]

Friendly infantry took positions on the south bank of the Cienka Creek; the 3rd Company of the 1st battalion screened from the southern edge of Tluszcz.

On the two days that followed, with the exception of some low-level reconnaissance probes, it was relatively quiet. Both sides improved their positions. The 5th Company relieved the 3rd Company along the southern part of Tluszcz, which then returned to the 1st Battalion. The 8th Company was pulled out of the line in the *"Westland"* sector, to return to the 2nd battalion as its ready reserve.

---

12. Author's Note: Daily logs of the *I./SS-Panzer-Regiment 5.*

The relief of a *Wehrmacht* infantry battalion by *Panzergrenadiere* of "*Wiking*."

1944, an area northeast of Warsaw: *SS-Obersturmführer* Jessen, the commander of the 5th Company, and *SS-Hauptsturmführer* Hannes, the commander of the armored company of *SS-Panzer-Grenadier-Regiment "Germania,"* coordinate.

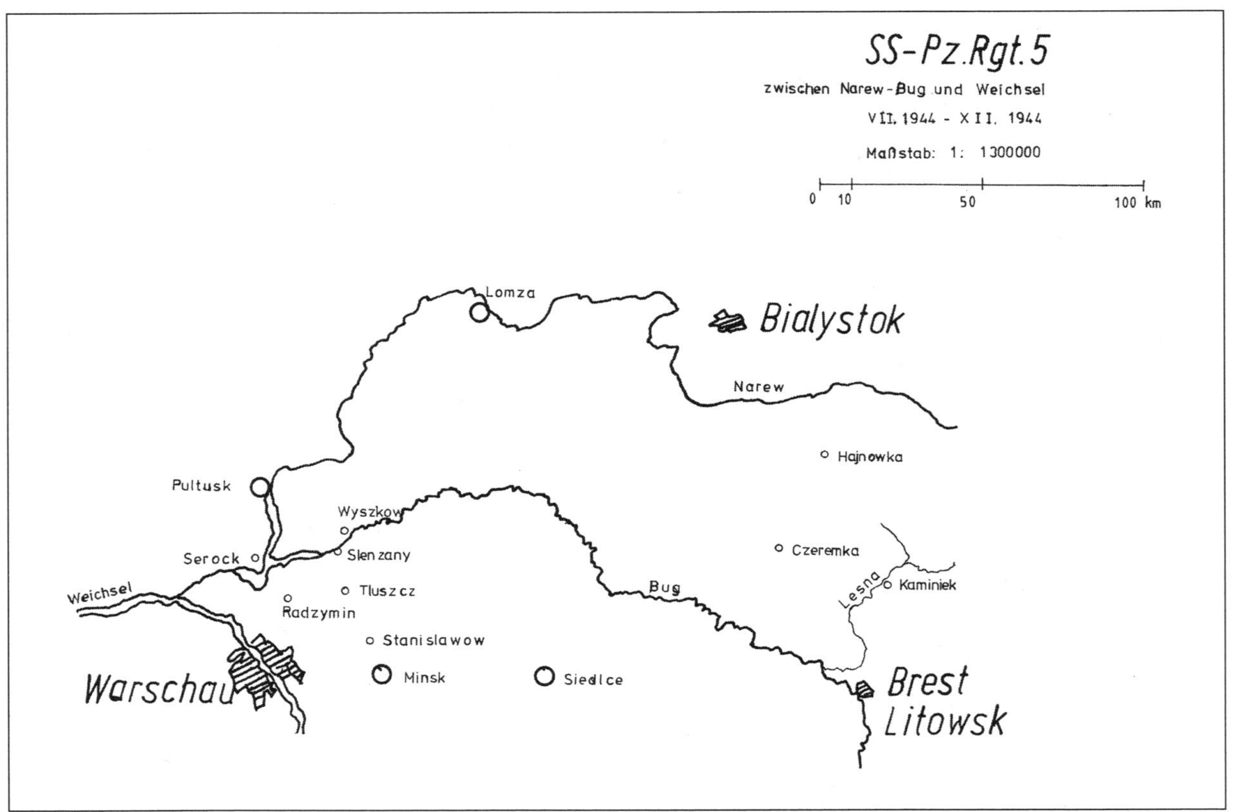

SS-Panzer-Regiment 5 between the Narew, Bug and Vistula during the period from July to December 1944.

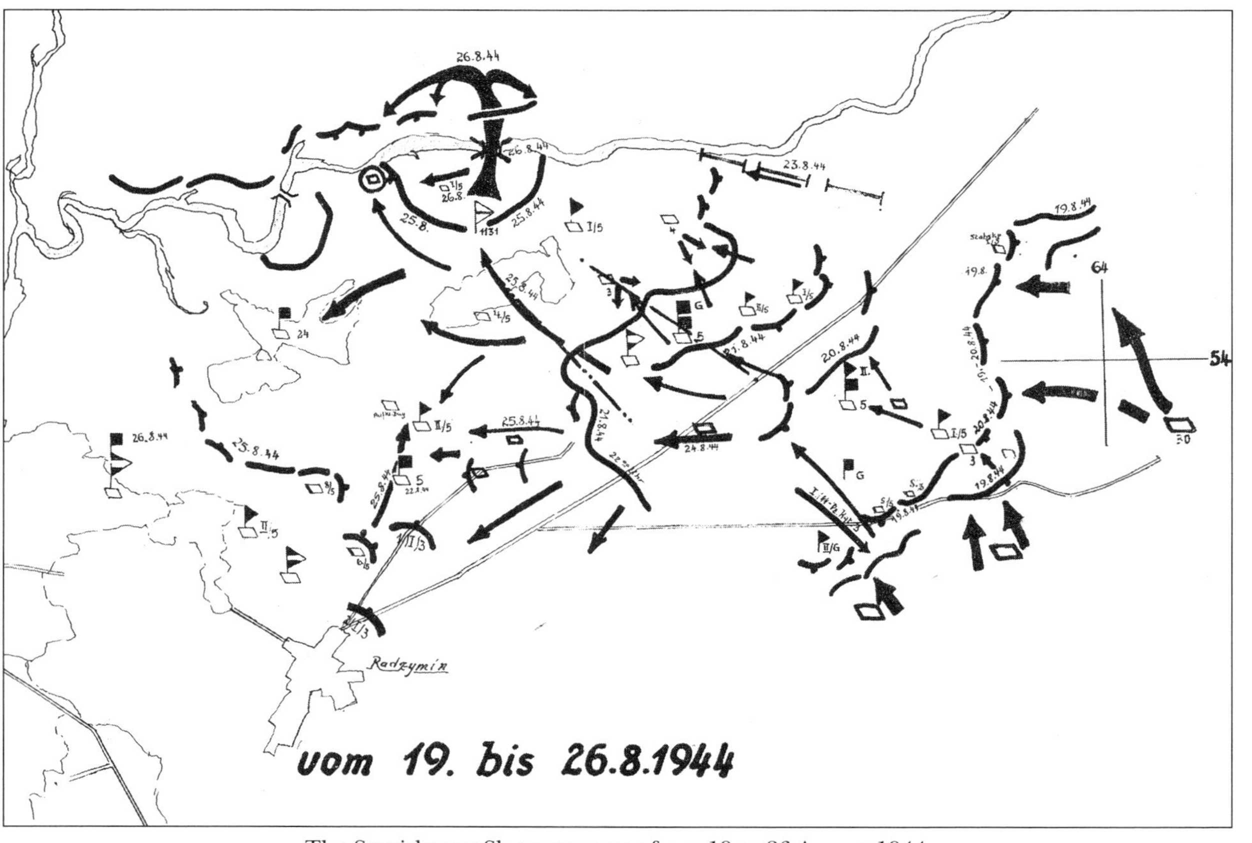

The Stanislawow-Slenzany sector from 19 to 26 August 1944.

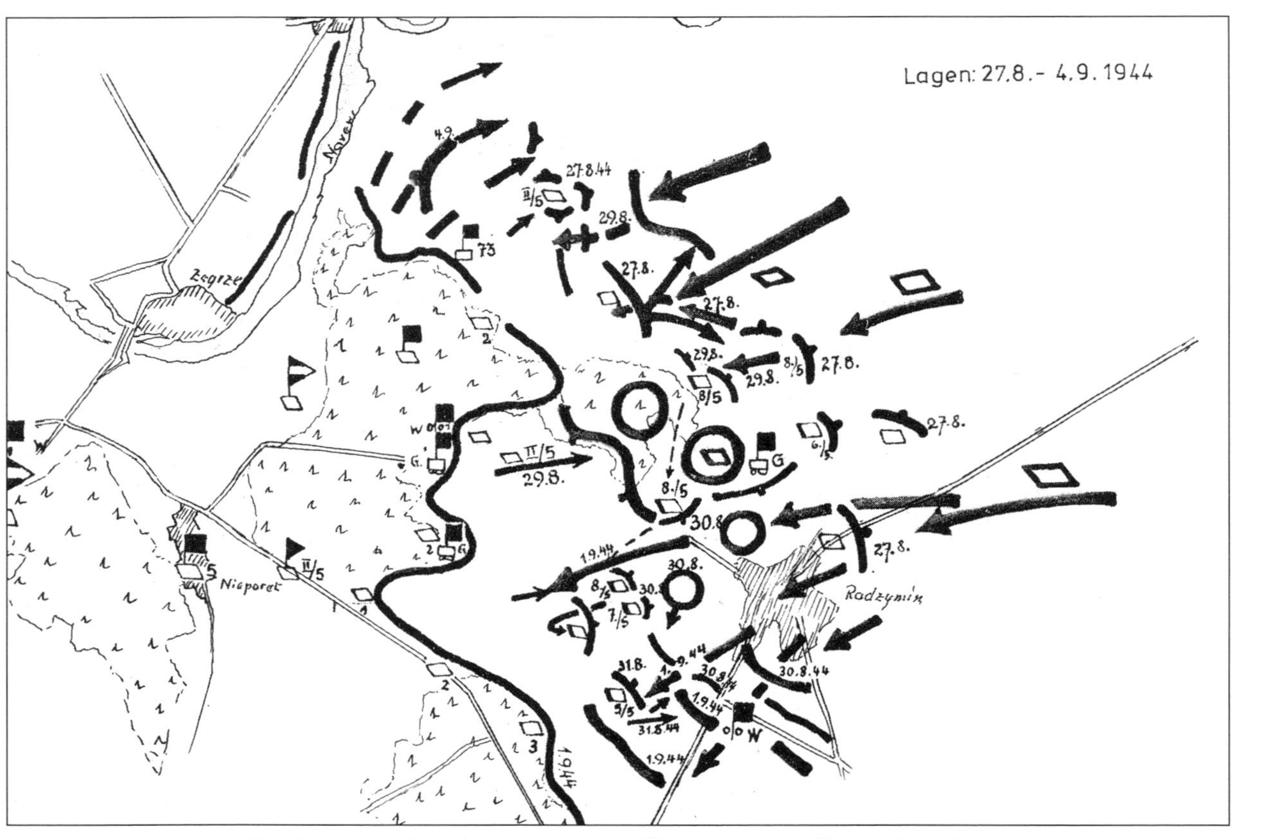

The Radzymin-Serock sector between 27 August and 4 September 1944.

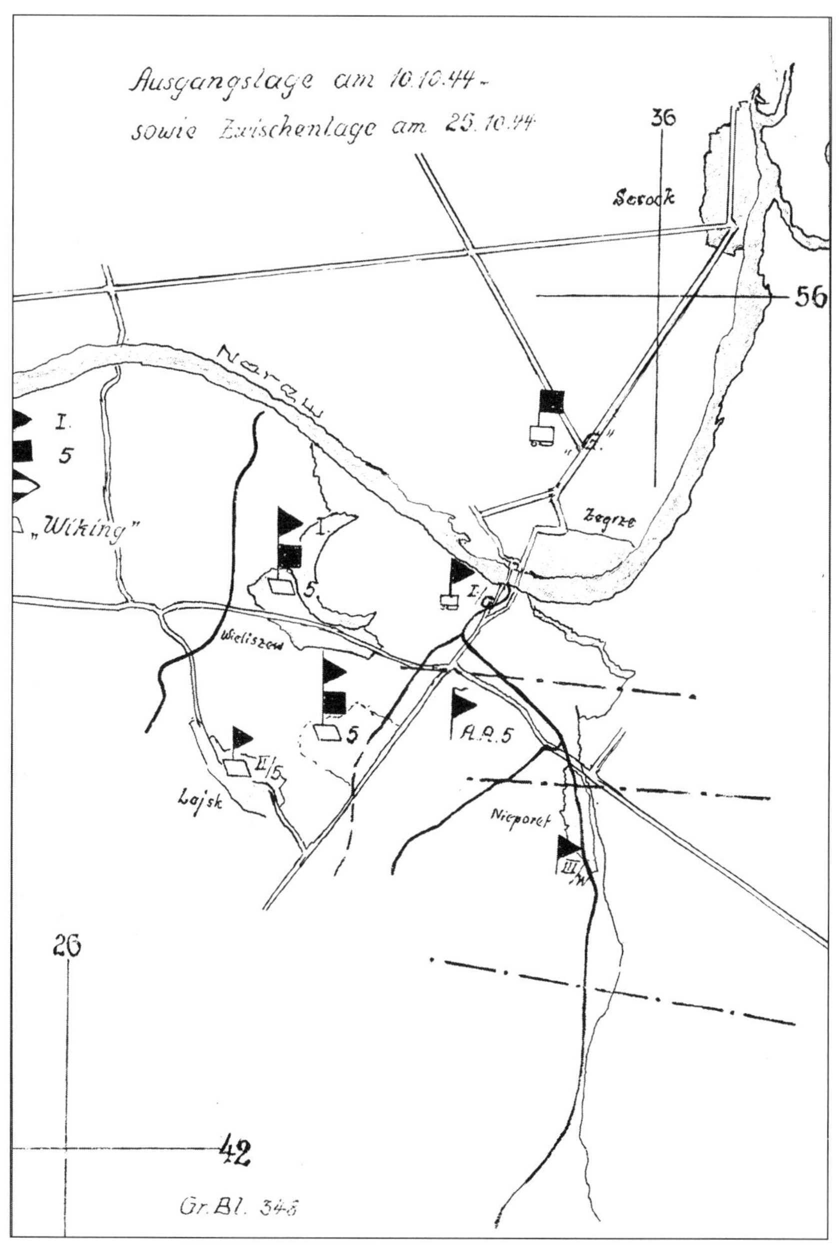

The situation along the Narew south of Serock in October 1944.

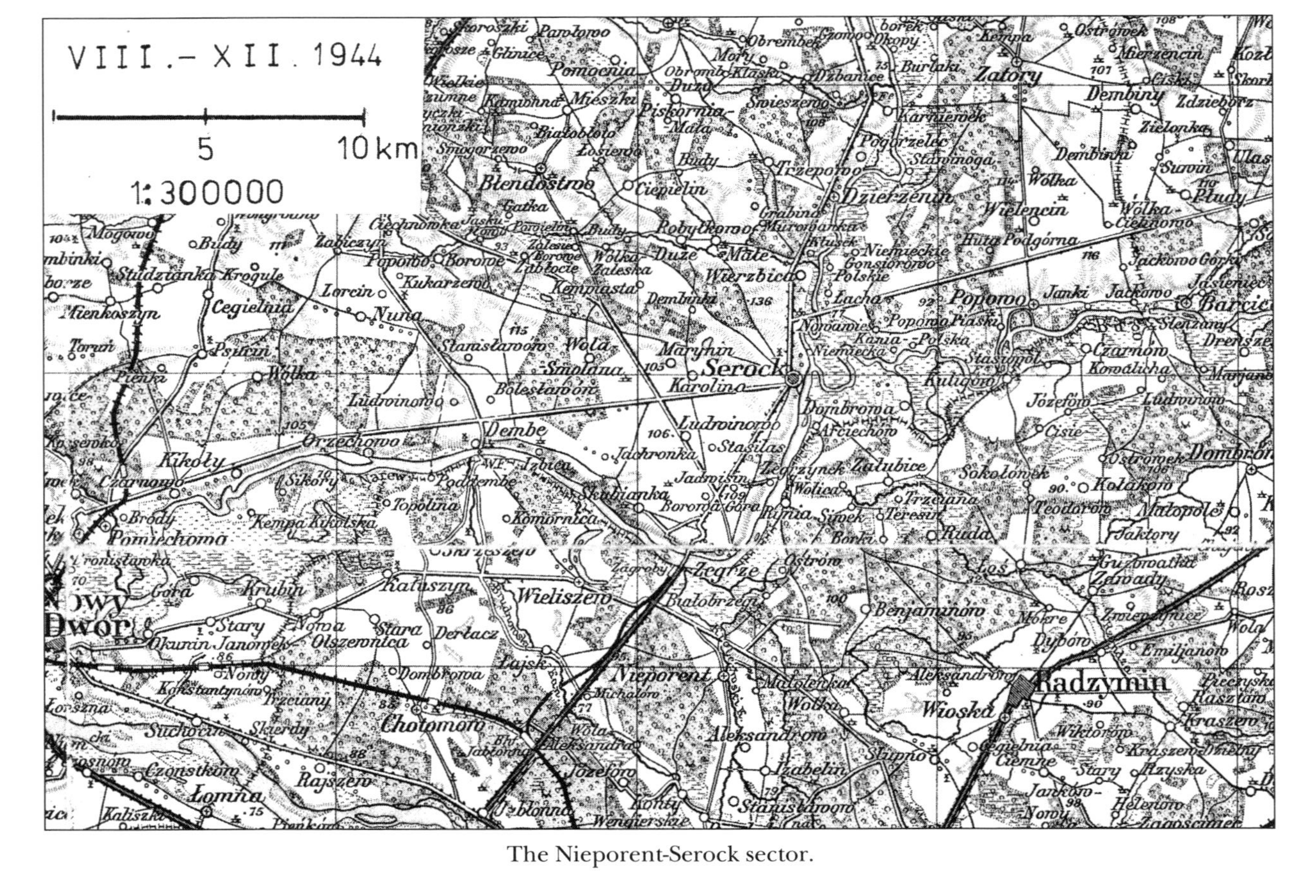

The Nieporent-Serock sector.

CHAPTER 7

The First Battle of Warsaw

At 0900 hours on 18 August, the anticipated major offensive of the Soviets started with artillery barrage fire across the entire divisional sector. With only a few short breaks to catch its breath, the division fought heavily and continuously for the next four weeks and underwent a huge test. Although the enemy succeeded in gaining some ground, he still failed in garnering the decisive success he wanted—that is, a breakthrough to the northeast. The tankers of *SS-Panzer-Regiment 5* contributed greatly to that success. With their last reserves of strength and the final few tanks remaining to them, they supported the hard fighting and continuously dwindling number of grenadiers against an oppressive superiority in numbers. In some cases, the tankers went in their place.

✠

The main efforts of the enemy were directed to the two wings of the division. Although the positions of the 1st Battalion of *"Westland"* could be held on the right and in the center of the regimental center, the Soviets were able to penetrate in the sectors of the 5th and 6th Companies on the left. With 15 minutes of the start of the attack, Soviet infantry was outside of the command post of the 1st battalion of the tank regiment and had to be eliminated in close-in fighting. The 3rd Company was positioned with three of its tanks (under the command of *SS-Obersturmführer* Schumacher) at the command post of the 2nd Battalion of *"Westland"* (*Bataillon Schmidt*) at Wymysly, to the northwest of Sulejow; four tanks under *SS-Oberscharführer* Ruf were in at the edge of the woods northwest of Sulejow.

Around noon, enemy forces that had penetrated into Wolka Sulejowka, northeast of Sulejow, were pushed back in an immediate counterattack conducted by the 3rd Company, Lüthgarth's assault gun platoon from the 4th Company and mechanized infantry on *SPW's*. *SS-Obersturmführer* Lüthgarth's assault gun was knocked out along the southeast edge of Wolka Sulejowka, and the officer was badly wounded.

Contact was lost with *SS-Oberscharführer* Ruf's platoon. Elements that pulled back to the command post reported that all of this platoon was lost while defending against the Soviets and after having knocked out nine enemy tanks.

After enemy forces attacking the command post were turned back in the afternoon, it was moved back to the wood line south of Wymysly along with two operational assault guns of the 4th Company.

Late in the afternoon, *SS-Obersturmführer* Schumacher attacked Wolka Sulejowka one more time using two *Panzer IV's* and two assault guns. The effort was under the direct command of the battalion commander. The armored vehicles entered the village and observed heavy vehicular traffic moving from Sulejow to the north.

On the first day of fighting, the 1st Battalion suffered heavy losses, but it also accounted for 17 enemy tanks—6 Shermans, 6 T-34's, 4 T-43's[1] and 1 flamethrower tank—and 10 antitank guns.

✠

On the right wing of the division, the enemy succeeded in breaking through at Point 99 by attacking behind a wall of smoke. The 2nd Battalion of *"Germania"* was unable to prevent two enemy companies from entering Tluszcz. Hill 107 was also lost. In heavy fighting around the Jasienica area, the 7th and 8th Companies knocked out 12 Soviet tanks and brought the enemy advance to a standstill, inflicting heavy casualties on the Soviet infantry. The friendly infantry were beaten back, however, and the tanks remained without infantry support.

Because the Soviets attacked again in the afternoon to the north from Tluszcz, the regimental command post set prepared a close-in defense. Based on the uncertain situation in the sector of the friendly forces to the left, the regiment's reconnaissance platoon reconnoitered to the northeast in the direction of Mokrawies. Towards evening, under the command of *SS-Untersturmführer* Renz, it assumed screening duties to the south in the direction of Tluszcz.

In the sector of the division to the right, where the *3. SS-Panzer-Division "Totenkopf"* was positioned, the enemy also succeeded in making penetrations with heavy infantry and armor forces. Initially, the penetrations could not be sealed off. The battle staff of the *II./SS-Panzer-Regiment 5* and the 7th Company—*Panzergruppe Flügel*—were enveloped and cut off. They were able to hold their positions until evening, however, before pulling back.

1. Editor's Note: The Germans referred to the T-34/85, an up-gunned version of the T-34 with an 8.5-cm main gun, as a T-43. This is not a Soviet designation.

New, intense fighting developed and was concentrated along the boundary between *"Totenkopf"* and *"Wiking"* along the main line of resistance running Klembow—Rzonza River—south of Krusze—Wolka Kozlowska—Postoliska—Mokrawies, which had been occupied during the night of 18–19 August. *Panzergruppe Flügel* succeeded in "fighting its way back across the railway embankments southwest and west of Tluszcz."[2] *SS-Hauptsturmführer* Flügel has provided amplifying comments to the single-line entry from the regimental chronicle:

> Before the barrage fire of the Russians commenced, all of the company commanders were summoned to the battalion command post to receive important orders. Reporting were Nicolussi-Leck, Großrock, Schneider with Olin and the Battalion Surgeon, Dr. Kalbskopf.
>
> My tank was off to the side with differential problems and was being repaired by the maintenance team.
>
> There was no time at the conference to say a proper good-bye. With the sudden onset of the Russian barrage fire, all options for coordinated command and control were immediately taken out of my hands. The commander of the 8th Company received shrapnel in his right hip, removing him from the picture. He was placed aboard my tank.
>
> The commander of the 6th Company, Martin, had been killed on 14 August by enemy action. He had brought prisoners on his tank to the command post to identify them. In the process, one of the prisoners blew himself up with a hand grenade, whereby Martin was mortally wounded. The company was then taken over by Großrock.
>
> The Russians were launching one aerial ground attack after the other. They dropped parachute bombs[3] between our tanks, in the process of which several were considerably damaged in the running gear. We took some losses and were all on our own, since the escort infantry was no longer with us. The enemy then advanced across Hill 99 with infantry and tanks against us. The 7th Company, under Schneider and Olin, deployed so as to hold our defensive position for

2. Author's Note: *Chronik Pz.Rgt. 5.*

3. Translator's Note: The German term used—*Luftmine*, literally aerial mine—is a bit unclear. It is generally interpreted as parachute bomb, but the effects described do not correspond exactly. A parachute mine is also similar in nature to the British or American "Blockbuster." Editor's Note: These were probably sea mines converted for use as an aerial bomb and dropped by parachute. These mines had a thin-walled casing, were packed with high explosive and were very effective weapons. The Germans used similar weapons.

as long as was needed until we had a clear idea of what had happened to the left and right of us. Thank God that we had conducted terrain reconnaissance a few days previously so as to be prepared for all eventualities. It was not intended to fall back across the river, which was an impassable obstacle for tanks.

The Russian infantry entered the patches of woods behind us, after the enemy had taken the bridgehead over the river, which was supposed to have been held by our neighbors, *"Totenkopf."* We were exposed to every pistol round at that point and could only conduct small movements. There was no thought given to attacks, either ours or in relief. Fortunately, radio contact with both the regiment and the division was still good. I was able to render a situation report. Relief was promised by the regiment, the division and even the artillery. Everything was unsuccessful, however.

Towards the afternoon, we were almost in the hands of the Russians. I ordered that no one was to leave their tank. All of the patrols being conducted by the tank crews were called off. Our only mission was to cover each other.

Around 1400 hours, we heard a detonation in the direction where my non-operational tank had been located. We immediately took off with two tanks to determine what had happened. We determined that after the crew had fired off the last of its ammunition, it had blown itself up in the air along with the tank.

We had our hands full trying to remain in firing positions and holding out. With the last bit of sending power left in the radios, we arranged with the division through the regiment to disengage from the enemy in the evening, around 1900 hours.

The time passed extraordinarily slowly. The amount of ammunition steadily dwindled; the fuel was also being increasingly reduced. We notified each another to only fire if it was absolutely necessary.

The Russians marched past us in column on the railway embankment. Everyone moving up above along the embankment took what he had—whether hand grenade or submachine gun—and fired at us. Our crews had to sit by and clench their teeth, since they were only allowed to fire in extreme necessity.

Around 1900 hours, it started to turn dark. The division had promised to fire artillery across Hill 99, on [it] and in front of [it] to support the first breakout attempt in the direction of Tluszcz. We had no other choice but to roll along with the Russian tanks in attack formation in the direction of our own lines.

To the left of us was a railway underpass that we had to go through. *Untersturmführer* Großrock was given the mission to advance with two tanks, pass through the underpass, thin out the ranks of the Russians once there and guide our tanks through. Following that, we wanted to deploy for combat and aggressively move towards our own lines together with the Russians.

Großrock took the lead, as was his norm. After he had barely passed through the underpass, his tank was knocked out by a direct hit. I assume it was a special charge with high penetrating capability. The tank was almost glowing. Großrock got out of his vehicle, 50 percent burned. The men of the crew were also able to save themselves and were taken aboard the other tanks.

The breakout attempt had failed. The rest of my tank battalion was positioned tank to tank, discussing the next breakout attempt on the radio. We were well camouflaged though; we had time, after all, since there was no longer anyone in a position to help us.

The friendly artillery fire did not come. As we later found out, the artillery was already back in its next firing position.

The second breakout attempt headed in the direction of our former neighbor, the "*Totenkopf*" Division, in the direction of the Cienka Bridge. The Russian tanks had already advanced across it and were on the far side of the river in our rear.

Untersturmführer Schicker, my adjutant, took the lead. I moved right behind him. He had barely moved 100 meters, when his tank nosed into a large bomb crater. His turret jammed. Schicker got his hand caught in the turret race and was badly injured. This breakout attempt also failed. A recovery was not possible. The tank had to be left behind. It was blown up. Schicker was taken aboard my tank. My tank was slowly becoming full with Großrock and Schneider and their crews. There was only one option left: Advance through the river with the tanks in the direction of Tluszcz to reach our own lines. There was no longer any radio contact.

The decision concerning the last breakout effort was made about 0200 hours and discussed in great detail. We had coupled together our tanks with their sideskirts—steel plates designed to protect the running gear—one tank with the other. We arranged to sink the sideskirts in the river to provide a good foundation for the tracks.[4]

---

4. Translator's Note: Apparently, Flügel's memory did not serve him well at this point, since he states the tanks were joined together by their sideskirts. He actually meant that they were coupled together by tow cables. The former might have been theoretically possible, but it would not have allowed the tanks to move. As indicated in the passage, the tanks were linked via tow cables, which helped them stay together when moving to the river. Undoubtedly, the sideskirts were loosened for easy and quick removal at the river.

The crossing over the river was to be covered by two quad *Flak*.

During the night, there was heavy armor movement in our vicinity. Aerial pyrotechnics of every color were fired above us by the Russians, and we were happy when some fog, attracted by the river, descended. Under its concealment, we would be able to conduct a detailed reconnaissance on foot. Using heavy flank security, we felt our way through the Russians to find a place where we could ford the tanks. I dismounted at the river along with a few platoon leaders and company commanders to find the exact crossing point. We did not get too far, because a Russian battalion had set up camp for the night on the far side. As I later discovered, it was there to follow the attack of the lead Russian elements, that had already taken Tluszcz.

At that point, the quad *Flak* were brought forward. They were placed off to the side, and a few sideskirts were dropped in the river. It was a total free-for-all. The Russians did not know who was their enemy or who was their friend, when the quad *Flak* opened up upon a pre-arranged signal and cleared a path for the crossing. The element of surprise and the panicky behavior of the Russians worked to our advantage, allowing the first few tanks, each coupled to the following one with a tow cable, to ford.

When the first ones reached the far side, they created some breathing room for us, and all of the other vehicles followed behind. We still had nine tanks left. After fording, we stopped and attempted to get over the railway embankment, which was paralleled by a very good road that lead to Tluszcz.

Förster's tank was sent forward to reconnoiter across the embankment. Everything proceeded very slowly and carefully. We had some time until first light, after all.

When Förster reached the embankment after about 300 meters . . . his tank detonated with a mighty crash, which literally lifted it into the air. He flew head over heels across the embankment and remained there, motionless. Without regard for what might happen, we moved forward and covered Förster's tank. Förster looked pretty bad. Several charges had been tossed up on his vehicle. The tank had rolled off of its tracks, and Förster was sitting there without his legs. They had been shredded. He said to me: "*Hauptsturmführer*, it's all over. I'm checking out."

We had to continue reconnoitering in the direction of Tluszcz with one of the remaining eight tanks. At first light, the 7th Company pushed one tank forward to check a small bridge in the vicinity for its load-bearing capacity. When the tank reached the bridge, Russians suddenly jumped out of the vegetation and knocked out the tank with demolition charges. The crew was able to dismount under cover of the remaining tanks and reach our lines.

Our ammunition started to run out. I personally only had a few aerial pyrotechnic signals left. From our position, we could observe how the Russians were marching at first light in the direction of Tluszcz; there were several tanks with infantry mounted on them. We had no other choice but to move though the vegetated terrain in the same direction in order to reach our own lines. My last pyrotechnic was intended to warn our comrades that they were dealing with their own tanks and not those of the Russians. Our seven tanks were overcrowded with wounded and the remaining other crews. Moving quickly, we headed in the same direction as the Russians towards our own lines. As we got closer, we heard the sound of fighting about 2 kilometers away.

I immediately ordered the recognition panel to be raised. Fortunately, our infantry identified us immediately. We succeeded in reaching our main line of resistance without taking any additional casualties. None of our company commanders were available; in some cases, they were wounded. We had succeeded in taking along all of our dead and wounded.

After two hours, I was headed out again with a new mission. The 5th Company, which was under the command of *Obersturmführer* Lichte at that point, was in a jam. My own tank had problems and was in the maintenance facility because of it. As a result, I took a tank from the regimental headquarters to allow our formations a little breathing room in their withdrawal movements.

✠

Who could capture the scope and the number of all of the individual accomplishments that took place daily on the battlefield? No chronicle could contain them all. What *SS-Untersturmführer* Seebode, an acting company commander, wrote to the father of a radio operator who was killed on 28 August 1944 may be considered illustrative of countless untold others:

For a few weeks now, the *"Wiking"* Division has thwarted all of the efforts by the Soviets to break through northeast of Warsaw. The tank regiment, in which your son, *SS-Sturmmann* Hendrik Ponse, radio operator, serves along with his brother, has played a significant role in this success. On 18 August, *Funktrupp Ponse* was hit by artillery fire, whereby your son, Hendrik Ponse, found his death, and his brother was badly wounded. *Funktrupp Ponse* was a household name throughout the regiment, and its loss hits us hard. In the most miserable of situations, *Funktrupp Ponse* provided the regiment with command and control by means of radio by its unstinting devotion to duty. Whenever it appeared to be impossible to establish radio communications with the tank companies, it was *Funktrupp Ponse* that established the connection.

The radio section was full of terrific camaraderie and was held in respect by all superiors. Even though badly wounded, *SS-Unterscharführer* Ponse made his report to his platoon leader: "*Funktrupp Ponse* not combat ready; two men killed; I myself badly wounded."

That was the spirit and attitude of your boys, and you can truly be proud of them. Exemplary in the fulfilling of his duty, Hendrik Ponse remained true to his German homeland unto his death. Loved and respected among his comrades, he will remain unforgotten by all of us.

Sturmmann Ponse was laid to rest at the military cemetery in Modlin.

The Soviets appeared to want to increase the offensive tempo. At the same time that the elements of the *II./SS-Panzer-Regiment 5* escaped the mousetrap at Tluszcz, 15 enemy tanks and infantry advanced out of the woods south of Kozly (3 kilometers north of Tluszcz) and crossed the road north of Krusze. They were then stopped by the regiment's 5th Company. By 1300 hours, the 5th Company had knocked out five enemy tanks. The number of tanks kept appearing to grow larger, however, as did the number of infantry. It seemed that for every tank knocked out, two took its place.

In the armored engagement that developed that afternoon between Kozly and Wolko Kozlowska, the 5th and 8th Companies knocked out an additional 13 Shermans and T-34's, supported by the *Panther* battalion of the *"Totenkopf"* Division. Late in the afternoon, friendly infantry pulled back from enemy armor advancing to the north against the positions of the *"Westland"* Regiment from Wolka Kozlowka. The *3./SS-Panzer-Regiment 5* fought it out there with 13 enemy tanks. The 4th Company of the tank regiment, employed in support of the 2nd Battalion of *"Westland,"* lost *SS-Untersturmführer* Harwik and two vehicles at Wolka.

On the division's left boundary around Przykory, the regimental reconnaissance platoon was involved in fighting against Soviet infantry and armor on the road heading from Mokrawies to the north. Strong Soviet forces that were brought forward the following night to the north through Tluszcz to the Jarzambiadonk area attacked further north at first light and forced the evacuation of the village of Debinki by *"Westland"* at 0800 hours. The 4th Company of the tank regiment succeeded in blocking the enemy force and preventing a threatening breakthrough along the almost exposed left flank of the division. At the same time, the 3rd Company was involved in heavy fighting along the boundary between the *"Westland"* and *"Germania"* Regiments against enemy forces that were pressing northwest from the Kozly area. For a while, the tank company held the position without infantry support, until elements of the grenadiers reorganized around the battalion command post and occupied a new defensive line along the field trail running from Chrosciele to Roszczep. It was only at that point that the 3rd Company was able to pull back to a new position around Fabianow.

Constantly fending off enemy tanks and infantry, the 5th Company, which was being supported by greatly weakened infantry elements, pulled back to Trojany along the Radzymin-Wyskow road. The regimental command post, which was practically in the front lines on occasion, moved to Karpin, to the north of that road. On that day of fighting, the 1st Battalion knocked out 5 tanks and the 2nd battalion accounted for 15.

✠

The danger of being enveloped on the division's left-hand boundary and the consequent result—being cut off from the rearward lines of communications—could only be achieved on the previous two days by the employment of the final reserves and the decisiveness of individual brave elements.

An enemy infantry and armor thrust from the east out of the Mieczyslawow area hit a gap in the front. It was the decisiveness and the tactical sense of the commander of the Headquarters Company, *SS-Obersturmführer* Senghas, that deprived the enemy of a victory that was almost within his grasp. In an after-action report on 29 August, Senghas wrote:

> On 18 August 1944, all of the trains elements, including the Headquarters Company, were under my command in Zabrodzie,

about 1 kilometer east of the Wyskow-Warsaw road. Around 1100 hours, a messenger from the German Armed Forces arrived at my location and said that the Russians had broken through 1 kilometer east of the rail line at Zabrodzie and that tanks were already outside the village. Friendly infantry, which had been positioned to the front, had pulled back and also scattered, with the result that a gap of about 3 to 4 kilometers existed at the front. I immediately had all the drivers man their vehicles and immediately alerted my tank hunter/killer teams. When that happened, I took my staff car to the east across the rail line to determine how strong the enemy was and from what direction he was attacking.

About 1 kilometers east of Zabrodzie, I ran into the lead elements of a Russian cavalry element and also saw a mass of enemy infantry widely dispersed moving from east to west towards the railway line. I immediately moved back to assemble combat elements of the trains and defend, along with two non-operational tanks, which were with the maintenance team. It was immediately apparent to me that the Russians had identified the gap in the front and were taking pains to get to the main road as soon as possible in an effort to hamstring the entire logistics effort of the division.

In the meantime, I held up scattered elements of an engineer battalion and a few noncommissioned officers and enlisted personnel of a penal company, who were fleeing back, and formed them into a company along with my trains elements. It was outfitted with submachine guns, rifles and pistols and had 58 men.

As we were going into position along the railway embankment, the enemy started firing artillery, antitank guns and mortars, which were in position 1.5 kilometers east of the railroad line. Around 1430 hours, a horse-mounted patrol came riding towards us—about 8-men strong—but it immediately turned off to the north when engaged and disappeared in the heavily vegetated terrain.

An hour later, I noticed movements along the western edge of the woods, approximately 1 kilometer east of the railway line, and immediately had the movements covered in fire by the two *Panzer IV's*, which I had had emplaced somewhat offset west of the railway line. A short while later, the enemy initiated heavy artillery and mortar fire and then moved out to attack in the direction of the railway embankment with approximately two companies, each composed of about 50 men. I had ordered the men not to open fire until pointblank range, since we were short of submachine gun ammunition. As a result, the fire had very good effect.

The two *Panzer IV's*, which I had set back somewhat, had to pull back right at the start of the attack, since they were receiving well-directed antitank gun fire. The Russian attack bogged down 200 meters in front of us. Because the enemy realized he was not going to be able to advance that way, he pulled back to the woods, leaving a lot of wounded out in the open . . .

Around 0830 hours, the enemy attacked again, this time out of the patch of woods east of the railway embankment and more in a northwesterly direction. He had probably reconnoitered during the night and determined that there was a gap of about 800 meters to the left of my company to the friendly forces on the left. There was a security regiment of the [Army] positioned there, with the mission to defend to the south.

The Russian attack was repeated twice that day and was turned back each time, with the enemy suffering bloody losses. Friendly losses were two badly and four slightly wounded men.

The night that followed also passed quietly. The next morning, however, the Russians laid down barrage fire with artillery and mortars for half an hour on our positions but concentrating on the friendly forces to the left. Towards 1000 hours, four enemy tanks moved north and quickly disappeared in the vegetated terrain.

An hour later, the enemy attacked our positions once more form the woods. Since my men did not have any machine guns, I had the radio operator machine guns taken off the tanks and had them emplaced in our positions to good effect.

When the Russian infantry had closed to about 600 meters, three of the four tanks suddenly appeared that we had seen previously, apparently wanting to support the Russian attack. One of my *Panzer IV's* knocked out all three in a short span of time; the fourth one was eliminated by the infantry on the left wing.

The enemy tanks—T-34's and Shermans—immediately caught fire and blew apart a short while later. The Russian attack then bogged down forward of our positions. When the enemy attacked again two hours later, a heavy antitank gun was destroyed.

Towards 1600 hours, a report was received from the right that the Russians had broken through in the sector of the *"Westland"* Regiment. I was then able to explain why we had been continuously receiving fire from the rear for more than an hour. When we ran out of ammunition at 1900 hours—the tanks had long since shot off their ammunition—and the front lines in the sector of the friendly forces to the left were being pulled back, we pulled back by circuitous

> routes. The village of Zazdros, which was right behind us, had been occupied by the enemy for some time.

For his initiative and well-thought-out actions, *SS-Obersturmführer* Senghas was awarded the Knight's Cross to the Iron Cross on 11 December 1944.[5]

During the night of 20–21 August, the greatly weakened battalions of the *"Westland"* Regiment were pulled back to Laskow, north of the Radzymin-Wyskow road, and reorganized. The 3rd and 4th Companies of the tank regiment covered the withdrawal movements and the reorganization and were engaged in combat with the enemy, who started attacking at 0400 hours. Under the heavy pressure exerted by the enemy, the main line of resistance was pulled back to the woods high ground southwest of Slopsk, including Points 103 and 106. The repeated enemy attacks, which were supported by fighter-bombers and heavy weapons, were driven back. The daily logs of the *I./SS-Panzer-Regiment 5* noted:

> The 3rd and 4th Companies are covering the reorganization of friendly grenadiers from good positions against the pressing enemy. Surrounded by Russian infantry and without infantry support in the woods, the crews are offering resistance and enabling friendly grenadiers the necessary time to reorganize and go into position on Hills 106 and 103 near Slopsk.

The character of the fighting to defend the main line of resistance, which was only occupied in strongpoint fashion, is reflected in this after-action report submitted by Senghas concerning the operations of the antiaircraft platoon of the 1st Battalion:

> The battalion headquarters was in front of the line of infantry; the *Flak* platoon secured in the direction of Wolka-Slopska with its No. 2 gun. There were no more infantry up front. The outpost of Gun No. 2 observed Russian infantry entering the southeastern portion of Wolka-Slopska, first with 20 men and then, 100 meters farther back, 25 to 30 men. Well-placed constant fire with all four barrels forced the Russians to pull back in a panic. In any case, the Russians suffered casualties as a result of the ambush by fire.

5. Translator's Note: Scherzer lists Senghas as being the acting commander of the *I./SS-Panzer-Regiment 5* on the award. (Veit Scherzer, *Die Ritterkreuzträger*, Scherzers Militaire-Verlag, Ranis/Jena: 2005, 674.)

> After about two hours, the enemy felt his way forward again with a few squads. In the process, he succeeded in placing a mortar into position. After our fire opened up again, the enemy covered our position with mortar fire. Within one or two minutes, Gun No. 4 had four casualties. The gun had to change position immediately.
>
> The only one left at the battalion command post was the commander and his tank. There was nothing else left there. The command post moved to Marjanow.

In the righthand sector of the division, where the *"Germania"* Regiment was committed, the enemy succeeded in taking Trojany along the Radzymin-Wyskow rail line after attacking all day. The tank regiment command post was northwest of Dombrowka, collocated with the command post of the infantry regiment. The *I./SS-Panzer-Grenadier-Regiment "Eicke"* of the *"Totenkopf"* Division, which was employed there as reinforcements, pulled back to new positions just 500 meters from the command post of the tank regiment.

When the lefthand division sector was assumed by the *1131. Infanterie-Brigade* of *Oberst* Söth in the afternoon, the *"Wiking"* Division swung into a north-south defensive line northwest of Radzymin. The Army infantry brigade was positioned in a line running Slopsk—Points 103/106—Malopole. That evening, the tank regiment command post moved to the northern edge of Gutzowatka, southwest of Dombrowka.

While the 2nd Battalion assumed the screening mission southwest of Dombrowka, the 1st Battalion remained as the ready reserve behind the Army infantry brigade in the east part of Marjanow, half way between Dombrowka and the south bank of the Bug at Slenzany.

The fighting of 23 and 24 August was characterized by enemy efforts to cross the road to the north with stronger forces. After successful immediate counterattacks by the 1st Battalion at Hill 103 and the 2nd Battalion at Hill 106 and Malopole, the main line of resistance remained firmly in German hands. Malopole changed ownership three times, however.

The 24th of August was also marked by efforts to improve and establish friendly positions in anticipation of the expected Russian advance to the Bug crossings.

SS-Obersturmführer Metzger assumed command of the 4th Company on 23 August. The relative quiet allowed the presentation of deserved awards. The commander of the 6th Company, *SS-Untersturmführer* Großrock, received the Knight's Cross to the Iron Cross from the acting division commander, *SS-Standartenführer* Mühlenkamp, at the regimental command post, which had moved in the meantime to the forestry buildings 1.5 kilometers west of Cisie.

At the command post of the 1st Battalion, *SS-Untersturmführer* Meyer received the Iron cross, First Class for his fearless actions. *SS-Schütze* Wieser received the same award. Although a messenger, Wieser quickly assumed the duties of tank gunner, who was not available, during the fighting at Fabianow on the battalion commander's tank and knocked out a T-34 with his first round.

✠

Starting at 0300 hours on 25 August, the Russians placed barrage fires of all calibers on the positions of the *1131. Infanterie-Brigade.* The 1st Battalion of the tank regiment had moved all non-essential vehicles of the battle staff across the bridge over the Bug at Slenzany to the north bank. This proved to have been a prudent measure, since the battalion commander discovered at the brigade command post an hour after the barrage started that the Soviets had penetrated the main line of resistance along the boundaries between the brigade's 1st and 2nd Battalions and had already infiltrated into the patch of woods 2 kilometers south of the command post.

While the 4th Company attempted to win back Hill 97 south of Ludwinow, the 3rd Company was committed against the enemy in the 1st Battalion's sector of the infantry brigade.

When the woods southeast of Ludwinow were lost, the 3rd Company was directed to the village in an effort to hold it. The general murkiness of the situation was reflected by the statement of a captured Soviet soldier, who stated that his mission had been to determine whose vehicles were actually moving around in Ludwinow. The 3rd Company discovered from the same soldier that five KV(SU)-85[6] assault guns were positioned to the south right outside of the village.

✠

After the loss of Jaktory, Malopole and Gutzowatka, the 8th Company was positioned at Point 104 southeast of Kolakow in the right-hand sector of the division. In the fighting for the villages, the company had knocked out five Shermans and T-34's and immobilized another seven. Of that number, eight were attributed to *SS-Unterscharführer* Tausend alone.

During the evening of 25 August, the 6th and 8th Companies, together with tanks from the *"Totenkopf"* Division, screened in a triangle defined by

6. Editor's Note: The KV-85 was a KV chassis mounting a fully-rotating turret with an 8.5-cm main gun. The SU-85 assault gun had a fixed superstructure mounting an 8.5-cm gun, with limited traverse, on the chassis of a T-34.

Zawady-Los-Mokry. Farther to the north, Soviet tanks advanced as far as the south bank of the Bug at Czarnow, after bypassing Ludwinow. As a result, they had positioned themselves between the *"Wiking"* Division and the *1131. Infanterie-Brigade* by that evening. The infantry's weak forces appeared to be exhausted, and they were withdrawn during the night to a smaller bridgehead around Slenzany.

THE SLENZANY BRIDGEHEAD

The main line of resistance of the *I./Infanterie-Brigade 1131* ran from the south bank of the Bug east of Slenzany to the south to the southern edge of Kowalicha. It formed its boundary there with the 2nd Battalion of the brigade—*Bataillon Augustin*—whole lines extended to the southwest to the southern edge of Ludwinow and then to the northwest as far as the patch of woods about 1.5 kilometers northwest of the village. Recognizing the danger present along the uncovered southwest flank due to the enemy armor forces that had already reached Czarnow, *SS-Hauptsturmführer* Säumenicht, the commander of the 1st Battalion of the tank regiment, decided to conduct a reconnaissance-in-force in the direction of the latter village. It was intended to destroy the four Shermans reported there, occupy the locality and then establish contact to the southeast with the right wing of *Bataillon Augustin.* Although the operation did not succeed in its intended objectives, it was determined that there were no German outposts for a stretch of 2 kilometers between the northern edge of Ludwinow and the southern edge of Czarnow. Säumenicht ordered his 3rd Company to occupy positions along the southern edge of Slenzany—2 kilometers from its then current positions southeast of the village—to defend against an anticipated enemy armored thrust from Czarnow.

At almost the same time as the 3rd Company started to change positions—around 0400 hours—the Soviets also advanced. Although the enemy was turned back, he achieved notable success in detonating the charges placed on the nearby 24-ton bridge by means of a direct hit. The bridge was destroyed. Traffic in and out of the threatened bridgehead was stopped.

Since there was no longer any direct contact with the tank regiment north of Benjaminow, some 13 kilometers southwest of Slenzany, as a result of the Soviet wedge on the south bank of the Bug as far as Czarnow, Säumenicht directed his adjutant, *SS-Obersturmführer* Mittelbacher, to rope across the destroyed bridge to the north bank, establish contact with *Oberst* Söth and then inform the commander of *SS-Panzer-Regiment 5* about the situation and request orders. *Oberst* Söth requested the bridge be restored. While he was requesting the repairs, the acting commander of the division, Mühlenkamp, issued orders at his command post to the regimental commander, *SS-*

Obersturmbannführer Darges, affecting the 1st Battalion. The commanding general, Gille, was present:

> On order of the division, the *I./[SS-Panzer-Regiment 5]* attacks the enemy armored force at Czarnow and eliminates it. It then breaks through to the west into the Stasiopol Kuligow bridgehead. [Establish] an armored bridgehead at the Popowo-Koscielne Bridge.
>
> In case *Brigade Söth* receives orders from the Commanding General, *SS-Gruppenführer* Gille, to pull back from its current bridgehead, it is to destroy the bridge in such a manner that an infantry attack on Jackowo will be impossible.

In addition, Mittelbacher received a directive from the regimental commander to ford through the Bug to the north in case the division order could not be carried out. It was then to move to the Kuligow Bridgehead via Popowo.

After establishing contact with the on-site commander at the Kuligow Bridgehead, *SS-Hauptsturmführer* Schlette, Mittelbacher returned to the 1st Battalion's command post in the patch of woods 3 kilometers north of Barcice and briefed the battalion commander, who was south of the Bug, by radio.

After the five KV(SU)-85's that were in Ludwinow the previous day also broke through to the north and linked up with the enemy tanks in Czarnow, Säumenicht entertained doubts concerning the chances of success for the ordered attack on Kuligow, where there were another eight tanks.

Nevertheless, the 1st Battalion launched its attack at 1330 hours in accordance with its orders. The four assault guns of the 4th Company pushed forward under the covering fires provided by the 3rd Company and quickly reached the edge of Czarnow. It was there at 1400 hours that a round from a Soviet sniper mortally wounded Säumenicht. The German attack wavered and was unable to make any further progress. Receiving fire from the numerically superior enemy force, the 1st Battalion pulled back to Slenzany.

The commander of the 4th Company, *SS-Obersturmführer* Metzger, wrote the following after-action report on 1 September:

> I initially made good progress with my four assault guns and placed several salvoes on the eastern edge of Czarnow from firing positions 400 meters west of Slenzany. In the continued attack, I got to within 400 meters of the east side of Czarnow; then had to swing out to the left to reconnoiter for a dry patch of ground, since the terrain in front of me was very marshy. Finding a path 300 meters further to the south, I got to within 50 meters of the east side of Czarnow. Looking

> for my wing vehicles, I saw that both of them were 300 meters behind me to the right and stuck in the marsh.
>
> Directly behind me was my wingman and the *Panzer IV's* of the 3rd Company.
>
> As I advanced with my assault gun towards the edge of the locality, pulling out from behind high ground, I was suddenly in front of two enemy tanks, a Sherman and a T-34, moving across my front.
>
> Right after my first round, I had a misfire and was just able to get my assault gun backed up and under cover thanks to the quick thinking of my driver. I was unable to observe the effect of my round, since the scissors scope and the vision blocks were shot in two in short order.
>
> At the same moment, I heard on the radio about the severe wounding of the battalion commander and received orders to pull back.
>
> The withdrawal succeeded despite difficult circumstances (a few *Panzer IV's* and one assault gun were stuck in the marshland off to the sides of the road) as a result of the fabulous teamwork of the tank crews. I moved in my assault gun to the two stuck assault gun in order to pull them loose. The pulling effort did not succeed. Under covering fire from my assault gun, the two crews were able to be recovered, including one badly wounded man. The two assault guns were then blown up.

According to Metzger, the failed attack and the slow withdrawal of the dwindling infantry towards Slenzany led to the following situation at 1600 hours:

> The enemy moved out against the bridgehead that extended in the direction of Slenzany with fire support from all of his weapons and attacked from the east, south and west with armored support.

The desperate attempt to find a ford site suitable for tanks through the Bug remained without success. Two *Panzer IV's* that sank while attempting to ford were blown up. The remaining six *Panzer IV's* and two assault guns, which were then under the command of *SS-Obersturmführer* Senghas, covered the retreat of the grenadiers across the Bug with their remaining ammunition. Once it was expended, they were blown up. Metzger's report continues:

> Since one of the assault guns had already expended its ammunition, the other one, along with the *Panzer IV's* of the 3rd Company, helped

> suppress the enemy, who was pressing hard from the south and the southwest. While the friendly infantry crossed the Bug to the north, the tank crews were still fighting. With the approval of *Obersturmführer* Senghas, the guns and the *Panzer IV's* were blown up after they had fired their last ammunition, the bridgehead had been reduced and the enemy infantry had closed to within 50 meters. *Obersturmführer* Senghas and I were the last to leave the bridgehead with the remaining tank crews.

A final attempt to help came when *SS-Obersturmführer* Schumacher hurried towards the battalion's location with two *Panthers* and two *Panzer IV's* from the maintenance facility. But it was too late.

The results of the day were depressing. The losses suffered were especially difficult to take when every tank was needed to help contain the Soviet onslaught. In addition to irreplaceable men and equipment, the battalion also lost its commander. Eight *Panzer IV's* and four assault guns were complete losses.

Enemy losses were registered as 3 Shermans, 2 T-34's, 2 antitank guns and 10 light infantry guns, in addition to numerous casualties in the form of dead and wounded.

It is understandable that there were intimations of guilt when the men were under such extreme physical and mental stress and that recriminations were heard against all parties. After-the-fact determinations came to be mixed in with the flow of events of that day.

The Soviet efforts had been directed towards the destruction of the enemy armor positioned at Slenzany, at the access point to the bridge and the crossing itself. Although the defenseless tanks that had run out of ammunition in front of the bridge could still move, there were no fording sites and the grenadiers would have been able to hold out against such massive numbers of enemy for only so long. The tanks were no longer capable of fulfilling a combat mission. Forced to abandon the bridgehead, the tanks had to be blown up.

The enemy was so content with his success, that the infantry forces east of Slenzany and still on the south bank of the Bug—the 1st Battalion of *Infanterie-Brigade 1131*, whose right wing was only about 400 meters east of Slenzany—were able to remain in its positions until that evening. It was not until around 2100 hours that the battalion evacuated its positions and moved across the river to the north bank.

The Army brigade commander, *Oberst* Söth, wrote the following in an after-action report to the division written on 27 August:

> The withdrawal movement was magnificently support by the tank battalion of *Hauptsturmführer* Säumenicht; The coordination with the battalion could be characterized as exemplary on the preceding days as well . . .
>
> In my opinion, the tank crews did not want to leave the hard-pressed grenadiers until every last one of them had crossed and then, after the last round had been fired, blown up the vehicles to prevent the tanks from falling into the hands of the enemy. A withdrawal towards the 1st Battalion [of the infantry] might have possibly kept the tanks, but strong pressure by a superior enemy would have caused heavy casualties to the [infantry] battalion.
>
> Therefore, I absolve the tank crews, whom I had come to know as unflappable warriors, of any question of guilt.

✠

Following the withdrawal from Slenzany, an outpost line was established on the north bank of the river using trains elements and rear-area services personnel. The backbone of the line was formed by the two *Panzer IV's* and an assault gun of Kampe's platoon from the 3rd Company. A second group, consisting of three *Panthers* and one assault gun, performed the same mission at the 70-ton bridge at Popowo, 5 kilometers further to the west. It was under the command of *SS-Oberscharführer* Müller of the 7th Company.

It was imperative that the enemy be prevented from crossing over to the north bank of the river.

✠

During the night of 26–27 August, what remained of the 1st Battalion of the tank regiment (minus Kampe's platoon) was pulled out of the line and moved to Marynin, 4.5 kilometers west of Serock on the west bank of the Narew, with the intent of regrouping and maintaining tanks, vehicles, weapons and equipment.

On 28 August, which passed relatively quietly, the battalion took its leave of its dead commander. Each company provided a detail of three enlisted and two noncommissioned officers to join the officer corps of the battalion in paying its final respects in the citadel at the Modlin Fortress, where he was laid to rest.

The lost of the south bank of the Bug between Wyskow and Serock signaled the end of the first phase of the Soviet operation breakthrough to the northwest in the sector of the division. The success of the defensive fighting, in which the tank regiment played a significant role, was the fact that the large-scale Soviet breakthrough operation was slowed down. Following its crossing over the Bug at Wlodawa, the 1st White Russian Front took more than 170 kilometers of ground—as far as the area south of Stanislawow—in 10 days. It took more than 30 days of extremely hard fighting to take the next 40 kilometers as far as the line running Bug-Serock-Nieporent-Vistula (northwest of Warsaw)—that is, one quarter of the area in three times the time.

The Soviet offensive, conducted with a 10-to-1 superiority in numbers, could initially be stopped in the line described above. In the 60 days that followed, from 31 August to the end of November 1944, the enemy was only able to push the cohesive front of the division another 20 kilometers back—one meter at a time—in the hard fighting in the so-called "wet triangle" between the Narew and the Vistula.

The unusual harshness of the fighting was determined by the oppressive superiority of the enemy in terms of materiel and personnel on the one hand and the iron will of the individual warrior to assert himself and the moral strength of the formations in the defense on the other hand.

The fighting was also characterized by another factor, the unusual terrain features of the combat area of operations. The south bank of the Bug was bordered by a band of dunes and marshes that extended anywhere from 2 to 3 kilometers. Adjoining it and running parallel was a band of continuous woodland that also ran from 2 to 3 kilometers in width. The east bank of the Narew was similar in character.

The entire area of operations south of the Bug and the Narew was broken up and covered by creeks, patches of woods and forests of a wide variety of expanse. The "wet triangle" is also cut up by canals and dead tributaries to a large extent. Terrain of that nature hinders the combat operations of a tank regiment or an armored division. Tank maneuverability and the employment of weapons to maximum effective range is greatly reduced. By the same token, the danger to tanks, whose visibility is reduced, is increased by their exposure to close-in infantry assault. The main strength of armor—massed employment as part of a large formation—is hardly possible.

The same conditions were of decisive advantage to the massed Soviet rifle divisions. The woods allowed a rapid infiltration of the infantry swarming through them like bees and a corresponding infiltration through the German formations, which had shrunk to almost nothing in some cases.

The ability of the Soviets to mass artillery at will, coupled with the unimpeded employment of close-air support, acted as combat multipliers for the Soviets, who were already massively superior in numbers.

THE SECOND RECONSTITUTION OF THE *I./SS-PANZER-REGIMENT 5*

After eight weeks of uninterrupted operations, the tank regiment's 1st Battalion only had its 4th Company still committed against the enemy. The battalion, which had already been pulled out of the line once before for reconstitution—six months previously after the Tscherkassy Pocket—was once again no longer combat effective after the conclusion of the fighting for the crossings over the Bug at Slenzany.

Two of the companies, the 1st and 2nd, did not even see the initial round of fighting described in the previous section, since they had been moved to the Heidelager/Debica Training Areas at the end of July. At the end of August, the were in the Litzmannstadt (Lodz) area for training and under the command of *SS-Hauptsturmführer* Hein. They still did not have any tanks to train with, however.

The elements of the battalion that had been committed were pulled back to Marynin on the west bank of the Narew, where they were given a rest period and given the opportunity to maintain weapons, equipment and vehicles. Visits to the movies in Ostenburg (Pultusk) helped provide some recreation.

The tireless truck drivers received a seemingly odd mission, given the current situation at the front: They moved Hungarian forces from the area around Zegrznek to Struga. Based on agreements with the Hungarian government, the *Honved* forces were being sent back to Hungary.

On 6 September, the elements of the battalion being reconstituted were moved into the Bugmünde (Nowy-Dwor) area, because they would be allowed undisturbed training, removed from the direct influence of the front. That was made all the more necessary, since the personnel replacements were primarily coming from forced transfers from the *Luftwaffe*. Their basic training for ground combat left a lot to be desired.

In addition to the military requirements, personal needs were also met. For instance, the commander of the regiment, *SS-Obersturmbannführer* Darges, officiated at the proxy wedding of *SS-Unterscharführer* Schlegel of the 3rd Company on 7 September. The wedding ceremony served as inspiration for an extended celebration by the company afterwards.

As part of the organizational changes that came with the reconstitution effort, *SS-Untersturmführer* Weise assumed command of the tank maintenance company on 7 September. On 17 September, the regimental armored engineer company was deactivated in Zakrozym. Each battalion received a platoon of engineers in its place.

To continued the undisturbed training, the battalion was moved to Naruszewo (12 kilometers south of Plöhnen/21 kilometers northwest of Modlin) that same day. At the same time, *SS-Obersturmführer* Senghas assumed command of the 1st Company in Horschowitz.

As part of the major reorganization within the armored forces in 1944, the battalion also formed a logistics company. Its command was assumed by the battalion adjutant, who was simultaneously also the commander of the battalion's headquarters company. In addition, the adjutant was also entrusted with command of *Alarm-Bataillon II*, an *ad hoc* alert element.

In the meantime, the 2nd Company, which received 17 *Panzer IV's* from Linz on 17 September, arrived in Bugmünde, where it was able to continue its training until 25 September. The next day, the training and reconstitution period was over for it, the headquarters company and the battle staff. Coming in from Bugmünde and Naruszewo, the units arrived in the new area of operations around Zagroby—Wieliszew—D. Poniatow, south of the large bend in the Narew, where they linked up with the 4th Company, which had been in constant combat during this period.

SS-Obersturmführer Hain had this to say about his elements in a report prepared for the tank regiment headquarters on 5 October:

> The general health of the men is good. As a result of the activities of the battalion surgeon and the attentiveness of the unit leaders, incidents of illness have only surfaced individually . . .
>
> Soldier support for the men whose homelands have since been occupied by the Allies (ethnic Germans from Rumania, Flemish and Dutch) need to be developed even more . . .

In his summary, he wrote:

> After issuance of the missing armored fighting vehicles, the battalion has become operational in an extremely short period. The battalion has reached an excellent standard in all areas.

The continued separate employment of individual elements of the battalion is detrimental to the cohesiveness of the men. It makes command of the battalion more difficult, results in greater losses to the smaller number of vehicles the battalion can send into action and does not bring the heretofore accustomed success . . .

CHAPTER 8

The Second Battle of Warsaw

While the main body of the 1st Battalion was undergoing reconstitution for four weeks, the regimental headquarters, the 2nd Battalion and the 4th Company were continuously involved in defensive fighting in the so-called Second Battle of Warsaw as part of the division.

On 29 August, Kampe's platoon was positioned on the north bank of the Bug at the 70-ton bridge at Popowo with its three *Panzer IV's*; *SS-Unterscharführer* Sander had his three assault guns at the 24-ton bridge at Slenzany. Until 2 September, the enemy did not attempt to undertake any crossing attempts. Instead, he concentrated his efforts in the direction of the bend on the Narew south of Serock and on the Radzymin area, where he succeeded in penetrating into the northwestern portion on 29 August. During that fighting, the 8th Company knocked out five enemy tanks. The enemy also penetrated into Trzciana and Ruda, 6 kilometers northwest of Radzymin, but the 6th Company was able to eject the enemy from Trzciana. Further to the north, the 5th Company held the eastern edge of Zalubice.

A counterattack launched against Regentowka by the 2nd Battalion (three tanks) and supported by tanks from the 1st Battalion of *SS-Panzer-Regiment 3 "Totenkopf"* and the 2nd and 3rd Companies of the divisional reconnaissance battalion never got anywhere, however.

Over the next two days, the 2nd Battalion eliminated 20 enemy tanks. Despite that, the enemy pressure on Alezxndrow, west of Radzymin, and Borki, 7 kilometers to the northwest, remained unabated. In that fighting, the 2nd Battalion was supported by the 5th and 6th Companies of *SS-Panzer-Grenadier-Regiment "Eicke"* of the *"Totenkopf"* Division. Gegielnia, a village on the road to Warsaw, was lost. It was apparent that the enemy was concentrating his efforts in that sector. After strong artillery and mortar preparation along the entire division sector, he moved out at 1000 hours on 1 September with strong armor and air support in the direction of Radzminiek and Slupno on the major road to Warsaw.

The 2nd Battalion of *"Westland"* and the 5th Company of the tank regiment were overrun, resulting in the loss of a *Panther* and two *Panzer IV's*. Slupno proper was lost. A breakthrough by the enemy tanks was prevented in the tank engagement that took place, however. Despite heavy friendly artillery fire on Slupno, the Soviets attacked from there to the southeast at 1830 hours. Forty Soviet bombers churned up the ground around the hotly contested Point 104. The defenders continued to hold however, even after a second vehemently conducted attack. Among the 24 enemy tanks destroyed were Shermans, Valentines, T-34's, T-43's and KV-I's.

✠

The intensity of the attacks abated in the next two days. The enemy then attempted his luck in three night attacks, each preceded by an hour of barrage fire, against Borki. *Panzergrenadier-Regiment 73* (*19. Panzer-Division*) turned back the attacks. Although Borki was lost the following afternoon, an immediate counterattack launched by a penal battalion—*Bewährungs-Bataillon 560*—and *Bataillon Ridder* regained the village by 2200 hours.

A penetration at Point 104 was sealed off and eliminated by the 5th Company of the tank regiment.

On 4 September, *Bataillon Ridder*, supported by the *7./SS-Panzer-Regiment 5*, ejected enemy forces that had penetrated into the area marked by dunes at Dombrowa and Arciechow, in the vicinity of the mouth of the Bug southeast of Serock. In the Borki area, the regimental reconnaissance platoon reported knocking out two assault guns and a T-34.

✠

The reduction in fighting the preceding two days in the division's sector was explained during the evening of 4 September. At Wyszkow, an important road and rail hub with crossing points over the Bug some 50 kilometers northeast of Warsaw, the Soviets had broken through the positions of the *35. Infanterie-Division* and the *5. Gebirgsjäger-Division* and was pressing forward in the direction of Ostenburg (Pultusk), supported by about 12 tanks.

The 4th Company of the tank regiment was ordered to Wola-Mystowska at 1900 hours with four assault guns to interdict the enemy forces that had broken through. After knocking out two enemy self-propelled guns and a truck, darkness prevented further operations.

At 2030 hours, new orders sent the company to the Wyskow-Serock road, north of Somianka, to cover the withdrawals of the *1131. Infanterie-Brigade* and the *35. Infanterie-Division* across the Narew at Serock. In an after-action report submitted on 10 September, *SS-Obersturmführer* Metzger, the company commander, reported:

> The withdrawal movements of the friendly infantry were screened by four assault guns, screening to the east. The four assault guns leapfrogged from one terrain feature to the next, picked up stragglers and wounded and reached the bridgehead northeast of Serock around 0500 hours the next day without major combat activity. From there, they continued to screen the continued withdrawal of the infantry until 0630 hours.
>
> At 0635 hours, I advanced with the four assault guns towards the east on the road another 2 kilometers and identified pursuing enemy infantry, antitank guns and horse-drawn elements in the patch of woods northeast of Serock. After shooting individual infantry sections to pieces, I withdrew to the bridgehead under heavy antitank gun fire and crossed the Narew at 0705 hours as the last unit. Five minutes later, the bridge was blown up by order of *SS-Obersturmbannführer* Braune.

As a result of the loss of the east bank of the Narew north of Serock, the possibility of a northern envelopment of the positions between Warsaw and the bend in the Narew south of Serock became apparent. As a result, a direct countermeasure after the evacuation of the friendly bridgehead was to send Olin's platoon of 4 *Panthers* of the 7th Company to Karolino, west of Serock, to act as a ready reserve. The regimental maintenance company was moved further to the rear and the regimental command post was shifted to Nieporent.

During the night of 4–5 September, while the German withdrawals across the Narew were taking place, the enemy succeeded in also crossing the Narew, 7.5 kilometers further north at Pogorzelec. The 600 men were assisted in their effort by the flanking opportunity afforded by a broad bend in the river that opened to the west. Despite immediate counterattacks by the 4th Company of the tank regiment, supported by an *SPW* company of the divisional engineers and, later on, Olin's platoon from the 7th Company, the enemy could not be eliminated, even after the 4th Company reached Pogorzelec.

In Metzger's after-action report, the following can be read:

> After being resupplied, the company moved out at 0835 hours with three assault guns and reached Point 81, west of Dsierzenin, without enemy contact. But after crossing the high ground, it started to receive heavy artillery fire. The *SPW* company swung to the left in an enveloping maneuver. The assault guns advanced frontally against

> the southwestern portion of Pogorzelec and reached a line 500 meters from the southern edge of Pogorzelec.
>
> Two assault guns became mechanically disabled there, but they were towed to the rear under extremely heavy infantry fire. I changed vehicles and reached Hill 108 in Pogorzelec and continued to advance another 1,000 meters east. Since there were no friendly infantry to provide security, enemy infantry pressed forward around 1200 hours after I had withdrawn (due to receiving a new mission) and expanded their bridgehead to the west in the course of events.

The new mission took the company to Dsierzenin, which the enemy, who was pressing towards the south, had already reached after also blocking the Ostenburg (Pultusk)–Serock road. Metzger: "We advanced as far as Hill 110.5, but the infantry that followed did not come forward, with the result that the attack was denied even greater success."

The enemy forces, which were being reinforced with heavy weapons and armor, were already being reported at 1500 hours with large infantry elements in Dzbanice, 3 kilometers northwest of Pogorzelec. During the afternoon of that 5 September, the following German forces were introduced against the enemy bridgehead that was expanding to the northwest, west and south: From the north, an armored brigade with lead elements at Gzowo on the Narew, approximately 4 kilometers north of Pogorzelec; from the west with *Panzergrenadier-Regiment 1007*[1] of the *19. Panzer-Division;* and, from the south, the *1131. Infanterie-Brigade.*

In addition to the elements of the 7th and 4th Companies at Dsierzenin, there were four *Panthers* of the 8th Company (*SS-Untersturmführer* Bauer) at Trzepowo 3 kilometers west of Pogorzelec. The fighting that was conducted with great bitterness on both sides at first light on 6 September did not bring success to the German formations. Both of the battalion commanders of *Panzergrenadier-Regiment 1007* were killed.

A certain amount of disappointment and criticism can be read in Metzger's after-action report of 10 September. His attack objective, together with the regiment's 7th Company, had been the bridge over the Narew at Karniewec:

> As ordered, the company moved out at 0430 hours with four assault guns and one *Panzer IV*; it reached a general line 500 meters north of the cemetery to the left of the road.

1. Translator's Note: There is no record of a *Panzergrenadier-Regiment 1007*, either organic to the *19. Panzer-Division* or exclusive of it. It is not certain where the author got this information. The organic mechanized infantry regiments of the *19. Panzer-Division* were *Panzergrenadier-Regiment 73* and *Panzergrenadier-Regiment 74*.

> The friendly infantry, which only followed the guns hesitantly, lacked an aggressive spirit, and after casualties were taken after the first few hundred meters, it no longer advanced.
>
> I engaged heavy machine-gun nests and antitank rifles with the guns. The *Panzer IV* received an antitank gun hit in the right drive sprocket and, after an unsuccessful attempt to retrieve it, received another hit in the fighting compartment, which resulted in a total loss of the *Panzer IV*.
>
> While the company attempted to rally the friendly infantry forward once more by holding on to the line described above, two tank commanders and four men of the company were wounded. I personally was slightly wounded and pulled back to the line of departure at 0520 hours as the last assault gun.
>
> In summing up, Metzger wrote:
>
> The attack, which was conducted after a preceding friendly artillery preparation of only 20 to 30 shells against well-constructed field fortifications of the enemy, could not be crowned with success due to the numerical inferiority (Force ratio: 1:20). I had the impression that the attacks on the bridgehead were not properly prepared from on high. In any event, there was no cohesiveness in the command and control to any great degree.

For his part, the enemy charged south twice in vain against tanks positioned there.

✠

Recognizing the necessity to coordinate the friendly attacks, the command post of the regiment's 1st Battalion moved to Marynin, northwest of Serock, during the afternoon. Likewise in recognition of the enemy's shifted main effort (north of the Narew), the elements of the 2nd Battalion that were positioned southwest of Radzymin at Point 104 were pulled back into the woods south of Nieporent behind the Krolewski Canal.

During the night of 6–7 September and during the following morning hours, the enemy expanded his established bridgehead to the north and west so as to create the prerequisites for breaking through to the south at 1600 hours with strong tank forces into the left flank of the division and, in case the effort succeeded, in turning out the division from its then current positions along the Narew.

Twenty enemy tanks succeeded in breaking through in the direction of Male, 5 kilometers northwest of Serock. At the same time, Soviet infantry pressed the right wing of *Panzergrenadier-Regiment 73* (*19. Panzer-Division*) back along the road towards Serock.

While tanks from the *"Totenkopf"* Division were able to master the situation there, the regiment's 7th Company (*SS-Untersturmführer* Olin) was committed against the 20 enemy tanks that had broken through. Four *Panthers* faced the enemy at Murowanka, northeast of Male; 2 *Panthers* fought 10 enemy tanks at Male. The commander of the 2nd Battalion, *SS-Hauptsturmführer* Flügel, hurried with his command tank and an assault gun to Dembinki, south of Male, to size up the situation.

Olin was able to achieve victory in the Male area with the *Panthers* of this 7th Company. Eleven of the tanks that had broken through were destroyed. One of them turned out to be a milestone for the regiment: It was the 500th tank "kill" the regiment had claimed in five months of operations, commencing in April 1944. In addition, Olin's men captured two tanks.

On that 7 September, the 4th Company also proved unshakeable in the maelstrom, even though it only had three operational assault guns, meaning that its over-all combat power was less than that of a fully equipped platoon. Metzger wrote about the actions of his company in his after-action report:

> The company was positioned with three assault guns 1 kilometer west of the cemetery at Dzierzenin, screening in a generally northerly direction. A massed large-scale attack by the enemy, which took place at 1000 hours, was finally defeated through massed fires at 1100 hours, in conjunction with the 7th Company.
>
> The enemy marched past us, about 1,500 meters in front of our eyes, in a west-southwest direction with strong infantry forces.
>
> At 1200 hours, enemy tanks were reported in the Male area. The 7th Company headed in that direction with 5 *Panthers*. I continued to block to the north with my three assault guns and, at 1700 hours, defeated another strong enemy attack in front of my position. In the process, one assault gun suffered bad track and final drive damage. Under heavy enemy fire, the assault gun was repaired to the extent that it could be towed. The recovery took place in the middle of strong enemy infantry forces around Male.
>
> After I changed vehicles, I was in my old position with my assault gun and attempted to turn back a new enemy attack at 1745 hours. The enemy, who was vastly superior (1:30), gained ground and was soon directly along the left flank of my position.

While engaging enemy infantry, I suddenly caught sight of 2 T-43's 200 meters off my right flank. Their commanders were being briefed at the moment. Both of the tanks were knocked out in 20 seconds with two rounds.

The entire attack stopped at the moment the two enemy tanks detonated and portions of the attacking forces streamed to the rear.

Ten minutes later, the right track on my assault gun broke. The damage was repaired in an hour of work under heavy enemy fire. I covered the withdrawal of the infantry from the enemy with my assault gun. At 2100 hours, I linked up with the *Panthers* of the 7th Company and screened north until 0200 hours in the Male area.

✠

In the division sector south of the Narew, the enemy was quiet. Within the framework of the Soviet 28th Army, which was positioned across from the *IV. SS-Panzer-Korps* north of Warsaw, the division was facing the XX Rifle Corps with four Guards rifle divisions (76th, 20th, 42nd and 55th) ever since the beginning of September. The rifle corps had replaced the VIII Guards Tank Corps, which had been pulled out of the line. The materiel superiority of the enemy came into sharp focus through aerial reconnaissance, which showed that there were 130 enemy batteries in position around Radzymin, ten times as many as the *"Wiking"* Division could muster.

✠

In the days that followed, the enemy limited himself to local attacks, which generally could be turned back. Only the penetration into the northern portion of Serock could not be completely eliminated. The enemy attempted to repair the bridge north of the city for his forces.

On 9 September, enemy concentrations in the Duza area, 7.5 kilometers west of the Narew, were scattered by fire missions from friendly artillery. The fighting to contain the Soviet bridgehead died down.

✠

On 13 September, an enemy offensive east of Warsaw, which overran the *73. Infanterie-Division,* also changed the situation for the *"Wiking"* Division. When Praga was lost once and for all on the east bank of the Vistula the next day, the main line of resistance of the division, together with the *"Totenkopf"*

Division, had to be pulled back to a general line running Alexandrow (Krolewski Canal)—crossroads southwest of Nieporent—Zegrze—Serock.

Minus the elements committed north of the Narew, there were two *Panzer IV's* of the regimental reconnaissance platoon southwest of Nieporent and five *Panthers* behind the main line of resistance in Nieporent. Five *Panthers* of the 5th Company under *SS-Obersturmführer* Lichte served as the regimental reserve at the regiment's command post, which had moved to Wieliszew in the meantime.

In addition to the aforementioned forces of the XX Rifle Corps, two additional divisions—the 413th and 165th Rifle—were identified across the sector from the *"Wiking"* Division.

During the last half of September and during the first 10 days of October, positional warfare was conducted along the entire defensive sector of the division. The combat operations on both sides served to improve the forward lines, build up positions and conduct reconnaissance and combat patrols. Building on aerial and radio reconnaissance, the latter operations were designed to determine the enemy's intentions and prepare for them. The Soviets also established a deeply echeloned trench and bunker system.

The engineer squads of each battalion supported the grenadiers in constructing their positions by cutting down wood for bunkers and emplacing mines in front of positions, in some cases only 30 meters from the enemy lines.

The tank companies changed their positions in accordance with the changing interpretations of enemy intentions.

The 2nd Battalion had its 7th and 8th Companies and battle staff north of the Narew. Its 5th and 6th Companies were to the south of the river.

The assault guns of the 4th Company were moved from Dembiunki to the south. Initially, they were placed behind *Bewährungs-Bataillon 560* and, later on, behind the divisional reconnaissance battalion. On 23 September, the *II./SS-Panzer-Grenadier-Regiment 10 "Westland"* assumed the sector of the penal battalion, which was pulled out of the line to serve as a field-army reserve.

The tank regiment moved its trains and the maintenance company to the area designated for it around Zakrozym, west of Modlin. As had already been done in the battalion, an alert company was established and placed under the command of *SS-Untersturmführer* Seebode.

Two days after the arrival of the 2nd Company in Wieliszew on 26 September, *SS-Standartenführer* Mühlenkamp officially handed over command of the regiment to *SS-Obersturmbannführer* Darges. Darges had been the acting commander for some time (ever since 10 August), while Mühlenkamp had held acting command of the division. A few days prior to the change-of-command ceremony, which was held in front of the assembled 2nd Company and all of the officers and senior noncommissioned officers of the regiment, Mühlenkamp had received the Oakleaves to the Knight's Cross to the Iron Cross. It was an award that the entire regiment perceived as an honor for it.

The Soviets employed two additional methods of conducting the war during those weeks. On 18 September, the partisans operating in the woods south of Modlin were supplied at noon by 120 Soviet bombers. In additional to supply containers being dropped, paratroopers were also added to the mix. A number of supply containers fell among friendly forces in the Poniatow–Kaluszum–Krubin area.

On 29 September, the "Free Germany" Committee[2] made its first appearance in the sector of the 3rd Battalion of the *"Westland"* Regiment. The loudspeakers called for the soldiers to give up the fight and desert. The loudspeaker propaganda was repeated on 6 October.

Since the situation north of Warsaw did not allow for any offensive operations, the two bridges over the Krolewski Canal north of Nieporent were blown up on 2 October. In contrast, elements of the *9. Armee* brought to the front north of the Narew attacked the Soviet bridgehead at 0510 hours on 4 October. In two days of fighting, in which the 7th and 8th Companies of the regiment participated, the German forces succeeded in reducing the Soviet bridgehead to a small area in which only small enemy elements were still capable of operating.

---

2. Translator's Note: *Nationalkomitee "Freies Deutschland"* was an anti-Nazi group formed by the Soviet Union enlisting disaffected German military prisoners to agitate against the Hitler regime.

CHAPTER 9

Fighting in the "Wet Triangle"

During the first few days of October, the headquarters of the *IV. SS-Panzer-Korps* came to the conclusion that a large-scale Soviet offensive could be expected any day. That conclusion was based on a careful analysis of the enemy situation, intercepted radio message traffic and direct observations to the immediate front, such as the clearing of minefields and the creation of new firing positions. For the 42 artillery batteries available in the SS corps sector, the enemy had 235.

General von Lüttwitz's *9. Armee*, which received the reports and estimate of the situation prepared by the corps, both telephonically and telegraphically, came to a diametrically opposite conclusion and reported to the field-army group that there were no signs of an offensive in the SS corps sector.

There were two serious consequences that resulted from the conclusions drawn by von Lüttwitz: The *19. Panzer-Division* was withdrawn from the sector, which resulted in the defensive sector of the corps being increased, and the denial of requests for increased ammunition.[1]

The conclusions drawn by the corps were confirmed on 10 October, when the Soviet offensive started. Because of concentrated pre-emptive artillery missions and fires-for-effect on enemy command posts near the front, on artillery positions and areas of concentrations for Soviet infantry, the enemy offensive was pushed back for at least 24 hours.

On the day before the Soviet offensive started, the division received a change of command. Mühlenkamp was transferred to Berlin, to assume duties as the Inspector general of Armored Forces for the *Waffen-SS*. Replacing him in acting command was *SS-Standartenführer* Ullrich, who came from the *"Totenkopf"* Division.

Starting at 0900 hours on 10 October, Soviet artillery batteries placed barrage fire on both the *"Wiking"* Division and its neighbor to the right, *"Totenkopf."* At 1030 hours, the Soviet command considered the German

1. Author's Note: *Europäische Freiwillige*, 301.

positioned to be suitably softened up and the rifle divisions started to attack, with the main effort directed against the divisional boundary, which was formed between the 3rd Battalion of *"Westland"* and *"Totenkopf."*

The enemy succeeded in scoring a deep penetration, but he was unable to break through. The woods at Konty-Wengierski, 5 kilometers west of the Krolewski Canal, was lost.

Within the sector of *"Westland"* the enemy also succeeded in penetrating south of Nieporent and at Alexandrow. He crossed the Krolewski canal and entered the woods east of Michailow. The positions of the 3rd Battalion (Nedderhof) were overrun, the battalion was scattered and all of the company commanders were killed or wounded.

In an immediate counterattack, five *Panthers* and an assault gun of the 4th Company, along with some scattered forces that could be rounded up, stopped the advancing enemy in the vicinity of the Nedderhof's command post and allowed the main line of resistance to be re-established.

Further to the north, enemy forces that had been able to reach the railway embankment in the sector of *SS-Panzer-Aufklärungs-Abteilung 5*, were ejected in an immediate counterattack. The 9th Company of *Westland,* "which had been practically buried after two hours of barrage fires, was shoveled out after a successful immediate counterattack. Elements occupied the communications trenches between the 3rd Battalion of *"Westland"* and the reconnaissance battalion in an effort to prevent further advances of the Soviets to the north.

The commander of the 4th Company decided to divide his forces. He left four assault guns at Nedderhof's command post to assist in preventing further enemy advance to the west. With his remaining four assault guns, he reached the northern edge of the woods and advanced from it, heading north to south, into the flank of the advancing Soviets. Together with the remnants of what was left of a company from *"Westland"* that had been positioned there, the attack gained ground and approached the outskirts and church of Nieporent. At 1530 hours, the assault guns, which were engaged with enemy forces along the right flank, were passed by advancing forces of the division reserve—the *2./SS-Panzer-Regiment 5* and the 10th (*SPW*) Company of *"Germania"*—which were attacking out of the sector of the divisional reconnaissance battalion. The attack force covered the short distance to the first houses of Nieporent, but the edge of the village was packed with antitank guns. Two of the *Panzer IV's* on the main village street were destroyed, followed shortly thereafter by an *SPW.* After the company commander was incapacitated, three more *Panzer IV's* were lost during the subsequent pullback to the north. They were destroyed by Soviet antitank guns and tank hunter/killer teams.

✠

Siegfried Melinkat, assigned to the 2nd Company, summed up his impressions of the day in a poem:

Nieporent
Die Erde bebt im Feuerschlag
massierter Batterien.
Gewaltig Dröhnen füllt die Luft,
vorne wird Hurrääh geschrien.
Wir hören es im Funkverkehr,
Wortfezen, hart und schnelle.
Der Russe trommelt seit neun Uhr,
durchbrach die HKL.
Ein Kradmelder bringt den Befehl:
"Die Zweite greift jetzt an!"
Rückwärts gestaffelt fährt sie vor,
rollet an den Feind heran.
Lenkbremsen kreischen, Ketten klirren,
Motore heulen auf.
Granaten schlagen um uns ein,
wir fahren dichter auf.
Die Infanterie in SPW's,
noch hüllt der Staub sie ein.
Der Spitzenzug bleibt vorne stehn,
schießt in die Gräben rein.
Da! Grelle Lohe, harter Knall
und roter Feuersturm.
Paktreffer bei dem Wagen vorn,
drei springen aus dem Turm.
Dem Fahrer sperrt das Rohr den Weg,
wir hören noch sein Schrei'n,
als ihn die helle Flamme faßt,
es ging durch Mark und Bein.
Der Funker?———Keiner sah ihn mehr.
Sein Spruch klingt noch im Ohr:
"Achtung! 2 Uhr, Pak im Gehölz!"
Dann blitzte es davor.
Der Panzer steht in heller Glut,
wir feuern, setzen ab,
erreichen eine Nebelwand———
fast was es unser Grab.

Und Schlag auf Schlag traf dann die Pak,
zerschoß die Kompanie.
Manch' Kamerad von mir blieb dort,
den Tag vergeß' ich nie.

Nieporent
The earth shook in the blows
of massed batteries.
Powerful booming fills the air,
up front, *Hurrääh* is screamed.
We hear it in the radio traffic,
scraps of words, hard and quick.
The Russians have been pounding since 9 o'clock,
broke through the MLR.[2]
A motorcycle messenger brings the order:
"The 2nd is to attack now!"
It advances echeloned to the rear,
rolls towards the enemy.
Steering brakes screech, tracks rattle,
engines scream.
Shells impact next to us,
we close ranks.
The infantry in *SPW's*;
the dust continues to cover them.
The lead platoon stops up front;
firing into the trenches.
There! Brilliant flame, hard crash
and red stream of fire.
AT hit on the vehicle up front,
three jump out of the turret.
The gun blocks the way for the driver;
we still hear his screams,
as the brilliant flame grabs him;
it goes right through us.
The radio operator?———No one saw him any more.
His message still echoes in our ears:
"Watch out! 2 o'clock; AT in the woods!"
Then there was a flash in front.
The tank was engulfed in brilliant embers;
we fire, pull back,

2. Translator's Note: Main line of resistance.

reach a wall of smoke———
It was almost our grave.
And then the AT hit blow after blow;
shot up the company.
A few comrades of mine remained there;
I'll never forget that day.

✠

As it turned dark, in a screening line running from east to west, the 2nd and 4th Companies prevented the Soviets that had penetrated from expanding their toehold to the north. The 5th Company was pulled back to Michailow towards evening to serve as the division reserve.

✠

After an unsuccessful night attack by the 1st and 3rd Battalions of *"Westland"* in the broken up dunes, the enemy continued his attacks the next day against the positions of the reconnaissance battalion and *"Westland." Panzerkampfgruppe Hain*—the 2nd Company of the tank regiment—turned back four enemy attacks, supported by the grenadiers.

✠

Late in the afternoon, the Soviets attacked from the church in Nieporent to the north. They overran the 9th Company of *"Westland"* and got to the rear of the 3rd Company of the reconnaissance battalion. Under the pressure exerted by a concurrent attack against the right wing of the reconnaissance battalion, the German units pulled back to the railway embankment northwest of Nieporent.

Further to the south, the 5th Company supported the 3rd Battalion of *"Germania"* in the Michailow with 11 of its *Panthers.*

✠

On 12 October, the pressure exerted by the enemy on the boundary between the reconnaissance battalion and the *"Westland"* Regiment continued unabated. At 0900 hours, a battalion-sized attack was turned back by *SS-Panzer-Aufklärungs-Abteilung 5.* Then, from 1200 to 1230 hours, barrage fires were placed on the positions of the reconnaissance battalion, the *"Westland"* Regiment and the 2nd and 4th Companies of the tank regiment. Tanks 224 and 225 of the 2nd Company, positioned north of the railway embankment, received direct hits and were destroyed. After a casualty-intensive struggle, the Soviets, who appeared to be immune to losses, reached the railway embankment at the Wieliszew church in the *"Westland"* sector.

The enemy continued to send forward reinforcements to the rear of the 5th Company of the tank regiment, which was screening in the direction of Wola-Alexandra along with elements from *"Westland,"* about 4 kilometers further south. As it turned dark, more elements were employed against the left flank of the tank company. After six enemy tanks reached Fw. Michailow, the sounds of many tracks could be heard in the woods.

Under the impression that the enemy sought to reach the decision in the sector of the *"Westland"* Regiment—because of all the reinforcements flowing into the area—Darges moved the 7th and 8th Companies of the 2nd Battalion, which were north of the Narew at Marynin, to Lajsk on the Brudnowski Canal, some 3 kilometers south of Wieliszew, behind the threatened sector on the evening of 12 October. The command post of the 1st battalion was moved from Lajsk to Poniatow.

As expected, the enemy attacked with strong forces early in the morning of 13 October in the direction of the road overpass over the railway line northeast of the Wieleszew church. He reached the cemetery to the north of the village with elements; over the next few days, it would become the scene of a hotly contested fight. The Red Air Force conducted rolling attacks the entire day, especially against the rearward lines of communications and the command posts. During one sortie flown by 14 Il-II's,[3] *SS-Oberscharführer* Aumeyer of the *Flak* platoon shot one down.

Starting at 0800 hours, the 2nd Battalion of the tank regiment attacked east from Lajsk, reaching Points 94.5 and 87 on the major road from Zegrze to Jablonna. Adjoining to the north, in the sector of the reconnaissance battalion, where the 4th Company of the tank regiment was also employed, Soviet infantry pressed through the German lines, which were no longer being held continuously, and headed west and northwest to the rear of the defenders. The main line of resistance and the armored outpost line had to be pulled back to the railway embankment , where screening needed to be conducted not only to the east, but also to the north and the northwest. The

3. Editor's Note: The Il-2 "Sturmovik" was the principal Soviet ground-attack aircraft and greatly feared by German troops. Very heavily armored, it was extremely difficult to shoot down.

enemy appeared to be everywhere. One of the assault guns was hit by artillery, resulting in two crewmembers being killed.

Early in the afternoon, the reconnaissance battalion, together with elements from the right wing of the 1st Battalion of the *"Germania"* Regiment, took back the main line of resistance along the railway embankment north of the Wieliszew church by means of an immediate counterattack. Both sides were fighting with utmost bitterness.

At the same time, it appeared that the enemy, who was being reinforced with armor at that point, was going to succeed in breaking through south of the Wieliszew church. The enemy's lead elements reached the railway station in Wieliszew.

The armed group of the 4th Company of the tank regiment assembled at the east side of the village. Scattered elements of the *"Westland"* Regiment and the reconnaissance battalion were also collected there and reorganized for an immediate counterattack. The grenadiers, together with the tanks of the 1st and 2nd Battalions, then took back their old positions, with the exception of the area around the cemetery. An after-action report of the tank regiment's 2nd Company covers the fighting of 13 October:

> The enemy had succeeded in breaking through west of the security line of the company during the morning hours and establishing himself just short of the Wieliszew—Nieporent rail line. By doing so, the enemy succeeded in cutting off the company and elements of the infantry with his strong forces.
>
> At 1100 hours, orders arrived from the battalion commander to pull back with the remaining infantry forces and occupy new positions behind the railway embankment in the sector of the reconnaissance battalion. The enemy positions were overrun in a short engagement and a new security line was established. As a result of additional attacks by the enemy to the right of us, he succeeded in breaking through all the way to the rail station in Wieleszew and, as a result, cutting off the retreat route for the battalion, the remaining elements of the infantry and the reconnaissance battalion. As the result of the sudden appearance of several enemy tanks, a great deal of hubbub arose among the infantry, which immediately pulled back to the location of our tanks. As the result of heavy enemy artillery fire, one tank was set alight by a direct hit; in addition, one vehicle with front differential problems was set alight by our own vehicles, because there were no recovery means available.
>
> Since the enemy pressure continued to increase, the battalion, together with the remnants of the infantry and the reconnaissance

battalion, had to pull back to Wieliszew. After reaching our own positions, the company was committed to an immediate counterattack against the patch of woods south of Nieporent to restore the old main line of resistance along the railway embankment. After completing the mission, the company pulled back as far as the edge of the woods and screened to the east. Destroyed were 2 4.7-centimeter antitank guns, 2 trucks, 10 machine guns; enemy losses: 30-40 men.

On the next two days, the fighting continued with undiminished harshness at the Wieliszew church and at the cemetery to its northeast. After being pounded by the enemy's murderous barrage fire and subjected to the pressure of his tanks and fighter-bombers, the infantry pulled back to the outpost lines of the tanks. The tanks then rallied the infantry by means of an immediate counterattack and ejected the enemy that had advanced into the vacated German positions, destroying five T-34's in the process. *SS-Oberscharführer* Weiß and his crew accounted for four enemy tanks and several antitank guns on that 15 October.

For the first time, the enemy attacked with tanks along the left wing just south of the bend in the Narew at the crossroads southwest of Zagroby. He was ejected by the tanks of the regimental reconnaissance platoon, however.

On the evening of 15 October, the cemetery was back in German hands after an extremely heavy artillery preparation and the employment of rocket-launcher batteries. As a result, contact was re-established between the divisional reconnaissance battalion and the 1st Battalion of the *"Westland"* Regiment. The 4th Company of the tank regiment, launching repeated immediate counterattacks in the direction of the railway embankment from out of the box-shaped patch of woods, attempted to provide relief to *Kampfgruppe Heder*, an *ad hoc* formation composed of alert units. Several antitank guns and two enemy tanks were knocked out.

After a failed night attack on the embankment, *Kampfgruppe Heder* was relieved by the 2nd Battalion of *"Germania"* on 15 October. It was not possible to prevent the enemy from infiltrating into the box-shaped patch of woods, however.

After the enemy employed rolling air attacks at first light on 16 October, he launched an attack at Zagroby, but it was turned back. A powerful counterpunch by the Germans in the form of rocket launchers ensured noticeable quiet in the sector.

Late in the afternoon, a German counterattack, accompanied by preparatory supporting fires from all available heavy weapons, hit any enemy attack force, which was moving on the woods at K. Wieliszew after preparatory barrage fires. The German grenadiers, who had been pulling back under the blows of the enemy attack, were rallied by the personal appearance of the tank regiment commander on the battlefield. Darges personally led an immediate counterattack with two *Panzer IV's* and an *SPW.* Positions northwest of the cemetery were retaken and, in the course of the following night, the cemetery proper was retaken.

The counterattack of the 2nd Battalion of *"Germania,"* working together with the 4th Company of the tank regiment, was able to advance as far as the railway embankment, which was then held.

Apparently, the Soviet forces were not without their limits, either. In the next two days, 17 and 18 October, it was relatively quiet along the entire sector. Of course, it was just the calm before the new storm, which broke loose at 0745 hours on 19 October with barrage fire, with the main effort on the woods at the Wieliszew church. The inferno lasted one and one-half hours, before the brown-clad figures assaulted. Klein's platoon in the 4th Company lost two fighting vehicles; Klein himself had to dismount his tank due to damage to the track.

Even while the barrage fire was still underway, there were Soviet infantry outside the command post of the 2nd Battalion of *"Germania,"* whose lines had been overrun and broken through. The commander of the 4th Company of the tank regiment, *SS-Obersturmführer* Weerts, was wounded while occupying a blocking position.

The 2nd Company of the tank regiment, together with the assault gun and infantry still available, conducted an immediate counterattack at 1020 hours and was initially able to prevent the enemy from exiting the woods to the west.

At 1600 hours, a counterattack was launched by the 1st Battalion of the tank regiment (*SS-Obersturmführer* Schumacher) and the 1st Battalion of the *"Westland"* Regiment, which showed good effect. The enemy was ejected from his advanced positions and, by evening, the tanks were at the railway embankment again, although there was no infantry with them in certain sections.

The resupply of the tanks, especially the refueling and rearming, proved to be extraordinarily difficult during those days of uninterrupted combat. It was only possible during the night and was made all the more difficult by the occasionally murky situation along the flanks and in the rear of the forward elements. The maintenance services worked tirelessly under the most difficult of circumstances. The morale of the men of the tank regiment during that period was characterized by the following entry in the daily logs of the 1st Battalion on 21 October: "The fighting is very difficult; morale continues to remain high."

To safeguard against surprise enemy armor moves, the road embankment west of the Wieliszew crossroads was blown up during the early morning hours of 20 October. The friendly infantry outposts there were even too weak to keep the enemy from infiltrating into the southern flank of the screening tanks.

Leaving behind two each *Panzer IV's* and assault guns to screen against the railway embankment and the cemetery, which had been reoccupied by the enemy in the meantime, the 2nd and 4th Companies were pulled out of the woods east of Wieliszew. The enemy pursued and occupied the woods, immediately bringing heavy antiarmor weapons forward. When the 2nd and 4th Companies launched an immediate counterattack at 1030 hours, they were turned back, since the tanks were unable to advance along the cuts in the woods, which were covered by antitank guns, without escort infantry. A counterattack supported by infantry and conducted by the 1st Battalion also failed, however.

On the following night, the 2nd Company lost its company commander, *SS-Untersturmführer* Bauer, by a wound to the head when the company pulled back from an unsuccessful attack.

The pressure the enemy exerted on Wieliszew, especially in the sector of the 1st Battalion of the *"Germania"* Regiment, continued the following day. The command and control tanks of the 1st Battalion headquarters had to be committed to reinforce the weakened companies in the blocking positions east of the village, since the 2nd Company only had four operational tanks and the 4th Company three operational assault guns. Basically, each company was reduced in combat power to that of a platoon.

It came as no surprise when division orders arrived that evening to start to pull back that night to the "Marder-Dachs" Position along the Brudnowski Canal. The command posts of the regiment and the 1st Battalion moved to Skrzezew, to the north of the village of Poniatow, 6 kilometers northwest of Wieliszew.

The combat outposts, reinforced with tanks, covered the withdrawal movements and were themselves forced to pull back by the following morning, in some cases. The enemy attacks were concentrated against Wieliszew, which was initially defended. After the enemy occupied the village, German infantry and tanks attacked it during the day and the following night in a series of combat raids. The attacks disrupted the enemy's efforts to concentrate and inflicted heavy casualties on him.

The enemy seemed to be paying special attention to the left wing of the newly formed defensive sector "Darges." The tanks of the 2nd Company, together with the grenadiers of the 1st Battalion of *"Germania,"* gradually started to defend more to the north in the direction of the Narew than to the east. The enemy had started to attack Izbica on the north bank in the meantime, and he was already outflanking the positions on the south bank. Based on the situation, the command post of the 2nd Battalion was also pulled back to Skrzezew.

Friendly movements were being made increasingly difficult by the enemy presence on the north bank by antitank guns and snipers. The coordinated movements of the enemy on both riverbanks fragmented the already weakened efforts of the defenders.

Although attacks that were preceded by barrage fires against the positions of the 1st Battalion of *"Germania"* and the divisional reconnaissance battalion were turned back on 24 October, a crossing in broad daylight by the enemy in battalion strength from north to south in the vicinity of Izbica could not be stopped. As was their practice, the Soviets immediately dug in in the woods and heavily vegetated areas and could not be driven out, since there were no reserves available. The 1st Battalion of *"Germania"* bent its left wing to the west and attempted to keep the situation under control with the help of two tanks.

On 26 October, an even more serious threat started to emerge as the Soviets launched a twin-pronged attack on both sides of the Narew. After an hour of barrage fires, the enemy attacked west on the north bank at 1020 hours in the direction of Dembe with an infantry battalion supported by tanks. At the same time, the forces that had crossed the river attacked to the southwest and pushed the German grenadiers back to the area of the command post of the 1st Battalion of *"Germania."*

Of the five enemy tanks attacking in the direction of Dembe, *SS-Oberscharführer* Fischer, a platoon leader in the 2nd Company, knocked out three of them from the south bank of the Narew in the space of 30 minutes. At 1150 hours, the enemy put another force—some 150 men—across the river in rubber rafts in the vicinity of Point 71. The reinforced forces succeeded in scoring a penetration 400 meters east of Point 86 a short while later. The tireless tankers cleaned up the situation once again. The after-action report of the 2nd Company recorded:

> Our vehicles, together with the attached *SPW's,* shattered the enemy's attack in an aggressively led immediate counterattack and pushed him back to his lines of departure behind the sand dunes at Hill 86. After the infantry was back in its old positions, the fighting vehicles pulled back a bit. Around 1500 hours, the friendly infantry had pulled back again. At the onset of darkness, it was brought back to the hill through another immediate counterattack. During the night, the former screening lines from the previous day were occupied.

The delaying actions, which took on the character of defensive fighting in some cases, demanded the utmost from the employed forces in the days that followed as well. The main battle area shifted each day more and more towards the area of the former fortress of Modlin, the increasingly narrow area between the confluence of the Vistula and the Narew.

When the German forces entered the area of the so-called "wet triangle" to the south of Zegrze, the north-south frontage of the main line of resistance was 18 kilometers. At this point, it was not even 12 kilometers. As a result, forces became available from the front lines of the *"Wiking"* Division and the sector of the *"Totenkopf"* Division was lengthened.

As a part of the continued withdrawal of the main line of resistance into the so-called "Fox" Position on 27 and 28 October, both *"Germania"* and the tank regiment were moved from the south bank of the river to the north bank. The grenadiers of *"Germania"* assumed the positions vacated by the *19. Panzer-Division*, with *SS-Panzer-Regiment 5* assuming the missions of *Panzer-Regiment 27.* During the afternoon of 27 October, the tanks and assault guns of the 1st Battalion supported the withdrawal of *Kampfgruppe Oeck.* Late that same afternoon, strongly pressing enemy forces were stopped by effective fires from rocket launcher batteries.

Movements were less hampered by enemy actions, although signs of exhaustion were becoming apparent, than by technical difficulties. For instance, the knocked-out tank of *SS-Unterscharführer* Schnell was able to be recovered, but the one of *SS-Unterscharführer* Juhr had to be blown up. The breaking of track, including those on recovery vehicles, forced the "wagons to be circled" while the recovery work commenced. During the night of 27–28 October, the 1st Battalion reached Janowek by way of Skrzeszew. From there, it went to Bugmünde to then take up quarters in Kikoly on the north bank of the river. After a short maintenance period, the tanks of the 2nd Company relieved the 2nd Battalion and screened from the palace grounds at Dembe to the south and east. The rest of the battalion was positioned near the command post 400 meters east of Orzechowo or remained in Kikoly.

The heavy fighting in the "wet triangle" slowly came to an end during the last days of October and the beginning of November when the forces reached the fortress area of Modlin and regrouped.

Together with the two battles of Warsaw that preceded it, the enemy had been able to gain ground in almost 10 weeks of uninterrupted combat that involved large amounts of personnel and materiel. It was thanks to the unbroken will of the *"Wiking"* Division, along with that of the comrades from the *"Totenkopf"* Division, that the enemy's operational intentions were thwarted, however. He failed to break through to the northwest and outflank the remnants of both *Heeresgruppe Mitte* and *Heeresgruppe Nord.* To that end, the tanks of *SS-Panzer-Regiment 5* also contributed a great deal.

The villages of Janowek and Czarnowo on both sides of the Narew were the outer forts of what was once the strongest fortress of imperial Russia. In August 1915, some 29 years previously, the fortress of Nowo Georgiewsk (Modlin) fell to the bold attack of German militia divisions under the command of *General* von Beseler. At that time, 90,000 Russian soldiers were forced to capitulate. In addition, 30 general officers were taken prisoner.[4]

At the beginning of November 1944, the fighting in the same area ended not with the capitulation of the defending forces—this time, German—but rather with a flood of a vastly superior forces dashing themselves against numerically vastly superior but determined defenders.

The fighting in the month of November and December 1944 have been characterized as positional warfare without any major events. In the foreground of all of the efforts during the well-earned breather was the battlefield reconstitution of *SS-Panzer-Regiment 5,* which was undertaken immediately. The combat elements of the regiment were divided into two. Elements of the 2nd, 4th, 5th and 6th Companies remained at the front. The regimental reconnaissance platoon joined those elements of the 1st Battalion remaining in action with its two *Panzer IV's.*

The 1st, 3rd, 7th and 8th Companies—along with some elements of the 2nd and 4th Companies—were consolidated into an instructional battalion under the command of *SS-Obersturmführer* Nikolussi-Leck. The *ad hoc* element quartered at the Schieratz Training Area, south of Litzmannstadt (Lodz), and took up a training program starting on 13 November. The first train there had left Modlin at 1400 hours on 9 November. The 3rd Company linked up at Plöhnen and the 1st Company at Lowic; both of those companies had been conducting training for weeks there. The third *Panzer IV* of the reconnaissance platoon was used as a training tank.

For those elements of the 1st and 2nd Battalions that remained at the front, they were involved in positional warfare. Shortfalls of tanks were covered by the use of "dummy" vehicles. They often became the preferred

4. Author's Note: Gerhard Stalling, *Schlachten des Weltkrieges,* Oldenburg, 1926, 108.

targets of the Soviets and admirably fulfilled their purpose in deceiving the enemy. In the remaining two months of 1944, the front lines of the division barely moved.

Four years previously, orders had been issued creating the division. A world of military experience had inserted itself in the intervening years. The division command used the relative quiet to look back on those times during a solemn ceremony. In the veteran's journal, *Wiking Ruf (Viking Call)*, some eight years later, the ceremony was described:[5]

> The best example of that Germanic fidelity, which was kept alive not only in happy circumstances but also during bleak, unhappy hours and proudly maintained an unchanged attitude, was offered by the men of the *SS-Panzer-Division Wiking*, who gathered in December 1944 in the walls of the fortress of Modlin—a Polish fortress that was in the thick of the fighting—and commemorated the 4th anniversary of the existence of their European formation . . .
>
> While an icy storm whipped around the walls—the front was preparing itself for new, difficult days under a deep cloud cover—the command of the *"Wiking"* Division held a short ceremony.
>
> The division commander, *SS-Standartenführer* Ullrich, and the Commanding General of the *IV. SS-Panzer-Korps, SS-Obergruppenführer und General der Waffen-SS* Herbert Gille, spoke briefly to the assembled "Vikings" between the sounds of Beethoven and Richard Wagner. In their words were reflected that run on the goal, which had Norwegian, Danish and Dutch peasant sons and youthful Flemish workers and students marching through the Ukraine along with their German and other comrades—across the Dnjepr and all the way to the Mius. The days and nights in the iced-over *balkas* during that 1941–1942 winter in the east came alive in everyone's thoughts. Then the many battles and engagements up to the fighting in the shadows of the icy peaks of the Caucasus.
>
> Who among the "Vikings," who were drinking in the words of their leaders in the vast hall of the fortress, could not help but remember the grim expanse of the Kalmuck Steppes, when the division secured the rear and flanks of the Caucasus Army.
>
> The first in the attack against the enemy and the last during the retreat—that's how the division etched its deeds in the bloody history of the campaign in the east. It was a captivating picture: The gloomy Polish fortress, the volunteers assembled in it from practically all European countries. Men, whose families were being interned

5. Author's Note: *Wiking Ruf*, No. 4, February 1952.

in many instances, who were being persecuted and hated by those around them in their homeland because of their righteous behavior. Men, scoffed and scorned, who left everything behind for four years, placed their young lives on the line, buoyed by a belief in a better future . . .

CHAPTER 10

The Development of the Military Situation along the Danube from August to December 1944

Around 1800 hours on Christmas Eve 1944, the *IV. SS-Panzer-Korps* received orders moving it to Hungary to the area west of Budapest.

That meant that the tank regiment was to see a new theater of war. The final difficult fighting in the last phase of the war between the Danube, on both sides of Budapest and the Eastern Alps between Graz and Vienna would once again demand the utmost of men and materiel, coupled with the added burden of the almost certain knowledge that the war was lost.

In order to understand the fighting in the Danube area, an effort will be made to provide an overview of the events on the Eastern front since the beginning of the large-scale offensive operations in the summer of 1944.

The Soviet offensives in the spring of 1944 had led the field armies of the 1st and 4th Ukrainian Fronts to a general line running Kowel–Lemberg–east of Stanislau at the eastern foothills of the High Tatras. The field armies of the 2nd and 3rd Ukrainian Fronts adjoined to the southeast—via Kolomea west of the Sereth—to north of Roman, then turned in an eastward direction north of Jassy as far as Cornesti and then to the southeast north of Kishinew to the Dnjestr. The 3rd Ukrainian Front had established two bridgeheads across the river as far as the Black Sea, with the bigger one being around Tiraspol.

The operational objective of those Soviet forces north of the Black Sea was the collapse of the three governments still allied with Germany—Rumania, Bulgaria and Hungary—the breakthrough to the partisan armies of Tito and the interdiction of the rearward lines of communication of the German forces still positioned in the Balkans.

The movement of modern field armies in that area was decisively influenced by the two large mountain ranges along the flanks of the great river networks of the Moldau and the Danube in Rumania. The Carpathians, which run north-south and their almost right-angled continuation east-west in the form of the Transylvanian Alps, surrounded the Transylvanian uplands, whose possession is of decisive importance for an attack into the Hungarian lowlands along the Theiß (Bega) and the Danube.

Prior to the start of the Soviet's summer offensive, more than 800 kilometers separated the field armies positioned along the Dnjestr and the Danube south of Budapest. To defend the Rumanian area, *Heeresgruppe Südukraine*, which was redesignated as *Heeresgruppe Süd* on 15 September, had Field-Army Group "Dimitrescu" with the Rumanian 3rd Army and the *6. Armee* in the Dnjestr Position and the *4. Armee* and the Romanian 4th Army coverings the area defined by Cornesti—Roman—eastern edge of the Carpathians.

On 20 August 1944, the field armies of the 3rd and 2nd Ukrainian Fronts initiated their offensives after a two and one-half hour artillery preparation. At the same time, the *5. SS-Panzer-Division "Wiking"* was decisively engaged in the first battle of Warsaw. In that day, the Falaise Pocket was formed in Normandy. Most of the *7. Armee* was eventually lost there, thus clearing the way through France for the Western Allies. Five days previous to that, the US 7th Army landed in southern France in the area around Marseilles. In Italy, the Allies were already north of Florence; barely a year previously, the Italians had become enemies.

War was approaching the borders of the *Reich* with ever greater speed and from all sides at the time the operations in Rumania started.

The divisions of the *6. Armee* and the *8. Armee* were able to hold out against Tolbuchin's field army (3rd Ukrainian Front) and Malinovski's (4th Ukrainian front) for three days. The allied Rumanians were their target: "Just about everywhere that the Russian attack hit the Rumanian formations, they gave up fighting from the very start."[1]

During the evening of 23 August, the Rumanian king announced a ceasefire. The Rumanian forces switched to the Soviet side. Von Tippelskirch: "The front lines were transformed into chaos. Everywhere the Rumanian

1. Author's Note: von Tippelskirch, 482, 484–85 (this passage and the next).

formations had been positioned, the lines opened up with the result that the Russians found the path open even in sectors they had not previously attacked."

The 2nd Ukrainian Front, advancing via Jassy on both sides of the Pruth to the south, linked up with the advanced elements of the 3rd Ukrainian Front in the Vaslui-Husi area, after they had moved westward from their bridgehead at Tiraspol. That sealed the fate of the German divisions that had not withdrawn fast enough from the bend in the front at Kishinew-Cornesti.

> In order to prevent a total collapse and escape destruction, an immediate retreat and the rapid occupation of the Danube bridges would heave been necessary. Since that did not happen, the Rumanians beat the Germans there, blocked the crossing points and handed the German formations over to the Russians. Sixteen German divisions were completely lost, an irreplaceable loss in our already difficult situation.[2]

It should be noted that only a few weeks previously, at the beginning of July, 25 German divisions had already been lost in the maelstrom of the collapse of *Heeresgruppe Mitte.*

After the collapse of the front along the Dnjestr, from which elements of the *8. Armee* and only small elements of the *6. Armee* were able to force a retreat across the Sereth and reach the Carpathians, Malinovski's forces north of the Danube moved on Bucharest, advancing to the south via Ploesti. On 8 September, they crossed the Danube and entered Bulgaria.

By 6 September, elements that had been attacking westward at Turnui-Severin established contact with Tito's forces after crossing the Walachei.

At the same time, Tolbuchin's forces raced through the Dobrudscha and reached the Black Sea on 30 August. They then advanced to Warna on the Bulgarian border.

On 7 September, Bulgaria also broke ranks officially with the Germans and declared war against its former ally. Bulgaria was forced by the Soviets to place its 10 divisions, which had been well equipped by the Germans, under Soviet command. Malinovski's forces pressed from the south into Transylvania through the passes of the Transylvanian Alps. On 5 September, Kronstadt fell. The Rumanian field army that had been formed in the Kronstadt-Herrmannstadt area poured into the gap that had formed between

2. Author's Note: Heinz Guderian, *Erinnerungen eines Soldaten,* 1951, 332.

the remnants of the *6. Armee* employed there and the Hungarian 2nd Army. The strong Soviet forces that followed them pushed the Hungarian 3rd Army back to the west. By the beginning of October, the Hungarian forces had pulled back to behind the Theiß.

The *8. Armee* was unable to prevent the right wing of the 2nd Ukrainian Front from moving out of the mountains. The casualty-intensive armored engagements on the *puszta*[3] came to an end. At the end of October, the cities of Großwardein and Debreczen were lost.

At the end of October, the *8. Armee* was also behind the Theiß, with its forces arrayed around Tokai. The Hungarian-German alliance also fell apart under those circumstances. On 15 October, the Imperial Vicar of Hungary, Admiral von Horthy, requested a ceasefire from the Soviets. General Miklos, the former military attaché in Berlin and the then current Commander-in-Chief of the Hungarian 1st Army, crossed over to the Soviets the same day, along with a few other generals. After Belgrade was encircled by formations from the southern wing of the 2nd Ukrainian Front and elements of Tolbuchin's forces from the south, the city fell on 18 October.

On 29 October, Malinovski's forces along the Theiß broke though in the sector of the Hungarian 3rd Army and pressed on Budapest.

Four weeks later, on 24 November, elements of the 3rd Ukrainian Front crossed the Danube at Mohacs, 180 kilometers south of Budapest. Fünfkirchen (Pécs) was lost. At the same time that the lead Soviet elements were only 270 kilometers southeast of Vienna, German forces were still in Saloniki and Durazzo, some 600 to 800 kilometers away.

A new thrust by Malinovski to the north in the middle of December broke through the German blocking position between the Theiß and the Danube. His lead elements in the north reached Eipel Valley. Further to the south, they advanced to the city of Waitzen on the great bend in the Danube.

A few days later, Tolbuchin's forces south of the Danube shattered the German positions north of Lake Velence. By then, Tolbuchin had also received the Soviet 37th Army, which had taken over the mission of the Bulgarian forces in the field. In the north, its lead elements reached Gran (Danube) and the Tata area on the western edge of the Vertes Mountains in the northwest. The Vértes Range is a continuation of the Bakony Mountains to the northeast as far as the Danube on both sides of Gran. That meant that Budapest was encircled on Christmas Eve 1944 and cut off from all external lines of communications.

It was in that situation that the German government, fighting for its very existence, found itself without any operational reserves. In the fighting of the summer and fall of 1944, it had lost nearly 60 divisions in the European

---

3. Translator's Note: The Hungarian lowlands.

theaters of war. Of that number, about 40 had been lost in the east. In order to gain a better appreciation for those numbers, the reader is reminded that the number of lost divisions in 1944 was roughly equal to the entire strength of the German Army when the war started in 1939.

At the same time, the defensive effort in the Danube area was stripped naked overnight as a result of the loss of the previously allied nations' forces, which largely went over to the side of the Soviets.

The intention of preventing a Soviet south-to-north thrust into the Slovakian-Czech area from the almost completely exposed area in Hungary, which would have led to a southern envelopment at the operational level and the resulting collapse of the Eastern Front, led to the doubtful action of withdrawing the *IV. SS-Panzer-Korps* from the front lines north of Warsaw and committing it in the Budapest area. The seriousness of the threat of the Soviet offensive intentions in the Slovakian-Czech area is reinforced by the premature uprising in Slovakia at the end of October/beginning of November 1944, which had to be put down by German front-line forces.

THE FIRST BUDAPEST RELIEF EFFORT

As a result of the events of 24 December. Some 25,000 German and 40,000 Hungarian soldiers were encircled in the Budapest area.[4] On 1 January 1945, the first day of the German relief effort, the defensive ring of the fortress of Budapest had a north-south length of 21 kilometers and an east-west of 18.

The western defensive portion of the city on the west banks of the Danube-Buda had a line of only 4.5 kilometers from east to west at its widest part in the south.

On the evening of 24 December, the tank regiment and its two battalions were alerted. The same order was also sent to the tank training company of *SS-Obersturmführer* Nicolussi-Leck at the Schieratz Training Area. The combat elements were loaded on trains on 26 December, and the rail-loading operation was conducted without enemy interference. They left one of the 50 different rail-loading sites in the Modlin-Nasielsk area that same day. The commander of the 2nd Battalion, *SS-Hauptsturmführer* Flügel, made it back from homeland leave just in time to catch his battalion's departure. The march route and objective were not given. The entire operations was labeled "top secret."

In the midst of cold winter weather, the tankers moved in unheated rail cars through Slovakia and reached Komorn (Komarom) on the Danube—a

4. Author's Note: *Europäische Freiwillige*, 320.

distance of nearly 700 rail kilometers—about 70 kilometers northwest of Budapest. The elements that were brought in from the Schieratz Training Area were sent to Raab–Neu Raab (Györ), 40 kilometers farther west, where they took up quarters.

In their typically positive approach, the men celebrated New Year's in Komorn. The next day, at 0900 hours and under the beginning snowfall, they moved out in the direction of Tata after a concert on the Komorn marketplace. The trains followed on 2 January.

The elements of the division rapidly staged in the area east of Tata after their detraining to prepare for the first relief attack on the Hungarian capital. The friendly forces to the right were elements of the *6. Panzer-Division*, the *Gruppe Pape*[5] and a Hungarian cavalry division. To the left was the *"Totenkopf"* Division.

The attack time was scheduled for 1800 hours. Acting in place of the division commander, who had not yet arrived, was the commander of the *"Germania"* Regiment, *SS-Obersturmbannführer* Dorr. The tank regiment had 22 *Panthers* operational in its 2nd Battalion and 10 *Panzer IV's* in the 1st. That meant that the regiment barely had the combat power of two line companies, or about 20% of its authorized strength. Attack preparations were conducted with the greatest of urgency.

The mission of the division's armored group was to attack along the road leading from Tata to the east, break through the enemy position, reach Agostyan about 4 kilometers farther east and then take the high ground at Biecske by advancing along the road leading there in a bold thrust. The 1st and 3rd Battalions of *"Germania"* were positioned along both sides of the road at the east side of Tata to support the attack.

The attack, which was initiated in the gathering darkness, was launched without an artillery preparation in order to aid in the moment of surprise. It promptly ran into a heavily mined position. The infantry did not break through until about 2300 hours; the mines on the road were not cleared until 2400 hours. At midnight, the tank regiment's 2nd Battalion moved out to attack Agostyan. The lead platoon of the 6th Company was led by *SS-Untersturmführer* Hinz. Shortly before reaching the hill outside of Agostyn, he was hit in the head from the right rear, causing his immediate death.

The attack and breakthrough to Agostyn happened in such a surprising manner for the Soviets that they were unable to prevent the liberation of German prisoners-of-war that had been taken there a week previously. The

---

5. Translator's Note: *Gruppe Pape* (further attached to *Gruppe Breith*) consisted of the following elements: *3. Panzer-Division* (armored part); Hungarian 1st Cavalry Division; *8. Panzer-Division* (armored part); *6. Panzer-Division* (armored part); and *271. Volks-Grenadier-Division* (www.axishistory.com/index.php?id=2076).

continued attack over the hill just south of Agostyn at first light failed in the face of heavy Soviet defensive fires. The Soviet artillery even succeeded in knocking out a German tank from a camouflaged field position.

It was not until it started to turn dark that the 5th Company, which had taken over the lead, was able to force its way to the road leading to the southeast. Combat engineers moving with the lead tanks cleared the mines. Antitank gun obstacles had to be eliminated. Increasingly strong Soviet infantry elements started attacking out of the woods that abutted the road from the steeply rising slopes. The woods prevented the armored vehicles on the roads from responding properly to the threat. During the early morning hours of 3 January, the lead tank elements were in Vertestolna, 6 kilometers southeast of Agostyn. That same night, the 2nd Battalion of *"Germania"* of *SS-Hauptsturmführer* Pleiner, had reached the same village. Pleiner's men had also attacked from Tata but had swung considerably further to the south.

An armored patrol determined that there was a strong Soviet antitank-gun belt approximately 1 kilometer southeast of Vertestolna at the point where the main road from Tata to the southeast entered the woods again and was joined by the road leading in from Vertestolna. The Soviet antitank guns were dug in and oriented along the main road.

It did not appear possible to break through the antitank-gun defenses, since there was no friendly air support and, at the same time, the Red Air Force was active. Further, friendly artillery support was barely effective due to the considerable terrain difficulties.

The tanks then did the unexpected. They swung around through a defile and then attacked along the wood line, hitting the largely immovable antitank guns in the flank and eliminating them without taking any losses. The Soviets left 17 antitank guns and several tanks behind.

The lead tank element then had to force its way through the serpentines that led through the woods and destroyed individual Soviet tanks that were positioned at intervals along the road. Although the road through the woods and elevations was highly ill suited to the employment of armor, there was virtually no alternative. The woods, which climbed up to 400 meters on the right side offered no opportunities to bypass it. The rising terrain to the left was not covered with the same thick woods, but another situation made the attack there more and more difficult: The friendly forces on each flank were hanging further and further back. The open flanks, which were growing ever longer, were taking up the reserves that had been held back for the deep attack and weakening the over-all combat power. The enemy, who had recovered from his initial surprise, knew how to use the terrain to his advantage. The wooded ridgelines ran from the northwest to the southeast, and the armored attack force had to use the roads that were at the bottom of the high ground. The enemy's advantages in terrain were considerable.

✠

The division commander and the commanding general were with the lead armored elements and pressed for a quick breakthrough. The armored attack slowly ground its way forward to the far end of the woods, a few hundred meters from the village of Tarjan.

The lead element was composed of the 1st Platoon of *SS-Untersturmführer* Kerckhoff of the 5th Company. Shortly before Kerckhoff's tankers reached the open terrain, the platoon leader of the 2nd Platoon, *SS-Oberscharführer* Männer, who was moving behind the tank of the company commander, *SS-Obersturmführer* Lichte, was mortally wounded. A heretofore unidentified Soviet assault gun, which was to the right flank and rear of the lead elements, knocked out Männer's tank. The enemy assault gun was then destroyed.

At 1500 hours, Tarjan was taken, with the fighting along the southern edge of the village drawing out until it started to turn dark. But even while there was still fighting in the village, the division command post was brought forward at 1700 hours. It was intended to increase the tempo of the attack by doing so.

The terrain difficulties, the enemy's defensive measures and his aerial activity above the only available route of advance increased. There was hardly any sign of friendly air activity. The support capabilities of friendly artillery continued to be restricted.

To the southeast of Tarjan, the woods receded from the road along the rising slopes. They extended for about 3 kilometers at a distance of about 1.5 kilometers on both sides of the road. The regimental commander, *SS-Obersturmbannführer* Darges, decided to avoid a repetition of the "running of the gauntlet" such as the tankers had experienced at Malgobek more than two years previously. If they proceeded along the original route of advance, they would have to cross that section with exposed flanks, as a result of the friendly forces to either flank not being able to keep up with the "*Wiking*" tankers. Darges ordered his men to turn directly south, cross the ridgeline to reach the village of Tatabanya, which was on the south side of the ridge, so as to be able to attack across terrain that was more suitable for tanks. From Tatabanya, he hoped to reach the main road to Biecske again.

Reconnaissance reported that the terrain to be crossed southwest of Tarjan was clear of the enemy. Kerckhoff's platoon resumed the lead and the tanks struggled up the slopes in the darkness. The tanks joked that they would receive the alpine trooper badge as recognition for their feat. While conducting the movement that was now heading perpendicular to the original direction of attack, the tanks mounted up the soldiers of the Norwegian battalion, under the command of *SS-Hauptsturmführer* Vogt, which had been able to advance as far as the tankers by then.

Just outside of Tatabanya, Kerckhoff's tank was hit by a Soviet antitank-gun round in the running gear. Kerckhoff headed back on foot. The regimental commander, who was following behind the lead elements in an *SPW*, made some pointed comments to Kerckhoff about "general conduct of a soldier while in the open," whereupon the young officer took cover in the roadside ditch. The maintenance company, which was following the combat elements, was later able to provide Kerckhoff with a repaired tank, with which he then rejoined his company north of Biecske.

The regiment finally reached Tatabanya, after the resistance of Soviet rearguard elements, which consisted of dug-in antitank guns and tanks, was broken. Up to that point, the Hungarian civilians had enthusiastically greeted the German soldiers wherever they had appeared along the route of march.

During the night of 4–5 January, the tank regiment continued its attack to the southeast across relatively open and slightly rolling terrain. By first light, it reached the Csabdi—Biecske road, about 3 kilometers north of the latter, where it surprised and eliminated a Soviet supply column. Just before reaching the road, the commander of the 2nd Battalion, *SS-Hauptsturmführer* Flügel, was wounded while reconnoitering on foot near the command post of the 2nd Battalion of *"Germania." SS-Hauptsturmführer* Pleiner brought his battalion forward to behind a hay barn.

Kerckhoff's platoon crossed the Hegyiks Estate on the southern edge of Csabdi and turned onto the road leading towards Biecske. After moving a few hundred meters, Kerckhoff's men started to receive unexpectedly strong antitank-gun fire from the direction of Biecske, which took out the two lead tanks. It was only thanks to the immediate use of smoke grenades by Kerckhoff and his company commander, *SS-Obersturmführer* Lichte, that their two tanks were able to pull back behind a swell in the ground unscathed.

The portions of the tank regiment that were still operational set up an all-round defense at the estate, together with the Norwegian battalion. Over the next few days, they would have to defend it like a fortress. The enemy force, which was constantly being reinforced by additional battalions and regiments, was receiving increasing artillery support and was attacking without interruption with tanks and from the air, had long since tied up the German reserves along the flanks. The wintery weather and the onset of a snowfall made movements more difficult. Although the friendly forces to the left, the

"Totenkopf" Division, was able to advance with its lead elements as far as Many-Zsembek, the friendly forces on the right were no where to be seen.

Despite the fact that the Soviets were reinforcing Biecske along its outer perimeter, the armored group attacked on 8 January as part of another push by both divisions and reached the cemetery on the northern edge of the village. At that point, however, it appeared that the combat power needed to push on to Budapest was exhausted.

From that point forward, the defenders of the Hegyiks Estate had their hands full with the constant attacks by the Soviets, which were conducted with armored forces and heavy artillery support. Issues arose with logistics. The wounded, who were tended to by Dr. Kalbskopf, could only be evacuated at night. At night, ammunition was resupplied in trucks that had been repaired by the maintenance company and were being brought forward.

The Soviet artillery forced the "guests" staying at the estate from the second floor to the first floor and, eventually, the basement. The defenders were no longer able to get any sleep. During the night, Soviet infantry frequently attacked, infiltrated through the fence around the estate and entered the inner courtyard, where they were ejected. During one such attack, the 1st Battalion Commander, *SS-Hauptsturmführer* Hein, was wounded in the lower leg by shrapnel from an exploding Soviet hand grenade as he stood in a doorway at the rear of a building talking to the 5th Company commander, *SS-Obersturmführer* Lichte. *SS-Obersturmführer* Bauer assumed acting command of the battalion.

The Norwegian battalion defended with extraordinary bravery and was able to seal off and clear every penetration. The Soviets evidently feared their battle cry—*Norge*—and the Nordic soldiers were able to eject all enemy intrusions. One example will perhaps serve to illustrate the élan of those men: An *SS-Oberscharführer* of the battalion, who had already lost one arm and, despite that, reported back for frontline service, was shot through the mouth during the fighting within the estate. Since he could not speak, he wrote on the door of the room where the wounded were being treated: "Am I going to die?" Dr. Kalbskopf calmed his patient: "If you keep your mouth closed, perhaps not!"

The men of the tank regiment defended at the estate until 12 January. By then, however, the first attempt to relieve the defenders of Budapest by way of Biecske was called off. Starting on 9 January, the main body of the division was pulled out of the line, often under enemy observation, along the iced-over roads and field paths. The division was directed further north and staged in the Gran (Estergom) area for a second effort—by way of the Pilis Mountains—to relieve the beleaguered city.

For the tankers outside of Biecske, the calling off of the first relief effort did not make any sense. They were only 27 kilometers from the western outskirts of Budapest. They did not participate in the second effort, however. Instead, they marched to Raab, where they were loaded on trains and sent via Papa to the Vesprem area.

✠

Generaloberst Guderian, who had assumed duties as the Army chief of staff in July 1944, visited the command posts of *General der Panzertruppen* Balck (*Armeegruppe Balck*) and *SS-Obergruppenführer* Gille. Guderian later wrote down his impressions of those visits conducted during the first relief attempt of Budapest in his memoirs:

> It is most likely that the failure of the attack lies in the fact that the initial success of the fighting conducted during the evening of 1 January was not exploited the following night by a ruthlessly conducted breakthrough. We no longer had the leaders and forces of 1940; otherwise, we might have been blessed with a success there . . .[6]

✠

The tough criticism of the tanks and their leaders who were employed there appears incomprehensible and unjustified.

Generaloberst Guderian was able to be convinced by the commander in chief of the field-army group, Balck, of the unfavorable nature of the terrain that had been selected for the attack during a fleeting glance at the situation maps at the headquarters he visited. It was not reconcilable with the doctrinal principles in force back then to allow an armored formation to attack through extensive mountain woods along serpentines in the dead of winter against an opponent prepared for the defense.

There were officers and noncommissioned officers among the tankers of the regiment and within the elements of the division that were familiar with the way things had been in 1940. They knew that tank formations in 1940 never attacked with only 20 percent of their authorized strength. They fought in 1940 with artillery that offered sufficient support and a friendly air force that possessed air superiority and was able to attack point targets of the enemy

6. Author's Note: Guderian, 350.

with heretofore never before seen accuracy along the routes of advance with *Stukas*, clearing the way for the armor. The first relief attack on Budapest was conducted by brave and battle-experienced soldiers, but it was not planned properly.

✠

On the same evening of 12 January that the tank regiment marched to Raab to be loaded on trains, the second relief effort , which had started during the evening of 10 January—moving from Gran to the southeast—was also called off.

During that effort, the *"Germania"* and *"Westland"* Regiments found a completely surprised enemy force in front of them, and the weakly manned enemy defensive positions pulled back when attacked. The field messes were already cooking meals for the soldiers in Budapest, who would be breaking out. The church towers of Budapest, only 17 kilometers away, could be seen from Pilisszentkereszt, which the *"Wikings"* had taken. At 2000 hours, the fighting forces, which were full of confidence, received incomprehensible orders from *Armeegruppe Balck* to call off the attack. All of the arguments of the commanders on the ground went unheeded. The men headed north the next morning, having given up their trump card. The feeling of victory had been palpable; the men had been confident in their ability to rescue their encircled comrades. As they headed north, they went though the spa at Dobogekö so as to be able to see the church towers of Budapest one more time.[7] Grumbling and loud, the talk was of treason that would cost the lives of tens of thousands.[8]

THE THIRD BUDAPEST RELIEF EFFORT

The march objective of the tank regiment, which was loaded on trains at Raab under icy cold conditions, was the area east of Vesprem, some 70 kilometers to the southeast and 5 kilometers north of the tip of Lake Balaton. The division was staging there, along with the rest of the *IV. SS-Panzer-Korps*, for a renewed attempt to relieve Budapest. The mission dictated a thrust through to the Danube, then a pivoting to the north and a relief of the city from the south.

It was to be the third and last relief effort.

The forces of the division that had assembled in the area over the previous week—with the exception of those involved in the abortive second relief effort of 10–12 January—had covered some 250 kilometers to get there,

7. Author's Note: Jahncke's diaries.

8. Author's Note: Account provided by Kerckhoff.

often moving perpendicular to the front lines and sometimes under enemy observation.

The fighting around Biecske and the road march to Raab, some 80 kilometers, shrunk the operational strength of the tank regiment even further. The men of the maintenance company gave their all in trying to get the vehicles road-worthy and combat-ready again. The 2nd Battalion was reduced to about 10 to 12 operational *Panthers*, which were divided among the 5th and 6th Companies. Together with the 1st battalion, it moved at the onset of darkness on 17 January into staging areas east of Vesprem and behind the *"Germania"* Regiment, which was on the division's left. The combat power of the two tank battalions was less than one full-strength company apiece. It has been impossible to determine the exact number of operational combat vehicles. In order to maintain secrecy for the upcoming offensive operations, the commanders reconnoitered the assembly areas in Rumanian uniforms. They also established contact with the forces in position at the front wearing the same uniforms.

✠

The attack, launched at 0430 hours on Thursday, 18 January, ran into stubbornly defended Soviet main line of resistance. Minefields and antitank-gun belts were reinforced for the first time with electrified barbed-wire obstacles.

Since the attack did not achieve the desired breakthrough by the afternoon, the armored group of *SS-Obersturmbannführer* Dorr, which had been held in reserve up to that point, was committed. By evening, it had penetrated the heavily improved Soviet defensive positions and gained ground to the east.

SS-Untersturmführer Kerckhoff provides perspective from the vantage point of the 5th Company:

> Berhida was taken in the afternoon; by evening, we were outside of Nadesdladany. The morale had turned optimistic, especially since we were going forward.
>
> The night was bitterly cold; it rained and snowed; the roads were slick; resupply worked.
>
> 19 January 1945: Moved out early; initially, the attack proceeded slowly; the 5th left, the 6th right; *SPW's* followed in the middle. After taking some ground, the Russian arty fire increased, and they employed fighter-bombers. Despite it all, we continued to advance.
>
> The Russians started to waver; it snowed less; the terrain opened up some; there were no open flanks as had been the case in the

> Vertes Mountains. Good visibility; slightly rolling terrain. We crossed the canal[9] . . . and were almost 35 kilometers east of the day we moved out. Morale climbed.

On 20 January, Hungary signed a ceasefire agreement with the Soviets. The Hungarian chief of staff, General Vörös, had also changed sides in the meantime. He used the staff car that *Generaloberst* Guderian had presented him with after he has made assurances of his loyalty to the alliance to drive to the Soviets.[10] Kerckhoff continues:

> 20 January 1945: Moved out very early. The previous organization for combat was maintained. Our progress was slower. The Russians had established antitank-gun belts in extreme haste. Blocking divisions made life difficult for us. On top of everything else, we lost the commander of the 5th Company, *Obersturmführer* Lichte. His tank was knocked out during the attack on Sarosd and he was badly wounded. *Untersturmführer* Kerckhoff assumed [acting command of] the 5th Company.

During the attack on Sarosd, the tanks, together with engineers, attacked a broad rising slope that was covered with cornfields towards a farmstead on the crest. The farmstead was captured; prisoners were taken. From the depths of the Soviet positions, tanks advanced to launch an immediate counterattack. They set the farmstead on fire. As a result of the heavy smoke that developed, the German forces had to pull back.

After the wheeled vehicles had withdrawn, the tanks of the 5th Company offered battle. The numerically vastly superior enemy tank force enveloped the *Panthers* and hit them in the flank. One of the *Panthers* was knocked it; it had been manned by the administrator of the 2nd Battalion, who had been filling in for a tank commander.

Kerckhoff ordered his tanks to disengage from the enemy. In order to deprive the enemy of visibility and allow his tanks to pull back, he set off a smoke grenade. At the same instant, Kerckhoff's tank was hit in the turret and the acting company commander was wounded. After losing consciousness temporarily, Kerckhoff was able to evade the aimed rifle fire of the advancing Soviet infantry and get picked up by the tank of *SS-Untersturmführer* Großrock, the acting commander of the 6th Company. We continue with Kerckhoff's account:

---

9. Author's Note: The Savitz Canal south of Stuhlweißenburg (Székesfehérvár).

10. Author's Note: Guderian, 343.

21 January 1945: Although Sarosd was clear of the enemy, Dorr could not decide whether to take the locality that evening. The enemy was reinforced during the night and occupied the locality.

The Russians broke through with a strong formation behind the armored group. *Gruppe Dorr* was cut off from the division.

Großrock and his 6th Company screened west and south; the 5th company to the north and east. During the night, the *SPW's* were positioned between the tanks. The division commander was making his way to the lead elements.

During the night, a direct hit on the *Germania* command post. A few officers were killed; Dorr was badly wounded. *Sturmbannführer* Müller assumed command of *Germania.*

22 January 1945: *Gruppe Dorr* moved out after a good arty preparation and made good progress. Objective of the day: Through Seregelyes to Psz. Szabolcs. One antitank-gun belt after the other overcome. After the tanks (14 vehicles) eliminated the antitank gun belts, the *SPW's* advanced with them. Attack on Stuhlweißenburg ordered by the corps today. During the afternoon a counterattack reinforced with tanks. 12 T-34's burned out along with a number of horse-drawn wagons and trucks. The attack made good progress. That evening, we were in the village of Psz. Szabolcs. We took our day's objective.

Our left-hand neighbor, the [*Totenkopf*] Division, hung back, as did the *3. Panzer-Division.* Fuel and ammunition needed to be brought forward. Not so simple for the wheeled vehicles, since the roads were heavily iced over.

23 January 1945: With clear visibility and under bitterly cold conditions, we turned east and attacked. We made slow progress against tough resistance. The 5th Company eliminated an antitank-gun belt at Som and started screening. The weather turned worse; rain and snow alternated and reduced visibility.

24 January 1945: We heard that the concentric attack on Stuhlweißenburg by the Army, *Waffen-SS* and Hungarians was making good progress; we were in a good mood. Fuel and ammunition had also been brought forward during the night. The rations requirements of the men were also met.

Consequently, we moved out and, by the afternoon, we were already at Adony on the Danube after facing tough resistance by the Russians. We started screening. We were out there all by ourselves.

The *SPW* Battalion was ordered to Lake Velence to screen the left flank of the division. In the south, the Russians were pressing into our rear at Perkata. It was the same strong forces that had cut off the lead elements of the division on 21 January. The *3. Panzer-Division* needed to finish off its small portion of things!

It snowed a lot in the evening. What was to the night going to be like without infantry?

That same day, the division attack to the north only made slow progress. The *"Germania"* Regiment, employed along the banks of the Danube, and the *"Westland"* Regiment attacking to its left were encountering stiff resistance. Kerckhoff wrote the following about 25 January:

> No attack; we screened. The weather turned worse and, as a result, the visibility. Late in the afternoon, we heard noise; the wind was in our favor. Just before dark, the Russians attacked with tanks and infantry. Seven Russian tanks, almost all of them T-34's, were burning and gave us a view into the intentions of the Russians. We suffered no losses and still had 11 *Panthers* screening (the 5th and 6th Companies together). Morale was good.

As a result of the increasing enemy resistance and the fact that the friendly forces on the left were still hanging considerably back, the division broke off its attack on 25 January and transitioned to the defense. At the same time that there was little enemy contact to the front, concerns grew about developments along the right (southern) flank.

The alert battalion, which had been formed out of personnel from the supply elements, had to be committed in Adony. Perkata, 9 kilometers to the southwest, was lost on 27 January. The Soviet attacks along the left flank also increased in intensity. They continued on 28 January.

On 29 January, a strong Soviet attack was launched from the north, hitting the elements of the division that had been preparing to attack, as well as the *"Totenkopf"* Division to the left, just before the intended start of the German attack.

Based on the statements of the assistant operations officer of the *"Wiking"* Division, *SS-Hauptsturmführer* Jahncke, and the Chief-of-Staff of the *IV. SS-Panzer-Korps*, *SS-Obersturmbannführer* Schönfelder, both of which generally agree with one another, the following can be offered as a summary of the dramatic events associated with the third relief attempt on Budapest: The attack that had started on 18 January had advanced the lines of the *"Wiking"* and *"Totenkopf"* Divisions about as far as the Vali Canal by 29 January, following the capture of Stuhlweißenburg. From the positions reached north of Adony on the Danube, the lines extended about 25 kilometers to the northwest along the canal. Since the canal continued to run northwest and the friendly forces to the left continued to hang back, the front was distancing itself more and more from Budapest. The closest distance to Budapest—about 24 kilometers—was at a point 10 kilometers northeast of Lake Valence between Kajaszo and Baracska. From there, the avenue of advance moved along the straight main road through Tarnok (another 10 kilometers to the northeast) to Budapest. According to Jahncke's diary:

> The attack on Budapest was set for 0700 hours (?). According to information from the field army intelligence officer, the enemy only had a battered cavalry division in front of *Wiking*. We were directed to break through to Budapest in a single move. The attack was pushed back twice—at 0800 hours and 0900 hours—due to fog.
>
> Just before the final attack time, the enemy moved out. The Russians attacked along all fronts with heavy air support . . . The division was surprised by the massive tank attack and was upset about the inadequate enemy intelligence.

According to Schönfelder:

> 25 January: All divisions arrayed along the canal; small bridgeheads. Enemy constantly being reinforced and attacking without interruption along the entire front. Despite that, it was intended to cross the canal at Kajaszo, since the resistance was the least there, turn south and hit the enemy along the canal in the rear, thus clearing the avenue of advance to Tarnok again.
>
> 26–28 January: Renewed orders from the field army to call off the attack there and instead attack north, then northwest and, finally, west to hit the enemy in front of the left-hand neighbor in the rear.
>
> All of the elements set up for the defense. The intelligence officer reported that a strong enemy armored force, a tank corps, was staging to the north. The field army disagreed and insisted on a continuation of the attack to the west. We prepared to defend against the enemy attack, which then took place on 29 January. About 250 enemy tanks attacked and advanced all the way to the main road. Large tank engagement at Pettend, during which 140 tanks were eliminated on that day alone.
>
> *Bataillon Norge*, consisting almost entirely of Norwegians, defended there and held its positions. The commander, *Hauptsturmführer* Vogt, personally knocked out six tanks with the *Panzerfaust*.

> Because of the brave stance of the battalion, a rolling up of the front was prevented. In the days that followed, an additional 60 enemy tanks were destroyed.

In both statements, almost the same remark is found at the end: "Two days later, the intelligence officer of the field army was picked up for collaborating with the Russians and shot."

The fighting continued on the next two days with unabated ferocity. The number and intensity of enemy attacks increased. Kerckhoff wrote the following concerning 30 January:

> All hell broke loose around noon. Infantry attack in battalion strength. We and the artillery were able to turn it back. Then, like a phoenix rising from out of the ashes, 30 enemy tanks—T-34's and T-43's—appeared out of the light fog. By evening, 17 enemy tanks and 2 trucks were burning. Grenadiers needed to come forward for the night. Regiment attempted to help . . .

On 31 January, according to Jahncke, the enemy obtained

> several penetrations into *Westland* that could no longer be contained. The situation was completely cloudy in the south; or was there no German front there at all? There could be no more thoughts of an attack . . .

According to the daily logs of *Heeresgruppe Süd*, "strong enemy forces" pushed back "the left wing of the *1. Panzer-Division* at Radicsa psz. [6 kilometers south of Adony] back to the northwest along the Dunapentele-Adony road" on the next day, 1 February.

The *Panthers* of *SS-Panzer-Regiment 5* were once again able to master the situation. In another entry of the field-army group's daily logs, we find:

> Elements of the *5. SS-Panzer-Division Wiking* positioned in Adony were pushed back to the northwest by enemy forces in battalion strength supported by 14 tanks; however, in an immediate counterattack, they were able to take back the western edge of the locality after hard house-to-house fighting and knocking out five enemy tanks and one self-propelled gun. At the mouth of the Vali [6 kilometers north of Adony], the enemy infiltrated in company strength through the gaps in the main line of resistance of the *I./[SS-]Panzer-Grenadier-Regiment Germania* to the south . . .

Kerckhoff noted on 1 February:

> It became clear to us that this attack on Budapest was also over. Every hour, we noticed the enemy being reinforced . . . The weather grew worse hour by hour. A heavy snowfall ensued. Fog surrounded out position. What would the night bring? We were still in Adony.

That night, the front lines of the hard-pressed divisions were pulled back. According to the daily logs of *Heeresgruppe Süd*, permission was granted at 1750 hours for the

> request by *Armeegruppe Balck* to pull back its forces positioned east of the lakes to a line that would conserve forces from the Sio through Degh and Sarosd as far as the middle of the south banks of Lake Velence.

The field-army group had received permission from the German Army High Command to execute that maneuver at 1745 hours. It was obvious at the field army command level that this decision also meant that the road paralleling the Danube was being handed over to the enemy. Jahncke summarized the events of the day as follows: "Division had to disengage from the Danube and pull back to the west. The enemy only followed hesitantly."

On 2 February, the formations continued to pull back in accordance with their orders. There was a heavy fog. The enemy started to exert more pressure in pursuing the withdrawing forces after noon. The division command post, which had been on the east side of Seregelyes at 0800 hours, had to pull back under enemy pressure to the middle of the village.

The daily logs of *Heeresgruppe Süd* made the following notations concerning the withdrawal movements:

> Movements of the *5. SS-Panzer-Division Wiking* also not interfered with. Enemy closed on the new line rapidly; pushed the rearguards at Psz. Szabolcs back to the main line of resistance after attacking with infantry and 30 tanks; broke through on both sides of the Psz. Szabolcz–Seregelyes rail line with 15 tanks; and advanced to within 2 kilometers east of Seregelyes. Counterattack by the ready reserve of the *3. Panzer-Division* and the *5. SS-Panzer-Division Wiking* launched . . .

The operations officer of the *IV. SS-Panzer-Korps, SS-Sturmbannführer* Rentrop, ran into one of the enemy forces—60 men and 2 tanks—that had broken through. Schönfelder comments:

> Movement of command posts from Seregelyes to Stuhlweißenburg. Rentrop went as the advance party. Heavy fog. I followed a short while later and ran into the evidence of the attack on the road—empty vehicles with traces of blood in them. Hungarian eyewitnesses stated that Rentrop and his party had been wounded and taken into captivity. The documents that the enemy was able to capture were daily reports concerning ammunition and fuel status within the corps.

Jahncke characterized the day as follows: "There was a bit of confusion. The withdrawing forces were coming into the locality from all sides."

The next day—sometimes in fog, sometimes in clearer weather—the enemy charged Seregelyes in vain. Of the 27 attacking tanks, 12 were knocked out. An enemy force advancing to the northwest succeeded in encircling elements of *SS-Panzer-Grenadier-Regiment "Germania"* and the divisional artillery, which were in the process of changing firing positions. The daily logs of *Heeresgruppe Süd*:

> The enemy moved out to attack with strong infantry forces and approximately 50–60 tanks against the left wing of the *3. Panzer-Division* and the front of the *5. SS-Panzer-Division Wiking* and broke through in numerous places along the thinly held main line of resistance. Seregelyes and Dinnies were held in hard fighting . . . *Bataillon Norge*, supported by some individual tanks, attacked out of Seregelyes and relieved an encircled friendly force; by evening it was continuing to advance on Dinnies. The enemy bypassed many friendly, widely dispersed strongpoints—in some instances, without a fight—in the fog, which made command and control extremely difficult, and advanced west.

On the evening of 3 February, all hopes of relieving the defenders of Budapest disappeared, thanks to the renewed pressure of the enemy and the displacement of the division command post to Belsöbarand, 5 kilometers west of Seregelyes. According to the daily logs of the field-army group:

> The struggle for the imperial palace and the portions of the city to the south continued. The forces in the city, which had been reduced to a

small area and suffered under an extremely difficult supply situation, offered bitter resistance against the enemy, who was advancing house by house.

At 1755 hours, *Armeegruppe Balck* received permission to send the following to the encircled forces in the city: " . . . that its intentions remained to conduct the relief, but that it was not possible at the time due to the strong enemy counterattacks."

✠

The options available to conduct a relief worsened the following night and again on 4 February. The *"Germania"* Regiment was pushed back from north of Seregelyes to the "Margarethe" Position. Sarosd and Seregelyes were lost. The new main line of resistance ran between Seregelyes and Belsöbarand at that point. At 2300 hours, the division command post moved to Falubattian, 15 kilometers west of Seregelyes.

According to the daily logs of *Heeresgruppe Süd*, *Armeegruppe Balck* requested the following in light of the worsening situation: " . . . to pull the main line of resistance back from in front of the Stuhlweißenburg bottleneck to a shorter line approaching the Margarethe Position."

The field-army group forwaded an appropriate request at 1905 hours and "the *OKH* granted the freedom to make that decision at 0040 hours inasmuch as the situation of the forces and the enemy attack forced it." The decision by the Army High Command stated:

> The *Führer* accepted the fact that the most important thing was to hold the front north of Stuhlweißenburg. He granted the field-army group the freedom to decide to withdraw the salient in front of the Stuhlweißenburg bottleneck as far as the Margarethe Position. That should only happen, however, if the friendly situation and the enemy's attack activities necessitate it.

In the meantime, the defenders of Budapest continued their struggle, despite sinking hopes for a relief and the ever-intensifying Soviet attacks. Again, from the daily logs of *Heeresgruppe Süd*:

> Superb performance on the part of the forces and their command in the face of extreme physical and mental stress. Vast enemy superiority in materiel and war-related events on the home front exert a tremendously depressing effect on the forces in the field.

> A slice of bread and some horsemeat is the only daily nourishment for the troops. Every movement is difficult due to physical weakness. Despite all of that and despite six weeks of promises for relief, the men continue to fight toughly and bitterly and continue to obey. Cases of typhus are on the rise due to the miserable confinement in the dug-outs and casemates, without any appreciable countermeasures being able to be taken.

✠

The combat power of the offensive enemy forces facing the *"Wiking"* Division proved to be undiminished the following day. Penetrations along the northwestern side of Seregelyes and 4 kilometers southwest of Dinnies along Lake Velence could be sealed off and cleared, in some cases using the advantages of darkness.

On that 5 February, Hitler denied permission for the men of Budapest to attempt a breakout. He decided that the city was to continue holding out.

On 6 February, the enemy forced a larger penetration in the front, which was stretched to the breaking point, between Seregelyes and Lake Velence. The daily logs of the field-army group:

> The enemy, supported by 20 tanks, moved out for the attack from Seregelyes to the northwest along both sides of the road, took Janos mjr. and advanced with 12 tanks as far as Börgond. Repeated enemy attacks on Dinnies were turned back.

The division's armored group was committed against the 1.5- or 2-kilometer gap in the lines that was created around Janomjr. Max Juhr, a tank commander in the 2nd Company, has provided this firsthand information:

> The battle group consisted of four *Tigers*, 2 *Panzer IV's* and *Obersturmführer* Bauer. I believe he was in a *Panther*. The codename for the battle group was *"Flieder"* ["Lilac"]. I can still hear the radio message to this day: "Do you want to leave Lilac all alone?" The *Tigers* had remained stationary. I was to the left of the locality at a cemetery; was able to knock out an antitank gun and was also knocked out myself. My gunner, Renkewitz, was badly wounded.

Jahncke summarized the day's events as follows: "Constant enemy attacks. Hills 122 and 130 northwest of Seregelyes were lost. Division was too weak to launch an immediate counterattack."

The daily logs of the field-army group reported on the worsening prospects for relieving the encircled forces in Budapest:

> Splitting of the pocket unavoidable in the short term; supply situation already reported enough. Continuing extremely heavy friendly losses. 11,000 wounded receive 15 grams of legumes and half a slice of bread. Those quantities are only available for another two days.

The lost hills northwest of Seregelyes were the object of a combined attack by the *1. Panzer-Division* and the *"Wiking"* Division on the next two days. The attacks only gained momentum slowly; late in the afternoon, however, it pushed the Soviets back across the high ground. The "Vikings" knocked out 13 enemy tanks. That appeared to break the offensive combat power of the Soviets for the time being. A cohesive main line of resistance from west of Seregelyes to the southern edge of Lake Velence was maintained and improved in the days that followed.

An additional weakening of the combat power of the division nearly came about when the SS Main Office ordered the release of the members of the Danish and Norwegian battalions back to their original headquarters. At the request of *Armeegruppe Balck*, the Army High Command prevented that from happening and dictated that the two battalions were to remain with the division.

The break in the fighting that ensued also signaled the end of the attacks conducted to relieve Budapest. The major Soviet offensive that had started on 29 January had thrown the German relief forces back to the west and also considerably weakened them.

The tragedy associated with the encircled forces of Budapest, whose hopes in being relieved had been dashed and whose fate had been sealed, ended with a breakout attempt on the night of 11–12 February. Approximately 700 of those still capable of fighting reached the German lines. As late as 8 February, *SS-Obergruppenführer* Pfeffer-Wildenbruch, the commanding general of the *IX. SS-Gebirgs-Korps* and the commander in chief of the encircled forces in Budapest, and *General der Panzertruppen* Balck attempted to get permission to break out. The final denial of the request was relayed through the commander in chief of *Heeresgruppe Süd, General der Infanterie* Wöhler, at 1950 hours on 8 February:

> At 1950 hours, the [commander in chief] notified the chief of staff from the *Führer* Headquarters that the *Führer* had again denied permission for the *IX. SS-Gebirgs-Korps* to break out, even in the case

> of the start of a new friendly [relief] operation. He was of the opinion that a breakout would not succeed.

With the extension of the division sector to the southern edge of Stuhlweißenburg, the *"Wiking"* Division again came under the command and control of the *IV. SS-Panzer-Korps.* After another 10 days of no appreciable combat activity, the division assumed the sector of the *3. SS-Panzer-Division "Totenkopf"* on 23 February. The sector ran from the southern edge of Stuhlweißenburg to Moha, about 7 kilometers northwest of the city. The *"Westland"* regiment was employed on the right and the *"Germania"* Regiment on the left. The 2nd Battalion of the tank regiment was employed along the left wing of the division sector. Combat activities over the next few weeks was restricted to minor patrol activity on both sides, occasional artillery fire and no aerial activity. The rest period lasted until 16 March and was enthusiastically received and enjoyed by all.

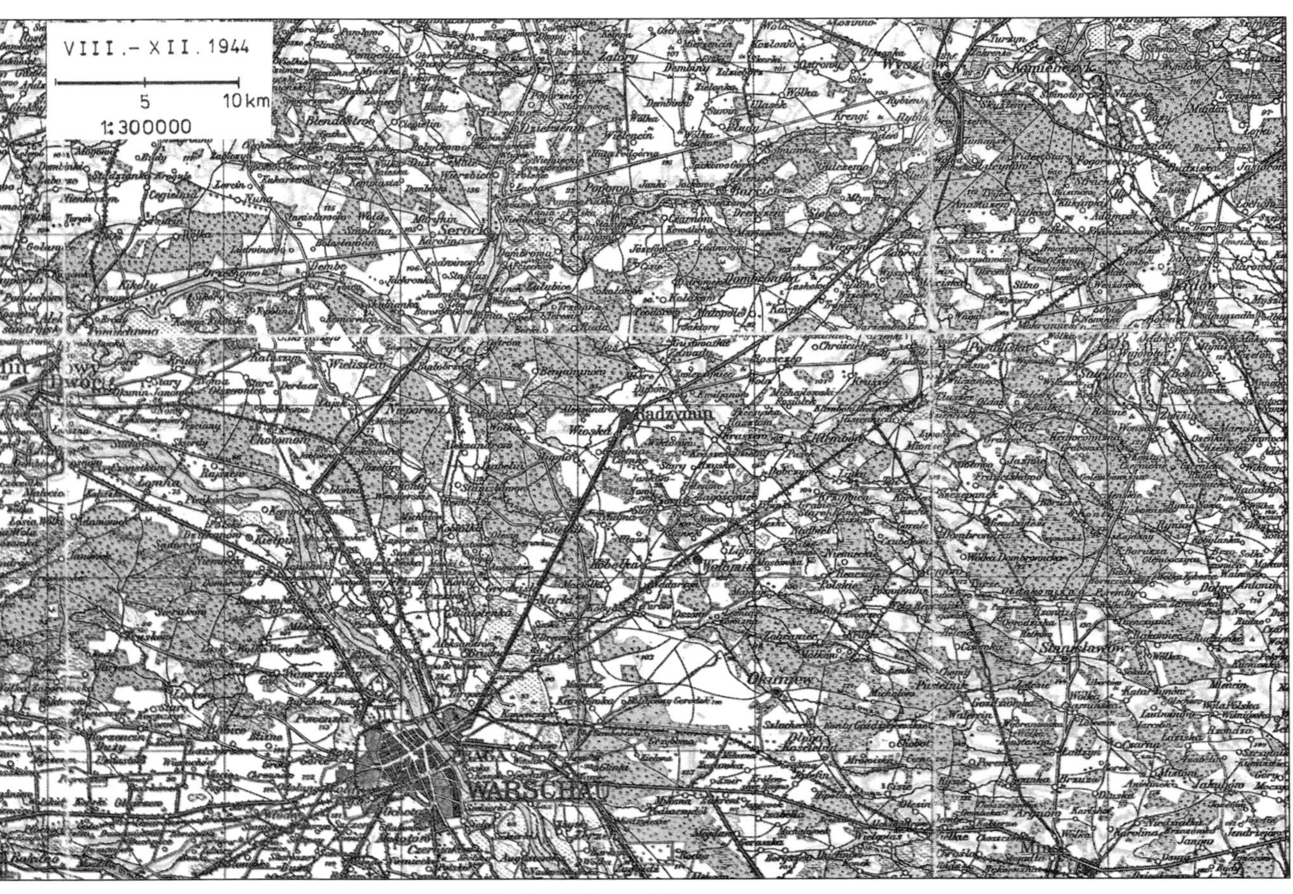

The Stanislawow-Warsaw sector.

M = 1 : 15000

← Bug

zerstört am 26.8.44

Slezany

Czarnów

Skizze zum Angriff der 3. u. 4. Kp. auf CZARNOW (zugl. Lagemeldung der gesprengten Sturmgeschütze) am 26. 8. 44

zu ①: Ausgangsstellung der 3. u. 4. Kp. zum Angriff
zu ②: Einbruch in die Feindstellungen am Ostrand CZARNÓW, da jedoch zu starker Pak- u. Panzerfeind ③ und außerdem schwieriges Gelände, sofortiges Absetzen in die Ausgangsstellung.
zu ④: Lage der im Sumpf festgefahrenen, anschließend gesprengten Sturmgeschütze 431 u. 432
zu ⑤: Stellungen der am Südrand des Brückenkopfes stehenden u. nach Zurückgehen der eigenen Infantrie über den Bug gesprengten Sturmgeschütze 422 u. 443

The attack of the 3rd and 4th Companies on Czarnow (encompassing the report of the blow-up assault guns)

Legend:
1: Initial line of departure for the attack of the companies.
2: Entering the enemy position along the eastern outskirts of Czarnow. The enemy antitank and armor forces were too strong (3) and the terrain too difficult, hence an immediate withdrawal to the lines of departure.
4: Position of assault guns *431* and *432*, which bogged down in the marshland and had to be blown up.
5: Positions of assault guns *422* and *443*, which were located at the southern edge of the bridgehead and had to be blown up after the withdrawal of friendly infantry across the Bug.

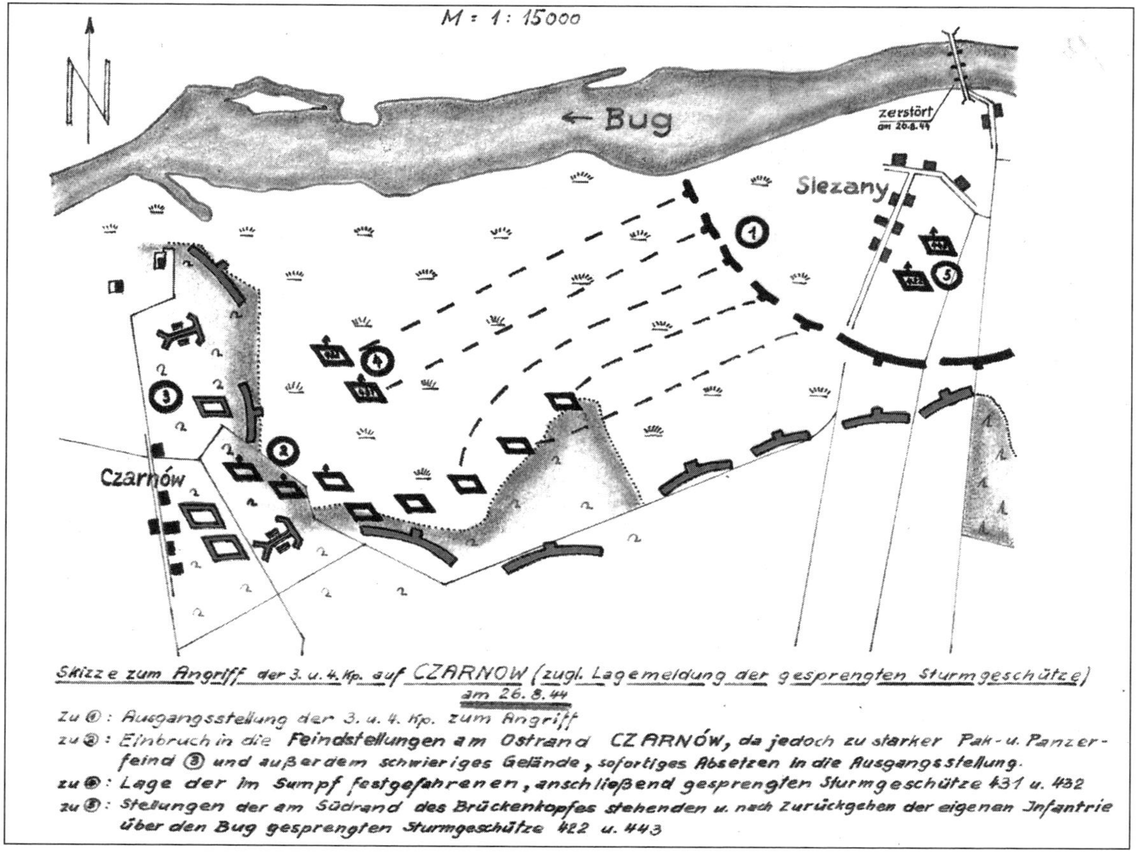

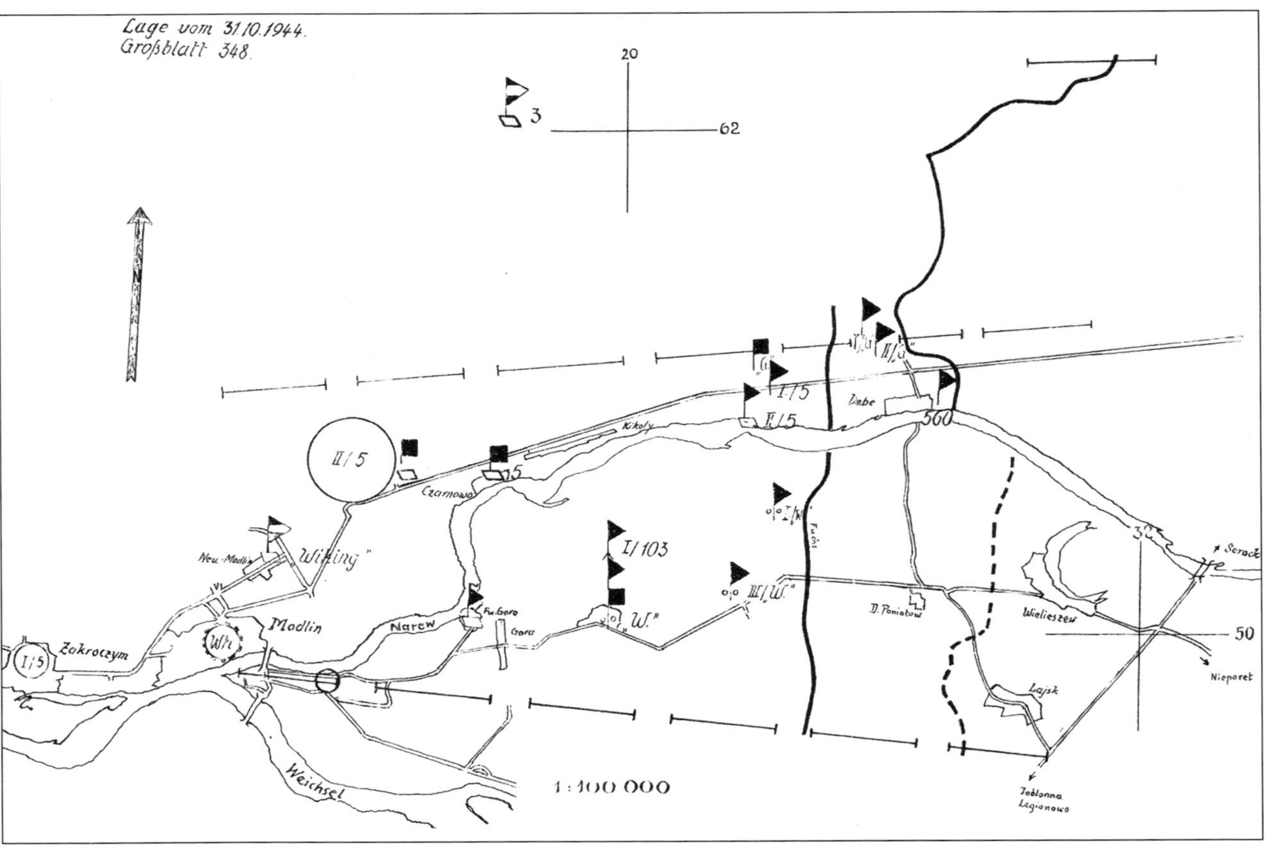

Divisional situation on 31 October 1944.

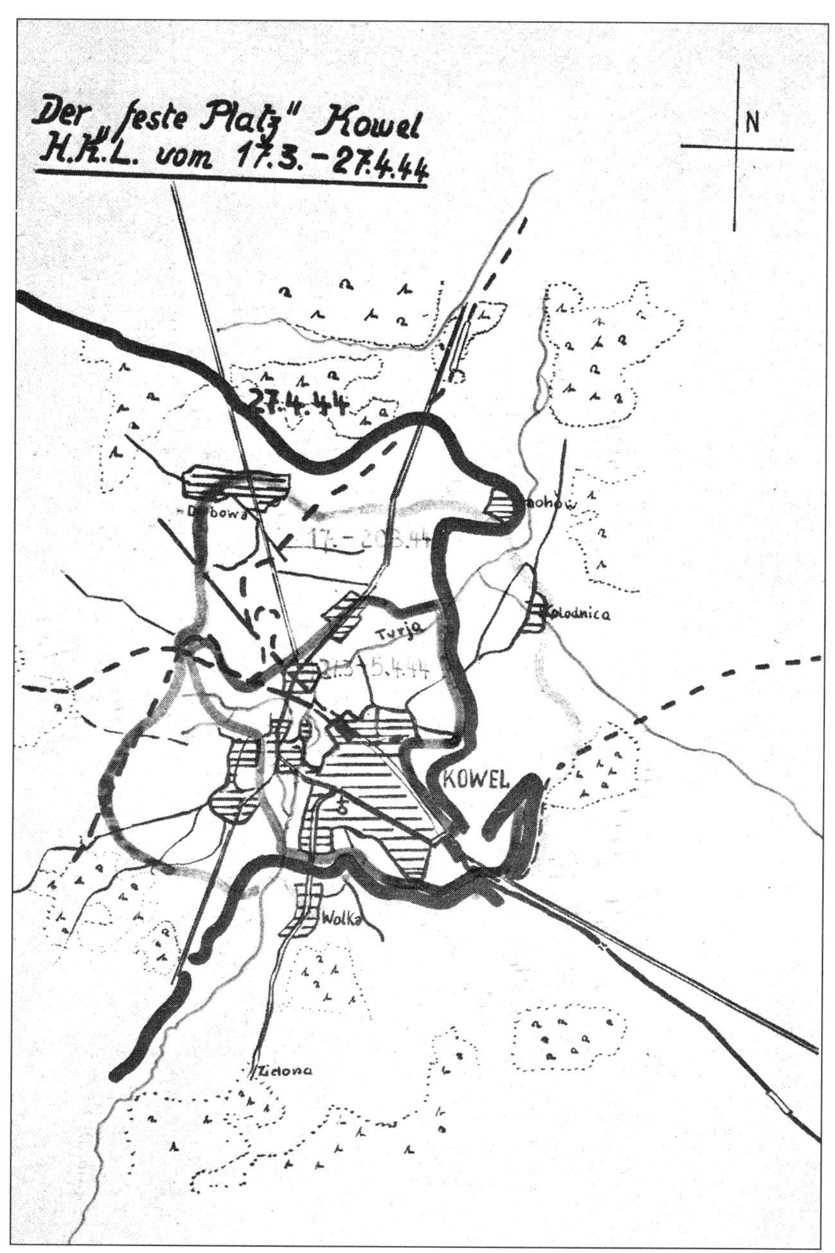

The "Fortress" of Kowel from 17 March to 27 April 1944.

The *Panther*, one of the best tanks of the Second World War.

SS-Obersturmbannführer Darges, the last regimental commander, in field positions in Hungary in the spring of 1945.

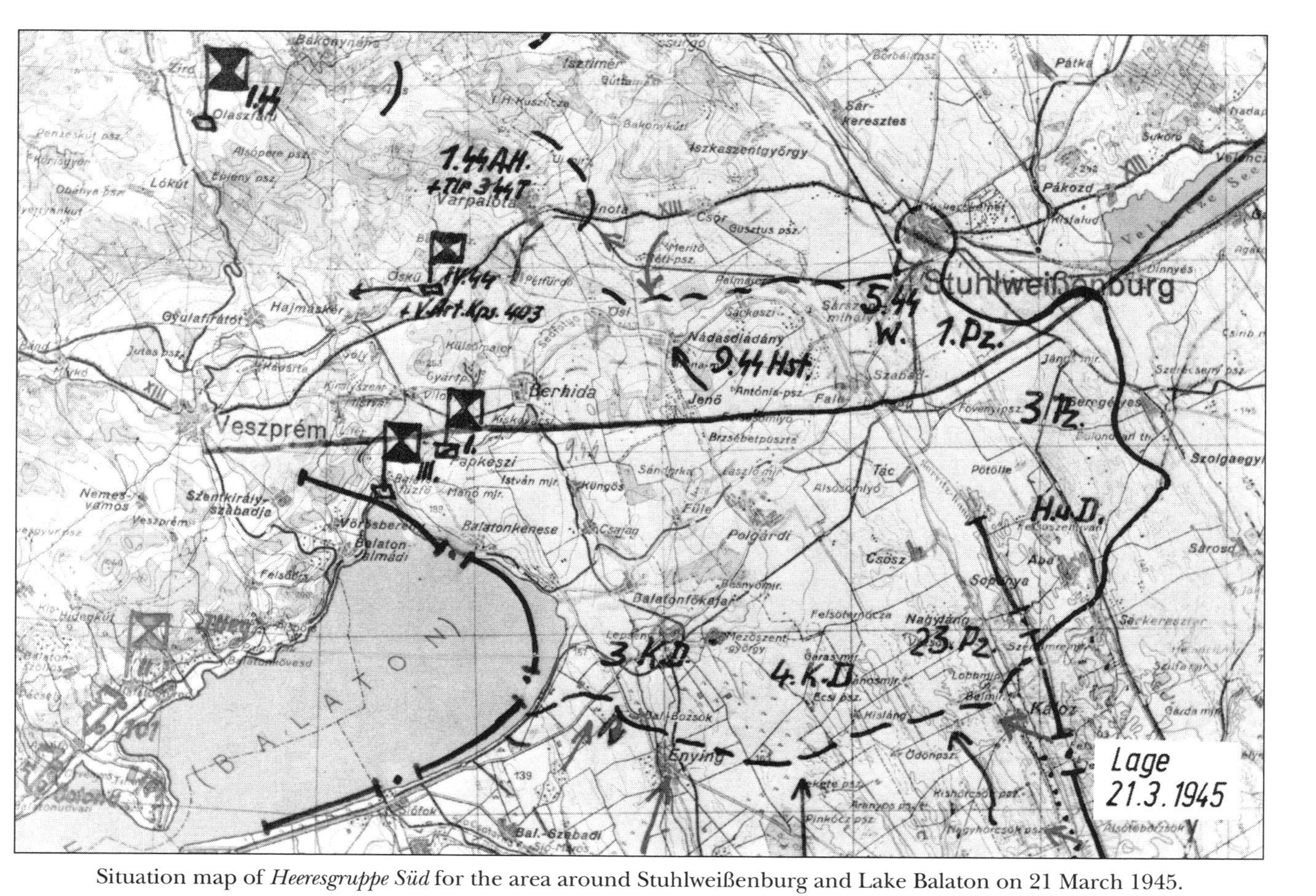

Situation map of *Heeresgruppe Süd* for the area around Stuhlweißenburg and Lake Balaton on 21 March 1945.

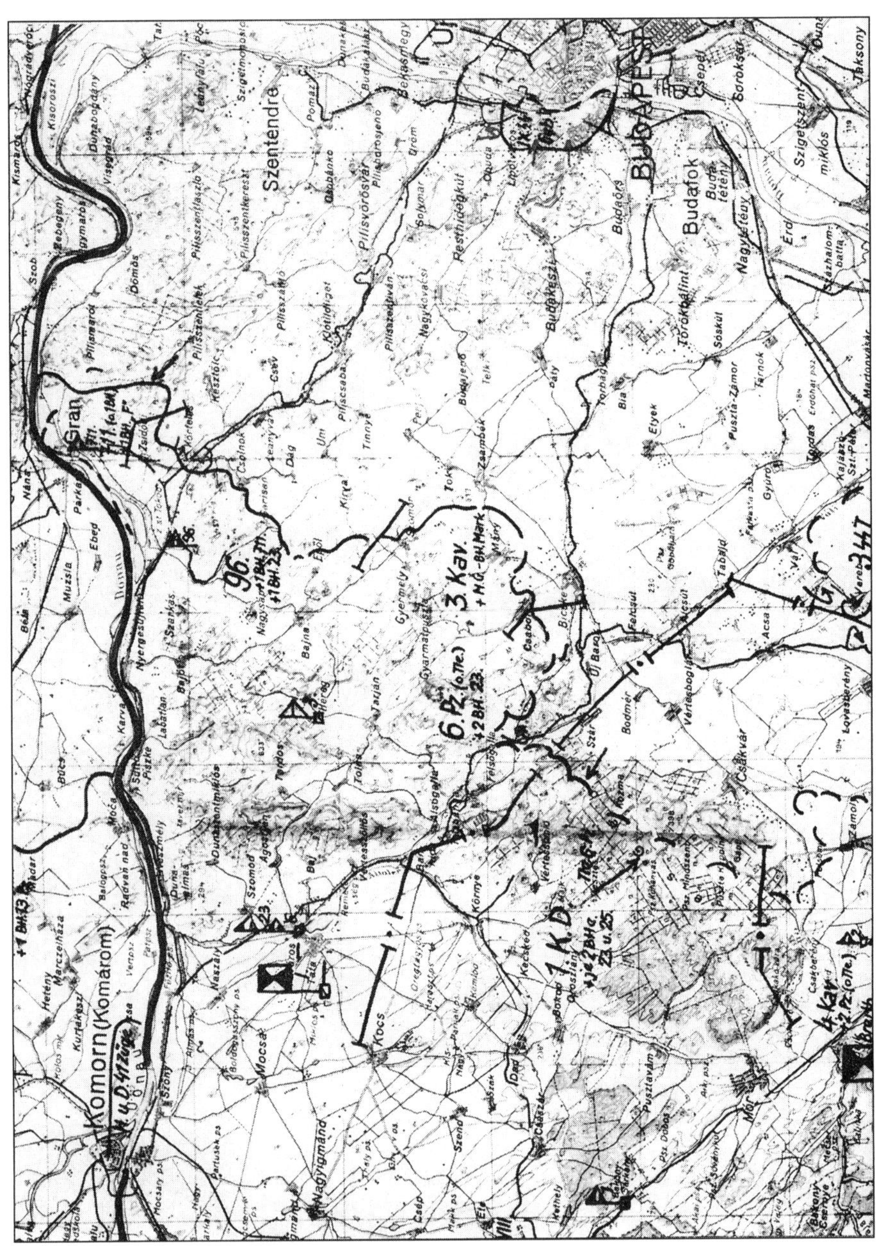

Situation map of *Heeresgruppe Süd* between Komorn and Stuhlweißenburg on 27 January 1945.

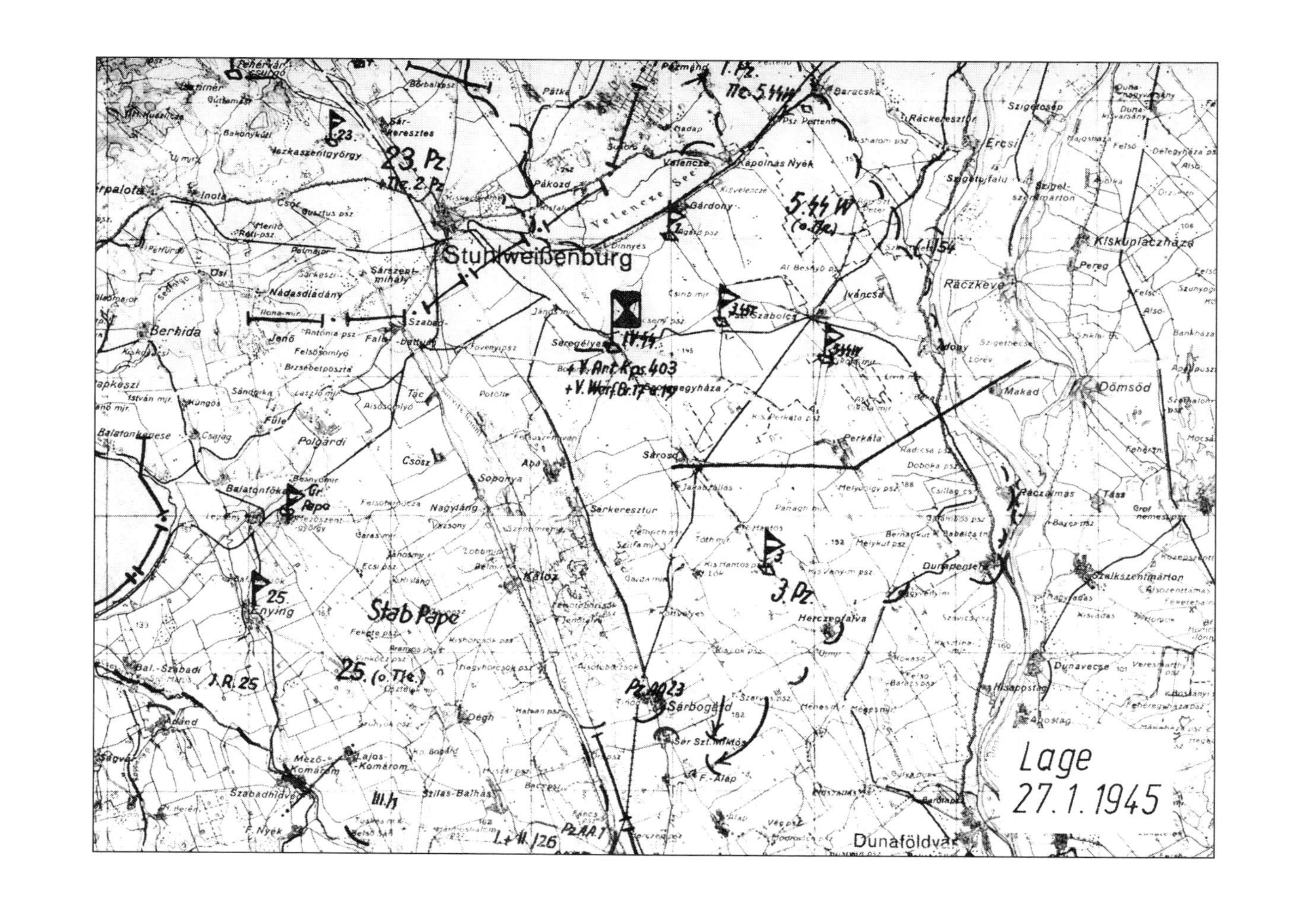
Lage
27.1.1945
Stuhlweißenburg
23. Pz.
1. Pz.
5. SS W
3. Pz.
Stab Pape
25. (o. Tle.)
Dunaföldvár
Dömsöd
Ráczkeve
Ercsi
Kiskunlaczháza
Sárbogárd
Enying
Berhida
Polgárdi
Velencze See
Gárdony
Kápolnas Nyék
Baracska
Seregélyes
Perkáta
Herczegfalva
Dunapentele
Szalkszentmárton
Dunavecse
Szabadhidvég
Sárkeresztur
Káloz
Soponya
Nagydáng
Csősz
Adony

Heavily armed *Wiking Panzergrenadiere*, with an *MG 42* and *MP 44* assault rifles.

Commanders conference with the 5th Company of the *Panzer* Regiment.

5th Company *Panthers* approach Kowel.

CHAPTER 11

The Final Fighting

STUHLWEISSENBURG—THE FINAL BATTLE

The birthday of the new battalion commander of the 2nd Battalion, *SS-Hauptsturmführer* Berndt, was celebrated at his command post in Sarkeresztes, 6 kilometers north-northwest of Stuhlweißenburg, on 11 March. It was still quiet in that sector of the front. On the far side of the bottleneck between Lakes Velence and Balaton, the offensive of the *6. Panzer-Armee,*[1] had passed its culminating point. The field army was forced to go over to the defensive. The final battle in Hungary had started, decisively influenced by the terrain features of the area.

The area of operations in Hungary west of the Danube is compartmentalized by a diagonal in the form of the Bakony Woods that runs from the southwest to the northeast. It is joined in the northeast by the Vertes Mountains. The mountain belt has an average width of 40 kilometers and extends some 180 kilometers in length. At the southern tip of the Bakony Woods, extending to the southeast, is Lake Balaton, which is approximately 80 kilometers long and about 9 kilometers wide on average. Lake Velence, 10 kilometers long, is found to the northeast, separated from Lake Balaton by a land mass of about 35 kilometers.

The operational importance of this natural obstacle is supplemented by the military/industrial in the form of the industrial area of Berhida-Tatabanya, 40 kilometers north of Stuhlweißenburg.

The cities of Vesprem on the northwest corner of lake Balaton and Stuhlweißenburg on the southwest corner of Lake Velence block passage through the land mass separating the lakes as well as access through the Bakony Woods to the northwest. While Stuhlweißenburg is connected via Mor and Kisber to Komorn in the north by means of rail and road, Vesprem is the starting point for the three major passage points to the northwest, west

1. Translator's Note: Often referred to as the *6. SS-Panzer-Armee* as well, although the *SS* was never officially part of its designation. (See Georg Maier, *Drama between Budapest and Vienna,* JJ Fedorowicz Publishing, Winnipeg: 2004.)

and southwest. The exit point from the Bakony Woods in the northwest south of papa is only about 70 kilometers from the Austrian border.

The Bakony Woods are located in highlands. Mina Hill, some 20 kilometers south of Vesprem, has a 601 meter high summit. Cross Mountain, 20 kilometers northwest of Vesprem, is 713 meters high. Those are the two highest hill masses.

The *6. Panzer-Armee* initiated its offensive in that area on 6 March. Its basic avenue of advance was directed through the land mass between the two lakes, but its attack southeast ultimately failed. After 10 days of offensive operations, the Soviet countermeasures forced it to be called off, thus initiating a round of decisive defense fighting in Hungary for the German forces. In the crosshairs of the Soviet intentions were the *6. Armee* (Balck) and the *6. Panzer-Armee* (Dietrich), positioned along the inter-lake land "bridge" and to both sides.

Prior to the start of the Soviet offensive, continuous enemy reinforcements along the front lines of the *"Wiking"* Division left no doubt that there would soon be combat operations again. On 16 March, there was a light snowfall along the front. At 1230 hours, the Soviets unleashed a 1-hour barrage fire that was not unexpected but also whose severity was not anticipated. Kerkhoff again takes up the narrative:

> Towards noon, the Russians put down a barrage with all available calibers like they had at Warsaw and Kowel. We fired up the engines, slammed the hatches shut and remained alert. After a good hour, the Reds attacked. The grenadiers stood their ground; we provided high-explosive rounds to good effect. Together, the attack was turned back and abated towards evening.

After a quiet 17 March, he continued:

> 18 March 1945: The Russians started the dance really early with arty and mortar fire. That was followed by support from fighter-bombers. Ivan was setting off fireworks like the good old days. Infantry and tanks then attacked. There were nine of us *Panthers* and we were positioned under good cover right on the Stuhlweißenburg—Mor road. The 5th and 6th Companies initially concentrated on the enemy tanks, some 50-60. In short order, we knocked out six of them. That motivated the grenadiers and gave the Russians weak knees.
>
> Towards noon, the sounds of battle swelled back to a hurricane. It appeared to me that the Russians were trying to force a decision. Just like *Wiking*, *Totenkopf* and the *1. Panzer-Division* and the *3. Panzer-Division* were greatly weakened. The enemy knew that as well;

consequently, forces were massed to force a breakthrough. A crisis started to arise in the sector around Stuhlweißenburg. Wave after wave of fighter-bombers came in. We had the impression that the barrage fires of the arty were getting even stronger.

The Russians had formed up their tanks and started to attack. We opened fire at 1400 meters. After working it out with Großrock, the 6th Company took the Russians from the right to the left and the 5th Company from left to right. In short order, seven enemy tanks were immobilized on the battlefield; another six had been destroyed by direct hits. By 1600 hours in the afternoon, we had suffered only one loss.

Around 1700 ours, it started to turn dark and, with it, enemy tanks suddenly surfaced along the left flank on the Mor—Stuhlweißenburg road. We gave battle immediately, and the first three enemy tanks were knocked out surprisingly quickly.

Großrock then concentrated on the enemy attacking to the front and the 5th Company on the flank attack of the Russian tanks . . .

Kerkhoff's account breaks off at that point, since his tank was knocked out while conducting a change in position and Kerkhoff himself was wounded.

The possibility of a Soviet flank attack along the road from Mor to Stuhlweißenburg had already been established the previous day, when the Soviets had achieved deep penetrations in the sector of the friendly forces to the left. By evening of the previous day, the enemy was already at Moha along the left flank of the division.

The resistance of the steadily shrinking armor and infantry forces of the division north of Stuhlweißenburg could not prevent the deep penetrations of the enemy to the left and his advance to the west. On 18 March, strong enemy armored forces advanced as far as the division command post in Iszkaszentgyorgy. The left wing of the division had to be pulled back to the northern edge of Stuhlweißenburg. The left flank of the division was exposed, since there were no friendly forces there. The *"Germania"* Regiment attempted to conduct a strongpoint defense on the Stuhlweißenburg-Gor-Varpolota road and screen to the north. The right wing of the division was thrown back to the rail station on the southeastern edge of Stuhlweißenburg. Although the Soviets were able to penetrate as far as the city center with tanks late in the afternoon of 19 March, the city was held. To the northwest of the city, however, there was a "gap of 8 kilometers, through which the enemy had advanced, crossing the creek."[2]

In the sector of the friendly forces to the left, the localities of Csor, Isztimer and Bodayk—all west of the Mor—Stuhlweißenburg road—were lost.

2. Author's Note: Daily logs of *Heeresgruppe Süd.*

Even though the Soviet offensive north of Stuhlweißenburg had not come as a surprise, the power of it far exceeded expectations. There was no time available for the necessary countermeasures: Pulling back the badly stretched front southeast of the land "bridge" with the objective of releasing forces, forming reserves and pushing them into the threatened areas of penetration north of Stuhlweißenburg.

The decision to conduct a major withdrawal, which, in hindsight, was the necessary and proper solution, was not immediately made. The next few days were marked by uncertainty about the development of the situation, insufficient clarity concerning the enemy's intentions, doubt and hesitation, coupled with the well-known difficulties of executing the movement of large formations and the unexpectedly fast deterioration of the situation north of Stuhlweißenburg.

The *356. Infanterie-Division,* which was pulled out of the line south of Lake Velence during the night of 18–19 March, had to cut a wide arc through Raab to get to its new area of operations around Komorn. The march route was more than 150 kilometers. After the *2. SS-Panzer-Division "Das Reich"* was pulled out of the line, it staged in the Nadesdladany area so as to move expeditiously to its new area of operations on the left wing of the *IV. SS-Panzer-Korps.* The *I. SS-Panzer-Korps,* moving through the land "bridge" between the lakes, assembled behind the area that had been penetrated in the sector of the *3. SS-Panzer-Division "Totenkopf."* The corps became committed in difficult fighting to the northwest of Stuhlweißenburg just in its effort to occupy the assembly areas for the attack it had been ordered to make to the east.

The *I. Kavallerie-Korps,* which had previously been positioned along the east banks of Lake Balaton, was directed to disengage its initial elements during the night of 19–20 March and move behind the left wing of the *I. SS-Panzer-Korps* in order to block the Soviet penetrations northwest of Stuhlweißenburg. The cavalry corps had the infantry that was needed and was more effective in fighting in the trackless wooded areas than armor formations.

Instead of carrying out that mission, however, the cavalry corps, which was in the process of attempting to disengage, was committed to a counterattack along the east banks of Lake Balaton, because the Soviets had overrun and scattered the Hungarian 25th infantry Division, which had been positioned there.

The dilemma caused by a lack of infantry in the Bakony Woods is reflected in this daily log entry for *Heeresgruppe Süd* on 20 March:

> At least one mounted regiment needs to be pulled out of the line. The disengagement of the entire corps is even more desired, since the enemy's vast numerical superiority, which even today had

threatening consequences in the mountainous and wooded terrain, cannot be eliminated by armored forces but only by our own infantry . . .

The *I. Kavallerie-Korps* remained fixed along Lake Balaton, however.

✠

The road network to and from the front, which was already being heavily burdened by supply and logistics traffic in the land "bridge" around Stuhlweißenburg, was being further jammed by the movement of the major formations and, in addition, the movements of refugees and interference by the enemy. The bridge over the Sarvitz Canal was destroyed by bombs.

Command and control relationships were changed to reflect the circumstances. At 1400 hours on 19 March, the *6. Panzer-Armee* assumed the sector of the front from the southern tip of Lake Velence to Komorn on the Danube. The *6. Panzer-Armee* also retained command and control of the forces southeast of the land "bridge."

Changes in command and control relationships that resulted from the above could not be executed or were delayed in their punctual execution by enemy actions. In some cases, the consequences were less than could be desired. Just as the *I. Kavallerie-Korps* could not be pulled out without endangering the Lake Balaton sector, the *9. SS-Panzer-Division "Hohenstaufen"* was likewise not released by the *6. Armee,* despite the urgent requests from the *6. Panzer-Armee* and the pressing directives of *Heeresgruppe Süd.*

The uncertainty of the senior commands concerning the scope and intentions of the enemy were demonstrated once again on 19 March when permission arrived from the Army High Command at 1410 hours to shorten the front in a line running Lake Balaton–Seregelyes–Dinnies (southern tip of Lake Velence) but a denial by the field-army group at 1800 hours of the request of the *III. Panzer-Korps* to evacuate the bridgehead at Seregelyes in order to free up the *1. Panzer-Division.* The field-army group was of the opinion that such an action would invite the enemy to break though in that sector.

On 20 March, the enemy continued to advance and fight for the eastern entrances to the Bakony Woods. The daily logs of *Heeresgruppe Süd* recorded: "As was the case in the first two days of fighting, the enemy committed massed infantry to battle, taking possession of the wooded hills and enveloping the friendly strongpoints."

To the west of Stuhlweißenburg, the *1. SS-Panzer-Division "Leibstandarte SS Adolf Hitler"* defended against heavy armored attacks from the area around Inota and Reti pcs. north of the Stuhlweißenburg-Varpolata rail line. Thirty enemy tanks were knocked out. Further to the southwest of Stuhlweißenburg, in a line running northern edge of Nadasdladany—northern edge of Ösi—northern edge of the patch of woods northwest of Ösi, the elements of the *"Hohenstaufen"* Division, which had been pulled out of the line the previous night south of Seregelyes, were employed screening north. The elements included the divisional reconnaissance battalion and the 2nd Battalion of *SS-Panzer-Grenadier-Regiment 19.* They were placed along the open left flank of the *"Wiking"* Division and, by extension, the *III. Panzer-Korps,* to which the division had been attached since 20 March.

The enemy's pressure south of Lake Velence continued to increase. According to the daily logs of the field-army group: "In heavy fighting, strong enemy forces ejected the *II./SS-Panzer-Grenadier-Regiment Westland,* which was in a forward position just west of Seregelyes, from Börgesd, 3 kilometers south of Dinnies." The *1. Panzer-Division,* which had been pulled from the line, was able to "restore contact with the elements of the *5. SS-Panzer-Division Wiking,* which were stubbornly holding the city of Stuhlweißenburg."

The "Vikings" continued to hold the eastern outskirts of the city and push back the enemy forces advancing along the rail line to the west. They were able to retake the suburb of Kiskekskement in an immediate counterattack and engaged in intense urban fighting against enemy armor that had penetrated to the middle of the city. Stuhlweißenburg had become the lynchpin of the entire front.

Analyzing the situation in a sober fashion, the *6. Armee* considered shortening the front as follows: Balatonfökajar—Polgardi (southwest of Stuhlweißenburg)—Sarvitz sector (west of Stuhlweißenburg). With regard to the intended evacuation of Stuhlweißenburg, the Chief-of-Staff of the field-army group replied at 1935 hours:

> If one gives up contact with Lake Velence and Stuhlweißenburg, then the enemy would have the opportunity to attack west along a narrow front with his 22 freed-up rifle divisions as his main effort. That would be a massing of forces that one could only tough out with difficulty.

The possibility of 22 freed-up divisions was influencing the decisions of the field-army group!

General confusion and a lack of focus were increasing in the higher levels of command. On the evening of 20 March, the *"Wiking"* Division had no contact with the *III. Panzer-Korps.* The division's assistant operations officer believed the Soviets were already further north in the vicinity of papa, 20 kilometers west-northwest of Stuhlweißenburg. In actual fact, Papa was not lost until five days later. Nonetheless, the slow isolation of Stuhlweißenburg was making progress, as evidenced in the account that follows that was written by the tank regiment commander, *SS-Obersturmbannführer* Darges, who was on his way to the division command post during the evening of 20 March:

> After a short cure for bronchial pneumonia, I wanted to report back to the division and went in the division physician's *Kfz. 15* from Vesprem towards Stuhlweißenburg.
>
> Since a withdrawal movement had been initiated by the division, it could not be determined where the division command was located. Consequently, *Obersturmbannführer* Dr. Thon and I rode in the staff car along with two medical personnel in a convoy in the direction of Stuhlweißenburg, along with a *VW-Kübelwagen*, which had the general-staff officer candidates and "Schlieffen show-offs," *Obersturmführer* Schumacher and *Obersturmführer* Glanert, in it.
>
> We encountered the typical picture of withdrawing units and jammed roads, when the stream suddenly ended and the road became clear. It had already started to turn dark and a number of burning vehicles marked the road.
>
> A problem with a tire on the *VW* moving ahead of us, forced the occupants to stop briefly, while we continued on in the direction of what we assumed was the division command post. Moving around a curve that offered little visibility, we saw three tanks staggered on both sides of the road. Assuming that they were tanks from the neighboring division to the north—our own division's tanks were not expected at this location—we approached closely to the right-hand side of the first tank. Standing in the staff car, I leaned slightly on the tank and asked the commander inside what his unit was. I had just finished saying the last word when the commander surfaced out of the tank and I realized it was the silhouette of a Russian T 43. I called to *Dr.* Thon: "It's Ivan!" The staff car shot forward only for us to see in the turned-on headlights that there was tank after tank lined up in the next village.
>
> Everything else took place in the fraction of a second: Stop . . . jump out of the vehicle . . . drop our overcoats . . . take our pistols in our hands . . . and run, crawl and jump towards our own forces. The bursts of submachine-gun fire cordially sent our way put holes in our uniforms and slightly wounded two men. In the garish light of the aerial flares that were sent up without interruption and in the fire of submachine guns and machine guns, we completed the fastest run of our lives. While catching our breath in a depression, we heard the *VW* we had left behind on the road drive into the assembly area

> of the Soviet armored formation without us having any way to give a warning.
>
> Ivan, who had been alerted by us, received the *VW* with bursts of submachine-gun and machine-gun fire, whereby two of the occupants were badly wounded. *Obersturmführer* Glanert, bleeding profusely, was able to drag himself away and was found by chance in an unconscious, badly weakened state by a military policeman—he stepped on him in the dark—and was sent to a hospital.
>
> *Obersturmführer* Schumacher, brave and highly decorated, liked by both officers and enlisted, who had proven himself in more than a hundred armored engagements, has been reported as missing ever since.

That meant that the only road connecting the division in Stuhlweißenburg to the west had been blocked by the Soviets. The corridor the division found itself in was perhaps 15 kilometers long and, at the most, 3 to 4 kilometers wide. Despite that, the orders for the division continued to remain to hold Stuhlweißenburg.

The 21st of March saw the enemy score continued, decisive success in the main areas of the fighting. In the sector of the left-hand neighbor of the division, the *1. SS-Panzer-Division "Leibstandarte SS Adolf Hitler,"* Varpalota, 20 kilometers west of Stuhlweißenburg, was lost around noon. In the process, the enemy, who was attacking from the southeast, east and north, lost 46 tanks. According to the daily logs of *Heeresgruppe Süd*, strong enemy forces supported by tanks took Ösi

> and threw the elements of the *9. SS-Panzer-Division*, which had been trying to flank [the enemy], back to the south. In continued advancing to the southwest and west, the enemy reached the vineyards country east of Berhida [about 20 kilometers southwest of Stuhlweißenburg]. *Reiter-Regiment 41* [*4. Kavallerie-Division*] was able to hold out on the northern and eastern outskirts against enemy attacks in regimental strength conducted from the northeast and north.

In the sector of the friendly forces to the right, the *1. Panzer-Division*, the enemy was turned back with the exception of some minor penetrations.

On the northeastern tip of Lake Balaton, the enemy advanced into the wooded terrain around Füle. That meant that the lead Soviet attack elements were only separated from east to west by about 5 kilometers. It looked as though there was to be no way of averting an encirclement of elements of the

1. Panzer-Division, the *3. Panzer-Division*, the *44. Reichs-Grenadier-Division "Hoch- und Deutschmeister"* and the *"Wiking"* Division.

The daily logs of the field-army group:

> During the night, the defenders of Stuhlweißenburg sealed off and cleaned up deep penetrations in the northern and southwestern portions of the city and held the following line in the morning: West of the small lake to the south of Stuhlweißenburg—Railway facilities—western vineyard area—southern portion of the city (Kiskekskement)—rail line to Mor as far as the fork in the line southwest of the city.

Jahncke, the assistant division operations officer, noted the following on 21 March:

> As a result, the situation in Stuhlweißenburg is very serious and a continued holding appears to be pointless . . . Farther to the rear, the situation is completely unclear. Contact with the *III. Panzer-Korps* has also been broken...
>
> Towards noon, for the first time: *Führer* Order—Stuhlweißenburg is to be held. We consider this order to ne sheer madness, since only a few [enemy] forces were being fixed by us.

As far as conditions in the city were for the defenders, we get a glimpse from a letter written in 1953 by the former battalion physician of the 2nd Battalion of the tank regiment, Dr. Kalbskopf, to the parents of *SS-Untersturmführer* Jensen, the battalion adjutant, who was reported missing. Although conditions were still relatively bearable up through 15 March in the headquarters of the city military administration, he wrote:

> Around 15 March, that status changed abruptly. All at once, contact was lost with our neighbors. Through binoculars, we could see Russian columns heading west to the left and right of us out of range. We received orders to hold the city under all circumstances. I can certainly claim that the days up to the afternoon of 21 March were the worst ones that I experienced during the war.
>
> During those days and night, I came to admire your son. Telephone connections were no longer available. Every report,

every bit of information concerning the situation had to be fetched personally. I can still see your son getting up during those nights and heading out into the uncertainty of the darkness so as to find out what was absolutely necessary for the well-being of all.

We always awaited his return anxiously and tried to determine from his expression, when he returned, whether the "mail" he brought was good or bad.

Our situation in the city grew ever more desperate approaching 21 March. The Soviets had pushed us back into the city center, where we were sitting in a mousetrap. There were still no orders for the division to pull back.

During the night of 20–21 March, we sat together in the entryway to a massive vault in the city center—completely surrounded. Everyone hesitated to say even a single word about our fate. I was fearful of what might happen to the many wounded in the cellar below. It was clear to us that under these circumstances it was going to be a fight to the last man or the final sacrifice, since no one wanted to fall into Russian hands alive. Like a miracle, we received a radio message on the afternoon of 21 March that we were to immediately pull back to the west. It was only an unbridled will to survive after those nights of doubt that the risky move met with success. After the ring was broken with the last of our operational tanks, the evacuation started, which demanded all of my attention with regard to the wounded. It was not until darkness started to fall that we gathered together again a few kilometers west of the city along the withdrawal route. When that happened, a rumor surfaced that we were already in another pocket that stretched 30 kilometers in a very thin corridor from Stuhlweißenburg as far as the northern shore of lake Balaton and only had a very small outlet. On the evening of 21 March, when we started moving westward, I saw your son for the last time.

The losses in the pocket were horrific. In my case, my medical *SPW*, fully loaded with wounded, was blown sky high by an antitank-gun round. No one inside remained alive. Just before I left the pocket, someone told me that the Adjutant, Jensen, and the signals officer had been killed in a Stalin organ salvo . . .

The Commander-in-Chief of the *6. Armee*, *General der Panzertruppen* Balck, considered the situation so serious that he had requested a shortening of the front at 1055 hours that morning of 21 March. He wanted the new line to run Lake Balaton–Falubattian–Nadesdladany–Varpalota. The line ran west of Stuhlweißenburg and meant that the city would be given up.

At 1320 hours, he intended to execute that plan without waiting for the decision of the Army High Command. Discussing the matter with the field-army group headquarters, he once again came out against the holding of Stuhlweißenburg. At 1655 hours, the field army's chief-of-staff repeated the request, as recorded in the daily logs of *Heeresgruppe Süd*: "The *5. SS-Panzer-Division Wiking* [in Stuhlweißenburg] would already have to fight its way free through Nadesdladany."

At 1640 hours, the field-army group received permission to allow the *6. Armee* to shorten its frontage, with the caveat that Stuhlweißenburg still had to be held.

Later on that afternoon, Hitler was presented with the issue of Stuhlweißenburg one more time and decided at 1750 hours that the city was to be held. It was most likely that order that caused *Generaloberst* Guderian in a telephone conversation at 2105 hours to emphasize the holding of Stuhlweißenburg: "If one were to give up there, then one would start to waver and lose his footing all the way to Komorn."[3]

Faced with the impending encirclement, the division commander struggled with the decision that evening to give up the city, allowing his division to escape a death sentence. Based on the rapidly worsening situation in the sectors of the friendly forces on his flanks, he thought hopes for relief, once encircled, to be illusory and impossible to execute. According to Schönfelder, the corps sent him the following message: "Assemble vehicles and pull back to the west; channel the wounded through to the west." The message was more of a moral reinforcement, however, since the division did not report to it at the time.

When only the southwestern portion of the city continued to be held late in the afternoon, the chief of staff of the *6, Armee* informed the field-army group at 2010 hours "that the city of Stuhlweißenburg was no longer in our hands, according to a report from the *1. Panzer-Division* positioned to the south."

At 0010 hours, the field army operations officer of the *6. Armee* informed the operations officer of the field-army group that

> he had received message traffic from the *5. SS-Panzer-Division Wiking* at the tactical time of 2220 hours that the Stuhlweißenburg rail station was in enemy hands and the division was positioned on the southwestern portion of the city.

3. Translator's Note: This passage, again from the daily logs of *Heeresgruppe Süd*, is written in the subjunctive in German, which is the standard way of paraphrasing quotations, hence the fairly stilted manner of writing, which is generally rendered in the indicative in modern English.

The field-army group reacted by stating that the giving up of the city contradicted the directive received from *Generaloberst* Guderian, which meant that in following the intent of the directive, the southwestern portion of the city still had to be held. The field-army group directed that the *1. Panzer-Division* needed to try to establish contact.

According to the daily logs, at 1245 hours, 12 hours previously, *Generaloberst* Guderian had emphasized:

> The situation west of Stuhlweißenburg had to be restored by means of attack and, by doing so, contact with the city established. What was imperative was that no one be cut off.

✠

For soldiers on the ground, the situation on both sides of Stuhlweißenburg on the afternoon of 21 March no longer justified any expectation of restoring the situation west of the city by means of an attack nor the forced re-establishment of contact with the city.

The massive attacks in the sector of the *I. Kavallerie-Korps* continued during the night of 21–22 March and increased in intensity the following day. In the daily logs of the field-army group, the following was written concerning the sector of the *III. Panzer-Korps* south of Stuhlweißenburg:

> Elements of the *1. Panzer-Division* and the *44. Reichs-Grenadier-Division Hoch- und Deutschmeister* were still engaged in hard defensive fighting on the high ground west of Falubattian on the afternoon of 21 March.

When Falubattian fell, however, the front, which had been in the process of being re-established, was ripped open again.

✠

The division commander, *SS-Standartenführer* Ullrich, decided on his own initiative to prevent the threatened encirclement or cutting off of his forces. Jahncke provides the following insight from his diary:

> The division commander decided at 2000 hours—in contravention of the *Führer* Order—to order the withdrawal from Stuhlweißenburg so as to save at least the majority of his soldiers and weapons.

That order, in defiance of a repeated and emphatic directive, found the division commander in agreement with an option discussed in German regulations that concerned such situations. According to the *Exerzierreglement für die Infanterie*[4] of the Imperial German Army of 26 May 1906, paragraph 304 states the following:

> The highest quality of leadership remains the willingness to accept responsibility. That quality would be falsely understood if it only sought to allow decisions to be independently made without regard to the over-all situation or not to follow issued orders to the letter whenever feelings of knowing it all better take the place of obedience.
>
> But in cases in which the subordinate has to say that the person giving the mission does not fully understand the situation or the order has been overcome by events, it is the duty of the subordinate to either not obey them or change them accordingly and to report that to the superior. He is still fully responsible for not obeying the order.

In the manual *Die SS- und Polizeigerichtsbarkeit*[5] of 1 July 1944, the following is formulated:

> An order can sometimes be overcome by events that have occurred since it was issued. If the subordinate gains the impression after carefully examining all of the information available that the conditions under which the order was issued have changed or are quite different from what the officer issuing the order assumed, with the result that the issued order is no longer appropriate and in the interest of the matter at hand can no longer be executed, then he needs to act on his own initiative, if no time remains to render a report or request new orders. The subordinate must constantly ask himself whether the superior in his position would insist on the order or issue a different order.[6]

The turbulent situation of 22 March, in which orderly command and control threatened to derail, was noted in the field-army group daily logs as follows:

4. Translator's Note: *Drill Regulations for the Infantry.*

5. Translator's Note: *SS and Police Jurisdiction.*

6. Author's Note: See also *Heeresdienstvorschrift 300, Truppenführung,* paragraph 37.

> In the area southwest of Stuhlweißenburg, the enemy continued his massed attacks, focusing his main effort of the area just northwest of Lake Balaton. Despite heavy casualties in personnel and armor, he succeeded in pushing back the friendly defensive sector several kilometers to the northwest. Further to the north, the enemy advanced between the battle groups southwest of Stuhlweißenburg, some of which were still moving in an effort to break out to the west. During night attacks, Ösi, Nadasdladany and Berhida were lost to enemy forces advancing from the north; during the morning, Jenö and the patch of woods to its northeast were also lost. The *3. Panzer-Division* and the *5. SS-Panzer-Division Wiking*, employed in the Stuhlweißenburg area, fought through those enemy forces in a generally west-southwest direction and reached Balatonfüzfö with their lead elements...
>
> The enemy attacked with massed infantry and armor forces from the Varpalota area towards the southwest and reached a line running Gyarts-Soly-Kadarta-Gyalafiratot. Enemy tank elements 3 kilometers east of Vesprem were turned back, with three enemy tanks knocked out...
>
> The *9. SS-Panzer-Division* [*Hohenstaufen*] and elements of the *4. Kavallerie-Division* established a blocking position running south of Berhida–Papkeszi North–Volonya North–Sita north. They turned back enemy attacks supported by tanks.

Late in the afternoon, at 1745 hours, the *6. Panzer-Armee*, in the sector to the north, reported: "The *1. SS-Panzer-Division* [*Leibstandarte SS Adolf Hitler*] has been split into several groups as a result of constant main-effort enemy attacks since yesterday afternoon."

The Commander-in-Chief of *Heeresgruppe Süd*, visiting the command post of the *6. Armee*, had "the impression that absolute confusion reigns there. Since there are no telephonic communications, it is difficult to get a clear picture."

Let us now turn our attention back to the breakout efforts of the *"Wiking"* Division, as recorded in the diary of *SS-Hauptsturmführer* Jahncke, the division's assistant operations officer:

> Disengagement from the enemy during the night without a hitch and without significant enemy contact. By first light, all elements of

the division assembled in a small area around Urhida. The division intended to split up into two battle groups and push through to the southwest in the direction of the northern edge of Lake Balaton. We assumed that at least the southern front still has some sort of cohesion.

Gruppe Hack (*Westland*) was directed to screen to the north in the direction of Nadasdladany, and the main group—all armored elements—was to force a penetration through to the southwest.

In the morning, however, the southern front collapsed. All of the divisions, including the encircled *Tiger* battalion, were fleeing west towards Vesprem. Despite strong enemy thrusts from the south, the division succeeded in continuing to advance southwest. It should be noted, however, that all of the armored elements—such as tanks, assault guns, *SPW's*, the *II./SS-Artillerie-Regiment 5* (self-propelled battalion)—were lost in the constant fighting against new enemy groups that kept appearing. The individual units fought their way through in combat patrol fashion.

At noon, we ran into the elements of the southern front that were fleeing in a panic to the west. It was only thanks to the tight control of the leadership and the old discipline that was still intact that no panicky flight ensured in our ranks.

In addition, we owed thanks for our successful breakout to the *Hohenstaufen* Division, whose commander, *Standartenführer* Stadler, violated orders and extended his front lines as far as possible towards the northern portion of Lake Balaton so as to leave a passage point open for us.

With regard to the demise of *SS-Panzer-Regiment 5* in the fighting for Stuhlweißenburg and Vesprem, we have a first-hand account from the command of tank 201, Siegfried Melinkat:

On 21 March 1945, after I had been knocked out in Tank 201 in the last battle group of the regiment—one *Panzer V* and two *Panzer IV's*—just behind Vesprem (Hungary), I moved with my crew to the trains of the 2nd Company. Witness to my being knocked out was none other than our last division commander (Ullrich), whose command post was nearby. He was the first one to congratulate us on getting out in one piece.

The lead elements and command staff of the division, which also had to fight its way through without being able to exert any influence on the fighting, arrived at 1600 hours at the command post of the *"Hohenstaufen"* Division in Papkeszi and at 1700 hours at the command post of the *III. Panzer-Korps* in Balatonfüzfö.[7]

The *I. Kavallerie-Korps,* still positioned along the northern banks of Lake Balaton, was resupplied with nine tons of munitions during the night by 10 *Ju 52's.* According to the daily logs of the field-army group, the *23. Panzer-Division,* which reported to the corps, moved out

> during the night of 23–24 March from the area north of Balatonkenese (southeast of Papkeski) and attacked east, advancing as far as and through Küngös, knocking out 15 enemy tanks in the process and passing the elements of the *1. Panzer-Division,* the *3. Panzer-Division* and the *44. Reichs-Grenadier-Division Hoch- und Deutschmeister,* which were fighting their way back in a generally westward direction…

By passing those formations, coupled with the breakout of the *"Wiking"* Division the previous day, the intermediate operational-level objective of the Soviets—to encircle and eliminate strong German forces along the land "bridge" around Stuhlweißenburg—was not obtained. On the other hand, according to *Heeresgruppe Süd,* "the lynch pins of the defense—Stuhlweißenburg, Varpalota, the industrial area of Tatabanya and Gran—were lost, however."

The *"Wiking"* Division had escaped encirclement and destruction. The loss of the greater part of the heavy weapons and equipment meant that the division was unable to operate the way it had previously. The tank regiment, for instance, basically had no tanks left.

In order to judge the performance of the forces in doing their utmost to execute their assigned combat missions, it may be useful to look at losses sustained in that last round of major fighting. Numbers are not available that

7. Author's Note: According to the daily logs of *Heeresgruppe Süd.*

directly address *SS-Panzer-Regiment 5*, but the numbers given for the division should be meaningful enough.[8]

In the difficult fighting north of Warsaw, the number of dead, wounded and missing in October 1944 came to 4,072. The numbers in November and December were lower, only to start climbing again in Hungary in January to 2,787 and, in March, to 3,534. The total losses of the division in the six months from October 1944 to March 1945 were 12,136 men. That represents—at 67.6 percent—more than two-thirds of the authorized strength of 17,797 men. Following Stuhlweißenburg, the division had been bled white to its core. To make up for those losses, the division received 9,813 men as replacements between that same October and March. For the most part, however, those replacements were transferred air force and naval personnel, who had no ground combat experience.

During the same period, 407 convalescents returned to the division, 5.1 percent of all of the wounded.

The number of missing increased considerably during that 6-month period in comparison to other time periods. During the five months of defensive fighting between the Dopnez and the Dnjepr from August to December 1943, the total number of missing was recorded at 281. From May to September 1944, the number was 284. In the last three months of 1944, the number grew to 883. From January to March 1945, the number shot up to 1,255, a many-fold increase over previous numbers reported as missing.

If one assumes that the combat elements were generally more strongly affected by casualties than the trains and the rear-area services, then the significance of the numbers becomes apparent.

In judging the operations and their leadership on the German side in Hungary in March 1945, the daily logs of *Heeresgruppe Süd* are an authoritative source. The daily logs and other documents of equal importance for the subordinate organizations and formations, such as the *6. Armee*, the *III. Panzer-Korps*, the *IV. SS-Panzer-Korps*, the *"Wiking"* Division or *SS-Panzer-Regiment 5*, are not available. That circumstance undoubtedly reduces the ability to accurately portray what happened significantly. Without considering the after-the-fact accounts and conclusions concerning the decisions and the orders—all formed from different perspectives—the following remarks are based on a thorough study of the appropriate sections of the field-army group's daily logs.

8. Author's Note: These figures are extracted from the status reports submitted by the division.

In hindsight, the repeating of attack orders and the preoccupation with new offensive actions by the field-army group come across as illusionary and out of step with the overall situation along the front between the Danube and Lake Balaton, which was increasingly worsening, especially in light of the decimation and, in part, destruction of friendly forces, whose combat power was not even sufficient to mount a proper defense. Those portions of the daily logs of the field-army group that were evaluated do not give the impression that the unanimous opinion of the commanders at the front concerning the catastrophic situation, the destruction of friendly forces and the pressing consequences for the conduct of combat operations were forwarded to the German Army High Command in an unvarnished and forceful way.

In March 1945, the area left to the Germans offered only restricted operational decisions. Giving up the western Hungarian area of operations to construct a new, stable front along the borders of the *Reich* was tantamount to also giving up those limited operational options. Adopting such a position would have also meant curtailing the already precarious influx of raw materials. Prudent leadership could not expect a successful defense in a new position, such as one along the *Reich* borders, that was neither prepared nor improved when conditions continued to worsen. After all, retreats also bring materiel and personnel losses with them.

A new position based on the eastern slopes of the Alps would have restricted the use of mechanized forces on both sides. The enemy would have then maintained his decisive superiority in masses of infantry, which had already swarmed through the Bakony Woods and the Vertes Mountains. The Germans' lack of infantry had already forced the abandonment of those two areas.

In such a situation, there were hardly any military alternatives any more. Unconditional surrender, which was demanded by the enemy and which was without precedent against honorable opponents in modern European history, was the alternative.

As a result, a virtually unsolvable conflict arose involving military honor in its hitherto practiced and accepted norms and the equally understandable feeling of responsibility for the soldiers, whose lives were entrusted to the commanders.

The almost stereotypical recital of the field-army group of orders from the Army High Command and the *Führer* causes one to reflect. On the other hand, the thought process may have prevailed that the Soviet forces needed to be prevented under all circumstances and even with taking large numbers of casualties from crossing the last natural barrier in the Hungarian area of operations—an area rich in wooded terrain and pathless mountain obstacles—

so as to slow down the Soviet flood one more time before it reached the borders of the *Reich.*

The present-day scribe, seeing all of the circumstances, understands the logic of what happened. The military commander on the ground, however, must make his decisions under the weight of many imponderables, not unlike between Scylla and Charybdis.

TANKER INFANTRY BATTALION—TANK ACCEPTANCE DETAIL AT CAMP SENNE—CAPITULATION

The remnants of the division, including the tankless tank crews of the regiment along with its trains and rear-are services, reorganized on 24 March, established blocking positions against the advancing Soviets on both sides of the road leading south from Vesprem to Tapolca and attempted to establish contact to the right and left. By the evening of 25 March, they had reached the area around Kapolcz, after leapfrogging through Totnaszony and Voröstö. Jahncke provides some insight into the movement:

> It was only through the personal efforts of all the commanders in their *SPW's,* including that of the division commander, that is was possible to hold the front in strongpoint fashion and prevent the Russians from flooding us. The small troop elements that were still functional clustered around the few *SPW's,* which were the only heavy weapons. A loose defensive network as a result. Forces are overtaxed.

The general retreat, which had previously run in about 10-kilometers parallel intervals from the northern banks of Lake Balaton to the southwest, then took on a west-northwest direction and reached the bridgehead over the Raab at Vasyar in a big jump on 29 March. The distance between Vesprem and Vasyar is some 50 kilometers. The blocking positions on the way there were held by the only intact combat formation the division had left after Kapolcz, the reconnaissance battalion, under its new commander, *SS-Sturmbannführer* Vogt.

Since the Soviets had already thrust far to the west north and south of Vasyar, the division pulled back to the so-called *Reich* Defensive Position on 29 and 30 March, entering the area around Fürstenfeld by way of Körmend.

The remnants of the tank regiment entered Heiligenkreuz on the German-Hungarian border and assembled at the Hartbergen bei Ilz Palace, north of the Fürstenfeld-Graz road. The 2nd Company was assigned quarters in Eichberg.

The last tank of the regiment—a *Panzer IV* under the command of *SS-Unterscharführer* Lasch—is said to have been blown up by Army engineers on a bridge in the vicinity of the border.

Exactly three years earlier, those men had been the first soldiers of the *Waffen-SS* to receive tanks. They had led them honorably across the Don and into the Caucasus, from the area of operations west of Stalingrad, through Tscherkassy and Kowel and on into the defense of Warsaw. In vain they had attempted to relieve their encircled German and Hungarian comrades in Budapest over the previous few weeks. Thrown back to the borders of the *Reich,* they literally had to leave behind their last combat vehicle, destroyed on the battlefield. They would only be able to surrender themselves to the victors.

The division then attempted to occupy its designated positions along a line running from Jennersdorf to Fürstenfeld. It trucked the men to their positions, in some cases having to eject Soviet forces that had already penetrated that far. The division ordered a "tanker" infantry battalion to be formed from the tankers who no longer had tanks.

Four companies—outfitted with submachine guns, rifles and machine guns—were formed under the overall command of *SS-Hauptsturmführer* Schneider, the former commander of the 7th Company. The platoons consisted of three squads with 10 to 15 men each. A heavy company was also formed. It had a heavy machine-gun platoon, an 8-centimeter mortar platoon, a flamethrower section and an *Ofenrohr* section.[9] They were given infantry training for a week.

The initial fighting in April 1945 concerned itself with the possession of the *Reich* Defensive Position, which had been improved in sectors with field positions and was occupied in strongpoint fashion by the *Volkssturm.*[10] To the south of Fürstenfeld, Hill 385 was contested for a while due to its status as a dominant terrain feature.

There was a deep penetration at Jennersdorf and the friendly forces to the left of the division pulled back to a line running along the Lafnitz. The division was forced to also pull back, and the fighting alternated between enemy penetrations and immediate counterattacks in an effort to maintain

9. Author's Note: Jakubetz's account. Translator's Note: "Stovepipe," which was the slang term applied to the German equivalent of the American bazooka.

10. Translator's Note: The *Volkssturm* was a "people's" militia, largely composed of overage men and underage youths that was formed as a last-ditch effort to defend the *Reich.*

and shorten the front. The division assistant operations officer noted in his diary:

> the tank battalion especially proved itself...The battalion, composed of frontline, decorated soldiers, left a terrific impression. Like child's play, the battalion sealed off a few penetrations with great élan and without taking any losses. The battalion has been committed ever since 13 April and cannot be differentiated from well trained and well-proved frontline [infantry] soldiers. It's a joy!

Tank commander Melinkat, whose tank had been knocked out in the last armored group of the regiment east of Veszprem, was a squad leader in the 2nd Company. His platoon leader was *SS-Untersturmführer* Lasch, whose *Panzer IV* had been the last tank of the regiment. It was the one that had been blown up on the bridge in an effort to slow down the Soviet advance. Melinkat notes:

> It's stayed in my memory for a long time how our platoon was without any [external] contact for three days at one point—fighting close combat engagements at night, hardly any ammunition left and already considered to be missing by the battalion. Through the courageous effort of a messenger, contact was reestablished, and the platoon was able to fight its way to a passage point maintained by the *1. Panzer-Division.*

The events that occurred before and during the expected capitulation were more or less similar for the remaining committed elements of the tank regiment. The path led to either captivity by the Western Allies or personal freedom in the underground. Melinkat's story continues:

> We occupied our last position above Feldbach in Untersteirmark.[11] We received news of the capitulation there.
>
> Around 1100 hours on 8 May, the 2nd Company pulled back in accordance with its orders and was loaded on trucks. The journey took us through Graz, which we passed through singing during the night, and in the direction of Judenburg.
>
> During the morning of 9 May, we reached Leoben and received infantry fire just in front of a bridge. My squad dismounted. The

11. Translator's Note: An Austrian province.

machine-gun section held down the partisans, who had holed up in a multi-storied building outside of the bridge and fired at everything that was moving past.

A short while later two *SPW's*—cannon vehicles with 7.5-centimeter short-barreled cannon—approached and took the building under fire. At that point, the partisans gave up their resistance.

It should also be noted that on that same morning of 9 May we were attacked by Russian fighter-bombers—after the capitulation, of course—and took losses.

Outside of Leoben, my squad broke up. We continued to carry small arms. In groups of two and three we made our way along mountain paths and less-travel roads through Bas Aussee, where we said goodbye to *Hauptsturmführer* Hein, who was in the hospital there, and on through Bad Ischl, as far as Bavaria. At Braunau, we intended to cross the Inn, which the locals said was being closely guarded by the Americans. During an effort to try my luck in crossing a bridge in broad daylight, I was taken prisoner along with two of my soldiers by an American reconnaissance unit.

Melinkat wrote these words of farewell to one of the last tankers to fall from the 2nd Company of the tank regiment, *SS-Oberscharführer* Gerhard Hosan, who had been assigned to the 3rd Company of the tanker "infantry" battalion:

Gerd
Im Tod noch lachte sein Gesicht,
die blauen Augen klar und offen,
als wollt' er sagen: fraget night,
wir werden alle mal getroffen.
Sein blonder Haarschopf lag im Staub,
die linke Hand hielt noch die Karte.
Am Fuß der Böschung schwarzer Rauch
vom Einschlag einer Sprenggranate.
Der Hohlweg war hier einzusehen.
Weit hinten hat die Pak gestanden.
Ganz plötzlich, ohne sein Verstehn,
zerschnitt der Tod des Lebens Bande.
Ich kannte ihn von früher her,
Freiwilliger meines Jahrgangs,
Als Panzermann im großen Heer,
jetzt Infanterist wie anfangs.

Wir robbten Mann für Mann vorbei,
mit Sturmgepäck und Waffen.
Ich wischte mir den Schweiß dabei
und sah———sein letztes Lachen.

Gerd
In death, his face still had a laugh,
his blue eyes clear and open,
as if he wanted to say: Don't ask,
All of us get hit sometime.
Locks of hair in the dirt,
a map was still in his left hand.
At the base of the vegetation was black smoke
from the impact of a high-explosive round.
The defile could be observed at that point.
The AT gun was far to our rear.
All of a sudden, without him noticing it,
death cut the bonds of life.
I knew him from early on,
A volunteer my age,
A tanker in the field army,
now an infantryman again.
We crawled past man by man,
with assault packs and weapons.
I wiped the sweat away in the process
and saw———his last laugh.

In the fighting for Stuhlweißenburg, *SS-Untersturmführer* Jakubetz, had to turn over his tank, *Panther 612*, to the company commander, *SS-Untersturmführer* Großrock, after the latter had his own tank knocked out from under him. In Kirchberg in the vicinity of Feldbach, he became the adjutant of the tanker "infantry" battalion.

He has also stated that the battalion disengaged from the enemy northwest of Feldbach and was loaded on trucks, moving through Graz and Leoben to reach the demarcation line at Enns. North of Selzthal, the weapons were tossed into the river. Prison camp awaited them.

Seven hundred kilometers farther north, in the northern part of Westphalia, the end greeted those elements of the tank regiment that had gone to the Neu-Raab area in January 1945 and then moved by rail to Camp Senne in February under the command of *SS-Hauptsturmführer* Nicolussi-Leck. After an adventurous train journey, including a bombing of the train in Czechoslovakia, some 200 tankers without tanks reached the designated area where they were supposed to receive approximately 40 new *Panthers*. The unit was put up in the Warendorf-Versmold area, where they waited in vain for the tanks. The days were then spent conducting drill and infantry training.

Nicolussi-Leck's men never had any contact with either the regiment or the division when the war ended. As it turned out, that half of the tank regiment wound up ending the war being employed as infantry.

On 31 March, Nicolussi-Leck's 1st Company, quartered in Oesterweg, 2 kilometers southeast of Versmold, was alerted. It received the mission of conducting combat reconnaissance in the direction of Warendorf against lead enemy tank elements that had been reported.

SS-Obersturmführer Senghas, whose company command post was in the *Gasthaus Margenau*, pushed his 1st and 2nd Platoons forward in the direction of Freckenhorst, 2 kilometers to the south. *SS-Untersturmführer* Fischer reconnoitered in the direction of Hoetmar, where Waller's squad encountered the enemy and pulled back in the direction of Freckenhorst. Senghas has written about his last combat operation:

> On the morning of 1 April 1945, around 0200 hours, I received orders from the battalion to check out the situation in the direction of Warendorf. To that end we requisitioned a *DKW-Meisterklasse* [civilian car], which belonged to a dealership, which we promised to return with a full tank of gas when we got back.
>
> I rode with three other men, sitting on the left front bumper (*Unterscharführer* Klein was on the right front bumper), through Warendorf, where there were already white flags hanging out of the windows, that night so as to reconnoiter west. While doing that, our vehicle was knocked out by a Yank armored car that had gone into position during the night. I fell into the roadside ditch, badly wounded. Round embedded in the thigh; round through the left foot; and a ricochet through my left lower arm, grazing the artery and damaging the nerves.

> My messenger, who had jumped into the ditch, dressed my left arm. After a short while, we were taken prisoner by American soldiers who searched the terrain at first light.
>
> The operations, experiences and turns of events of those final days were all very similar. A tank radio operator, Overbeck, had this to say:
>
> On Easter Monday, I went with my comrades, Hans Schweinfurth and Max Kuder, on patrol in the direction of Sassenberg. The enemy went past us, and when we returned to Versmold late in the afternoon after having had enemy contact, the locality was already occupied and our forces had pulled back to Borgholzhausen from Versmold.

A tank commander from the 2nd Company, Walter Fröbe, has contributed this account:

> I was one of the knocked-out crews from Hungary, which was supposed to pick up the new tanks at Camp Senne. As an aside, I'd like to mention that I was knocked out for the last time at Lake Balaton. So we waited for our new tanks. It was said that the Americans were on the way towards Borgholzhausen. We borrowed bicycles from the civilian populace of Oesterweg and its environs and pedaled off in the direction of the Yanks.
>
> We dug in at the entrance to the village; some were still in the process of doing so. All of a sudden, we saw American tanks. But it wasn't just us who saw the American tanks, they had also seen us.
>
> In the same instant, there was a crash next to us. The Americans had sent over a couple of high-explosive rounds. That was the moment that it got all of us. That's what I'm assuming, at least. Then, everything was quiet. Sepp was mortally wounded next to me. I got it in the leg and thigh; I was incapable of walking. I lost consciousness as the result of losing too much blood and did not come to until later in a cellar in a farmhouse, where they had hidden me. Then I went to a military hospital. The shrapnel had to be removed. That was followed by two years of captivity.

The leader of the 3rd Platoon of the 1st Company, *SS-Oberscharführer* Putensen, noted the following in his diary on 1 April: "*Sturmmann* Stenzhorn missing; *Unterscharführer* Döllner most likely killed in action."

Putensen, who had been entrusted with screening four bridges and waterway footpaths over the Ems, received two shoulder boards belonging to his wounded company commander from a comrade he no longer remembers.

He stuffed them in his "butt pack" and made the following entry in his diary:[12]

> And so they wandered with me, after we had pulled back by foot from Warendorf—long since bypassed or overrun by the enemy, in the rear of the English and the Americans—through the Teutoburg Woods, the Wiehen Mountains, across the Midland Canal, the Weser and the Aller, until we set up in the ranks of German forces again on the north bank in the vicinity of Reuthen. We continued on through a "passage point" established by the *Luftwaffe* at Winsen/Luhe and on through the military facility at Langenhorn (Hamburg), where I found the remnants of our battalion in the vicinity of Gadebusch and Mecklenburg on 28 April 1945.
>
> On 29 and 30 April and 1 and 2 May 1945, we put together a combat unit. *Untersturmführer* Fischer took one company; I assumed command of a *SPW* platoon in it.
>
> Alerted on 2 May! Americans in Gadebusch; departure for Carlow; in the evening, disbanding of the entire combat unit. On your own to the west.
>
> On 4 May, captured in an open field by the Americans, along with comrades Hans Fischer and Hans Wallner. Taken to the military facilities in Ratzeburg that evening.
>
> Hans Fischer and I escaped the next day; crossed the Elbe-Trave Canal with some difficulty and all sorts of luck during the night of 5–6 May and then crossed the Elbe at Stove on 7 May. On 8 May, I reached my home town with Hans Fischer, but noted to my sorrow that my parent's house had been set alight when the English forces had marched in and was completely destroyed.

The efforts of the German command to change the fate of the north German area by means of improvisation were doomed to failure. The provisional nature of the measures could not be transformed into defensive measures that suited the situation and the forces of the enemy. Von Tippelskirch notes the following in his history of the war:

> The advance of the English 2nd Army and the Canadian 1st Army brought those illusions in the north German area to a quick end.

12. Author's Note: Putensen presented his former company commander with the shoulder boards at an annual reunion in Jagsthausen in 1977, some 32 years later.

> The 2nd Army was delayed along the Ems, the Weser and the Aller by the non-uniform resistance of German forces and the substantial destruction of bridges. Its southern wing reached the Aller at Celle by 7 April, however.[13]

On the northern wing of the American forces, its 9th Army pressed on Hameln and crossed the Weser during the first few days of April. Some details of von Tippelskirch's "non-uniform resistance" are provided by *SS-Oberscharführer* Karl Jauss, who was a platoon leader in the detail that originally been sent to Camp Senne to pick up new tanks:

> After being alerted on Easter Sunday 1945, we blocked the access roads into our quartering area with hastily constructed antiarmor obstacles. From the standpoint of a tanker, our work was pathetic. We had no mines, no demolitions, only a few hand grenades and no long-range anti-armor weapons. It didn't make much sense.
>
> Just before noon, the outpost on a field path coming from Harsewinkel reported the lead tank elements. Our meager resistance didn't even force the lead elements to deploy. Turning their barrels to the right and left, moving slowly (5 kilometers an hour) and firing, the enemy column passed through our billeting area, approximately two tanks battalions and a battalion of motorized infantry.
>
> The only thing we could do was take cover! After it turned dark, we gathered in a nearby patch of woods. A patrol to Melsbach was interdicted early in the morning.
>
> We had to leave our wounded behind under the care of the local populace. For the first time, we saw white flags on the houses.

The battle group reached Minden on foot, moving through Borgholzhausen:

> The enemy was not there yet; but there weren't any friendly forces, either, with the exception of the local military administrative authorities. We occupied the east banks of the Weser at the bridges. To blow them up, we were given 50 kilograms of bombs, but without mechanical or electrical igniters. To ignite the bombs, we prepared a bundled charge made out of hand grenades.
>
> The following night, we were picked up by natural-gas-powered trucks, which took us to a large Army vehicle yard in a well-camouflaged

13. Author's Note: von Tippelskirch, 566.

area of a river flood plain. There were a lot of factory-new vehicles there, including *SPW's*, with and without 2-centimeter cannon.

[Nicolussi-Leck] had found the vehicle yard and made things happen so that we were immediately able to get 10 to 12 *SPW's*, some with 2-centimeter cannon. After we took them, we moved right to the Hanomag works in Hanover. There were even able to get seven brand-new *Jagdpanther's* with long-barreled main guns and a recovery vehicle, along with some spare parts. The main guns had not yet been fired or calibrated. There was little fuel there; no ammunition at all. During the course of the day, however, all of the issues were resolved.

We operated in two groups. A front had not been established around Hanover. We never had any neighbors that we knew about. Our operations orders came directly from the local military authorities or were decisions personally made by [Nicolussi-Leck]. Our supply depots had been plundered in part by the foreign workers.

The first day of fighting with the armored groups brought some success. For instance, one tank commander (Andörfer) was able to knock out six tanks in the space of a few minutes before he was also hit.

At Ricklingen, at least 20 armored vehicles, ranging from Shermans to armored personnel carriers, were destroyed, along with an equal number of trucks and smaller wheeled vehicles. Our losses: One *Jagdpanther* and one *SPW* (total losses), with both crews wounded.

Even though we visibly abandoned the area after our successful action, the enemy plastered the small village with heavy artillery fire. That same day, we were employed to screen along the northwestern roads leading into the city, where one of our groups had to survive a sharp armored engagement. Some five to eight enemy tanks were destroyed during it. Through tricks or adverse circumstances, the enemy split up our tanks and also eliminated a portion of the leaders. One of the officers was captured.

During the night, large elements of enemy infantry on light wheeled vehicles infiltrated into Hanover. At first light, the masses of enemy armor started to roll out. [Nicolussi-Leck], with three tanks and a few *SPW's*, was wedged in between the tank columns rolling past him. In a true cavalry charge, he raced past the surprised armored formations and made it to Lehrte without a lot of firing.

It was possible to reassemble the scattered and separated groups in Lehrte. *Kampfgruppe Nicolussi-Leck* moved in the direction of Celle, seeking enemy contact all the way. In the process, the men were able to resupply themselves without taking casualties. But they were unable to establish contact with German forces:

> There were repeated smaller skirmishes, which we only accepted in order to hide our "strength" or to gain a little respect for us. It was certainly annoying for our enemies, usually Yanks but also Tommies, since we continued to set tanks and trucks alight over and over again. Our trains consisted of Yank trucks. We also had a Yank armored car, which we used to conduct aggressive battlefield reconnaissance. Often times, the vehicle approached entire columns. During the day, we captured up to 50 prisoners, whom we released at night, far away from where they had been captured.
>
> At night, we strengthened our infantry element by adding scattered elements of all branches, including *RAD.* Our combat power was not appreciably improved by doing that, however. Most of the men scrammed over the following nights.
>
> As a result of the constant withdrawals, we were pushed back into the Celle-Gifhorn area. The Aller was in front of us. Our own reconnaissance revealed increasing tank movement along the roads in our vicinity. All of the bridges were being screened with heavy [enemy] antiarmor weaponry and, in some cases, covered in depth. While reconnoitering, we made the acquaintance of the 9.1-centimeter antitank gun—an unpleasant encounter!
>
> In a area measuring only a few hundred meters, we counted about 80 enemy tanks one time.
>
> With the help of a *BDM* girl,[14] we reconnoitered a crossing point over the Aller, which was in a high-water stage in the middle of April. All of the wheeled vehicles had to be left behind. While we were staging to cross, a reconnaissance aircraft discovered us. Since it flew very low, it was shot down by a 2-centimeter cannon, which had as a consequence the appearance of two more a few minutes later. Not as low, however. Well-placed artillery fire started.
>
> The *SPW's* were hitched to the *Jagdpanthers* and towed through the river. The infantry held on to the vehicles. We took considerable casualties in wounded. While recovering our wounded from the river, a captured American officer comported himself well.

14. Translator's Note: *Bund deutscher Mädel* = Organization of German Girls, which was somewhat the female equivalent of the Hitler Youth.

He helped recover our people to the riverbanks. We left our wounded under cover with the American officer and a few volunteers.

When we unhitched the *SPW's*, we discovered that a few had been flooded and the engines would no longer start. For those who were left, it was high time to get moving. The main road from Celle to Wittlingen had to be crossed before the enemy could occupy positions there. We almost did it. But a meddlesome rifleman alerted the Sherman's about 600 meters away on the right flank through some unnecessary shooting. They did not have much trouble in extinguishing the light on two of our five armored vehicles, including the recovery vehicle. Apparently, no one got out of the one tank; on the other vehicle, the crew escaped with bad burns.

During that encounter with the enemy, the lack of a turret on the *Jagdpanther* proved to be a big disadvantage.

We bivouacked and holed up in a patch of woods about 5 kilometers away from that last event. Reconnaissance was necessary. We needed wheeled vehicles again, along with rations and fuel.

By evening, we had two trucks and a jeep, rations, fuel and about 30 prisoners, including 20 MP's. Some of them made a very bad impression...

Our combat operations were over at that point. During one of the next few days, Nicolussi-Leck was captured. It was all over anyway!

On 16 April, we had the last two tanks roll into the moor in first gear. Within a few minutes, they sank, covering the running gear. We still had about 10 rounds for the main guns. We buried them at a different location. We did not want to blow them up, since the enemy would have easily found us. Towards evening, the little group said goodbye to one another with long handshakes and the prospect of an uncertain future.

The two trucks were rolled onto a railway line during the night by a detail and blown up. The practically new jeep was loaded with close-in combat weapons, rations and fuel and used by four comrades (the last detail) to drive home. The trip ended in Winterbach in Rems Valley on 20 April 1945 after an adventure-filled journey, oftentimes riding along with enemy columns for kilometers at a time and several times leaving behind enemy outposts in a burst of infantry fire.

The leader of the detail assigned to pick up the tank, *SS-Hauptsturmführer* Nicolussi-Leck, has provided his impressions of what happened during that period through the final collapse:

After the collapse of the Ruhr Pocket and the suicide of *Generalfeldmarschall* Model, *Generaloberst* Student assumed command. He gave me the sector of the front from Camp Senne to Münster and also attached the *Volkssturm* there to me. At Versmold, I relieved the leaders of the *Volkssturm* from their obligation not to release the large number of *Panzerfäuste* available and started a delaying action against the advancing English and American forces towards a line running Teutoburger Woods–Minden–Hanover.

We got *SPW's* and American vehicles for ourselves. A *U-Boot* crew that wanted to fight also joined us, as well as a battery of self-propelled guns. At Hanomag, we were even able to procure seven *Jagdpanthers* and employ them.

When the Americans advanced from Hildesheim towards Hanover, we were able to knock out 60 armored and other vehicles with the help of the *Jagdpanthers.* A few days after that defensive success, however, Hanover was surrendered to the Americans without our knowledge. We were able to successfully move through Hanover, but then had to blow up the *Jagdpanthers* in the Gifhorn area, since we no longer had any ammunition. I wound up in American captivity there, along with my adjutant, whereupon the battalion disbanded between Gifhorn and the Elbe.

✠

After the capitulation of the Armed Forces of the Greater German *Reich* on 8 May 1945—after years of see-saw fighting, where the last tank of the regiment remained on the battlefield—the men of *SS-Panzer-Regiment 5* marched into captivity, as they had been ordered.

Elements of the regiment fought until the very end between the Weser and the Elbe and fought until captured or were able to escape captivity.

Those men were unable to stave off the fate of the *Reich* and its collapse. Those men—unbroken and ready to master whatever fate threw their way—faced a dark future. Each had to face it to the best of his ability and on his own.

They were faithful and loyal, proud, brave and obedient. They were the tankers of *SS-Panzer-Regiment 5 "Wiking."*

APPENDIX A

Rank Comparisons

U.S. ARMY	BRITISH ARMY	GERMAN ARMY
Enlisted Men		
Private	Private	*Schütze*
Private First Class	Private 1st Class	*Oberschütze*
Corporal	Lance Corporal	*Gefreiter*
Senior Corporal	Corporal	*Obergefreiter*
Staff Corporal		*Stabsgefreiter*
Noncommissioned Officers		
Sergeant	Sergeant	*Unteroffizier*
	Staff Sergeant	*Unterfeldwebel*
Staff Sergeant	Technical Sergeant	*Feldwebel*
Sergeant First Class	Master Sergeant	*Oberfeldwebel*
Master Sergeant	Sergeant Major	*Hauptfeldwebel*
Sergeant Major		*Stabsfeldwebel*
Officers		
Second Lieutenant	Second Lieutenant	*Leutnant*
First Lieutenant	First Lieutenant	*Oberleutnant*
Captain	Captain	*Hauptman*
Major	Major	*Major*
Lieutenant Colonel	Lieutenant Colonel	*Oberst Leutnant*
Colonel	Colonel	*Oberst*
Brigadier General	Brigadier General	*Generalmajor*
Major General	Major General	*Generalleutnant*
Lieutenant General	Lieutenant General	*General der Fallschirmjäger, etc.*
General	General	*Generaloberst*
General of the Army	Field Marshal	*Feldmarschall*

APPENDIX B

Activation and Chronological Overview of *SS-Panzer-Regiment 5*

Year/Date	Formation		
	SS-Panzer-Regiment 5 (Headquarters and Headquarters Company)	*SS-Panzer-Abteilung 5* (*I./SS-PR 5*)	*II./SS-PR 5*
1942			
11 February		Activation orders at Wildflecken Training Area	
12 April		Assignment to *SS-Division "Wiking"*	
9 June		Transport to the Eastern Front	
21 July		Start of Operations at Rostow	
1943			
28 February	Start of activation at the Altneuhaus Training Area	Re-designated as the *I./SS-PR 5*	Start of activation at the Altneuhaus Training Area
August	Transport to Croatia		Transport to Croatia
December	Transport to Erlangen		Transport to Erlangen
1944			
6 February	Transport to the Mailly Training Area (France)		Transport to the Mailly Training Area (France)
18 February	Transport to Cholm (Poland)		Transport to Cholm (Poland)

27 March	Start of relief operations at Kowel		Start of relief operations at Kowel
4 June		Transport to Debica (Yugoslavia)	
10 July		3rd and 4th Companies operational; 1st and 2nd Companies in Debica	
6 September	Addition of Armored Engineer Company	Reconstitution of the 3rd Company	
25 September		1st and 2nd Companies operational	
13 November	Reconstitution, re-designation and reorganization as the *SS-Panzer-Lehr-Abteilung*. Reconnaissance platoon to the 1st battalion	Reconstitution, re-designation and reorganization as the 1st and 3rd Companies of the *SS-Panzer-Lehr-Abteilung*; Elements of the 2nd and 4th Companies as part of the SS-Lehr-Abteilung; remainder of the 2nd and 4th Companies operational.	Reconstitution, re-designation and reorganization as the 7th and 8th Companies of the *SS-Panzer-Lehr-Abteilung*; 5th and 6th Companies operational.
26 December	Transport to Hungary	Transport to Hungary	Transport to Hungary
1945			
1 January	Fighting for Budapest	Fighting for Budapest	Fighting for Budapest
February		Instructional Battalion at Camp Senne	Instructional Battalion at Camp Senne
April	Infantry Battalion (Armored Personnel)	Infantry Battalion (Armored Personnel)	Infantry Battalion (Armored Personnel)
8 May	Capitulation	Capitulation	Capitulation

APPENDIX C

Authorized Strengths of *SS-Panzer-Abteilung 5* and *SS-Panzer-Regiment 5*

Formation		Personnel			Vehicles			
SS-PR 5	TO&E	O	NCO's	Enlisted	Motorcycles (sidecars)	Wheeled Vehicles (Trucks)	Half-tracked vehicles	Tanks
Regimental Battle Staff	1103 (1 November 1944)	5	4	8	4	3		
Headquarters Company	1103 (1 November 1944)	2	36	54	3	4 (11)	1	8
Armor Maintenance Company	1187 (1 November 1944)	6	35	153	3 (1)	7 (42)	7	
1st Battalion Battle Staff	1107 (1 April 1943)	8	4	11	2	6 (1)		
Headquarters Company	1150 (1 November 1941)	7	49	169	26 (13)	7 (42)		
Armor Maintenance Platoon	1185 (1 June 1942)	4	22	86	4 (4)	3 (21)	4	
1st Company (Light) (*Panzer III's*)	1171 (1 November 1941)	5	63	77	7 (4)	3 (7)	2	17

2nd Company (Light) (*Panzer III's*)	1171 (1 November 1941)	5	63	77	7 (4)	3 (7)	2	17
3rd Company (Medium) (*Panzer IV's*)	1175 (1 November 1941)	8	60	77	7 (4)	3 (7)	2	17
2nd Battalion Battle Staff	1107 (1 April 1943)	8	4	11	2	6 (1)		
Headquarters Company (including a Maintenance Platoon)	1150 (a) (1 June 1943)	7	71	277	13	20 (70)	4	13
5th Company (*Panzer V's*)	1177 (1 November 1943)	3	66	78	3	7 (9)	2	17
6th Company (*Panzer V's*)	1177 (1 November 1943)	3	66	78	3	7 (9)	2	17
7th Company (*Panzer V's*)	1177 (1 November 1943)	3	66	78	3	7 (9)	2	17
8th Company (*Panzer V's*)	1177 (1 November 1943)	3	66	78	3	7 (9)	2	17
Totals		**77**	**675**	**1312**	**90 (30)**	**93 (245)**	**30**	**152**

APPENDIX D

The Maintenance Company of an Armored Regiment

In accordance with KStN 1187, dated 1 November 1944[1]:

Organization	Officers	NCO's	Enlisted
Command Group	3		8
1st Platoon	1	9	49
2nd Platoon	1	9	49
Recovery Section		3	13
Armaments Section	1	2	7
Signals Repair Section		4	8
Spare Parts Section		1	5
Trains		7	14
Totals	6	35	153

Specialists authorized for the company:

Specialty / Function	Officers	NCO's	Enlisted
Foreman	2		
Tank mechanic (engine)		6	12
Tank mechanic (automotive)		6	12
Tank mechanic		4	12
Automotive mechanic			12
Electrician (tank)			4
Tank arc welder			4
Lathe operator			2
Blacksmith			2
Metalworker			2
Saddler			2
Carpenter			2
Recovery specialist		3	2
Towing specialist			5
Armorers	1	2	
Assistant armorers			5
Signals specialists		2	
Signals repairman		2	4

1. The figures given are for a maintenance company organic to a "mixed" tank regiment consisting of one battalion of *Panzer IV's* and one battalion of *Panthers*. The organization was constantly being modified, so these strength figures only represent a "snapshot" in time.

APPENDIX E

On-Hand Tank Strengths of the Battalion and Regiment Based on Status Reports in 1943, 1944 and 1945

Date	Area of Operations	Panzer III			Panzer IV			Panzer V			StuG		
		A	O	%	A	O	%	A	O	%	A	O	%
1 July 1943	Between the Donez and the Dnjepr	35	24	70	14	17	120	-	-	-	-	-	-
1 September 1943	As above	35	8	23	14	8	57	-	-	-	-	-	-
1 October 1943	Tscherkassy	35	8	23	14	5	36	-	-	-	7	5	70
1 January 1944	As above	55	13	24	121	6	7	-	-	-	45	4	9
1 April 1944	Kowel	7	-	-	73	21	29	75	58	77	31	19	61
1 August 1944	East of Warsaw	2	-	-	101	12	12	79	42	53	-	11	-
1 September 1944	Northeast of Warsaw	2	-	-	101	4	4	79	19	24	-	4	-
1 November 1944	"Wet Triangle"	2	-	-	101	7	7	79	15	19	-	4	-
1 January 1945	Hungary	4	-	-	114	10	9	79	22	29	-	4	-
1 February 1945	As above	4	-	-	114	3	3	79	6	8	-	-	-
1 March 1945	As above	4	-	-	114	3	3	79	9	11	-	2	-
1 April 1945	As above	4	-	-	114	-	-	79	2	3	-	-	

Figures based on periodic status reports submitted by the division to higher commands

APPENDIX F

Comparisons of Various Tank Characteristics

Characteristic[6]	*Panzer II* (Model F)	*Panzer III* (Model J)	*Panzer IV* (Model F)	*Panzer V* (*Panther*)	T-34	Sherman (M4A3)
Weight in tons	9.5	21.6	22.3	45.5	26.5	33.5
Armor in millimeters	20–35	30–50	40–70	80–110	60	92
Horsepower	140	265	320	650	500	450
Maximum speed in kilometers per hour	55	40	42	54	53	45
Main gun in centimeters	2	5	7.5	7.5	7.62	7.62
Crew	3	5	5	5	4	5

APPENDIX G

Telegraph from the Division to the *LII. Armee-Korps* on 26 September 1942 (Tank Ditch at Osemyj)

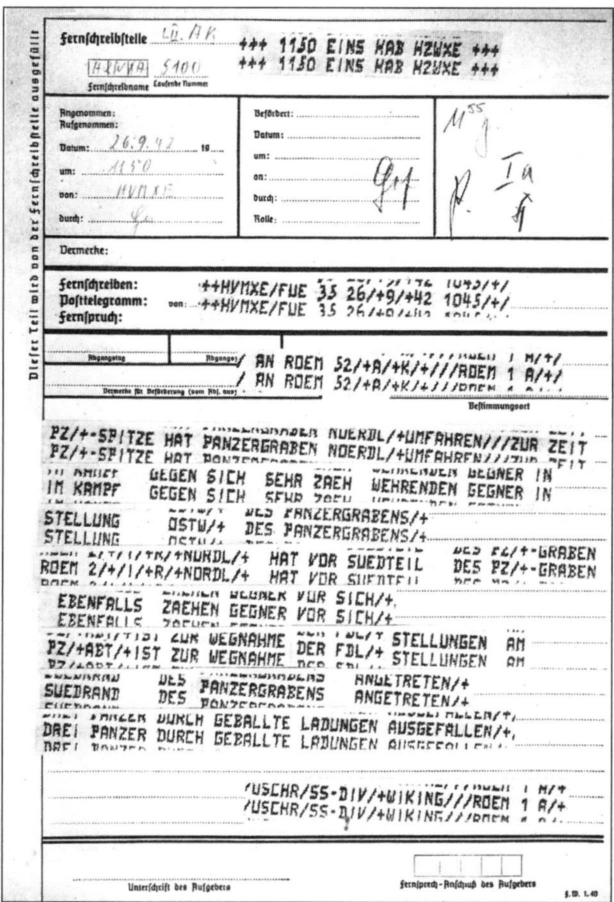

Dieser Teil wird von der Fernschreibstelle ausgefüllt

Fernschreibstelle LII. AK

+++ 1150 EINS HAB HZWXE +++

HZWXA 5100

Fernschreibname Laufende Nummer

Angenommen:
Aufgenommen:
Datum: 26.9.42 19
um: 1150
von: HVMXE
durch:

Befördert:
Datum:
um:
an:
durch:
Rolle:

Vermerke:

Fernschreiben:
Posttelegramm:
Fernspruch:
von: ++HVMXE/FUE 35 26/+9/+42 1045/+/

Abgangstag
Abgangszeit
Vermerke für Beförderung (vom Abs. aus)

/ AN ROEM 52/+A/+K/+///ROEM 1 A/+/

Bestimmungsort

PZ/+-SPITZE HAT PANZERGRABEN NOERDL/+UMFAHREN///ZUR ZEIT
IM KAMPF GEGEN SICH SEHR ZAEH WEHRENDEN GEGNER IN
STELLUNG OSTW/+ DES PANZERGRABENS/+
ROEM 2/+/I/+R/+NORDL/+ HAT VOR SUEDTEIL DES PZ/+-GRABEN
EBENFALLS ZAEHEN GEGNER VOR SICH/+
PZ/+ABT/+IST ZUR WEGNAHME DER FDL/+ STELLUNGEN AM
SUEDRAND DES PANZERGRABENS ANGETRETEN/+
DREI PANZER DURCH GEBALLTE LADUNGEN AUSGEFALLEN/+,

/USCHR/SS-DIV/+WIKING///ROEM 1 A/+

Unterschrift des Aufgebers

Fernsprech-Anschluß des Aufgebers

F.W. 1.40

Translation of main body of telegram:

Armored spearheads have bypassed the tank ditch to the north. Currently engaged against toughly defending enemy in position east of the tank ditch. Likewise tough enemy in front of us to the south of the tank ditch. Tank battalion has moved out to take the enemy positions along the south side of the tank ditch. Three tanks lost to bundled charges.

APPENDIX H

Radio Message from the Division to the *LII. Armee-Korps* on 27 September 1942

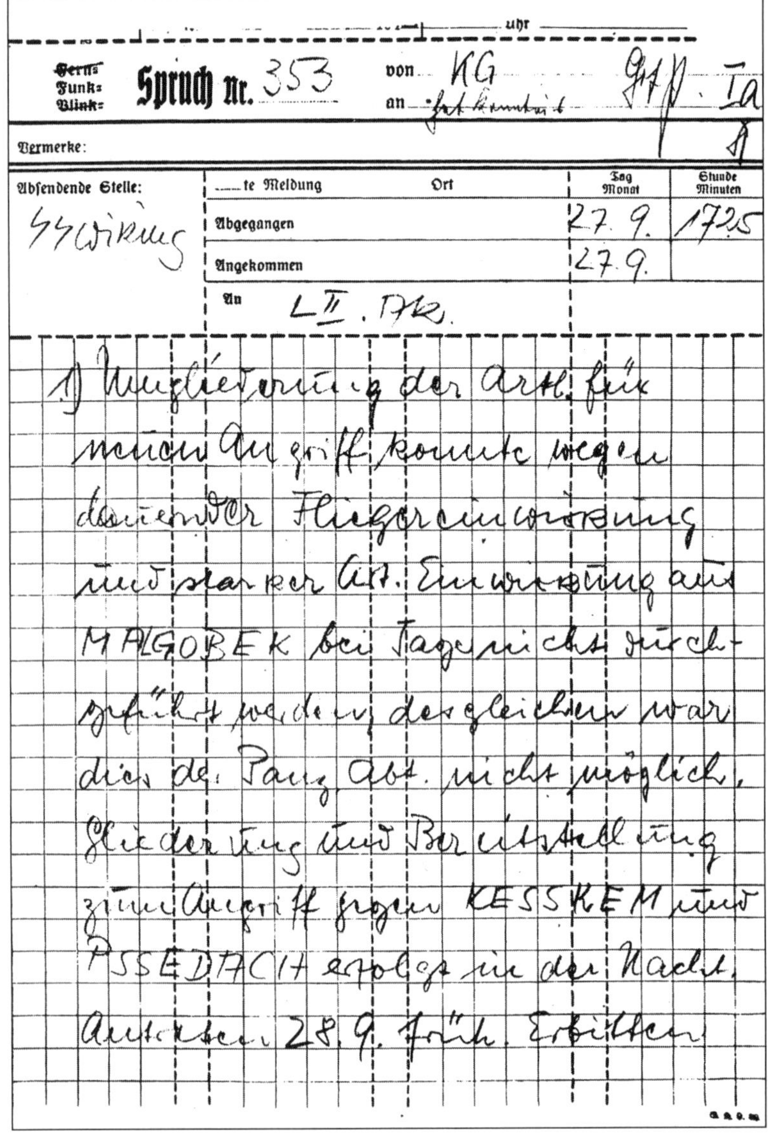

Fern- Funk- Blink- **Spruch Nr.** 353 von KG an ... Ia

Vermerke:

Absendende Stelle:	...te Meldung	Ort	Tag Monat	Stunde Minuten
SS Wiking	Abgegangen		27. 9.	17²⁵
	Angekommen		27. 9.	
	An LII. AK.			

1) Umgliederung der Artl. für
neuen Angriff konnte wegen
dauernder Fliegereinwirkung
und starker Art. Einwirkung aus
MALGOBEK bei Tage nicht durch-
geführt werden, desgleichen war
dies der Panz. Abt. nicht möglich.
Gliederung und Bereitstellung
zum Angriff gegen KESSKEM und
ASSEDACH erfolgt in der Nacht.
Antreten 28. 9. früh. Erbitten

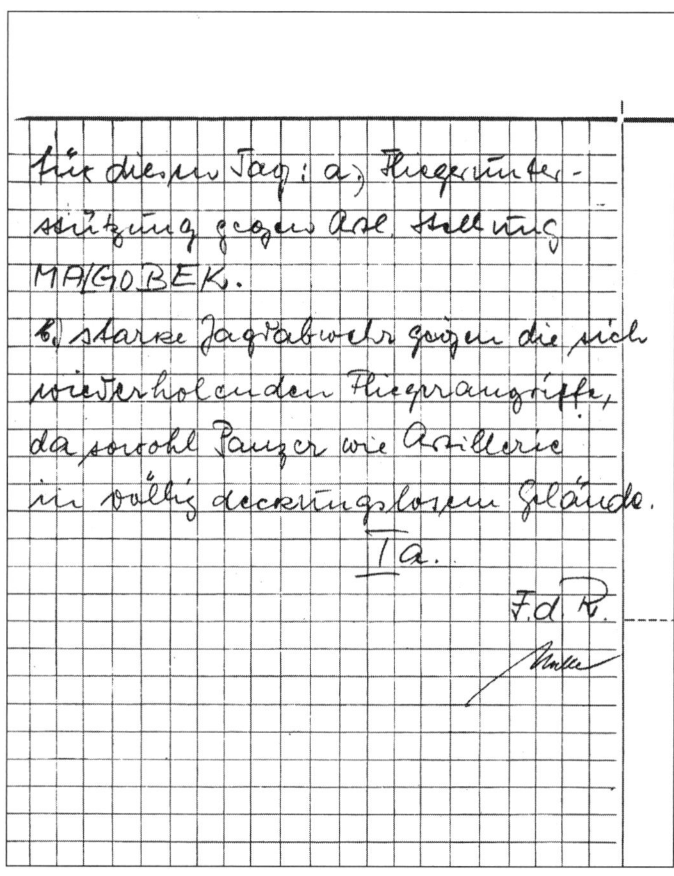

für diesen Tag: a.) Fliegerunterstützung gegen Art. Stellung MALGOBEK.
b.) starke Jagdabwehr gegen die sich wiederholenden Fliegerangriffe, da sowohl Panzer wie Artillerie in völlig deckungslosem Gelände.

Ia.

F.d.R.

Text of main body of message:
1.) Reorganization of the battalion for the new attack could not be executed during the day due to constant enemy air activity and heavy artillery fires from Malgobek, and the tank battalion was incapable of responding in kind. Reorganization and occupation of assembly areas for the attack on Kesskem and Pssedach to take place at night. Moving out early on 28 September. Request for this day: a.) Air support against the artillery position at Malgobek. b.) Heavy fighter cover against the repeated enemy air attacks, since the tanks as well as the artillery are in completely open terrain.

APPENDIX I

Annex 4 to Order by Headquarters, *1. Panzer-Armee*, Operations (Field Army Quartermaster), No. 965/42 (SECRET COMMAND MATTER)

It is intended to distribute the scheduled and already arrived winter equipment and uniform items as follows:

Designation	*III. Panzer-Korps*			*LII. Armee-Korps*		*XXXX. Panzer-Korps*
	13. PD	*23. PD*	*370. ID*	*SS-Wiking*	*111. ID*	*3. PD*
Winter equipment						
Sled, Type Hs 1 (E41)	130	130	170	130	170	130
Sled, Type Hs 3 (500 Kg)	600	600	400	400	400	600
Sled, Type Hs 5 (1000 Kg)	100	100	70	30	70	100
Sled, Medical, Type G	30	30	25	35	25	30
Sled, Medical, Type E41	10	10	10	15	10	10
Sled, Ambulance, Type HS 3/1	25	25	22	30	22	25
Light Akja	500	500	300	500	500	
Weapons Carrier Akja	170	170	170	100	170	170
Boat-type Akja	210	210	210	210	210	210
Skis	900	900	900	900	900	900
Snow tires	1000	1000	1000	1000	1000	1000

Plywood tents	200	200	160	240	160	200
Tent heaters	200	200	160	240	160	200
Firing supports for Mortar, Type 36	30	30	30	30	30	30
Snow supports for Mortar, Type 36	20	20	20	20	20	20
Wooden skids for the Model 41 antitank rifle	6	6	-	6	-	6
Set of ski skids	83	83	72	60	72	83
Set of mounts for the 3.7cm Antitank Gun for the Hs 3 sled	-	-	30	-	30	-
As above for the Model 18 Light Infantry Gun	4	4	8	8	8	4
As above for the Model 38 Antitank Gun	9	9	3	-	3	9
Set of ski skids	-	-	45	-	45	-
Snow plate for machine gun	400	400	500	600	500	400
Fur pelts	50	50	50	50	50	50
Brake fluid (arctic); winter oil and grease; ski wax; white paint	As needed					
Winter uniform articles						
Padded trousers	2300	2300	1700	2100	1700	2300
Padded jackets	2300	2300	1700	2100	1700	2300
Felt boots	2300	2300	1700	2100	1700	2300
Toques	2300	2300	1700	2100	1700	2300
Mittens with extensions	2300	2300	1700	2100	1700	2300

APPENDIX J

Soldbuch Page with Engagement Entries

Eins. Tage:	Datum:	Ort nach Rgts.- bzw. Abtlgs.-Bef.:	Bescheinigung:
37	4. 9.	Hf. Butzki	
38	6. 9.	Schljach	
39	7. 9.	Bolgar	
40	8. 9.	Sochw. 8 Marta	
41	lo. 9.	Tawarowka	
42	11. 9.	Walki	
43	16. 9.	Ssnoshkoff-Kut	
44	19. 9.	Sarudka	
45	21. 9.	Bol. Lipnjagi	
46	22. 9.	Bol. Lipnjagi	
47	23. 9.	Tolstaja	
48	2.lo.	Chutor Kresch-tschatik	
49	7.lo.	Fuchsschwanzinsel	
50	8.lo.	Fuchsschwanzinsel	
51	17.lo.	Kreschtschatik	
52	13.11.	Sswidowok	
53	14.11.	Sswidowok	
54	15.11.	Ssekirna	
55	16.11.	Ssekirna	
56	17.11.	Sswidowok	SS-Hauptsturmführer und
57	5.12.	Chatzki	Abteilungs-Führer
58	7.1.44	Mal. Starolselje	
59	8. 1.	Buda-Orlowezkaja	
60	24. 1.	Butki	
61	25. 1.	Ossitnjatschka	
62	26. 1.	Pastorskoje	
63	27. 1.	Pastorskoje	
64	28. 1.	Pastorskoje	

Eins. Tage:	Datum:	Ort nach Rgts.- bzw. Abtlgs.-Bef.:	Bescheinigung:
65	29.1.44	Olschana	
66	3o. 1.	Leninna-Melnikowka	
67	31. 1.	Olschana	
68	1. 2.	Olschana	
69	12. 2.	Nowo-Buda	
70	15. 2.	Nowo-Buda	
71	17. 2.	Lissjanka	Hauptsturmführer Abteilungs-Führer

Soldbuch page with days of engagement. The legend at the top of the page reads: Running days of engagements; date; location according to the regimental or battalion order; certification. The running list of days was maintained to make it easier to track combat awards, especially numbered assault badges or the close-combat clasp.

APPENDIX K

Days of Combat That Can Be Counted for the Award of the Armored Combat Badge, 29 March to 15 April 1944

1122 Anlage: 2/

ϟϟ-Panzer-Regiment 5
Ia / IIa / Li. / No.

Rgts.-Gef.St., den 17.4.1944

Betr.: Anzurechnende Gefechtstage für die Verleihung des Panzerkampfabzeichens für die Zeit vom 29.3.-15.4.44.

Verteiler: bis Kompanien

Für die Verleihung des Panzerkampfabzeichens werden nachfolgende Gefechtstage festgelegt:

29.3.1944	Angriff auf Czerkasy	8. Kompanie
3o.3.1944	Durchbruch nach Kowel	8. Kompanie
31.3. = 5.4.1944	Einsatz in Kowel	8. Kompanie
1.4.1944	Gegenstoß zur Wiedereinnahme von Czerkasy	7. Kompanie
4.4.1944	Unterstützung des Angriffs II./ϟ-Pz.Gren.Rgt."Westland" ostwärts Stare Koszary	5. Kompanie
5.4.1944	Angriff auf Dubowa Durchbruch nach Kowel	Rgts.-Stab Stab II./5 6. u. 7.Kp.
6.4.1944	Unterstützung des Angriffs I./ϟ-Pz.Gren.Rgt."Germania" an Bahnlinie Kowel - Czerkasy	6. Kompanie
1o.4.1944	Unterstützung des Angriffs des Pz.Gren.Rgt. 33 auf Bachow und Höhe 179	6. Kompanie
12.4.1944	Panzergefecht bei Höhe 179	6. Kompanie

i.E. gez. M ü h l e n k a m p

F.d.R.
[signature]
ϟϟ-Obersturmführer und
stellv.Rgts.-Adjutant

This document specified which days could be counted as engagements for the award of the Armor Assault Badge. It was distributed down to company level. The main body reads:

29 March 1944	Attack on Czerkasy	8th Company
30 March 1944	Breakthrough to Kowel	8th Company
31 March to 5 April 1944	Operations in Kowel	8th Company
1 April 1944	Immediate counterattack to retake Czerkasy	7th Company
4 April 1944	Support of the attack of the II./*SS-Panzer-Grenadier-Regiment "Westland"* to the east of Stare Koszary	5th Company
5 April 1944	Attack on Dubowa; breakthrough to Kowel	Regimental headquarters; headquarters of the 2nd Battalion; 5th, 6th and 7th Companies
6 April 1944	Support of the attack of the I*I./SS-Panzer-Grenadier-Regiment "Germania"* along the Kowel—Czerkasy rail line	6th Company
10 April 1944	Support of the attack of *Panzer-Regiment 33* on Bachow and Hill 179	6th Company
12 April 1944	Armored engagement at Hill 179	6th Company

APPENDIX L

Telegraph from the Headquarters of *Heeresgruppe Mitte* to the Headquarters of the *2. Armee* Dated 16 July 1944 (Allocation of the Division)

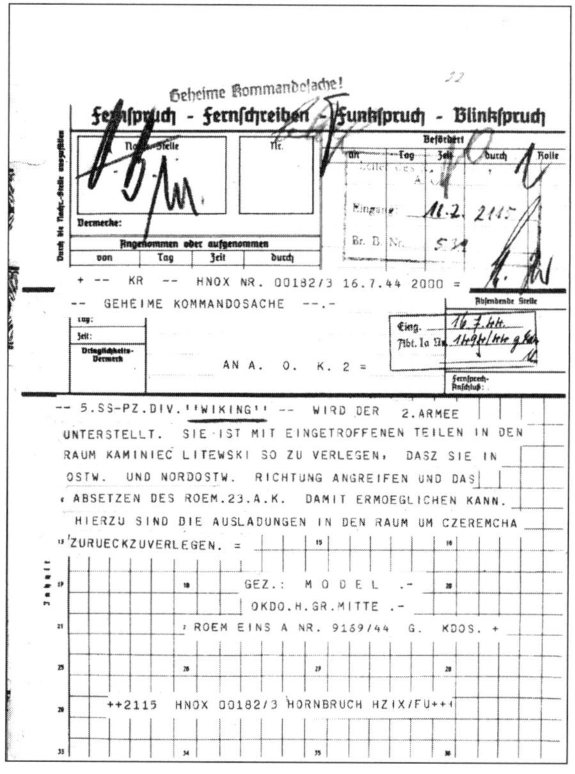

Geheime Kommandosache!

Fernspruch - Fernschreiben - Funkspruch - Blinkspruch

+ -- KR -- HNOX NR. 00182/3 16.7.44 2000 =

-- GEHEIME KOMMANDOSACHE --.-

AN A. O. K. 2 =

-- 5.SS-PZ.DIV.''WIKING'' -- WIRD DER 2.ARMEE UNTERSTELLT. SIE IST MIT EINGETROFFENEN TEILEN IN DEN RAUM KAMINIEC LITEWSKI SO ZU VERLEGEN, DASZ SIE IN OSTW. UND NORDOSTW. RICHTUNG ANGREIFEN UND DAS ABSETZEN DES ROEM.23.A.K. DAMIT ERMOEGLICHEN KANN. HIERZU SIND DIE AUSLADUNGEN IN DEN RAUM UM CZEREMCHA ZURUECKZUVERLEGEN. =

GEZ.: M O D E L .-

OKDO.H.GR.MITTE .-

ROEM EINS A NR. 9169/44 G. KDOS. +

++2115 HNOX 00182/3 HORNBRUCH HZIX/FU++

The main body of the telegram reads:
The *5. SS-Panzer-Division "Wiking"* is attached to the *2. Armee*. It is to position itself with its arrived elements in the Kaminiec Litewski area in such a way that it can attack to the east and northeast, thus enabling the withdrawal of the *XXIII. Armee-Korps*. To that end, the offloading is to be moved back to the area around Czeremcha.
/signed/ Model
Headquarters, *Heeresgruppe Mitte*

APPENDIX M

List of Combat Engagements for the Period from 7 to 26 July 1944

Day	Unit	Description of Engagement
7 July 1944	*II./SS-PR 5*: Headquarters, Headquarters Company; 5th, 6th and 8th Companies	Armored engagement and immediate counterattack at Hill 197.2, 2 kilometers northwest of Kruhel
8 July 1944	*II./SS-PR 5*: Headquarters, Headquarters Company; 5th, 6th and 8th Companies	Armored engagement on Hills 206 and 220, east of Maciejew
9 July 1944	*II./SS-PR 5*: Headquarters, Headquarters Company; 5th, 6th, 7th and 8th Companies	Immediate counterattack and screening on Hills 212 and 220, east of Maciejew
10 July 1944	*II./SS-PR 5*: Headquarters and 6th Company	Defense along Hill 212.2, east of Maciejew
11 July 1944	*II./SS-PR 5*: 5th Company	Immediate counterattack on Hill 220.8, southeast of Maciejew
16 July 1944	*II./SS-PR 5*: 5th Company	Attack at Kamieniec Litewski
	Headquarters Company, 7th Company, Regimental Headquarters, Regimental Headquarters Company and Armored Engineer Company	Fighting at Ranie and the Szczerbowo crossroads
17 July 1944	*I./SS-PR 5*: Battle Staff; 3rd and 4th Companies	Reconnaissance-in-force in the direction of Widlowla; armored engagement at Hill 171.6, north of Widlowla
	II./SS-PR 5: Headquarters, Headquarters Company; 7th Company	Capture of Szczerbowo, Podbrodziany and Hill 178.4
	8th Company, Regimental Headquarters, Regimental Headquarters Company and Armored Engineer Company	Attack and screening at Kamieniec Litewski
18 July 1944	*I./SS-PR 5*: 4th Company	Attack on Toploje

	II./SS-PR 5: Headquarters, Headquarters Company; 7th Company. Regimental Headquarters, Regimental Headquarters Company and Armored Engineer Company	Fighting on Hill 178.4, at Czemery and at Toploje
	II./SS-PR 5: 8th Company	Attack on Ranie
19 July 1944	*I./SS-PR 5*: 4th Company	Attack on and taking of Sziszowo; defensive operations at Hill 162.4
	II./SS-PR 5: 8th Company; Armored Engineer Company	Attack on and screening at Hill 162.4
20 July 1944	*II./SS-PR 5*: 5th Company	Attack on Kalenkowicze and Podborze
	6th Company	Immediate counterattack on Hill 178.4 and Czemery
	7th Company; Regimental Headquarters, Regimental Headquarters Company and Armored Engineer Company	Fighting at Dolbizna and Chlewiszcze
21 July 1944	*II./SS-PR 5*: 6th Company	Attack at the Awuls Collective farm
	7th Company; Regimental Headquarters and Armored Engineer Company	Immediate counterattack at Dolbizna
	8th Company; Armored Engineer Company	Attack and screening at the Nurzec Collective Farm and Hill 180
22 July 1944	*I./SS-PR 5*: Elements of the battle staff and the 3rd Company	Attack on and capture of Zubackze
	II./SS-PR 5: 5th Company	Attack on Zerczece
	6th Company; Regimental Headquarters, Regimental Headquarters Company and Armored Engineer Company	Attack against Tymianka
	8th Company	Attack through Borka and the railway crossing southwest of Czeremcha
23 July 1944	*I./SS-PR 5*: Battle staff and the 4th Company	Attack against the rail station at Czeremcha
	II./SS-PR 5: 5th Company	Breakthrough at Augustynko

Day	Unit	Description of Engagement
	6th Company	Screening at Hill 181.2 and establishing contact with the *4. Panzer-Division* at Kleszczele
24 July 1944	*I./SS-PR 5*: 4th Company	Armored engagement at the Czeremcha rail station
	II./SS-PR 5: 6th Company	Screening at Hill 180 and reconnaissance-in-force against Hill 178, southeast of Rogacze
	7th Company	Fighting at the Czeremcha rail station and immediate counterattack to eliminate Chklewiszcze.
	8th Company, Regimental Headquarters, regimental Headquarters Company and Armored Engineer Company	Immediate counterattack on Hill 181.2 and Kleszczele
25 July 1944	*I./SS-PR 5*: 3rd Company	Immediate counterattack in Czeremcha and on Hill 184
	Battle staff, antiaircraft platoon, 3rd and 4th Companies	Armored engagement west of Czeremcha
	II./SS-PR 5: 7th Company	Fighting at Kostycze
	8th Company and Armored Engineer Company	Immediate counterattack on Czeremcha and Hill 181.2
26 July 1944	*I./SS-PR 5*: 3rd Company	Defensive fighting in Czeremcha and immediate counterattack on Hill 184
	4th Company	Armored engagement west of Czeremcha
	II./SS-PR 5: 5th Company	Immediate counterattack on Hill 176, north of Werpol
	6th Company	Immediate counterattack on the Biala—Podlaska—Terespol road
	7th Company and Armored Engineer Company	Fighting at Kostycze

APPENDIX N

Regimental Special Order Dated 7 September 1944

SS-Panzer-Regiment 5
Commander

Regimental Command Post, 7 September 1944

Regimental Special Order

During the period from 29 March 1944 to 7 September 1944, SS-Panzer-Regiment 5 scored its

500th Tank Kill

During that time, the following were also destroyed or captured:

4	Armored Cars
71	Antitank rifles
787	Heavy Antitank Guns
363	Light Antitank Guns
34	Combination antitank/antiaircraft guns
38I	nfantry guns
10	Heavy mortars
44	8.5cm antiaircraft guns
3	2cm antiaircraft guns
6	Heavy gun carriages
3	17.2cm guns
11	Medium caliber guns
15	Heavy machine guns
14	Light machine guns
4	Aircraft
26,735	Enemy dead
125	Trucks
1	Prime mover
1	Armored personnel carrier

The regiment is proud of its unique successes. It will serve as an inspiration to us so that we can soon report our 1,000th tank kill.

/signed/ Darges
SS-Sturmbannführer and Regimental Commander

APPENDIX O

German Army High Command Orders Dated 16 September 1944 Concerning the Personnel Reconstitution of the *5. SS-Panzer-Division "Wiking"* and the *3. SS-Panzer-Division "Totenkopf"*

Text of message:

SUBJECT: Personnel Reconstitution of the *SS-Panzer-Division Wiking* and *Totenkopf*

1.) For the reconstitution of *SS-Panzer-Division Wiking* and *Totenkopf*, 10,000 men are being provided by the Luftwaffe. Transfer is anticipated by 19 September.

2.) The personnel consist of ground organization personnel and soldiers the *Luftwaffe* considers fully trained in aviation specialties.

For ground-combat operations, a general retraining period of 3-8 weeks, respective of the state of individual training, will be necessary.

3.) The SS Main Office intends to transport the 10,000 men to the field replacement battalions of the two divisions and for the training to be conducted in these battalions.

APPENDIX P

Organization Chart for the Division on 21 February 1944

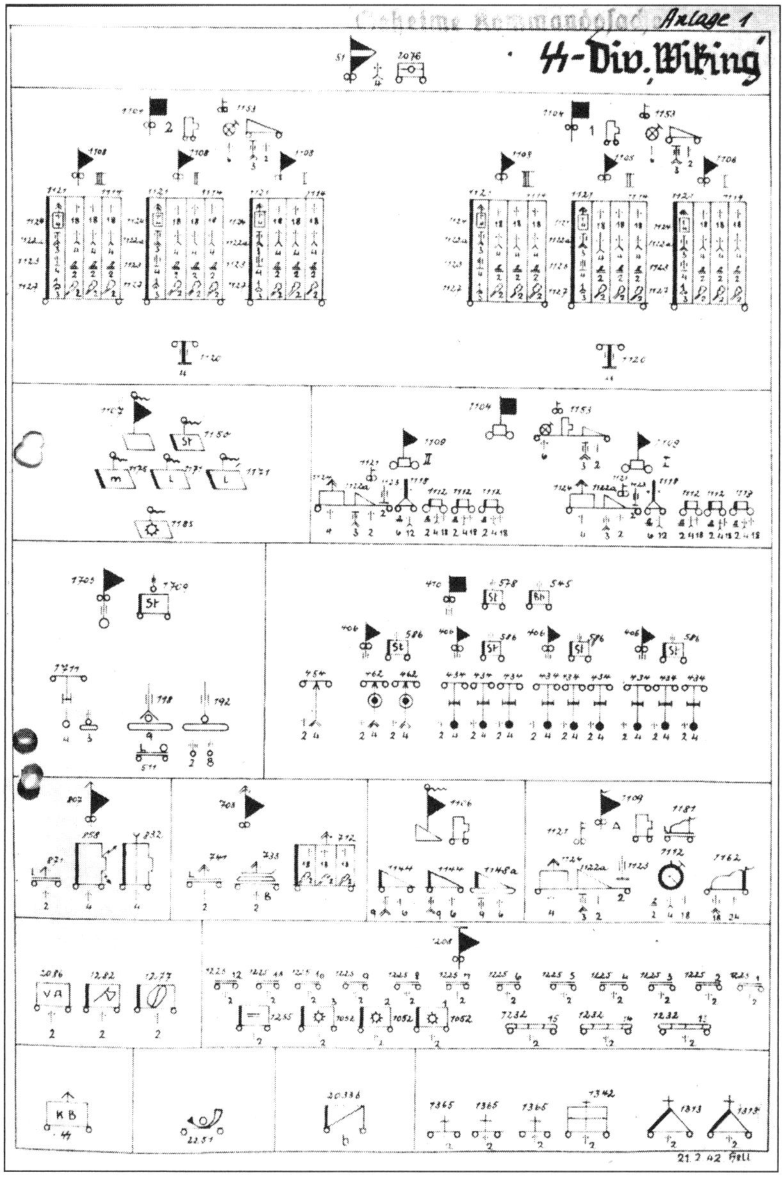

APPENDIX Q

Organization Chart for the Division on 1 June 1944

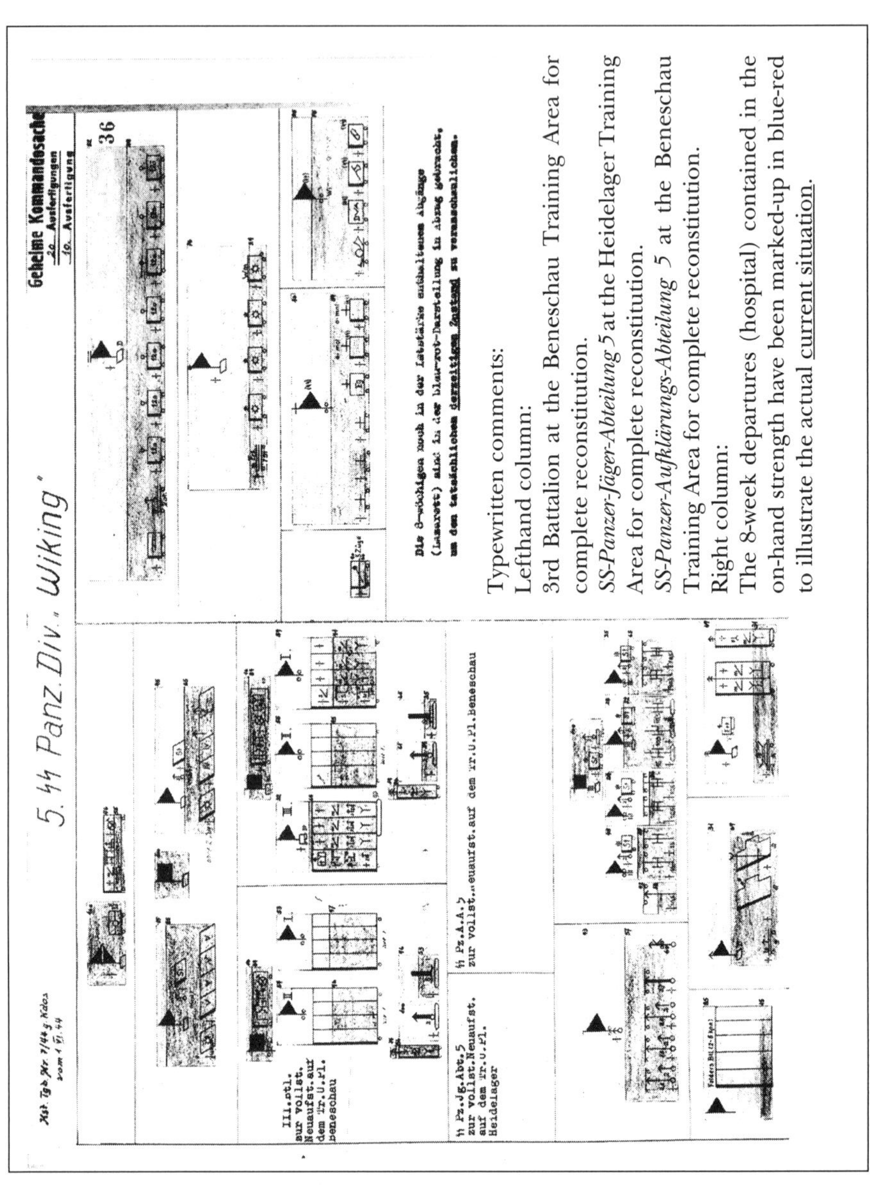

APPENDIX R

Status Report for the Division on 1 June 1944

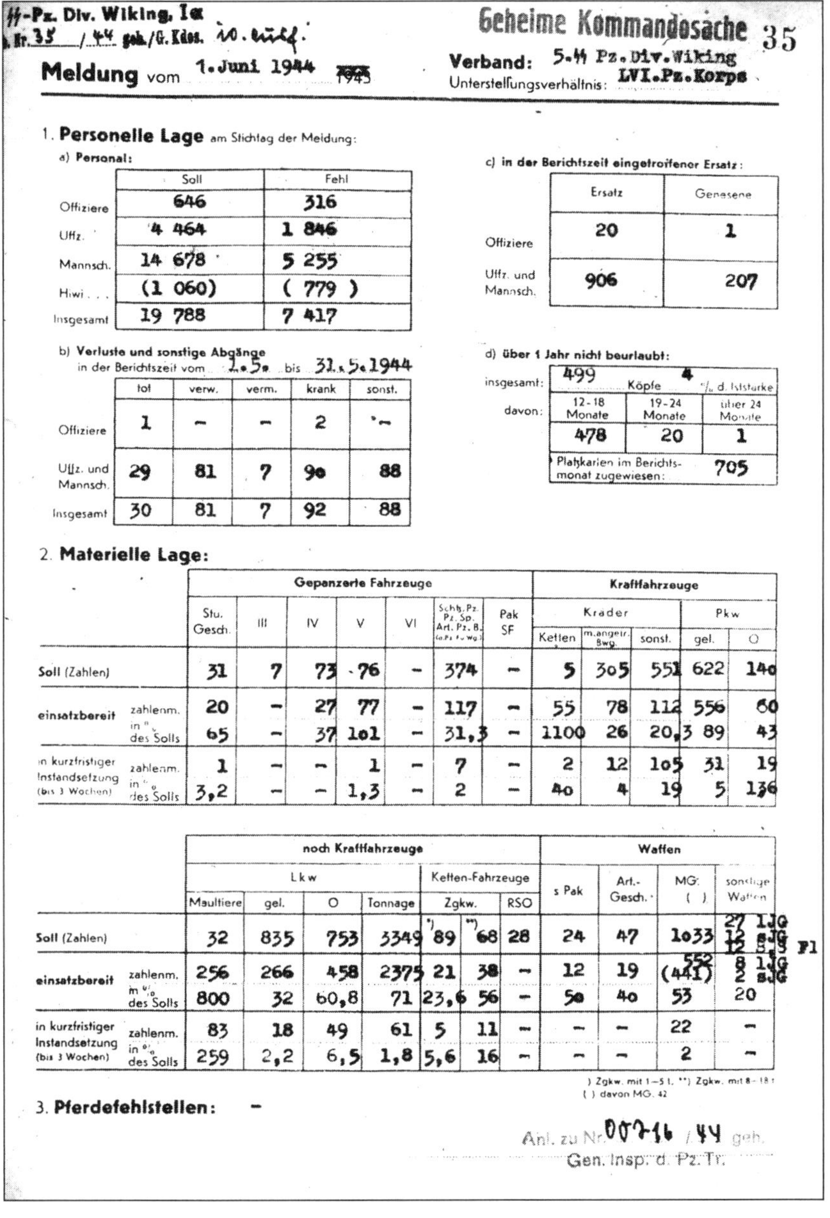

SS-Pz. Div. Wiking, Ia
Nr. 35 / 44 geh./G. Kdos. 10. Ausf.

Geheime Kommandosache 35

Meldung vom 1. Juni 1944

Verband: 5. SS Pz. Div. Wiking
Unterstellungsverhältnis: LVI. Pz. Korps

1. **Personelle Lage** am Stichtag der Meldung:

a) **Personal:**

	Soll	Fehl
Offiziere	646	316
Uffz.	4 464	1 846
Mannsch.	14 678	5 255
Hiwi . . .	(1 060)	(779)
Insgesamt	19 788	7 417

b) **Verluste und sonstige Abgänge** in der Berichtszeit vom 1.5. bis 31.5.1944

	tot	verw.	verm.	krank	sonst.
Offiziere	1	–	–	2	–
Uffz. und Mannsch.	29	81	7	90	88
Insgesamt	30	81	7	92	88

c) **in der Berichtszeit eingetroffener Ersatz:**

	Ersatz	Genesene
Offiziere	20	1
Uffz. und Mannsch.	906	207

d) **über 1 Jahr nicht beurlaubt:**

insgesamt: 499 Köpfe 4 % d. Iststärke

davon:	12-18 Monate	19-24 Monate	über 24 Monate
	478	20	1

Platzkarten im Berichtsmonat zugewiesen: 705

2. **Materielle Lage:**

		Gepanzerte Fahrzeuge							Kraftfahrzeuge				
									Krader			Pkw	
		Stu. Gesch.	III	IV	V	VI	Schtz. Pz. Pz. Sp. Art. Pz. B. (o. Pz. Fu. Wg.)	Pak SF	Ketten	m. angetr. Bwg.	sonst.	gel.	O
Soll (Zahlen)		31	7	73	76	–	374	–	5	305	551	622	140
einsatzbereit	zahlenm.	20	–	27	77	–	117	–	55	78	112	556	60
	in % des Solls	65	–	37	101	–	31,3	–	1100	26	20,3	89	43
in kurzfristiger Instandsetzung (bis 3 Wochen)	zahlenm.	1	–	–	1	–	7	–	2	12	105	31	19
	in % des Solls	3,2	–	–	1,3	–	2	–	40	4	19	5	136

		noch Kraftfahrzeuge							Waffen			
		Lkw				Ketten-Fahrzeuge			s Pak	Art.-Gesch.	MG ( )	sonstige Waffen
		Maultiere	gel.	O	Tonnage	Zgkw. *)	Zgkw. **)	RSO				
Soll (Zahlen)		32	835	753	3349	89	68	28	24	47	1033	27 lJG 12 sJG 12 8,8 Fl
einsatzbereit	zahlenm.	256	266	458	2375	21	38	–	12	19	552 (441)	8 lJG 2 sJG
	in % des Solls	800	32	60,8	71	23,6	56	–	50	40	53	20
in kurzfristiger Instandsetzung (bis 3 Wochen)	zahlenm.	83	18	49	61	5	11	–	–	–	22	–
	in % des Solls	259	2,2	6,5	1,8	5,6	16	–	–	–	2	–

*) Zgkw. mit 1–5 t, **) Zgkw. mit 8–18 t
( ) davon MG. 42

3. **Pferdefehlstellen:** –

Anl. zu Nr. 00716 / 44 geh.
Gen. Insp. d. Pz. Tr.

The Division Status Report was submitted monthly and offered higher command elements a "snapshot" of the personnel and materiel status of the division as well as the commander's assessment of its combat capabilities. The commander's evaluation is not included here. This report is dated 1 June 1944, when it was attached to the *LVI. Panzer-Korps*. It was classified as a SECRET COMMAND MATTER.

Section 1 (*Personelle Lage*) covers the personnel situation of the division. Subsection (a) lists the authorized strength (*Soll*) and shortages (*Fehl*) by officers, noncommissioned officers, enlisted personnel, *Hiwis* and an aggregate. Subsection (b) details losses and other departures from end strength during the reporting period (1 to 31 May 1944) by officers, noncommissioned officers & enlisted personnel and an aggregate. Subsection (c) lists replacements (*Ersatz*) and convalescents (*Genesene*) received during the reporting period by officers and noncommissioned officers and enlisted personnel. Finally, subsection (d) lists the number of personnel who have not had leave in more than a year. The total number (499) is presented as a percentage of end strength. The figures are further broken down by those who have not had leave during the last 12–18 months, 19–24 months and more than 24 months.

Section 2 (*Materielle Lage*) covers the materiel status of the division, based on armored vehicles (*gepanzerte Fahrzeuge*), motor vehicles (*Kraftfahrzeuge*), additional motor vehicles (*noch Kraftfahrzeuge*) and weapons (*Waffen*). The vehicles and weapons are listed in terms of authorized levels (*Soll*), operational status (*einsatzbereit*) in terms of numbers and the percentage of authorized strength they represent and, finally, the number and percentage of vehicles in short-term maintenance (up to three weeks) (in *kurzfristiger Instandsetzung*).

APPENDIX S

Organization Chart for the Division on 1 January 1945

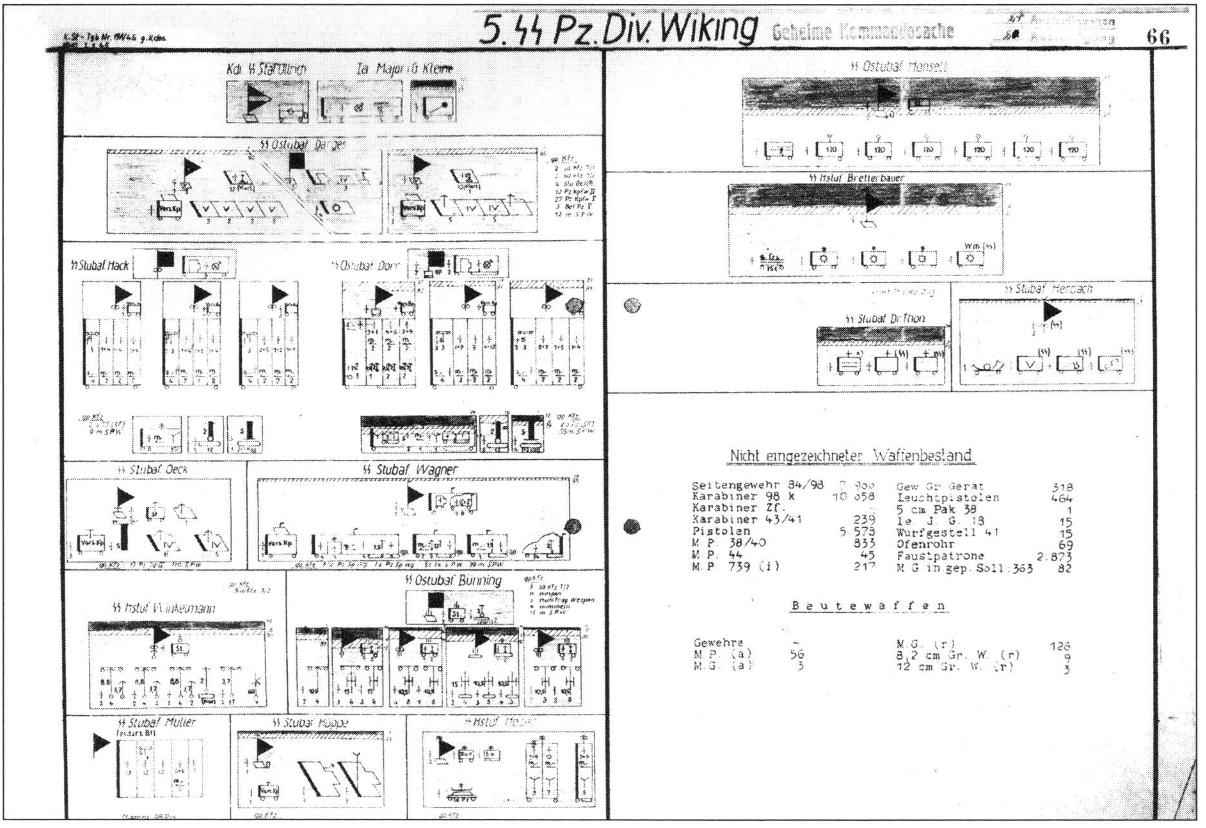

The typewritten comments refer to weapons not listed on the chart (*Nicht eingezeichneter Waffenbestand*) and the numbers of captured weapons employed (*Beutewaffen*).

APPENDIX T

Status Report for the Division on 1 January 1945

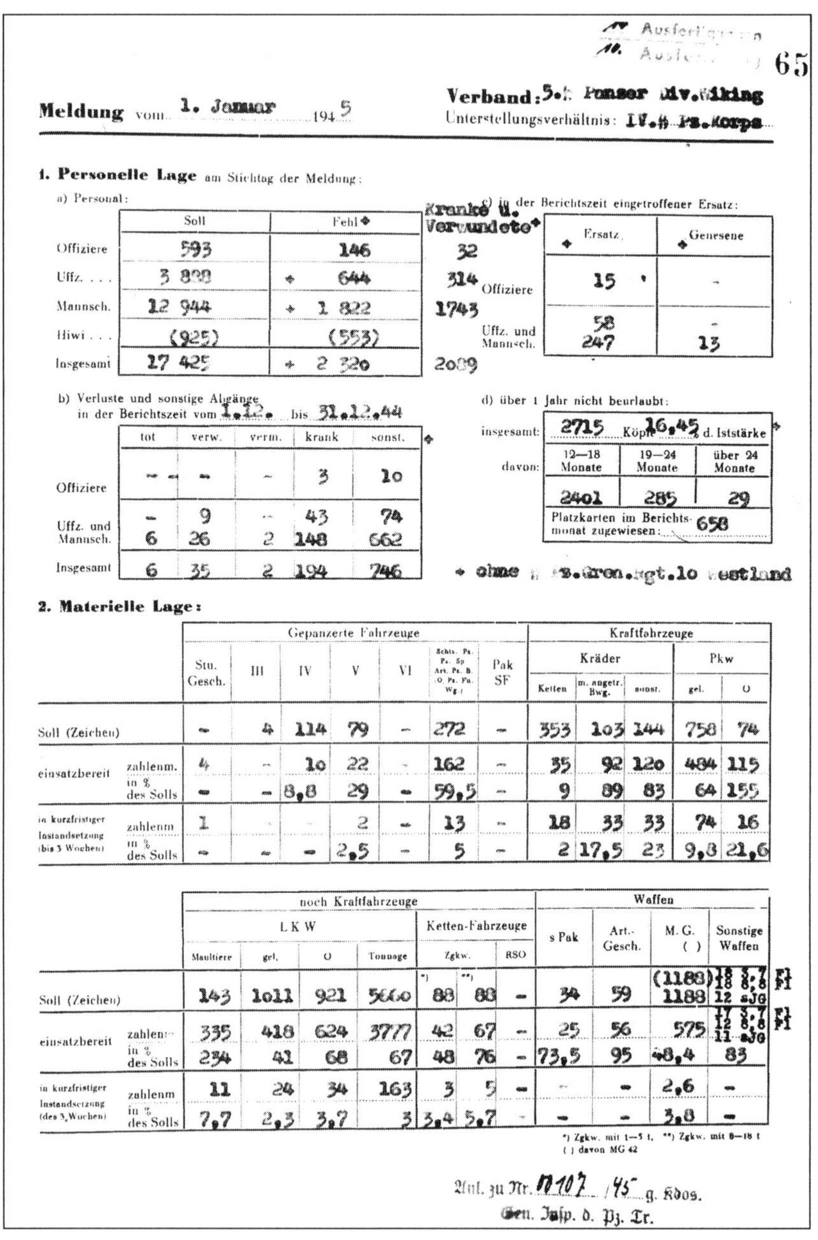

Ausfertigung
Ausfertigung 65

Meldung vom 1. Januar 1945

Verband: 5. SS Panzer Div. Wiking
Unterstellungsverhältnis: IV. SS Pz. Korps

1. Personelle Lage am Stichtag der Meldung:

a) Personal:

	Soll	Fehl +	Kranke u. Verwundete +
Offiziere	593	146	32
Uffz. . . .	3 808	+ 644	314
Mannsch.	12 944	+ 1 822	1743
Hiwi . . .	(925)	(553)	
Insgesamt	17 425	+ 2 320	2089

c) in der Berichtszeit eingetroffener Ersatz:

	+ Ersatz	+ Genesene
Offiziere	15	-
Uffz. und Mannsch.	58 247	- 13

b) Verluste und sonstige Abgänge in der Berichtszeit vom 1.12. bis 31.12.44 +

	tot	verw.	verm.	krank	sonst.
Offiziere	- -	-	-	3	10
Uffz. und Mannsch.	- 6	9 26	- 2	43 148	74 662
Insgesamt	6	35	2	194	746

d) über 1 Jahr nicht beurlaubt:

insgesamt: 2715 Köpfe 16,45 % d. Iststärke +

davon:	12–18 Monate	19–24 Monate	über 24 Monate
	2401	285	29

Platzkarten im Berichtsmonat zugewiesen: 658

+ ohne SS Pz. Gren. Rgt. 10 Westland

2. Materielle Lage:

		Gepanzerte Fahrzeuge							Kraftfahrzeuge				
		Stu. Gesch.	III	IV	V	VI	Schtz. Pz. Pz. Sp Art. Pz. B. (O. Pz. Fu. Wg.)	Pak SF	Kräder Ketten	Kräder m. angetr. Bwg.	Kräder sonst.	Pkw gel.	Pkw O
Soll (Zeichen)		-	4	114	79	-	272	-	353	103	144	758	74
einsatzbereit	zahlenm.	4	-	10	22	-	162	-	35	92	120	484	115
	in % des Solls	-	-	8,8	29	-	59,5	-	9	89	83	64	155
in kurzfristiger Instandsetzung (bis 3 Wochen)	zahlenm	1	-	-	2	-	13	-	18	33	33	74	16
	in % des Solls	-	-	-	2,5	-	5	-	2	17,5	23	9,8	21,6

		noch Kraftfahrzeuge							Waffen			
		LKW Maultiere	LKW gel.	LKW O	LKW Tonnage	Ketten-Fahrzeuge Zgkw. *)	Ketten-Fahrzeuge Zgkw. **)	Ketten-Fahrzeuge RSO	s Pak	Art.-Gesch.	M. G. ( )	Sonstige Waffen
Soll (Zeichen)		143	1011	921	5660	88	88	-	34	59	(1188) 1188	18 3,7 Fl 18 8,8 Fl 12 sJG
einsatzbereit	zahlenm.	335	418	624	3777	42	67	-	25	56	575	17 3,7 Fl 12 8,8 Fl 11 sJG
	in % des Solls	234	41	68	67	48	76	-	73,5	95	48,4	83
in kurzfristiger Instandsetzung (des 3. Wochen)	zahlenm	11	24	34	163	3	5	-	-	-	2,6	-
	in % des Solls	7,7	2,3	3,7	3	3,4	5,7	-	-	-	3,8	-

*) Zgkw. mit 1–5 t, **) Zgkw. mit 8–18 t
( ) davon MG 42

Anl. zu Nr. 10107/45 g. Kdos.
Gen. Insp. d. Pz. Tr.

APPENDIX U

Organization Chart for the Division on 1 April 1945

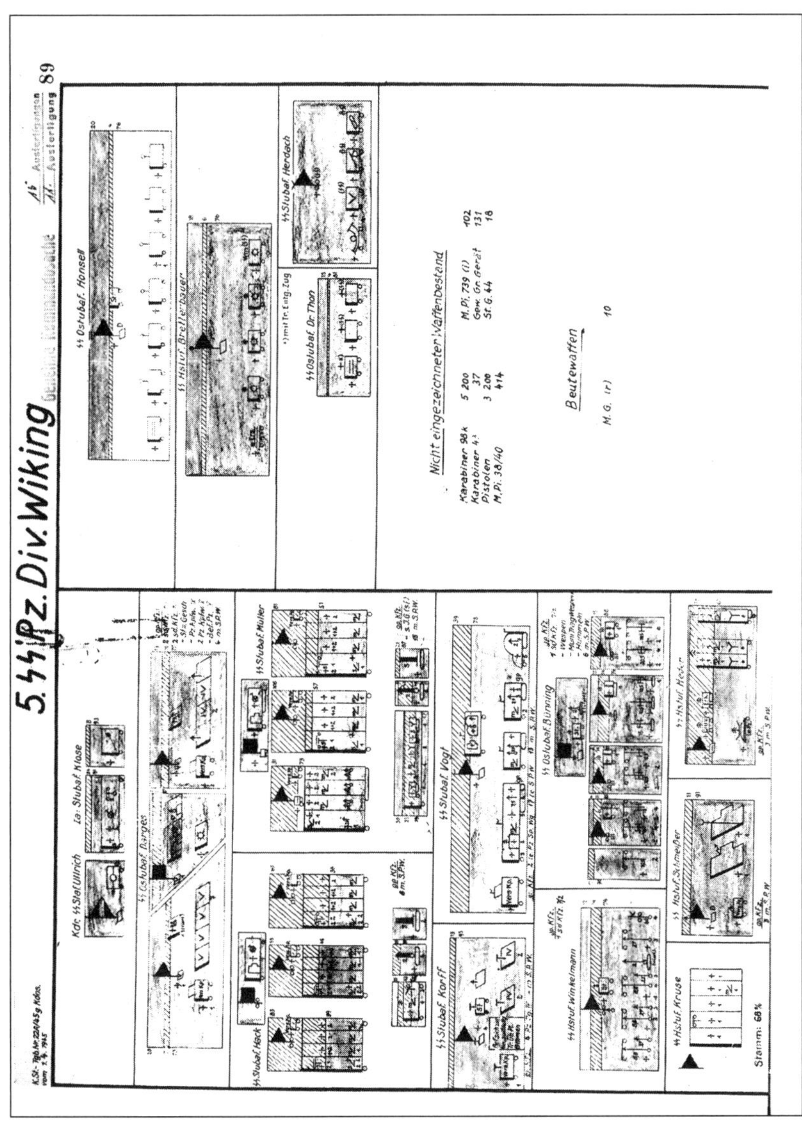

The typewritten comments refer to weapons not listed on the chart (*Nicht eingezeichneter Waffenbestand*) and the numbers of captured weapons employed (*Beutewaffen*).

APPENDIX V

Status Report for the Division on 1 April 1945

The reader is referred to Appendix R for an explanation of the report. This report was submitted on 1 April 1945, with the division still reporting to the *IV. SS-Panzer-Korps.*

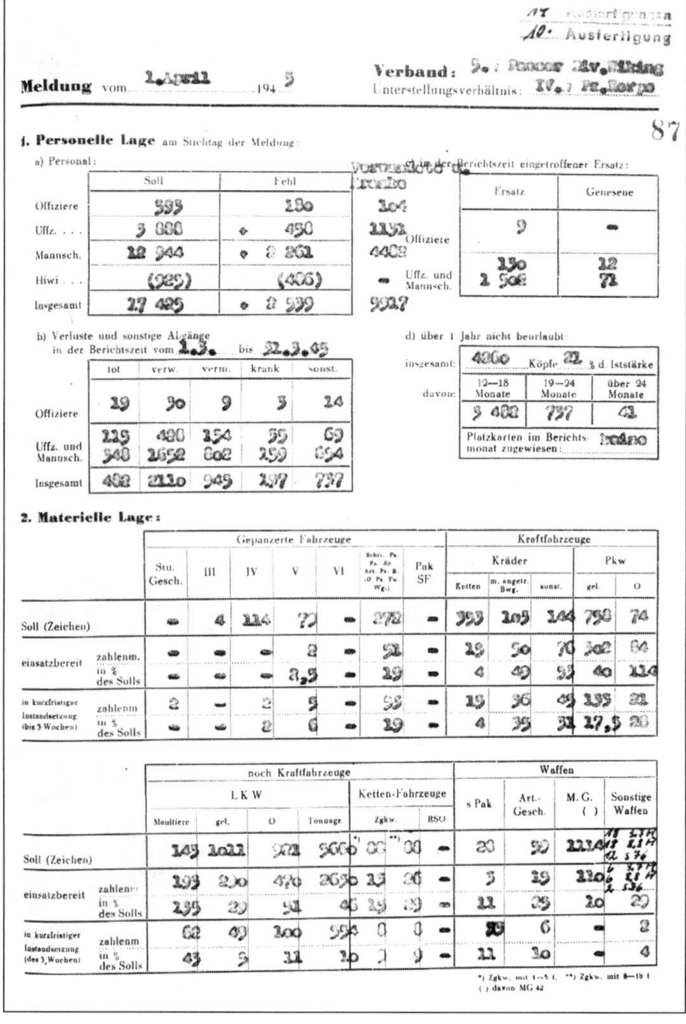

17 Ausfertigungen
10. Ausfertigung

Meldung vom 1. April 1945

Verband: 5. Panzer Div. Wiking
Unterstellungsverhältnis: IV. Pz.Korps

87

1. Personelle Lage am Stichtag der Meldung:

a) Personal:

	Soll	Fehl	[illegible]
Offiziere	599	180	304
Uffz. . . .	3 882	• 450	1132
Mannsch.	12 944	• 2 261	4402
Hiwi . . .	(925)	(406)	–
Insgesamt	17 425	• 2 539	9927

c) in der Berichtszeit eingetroffener Ersatz:

	Ersatz	Genesene
Offiziere	9	–
Uffz. und Mannsch.	150 1 508	12 71

b) Verluste und sonstige Abgänge in der Berichtszeit vom 1.3. bis 31.3.45

	tot	verw.	verm.	krank	sonst.
Offiziere	19	30	9	3	14
Uffz. und Mannsch.	125 348	428 1652	134 802	35 259	69 654
Insgesamt	492	2110	945	297	737

d) über 1 Jahr nicht beurlaubt:

insgesamt: 4260 Köpfe 22 % d. Iststärke

davon:	12–18 Monate	19–24 Monate	über 24 Monate
	3 482	737	41

Platzkarten im Berichtsmonat zugewiesen: [illegible]

2. Materielle Lage:

		Gepanzerte Fahrzeuge							Kraftfahrzeuge				
									Kräder			Pkw	
		Stu. Gesch.	III	IV	V	VI	Schtz. Pz. Pz. Sp Art. Pz. B. (O. Pz. Fu. Wg.)	Pak SF	Ketten	m. angetr. Bwg.	sonst.	gel.	O
Soll (Zeichen)		–	4	114	79	–	272	–	393	103	144	750	74
einsatzbereit	zahlenm.	–	–	–	2	–	51	–	15	50	76	302	84
	in % des Solls	–	–	–	2,5	–	19	–	4	49	53	40	114
in kurzfristiger Instandsetzung (bis 3 Wochen)	zahlenm.	2	–	2	5	–	53	–	15	36	45	133	21
	in % des Solls	–	–	2	6	–	19	–	4	35	31	17,5	28

		noch Kraftfahrzeuge							Waffen			
		LKW				Ketten-Fahrzeuge						
		Maultierr	gel.	O	Tonnage	Zgkw.*)	Zgkw.**)	RSO	s Pak	Art.-Gesch.	M. G. ( )	Sonstige Waffen
Soll (Zeichen)		143	1022	921	5660	80	88	–	28	99	1114	18 3,7 Fl 18 8,8 Fl 12 5,76
einsatzbereit	zahlenm.	193	200	470	2630	12	26	–	3	29	220	6 3,7 Fl 6 8,8 Fl 2 5,76
	in % des Solls	135	20	51	46	15	29	–	11	29	20	29
in kurzfristiger Instandsetzung (bis 3 Wochen)	zahlenm.	62	49	100	593	0	0	–	3	6	–	2
	in % des Solls	43	5	11	10	0	0	–	11	10	–	4

*) Zgkw. mit 1–5 t. **) Zgkw. mit 8–18 t
( ) davon MG 42

APPENDIX W

Letter to the Unit from the Father of *SS-Oberscharführer* Erwin Göpferich (*1./SS-Panzer-Abteilung 5*), Killed in Action on 24 December 1942.

Bauerbach, 29 March 1943

TO: Unit Field Post 09274

The news of the hero's death of our dear son, *Oberscharführer* Erwin Göpferich, hit us hard, and we thank you most gratefully for the heartfelt sympathy expressed by his field unit, which had become so dear to him. Fate deals horrible blows, and it is bitterly hard for a father and mother, when one of their children—in this case, our dear and only son—is torn from a young life so abruptly. But to mourn on his account would be out of place and purposeless, since he gave his life for Germany, for a better future, for all of us and, in this sense, our deep sorrow is also a source of pride and honor. His honor was certainly his loyalty.

We do have a wish, however: We would like to find out where and under what circumstance he found his hero's death, whether he is buried someplace or if there is anything else that should be known. Also, whether some of his personal belongings, such as a watch, a wallet, underclothes, etc. [might be available that] he wore or left behind. Should there be something else found from our son, we respectfully request that it be directed to us as a dear memento. After all, the heart of a father and a mother clings to even the smallest remembrance. His remaining military pay arrived last week.

Perhaps there are some of his closer comrades in the unit whom we could contact. Unfortunately, we do not have an address for any of his comrades, and we would like so much to establish written contact with the company or one of his former acquaintances.

We look forward to an answer to all of our questions soon and send our heartfelt greetings in proud mourning to the field unit of our dear dead son.

Heil und Sieg!
W. Göpferich Family

P.S. Request perhaps the address of one of his comrades as well.

Select Bibliography

PRIMARY SOURCES—DAILY LOGS

Headquarters, *1. Panzer-Armee* from 23 September to 31 October 1942; Headquarters, *2. Armee* from 12-22 July 1944 and 31 July to 2 August 1944; *LVII. Panzer-Korps* from 16 June to 30 September 1942 (Number 4) and 1 January to 28 February 1943 (Number 6); *XXXX. Panzer-Korps* from 1 to 28 February 1943 (Number 5); *LVI. Panzer-Korps* from 21 March to 27 April 1944; *LII. Armee-Korps* from 23 to 30 September 1942 and 1 to 31 October 1942; *I./SS-Panzer-Regiment 5* from 9 February to 30 November 1944.

PRIMARY SOURCES—AFTER-ACTION REPORTS

Rifle Company, *I./SS-Panzer-Regiment 5* (Wittmann), covering 11–17 February 1944.

Headquarters Company, I.*/SS-Panzer-Regiment 5* (Senghas), covering 18–22 August 1944.

Antiaircraft Platoon, *I./SS-Panzer-Regiment 5* (Aumeyer), covering 10–14 October 1944.

2./SS-Panzer-Regiment 5 (Paetow) covering 10–20 October 1944.

2./SS-Panzer-Regiment 5 (Bauer) covering 21–31 October 1944.

3./SS-Panzer-Regiment 5 (Metzger) covering 4 September 1944, 25 August 1944, 26 August 1944, 5 September 1944, 6 September 1944 and 7 September 1944.

4./SS-Panzer-Regiment 5 (Weerts) covering 10–19 October 1944 and 20–26 October 1944.

PRIMARY SOURCES—SITUATION AND STATUS REPORTS

I./SS-Panzer-Regiment 5 (Kümmel), dated 19 March 1944.

I./SS-Panzer-Regiment 5 (Köhler, Radio Operator Course), dated 24 April 1944.

I./SS-Panzer-Regiment 5 (Säumenicht), dated 3 July 1944 and 5 July 1944.

I./SS-Panzer-Regiment 5 (Hein), dated 4 October 1944 and 2 December 1944.

I./SS-Panzer-Regiment 5 (Frels), dated 28 April 1944.

1./SS-Panzer-Regiment 5 (Brand), dated 2 May 1944.

2./SS-Panzer-Regiment 5 (Hein), dated 21 May 1944.

3./SS-Panzer-Regiment 5 (Schumacher), dated 17 October 1944.

Grenadier-Brigade 1131 (Söth), dated 27 August 1944.

PRIMARY SOURCES—PERSONAL DIARIES

Jahncke, G. (Assistant Operations Officer on the Division Staff) from December 1944 until 4 August 1945.

Hein, W. (*4./SS-Panzer-Regiment 5*) from 26 January to 18 February 1944.

Schneider, W. (*1./SS-Panzer-Regiment 5*) from December 1942 to 2 September 1943.

Schönfelder, M. (Chief-of-Staff of the *IV. SS-Panzer-Korps*) from December 1944 to 8 May 1945.

Von Staden, Th. (*2./SS-Panzer-Regiment 5*) from January to June 1942.

PRIMARY SOURCES—REPORTS, MANUSCRIPTS AND OTHER SOURCES

Darges, F., *Abwehrkämpfe um Stuhlweißenburg* (manuscript).

Eckert, K. H., *HKL wird wieder ausgebaut* (manuscript).

Flügel, H., *Ausbruch Tlucz, August 1944* (manuscript).

Frels, E., *Ausbruch aus dem Kessel von Tscherkassy* (firsthand account).

Fröbe, W., *Einsatz Versmold* (firsthand account).

Hein, W., *Lagebericht 11./12.1.1943, Dschungelkampf mit Panzern* and *Anmerkung zum Tagebuch, 18.2.1944* (all manuscripts).

Hepp, J., *Mein tiefstes Erlebnis an der Front,* (Article in *Wiking Ruf*, Number 19, of May 1953).

Jakubetz, L., *SS-Panzer-Infanterie-Bataillon* 1945 (Recording)

Jauß, K., *Ausbildungsabteilung 5 Versmold* (manuscript).

Kalbskopf, Dr. E., *Untersturmführer Jensen in Stuhlweißenburg* (letter)

Kerckhoff, M., *Entsatzangriff auf Budapest, 14.1.-18.3.1945* (manuscript).

Klapdor, E., *Mit der Panzerabteilung 5 zum Kaukasus* (manuscript).

Lange, G., *Meldung beim Chef des Stabes der 2. Armee, Juli 1944* (firsthand account).

Lehni, H., *Ausbruch Tscherkassy* (firsthand account).

Lichte, K. H., *Maciejow, das Dorf der II. Abt.* (manuscript).

Melinkat, S., *Die letzten Kämpfe, Panzer-Infanterie-Bataillon, April/Mai 1945* (firsthand account).

Mühlenkamp, J., *Aufstellung der Panzerabteilung 5, Angriff auf Rostow, Kampf um Malgobek* and *Rückzug vom Kaukasus* (all manuscripts).

Neumann, W., *Panzertreffen vor Ssagopschin* (manuscript).

Nicolussi-Leck, K., *Zwischen Senne und Hannover, April 1945* (firsthand account).

Overbeck, H., *Einsatz Versmold April 1945* (firsthand account).

Ploen, G., *Tod Unterscharführer Trodler* (firsthand account).

Putensen, R., *Zwischen Versmold und Ratzeburg* (firsthand account).

Renz, Dr. M., *Chronik Pz.Rgt. 5, 26.3.-30-11.1944* (manuscript).

Richtet, ?, *Einsatz Kowel* (manuscript).

Standl, Dr. R., *Organization und Einsatz der Sanitäts-Staffel* (firsthand account).

Truppenkameradschaft Panzer-Regiment 5, *Entsatzangriffe Budapest* (recording).

W. K., *Tapfere Söhne Europas, treue Kameraden* (Article in *Wiking Ruf*, Number 4, of February 1952).

Waber, G., *Fünf Mann halten einen Kolchos* (manuscript).

SECONDARY SOURCES

Dilthy, *Der Einjährig-Freiwillige*, E. S. Mittler & Sohn, Berlin: 1913.

Federal Archives, *Die Eroberung von Nowo Georgiewsk*, Stalling Verlag: 1926.

Guderian, H., *Erinnerungen eines Soldaten*, Vowinckel Verlag: 1950.

Hausser, P., *Soldaten wie andere auch*, Munin Verlag: 1966.

Konew, I. S., *Aufzeichnungen eines Frontoberbefehlshabers 1943/1944*, Militärverlag der DDR, Berlin (East): 1978.

Lenz, Fr., *Stalingrad, Der verlorene Sieg*, Fr. Lenz, Heidelberg: 1956.

Liddell Hart, B. H., *Geschichte des Zweiten Weltkriegs*, Econ Verlag, Düsseldorf: 1972.

Mackensen, E., *Vom Bug zum Kaukasus*, Vowinckel Verlag: 1967.

Manstein, E., *Verlorene Siege*, Athenäum Verlag: 1955.

Moltke, H., *Ausgewählte Werke Feldherr und Historiker*, Rainer Hobbing Verlag, Berlin: 1925.

Moskalenko, K. S., *In der Südwest-Richtung*, Militärverlag der DDR, Berlin (East): 1975.

Rendulic, L., *Soldat in stürzenden Reichen*, Damm Verlag, Munich: 1965.

Speidel, H., *Invasion 1944*, Rainer Wunderlich Verlag: 1949.

Straßner, P., *Europäische Freiwillige*, Munin Verlag: 1968.

Stalling Verlag, *Bilanz des Zweiten Weltkriegs*, Stalling Verlag: 1953.

Shtemenko, S. M., *The Soviet General Staff at War*, Progress Publishers, Moscow: 1970.

Office of the Reichsführer-SS, *Die SS- und Polizei-Gerichtsbarkeit* (1 July 1944), Friedrich A. Wordel Verlag, Leipzig: 1944.

Thöle, H., *Befehl des Gewissens*, Munin Verlag: 1976.

Tieke, W., *Der Kaukasus und das Öl*, Munin Verlag: 1970.

Tippelskirch, K., *Geschichte des Zweiten Weltkriegs*, Athenäum Verlag: 1956.